Social Change and Education in Canada

Social Change and Education in Canada

Third Edition

Ratna Ghosh
McGill University

Douglas Ray
University of Western Ontario

HARCOURT
BRACE
CANADA

Harcourt Brace & Company, Canada

Toronto Montreal Fort Worth New York Orlando
Philadelphia San Diego London Sydney Tokyo

Canadian Cataloguing in Publication Data

Main entry under title:

Social change and education in Canada

3rd ed.
Includes bibliographical references and index.
ISBN 0-7747-3277-6

1. Education—Social aspects—Canada.
I. Ghosh, Ratna. II. Ray, Douglas.

LC191.8.C2S62 1995 370.19′0971 C94-931770-5

Publisher: Heather McWhinney
Editor and Marketing Manager: Joanna Cotton
Projects Co-ordinator: Laura Paterson Pratt
Director of Publishing Services: Jean Davies
Editorial Manager: Marcel Chiera
Supervising Editor: Semareh Al-Hillal
Production Editor: Celène S. Adams
Production Manager: Sue-Ann Becker
Production Supervisor: Carol Tong
Copy Editor: James Leahy
Cover Design: Opus House
Cover Photo: Tom Stewart/Masterfile
Interior Design: Dave Peters
Typesetting and Assembly: Compeer Typographic Services Limited
Printing and Binding: Best Book Manufacturers, Inc.

♾ This book was printed in Canada on acid-free paper.

1 2 3 4 5   99 98 97 96 95

PREFACE

*S*ocial Change and Education in Canada has been revised, updated, and rewritten as necessary for the third edition. It brings recent major social research affecting educational policies to the attention of teachers in their initial professional education. The volume identifies the major trends and issues in the relationship between social change and education in Canada, and the distinctive qualities and diversity within its education systems.

The authors of this book are broadly representative of Canada's regions and are nationally recognized for their scholarship in their particular fields. Most chapters are original essays but some are modified and updated versions from the second edition.

According to the Constitution Act (British North America Act, 1867), education is a provincial responsibility. In many respects, Canada's school systems are highly centralized at the provincial level — more comparable to the systems of continental Europe than to the decentralized traditions of the United States or Great Britain.

Canada does not have a national policy institution or central office of education. However, national forces are generated and expressed through political, bureaucratic, scholarly, and citizen groups that filter through to the provincial decision-makers.

The private sector in Canadian education, both at the level of schools and universities, is relatively small. Only five provinces (Quebec, Manitoba, Saskatchewan, Alberta, and British Columbia) give direct public aid to private schools, and their levels of funding vary considerably. Private schools are usually religious but may be non-denominational. In some provinces, such as Quebec, private institutions are largely Roman Catholic, while in others, such as Ontario, they are often non-sectarian. Universities all receive public support, and private institutions receiving public funding are neither entirely private nor fully independent.

The role of education in any society is determined by the kind of change desired by that society. Social Change and Education in Canada explores the critical dimensions involved in Canadian society, which has not yet resolved its constitutional problems. The book is divided into three major sections: The first explores the link between education and the multidimensional context of social change; the second examines Canadian policies relating to education; and the third deals with the rights of several groups within the educational system. The book concludes with an assessment of Canadian education: what is distinctive, what should be avoided, what is worth borrowing and adapting.

The structure and approach of Social Change and Education in Canada provide the reader with a systematic overview, rather than a theoretical critique, of the relationship between social change and education in this country. As such, it will have succeeded if it encourages further investigation into the field.

ACKNOWLEDGEMENTS

*S*ocial Change and Education in Canada would not have reached its third edition without the willingness of the contributors to revise their chapters or prepare new chapters for this volume. Special thanks are due to them and several other colleagues—in particular, Greg Dickinson, Andrew Blair and Gerry Paquette (University of Western Ontario), and Jacques Lamontagne (University of Montreal).

We also wish to thank our colleagues who reviewed the second edition and offered constructive comments. They are Ishmael Baksh (Memorial University), L. Handy (University of Toronto), Steven Rusack (University of Toronto), and Chris Thorpe (Lakehead University).

Financial assistance came from Acting Dean B.B. Kymlicka at the University of Western Ontario. Finally, special thanks for the continued support of Dien Tran at the University of Western Ontario, and Elaine Correa at McGill University.

Readers wishing additional information on data provided through the co-operation of Statistics Canada may obtain copies of related publications by mail from: Publications Sales, Statistics Canada, Ottawa, Ontario, K1A 0T6, by calling (613) 951-7277 or toll-free 800-267-6677. Readers may also facsimile their order by dialing (613) 951-1584.

A NOTE FROM THE PUBLISHER

Thank you for selecting Social Change and Education in Canada, Third Edition, by Ratna Ghosh and Douglas Ray. The authors and publisher have devoted considerable time to the careful development of this book. We appreciate your recognition of this effort and accomplishment.

We want to hear what you think about Social Change and Education in Canada. Please take a few minutes to fill in the stamped reader reply card at the back of the book. Your comments and suggestions will be valuable to us as we prepare new editions and other books.

CONTENTS

I CONTEXT

II POLICIES

III RICHTS

IV APPENDICES

PART I

CONTEXT

INTRODUCTION

Social change usually involves economic, political, and sociocultural dimensions. Education cuts across this multidimensional context. The chapters in the first section of this book deal with the link between education and aspects of this context in the process of social change, as discussed in Chapter 1.

The emergence and transformation of formal schooling have been related to societal attitudes toward the school and expectations of its role as a social institution. The need for transmitting knowledge and skills, and developing new skills in an increasingly complex society, led to the development of special institutions—schools. And just as schools were seen as the forum for this transmission and development, so teachers were viewed as agents with special responsibilities to carry out these functions. With industrialization and its social consequences (slums, unemployment), the school was also seen as a means of social control, replacing the family to a great extent for inculcating values and discipline. The expansion of schooling was perceived by some as necessary for improving the workforce by teaching certain values: efficiency and work ethics. The democratization of schooling to include the working class was viewed by others as a potential source of conflict, as it was likely to raise the consciousness and expectations of all the people. More recently, with a move toward equality legislation, education has come to be viewed as a human right.

Livingstone and Hart's chapter in this section looks at public attitudes toward schooling in Canada and the expectations of teachers as significant agents of social change in a democratic society. The authors discuss current perceptions of the school and what it is expected to do based on national and provincial opinion surveys, which are among several other factors that have an impact on educational policy-making. The authors also explore the extent of consensus among groups regarding schooling and suggest that differences in attitude should be carefully considered before major changes in education are implemented.

The information revolution and the rapid introduction of new technology in the contemporary Western world have resulted in profound changes in Canadian society with implications for considerable innovations in the educational system. Dien Tran considers the impact of recent technological transformations for the process of schooling. A rapid and complete transformation of information processing and retrieval has been made possible by computers, and the impact of these changes provides individual learners with new methods of learning as well as new sources of data.

John Young examines the major demographic changes that have taken place in Canada and their relationship to educational development. Canada has witnessed significant population changes due to fluctuations in immigration, and regional differences because of internal migration. The education system faces tremendous challenges in coping with the demands of a culturally and ethnically diverse population that is also aging due to declining birth rates.

Dennis Dibski charts the financial patterns that have recently characterized Canadian education: reasonable equity between individuals within a community, between rich and poor communities, and among provinces. He reviews the mechanisms that have promoted such equity, and discusses the current trends.

1

SOCIAL CHANGE AND EDUCATION IN CANADA

Ratna Ghosh

Education has always been shaped by economic, social, political, cultural, and historical forces, both globally and locally. Formal education also contributes to all these areas. It is tied to the ideology of the ruling elite of the country and is political at every stage because of competing demands by various groups. Although reforms in the educational system have consequences in the wider societal structure, educational policies are based on the socioeconomic and cultural context of a nation and influenced by global events.

The events of the recent past have unleashed unprecedented changes in Eastern Europe, South Africa, and the Middle East, indicating a larger struggle for democratic change, peace, and stability. Western democracies are affected by these changes, not only because instability in other areas of the world indicates global dangers (war) as well as domestic threats to secure living (terrorism), but also because we have come to recognize the importance of "one environment, one humanity."[1] Meanwhile, in the West, a shift in perspective suggests reconstruction of the *preconditions* for social change and the progressive modernist ideals of freedom, justice, and equality. These liberal ideals are central to democracy, and to realize them culturally and politically, peripheral groups must affirm and realize their human capacity to define their own location in the democratic world.

This chapter begins with a brief overview of theoretical explanations of the relationship between education and social change. Following this, a general description of the sociopolitical background in which education is embedded in Canada leads to an overview of the impact of education for social change toward democratic ideals of the Canadian state. Finally, the chapter identifies some challenges for education on the threshold of the twenty-first century.

EDUCATION AND SOCIAL CHANGE

Education in this volume is defined as deliberate, planned experiences designed to transmit certain values, knowledge, and skills. The term "education" involves three categories:

- *Formal education* refers to what is learned in institutionalized settings such as kindergartens, schools, colleges, and universities.

- *Non-formal education* refers to programs organized by groups outside the formal educational structure, such as clubs and associations.
- *Informal education* refers to what is learned from all other societal institutions.

Although the term education is not synonymous with socialization, it is important to recognize the part all forms of education play in the socialization process. Emile Durkheim defined education as "methodical socialization of the young generation." Several of the essays in this volume explore this role and the interaction of education with other agents of socialization, such as the family, media, religion, and peers.

Defining social change is a more elusive exercise because change is ubiquitous. Analyzing change has occupied great thinkers for centuries. Western theorists like Hegel, Compte, and Spencer developed *evolutionary* theories of change. They saw social change as a linear process, moving in stages from simple to more complex societies. One of the most important notions in evolutionary theory was the concept of "survival of the fittest," in which various societies or their champions claimed for themselves the top of the evolutionary ladder because of their socioeconomic condition at a particular moment in history. In education, the function of schooling was to change societies from primitive stages of evolution to complex and civilized stages, as if the process were linear. Colonialism was justified as an attempt to make the non-industrialized societies (which were seen as primitive) advance to a more developed stage.

Between the 1930s and the 1950s Talcott Parsons and Robert Merton criticized evolutionary theory and proposed a theory of *structural functionalism*. This theory, rather than focus on social change, saw society as a composition of interrelated parts (such as family, education, religion, politics) that continually interact to retain a measure of harmony by preserving aspects of society. In educational terms, the function of schooling was to maintain the class structure by preserving the opportunities and educational levels of privileged classes through sorting students and streaming them to different fields and levels.

The theory of *modernization* that emerged in the 1950s looked at change as a dramatic and complex shift from a traditional to a modern state. The emphasis was on modern attitudes and values. Proponents of modernity such as Inkeles, Smith, and McClelland emphasized the importance of education and the process of socialization in developing values conducive to modernization. The imposition of modernization concepts upon other cultural patterns and traditional forms of knowledge has been challenged as being biased and ethnocentric.

Human capital theorists, following the work of Schultz in the 1960s, saw education as a productive investment, not just as an agent for personal development. An educated labour force was seen as the most efficient way to bring about a desired form of social change — a prosperous society.

From the 1970s there was a radical departure in theoretical explanations of the role of schools. *Conflict* theories, rooted in the ideas of Marx and Weber, interpreted social change as a response to conflict underlying social conditions. They proposed societal conflict (such as class struggle and economic exploitation) as the prime agent of change. Influenced by Marx, who based this theory of society on Hegel's theory of the dialectic and on economic conditions in the late nineteenth century, Marxist theories have had a profound impact on thinking about social change. (*Dialectics* refers to change as a result of interaction between opposing forces—thesis and antithesis—resulting in synthesis.) For Marx, class struggle meant a conflict between those who own the means of production and those who do not (and who are therefore exploited); such conflict would inevitably result in structural social change. Education, as part of a superstructure that supports a given society, was regarded by Marx as important for bringing about the revolution that would ultimately create a classless society.

Based on Marxian philosophy, communism focussed on the redistribution of wealth rather than on its production. The neglect of incentive and profit motives in the communist system resulted in inadequate production and distribution of wealth and eventually to the dramatic recent change toward market economies in the countries of Eastern Europe.

Neo-Marxists made considerable theoretical advances by broadening their analysis from the economy and class to other factors. They focussed on the conflicts in relationships in social, political, economic, and cultural contexts. According to conflict theorists, one purpose of education is to strengthen exploited groups to overcome the injustices in society, whether these be racism, sexism, or class discrimination.

Reproduction theorists looked at the relation between content of knowledge and the structure of power. Social reproduction theories (Bowles & Gintis, 1976) viewed schools as reproducing the unequal social relations in the larger society. Cultural reproduction theorists analyzed the school's legitimating function in reproducing social hierarchies through "cultural capital" (Bourdieu, 1973) and the cultural bias of language and language codes (Bernstein, 1971). Sometimes referred to as the "new" sociology of education, these studies attempted to combine the evolutionary and conflict perspectives by relating content and the development of knowledge to social control. Both social and cultural reproduction theorists saw the control of the content of socialization by the dominant culture as hegemonic (i.e., something that functions to exclude certain groups). The significance of cultural reproduction theories was that they examined the hidden curriculum as a means of cultural domination, questioned the validity of what constitutes acceptable "knowledge," and demonstrated that knowledge is socially constructed and is, therefore, also subjective.

The theoretical work developed by the Frankfurt School is often called "critical theory" and provides a foundation for a theory of *critical pedagogy*. Critical pedagogy refers to a heterogeneous and complex variety of discourses. It is associated with "modernism," which is itself an ideologically and politically complex term. Simply put, modernism is based on a view of scientific and technological progress as well as on rationality. The Frankfurt School is perhaps the most forceful proponent of modernism. Theorists such as Adorno, Horkheimer, Marcuse, and Habermas emphasized culture and psychoanalysis to expose the hidden social relationships in the objective world, but their work was not limited to an analysis of the working class as in orthodox Marxism. Rather, it attempted to change the perspective of the role of culture in Western civilization. The Frankfurt School's contribution to psychoanalysis and the development of consciousness is crucial to contemporary understanding of the subjective dimensions of liberation and domination. Their work on racism and prejudice (e.g., Adorno's *The authoritarian personality*, 1950) made a significant impact. By pointing to the political, social, and economic means used to control the cultural sphere, they dispelled the notion of culture as neutral object but did not contrast it with the economic realm as did orthodox Marxism.

In the 1980s, an emerging critical pedagogy was based on the work of social theorists such as John Dewey, John Childs, Paulo Freire, and Antonio Gramsci (see Giroux & McLaren, 1989, p. xxi). This work combines their theories of culture, power, and hegemony in defining the nature and purpose of education. The purpose of schooling is seen as empowerment. The "language" of the school, then, must provide students with the skills that all students (not only those of the dominant group) will utilize to construct identity, meaning, and value, thereby becoming critical citizens. The focus, therefore, is on literacy and an education that raises consciousness, rather than on formal requirements.

Influenced by postmodern, poststructural, postcolonial literacy theories as well as critical feminism, educational theories of production have questioned the very nature of knowledge. By reconstructing the boundaries between traditional knowledge and power it raises new questions and suggests different ways of knowledge construction that would represent different world views. This stage of critical pedagogy is marked by its focus on the social construction of knowledge and analysis of consciousness as exemplified by the works of Freire (1970), Giroux (1983, 1991), Aronowitz (1985), and Simon (1992) among others. It involves programs such as anti-racist education. For its emancipatory potential in the teaching and learning process, critical pedagogy draws on the democratic elements of modernism but emphasizes the "cultural politics of difference" of postmodernist discourse, rejecting overarching philosophies and a view of culture as artifact (Freire & Giroux, 1989, p. xii).

There is a lively and fruitful debate about the link between education and social change. Can education initiate social change or does social change dictate educational transformation? In the early twentieth century Durkheim saw educational change as the result of social transformation. He viewed the expansion of schooling in Western countries as a result rather than the cause of industrialization. The importance of schooling grew with the need for increased industrial skills in the workforce.

Since 1945, education has been seen as a crucial agent for accelerated change. In Canada, human capital theory and the belief that an educated population was essential for improved production dominated educational policy in the 1960s and the early 1970s. Education was recognized as a major agent of social change. As a result, there was a dramatic increase in educational expenditure and facilities during this period (Ray, 1974). In general, Canadian educational policy reflects modernization and human capital theories that aim at economic returns and has promoted expansion of a "modern" educational system with high participation rates and a standard school curriculum, as well as demand for continuing education for all ages.

Social change, whether gradual or revolutionary, is inevitable and brings with it new patterns of social interaction. The place of education in this process is both complex and critical. In today's postmodern, postindustrial society, the Canadian social profile is changing radically and rapidly. Education has a significant role to play in this change, especially because of the pressing changes in the nature of the family and of work, and the needs of a technological society in an information age. While education alone cannot achieve all the desired changes, it would be a great mistake to ignore its potential for affecting change (see Carnoy, 1975) and to minimize the school's responsibility for influencing the needed outcomes. Not only can education be a significant force for change, it is essential for producing critical citizens and for maintaining a critical democracy.

THE CANADIAN CONTEXT

How can education be an effective instrument for social change? This question must be viewed in a geographical, political, economic, and sociocultural context. Canada is one of the wealthiest and most productive nations in the world. With around 27 million (1991 census) inhabitants, it has a lower population density than any other major nation and the world's second-largest territory (after Russia) of 9.22 million square kilometres studded with important minerals. Eighty-five percent of Canadians live in urban areas, 55 percent of them in metropolitan centres within a few hundred kilometres of the Canada–U.S. border.

Canada's constitution as a federal state is one of the oldest in the world (after the United States and Switzerland) and is now in its second century. Politically a constitutional monarchy, its ten provinces and two territories provide for variety in legislative and administrative detail. This earlier Canadian constitution was updated by the Constitution Act of 1982 with its addition of the Canadian Charter of Rights and Freedoms. Constitutional reform has not yet reached a conclusion on several matters: recognition of Quebec "as a distinct society," the status of the First Nations, and the role of ethnic groups other than English and French.

Economically, Canada has a regionally distributed modern industrial sector, a rich agricultural sector, and many resources such as minerals, oil, lumber, and hydroelectricity. The Canadian economy recently outperformed most other industrial countries to earn membership in the Organization for Economic Cooperation and Development (OECD) group of seven (G7) most industrialized nations, all of them with much larger populations.

As a capitalist industrial society, Canada is characterized by mostly private ownership and investment; social change in such a society is usually designed to increase wealth, and some Canadians are among the most wealthy individuals in the world. But the Canadian state also represents the interests of the people, because only the effective use of human resources will maximize productivity. For example, in the last few years, through its participation in such initiatives as the General Agreement on Tariffs and Trade (GATT), the Canada–U.S. Free Trade Agreement, and the North American Free Trade Agreement, Canada has sought to expand its markets on a global basis.

As a liberal democracy, the Canadian state attempts to ensure its citizens equality of access to various social benefits such as education, health care, old age security, and pension benefits. All citizens are guaranteed a long list of rights and freedoms through such legislation as the Constitution Act, 1867; the Bill of Rights, 1960; the Human Rights Act, 1978; the Canadian Charter of Rights and Freedoms, 1982; and numerous provincial codes.

While the number of immigrants has varied widely over its history, Canada continues to be one of the world's major immigrant nations. In the first decade of this century, the most intensive period of nation-building, there was an influx of 1.5 million immigrants. Immigration then dropped dramatically over the following two decades, but climbed after 1945, reaching a peak in 1957 (282 164). Recent immigration numbers have fluctuated considerably since the early 1980s. Immigrants to Canada now total nearly 250 000 a year, and represent diverse racial, ethnic, religious, and cultural backgrounds. Immigration numbers have been offset, however, by significant emigration (around 50 000 per year), which makes net immigration smaller than the actual numbers of new immigrants. In 1991, over one-half of all immigrants were living in the country's metropolitan areas: Toronto (38 percent), Vancouver (30 percent), Calgary (20 percent), and Montreal (17 percent).

The last census, taken in 1991,[2] revealed dramatic differences in the reported origins of Canadians. People of *single* European origins constituted about 60 percent of the population (20 percent British, 23 percent French, and 15 percent of other European stock). Visible minorities formed around 7.5 percent (2.1 percent Chinese, 1.55 percent South Asians, 0.35 percent Caribbean, and 0.31 percent of Latin American background); Native peoples accounted for 1.7 percent of the total Canadian population. People claiming multiple origins constituted 28.8 percent of the total, and of these over 11 percent claimed British and French origins. There are two major implications of these statistics: The dominant place of the "two founding peoples" is increasingly insecure, and many people are reporting multiple origins. Cultural pluralism may well follow this diversity of origins.

Canada has an official policy of multiculturalism within a bilingual framework. As a pattern of social organization, the "Canadian mosaic"[3] is complementary to political federalism. Multiculturalism is said to give identity to Canada and distinction to Canadian society (Lawson and Ghosh, 1986). The multicultural reality is significant for schools because educational institutions are responsible for preparing all students to participate fully in a multicultural society. Notwithstanding the fact that Canada is an immigrant country and has become increasingly heterogeneous, the provincial departments of education have historically had a policy of assimilation.

EDUCATIONAL TRADITIONS

British and French settlers set the patterns of education by the mid-nineteenth century and formalized them in the British North America Act of 1867, which made education a provincial responsibility. This was reiterated in the Constitution Act of 1982. Federal influence in education is mostly indirect (through equalization subsidies), and policy formulation is largely at the provincial level. Policies, programs, and structures vary from province to province because of regional differences in the context of education. In many respects, Canada's school systems are highly centralized at the provincial level, more comparable to the systems of continental Europe than to the decentralized traditions of the United States or Great Britain.

Canada has the distinction of being the only Western country with no federal office of education, no national educational policy, and neither adequate national data collection on schools nor a national mechanism for dissemination of educational information. For common educational concerns, the provinces co-operate through the Council of Ministers of Education in Canada (CMEC). The federal government facilitates programs such as bilingualism and multiculturalism, and plays a significant role in constitutional reforms (Canadian Charter of Rights and Freedoms, 1982) that affect education. Provincial responses to federal legislation vary, as in the case of the Young Offenders Act and the Multicultural Policy and Bill (the latter was rejected by Quebec in favour of "intercultural education"). Although the federal government still has control of the education of First Nations peoples who live on reserves, this responsibility is being gradually devolved to the band councils. At a time when education's role in society is acknowledged to be very important, the Constitution prevents the federal government from participating formally in important policy decisions and reform initiatives. Equally, provinces are constrained at international policy debates. However, national forces, generated and expressed through political, bureaucratic, scholarly, and citizen groups, filter through to the national and provincial decision makers. In recent years, policy co-ordination has begun at the provincial level between sectors, and at the national level among professionals.

By providing and controlling education, the state (provinces and school boards) legitimates the social order while at the same time making it theoretically possible for groups other than the dominant class (such as the poor and minorities) to promote their interests (Porter et al., 1982). Educational opportunity for all is provided through the federal Charter, various provincial policies, and formal protections against discrimination. The Constitution Act, 1867, confirmed the educational divisions based on Catholic and Protestant school boards, and this continues to the present. In June 1993, the Supreme Court of Canada ruled that the Constitution allowed Quebec to proceed with the creation of new linguistic school boards, French and English, that will be superimposed on the denominational split.

The private sector in Canadian education, both at the level of schools and universities, is relatively small, but increasing (now 4.6 percent of total school population). In Ontario many Roman Catholic schools were brought into the public sector in 1985–88. Only five provinces (Quebec, Manitoba, Saskatchewan, Alberta, and British Columbia) give direct public aid to private schools, but their levels of funding vary considerably. Private schools are usually religious but may be non-denominational. All universities receive public support, and private institutions receiving public funding are neither entirely private nor fully independent.

Canada is among the world leaders in terms of its support of its educational system. In 1990, educational expenditure was 7.4 percent of gross national product (GNP), equalled by Sweden (7.4 percent), and significantly above the United States (5.3 percent in 1989), the United Kingdom (4.7 percent in 1988), France (5.5 percent), Australia (5.1 percent in 1989), and Japan (4.7 percent in 1988).[4] Although educational funding is declining, education ranks as one of Canada's largest expenses and most important investments. In the early 1980s the average cost of educating a student was $3850, compared with $10 a hundred years before. In 1986, for the nearly six million full-time students in all three levels of education, the country invested $33.34 billion.

The rapid expansion in schooling that took place between 1960 to 1975 saw a 42 percent increase in enrollment and a 72 percent increase in the number of teachers. The growth in preschool (138 percent) and postsecondary (170 percent) enrollment was phenomenal in the 1960s. The student-centred schools of that decade gave way to community-oriented schools as the end of the baby boom sharply reduced school enrollments: some schools even had to close. This trend will continue because fertility rates (1.7) have sunk below the replacement level (2.1 per woman), creating a "demographic deficit." Quebec's birth rate (1.45 per 100 women in 1990) is one of the lowest in the industrialized world. Although trends can always change, at the present rate of birth and death rates, and without immigration, Canada's population would disappear 800 years from now (National Health and Welfare, 1989, p. 2, 44). Immigration is essential to Canada's survival. The decline in fertility rate has changed the age structure in Canadian society from a broad base of young people, to a rapidly increasing group of middle-aged and older people. This has tremendous implications for adult education. The example of Sweden has shown that proper planning of resources can make such a society dynamic and prosperous.

CHALLENGES FOR EDUCATION

During the last decade Canada was caught up in such global changes as an economic recession, the technological and information revolutions, and the changing family structure — all of which have had far-reaching implications for re-education. There were changes in technology such as computers in the classroom. There were also changes in expectations for special groups—such as children with disabilities and gifted children— resulting in new attitudes toward educating culturally different children. These various changes brought together many part-time students and adults for *learning* a living, and increased the participation of women in higher education and some professional areas. Over one-third of postsecondary students pursue part-time studies. Women now constitute 54 percent of college and 52 percent of university full-time enrollment. The "rhetoric of a democratic society demands that whatever the outcome in the selection process, all children and all adults ultimately have equal value" (Rex, 1981, p. 39).

The most important questions to be addressed regarding education are simply: How educated is Canadian society? Has education in Canada produced the desired changes in terms of increasing social and economic benefits? Has education decreased poverty and unemployment? Has it promoted social justice?

The educational level of Canadians ranks high in the world and has continued to grow steadily. By 1985, 81 percent of the 15+ age group had some high-school education (compared with 48 percent in 1951); 31 percent had some postsecondary education (10 per-cent in 1951); 20 percent had graduated from a tertiary institution (5 percent in 1951). The number of adults in various forms of educational activities rose from 426 340 (1960) to 3 170 900 in 1983. In 1991–92, 1.4 million Canadians were enrolled in postsecondary institutions (community colleges and universities). Immigrants have a higher-than-average level of education. The 1986 census indicated that in the age group 25–64, 25.3 percent of the foreign-born had some university education, compared with 20.4 percent of the Canadian-born, and women immigrants had higher levels of education than their Canadian-born counterparts both in university and school education. They also had above-average incomes, if not for their community, for Canada as a whole. Statistics indicate that immi-grants increase the average total income in Canada: In 1985, average incomes of immigrant men and women were, respectively, 11.8 percent and 5.6 percent higher than the average incomes of those who were Canadian-born.

Despite these figures, about four million Canadians (22 percent of the population) are "at risk" of illiteracy. About 16 percent are not functionally literate, and another 22 percent avoid reading. The cost to Canada of dropouts from secondary school is estimated at $4 billion in 1989 alone. The personal costs in terms of marginalization in society, and the powerlessness resulting from an inability to communicate, participate, and produce effectively, cannot be calculated.[5]

Poverty tends to be structural, to affect particular groups and particular regions. The relationship between education, poverty, and unemployment is a vicious circle: schools fail the children of the poor and extend the cycle of underachievement leading to unem-ployment and poverty from generation to generation. The profound implications for their education can be seen in dropout rates but remain invisible in their personal experiences of failure and impeded opportunities. Statistics show a clear link between inadequate edu-cation and poverty. The lower the level of education of the family head, the greater the chance that the family will fall into poverty. In 1986 the poverty rate was 16.7 percent for families headed by a person with only primary education, but only 4.2 percent for fam-ilies headed by a university graduate. Two recent studies published by Statistics Canada— Leaving school (1991), and Adult education and training survey (1990) — conclusively link high-school graduation to better social and economic conditions. School education level is correlated with adult participation in further training, and greater job choices and earning potential. Dropping out is linked to crime, delinquency, poverty, drug use, and a lower quality of life. In 1991 poverty affected 18.3 percent of Canadian children under 18 (5 percent in Sweden and France).

Illiteracy and unemployment are also directly related. A mid-1980s national survey, Employment opportunity for the 80s, revealed that 70 percent of Canadians with postse-condary education were employed, compared with only 33 percent with Grade 8 education, and that income rises with level of education so that the income of someone with a Master's degree is more than double that of a vocational school graduate. The report also linked the social cost of illiteracy to poverty, racism, and crime. Census data show that lower levels of education are associated with higher levels of unemployment (without identifying which is cause and which is effect). Education also makes a big difference to family income. Families headed by people with elementary education have half the average income ($30 792), compared with family heads who have university degrees ($61 183).

The survey pointed out that under-educated people lack the basic educational preparation to even enter training programs. This accounts for much of the structural unemployment in Canada. While the economic aspects of illiteracy, poverty, and unemployment are severe, the psychological dimensions—stigma and vulnerability—are tremendous.

Has educational expansion promoted social justice and resulted in equality of opportunity? Canada is looked upon as a land of opportunity. Education is one means to that opportunity. While education undoubtedly facilitates social mobility, lack of education is more a problem of certain groups: the poor, certain ethnic groups, Native populations, and females. Equality of educational access is only a theoretical proposition if people of various racial and ethnic communities, and women, do not actually participate equally in the educational process. While data indicate that there has been a democratization of educational opportunities for disadvantaged youth, the gap in group inequalities for adults remains almost unchanged. This is evident in educational outcomes and employment statistics. Education has been shown to be one of the most important factors affecting relative economic position in Canadian society (Balakrishnan, 1988, p. 56). Even when educational level is controlled, there are differences in the mean income of ethnic groups; for visible minorities income is comparatively lower. For all categories of education, women have higher levels of unemployment, lower levels of education, lower pay, and lower-status jobs than do men.

TOWARD THE TWENTY-FIRST CENTURY

What are the future prospects of education in Canada on the threshold of the twenty-first century? Although substantial gains in education have been made, it is evident that increased education has neither eliminated functional illiteracy, nor significantly altered the pattern of poverty and unemployment, nor markedly reduced inequalities in the system and its outcomes. While most adult Canadians continue to have faith in their formal educational system, high rates of unemployment have created in some youth a sense of hopelessness, driving them to drugs, crime, and even suicide. A 1993 UNICEF study puts the Canadian suicide rate among young people (age 15–24) at 15.8 per 100 000—below only Australia and Norway. Canada's homicide rate by young people is 3.1, or 121 murders in an average year, second only to the United States.

The challenges of the past decade will further transform the social context of education, but at an unprecedented pace. For example, environmental hazards are even more urgent; the lives of children are affected more and more by the diversification in adult living styles and labour force participation. On the one hand, a high-technology economy has underscored the significance of human knowledge, and information processing is creating the demand for a new type of worker, trained in new skills. On the other hand, a larger proportion of older people will shift the political, tax, and social service priorities. Education will likely need to utilize the most sophisticated microelectronics and communication media to meet labour market as well as leisure activity needs. As Marshall McLuhan predicted, the future of work may indeed consist of "learning" a living. In addition, the very concept of education as an *age-specific* process has had to give way to the notion of *lifelong learning*.

According to sociologist Daniel Bell (1974), postindustrial society will be controlled by those who master technological knowledge: scientists and technologists. In science education Canada lags behind other countries, and high-school students place low in science tests internationally. A 1990 survey of scientific literacy among Canadian adults by Einsiedal indicates low public awareness and an inadequate science and technology culture. In addition, the universities do not graduate sufficient numbers of scientists, engineers (only 4 percent of whom are women), and technologists for Canada to remain industrially competitive.

Although Canada has a good scientific infrastructure, eminent Canadian scientists have noted that, for an age in which innovations, technology, and knowledge are the basis of wealth generation, Canada produces much less than its share of the world's technology. The percentage of GNP devoted to research and development (R&D) has stagnated at about 1.3 percent, while Canada's competitors have forged ahead and taken the markets in the process. The national spending on R&D should be brought up to at least 2.5 percent; this means that the federal government would have to double its current spending of $5 million annually and industry would have to spend a lot more than it does (Kerwin, 1989). This increase is of paramount importance to ensure Canada's economic and social future in a world marked by rapid and unrelenting technological change (Blais, 1990). Recently, the Canadian public has been warned of its increasing disadvantage by rapid developments in global competition. Among the many studies presented on the topic, the federal government's Prosperity Initiative (Canada, 1992) has sought a consensus on the problem and challenged Canadians to develop a new "learning culture." A growing consensus among policy-makers (government, educators, and businesspeople) is that great improvement is required in the level of basic skills of all Canadians and that a substantial number must acquire advanced specialized skills if Canada is to remain internationally competitive.

Technology will tend to produce elitism, and one of the dangers for education is that, without proper planning, sections of society may be left behind—socially, economically, and politically. But reforms in education will not be brought about by educators, for changes in social institutions imply changes in power relations, and, therefore, involve the political process. The questions are fundamentally political. What kind of society do we want? Is it one in which all persons—of every race and ethnicity, of both sexes, and of all ages—can benefit from technological advances and other rewards that society has to offer? Or are we willing to tolerate a Canada where, despite its advances and advantages, there are pockets of poverty, unemployment, illiteracy, and discrimination? As MacKay (1991) points out, the educative value of the rights discourse has the potential to raise consciousness and promote justice, but the Charter of Rights and Freedoms will only be as good as the vision of the people who apply it. The extraordinary transformation of the social base has resulted in a new identity emerging in Canada. Societal changes imply redistribution of power; whether education will be used to manipulate this transformation remains to be seen. The educational system will be judged by its ability to create and implement new visions for society and its institutions.

With the widening dimensions of the educational experience, the challenges for policy-makers are considerable, not only for structural reorganization and budget reallocations within the educational system but also for social policy impinging on education. Educational expenditures, for instance, must ensure maximum efficiency for a labour force requiring new skills, re-education, resocialization, and high levels of education.

CONCLUSIONS

Canada has a tremendous challenge in the immediate future to solve its constitutional crisis. The claims of Quebec for special status or sovereignty and the rights of Canada's First Nations will have to be resolved. The language question in Quebec is, perhaps, one of the most thorny issues. Although Canada has been officially bilingual since the early 1970s, historically English has been the language for social and economic mobility even in French Canada (until language legislation in Quebec made French the language of education and work, a policy that has tremendous implications for the education of non-English and non-French cultural groups).

The human rights debate will continue to appear on the national agenda in the immediate future. Canada's Charter of Rights and Freedoms, which provides constitutional protection and adds to the provincial statutory protections, also redefines and shapes a new social and political order. Because the Charter gives the power of judicial interpretation to the courts, it may have a standardizing influence on educational policy. In education, some strides have been made in the recognition of rights and policies. But several areas still require more attention.

Surveys tell us that Canadian society is becoming more, not less, racist. The individual effects of racism are bad enough, but institutional racism has far-reaching consequences. While four-fifths of Canada's immigrants before 1967 were of European origin, now almost three-quarters are visible minorities. The education and employment opportunities of their children will be a major issue as these groups get politically organized. A multicultural policy that *only* helps them retain their cultural identities may be seen to satisfy these groups, but it neither develops a sense of nationhood nor gives them the skills, knowledge, or the power to control their destinies in the creation of and participation in a just society.

Ideally, educational opportunities would not be influenced by cultural, racial/ethnic, or gender differences. The education system, especially teacher education, needs to be altered to take into account racism and sexism in the classrooms.

The goal of education is to provide maximum opportunity for all Canadians without restrictions based on their sex, race or ethnicity, social class, birth place, citizenship status, or religion. While Canadian education will likely continue to be affected by province of residence, official language status, and often by religion, some developments will be widely welcomed, others will remain controversial, and political debates will sometimes be sharp.

DISCUSSION QUESTIONS

❏ What is social change? What is its relationship with education?

❏ What is the sociopolitical context of Canadian education? What are some important issues of the future?

NOTES

1. Former prime minister of India, Indira Gandhi, expressed concerns for the environment in a 1972 speech: "Will the growing awareness of 'one earth' and 'one environment' guide us to the concept of 'one humanity'?" (U.N. Conference on the Human Environment, Stockholm, 1972).

2. At the time of writing, not all relevant data were available from the 1991 census. The data in this chapter have been taken from Statistics Canada documents listed in the References section.
3. John Gibbon (1938) disussed Canadian differences from the American "melting pot" in romantic terms. Since then, the term "mosaic" has been used to refer to the notion of allowing ethnic or cultural groups to retain their distinctive characteristics and identity instead of conforming to the ways of other Canadians.
4. Public Expenditure on Education table of the *UNESCO statistical yearbook*, 1992.
5. Literacy is a comparative concept and does not mean the same in Canada as it does in developing nations. In Western societies Grade 8 education is considered to be a realistic threshold for functional literacy that enables one to perform basic tasks. In Canada, Grade 10 has become the level for most skilled jobs.

REFERENCES

Adult education and training survey (1990). Ottawa: Employment and Immigration Canada.

Adorno, T.W. (1950). *The authoritarian personality*. New York: Harper.

Aronowitz, S., & Giroux, Henry A. (1985). *Education under siege*. South Hadley, MA: Bergin & Garvey Publishers.

Balakrishnan, T.R. (1988). Immigration and the changing ethnic mosaic of Canadian cities. *The review of democracy and its implications for economic and social policy*. Ottawa: The Royal Society of Canada.

Bell, D. (1974). *The coming of post-industrial society*. London: Heineman Publishing Co.

Bernstein, B. (1971). *Class, codes and control*. London: Routledge and Kegan Paul.

Blais, R.A. (1990, June). The need to increase industrial R&D in Canada. *IEEE Canadian Review*, pp. 5–7.

Bourdieu, P. (1973). Cultural reproduction and social reproduction. In R. Brown (Ed.). *Knowledge, education and cultural change*. London: Tavistock.

Bowles, S., & Gintis, H. (1976). *Schooling in capitalist America*. New York: Basic Books.

Canada. (1992). *Inventing our future: An action plan for Canada's prosperity*. Ottawa: Prosperity Secretariat.

Carnoy, M. (1975). Education change: Past and present. In Martin Carnoy (Ed.). *Schooling in a corporate society*. 2nd ed. New York: David McKay.

Durkheim, E. (1938). *The rules of sociological method*. Glencoe, IL: Free Press.

Einsiedal, E.F. (1990). *Scientific literacy: A survey of adult Canadians*. Monograph, University of Calgary.

Employment opportunities for the 80s (1985). Federal Task Force Report. Ottawa.

Freire, P. (1970). *The pedagogy of the oppressed*. New York: Continuum.

Freire, P., & Giroux, H.A. (1989). Pedagogy, popular culture and public life. In H.A. Giroux and R.I. Simon (Eds.). *Popular culture: Schooling and everyday life*. Critical Studies in Education Series. Toronto: OISE Press.

Gibbon, J. (1938). *The Canadian mosaic: The building of a northern nation*. Toronto: McClelland and Stewart.

Giroux, H. (1983). *Theory and resistance in education: A pedagogy for the opposition*. London: Heinemann Educational Books.

Giroux, H. (Ed.). (1991). *Post-modernism, feminism and cultural politics*. Albany: State University of New York Press.

Giroux, H., & McLaren, P. (Eds). (1989). *Critical pedagogy, the state and cultural struggle*. Albany: State University of New York Press.

Giroux, H., & Simon, R.I. (Eds.). (1989). *Popular culture: Schooling and everyday life.* Critical Studies in Education Series, Toronto: OISE Press.

Kerwin, L. (1989, May). Rating Canada's IQ. *Canadian Chemical News, 44*(1), pp. 5–6.

Lawson, R.F., & Ghosh, R. (1986, August). Canada. *Education and Urban Studies* (Special issue on policy issues in the education of minorities), *18*(4), pp. 449–61.

Leaving school (1993). Ottawa: Human Resources and Labour Canada.

McLuhan, M., & Fiore, Q. (1967). *The medium is the message.* Toronto: Bantam Books.

MacKay, A.W. (1991). The rights paradigm in the age of the charter. In R. Ghosh & D. Ray (Eds.). *Social change and education in Canada.* 2nd ed. Toronto: Harcourt Brace Jovanovich.

National Health and Welfare. (1989). *Charting Canada's future: A report of the demographic review.* Ottawa: Ministry of Supply and Services.

Porter, J., Porter, M., & Blishen, B.A. (1982). *Stations and callings: Making it through the school system.* Toronto: Methuen.

Ray, D. (1974). *Cultural education and political unity.* London, ON: University of Western Ontario.

Rex, J. (1981). Aims and objectives. In M. Craft (Ed.). *Teaching in a multicultural society: A task for teacher education.* Lewes, Sussex: Falmer Press.

Simon, R. (1992). *Teaching against the grain: Text for a pedagogy of possibility.* Toronto: OISE Press.

Statistics Canada. (1982). *1981 census of Canada.* Ottawa: Statistics Canada.

Statistics Canada. (1992). *1991 census.* Ottawa: Statistics Canada.

Statistics Canada. (1993a). *The nation.* Cat. no. 93-315. Ottawa: Statistics Canada.

Statistics Canada. (1993b). *Population and dwelling counts.* Cat. no. 93-301. Ottawa: Statistics Canada.

U.N. Conference of the Human Environment, Stockholm (1972). U.N. Doc. No. A/CONF48/14/Rev/1973. New York.

UNESCO. (1992). *UNESCO statistical yearbook.*

UNICEF. (1993). *The progress of nations.* New York: UNICEF.

FURTHER READINGS

Brown, R. (Ed.). (1973). *Knowledge, education and cultural change.* London, Ravistock.

Feinberg, W., & Soltis, J. (1992). *School and society.* New York: Teachers College Press.

Giroux, H.A. (1981). *Ideology, culture and the process of schooling.* Philadelphia: Temple University Press.

Lynch, J. (1992). *Education for citizenship in a multicultural society.* London: Cassell.

2

POPULAR BELIEFS ABOUT CANADA'S SCHOOLS

D.W. Livingstone and Doug Hart

Since the mid-nineteenth-century origins of mass schooling in industrial capitalist societies, people have tended to turn to the schools for both solutions and scapegoats in hard economic times (e.g., Curti, 1935). These are hard economic times in Canada. Over the past two decades we have seen mounting company bankruptcies and plant closings, stagnant profit margins, growing structural unemployment and a workforce increasingly polarized into "good" and "bad" jobs, and the emergence of insupportable public debt provoking serious government cutbacks in entitled services (Economic Council of Canada, 1991). The focus on the schools has once more intensified.

The prevalent neoconservative and corporate business theme has been that schools are failing our children and must be reformed to return the Canadian economy to international competitiveness. National goals stress "developing a flexible labour force with excellent generic skills" (D'Aquino, 1990) and more rigorous selection standards to ensure excellence in the acquisition of more advanced or specialized skills. The proposed means include closer links between schools and the private sector, more streamlined curricula and standardized tests to monitor progress and produce desired learning results, and innovative management to use limited finances more effectively (Corporate–Higher Education Forum, 1992).

But what do most Canadian citizens in different social groups actually think about current schooling and the need for change? Their beliefs should be an important factor in public policy-making.

Popular beliefs remain difficult to measure. Mass opinion surveys are currently the most reliable means for sampling the general public's sentiments about major social issues and alternative policy options. As long as their limitations are taken into account, such surveys can enhance the general public's collective self-awareness (Livingstone et al., 1985).

This chapter provides recent attitudes of the Canadian public toward schools, on the basis of available national and provincial opinion surveys.[1] We will review popular beliefs regarding general confidence in schooling and other major institutions, school performance, funding support, testing and curricular priorities, educational equality, and public educational involvement.

PUBLIC CONFIDENCE

During the past five years, all ten provinces and the two territories have appointed committees or commissions to review how well they teach elementary and high-school students. While the findings conflict in many areas, they are virtually unanimous in one pessimistic conclusion: too many students are either drifting through schools that fail to teach them to read and write well, or they are dropping out of high school. The result has been a rising level of frustration on all sides with almost every aspect of pre-university education (Fennell, 1993, p. 28).

Public education faces a crisis of confidence in the 1990s. The unease, doubt, and even anger over the state of schools today reflect a general loss of faith in public institutions and officials in Canada. Across Canada, school systems are under fire for failing to produce the outcomes expected by employers and other critics, including some parents. The most common criticisms have to do with curriculum and "standards." Under this heading, we can group "traditional" criticisms about inadequate "basic skills" (the three Rs) and new criticisms about underdeveloped "problem-solving skills" and appropriate personality attributes such as a teamwork orientation. All these are rolled into the Conference Board of Canada's (1992) *Employability skills profile*. The *Profile* is one reference point for the Business Council on National Issues' proposed minimum competency test (with "high" standards) for entry-level job applicants (*Globe and Mail*, 1993, March 24). Testing to monitor and enforce "standards" is a major issue, reflected in the "School Achievement Indicators" testing program sponsored by the Council of Ministers of Education, Canada (see *CMEC school achievement indicators program bulletins*, beginning November 1991).

Those criticizing the "product quality" of the educational system sometimes argue that poor quality results from giving "voice" to women, ethnic and racial minorities, gays/ lesbians, and other disadvantaged groups in the curriculum, and promoting equity of outcomes for these groups.

Equity issues remain prominent in the politics of education. In some cases, most notably destreaming in Ontario grades 9 and 10, equity issues still "drive" policy. More generally, testing has been resisted on the grounds of equity. The increasing number of ESL (English as a Second Language) students in some jurisdictions has also focussed attention on differences in treatment and outcomes.

Educational authorities must respond to all these dissatisfactions, and more. Whether or not the roof falls in depends critically on public confidence. If schools retain the confidence of stakeholders, teachers retain their freedom to address problems by their own lights. If they lose the confidence of stakeholders, their autonomy is in grave jeopardy. Ontario, at the time of this writing, provides two pointed examples. First, a provincial government, already exploring local school boards in quest of efficiency, has flirted with the idea of eliminating boards altogether. Second, the provincial government has by stages introduced comparative testing, allowing jurisdictions to be held accountable for their own results against the standards others have achieved. This has come about under sustained pressure from elements of the media, employers groups, some parent groups, and evidence of strong public backing for testing in a series of well-publicized polls. "High stakes" testing is the increasingly common price of apparent loss of public confidence (see Lewington & Orpwood, 1993, pp. 44–45, 148–49).

Public confidence for education protects freedom of action. High levels of confidence discourage wider public involvement in decision-making and curb the influence of critical activist groups. Lewington and Orpwood (1993, pp. 42–52) see loss of confidence and its consequences as the result of an excessive autonomy held by "insiders" within the educational system.

There is more at stake than the freedom of action of those within the educational system. Confidence in educational institutions helps buttress the legitimacy of social institutions as a whole. Educational institutions help shape public response to the evident failure of other institutions. Weiler (1982, p. 11) suggests that loss of confidence in educational institutions can accelerate a decline in confidence in other institutions: "Public education is a prime candidate to share in this more general disillusionment. After all, education is the primary mechanism not only for socializing the young but also for allocating social status and the rewards that accompany it."

Over the past two decades, the ability of schooling to guarantee access to higher-status, better-paying work has declined markedly, as indicated by growing underemployment rates among postsecondary graduates (see Clark & Zsigmond, 1981; Livingstone, 1987). Individuals frequently regard such economic rewards as "entitlements." Where expectations are disappointed, the legitimacy of not only educational institutions but political and economic institutions is more likely to be questioned (see Derber, 1978; Lambert & Curtis, 1979; and Baer & Lambert, 1982; see also Johnston, 1986, pp. 54–59, for a more general treatment of interdependence among attitudes to different institutions).

Despite the job difficulties of the well educated, education has become the touchstone for national economic well-being. No less than Robert Reich (1991), economic guru and an important economic adviser to U.S. President Clinton, has argued that a well-educated labour force has become the primary basis of economic competition. This is the updated version of human capital theory. Productivity based on technology can be moved "offshore"; productivity based on the skills of a local workforce cannot. In Canada, government, business and labour leaders, as well as a series of recent commission reports have all identified a better-educated workforce as the key to greater competitiveness (Economic Council of Canada, 1992; Government of Canada, Prosperity Initiative, 1991).

On grounds of economic well-being, confidence in educational institutions should have collapsed at least a decade ago. Returns in terms of income or job status on educational investment for individuals have been declining in terms of both monetary and job status (see Vaillancourt, 1986; Blakely & Harvey, 1988; but see also Krashinsky, 1987). An increasingly better-educated workforce has not led to commensurate increased productivity, increased competitiveness, or increased economic growth. Yet declining confidence in education is a recent phenomenon in Canada. The key to understanding this is, in part, probably time frame. Political institutions are expected to produce "turnarounds" in a relatively short period of time, the space of an electoral term. Public expectations appear to give educational institutions a lot more slack. Our research in Ontario has shown that public evaluations of the importance of postsecondary education have little to do with perceptions of current labour force demand for postsecondary graduates but are anchored in perceptions of future demand (Orbit 1986 survey, p. 11). Moreover, at the individual level, there is some evidence (see Smith, 1986) that people's expectations of returns from personal investment in education have been quick to adjust to the decline in real returns.

Finally, the socializing role of the schools goes well beyond the pragmatics of ensuring an adequately skilled labour force. Schooling has to do with preserving (and sometimes modifying) core societal values. Thus, we should not necessarily expect confidence in schools to wax and wane with perceptions of economic relevance.

THE RECORD ON PUBLIC CONFIDENCE

In each of 1979, 1984, 1989, and 1993, Gallup Canada asked respondents how much confidence they had in eight Canadian social institutions: the churches, Supreme Court, public schools, House of Commons, political parties, newspapers, large corporations, and labour unions (see *Gallup Report*, Feb. 1, 1993). Over a decade, the rank order of institutions in terms of public confidence has remained essentially unchanged (see Figure 2.1). The churches, the Supreme Court, and the public schools have occupied a relatively privileged position. Up to 1989, majorities indicated at least "quite a lot of confidence" in each. In 1993, the figure was 50 percent for the Supreme Court and just over 40 percent for churches and public schools. Other institutions had lower levels of confidence to begin with in 1979, and often experienced proportionally sharper declines.

In other words, the public schools have remained above the fray to a greater extent than might have been expected. In spite of their greater practical relevance to material conditions, confidence in the public schools only began to erode at the end of the 1980s. The drop was then substantial, but still left public confidence in the schools on a par with the churches and second only to the Supreme Court.[2] Meanwhile, confidence in legislative and party institutions slowly declined through the 1980s, then plummeted in the early years of the current decade. The only systematic change in rank order has been the slow sinking in public esteem of the House of Commons. Confidence in the House of Commons dropped from 38 percent in 1979 to 30 percent in 1989 and then to 16 percent in 1993. This paralleled the decline for political parties (not shown in Figure 2.1): 30 percent in 1979, 18 percent a decade later, but only 9 percent in 1993. In 1993, about one in five indicated that they had a "great deal" or "quite a lot" of confidence in large corporations or labour unions. This represented a decline for corporations from 34 percent in 1979, but

---

FIGURE 2.1

Confidence in Institutions: Canada. % 'great deal' or 'quite a lot'

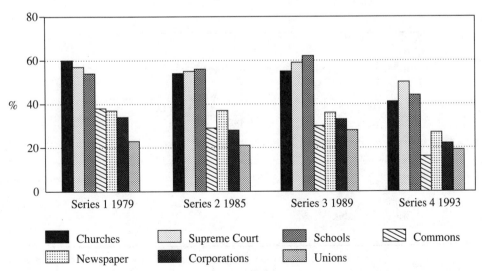

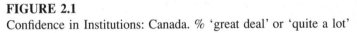

Source: *Gallup Report*, Feb. 1, 1993.

little net change over the period for unions. Business and labour, in 1993, rated somewhere above political institutions. The media, as represented by newspapers, also enjoyed somewhat higher public confidence than political institutions, despite a fall-off in the early 1990s. (National Decima Polls [Gregg and Posner, 1990, pp. 52–68] over the 1980s have also documented a pervasive decline in "trust," showing no net loss between 1980 and 1988, but a decline thereafter.) The recent decline in public confidence in the public schools has occurred across most regions of the country. The exception is Quebec, where there has been little change (see Table 2.1).

In the United States we find a different pattern. Confidence in the school system has consistently declined over the past decade. Figure 2.2 presents trends in American confidence ratings from 1979 to 1991 for seven institutions common to both the Canadian and U.S. Gallup surveys. As in Canada, the public schools were generally grouped with the churches and the Supreme Court on confidence ratings (but in 1979, also newspapers). But as the decade wore on, only the churches retained the confidence of the majority. Ratings of "quite a lot" or higher for the Supreme Court and the public schools dropped below the 40 percent level to rejoin newspapers. However, confidence ratings for Congress and for big business and labour were substantially lower in the United States both in 1979 and 1991. (Note: Figures for newspapers, business, and labour listed under 1989, are for 1988).

In the United Kingdom there is a different pattern (see Figure 2.3). Confidence ratings for the educational system evidenced a very gentle decline over the decade. Most other institutions, excepting major companies and unions, experienced a substantial decline in public confidence. What is striking about the pattern for the United Kingdom is the convergence of confidence ratings for different institutions (particularly if the press, increasingly notorious in the pursuit of sensationalism, is excluded). By 1989, not even the Church or the legal system commanded at least "quite a lot" of confidence from a majority. By 1993, there is no privileged "club" among the seven institutions for the educational system to belong to. It should be noted that majorities continued to have confidence in the armed forces and the police (a pattern found in the United States as well) and in the National Health Services.

TABLE 2.1
Confidence in the Public Schools by Region

| | % 'A GREAT DEAL' OR 'QUITE A LOT' | |
	1989	1993
Atlantic Canada	64	48
Quebec	59	54
Ontario	64	40
Prairies	67	42
British Columbia	57	32
Canada	62	44

Source: *Gallup Report*, Feb. 1, 1993. Unpublished provincial results were supplied to us by Gallup Canada.

FIGURE 2.2

Confidence in Institutions: U.S. % 'great deal' or 'quite a lot'

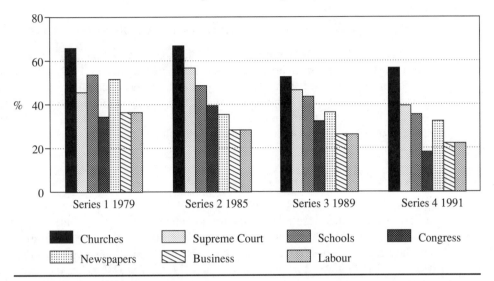

Source: Gallup Poll, Oct. 16, 1991.

FIGURE 2.3

Confidence in Institutions: U.K. % 'great deal' or 'quite a lot'

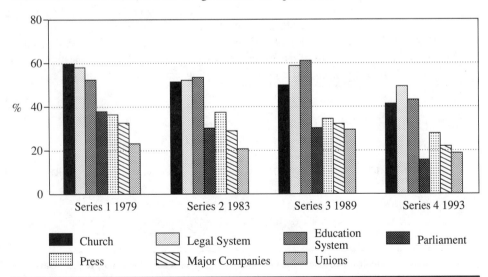

Source: Gallup U.K.

In summary, confidence levels in Canadian schools have held up longer than in the United States and in the early 1990s remain somewhat above levels in both the United States and the United Kingdom.

A NOTE ON PUBLIC VIEWS ON THE IMPORTANCE OF POSTSECONDARY

Over the past decade, the importance the public attaches to getting a university or college education has sharply increased (see Table 2.2). In Ontario, in 1992, three-quarters of respondents to the most recent OISE survey rated a university or college education as very important, compared with about one-third in 1979. Public opinion in the United States has followed a similar pattern. This can be taken as a vote of confidence in the continuing capacity of a higher education to promote well-being.

PERFORMANCE RATINGS

Performance ratings are a step back from confidence ratings. Confidence ratings entail a judgement about how educational authorities will do in the future. Performance ratings are judgements about how things are now. Performance ratings come in three common varieties. The first asks for grade ratings. In 1974, the *Phi Delta Kappan* adopted a letter grade rating system for local public schools (elementary and secondary) to be used in their annual U.S. Gallup poll of public attitudes toward the public schools. Respondents were asked to assign a grade to the quality of the work of the public schools—A, B, C, D, or Fail. This question has subsequently become a standard in public opinion polls of attitudes toward education. The second common measure of educational performance is the satisfaction rating. This asks respondents how satisfied or dissatisfied they are with schools. The third type of rating asks respondents to evaluate current school performance against some past standard. The standard can be one's own education or education at a fixed point in the past, for example, five or ten years ago. Respondents are typically asked if the education students receive has improved, stayed the same, or deteriorated.

Survey questions asking about confidence in institutions have had a standard form in most polls. In the case of performance ratings, however, different question formats are the rule. Apparently small differences in wording can make a lot of difference in the poll

---

TABLE 2.2
Rating the Importance of a University or College Education*

ONTARIO	% 'VERY IMPORTANT'	UNITED STATES†	% 'VERY IMPORTANT'
1979	34	1978	36
1986	61	1983	58
1992	75	1985	64

Source: *Ontario Ministry of Education. Livingstone, D.W., D.J. Hart, & L.E. Davie, 1987 and 1993; †A.M. Gallup, 1985.

results. In the case of satisfaction questions, whether or not a middle term ("neither satisfied or dissatisfied") is included can have a substantial impact on findings. In the case
of comparisons of present with past performance, the particular "benchmark" (one's own
schooling, 25 years ago, 10 years ago, etc.) chosen from the past is clearly important.

We will look at trend lines for all three types of performance ratings: grades, satisfaction
ratings, and change in quality measures referenced to the past. The main issue here is
whether we find patterns of deteriorating performance ratings that parallel or conflict with
trends in confidence ratings. If performance ratings drop in parallel with confidence ratings,
this suggests that confidence has been undermined by negative perceptions of the internal
workings of the school systems. If there is no clear parallel, this suggests that the decline
in confidence in schools mainly reflects perceptions of the relationship of the education
system to other institutions, in particular, the economy.

FALLING GRADES

Canadian Education Association (CEA) surveys in 1979, 1984, and 1992 have asked
respondents to grade the schools in the communities. The results by region and for Canada
as a whole are shown in Table 2.3.

There is no simple correspondence between the pattern of grades awarded to community
schools and the confidence rating in public schools in general. In particular, there is no
evidence of a downturn in grades in recent years corresponding to the decline in confidence
ratings. The proportion of A and B grades awarded nationally in 1984 and 1992 is virtually
identical. It was in the early part of the decade when confidence ratings showed no decline
that there was a fall-off in grades for community schools. As well, patterns of regional
differences for confidence and grade measures, and of changes over time, do not
correspond.

TABLE 2.3
Grades Awarded to Community Schools by Region*

| | % 'A' OR 'B' GRADES | | |
	1979	1984	1990
Atlantic Canada	67	60	48
Quebec	58	46	40
Ontario	62	48	46
Prairies	52	49	57
British Columbia	53	42	38
Canada	59	48	45

*'Students are sometimes given grades A, B, C, D, or F (for Fail) to denote the quality of
their work. Suppose schools in your community were graded in the same way. From your
knowledge, experience, or impressions of the schools in your area, what one grade would
you give these schools?'

Source: CEA, 1979; Flower, 1984; Williams & Millinoff, 1990.

SATISFACTION WITH SCHOOLS

Trends in grades awarded to local schools give little indication of a recent crisis in public evaluations. The same conclusion can be drawn from time series data on public satisfaction with "the education children are receiving today." This Gallup Canada series again shows an early drop-off in performance ratings, in this case, in the 1970s, followed by stability (see Table 2.4).

The OISE surveys have monitored satisfaction with "the school system in general" in Ontario throughout the 1980s. The results reveal a more complex pattern. Satisfaction ratings were stable in the early years of the decade, declined in mid-decade but began to recover after 1988 (OISE 1990 survey). Up to 1982, half of respondents indicated that they were satisfied with the school system. This fell to a little over a third in 1988, but recovered to almost 50 percent by 1990. The OISE question includes a middle option that operates to lower the proportions of respondents citing a definite opinion. An Institute for Social Research (ISR) survey conducted in 1990 without a middle option found 56 percent satisfied with "the education system in Ontario." If those not stating a definite opinion are excluded, the OISE and ISR polls yield identical results.

BETTER OR WORSE?

The grades awarded by the public schools and satisfaction ratings have no explicit baseline. A drop in performance assessments need not reflect views that schools are doing a poorer job. It may rather reflect rising expectations of what the schools should be doing. The results of a different type of question incorporating an explicit baseline allow some clarification of this issue. Since 1948, polls of educational opinion in Canada have asked respondents whether the schools have gotten better or worse. Question formats have not been consistent. We have two sorts of time series available, one based on comparison with the respondent's own schooling, the other on a specific prior point in time.

Looking first at comparisons with the respondent's own schooling (see Table 2.5), we see a very substantial decline between 1948 and 1976 in the proportion of the Canadian

TABLE 2.4
Satisfaction with Education Children Are Getting, by Region*

| | % 'SATISFIED' | | |
	1973	1978	1992
Atlantic Canada	63	44	41
Quebec	39	25	37
Ontario	56	36	30
Prairies	52	43	49
British Columbia		31	25
Canada	51	34	35

*'On the whole, would you say that you are satisfied or dissatisfied with the education children are getting today?'

Source: *Gallup Report*, Sept. 12, 1973; May 24, 1978; Sept. 7, 1992.

TABLE 2.5
'Do you think children today are being better educated or worse than you were?'

	BETTER/ IMPROVED	THE SAME	WORSE/ DETERIORATED	NOT STATED
1948	74	10	12	4
1971	63	12	20	5
1976	49	13	33	5
1981	47	9	38	6
1982	52	12	31	6
1983	41	13	41	5
1989	47	14	34	5

Source: *Gallup Report*, October 12, 1989.

public who think schooling has improved since their day, and a parallel increase in those who perceive deterioration. A large part of this decline is likely due to the additions of increasingly better-educated age cohorts (with correspondingly higher standards) to the adult population over the period. Many respondents have likely interpreted "better educated" as "more educated," that is, more years spent in school. However, the shift in national opinion between 1971 and 1976 surely cannot be ascribed mainly to demographic change but must represent increasing perceptions of real deterioration of the school system from a relatively fixed basis of comparison. After 1976 any shift in opinions as to whether children are better or worse educated is gradual. By the mid-1980s, opinion appears to have stabilized. But the last comparable survey was conducted in 1989.

The second sort of baseline ratings of school performance compared with a prior point in time is available mainly for Ontario. Respondents' assessments of the current quality of high-school education compared with the situation ten years previous are available through a 1976 Ontario Ministry of Education and Ministry of Colleges and Universities poll and OISE surveys between 1979 and 1990 (see Table 2.6). Between 1979 and 1984, the proportion of respondents who thought students were better educated declined slightly. Between 1984 and 1990 there was little change in opinion.

The OISE survey inaugurated a similar assessment for Ontario elementary schools (see Table 2.6). Between 1990 and 1992, the proportion who thought the quality of elementary-level education had deteriorated increased substantially from 30 to 46 percent. This did not, however, represent any decline in the proportion (30 percent) who thought quality had improved. Rather, fewer respondents in 1992 indicated that quality had remained the same, and fewer declined to offer an opinion. The 1990 survey had indicated somewhat harsher assessments of elementary schools compared with high schools. Nevertheless, it is very probable that assessments of high schools declined over the same period. A recent *Toronto Star*/Environics Poll (1993) also asked about whether "the education system in Ontario" had gotten better or worse over the past ten years. Unlike the OISE survey questions, respondents were not offered a "remained the same" option. Fifty-four percent thought education had gotten worse; 28 percent saw improvement. However, when we exclude those not stating a definite opinion, the *Star* poll results and the 1992 OISE survey results (for elementary schools) show similar levels of dissatisfaction.

TABLE 2.6

Have Schools Gotten Better or Worse?

	BETTER/ IMPROVED	THE SAME	WORSE/ DETERIORATED	NOT STATED
Ontario High Schools (Compared to 10 Years Ago)				
1976	31	16	46	8
1979	32	16	42	10
1984	28	17	37	18
1988	27	22	39	12
1990	25	24	39	12
Ontario Elementary Schools (Compared to 10 Years Ago)				
1990	29	26	30	15
1992	30	18	46	7
Ontario's Public Schools (Compared to 25 Years Ago)				
1986	45	24	32	
1993	25	15	50	10
Canadian Public Schools (Compared to 25 Years Ago)				
1986	42	22	35	
1993	30	17	46	7

Source: Ontario Ministry of Colleges and Universities/Ministry of Education (1976). [*Roles and responsibilities of secondary and postsecondary institutions secondary/postsecondary interface study, Project 1.*; Livingstone, D.W., D.J. Hart, & L.E. Davie (1991). "Public attitudes toward education in Ontario" (1990), *Orbit 22* (2); Angus Reid/Southam News (1993, February 5). School system failing 46% say. *Toronto Star.*]

In addition, Angus Reid/Southam News polls (1993) taken in 1986 and 1993 have used a 25-year time frame to assess the quality of public-school education across Canada. As Table 2.6 further indicates, on this criterion the proportion who perceive improvement fell substantially between 1986 and 1993, both in Ontario and Canada as a whole. Again, comparison of the OISE and Angus Reid/Southam News series suggests that the decline in performance ratings has been very recent. This recent erosion in public assessments of the schools appears deeper in Ontario than nationally. This may partly reflect the high degree of recent uncertainty over education policy in Ontario, in particular over issues of destreaming and curriculum reform aimed at a new common curriculum, as well as a protracted debate and major policy shifts on issues of testing.

Overall, trends in opinion on questions dealing with the performance of schools show declines in the mid-1970s or early 1980s but not in the last half of the 1980s. As we have seen, confidence ratings nationally were stable from 1979 to 1988 or 1989. We can conclude that erosion in performance ratings in the early part of the decade did not lead to a crisis of confidence. Moreover the recent (1989–1993) decline in confidence in schools has not been "led" by a prior decline in public evaluations of school performance. There is some evidence, however, that confidence ratings and performance ratings (at least those dealing with improvement or deterioration over the time) have fallen in tandem since 1990.

SUPPORT FOR EDUCATION FUNDING

T he past decade witnessed a concerted effort by the federal Conservative government and several provincial regimes, and by neoconservative regimes in the United Kingdom and the United States, to undermine the postwar pattern of state welfare provisions (health, education, and other welfare benefits) through program cuts, privatization of established services, and policies favouring private market forces. Polling data indicate that throughout this period the majority of Canadians have been willing to cut general government spending to reduce the deficit (Goldfarb Poll, 1984; Gallup Canada, April 22, 1989; Gallup Canada, April 24, 1993; Walker, 1993). However, the types of cutbacks that have drawn majority support are defence spending, subsidies to Crown corporations, and social benefits for the wealthy (Goldfarb Poll, 1984; Goldfarb Consultants, 1985; Speirs, 1990). At the same time, there has been very strong public support for maintaining or even *increasing* taxes and spending on health, education, and other established social welfare provisions (Goldfarb, 1984; Gallup Canada, Nov. 28, 1988; Speirs, 1990; Foster, 1990; Winsor, 1990).

Popular support for increased funding of education per se actually grew significantly during the early 1980s (see Hart and Livingstone, 1993). Since the mid-1980s, most surveys have found strong majority support for increased government funding of education in all regions, as Table 2.7 summarizes. In addition, internal government polls obtained

---

TABLE 2.7
Support for Increased Government Funding of Education by Region, 1986–1992

	% SUPPORTING INCREASED FUNDING								
	ELEMENTARY SCHOOLS			HIGH SCHOOLS			POST-HIGH SCHOOL		
REGION	1986	1991	1992	1986	1991	1992	1986	1991	1992
Atlantic	72	82	84	73	77	82	67	74	81
Quebec	60	71	74	64	72	78	72	68	75
Ontario	67	61	60	67	61	62	68	61	63
Prairies	66	65	69	68	61	68	61	63	67
B.C.	75	79	72	73	78	67	72	74	62
Canada	66	68	69	68	67	69	68	66	68

Source: Gallup Canada (1986, Dec. 1) "2 in 3 Canadians favour more funds for education." *The Gallup Report*. Gallup Canada (Bozinoff, L., & Turcotte, A.) (1992, September 7) "Canadians dissatisfied with the education children are receiving." *The Gallup Report*.

through the Access to Information Act showed strong majority opposition to the reduction of transfer payments to the provinces for postsecondary education both before and after the federal government took this step in early 1990 (Poitras, 1990), and most Canadians have recently expressed support for increased spending on education *even if* the deficit increases (*Maclean's*/CTV Poll, 1993).

So, in Canada, as in the United Kingdom and the United States (Taylor-Gooby, 1991; Cook & Barrett, 1988), the public's endorsement of the welfare state in general and government education funding in particular appears to have *strengthened* despite neoconservative ideology of provincial and federal political regimes committed to reducing government services. Of course, any political party that wishes to be elected in a liberal democratic state must demonstrate a certain "rhetorical elasticity" in its ideology, such as the campaign promises of the Mulroney Conservatives that universal social programs were a "sacred trust." Conversely, in a capitalist economy, any social democratic regime must also ultimately face hard spending constraints provoked by economic slumps, as even provincial NDP governments have done recently. In any event, the choice of restricting education funding rather than pursuing other options, such as progressive taxation measures, major defence expenditure cuts, or even deficit financing of education, clearly responds to the sentiments of a very small minority of the Canadian electorate. As Figure 2.4 reveals for the case of Ontario, since the mid-1980s majorities in all classes of non-agricultural employees have usually supported increased education funding. Employers generally have tended to be less supportive. But only among the tiny and powerful numbers of corporate executives was there consistent majority opposition to increased education spending as popular support grew. Even those demographic groups often presumed to have the least direct interest in education—the elderly and high-school dropouts —significantly strengthened their support for increased education funding during the 1980s

FIGURE 2.4

Educational Spending Preference. % increase spending

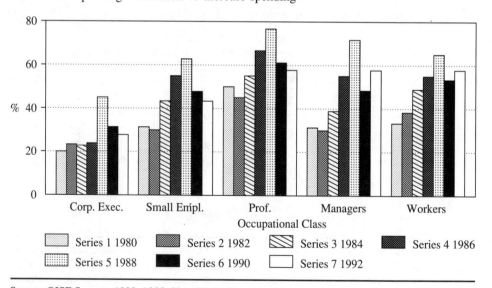

Source: OISE Surveys 1980–1992. Unpublished.

(Hart & Livingstone, 1993), leaving corporate business sentiments increasingly isolated on this issue.

It is in this context that public interest in educational privatization should be seen. There have been numerous recent calls for increased government funding of private schools and for voucher systems of financial credits for each child's education, which are designed to make parental choice of schools more like a consumer marketing decision. The Canadian public as a whole has been relatively tolerant of cultural diversity while also supporting the democratic right to individual choice in education (e.g., Holmes, 1992). According to the only available survey, Canadians are now more inclined to support than oppose a voucher system that would increase parental choice among government-approved schools (OISE 1992 survey). However, in spite of the significant growth of support for increased government funding of public schools during the past decade as well as growth in the still tiny minority who do send their children to private schools, only a stable minority of Canadians in general has continued to express support for government funding of private schools (OISE 1992 survey, pp. 8–10).

TESTING AND CURRICULUM

Accountability through testing is an issue of the day. It is hardly news that polls have consistently found strong majority support for testing. The public is now united on the desirability of comparative testing ("standardized tests"). Teachers' federations have generally been opposed. (Teachers themselves appear to be more divided and their views more nuanced. See King & Peart, 1992, pp. 79–81). Yet the contrast may be less drastic, or at least more complex, than it seems. While the public is strongly supportive of comparative testing, it does not support "test-driven" education. Teachers' federations have typically regarded comparative testing as automatically leading to "test-driven" instruction. This suggests that the public and teachers are united in regard to what happens in classrooms and in their view that testing should not determine curriculum. They may be divided over the need for "objective" measures of outcomes and over the prospect of such measures overriding the professional autonomy of teachers.

Recent evidence of public support for testing is readily at hand. In November 1991, 71 percent of respondents to an Environics Poll (1992, p. 12) agreed that "there should be nation-wide testing of Canadian school students." A recent Angus Reid/Southam News poll (1993, p. A1) found that 76 percent of Canadians would support "standardized testing in our educational system." In September 1992, 73 percent of Ontario respondents to the OISE survey agreed that 'province-wide tests should be used to assess the individual performance of elementary school students." This represented a sharp increase from 1990, when the figure was 59 percent. In May 1993, 91 percent of respondents to a *Toronto Star*/Environics Poll (1993, p. A1) said "yes" when asked, "Should Ontario elementary and secondary school students be required to take standardized test in literacy and mathematics?"

These questions are a mixed lot. Terminology varies: "national tests," "standardized tests," "province-wide test." Only the OISE question specifies what tests are to be used for (assessing individual students). The distinctions between low-stakes and high-stakes tests are not made, nor is it stated for whom the tests might be high stakes. As it stands at the time of writing, Ontario students will participate in four programs involving standardized testing: the Third International Math and Science Study, the interprovincial School Achievement Indicators Study, the Ontario Ministry of Education and Training Benchmarks Study, and the recently announced Grade 9 reading and writing tests to be taken by all Ontario Grade 9 students. None of these tests will be "high stakes" for students in the sense of affecting their marks or progress through the grades. They will, however, be "high stakes" for educational authorities identified as responsible for the results.

Testing issues inevitably lead to curriculum issues, if they did not start there in the first place. Comparative testing across jurisdictions (be these provinces or boards/districts within provinces) represents a force for standardization in the content areas tested and a force for prioritizing tested over untested content areas. Testing policy will drive curriculum if curriculum policy does not drive testing. Yet, while public views on testing are well documented, there has been little *systematic* research on the public's curriculum priorities at the elementary and secondary level. Lewington and Orpwood (1993, p. 113) note the conflict between "old basics" (reading, writing, and arithmetic), championed by some, highly vocal, parents' groups, and the "new basics," stressing "problem-solving" and team work, advocated by some business groups. These variants of neoconservative orientations to curriculum contend with liberal democratic curriculum objectives, notably representation of the histories, experiences, and viewpoints of disadvantaged groups. The Canadian public's views of the scope of the curriculum and curricular priorities have more often been imputed than solicited.

PROVINCE-WIDE TESTING AND ASSESSMENTS BY LOCAL TEACHERS

The OISE surveys provide evidence that public support for province-wide testing should not be read as support for an education system "driven" by non-local tests. While an overwhelming majority support province-wide testing, only a very small minority want such tests to be the most important means of assessing students. In 1990, only 9 percent of respondents to the OISE survey wanted provincial tests to be most important in judging the academic progress of *elementary* school students. Similarly small minorities in the 1979, 1982, and 1988 OISE surveys had supported giving priority to provincial tests in assessing students "in high grades" (OISE 1988 survey, p. 21). The 1988 OISE survey documented that these views on the *best* means of assessing students co-existed with majority support for the use of province-wide tests. In support of OISE survey results, a poll conducted by the Institute for Social Research (ISR) (1991, p. 4) found only 13 percent thought students' progress should be judged by province-wide tests alone. (This option is, admittedly, more extreme than the position taken by most proponents of testing.)

Public support for province-wide testing does not translate into an identification of accountability with meeting externally set standards. Issues of local input and influence on student assessment intervene. Both the OISE survey and ISR questions juxtaposed province-wide tests to local options. In the case of the ISR question, the alternative was "parents and teachers" as "best to judge a student's progress." Twenty-nine percent selected this option; 52 percent opted for both province-wide tests *and* the judgements of parents and teachers. The options for the OISE question are shown in Table 2.8.

Just over half of respondents — parents and the general public alike — supported a wholly locally based option as the best way to assess elementary students' academic progress. (The proportions were similar in 1979, 1982, and 1988 when the question was asked about students "in the higher grades.") One-third of respondents thought that the best way to assess progress involved joint local/provincial responsibility, while only a small minority

TABLE 2.8

'Which one of the following do you think is the best way of judging the academic progress of students in elementary school?' (Ontario, 1990)

	ALL RESPONDENTS %	PARENTS %	NON-PARENTS %
The Individual Teacher Should Have Sole Responsibility for Making Assessments.	20	20	20
Assessments Should Be Based on Tests Set Jointly by Teachers in The School.	34	37	31
Provincial Tests Should Be Used to Supplement Teacher-made Tests.	35	34	35
Provincial Tests Should Be Most Important.	9	7	11
Don't Know/Not Stated	3	3	3

Source: Livingstone, D.W., D.J. Hart, & L.E. Davie, 1991.

would hand the job to provincial tests alone. While the majority of the public were wedded to the test format as the best means of student assessment, local teacher-made tests alone or in conjunction with province-wide tests were seen as key.

The British Social Attitudes Surveys in 1987 and 1990 (Hasley, 1992, p. 54) have documented similar popular reservations over the dominance of formal examinations. In both years more respondents agreed than disagreed that "formal exams are the best way of judging the ability of students." However, the proportion who agreed fell short of 50 percent. In contrast, more than 60 percent in both years agreed that "a pupil's everyday classroom work counts for too little." (However, opinion did tilt somewhat toward exams and away from classroom work, over the period.)

TESTING AND TEACHING ORIENTATIONS

Public debates over testing have been closely linked to broader divisions in views on education. In these debates, neoconservative support for testing is related to support for a common curriculum concentrated on the "basics" and opposed to social democratic advocates' emphasis on autonomy to adapt curriculum to local conditions and the interests of students. Testing is also linked by neoconservative opinion leaders to support for a common standard of achievement (and, less consistently, to a positive view of competition as encouraging achievement), in contrast to child-centred approaches that stress individualized rates and ways of learning. These associations are tendencies, of course, to which exceptions could readily be found. Nevertheless, it is striking how frequently public views fail to follow these ideological or political definitions of consistency.

In 1984, when the OISE survey first asked whether province-wide tests should be used to assess the individual performance of (high-school) students, this was immediately preceded by a question on who should have the most influence on what is taught in local schools. Respondents were almost equally split over whether local groups (school board, local teachers, parents), or the provincial or federal government should have the most influence over curriculum. Those who chose one of the local options were less likely to support use of province-wide tests than others, but the difference was narrow: 63 versus 73 percent. In other words, a substantial majority of those who favoured a dominant local influence on curriculum also favoured province-wide tests, usually regarded in the ideologically charged debates as an instrument of centralized control over what is taught in local schools. (The 1992 OISE survey included a more general question asking whether the involvement of various groups in the operation of local schools should increase, decrease, or stay the same. While this question does not specifically reference curriculum, the results are instructive. Views on what should happen to the involvement of different groups in the operation of local schools had no bearing on opinion regarding province-wide testing. Those who wanted more involvement of teachers and parents in the operation of local schools were no less likely than others to support province-wide testing; those who favoured more Ministry of Education involvement were no more likely to indicate support for testing.)

The 1992 OISE survey also asked respondents to select the single most useful information to parents regarding how their child is doing in elementary school (see Table 2.9). The three options for standards of assessment (not necessarily through testing) were self-referencing to the individual student's own past performance, using the performance of other students as the norm and, finally, using explicit official standards or benchmarks of acceptable performance. The first is associated with child-centred education, the second with norm-referenced standardized testing, and the third with criterion-referenced testing. The survey found no consensus among the Ontario public as to which should take priority, but strongest support (49 percent) was for the child-centred option. Among corporate executives, however, there was a strong consensus (72 percent) on benchmarks. This is consistent with the priority of business groups on ensuring all students reach an acceptable level of literacy, numeracy, and other generic "basic" skills. Among the general public,

TABLE 2.9

Support for Use of Province-wide Tests at the Elementary Level by Views on Most Useful Information to Parents of Elementary School Students (Ontario, 1992)

MOST USEFUL INFORMATION TO PARENTS		% AGREEING WITH PROVINCE-WIDE TESTS		
	%	ALL RESPONDENTS	PARENTS	NON-PARENTS
How Their Child's Skills Compare to How They Were Doing Earlier.	49	64	63	65
How Their Child's Skills Compare to Those of Other Students.	16	76	73	77
How Their Child's Skills Compare to Official Standards or Benchmarks.	29	85	83	86
Don't Know/Not Stated	6	75	54	82

Source: Livingstone, D.W., D.J. Hart, & L.E. Davie, 1992.

those who selected the child-centred option were least likely to support province-wide testing. However, whether respondents held child-centred, norm-oriented, or benchmark-oriented priorities, a majority supported province-wide tests. This is the case for both parent and non-parents.

That public views are frequently, even typically, "inconsistent" when judged by the standards of opinion-leaders has been a common finding of opinion research (see Jennings, 1992). Minimally, the above results suggest that broad and growing support for testing does not signal wholesale public rejection of child-centred perspectives, nor do they suggest popular support for the *imposition* of a common curriculum.

CURRICULUM

The current wave of ideologically based criticism of the schools is mainly focussed on learning outcomes (although, as noted earlier, equity issues continue to be expressed). Yet there is little documentation of what outcomes the public wants the schools to teach beyond "basic" literacy and numeracy and, at the high-school level, occupational preparation. Here we use the limited data available to argue that public priorities for the curriculum are fundamentally pragmatic. This means they focus on "enabling skills" for work and for further education. These skills extend beyond the old "basics" (literacy and numeracy) to embrace both technological change, higher-level cognitive skills, and social skills.

In the five OISE surveys between 1978 and 1984 respondents were asked to select the educational objectives that should have the highest and second-highest priorities in high school. (This is, to our knowledge, the only time series on curriculum preferences for Canada.) In each year, job training was the most frequently cited objective; it was, in fact, the only objective that attracted majority support. There was, however, growing support for basic literacy and numeracy skills over the period.

Corporate executives were much less likely than the general public to make job training and career preparation a priority (see Table 2.10). In 1984, less than one-third of corporate executives cited job training as their first or second priority, compared with almost

TABLE 2.10
Curriculum Priorities at the High-School Level: The General Public and Corporate Executives (Ontario, 1984)

CURRICULUM OBJECTIVE	% RANKING AS FIRST OR SECOND PRIORITY	
	GENERAL PUBLIC	CORPORATE EXECUTIVES
Job Training and Career Preparation	64	30
Basic Reading, Writing, and Number Skills	40	63
Everyday Life Skills such as Money Management	26	7
Creativity and Imagination; Critical Thinking	22	81
Sense of Right and Wrong	11	5
Preparation for Future Roles as Parents	10	0
Ability to Get Along with Others	8	6

Source: Livingstone, D.W., D.J. Hart, & L.D. McLean, 1985.

two-thirds of the general population. Conversely, four in five corporate executives cited "creativity and imagination" or "critical thinking" as a priority, compared with little more than one in five of the public. For executives, generic skills related to problem-solving and flexible response to changing circumstances appear to take precedence over specific occupational skills.

In the 1984 OISE survey, respondents were also asked to indicate what subjects they would make compulsory in high school (see Table 2.11). Respondents were requested to provide separate tests according to the destination of students after high school: university, community college, or full-time employment. The two subjects that a majority agreed should be compulsory for all student streams were mathematics and use of the computers. Literacy (language study) received majority support for university-bound students, and near-majority support for other streams. However, while a majority would make business

TABLE 2.11

If you were the one to decide, what subjects would you require every high school student to take who plans to . . .?

				U.S.	
	GO TO UNIVERSITY %	GO TO COMMUNITY COLLEGE %	GET A FULL-TIME JOB %	GO TO COLLEGE %	NOT GO TO COLLEGE %
Mathematics	80	68	65	96	92
Use of Computers	57	57	54	68	68[a]
Language of Instruction (English or French)	54	48	43	94	90[b]
Science	46	32	21	84	61
Business and Vocational Studies	36	58	69	68/37[c]	76/83
Second Language (English or French)	35	24	27	57[d]	19[d]
History	33	21	15	84[e]	71[e]
Social Sciences	25	22	19	—	—
Geography	24	17	12	—	—
Physical and Health Education	17	16	11	43/52[c]	44/50[c]
Arts and Music	11	9	6	24/22[c]	18/18[c]

a. "Computer training" is an option on a second question in the U.S. survey concerning what additional areas should be required. No distinction is made regarding destination of students.

b. The U.S. option is "English."

c. Percentages are, in order, for separate options on the U.S. study.

d. The U.S. option is "foreign language."

e. The U.S. option is "history/U.S. government."

Source: George H. Gallup. "The 16th Annual Gallup Poll of the Public's Attitudes toward the Public Schools." *Phi Delta Kappan*, September 1984, pp. 30–31.

and vocational studies compulsory for students intending to enter community college or the workforce, this subject received minority support for the university stream, ranking well below science and on a par with second language learning and history. Thus, the overall priority for job training, indicated above, does not extend to the university-bound stream. However, the 1980 and 1986 OISE surveys also documented popular views that the university curriculum should become more oriented to labour force needs.

We draw two conclusions from these responses. The first is that there is consensus in the Canadian public on only a very narrow "core curriculum" at the high-school level: the old "basics," literacy and numeracy, and one new "basic," computer literacy. This core appears considerably narrower than that defined by the American public (see Table 2.11), particularly in excluding history and science. The subjects that receive majority support in Ontario appear to represent a pragmatic focus heavily influenced by employment concerns. This is suggested by the inclusion of computer literacy within "basics" and by majority support for compulsory business and vocational studies for all but the university-bound. For the university-bound stream, uncertainty over what are the pragmatic choices appears to have been translated into broader support for making more subjects compulsory. On average, respondents selected over four compulsory courses for students going to university, compared with less than four where the destination is community college, and only three where it is the labour force. In contrast to the general public, a majority of corporate executives favoured making history compulsory for all students, and science and geography compulsory for those going to college or university.

The 1988 and 1992 OISE surveys asked respondents to select priorities from lists (different in each year) *excluding literacy and numeracy*. In 1988, the list included a mix of subject areas (e.g., science, geography), generic skills (e.g., problem solving), and moral development (e.g., sense of right and wrong) options. Traditional subject areas received relatively little support. In 1992, the list of options was more narrowly focussed on content areas including traditional subjects, "use of computers," and career awareness. Once again, traditional subject areas (except science) did relatively poorly. "Use of computers" was the overwhelming priority, being the first or second choice of four in five.

The common factor in all these results was the relatively marginal position of traditional subjects. There was little indication of popular support for a "cultural literacy" priority encompassing a basic knowledge of history, for example (except among corporate executives). Beyond this, the incompatibility of question formats allowed few generalizations.

A recent national Environics Poll (1992, p. 10), however, provides some clues. Respondents were asked to rate the importance of each item in a short list of very general "goals of education." Learning skills and analysis skills, occupational and career-oriented knowledge and skills, and social skills (ability to get along and work with others) all garnered "very important"; just under half rated cultural values, including appreciation of the arts, at this level. There is a pragmatism here in the sense that all highly ranked areas involved "enabling" skills relevant to work. But it is a pragmatism far removed from the old "basics."

BELIEFS IN EDUCATIONAL EQUALITY

From the beginnings of mass schooling in Canada, advocates have frequently asserted the general capacity of schooling to provide equal opportunities for each individual to develop his or her abilities. In times of economic expansion, the schools' capacity to promote upward social mobility among the disadvantaged has also been proclaimed, while in tough times, such as the present period, there has been more public rhetoric about general upgrading of skills and selection for scarce positions through meritocratic "excellence" (see Carlton, 1984). In contrast to such ideological claims of educational equality, there is now a vast amount of research documenting systematic discrimination in the schools on grounds of class origins, race, and gender (e.g., Anisef et al., 1982; Gaskell & McLaren, 1991; Curtis et al., 1992). However, much of this discriminatory treatment is subtly embedded in language codes, curricular forms, and student selection criteria, and its consequences are most clearly expressed in unequal collective rates of educational attainment. Such inequities are often difficult for either individual students or teachers, let alone the general public, to comprehend fully in their daily experience.

At the most abstract level of belief, there has been near unanimity in Canadian public support for equal educational opportunities in general and for various social groups (e.g., Mason, 1984; Carleton Journalism School, 1985). There also appears to have been widespread acceptance of the claim that equality of opportunity prevails as a *general* operating principle in the schools. As Table 2.12 summarizes for Ontario in 1986, strong majorities expressed the view that students from all occupational class and ethnic backgrounds as well as both sexes have an equal chance of getting a higher education.

However, as Table 2.12 further suggests, public perceptions of equal opportunities may have declined somewhat in recent years, at least in terms of opportunities by class origins. Certainly on the experiential issue of the existence of bias in the schools against students from working-class families, more people now acknowledge class bias than deny it. Among occupational classes, only corporate executives strongly deny the existence of such a class bias (OISE 1990 survey, p. 13). School trustees in Toronto have recently responded to this growing popular perception by approving the first explicit Canadian policy against class bias in teaching materials (Duffy, 1993).

With regard to perceptions of gender bias, under the impetus of women's increased participation in paid labour and the feminist movement, a majority of Canadians now say that women have fewer general opportunities than men, and the proportion holding this critical view has grown across the country since the mid-1980s (Gallup Canada *Gallup Report*, 1993). There is also strong majority support for affirmative action in such matters

TABLE 2.12
Perceptions of Equality of Opportunity for Higher Education, Ontario

	% AGREEING		
	1979	1986	1988
Students from Families of All Occupational Backgrounds Have an Equal Chance of Getting a Higher Education.	75	72	62
Students from All Ethnic Backgrounds Have an Equal Opportunity of Getting a Higher Education.		82	
Both Boys and Girls Have an Equal Opportunity of Getting a Higher Education.		90	

Source: Livingstone, D.W., D.J. Hart, & L.E. Davie, 1987 and 1993.

as encouraging girls to take high-school math programs (OISE 1992 survey, p. 18). However, affirmative-action employment programs have begun to provoke backlash in these times of heightened economic uncertainty. For example, there has been declining general support since the mid-1980s for the hiring of more women elementary principals, as well as a growing gender gap on this issue. Corporate executives, the most predominantly male of all occupational classes, remain most strongly opposed to such programs. Women are generally both more perceptive of gender bias in education and more supportive of affirmative-action programs to overcome it (OISE 1992 survey, p. 19).

Similarly, visible-minority groups who have established themselves in this country are now expressing their perceptions that they have been treated in discriminatory ways in Canadian schools (*Toronto Star*, 1992). Both the mass media and Canadians in general appear to be becoming somewhat less tolerant toward immigrants as the economic slump has persisted (Watson, 1990; Thompson, 1993). However, the most distinctive ethnic bias in Canadian education involves French and English views on minority-language education (Bula, 1992).

CONCLUSIONS

There has been a nearly universal decline of public confidence in all major institutions since the 1970s in Canada, as in the United Kingdom and the United States, with scarcely any institution retaining the clear confidence of more than a minority by the early 1990s. The protracted economic slump left many institutions with a diminished capacity to "deliver the goods." But all three countries also witnessed the ascendancy of a dominant political ideology of neoconservatism, which criticized public institutions in terms of their denial of entrepreneurial initiative. The subsequent restructuring of public institutions appears to have provoked an even more substantial decline in confidence. Confidence ratings in Canada have remained higher and, in the case of public confidence in the schools, only began dropping at the end of the 1980s.

Declines in performance ratings for schools in Canada were registered in the 1970s and early 1980s. There was a substantial decline in grades awarded to local schools in the early 1980s, but virtually no net change between 1984 and 1990. Satisfaction with schools declined sharply in the mid-1970s, but by 1992 was no lower than in 1978. In terms of perceptions of changing quality in education compared with the past, the period of sharp decline in public evaluations of the schools occurred in the 1970s. We can conclude that erosion in performance ratings through the early part of the 1980s did not lead to an immediate crisis of public confidence in Canadian schools. However, confidence ratings and performance ratings have fallen in tandem since 1990.

Declining performance ratings and general public confidence in the schools have *not* translated into declining popular support for government funding of education. A growing majority of Canadians have expressed support for *increased* spending on education as well as for maintaining health and other established social welfare provisions. The general public appears to retain a basic belief in the potential of the schools to improve their performance and our lives if only they are given more adequate resources. At the same time, there is strong popular support in Canada for cutting government spending on such items as defence and social benefits to the wealthy in order to reduce the public debt.

Public opinion polls have consistently found majority support for comparative testing, but not "test-driven" education. The OISE surveys indicate that only a very small minority want such tests to be the most important means of assessing students. Public support is low for accountability by meeting externally set standards. Issues of local influence on student assessment intervene. Recent polls suggest that public consensus on curriculum at the high-school level in all highly ranked areas now involves "enabling" skills relevant to work. This pragmatism goes far beyond the old "basics" and is in line with the skill dimensions of the relatively broad-based "Employability Skills Profile" developed by the Conference Board of Canada. But for most people the main interest has been in well-defined training and preparation for secure jobs and careers.

Throughout the postwar era, Canadians have supported liberal democratic ideology, in particular the equality of educational opportunity, both as a desired goal and as a perceived operating principle in the schools. But public perceptions of educational inequalities along class, gender, and ethnic lines have increased, as has support for ensuring equal access to advanced education programs.

Popular demand for schooling is rapidly creating a "permanent education culture" especially through the expansion of continuing education programs. Over the past generation, Canadians have consistently supported greater public participation in running the schools. Support for greater parent, teacher, and student involvement has increased during the past decade, and there is also now majority support for increased involvement of business and labour groups.

These are some of the major trends and most general patterns of consensus and division that characterize public attitudes toward Canada's schools. The most significant finding is that the recently dominant Anglo-American neoconservative ideology of school reform reflects quite closely the views of most corporate executives but not those of the majority of the Canadian public on many educational issues. The general public increasingly tends to hold more democratic views on educational funding, testing, accessibility, and educational decision-making.

The views of the majority of Canadians will be reflected in their continuing threat to established educational provisions, their growing collective self-awareness of their own attitudes toward schooling, and the sustained public dialogue. But, as one of our most insightful political philosophers, Charles Taylor (1993), has observed, what has distinguished modern Canada as a political community has been the popular aspiration toward participatory democratic self-rule within the deep diversity of decentralized political cultures. At least in educational issues, this popular aspiration appears to be alive and growing. In light of declining public confidence in the condition of Canada's schools, can the assertion of a popular democratic educational ideology be far behind?[3]

DISCUSSION QUESTIONS

❑   Canadian education is well supported financially compared with most other systems, and opinion polls indicate that most people are more or less satisfied with the system. Explain why you agree or disagree with the public opinion expressed in the polls regarding the education system of your province.

❑   Despite the overall approval it receives, the education system contains some weak spots. As a teacher and as a taxpayer, how would you like to change the system to make it more responsive to the public's expectations?

❏   If the goal of education is to prepare a person to become a responsible and productive member of the society and an individual capable of realizing his or her destiny to the fullest of its meaning, then how would you explain the public perception of priorities in curriculum subjects, according to the destination of students after high school?

❏   Is elitism generally favoured in Canadian education system? If yes, how would you reconcile it with the principle of equality in education? If no, how would you explain the student selection criteria for admission to universities and/or colleges?

NOTES

1.   Since 1978, our own Ontario surveys have been the only regularly administered, publicly disseminated survey of public attitudes toward educational policy options in Canada. These surveys have all been published by OISE Press. They are as follows: D.W. Livingstone, *Public attitudes toward education in Ontario 1979*; Livingstone & Hart, *Public attitudes toward education in Ontario 1980* and *1981*; Livingstone, Hart, & Davie, *Public attitudes toward education in Ontario 1984, 1985, 1986, 1987, 1988, 1989, 1990, 1992,* and *1993*. The OISE surveys are also distinctive in their inclusion of supplementary representative samples of corporate executives, whose influence on provincial and federal educational policies has tended to far exceed their tiny numbers (see Arvay, 1984).

2.   A Gallup Poll conducted in April 1994 (see *The Gallup Report*, May 2, 1994) found little change in confidence ratings from a year earlier across institutions. A slight erosion in confidence in the Supreme Court has resulted in very similar levels of public confidence in the Court, the churches, and public schools.

3.   The emergence of a more popularly resonant ideology that *combines* liberal democratic equality concerns with a neoconservative market orientation is already discernible in customer-driven models of decentralized governance, which their advocates claim can empower disadvantaged local communities, particularly in terms of access to schooling (see especially Osborne & Gaebler, 1992).

REFERENCES

Abercrombie, N., Hill, S., & Turner, B. (1980). *The dominant ideology thesis.* London: Allen and Unwin.

Adams, M., et al. (1972). *Quality of education in Ontario: A survey of the parent's perspective.* Toronto: Environics Research Group.

Angus Reid/Southam News Poll. (1993, Feb. 5). School system failing 46% say. *Toronto Star,* p. A1.

Anisef, P., Okihiro, N., & James, C. (1982). *Losers and winners: The pursuit of equality and social justice in higher education.* Toronto: Butterworths.

Arvay, S. (1984). *The role of intra-capitalist class conflict in the development of education in Ontario.* Doctoral dissertation, Department of Sociology, York University.

Baer, D., & Lambert, R.D. (1982, May). Education and support for dominant ideology. *Canadian Review of Sociology and Anthropology, 19*(2), pp. 171–95.

Blakely, J.H., & Harvey, E.B. (1988). Market and non-market effects on male and female occupational status attainment. *Canadian Review of Anthropology and Sociology, 25*(1), 23–40.

Bradburn, N., & Sudman, S. (1988). *Polls and surveys: Understanding what they tell us.* San Francisco: Jossy-Bass.

Bula, F. (1992, Mar. 1). Attitudes, cash crunch threaten minority schools: Pollster. *Montreal Gazette*, p. A2.

Canadian Labour Market and Productivity Centre. (1990). *Business and labour leaders speak out on training and education.* Ottawa: CLMPC.

Carlton, R. (1984). Educational policies and the labour force: A historical perspective on the Ontario case. In A. Wipper (Ed.). *The sociology of work.* Ottawa: Carleton University Press.

Carleton Journalism School. (1985). Untitled survey of public attitudes toward Ontario universities. Ottawa: Carleton University Academic Staff Association.

Carnoy, M., & Levin, H. (1985). *Schooling and working the democratic state.* Stanford: Stanford University Press.

CEA Task Force on Public Involvement in Educational Decisions. (1979). *Results of a Gallup Poll of public opinion in Canada about public involvement in educational decisions* (Report No. 1). Toronto: CEA.

Clark, W., & Zsigmond, Z. (1981). *Job market reality for post-secondary graduates.* Ottawa: Minister of Supply and Services.

Cohen, M. (1994). New structures for training: Democratic potentials. Doctoral thesis, University of Toronto.

Conference Board of Canada (Maryann McLaughlin). (1992). *Employability skills profile: What are employers looking for?* Report 81-92-E.

Cook, F., & Barrett, E. (1988, Winter). Public support for social security. *Journal of Aging Studies, 2*(4), 339–56.

Corporate–Higher Education Forum. (1992). *Learning goals for K–12 education: To be our best.* Montreal: The Forum.

Council of Ministers of Education, Canada. (1991, *Bulletin* 1 issued in November). *CMEC school achievement indicators program bulletin.*

Curti, M. (1935). *The social ideas of American educators.* Paterson, NJ: Littlefield, Adams and Co.

Curtis, B., Livingstone, D.W., & Smaller, H. (1992). *Stacking the deck: The streaming of working class kids in Ontario schools.* Toronto: Our Schools/Our Selves Education Foundation.

D'Aquino, T.(1990). Business Council on National Issues remarks to the *Financial Post* conference, Building a competitive workforce. Cited in Government of Canada, 1991, p. i-2.

Derber, C. (1978, October). Unemployment and the entitled worker: Job entitlement and radical political attitudes among the youthful unemployed. *Social Problems 26*, 26–37.

Duffy, A. (1993, June 25). Toronto school trustees approve class-bias policy. *Toronto Star*, p. A21.

Economic Council of Canada. (1991). *Employment in the service economy.* Ottawa: Minister of Supply and Services.

Economic Council of Canada. (1992). *A lot to learn: Education and training in Canada.* Ottawa: Minister of Supply and Services.

Environics Poll. (1992, January 16). *Education in Canada: An overview of public attitudes.* A presentation to the Ontario Public School Boards' Association.

Fennell, T. (1993, January 11). What's wrong at school. *Maclean's,* pp. 28–32.

Flower, G.E. (1984). *Speaking out: The 1984 CEA poll of Canadian opinion on education.* Toronto: CEA.

Foster, J. (1990, August 29). Voters say they seek changes. *Toronto Star,* p. A11.

Gallup Canada (Canadian Institute of Public Opinion) (1973, September 12). Only half are satisfied with today's education. *The Gallup Report.*

Gallup Canada (CIPO) (1978, May 24). Majority are dissatisfied with today's education. *The Gallup Report.*

Gallup Canada (1986, December 1). 2 in 3 Canadians favour more funds for education. *The Gallup Report.*

Gallup Canada (Bozinoff, L., & MacIntosh, P.) (1988, November 28). Canadians against tax cut if services are reduced. *The Gallup Report.*

Gallup Canada (Bozinoff, L., & MacIntosh, P.) (1989, February 9). Confidence in political parties declines. *The Gallup Report.*

Gallup Canada (Bozinoff, L., & MacIntosh, P.) (1989, April 22). Selected budget cutbacks endorsed by Canadian public. *The Gallup Report.*

Gallup Canada (Bozinoff, L., & MacIntosh, P.) (1989, October 12). 47% believe children today receive superior education. *The Gallup Report.*

Gallup Canada (Bozinoff, L, & MacIntosh, P.) (1991, September 5). Vast majority of Canadians favour increased education funding. *The Gallup Report.*

Gallup Canada (Bozinoff, L., & Turcotte, A.) (1992, September 7). Canadians dissatisfied with the education children are receiving. *The Gallup Report.*

Gallup Canada (Bozinoff, L., & Turcotte, A.) (1993, February 1). Canadians are losing respect in their institutions. *The Gallup Report.*

Gallup Canada *Gallup Report* (1993, March 8). Cited in Women get raw deal, pollsters told. *Toronto Star,* p. A1.

Gallup Canada (Bozinoff, L., & Turcotte, A.) (1993, April 24). Canadians want to reduce the deficit. *The Gallup Report.*

Gallup, A.M. (1985, September). The 17th annual Gallup Poll of the public's attitudes toward the public schools. *Phi Delta Kappan, 67*(1).

Gallup, G.H. (1984, September). The 16th annual Gallup Poll of the public's attitudes toward the public schools. *Phi Delta Kappan, 66*(1).

Gallup, G. Jr. (1991, October 16). Confidence in institutions. In *The Gallup Poll, Public Opinion 1991.* Wilmington, DE: Scholarly Resources Inc.

Gaskell, J., & McLaren, A. (Eds.). (1991). *Women and education.* Calgary: Detselig Enterprises.

Globe and Mail. (1993, March 24).

Goldfarb Consultants. (1985, September). *Survey of attitudes in Ontario: A research report for the Ontario government.* Toronto: Government of Ontario.

Goldfarb Poll. (1984, September 19). Reported in 86% support cutting aid to wealthy, poll shows. *Toronto Star,* p. A2.

Government of Canada, Prosperity Initiative. (1991). *Learning well . . . Living well . . .* Ottawa: Minister of Supply and Services.

Gramsci, A. (1971). *Selections from the Prison Notebooks.* New York: International Publishers.

Gregg, A., & Posner, M. (1990). *The big picture: What Canadians think about almost everything.* Toronto: MacFarlane, Walter and Ross.

Halsey, A.H. (1992). Failing education? In R. Jowell et al. (Eds.). *British Social Attitudes: The 8th Report.* (pp. 43–58). Aldershot: Darmouth Publishing Co.

Hart, D., & Livingstone, D.W. (1993). Public support for university funding; Trends and determinants in Ontario, 1980–1990. *Canadian Journal of Higher Education, 23*(2).

Holmes, M. (1992). *Educational policy for the pluralist democracy: The common school, choice and diversity.* London: Falmer Press.

Hoy, C. (1989). *Margin of error: Pollsters and the manipulation of Canadian politics.* Toronto: Key Porter Books.

Institute for Social Research. (1991). *Opinions Ontario: A Semi annual survey.* April 23.

Jennings, M.K. (1992). Ideological thinking among mass publics and political elites. *Public Opinion Quarterly, 56,* 419–41.

Johnston, R. (1986). *Public opinion and public policy in Canada.* Toronto: University of Toronto Press.

King, A.J.C., & Peart, M. J. (1992). *Teachers in Canada: Their work and quality of life: A national study for the Canadian Teachers' Federation.* Ottawa: Canadian Teachers' Federation.

Kapron, D., & Stephan, W. (1991). Educational reform and the public: Two case studies of Poland and Saskatchewan (Canada). *International Review of Education, 37*(3), 319–34.

Krashinsky. M. (1987). The returns to university schooling in Canada: A comment. *Canadian Public Policy, 13*(2), 218–21.

Lambert, R.D., & Curtis, J.E. (1979). Education, economic dissatisfaction and nonconfidence in Canadian social institutions. *Canadian Review of Sociology and Anthropology, 16*(1), 47–59.

Lewington, J., & Orpwood, G. (1993). *Overdue assignment.* Toronto: John Wiley & Sons.

Livingstone, D.W. (1976). Images of the educational future in advanced industrial society: An Ontario inquiry. *Canadian Journal of Education, 1*(2).

Livingstone, D.W. (1979). *Public attitudes toward education in Ontario 1978.* Toronto: OISE Press.

Livingstone, D.W. (1983). *Class, ideologies and educational futures.* London: Falmer Press.

Livingstone, D.W. (1987). Job skills and schooling. *Canadian Journal of Education, 12*(1), 1–30.

Livingstone, D.W. (1992). Lifelong learning and chronic under-employment: Exploring the contradiction. In P. Anisef & P. Axelrod (Eds.). *Transitions: Schooling and employment in Canadian society.* (pp. 113–25). Toronto: Thompson Educational Publishing.

Livingstone, D.W., & Hart, D.J. (1980). *Public attitudes toward education in Ontario 1979.* Toronto: OISE Press.

Livingstone, D.W., & Hart, D.J. (1981). *Public attitudes toward education in Ontario 1980.* Toronto: OISE Press.

Livingstone, D.W., Hart, D.J., & McLean, L.D. (1983). *Public attitudes toward education in Ontario 1982.* Toronto: OISE Press.

Livingstone, D.W., Hart, D.J., & Davie, L.E. (1985). *Public attitudes toward education in Ontario 1984.* Toronto: OISE Press.

Livingstone, D.W., Hart, D.J., & Davie, L.E. (1986, December). Public attitudes toward education in Ontario 1986 (General issues). *Orbit, 17*(4), 19–26.

Popular Beliefs about Canada's Schools 43

Livingstone, D.W., Hart, D.J., & Davie, L.E. (1987, February). Public attitudes toward education in Ontario 1986 (School and work issues), *Orbit 18*(1), 3–13.
Livingstone, D.W., Hart, D.J., & Davie, L.E. (1989, February). Public attitudes toward education in Ontario 1988 (Special issue), *Orbit 20*(1), 1–36.
Livingstone, D.W., Hart, D.J., & Davie, L.E. (1991, April). Public attitudes toward education in Ontario 1990 (Special issue), *Orbit 22*(2), 1–28.
Livingstone, D.W., Hart, D.J., & Davie, L.E. (1993). *Public attitudes toward education in Ontario 1992.* Toronto: OISE Press.
Manitoba Education (Morrow, D.) (1985). *Public attitudes to education.* Winnipeg: Manitoba Education.
Mason, G. (1984). *Attitudes of the Manitoba population toward education in Manitoba.* Winnipeg: Institute for Social and Economic Research.
Maclean's/CTV Poll. (1993, January 4). Hope in hard times. *Maclean's*, pp. 14–17.
McQuaig, L. (1993). *The wealthy banker's wife: The Mulroney government's assault on equality in Canada.* Toronto: Penguin Books.
Mishler, W., & Clarke, H. (1990). Political participation in Canada. In M. Whittington and G. Williams (Eds.). (pp. 158–81). *Canadian politics in the 1990s* (Third Edition). Scarborough, ON: Nelson Canada.
Ontario Ministry of Education. (1979). *Attitudes of the public towards schools in Ontario.* Toronto: Ontario Ministry of Education.
Ontario Ministry of Colleges and Universities/Ministry of Education. (1976). *Roles and responsibilities of secondary and post-secondary institutions secondary/Post-secondary interface study, Project 1.* Toronto: Canadian Facts.
Osborne, D., & Gaebler, T. (1992). *Reinventing government: How the entrepreneurial spirit is transforming the public sector.* Reading, MA: Addison-Wesley.
Poitras, J. (1990, November 13). Canadians want bucks for education. *The Varsity*, pp. 1, 9.
Reich R. (1991). *The work of nations: Preparing for 21st century capitalism.* New York: Knopf.
Shor, I. (1986). *Culture wars.* Boston: Routledge and Kegan Paul.
Smith, H. (1986, April). Over-education and underemployment: An agnostic review. *Sociology in Education, 59*(2), 85–99.
Speirs, R. (1990, February 5). 79% still oppose sales tax despite lower rate, poll says. *Toronto Star*, p. A15.
Taylor, C. (1993). *Reconciling the solitudes: Essays on Canadian federalism and nationalism.* Montreal and Kingston: McGill–Queen's University Press.
Taylor-Gooby, P. (1991). Attachment to the welfare state. In R. Jowell et al. (Eds.). *British social attitudes: The 8th report.* (pp. 23–42). Aldershot: Darmouth Publishing Co.
Thompson, A. (1993, July 5). Report slams TV portrayal of immigrants. *Toronto Star*, p. A9.
Toronto Star (1992). Series on ethnic groups beginning June 7, 1992 and continued in the six subsequent Sunday editions.
Toronto Star/Environics Poll. (1993, May 29). Deep concerns about Ontario's schools. *Toronto Star*, p. A1.
Vaillancourt, F. (1986). The returns to university schooling. *Canadian Public Policy, 12*(3), pp. 449–58.
Walker, W. (1993, January 18). 60% say province should cut services. *Toronto Star*, pp. A1, 8.
Watson, P. (1990, February 16). Top pollster fears backlash looming over immigration. *Toronto Star*, p. A15.

Weiler, H.N. (1982, September). Education, public confidence and legitimacy of the modern state. *Phi Delta Kappan, 64*(1).

Williams, T., & Millinoff, H. (1990). *Canada's schools: Report card for the 1990s.* Toronto: Canadian Educational Association.

Winsor, H. (1990, February 12). Canadians show growing concern over unity. *Globe and Mail*, pp. A1, 2.

Wotherspoon, T. (Ed.). (1991). *Hitting the books: The politics of educational retrenchment.* Toronto: Garamond Press.

FURTHER READINGS

Hart, D.J., & Livingstone, D.W. (1993). Public support for university funding. *Canadian Journal of Education, 23*(2).

Johnston, R. (1986). *Public opinion and public policy in Canada.* Toronto: University of Toronto Press.

Kapron, D., & Stephen, W. (1991). Educational reform and the public. *International Review of Education, 37*(3).

Livingstone, D.W., Hart, D.J., & Davie, L.E. (1993). *Public attitudes toward education in Ontario 1992.* Toronto: OISE Press.

Osborne, K. (1991). *Teaching for democratic citizenship.* Toronto: Our Schools/Our Selves Education Foundation.

Williams, T., & Millinoff, H. (1990). *Canada's schools.* Toronto: Canadian Educational Association.

Wotherspoon, T. (Ed.). (1991). *Hitting the books.* Toronto: Garamond Press.

3

COMMUNICATION TECHNOLOGY AND EDUCATION IN CANADA

Dien Tran

> Modern technology is changing how and where we work, what work we do, how we communicate with others, how we play, and, at a deeper level, how we think, how we see ourselves, and what we value. It is also changing how, where, and when we learn, as well as why and what we need to learn. (Henchey, 1991, p. 37)

During the last three decades, with the appearance of computers, cellular telephones, fibre optics, and artificial intelligence, Canada has been undergoing the transition from an industrial society to an information society, thanks to developments in communication technology. To cope with the changes brought on by this transition, educational systems have undertaken new courses of action that have affected students, parents, educators—in fact, almost all members of our society.

In this chapter, we will discuss the characteristics, roles, and effects of communication technology in Canadian society. We will also consider the technology as tools, systems, and concepts, and address the dilemmas that communication technology poses for decision-makers, educators, parents, and students.

CHARACTERISTICS, ROLES, AND EFFECTS OF COMMUNICATION TECHNOLOGY

Communication technology includes such tools as radios, telephones, televisions, computers, satellite, fibre optics. At a higher level, it includes the structured systems of communication networks, and, at an even higher level, the management of such systems to share or disseminate information and knowledge.

CHARACTERISTICS

A main characteristic of communication technology is its ability to extend and expand human control over the communication environment. A human voice can be carried over the ocean or to remote areas depending on the transmitting power and the receiving devices. Teleconferencing is another example of extending human contact over distance.

Another important characteristic of communication technology, as Henchey (1991) has pointed out, is that it "has a reciprocal relationship with both science and culture." The telephone, for example is an application of acoustics and electricity. However, research and development in the telephone field, such as the carbon-button microphone at the turn of the century, have also benefited underwater sound, a specialized branch of acoustic science.

Communication technology, like other technologies, does not have a neutral impact on society. It has already caused displacement of workers, reorganization of many industries, and changes in our learning and working habits, as has been repeatedly stated by the Advisory Council on Adjustment, Canada (1989); the Council of Ministers of Education, Canada (1989); and the Economic Council of Canada (1990).

ROLES AND EFFECTS

Efficiency

As a tool or as a structured working system, communication technology tends to increase productivity—less human effort and time are needed to achieve the same amount of work. Word processors permit office clerks as well as managers to input data, edit, print, or electronically store the data with fewer errors and in a shorter period of time. Publishing a booklet or sending it to the printer across town can be done within a day. Newspapers can be edited in one place and printed in several different locations across Canada.

Achievements

Space discovery, medical research, and earth science all benefit from communication technology. Librarians can provide complete, accurate, and up-to-date information, retrieve articles, and send them to clients without delay. Hairdressers can project the customer's three-dimensional image on a screen before starting on a new hairstyle. Real-estate agents can plug a laptop into a television set and show the prospective buyer some of the current listings, letting the buyer walk through a home on screen in a few minutes without confronting traffic or inclement weather. Communication technology has indeed expanded human capacities to higher degrees of physical and intellectual achievements.

Effects on Jobs and Careers

As communication technology becomes increasingly rooted in our society, many jobs will be affected. At the simplest level of technological involvement, workers may not be affected at all and little or no training may be required. However, the productivity of new technology may make some jobs redundant, forcing a reduction in the workforce. Workers would also need to be retrained and perhaps relocated. If the level of the new technology is very high, a new generation of workers may be necessary as the jobs may become entirely different. Another important side effect of the new technology would be the decrease in daily interaction among people as more and more work is being done in the home.

REQUIREMENTS

Not all new technologies are received with the same enthusiasm. When changes are imposed merely to save money by reducing jobs, employee resistance is likely to be high.

Thus, when a company is considering introducing technology to its workplace, it must keep in mind the requirements of the end-users: accessibility, affordability, and acceptance.

Accessibility

Technology needs to be accessible. Although a period of tuning and refining may be necessary, the new technology should be understandable to those who have to use it on a regular basis. Accessibility must also be measured within a competent audience. A new computerized heart surgery technique would have a higher accessibility level for a group of surgeons than it would for a group of medical librarians. A technology that is inaccessible could be restricted in terms of popularity and therefore prevented from having a widespread impact.

Affordability

Next to being accessible, a new technology should also be affordable. Computers would not have become as widespread as they are today if they had not been made affordable to the general public. In this case, the realized affordability is the result of the ease that new computers brought to the transfer of ideas and concepts, which in turn lead to reduced labour and product costs.

Acceptance

Ease of use (user-friendliness) is also a key factor for public acceptance of a new technology. The learning curve of a new technology should not be too long: we would have no incentive to adopt a new technology if we believed that it might become obsolete before we could master it. It is also important that the new technology not be seen as a direct threat to existing jobs. In one case, the attempt to electronically transfer government cheques to recipients was fiercely opposed by the union of workers who processed the cheques by hand (*London Free Press*, 1993, Sept. 2).

It is clear that the impact of communication technology is twofold: It has improved productivity, enhanced human achievement, extended and expanded human control over the environment, but it has also eliminated many traditional jobs. While technology increases efficiency, it requires a highly trained workforce. How will our education system adapt to the challenges of the new communication technology? Are there roles or activities in education that will be adversely affected by the technological progress that permeates Canadian society?

IMPACT ON EDUCATION

Communication technology has introduced a large number of tools, systems, and concepts to the education system. Radios, cassette players, overhead and slide projectors, television, and programmed instruction have been used in the classroom for a number of years and continue to play a role in the schools. The appearance of computers and their related equipment and techniques raises new issues and gives a totally new perspective on the role, impact, and speed of change of technology in our education system.

THE INFRASTRUCTURE

Bill Gates, chairman of Microsoft Corporation, in a speech on August 19, 1993, at Toronto's Ryerson Polytechnic University, praised Canadian leadership in telecommunication technology. According to Gates, Canada has the highest percentage of cable television penetration in the world—at 80 percent—and an even higher penetration of telephones. This statistic clearly shows that Canada has a leading role to play in an increasingly digital world and that telecommunication systems now constitute the information infrastructure upon which communication technology can be built and nurtured to a healthy growth and development.

The Tools

Each school and education board in Canada has some computers and peripheral equipment such as printers and control units. Computer familiarization takes place very early in the student's life. Most children from Kindergarten on have access to some sort of computer programs. Many schools are equipped with computer labs, each accommodating 10 to 30 or more stations, all independent or linked together via a LAN (Local Area Network). The lab can be managed either by a computer teacher or by a non-teaching computer assistant. Some schools equip a number of classrooms with computers according to the homeroom teacher's proficiency in computer technique.

Another tool derived from the new communication technology is television. Canadian stations contribute a large proportion of their broadcasting time to educational programmes. According to UNESCO (1992) statistics, 88 000 hours of educational programming are broadcast in Canada each year; these figures compare with 2500 to 3000 hours in Europe.

The Systems

Integrated Learning Systems (ILS) provide a conventional approach to using computers to enhance the learning process. Often these systems are set up in a computer lab. Each session is self-contained and can be individualized to a certain degree. This reduces training costs and provides easy management with little expertise required. The teacher can turn over his or her class to the lab technician, thus allowing personal freedom for class preparation. The students work at their own stations and can receive individualized tutorial dialogue, a luxury often lacking in whole-class teaching. Most Integrated Learning Systems divide topics into well-defined subject areas and require no collaboration among teachers responsible for different subjects. The advantage of the ILS is that they fit well into the school structure and require very little change to the room allocation, the schedule, and the curriculum already in place (Newman, 1992). The drawback of this approach is that it offers little or no interaction among students and doesn't encourage cooperation and team work.

Other systems, taking advantage of the LAN technology, try to implement the teaching and learning process by "decompartmentalizing" the instruction. In these systems, the subjects are not totally isolated and students are requested to work in teams from the beginning to the final phases of an assigned project. The project may encompass many subjects. The main principle of these systems is a shared database, to which students can contribute, thus enriching the database. These systems involve classroom teachers and require collaboration at least from teachers of a department or from adjoining departments. Thus, a geology project may call on the expertise of the chemistry, biology, and math departments. Young children can pool together to draw, write, and store their work, using LOGO, HyperCard, or other programs available to the school. At a higher level, besides word processing, students may import different programs into their word processor or use their modems to communicate with other schools within their board, within their province, or even overseas. With these systems, the students are equipped to use technology to communicate, to collaborate, and to share knowledge in the way scientists do. However, such systems require a high degree of commitment from the school staff and flexibility in interpreting curriculum and education structure (Newman, 1992).

The Concepts

Another system that has become increasingly popular in educational settings is Instructional System Design (ISD), a systematic approach to instruction design. This system provides, through its intertwined steps, one of the most efficient and economical means of developing courseware. The strength of ISD resides in the evaluation process that is embedded in all its steps and that continues even after the training has ended with on-the-job follow-up evaluation. Applied with flexibility, this approach would help create effective courseware that economically fills a school's instructional needs.

As computer systems become more affordable, technologies like LAN, WAN (Wide Area Network), modems, and fax modems can maximize the link between schools, boards, businesses, and libraries. Geographic isolation is no longer a barrier, especially in Canada where telephone penetration is very high. International borders cease to be barriers as students from Canada can, via educational networks, communicate with students in Mexico, Hong Kong, or Europe. Computer-Assisted Learning (CAL), Computer-Based Training (CBT), ISD and Computer Managed Instruction (CMI) may also help developing countries provide maximum education to their populations at the most economical costs (Venezky & Osin, 1991).

A current pilot project linking Fanshawe College and the University of Western Ontario via two Bell dedicated telephone lines opens up new approaches to sharing resources between educational institutions and in improving distance education. Interaction between a teacher and a group of geographically dispersed students can be done on-line (interactively), in real time (instantly). Teachers and students can see and hear each other through the use of video cameras, microphones, and image scanners. Assignments can be graded, questions answered, and remedial tutorials made on the spot.

As CAL and CBT become more popular, authoring languages or programs also need to be upgraded and enhanced. PILOT, TENcore, NATAL II, and QUEST are among the few authoring languages developed or upgraded in the last ten years. These languages are described below:

- PILOT is a high-level programming language used to generate CAL, and is chiefly used to create question-and-answer types of courseware.
- TENcore is a sophisticated language that runs primarily on minicomputers of the DPS 6 series designed by Honeywell. It supports interactive video and the use of external video storage.
- NATAL1 II, derived from the work of the National Research Council Associate Committee on Instructional Technology (ACIT) in Ottawa, is further developed by Honeywell Limited in its North York facilities. A microNATAL was also developed as a C implementation by Softwords in Victoria. NATAL II is mostly main-frame-oriented and takes advantage of the powerful DPS-8 of Honeywell (Brahan & Godfrey, 1984).

- QUEST was successfully implemented to generate courseware for the Canadian Air Force in the Computer Based Electronic Warfare Training System (CBEWTS) using the then newly available IBM-AT and the laserdisc. It handles interactive video and is capable of allowing a free-play scenario where trainees actually interact with one another and not with the computer system alone.

At present, educational software abound as well as educational computer systems. This proliferation poses some dilemmas to all persons involved in public education, from decision-makers to Kindergarten pupils.

NEW DILEMMAS

DECISION-MAKERS

To get a niche within the educational market, computer makers donated their new products to school boards, anticipating that students would buy a system that is already familiar to them, or that they would need to buy a system that would permit them to toggle between school and home in doing their work or assignments. The first dilemma for decision-makers is to question the motive of such an arrangement. Without denying the beneficial contributions that business makes to our education system, we should realize that the primary goal of business is to increase profits and to compete in the marketplace. Cultural or societal impacts do not weigh heavily in business decisions. Educational choices must be motivated by factors other than those of the marketplace. As computer prices tumble, boards of education can now afford to acquire suitable equipment for their schools, even in these times of budget constraint.

The two established microcomputer operating systems are the IBM and IBM-compatibles and the Macintosh. Both systems have dedicated and loyal users in schools and in the business world. Although the two systems are becoming more and more compatible with each other, schools must still make a choice, based on the availability of human and financial resources within the board and on the intended use of the system. In the past, many schools have acquired systems claimed as education-dedicated only to be left with obsolete or unpopular systems that do not prepare students for the real world.

In times of budget constraint, another dilemma that decision-makers must face is the allocation of resources within the system. Robots have proved to be beneficial to autistic children, but at huge costs. Computers with appropriate software improve the learning paces of slow learners and act as remedial tools to children with attention deficits. However, due to the limited market, these systems are more expensive and would absorb a large part of the schools' already shrinking budgets. Should all children be allocated the same amount of taxpayer money for their instruction? Or should the balance be inclined toward those who need more help? The answers to these questions are not clear since the efficiency and usefulness of many systems are not or cannot be fully evaluated (Godfrey & Parkhill, 1980; Roblyer, 1993).

EDUCATORS

Educators must ask themselves some of the following questions when deliberating the pros and cons of introducing computers in the classroom:

- What is the goal of education? Does a computer system contribute to this goal?
- What would be the best approach to teaching students and training the teachers?

- What evaluation tools should be used?
- How should we interpret various learning profiles?
- What is the correlation between computer technology and other subjects?
- How far can we go into this new technology without destroying or undermining the true objectives of learning?

For educators who are not acquainted with the new technology, these dilemmas can be quite serious. When school boards began equipping the schools with computers, they very often neglected to supply the schools with personnel qualified to teach the students how to use the computers and software applications. When students faced problems learning a new program, they looked to their teachers for a solution, which, understandably, would not come. Many boards have offered upgrading courses and have encouraged their teaching staff to take advantage of them. However, because the trainers may not be well prepared or the course outline not well designed, quite a few upgrading courses not only fall short of their proposed goals but discourage the already shy or reluctant newcomers.

Educators need to distance themselves from the computer maze in order to answer the above questions. But can we withdraw ourselves completely to allow a global and objective view? If yes, do we have enough knowledge about the new technology to formulate our evaluation? Can we grasp the rapidly changing technology without being carried away on the very stream we are supposed to observe and to analyze? (Johnson, 1988)

PARENTS

In many cases, parents are enthusiastic about new communication technology. They share the vision that the computer is here to stay, and the more their children know about it, the better their chances of getting a job after school. But many parents are also sceptical about the long-term effects of computers on their children. They worry that their children may become computer-dependent or that they will not learn basic literacy and numeracy skills. Parents may have bought their children a computer with all the necessary software and discovered that their children do not get top marks, or still have problems with their homework and assignments. The tendency to blame the education system or the teachers is strong.

STUDENTS

Students are likely the least adversely affected by communication technology (Todman & Dick, 1993). Young children master computer skills quite quickly. Students develop a teamwork spirit through computer-based projects in which one student alone cannot manage all the requirements in the design of a project. However, children tend to see the computer as a toy, a game machine, and not as a tool to aid in learning. The computer cannot and will not replace the thinking process and cannot acquire for the user the necessary logic that maintains the human species above all other species on the earth (McLuhan & McLuhan, 1988).

CONCLUSIONS

Communication technology, by its rapid intrusion into the education world, has created a number of dilemmas. Its impact on the education system is important and is still being debated. Its presence in our daily life is no less of a reality. Preparedness, awareness of human factors, and open dialogue between the schools and the population they serve could solve some of these dilemmas. Educators, decision-makers, and parents should look at this new technology with a critical mind and with open eyes to set the proper priorities in preparing our students for a changing world. Isolating our children from the new technology, rejecting the changes, or restricting the import of new teaching media into our school system would not be the solution. Along with the openness and acceptance of new technology, we also need to participate if we are to understand how this technology works, in order to shape its outcome to suit our educational goals and to allocate our resources wisely. Thus the training of future trainers and educators should include communication technology, as tools, as systems, and as concepts to familiarize and to prepare them so that they in turn can manage, control, and apply this technology for the benefit of our society (Science Council of Canada, 1982).

DISCUSSION QUESTIONS

❏   Discuss the part that modern communication technology plays in providing solutions or being a contributing factor to society's problems?

❏   How would you change the educational structure to effectively use communication technology to expand access to learning to include people who now have limited opportunities (such as people with disabilities, those living in rural areas, adults, the populations of developing nations, and the gifted)?

❏   If communication technology is important in shaping our society, should it be part of the core curriculum of elementary and secondary schools? If yes, what changes should be made to the training of future teachers and educators?

❏   What aspects of a teacher's role (if any) can and should be replaced or enhanced by computers?

❏   How would you design the structure and organization of a school if all students and teachers had easy access to computer-based training systems?

REFERENCES

Advisory Council on Adjustment, Canada. (1989). *Adjusting to win.* Ottawa: Minister of Supply and Services Canada.

Brahan, J., & Godfrey, D. (Eds.). (1984). *Computer-aided learning using the NATAL language.* Toronto: Porcépic Books.

Council of Ministers of Education, Canada. (1989). *Education in Canada 1986–1988.* Toronto: Council of Ministers of Education, Canada.

Economic Council of Canada. (1990). *Good jobs, bad jobs: Employment in the service economy.* Ottawa: Economic Council of Canada.

Godfrey, D., & Parkhill, D. (Eds.). (1980). *Gutenberg two: The new electronics and social change.* Toronto: Porcépic Books.

Henchey, N. (1991). Communication technology and the transformation of learning. In R. Ghosh & D. Ray (Eds.). *Social Change and Education in Canada.* (pp. 37–48).Toronto: Harcourt Brace Jovanovich.

Johnson, W.B. (1988). Intelligent tutoring systems: If they are such good ideas, why aren't there more of them? *Proceedings of the 10th Annual Interservice Industry Training Systems Conference.* Alexandria, VA: National Security Industrial Association.

London Free Press (1993, September 2). Union wants new system for cheques put on hold. A6.

McLuhan, M. (1965). *Understanding media: The extensions of man.* New York: McGraw-Hill.

McLuhan, M., & McLuhan, E. (1988). *Laws of media.* Toronto: University of Toronto Press.

Newman, D. (1992). Technology as support for school structure and school restructuring. *Phi Delta Kappan, 74*(4), 308–15.

Roblyer, M.D. (1993). Technology in our time: Virtual, reality, visions, and nightmares. *Educational Technology, 33*(2), 33–35.

Science Council of Canada. (1982). *Planning now for an information society: Tomorrow is too late.* Ottawa: Minister of Supply and Services Canada.

Todman, J., & Dick, G. (1993). Primary children and teachers' attitudes to computers. *Computers Education, 20*(2), 199–203.

UNESCO. (1992). *Statistical yearbook.* Paris: UNESCO.

Venezky, R., & Osin, L. (1991). *The intelligent design of computer assisted instruction.* London: Longman.

World Commission on Environment and Development. (1987). *Our common future.* Oxford: Oxford University Press.

FURTHER READINGS

Dick, W., & Carey, L. (1985). *The systematic design of instruction.* Illinois: Scott, Foresman and Company.

Howard, D.C., & Kysela, G.M. (1993). Computer use in education: Current status and emerging issues in research and practice. In L.L. Stewin & S. McCann (Eds.). *Contemporary educational issues—The Canadian mosaic.* (pp. 442–58). Toronto: Copp Clark Pitman.

Ellul, J. (1964). *The technological society.* New York: Vintage Books.

Illich, I. (1973). *Tools for conviviality.* New York: Harper & Row.

Kroker, A. (1984). *Technology and the Canadian mind: Innis, McLuhan, Grant.* Montreal: New World Perspective.

Pelgrum, J.W. (1992). International Research on computers in education. *Prospect, 22*(3) pp. 341–9.

Polson, M.C., & Richardson, J.J. (1988). *Foundations of intelligent tutoring systems.* Hillsdale, NJ: Lawrence Erlbaum Associates.

Tobin, J., & Sharon, D. (1984). New technologies in education in Canada: Issues and concerns. Paper 17 in a series on "New technologies in Canadian education" prepared by TVOntario and the Canadian Commission for UNESCO.

4

DEMOGRAPHIC CHANGES AND EDUCATIONAL DEVELOPMENT

John Rowland Young

The right to an education for all Canadian children is well accepted and even reinforced by law. In a society such as ours, marked by a complex division of labour and increasing industrialization, education has always played an important role. It has been assumed that the quantity and quality of education would determine the economic and social potential of the nation. However, not all children experience the same amount or type of education. In Canada, the five factors of class, gender, ethnicity, region, and religion become major determinants of who gets the best education and, conversely, who is failed by the educational system. There are several perspectives one can use to determine the workings of a society. The approach taken in this chapter is to see the relationships between the changing demographic structure of Canada and educational development.

As Canada moves into its second century, one can look back on a history that can be described demographically as one marked by instability and change. There are probably three major reasons for this instability and change:

- Canada has experienced high levels of migration.
- Changes have occurred in the age distribution of the Canadian population.
- Natural increase, although declining for Canada as a whole, shows marked provincial differences.

From a period of massive growth half a century ago, Canada has reached a point where its population is growing slower, growing older, and showing uneven growth within the provinces. All of these factors have had profound influences on the nature of educational development.

Uneven growth of a population makes educational planning very difficult. Building schools, staffing them with qualified teachers, and developing curricula are costly and time-consuming. Rational planning is effective only when growth is even and predictable. According to Statistics Canada,

> the demographic accounts show that, as in 1990, the 1991 total growth was relatively high, at 1.5 percent. The total population increase of 402 000 persons is about equal to the population of the City of Ottawa. For the most part, this total growth is due to a still increasing number of births. . . . Since 1987, the annual number of births has risen progressively from 369 700 to 411 000 (an increase of 42 000). Annual deaths,

which are expected to rise in an aging society, have risen only by 11 100, reaching 196 000 in 1991. In terms of entrants into Canada, the 224 600 international immigrants who arrived in 1990 ranked second in number to only 1957 (282 144) since the all-time peak of 480 870 was reached in 1913—the year before World War I. Net international migration was therefore estimated at 186 300 given that 38 300 persons emigrated from Canada—the lowest number in the last 30 years. (Statistics Canada, 1992a, p. 7).

From the perspective of educational planning, the changes that occur *in* the age groups are more important than overall growth. During Canada's history, the unbroken trend has been an aging of the population. The median age for Canadians has increased from 22.7 years in 1901 to 33.5 in 1991 (Statistics Canada, 1983a; 1992b).

As shown in Table 4.1, the number of Canadians over 65 increased significantly from 1901 to 1991. Projections made by the National Council on Welfare (1985b) indicate that by 2051 nearly one in five Canadians will be over 65.

Perhaps more important from an educational perspective is that the proportion of the population under 5 is decreasing. In 1901, over 12 percent of the Canadian population was under 5 (Urquhart & Buckely, 1983, p. A78), whereas in 1991 the percentage had decreased to 7.2 percent (see Table 4.1). This smaller age cohort will be moving through the school system in the next twenty years, indicating a decreased need for classroom space and number of teachers. The percentage of children 5 to 19, most of whom are in some form of the educational system, has also declined during the century. Interestingly, from 1971 to 1991, the proportion in the 0–19 age group fell from 32.0 to 27.8 percent. This age cohort is not only declining as a proportion, but also in actual numbers. From 1961 to 1991 its numbers dropped by almost 100 000.

Another conclusion that can be drawn from this table is that we can project an increase in the aged dependency ratio, barring, of course, a major increase in immigration. As our population becomes more aged, a smaller percentage of Canadians in the workforce will be supporting a significantly larger number of elderly. This will require a more productive and efficient workforce.

However, if we regard the young under 19 and the elderly over 65 as dependents of the potential labour force (all persons between the ages of 20 and 65), we find an interesting phenomenon. Although the aged dependency ratio is increasing, it is sufficiently

TABLE 4.1
Distribution of Population for Selected Decades (Percentage)

	1901	1941	1961	1981	1991
0–4	12.0	9.2	12.4	7.3	7.2
5–19	32.7	28.8	29.5	24.7	20.6
20–64	54.2	55.6	50.6	61.7	60.6
65+	5.1	6.7	7.7	9.7	11.6

Sources: Adapted from Hiller (1986), Table 1.11, p. 30; *Postcensual annual estimates of population by marital status, age, sex and components of growth for Canada, provinces and territories.* Statistics Canada (Cat. 91-210), June 1, 1992.

offset by the decline in the proportion of the young such that Canada has an overall dependency ratio of 39.4 percent, which is an all-time low.

BIRTH RATE

A most significant demographic shift, from an educator's viewpoint, occurred in Canada between 1951 and 1966—the so-called baby boom. During this period our consistently declining fertility rate was reversed. The 1950s was a decade of relative prosperity and economic growth following two decades of depression and war. During the baby boom nearly one-half million children were born per year. John Kettle (1980) describes this generation:

> The Big Generation consists of the 6 715 000 people born between mid-1951 and mid-1966, plus the 260 000 people of the same age who immigrated to Canada during the period, minus the people of the same age who emigrated during the period, who were not counted but who must have numbered about 150 000, minus the 240 000 who died in infancy or youth. On Census Day, 1966, at the end of the explosion, the Big Generation numbered 6 591 700. That was 33 percent of the total population. One-third of all the people in the country had been born in the preceding fifteen years! (pp. 19–20)

This "Big Generation" of 6.5 million children required an educational system that would tax the provinces to the limit. But what was even more taxing was the fact that the boom would eventually burst and many of the classrooms built and the teachers prepared would not be needed within the short span of a generation.

It is interesting to look at the changing structure of the population during the boom–bust period; this can be seen in Table 4.2.

The baby boom–bust phenomenon is very evident. As can be seen, the school age population as a percentage of the total population has declined since 1961. Specifically, it was a decrease of 13.9 percent in the 30-year span. This means that fewer children will require the services of educational institutions. The demand for teachers, classroom facilities, and programs will continue to decrease. It can be projected that this decline will

TABLE 4.2
Population Distribution of Age Groups for Selected Years (Percentage)

	1961	1971	1981	1991	CHANGE 1961 TO 1991
Age Groups					
0–17	38.9	36.7	28.1	25.0	− 4.9
18–64	53.5	56.2	62.2	63.4	+ 75.3
65–74	4.9	5.0	6.1	6.9	+109.2
75+	2.8	3.1	3.6	4.7	+148.8

Sources: Adapted from *Current demographic analysis.* Statistics Canada, 1983, Table 11 (Cat. 91-209), p. 37; *Postcensual annual estimates of population by marital status, age, sex and components of growth for Canada, provinces and territories.* Statistics Canada (Cat. 91-209E) June 1991.

continue in the future, assuming that immigration rates remain stable. Table 4.3 shows actual numbers of students requiring places over a 60-year period.

One million fewer children required educational places in 1991 than in the peak year of 1971. Still, it is important to keep in mind, nearly one-fifth of all Canadians are enrolled in elementary and secondary schools.

Table 4.4 shows the effect of the "population bulge" on teacher demand. In the early part of the century the number of teachers increased by over 40 percent per decade. This was a period of high birth rate and high immigration. However, the greatest increase in the number of teachers occurred between 1951 and 1971, with the number increasing by over 70 percent and peaking in the mid-1970s. After this peak period, the ratio declined, and the number of teachers actually decreased in the last half of the 1970s; this decrease continued into the 1980s. During the last decade, however, the number of teachers has increased slightly by 8.4 percent.

Because the preparation of teachers takes approximately four years and is an expensive enterprise for both teachers and society generally, the apparent peaking of demand for teachers will have significant personal and economic consequences.

MIGRATION

Immigration has played a significant role in educational development. Canada is a multi-ethnic country and has exhibited cultural diversity throughout its history. According to the 1991 census (Statistics Canada, 1992a), the Canadian population was distributed as follows: 29 percent were of British extraction, 32 percent of French extraction, and 39 percent of approximately 30 other ethnic origins. If we look back to 1871, the distribution was 60 percent British, 31 percent French, and 9 percent of other backgrounds, which shows that Canada's cultural diversity has significantly increased throughout its history. The traditional origin of immigrants has been northern Europe and the United States. However, Table 4.5 shows some dramatic changes in immigration patterns.

TABLE 4.3
Total School Enrollment for Selected Decades

	NUMBER OF STUDENTS (GRADES 1 TO 12)
1921	1 807 702
1941	2 131 391
1961	4 192 000
1971	5 654 000
1981	4 640 000
1991	4 666 784

Sources: *Canada year book* (Cat. 11-402d) 1921; *Historical statistics of Canada* (Cat. 11-516) (2nd ed.); *Elementary education and secondary school education in Canada, 1936–48*, Dominion Bureau of Statistics; *Elementary and secondary school enrollment 1981–82* (Cat. 81-210), Statistics Canada, January 1983; *Elementary and secondary school enrollment 1990–91*, Statistics Canada, (Cat. 81-210c) December 1992.

TABLE 4.4
Full-Time Teachers in Public and Secondary Schools

	TOTAL NUMBER	% INCREASE FROM PREVIOUS DECADE
1900–01	27 369	—
1910–11	40 476	+47.9
1920–21	57 778	+42.7
1930–31	70 245	+21.6
1940–41	75 387	+ 7.3
1950–51	89 682	+19.0
1960–61	153 040	+70.6
1970–71	263 126	+71.9
1980–81	273 400	− 2.7
1990–91	296 500	+ 8.4

Sources: *Education in Canada: A statistical review for 1979–1980*. Statistics Canada (cat. 81-229) 1981; *Historical statistics of Canada*, (2nd ed), Statistics Canada (cat. 11-516) 1983. *Education in Canada: A statistical review for 1990–91*, Statistics Canada (Cat. 81-229) 1991.

TABLE 4.5
Percentage of Immigrants to Canada by Selected Places of Birth, 1961 and before to 1991

	BEFORE 1961	1961–70	1971–80	1981–87	1988–91
U.S.	5.0	6.7	7.4	5.7	3.1
Central America	0.1	0.3	0.9	4.4	4.5
South America	0.4	2.0	6.0	6.0	4.6
Caribbean & Bermuda	0.7	5.6	9.7	7.1	5.4
U.K.	26.5	21.6	13.5	7.5	3.8
Other Northern Europe	3.8	1.9	1.1	0.8	0.7
Western Europe	21.4	9.1	4.7	4.3	2.4
Eastern Europe	17.7	5.4	3.4	9.1	10.7
Southern Europe	20.7	31.1	13.1	5.0	5.0
Africa	0.5	3.3	5.8	5.1	6.9
Western Asia & Middle East	0.4	1.7	2.9	5.9	10.0
Eastern Asia	1.8	4.7	10.5	13.6	20.0
South East Asia	0.2	1.8	11.2	15.4	13.2
South Asia	0.4	3.6	8.2	8.7	8.8
Oceanic & other	0.5	1.2	1.7	1.2	0.8

Source: Adapted from *Immigration and citizenship: The nation.* 1991 Census. Statistics Canada (cat. no. 93-316) December 1992. Reproduced by authority of The Minister of Industry, 1994.

Although Canada's immigration reflects a degree of stability, what has changed are the areas from which immigrants have arrived. Before 1961, over 30 percent of immigrants came from the United States or Great Britain. By 1991 that number had dropped to under 7 percent. During that same period, the number of immigrants from Asian countries increased from 2.4 percent to 42 percent. The importance of this change in source is great, but one obvious fact is that for most Asian immigrants English or French will not be their first language. Two educational implications follow from this: schools will increasingly be faced with establishing English or French as a second language Programs and adult education in one of the two official languages will become more important.

Because of the political reality of Canada, where the responsibilities and rights of different institutions were allocated variously to federal or provincial governments by the BNA Act of 1867, internal migration also has a major effect on education. Provinces have the responsibility of providing educational resources to all those within their jurisdictions, usually for those between the ages of 5 and 16. If there is a high rate of internal migration, the rational planning in education is made difficult. As can be seen in Table 4.6, the interprovincial migration flow is very heavy and varies from year to year. Over one-third of a million Canadians move across provincial boundaries in any one year.

In the interprovincial exchange sweepstakes, Quebec, Manitoba, and P.E.I. have been losers in all years reported, while Alberta and British Columbia have been consistent winners. Alberta had a net gain of over 44 000 citizens during the year 1980–81, a period of boom in the Albertan economy, while British Columbia's gain was greater in the early 1990s, which corresponds to a later economic uprising. If one assumes that these statistics reflect the movement of workers with families, then the implications for education are profound.

One of the most obvious consequences for education is the difficulty of planning for classroom space and educational equality. Schools are expensive to build and staff, and a population mobility index as high as that in Canada means that many schools will not be located where they are required. If equality of educational opportunity is to be the goal for all Canadians, then the interprovincial movement of citizens makes regionally equivalent and equally distributed educational programs absolutely necessary. This is an exceptionally difficult outcome to achieve in Canada. Differences in educational staffing

TABLE 4.6
Balance of Internal Migration between Provinces for Selected Years

YEAR	NFLD.	P.E.I.	N.S.	N.B.	QUE.	ONT.	MAN.	SASK.	ALTA.	B.C.
1971	733	−129	−755	1 798	−25 005	18 508	−7 251	−17 986	2 408	25 034
1981	−6 238	−783	−2 465	−4 766	−22 549	−19 665	−3 621	−520	40 243	21 565
1991	−1 961	−1 553	987	−2 377	−12 259	−6 604	−7 663	−9 829	7 624	33 447
Total 1971 to 1991	−65 914	1 260	9 142	131	−373 736	229 478	−115 366	−131 752	178 095	391 505

Source: Adapted from *Current demographic analysis.* Statistics Canada, 1992, Table 42 (cat. 91-209), p. 78. Reproduced by authority of the Minister of Industry, 1994.

and curricula also make mobility for students problematic. Added to this problem is the decentralization of education within provinces, which further contributes to the problems of attaining equality in educational opportunity.

POVERTY

Perhaps the most important demographic trend in the early 1990s has been the slight decrease in the number of Canadians who have incomes below the poverty line. A recession and relatively high unemployment in the 1980s had pushed more than 4.2 million Canadians below the poverty line, as established by the National Council on Welfare (1992a). The most recent figures available indicate that around 4 million Canadians were poor in 1991. As to who are the poor, the Council states

> All Canadians face some risk of being poor, but the risks are relatively low for couples and two-parent families. The risks are relatively high for people living outside families, very high for older unattached women and incredibly high for single-parent mothers and their children. (National Council on Welfare, 1992b)

There has always been a clear relationship between education and poverty. The lower the education of the family head or the unattached individual, the greater the chance of falling below the poverty line. As can be seen in Table 4.7, in 1990 only 6 percent of those with university degrees are to be found in the category of the poor, compared with 16.5 percent for individuals with primary education only. However, the threat of poverty has increased for everyone during the last decade, and this is true for those who have university degrees or have graduated from other postsecondary institutions as well. Families headed by individuals with some postsecondary education registered the largest increase in their poverty rate. A high-school diploma is no longer a guarantee of an affluent future, free from the risk of poverty.

It is interesting to note that even in 1990, with all the emphasis on education, nearly one in three Canadians who were poor lacked a high-school certificate of some kind. According to the National Council on Welfare (1985b),

---

TABLE 4.7
Family Poverty Trends, by Education of Head, 1980–1990 (Percentage)

	PRIMARY	SOME HIGH SCHOOL	SOME POST-SECONDARY	POST-SECONDARY GRADUATE	UNIVERSITY GRADUATE
1980	18.8	12.2	7.5	6.6	4.5
1985	18.8	14.4	11.8	8.5	4.6
1990	16.5	16.6	14.1	8.7	6.0

Sources: *Poverty profile, 1985*, National Council on Welfare, October 1985; *Poverty profile, 1988*, National Council on Welfare, April 1988; *Poverty profile 1980–1990*, National Council on Welfare, Autumn 1992.

In the face of the clear value for future economic well-being of extended education, why do poor kids tend to aim lower and drop out first? Why do they tend to do less well than their mental ability would indicate? The answer is not a single simple one. What happens to poor kids in school is the result of one factor after another, none of them alone responsible, but each shifting the odds against success for a poor kid a little further than the last. (p. 20)

It is important to note that poor education may be both a cause and an effect of poverty. What this means for education is that qualitative changes may have to be made in educational programs if all children are going to benefit equally from their schooling experiences. Changes in teacher training, curriculum, and pedagogic practices may be required to help break the cycle of poverty that deprives so many Canadians from leading useful and fulfilling lives.

HUMAN CAPITAL

Another way of looking at the statistics concerning the levels of education of the Canadian population is to refer to the educational "stock" of the country—"stock" meaning the amount of trained human resources (often referred to as "human capital") available at any one time. The sum total of formal education received by students represents the country's educational stock. If we look at the educational stock of Canada in 1991 (see Table 4.8), we note that although there are differences between the provinces in median

TABLE 4.8
Educational Stock of Canadians over Age 15, 1991

	MEDIAN YEARS OF SCHOOLING	PERCENTAGE WITHOUT CERTIFICATION
Newfoundland	11.4	51.1
Prince Edward Island	12.2	45.4
Nova Scotia	12.2	45.1
New Brunswick	12.1	47.5
Quebec	12.2	40.9
Ontario	12.7	38.7
Manitoba	12.2	47.7
Saskatchewan	12.2	48.5
Alberta	12.6	39.1
British Columbia	12.7	37.2
Yukon	12.7	31.3
Northwest Territories	11.2	50.6
Canada	12.5	40.5

Source: Adapted from *Educational attainment and school attendance: The nation.* 1991 Census. Statistics Canada (cat. 93-328), May 1993. Reproduced by authority of the Minister of Industry, 1994.

years of schooling (the point where one-half the people have more schooling and one-half have less schooling than the median), the median is relatively high. The population includes those over 15 years of age.

Although the median for Canada as a whole is 12.5 years, we note that the pool of people with a degree, certificate, or diploma is relatively low: 40.5 percent of Canadians possess no such credential. Provincial differences are major, varying from 31.3 percent to a high of 51.1 percent of Newfoundlanders with no certification. If we assume that these credentials affirm a level of skill, knowledge, or competence that could provide entry into many occupations, then many Canadians will not have the entrance requirements for many jobs or professions. From this perspective one may conclude that the educational stock is not very high. Only 40 percent of the Canadian population had obtained an educational credential by 1991. However, these statistics may be interpreted differently. It may be like the idea of the wine bottle being half-full or half-empty.

Another way of looking at this phenomenon is that Canada is quickly becoming a "credential" society. By 1991, the latest census year, educational attainment had hit an all-time high. By this year, approximately 2.4 million Canadians possessed a university degree. Between 1961 and 1991, while the population 15 years and over increased by 63 percent, the number of persons with university degrees increased by 432 percent, or approximately seven times the rate of population growth. Another area where extensive growth has occurred is in other postsecondary institutions such as trade colleges, community colleges, CEGEPs in Quebec, and technology institutes. Nearly 5 million Canadians had participated at this level of education by 1991 and obtained certificates and diplomas.

As impressive as these statistics sound, it can be seen that educational credentials do not necessarily translate into successful employment, particularly for the young. Youth unemployment has always been relatively high in Canada. For youth between 15–24, 15.5 percent were unemployed in 1991, up from 13.7 percent in 1981. Provincial variations are profound. In 1991, Newfoundland's youth unemployment was a devastating 38.1 percent, compared with a low 11.8 percent in Alberta (Statistics Canada, 1991e). What has been shown here is that in the past Canada's "educational stock" was not large, but although there has been a significant increase in credentials over the past few years, it hasn't necessarily meant that the credential has ensured successful employment.

Ironically, the reality of these assumptions about human capital has been both successful and tragic. Although schools have increased the number of graduates with the requisite skills for a knowledge-based postindustrial society, education has not facilitated economic modernization, social mobility aspirations, or high rates of future economic returns on current investments.

Nor has the growth of education meant a concomitant increase in the growth of postsecondary school teachers. According to Mori and Burke (1986),

> between the 1965–66 and 1975–76 academic years, they increased by 295 percent, but between the 1975–76 and 1985–86 academic years, they increased by only 20 percent. This reflects the stabilization of the college systems which emerged during the late 1960s and early 1970s, which, in turn, were a partial response to the maturing of the post–Second World War Baby Boom Generation. (p. 23)

The demand for teachers tends to be greatest in postsecondary institutions. For example, while the number of all teachers, including postsecondary instructors, increased by

8.9 percent from 1981 to 1991, the increase for elementary school teachers was a lower 8.5 percent. The number of university teachers increased over 10 percent during that time (Statistics Canada, 1991b).

A look at the demographic changes in Canadian society shows us that the tide of increasing educational expenditures has not been quelled. Although poverty is increasing, unemployment is depressingly high, and the close fit between educational credentials and economic needs has not completely materialized. Canadians have not made major changes in the amount and proportion of money invested in education. A report by Statistics Canada (1991c) shows that

> expenditures on education reached 44.5 billion in 1989–90. From 1979–80 to 1989–90, they more than doubled, growing 8.3% annually on average. ... The cost of education per capita was $1697 in 1989–90, up about 100% over the 1979–80 level ($842). (p. 227)

What seems to be happening in the 1990s is a relative decrease in educational funding. Although the total educational expenditure in 1990–91 was over $44.5 billion, double the expenditure in 1980–81, it represents a decline in relative funding. For example, the ratio of expenditures to gross national product (money value of all goods and services produced in Canada) has actually decreased from a high of 8.6 percent in 1970–71 to a low of 6.9 percent in 1989–90 (Statistics Canada, 1991b). One conclusion that can be drawn from this is that Canadians tend to see education not in terms of job preparation, but rather in the sense of the contribution it can make to the personal development and growth of the individual. However, one can predict that future postsecondary expansion will not increase at the rates experienced in the 1960s and early 1970s. It appears that expansion will be geared less toward meeting the needs for immediate economic growth and more toward equality of opportunity and general citizenship goals.

One such general citizenship goal of education in Canada is bilingualism. Numerous measures have been taken by many agents of government to promote bilingualism. Has it been successful? The overall trend has been toward increased bilingualism. By 1991, 16 percent of Canadians, or more than 4.4 million, could conduct a conversation in both languages. What points to the success of schools in promoting this bilingualism is that the most rapid increases in bilingualism have occurred among persons under 25.

CONCLUSIONS

Contemporary Canadian society has evolved out of a history of major population changes in growth and movement. Growth has been uneven due to fluctuations in immigration and internal migration, both between provinces and within provinces (from rural to urban centres). The population has aged and the birth rate has declined, while cultural and ethnic diversity has increased. Although the educational stock of the country has consistently increased over the years, the promise of appropriate jobs for academic qualifications has not been successfully realized. This is our heritage today: a large country, relatively rich in resources, sparsely and unevenly populated, ethnically diverse, relatively well schooled, and moderately committed to social programs to equalize access to social and economic resources. This chapter has tried to show the difficulty that the educational system has experienced in meeting the needs and opportunities created by such profound demographic changes. What role can education play in the future of such a country? It is the writer's opinion that what is required is the fostering of a commitment to an ultimate national goal that will include the strengths and potential of all citizens regardless of region, religion, ethnicity, class, gender, or age. Schools must play the role of an integrative force in society, and with a more demographically stable future, changes of a qualitative nature could be made to the system. However, this goal will be as difficult to reach as it is desirable.

DISCUSSION QUESTIONS

❏   Why do you think politicians believed that increased educational expenditure was warranted?

❏   This chapter has focussed on how the needs of society influence educational development. In what specific ways can education meet peoples' needs?

❏   The overall educational level of the Canadian labour force is rising. What impact will that have on Canadian society?

❏   This chapter has dealt with only a few of the functions of education. What are some of its other functions?

REFERENCES

Canada yearbook. (1921). Ottawa: King's Printer.

Dominion Bureau of Statistics. (1950). *Elementary and secondary school education in Canada.* Ottawa: Dominion Bureau of Statistics.

Hiller, H.H. (1986). *Canadian society: A macro-analysis.* Scarborough: Prentice-Hall.

Kettle, J. (1980). *The big generation.* Toronto: McClelland and Stewart.

Mori, G.A., & Burke, B. (1986). *Educational attainment of Canadians.* Ottawa: Statistics Canada.

National Council on Welfare. (1985a). *Poverty profile, 1985.* Ottawa: National Council on Welfare.

National Council on Welfare. (1985b). *Poor kids.* Ottawa: National Council on Welfare.

National Council on Welfare. (1988). *Poverty profile, 1988.* Ottawa: National Council on Welfare.

National Council on Welfare. (1992a). *Poverty profile: Update for 1991.* Ottawa: National Council of Welfare.

National Council on Welfare. (1992b). *Poverty profile, 1980–1990.* Ottawa: National Council of Welfare.

Ross, L. (1986). *Canada's youth.* Ottawa: Statistics Canada.

Statistics Canada. (1981). *Education in Canada: A statistical review for 1979–80.* Ottawa: Statistics Canada.

Statistics Canada. (1983a). *Canadian statistical review.* Ottawa: Statistics Canada.

Statistics Canada. (1983b). *Elementary and secondary enrollment, 1981–82.* Ottawa: Statistics Canada.

Statistics Canada. (1984). *Schooling in Canada*. Ottawa: Statistics Canada.

Statistics Canada. (1988). *Education in Canada: A statistical review for 1987–88*. Ottawa: Statistics Canada.

Statistics Canada. (1991a). *Elementary and secondary school enrollment, 1990–91*. Ottawa: Statistics Canada.

Statistics Canada. (1991b). *Education in Canada: A statistical review for 1990–91*. Ottawa: Statistics Canada.

Statistics Canada. (1991c). *Occupations*: Ottawa: Statistics Canada.

Statistics Canada. (1991d). *Labour force activity*. Ottawa: Statistics Canada.

Statistics Canada. (1991e). *Postcensual annual estimates of population*. Ottawa: Statistics Canada.

Statistics Canada. (1992a). *Current demographic analysis*. Ottawa: Statistics Canada.

Statistics Canada. (1992b). *Elementary and secondary school enrollment 1990–91*. Ottawa: Statistics Canada.

Statistics Canada. (1992c). *Immigration and citizenship: The nation*. Ottawa: Statistics Canada.

Statistics Canada. (1992d). *Postcensual annual estimates of population*. Ottawa: Statistics Canada.

Statistics Canada. (1993). *Educational attainment and school attendance*. Ottawa: Statistics Canada.

Urquhart, M.C., & Buckley, K.A.H. (Eds.). (1983). *Historical statistics of Canada* (2nd ed.). Ottawa: Supply and Services.

FURTHER READINGS

Curtis, J., & Tepperman, L. (1988). *Understanding Canadian society*. Toronto: McGraw-Hill Ryerson.

Stewin, L., & McCann. (1993). *Contemporary education issues: The Canadian mosaic*. (2nd ed.). Toronto: Copp Clark.

Titley, B. (1990). *Canadian education: Historical themes and contemporary issues*. Calgary: Detselig.

5

FINANCING EDUCATION

Dennis Dibski

Canadians spent $48.2 billion in 1991 on education. Expenditures for all levels of education for 1990 were 7.0 percent of the gross national product (GNP), surpassing the United States (5.8 percent of its GNP), the United Kingdom (4.7 percent in 1988), France (5.5 percent), West Germany (4.1 percent in 1989), Japan (4.7 percent in 1988), Australia (5.1 percent in 1989), and most other industrialized countries where comparisons would seem appropriate. In 1990, only a few industrialized countries exceeded 7 percent: Sweden (7.3 percent), Norway (7.5 percent), and the U.S.S.R. (7.9 percent) (UNESCO 1992; Statistics Canada, 1992).[1]

Other statistics reveal how major an undertaking education is in Canada. Over five million students were enrolled full time in public, private, and federal elementary–secondary schools under the care of 334 300 teachers. The average annual expenditure per school student in 1990 was over $7300. In 1990, there were 1 363 250 full-time students enrolled in higher education and colleges. These were joined by very large numbers of part-time students in a lifelong learning system of training. Because education is constitutionally a provincial responsibility, most of the money for it comes from provincial and local school governments. In 1990–91, schooling and higher education accounted for 15.3 percent of all government (federal, provincial, municipal) expenditures in Canada. The elementary and secondary costs represented 63 percent of this total, while postsecondary education shared 28 percent, and the remaining 9 percent went to trade and vocational training programs (Statistics Canada, 1992).

Canadians and their governments allocate this share of their economic resources to education because they believe it to be an important investment. In addition to its economic benefits, it provides some glue to bind the country together, an important centripetal force in a nation of diversity.

In the more than 150 years since education began to be a public responsibility in Canada, various schemes have been developed to finance it. This chapter examines where the money comes from, the concept of "ability-to-pay" and its implications for educational financing (and its consequences for provincial and federal governments), the objectives of school financing programs and how governments have tried to solve them, and recent trends that may affect the future allocation of resources to education.

FINANCING AS A SHARED RESPONSIBILITY

Because the provinces have the responsibility for providing education, there are differences in their specific provisions, division of responsibility, and powers. In general, the ministries of education retain jurisdiction for establishing school districts, setting educational goals, developing curricula and courses of study, authorizing and sometimes providing textbooks, training and certifying teachers, providing support and consultative services to school boards, ensuring that school buildings and bus systems are used effectively, and similar functions. Each province does these things either directly or by providing grants-in-aid to school boards and perhaps to private schools. In some cases, provincial governments also are involved in collective bargaining with the teachers.

School boards are legally created by the province, so they may be controlled, changed, or even eliminated by the province. In most cases, boards are delegated responsibility for acquiring school sites, building schools, employing teachers and other staff, supplying instructional materials and resources, offering a full range of educational programs and services, busing students, preparing budgets, and raising revenue through local property taxes. The provincial government provides a stipulated part of these costs through grants to school boards. Boards may also have miscellaneous sources of revenue—tuition fees, rentals, and proceeds from the sale of assets—but these rarely total more than 10 percent of the budget.

Prince Edward Island and New Brunswick are exceptions to the standard provincial–local sharing arrangement. In these provinces, school boards receive all of their incomes from the provincial governments under a system called "full-state" funding. School boards in these provinces do not levy school taxes and have very restricted local sources of revenue (7.5 percent of total education budget). The province does the tax collecting associated with schooling.

SOURCES OF PROVINCIAL REVENUE

The money for provincial grants to education comes out of the general revenue fund of the province. This revenue comes from taxes and other sources. Personal and corporate income taxes, combined with retail sales tax (except for Alberta) and excise taxes on specific commodities such as gasoline and alcohol, account for the biggest percentage of most provincial revenue budgets. In some provinces, especially British Columbia, Alberta, and Saskatchewan, royalties on natural resources generate a great deal of revenue. Other revenue comes from the profits of Crown corporations and public utilities, and from fees collected by various government agencies for licences and services. Another major source of provincial revenue is federal transfer payments (more about these later). Provincial governments use the combined revenue from these and other sources to finance their public services and programs. They also share some of this revenue with local governments to help provide municipal and school services in their respective constituencies.

In 1990, provincial grants provided an average of 61.3 percent of total school board revenue, down slightly from the early 1980s. This ratio varied greatly from province to province, depending on the finance formulas. Newfoundland, Prince Edward Island, and New Brunswick relied almost exclusively on provincial funding for revenue (over 80 percent of total revenue). Conversely, boards in Ontario (49.6 percent), Saskatchewan (49.6 percent), British Columbia (59.3), and Alberta (59.4) received less than 60 percent of their funds from provincial grants and raised the rest from local property taxation and other local sources.

SOURCES OF LOCAL REVENUE

Besides grants, the other major source of school board revenue is the local property tax. Property for tax purposes consists mainly of land, buildings, business premises, and industrial and commercial developments such as mines, factories, refineries, and pipelines. Each province develops a standardized system, usually referred to as equalized assessment, in order to put some value on the property for tax purposes. The main factor in equalized assessment is market value, but other variables enter into the valuation as well. The total equalized assessment of all property (business and residential) in a school district or municipality forms the property tax base for local government.

To raise revenue from the property tax base, municipal councils and school boards first estimate their budgetary requirements. Then, using a common denominator called *mill*, they calculate the tax rate that must be applied to all properties, to generate the needed funds. One mill is the amount of property tax (in dollars) to be paid on $1000 of the assessed value (which may be on a different scale from the current market value) of a property. The common practice is to assess the value of a property according to the zoning area, the building and utilizable surface, the quality of the interior and the land surface. If the tax rate is 80 mills ($80 per $1000 assessed value), a property assessed at $10 000 would have a property tax amounting to $800. Municipal authorities generally collect the tax for both the municipality and the school district, a practice that reduces the cost of collection and administration. The education portion is then paid over to the school district.

FEDERAL CONTRIBUTION

Because education is a provincial responsibility, one might assume that the federal government does not share in the financing of education. This is not so—the federal government is involved in two major ways. First, it is directly responsible for providing educational services to the following groups: Native students residing in both the provinces and the territories; children resident in the non-provincial parts of Canada, that is, the territories and Arctic islands; children of armed forces personnel both at home and abroad; and inmates of penitentiaries. These programs fall outside the jurisdiction of the provinces, but where the children affected are residents within provincial boundaries, the federal government often enters into agreements with provincial or local school systems to buy services from them. At present, federal expenditures for these programs constitute about 3 percent of all expenditures on elementary–secondary education in Canada.

The federal government is also involved in financing education because of the nature of Canadian federalism. Since Confederation, federal governments have made various fiscal arrangements or have entered into various agreements to make transfer payments to the provinces out of the general federal revenues. The two major purposes of these payments have been equalization of provincial fiscal capacity and joint cost-sharing of specific social programs such as health, welfare, and postsecondary and vocational education. The general spirit underlying federal transfers has always been to preserve the autonomy of provincial governments. Federal funds, once received, become part of the provincial treasury and are expended according to provincial priorities (Carter, 1988). There is no doubt, however, that by increasing the fiscal capacity of the provinces, the federal government indirectly contributes to or affects the allocation of resources to education. In 1990, the federal government contribution to the provinces' education expenditures averaged 9.8 percent and varied between 6.8 percent for Ontario, 8.6 percent for Quebec, to 12.1 percent for New Brunswick.

Several federal programs result in higher educational costs, which are usually defrayed either directly through grants or indirectly through the salaries of federal employees associated with some of these programs. Examples are programs in official languages (schools and courses), multiculturalism, citizenship, and training. In general, communities are eager to secure these services and the potential revenue from them.

CONSENSUS ON SHARING EDUCATIONAL OBLIGATIONS

Federal, provincial, and local governments all share the responsibility for financing public education. The provincial governments and their respective school boards are the major partners in the design, since the federal government has only a few direct responsibilities in education that represent a small fraction of total spending. Indirectly, however, through the process of financing a federated state, the federal government becomes a major contributor to all public services of which education is a part.

THE CONCEPT OF ABILITY-TO-PAY

In Canada there are rich and poor people, rich and poor school systems, and rich and poor provinces. The following sections deal with the concept of ability-to-pay as it applies to education funding and with the processes that have been developed politically to overcome the great disparities in ability-to-pay that exist between the rich and the poor.

ABILITY-TO-PAY APPLIED TO SCHOOL SYSTEMS

The ability-to-pay of a school system refers to its capacity to raise revenue from its own sources to pay for educational programs. Two factors determine ability-to-pay: the equalized assessment of the school system and the number of pupils to be educated, or more succinctly, assessment per pupil. The difference between a rich school district and a poor school district may be illustrated with the following example.

District A is comparatively wealthy; its total equalized assessment divided by the number of pupils it has to educate is equal to $80 000 per pupil. With one mill of tax, therefore, it can raise $80 for every pupil in its schools. District B is relatively poor, having a tax base of $20 000 per pupil. Thus, District B can raise only $20 of revenue per pupil at the rate of one mill. What this means is that the rich district can raise four times as much money per pupil as the poor district. District B would have to carry four times its current tax rate to raise the same amount of money per pupil as District A. Consequently, poor districts by themselves cannot compete with rich districts in the quality of the programs they offer. If school districts were limited to their own revenue sources, poorer districts would have programs inferior to richer districts. This is where equalization comes in.

The inequality illustrated in this example is not acceptable in a democratic society. The concept of universality demands that quality of education should not depend on whether a child lives in a rich or a poor district. Overcoming the disparities created by variations in ability-to-pay is one of the main reasons why the financing of education in Canada is a responsibility shared by both provincial governments and school boards.

Each provincial government in Canada structures its school grants system to compensate for the varying fiscal abilities found at the local level. Grants are paid on a different basis to take into account local ability-to-pay. Thus, the grant received by a poor school district constitutes a higher percentage of that board's total revenue than would be the case for a rich district. Some districts may be so wealthy that they receive little or no grant. The grants system is designed so that the total amount of revenue per pupil from grants and taxes, and the mill rates for school taxes, are more or less equalized across the province.

Provincial–local sharing of the responsibility for financing education makes it possible to overcome the inequities in educational opportunity and taxation that arise from differences in local ability-to-pay. Two other justifications for shared responsibility may also be mentioned. First, the province, with its superior access to tax revenues, is in a position to ensure that the amount of money spent on education is sufficient to provide programs of quality throughout its jurisdiction. Second, there is an economic rationale, sometimes labelled the "Dutch-treat effect," that holds that if two levels of government help pay for education, the amount of money spent on this service, and therefore the level of quality, will be higher than if only one government were involved.

PROVINCIAL ABILITY-TO-PAY

Provinces in Canada differ in their ability-to-pay in the same way that school systems differ. A rich province can more easily raise a given amount of money per capita from its own sources than can a poor province. The fiscal capacity of a province, therefore, affects the quantity and the quality of public services it can produce and the standard of living its residents can enjoy. The effect of ability-to-pay on the provincial tax burdens is the same as the effect on local school governments. Taxpayers in poor provinces bear a much heavier tax burden and yet have access to an inferior package of social programs relative to rich provinces.

If provinces were left to their own sources, great interprovincial disparities would arise in public programs, tax burdens, and standards of living. To ensure that each province can at least meet the most basic needs of all its citizens, the federal government, in co-operation with the provinces, redistributes the wealth of the nation. The primary instrument in this redistribution function is *equalization payments*.

Since 1867, the federal government and the provinces have made various arrangements to share major sources of taxation and other public revenue in order to give all levels of government an adequate revenue base. Beginning in 1957, arrangements were made to include a system of equalization transfers from the federal treasury to those provinces whose own sources of revenue fell below a certain level. The amount of equalization that each province received depended on the shortfall between its own revenue and the agreed-upon norm. Thus the equalization payments on a per capita basis were much higher for poorer provinces and represented a greater percentage of the total revenue of these provinces. Those provinces whose own revenues equalled or exceeded the norm received no equalization. Equalization payments became a part of provincial revenue and their ultimate use was determined by the provincial government, free from federally imposed conditions.

The latest federal–provincial fiscal arrangement was negotiated in 1987 by the Mulroney government. The concept of equalization was maintained, but the norm for equalization was changed to a standard based on the ability-to-pay of five "representative" provinces: Ontario, Quebec, Manitoba, Saskatchewan, and British Columbia (Macdonald Commission, 1985, vol. 3, p. 189). Alberta was omitted because its natural resource revenue was so high that it distorted the "representativeness" of the norm. In 1985–86, the federal government was expected to make equalization payments totalling an estimated $5 billion to all provinces except British Columbia, Ontario, Alberta, and Saskatchewan (Macdonald Commission, 1985, vol. 3, p. 181).[2]

Revenue sharing refers to arrangements that have been made between the provinces and the federal government to share the use of the personal and corporate income tax base. Federal income tax rates leave room for the provinces to use this tax base for their own revenue-raising purposes (see Lipsey, Purvis, & Steiner 1988, ch. 25).

Conditional grants are federal payments made to provinces to share the costs of providing services in specified areas such as health, welfare, postsecondary education, regional development, and official languages. Before the current shared-cost programs, the amount a province received depended on how much it spent in the first place. This type of matching arrangement stimulated the allocation of resources to the specified programs, but it also brought the criticism that the federal government was setting priorities and was thereby interfering with provincial autonomy. Since the 1960s, successive federal governments experienced problems with the matching feature because they could not restrict the provincial requests, which depended in large part on what the provinces had spent. The Fiscal Arrangements Act of 1977 changed the basis for determining the amounts of many conditional grants to a per capita basis that would increase yearly in relation to the growth in GNP rather than to growth in provincial costs.

The method of administering conditional grants to help pay for the costs of health care and postsecondary education was changed in 1977 by the Established Programs Financing Act, which broke the link between federal grants and provincial expenditures. This act gave the federal government more control over the amount of payment—control that it badly needed because of increasing costs in these two fields and decreasing federal revenues. Transfers for health and postsecondary education are now calculated by reference to costs in a base year adjusted by increases in GNP, and payments are made in the form of both cash and tax-room concessions. This formula may soon be changed.

Equalization payments, revenue sharing, conditional grants, and Established Programs Financing have become increasingly important in Canada's federal system. Many of the social responsibilities that lie within provincial jurisdiction are clearly beyond the financial capacity of most provincial governments. Federal assistance is, therefore, required in order to establish social programs. The equalization effect of federal transfers is of paramount importance, since these payments make it possible for all provinces to provide reasonably comparable levels of service with reasonably comparable levels of tax burden, in spite of interprovincial differences in ability-to-pay. The concept is recognized in the Canadian Constitution (Constitution Act, 1982, section 36).

Statistics show that equalization and other transfer payments grow year by year and constitute an increasingly important source of revenue for most provinces. At present, approximately 18 percent of all provincial revenue comes from this source; for certain provinces in the Atlantic region the percentage is near or over 50 percent. The cost is nearly 20 percent of total federal expenditures. As Canada progresses into the 1990s, the fiscal interdependence of the federal government and the provinces becomes greater and greater.

This formula is gradually changing. The federal government wants to reduce the current annual deficits (over $40 billion) and has done so partly by reducing cost-sharing payments to the provinces starting in 1990 (Canadian Teachers' Federation, 1990a). The richer provinces are able to finance their own programs and the objections of the poor regions can be reduced by alternative grants that total less than the cuts imposed on equalization payments.

PRINCIPLES OF EDUCATIONAL FINANCE

The discussion on the concept of ability-to-pay and its implications for the roles of local, provincial, and federal governments in education contains some implicit normative assumptions about the provision of public services in Canada. The assumptions arise out of the beliefs, values, and experiences of Canadian society. This section articulates more explicitly a number of value premises, or principles, that should guide the financing of education within provincial school systems. They are particularly applicable in a political system where there is intergovernmental sharing of the responsibility for public services. The principles deal with the equalization of educational opportunity, the equalization of educational tax burden, the preservation of local autonomy, and the provision for provincial control.

EQUALIZATION OF EDUCATIONAL OPPORTUNITY

Many attempts have been made to define "equality of educational opportunity" (Nwabu-ogu, 1984). The traditional definitions have been expressed in terms of equal access to education, or in terms of equal allocation of resources. More recent definitions of equality have referred to equality of outcomes or achievement and to equal benefit. In educational finance, equality of opportunity has generally referred to resource inputs and to horizontal and vertical equity. These terms have particular meanings.

Translated into fiscal terms, equality of educational opportunity means that the province and the local school systems collectively ensure that equal dollars are available to educate every pupil. To illustrate for a given province, Saskatchewan (in 1988) could guarantee that the combination of local property tax revenue and provincial grant would provide $5000 for every child enrolled in school. Such a scheme would provide horizontal equity only. Equal dollars would translate into equal opportunity only on the condition that every child had educational needs of similar costs.

Because children differ in many ways, the cost of instruction varies. The educational environment that differs from school to school also influences costs. In sparsely populated regions where costs of transportation, utilities, goods, and services are high, the guaranteed $5000 would not buy the same quality of education available to students in wealthier areas (cities). In other words, equal dollars per pupil would not provide vertical equity. Achiev-ing *vertical equity*, or equality of opportunity, for children with different needs and in different circumstances requires differential amounts of money per child. Only in this way can a province and its school boards achieve equality of educational opportunity.

The finance formulas used by provincial school systems today are designed to achieve both horizontal and vertical equity. Differences in ability-to-pay among school districts are levelled out, and differential financial provisions are made to take differential needs and costs into account.

EQUALIZATION OF TAX BURDEN

The principle of equalization of tax burden holds that the financial burden incurred by those paying taxes to finance education should be equal. When the application of this principle is made within the confines of a provincial school system, it means the admin-istration of the property tax. The question then becomes: How can the property tax burden be equalized for all taxpayers in the province?

The provincial government has the power to implement a threefold solution to this question. First, the provinces can impose equalized assessment for all school systems within their jurisdictions. Second, the province can use a system of grants and controls of tax rates that keep local mill rates roughly the same. Third, when cities or counties have very high assessments and relatively small school populations, they do not require provincial grants. If their wealth is great, the province might even tax them to help pay for social programs elsewhere. Toronto and Ottawa have now no need for grants for education but have not yet been surcharged. If these three courses of action are followed, then equity in tax burden is assumed to be achieved, at least as far as property tax is concerned. Whether they actually do result in equality as measured by a personal income standard is another question.

PRESERVATION OF LOCAL AUTONOMY

The tradition of local self-government in education is strong in Canada. Inherent in this tradition is the belief that local governments should possess the highest degree of freedom possible to make decisions and to govern their local affairs.

Local autonomy applied to educational finance consists of two components: local control and local leeway. Because provincial governments in Canada pay substantial grants to school boards, there is a natural tendency for control to follow dollars. But local control means eliminating any conditions that must be satisfied before qualifying for payments. Once the grants are received, they should become part of the board's revenue, to be used according to local priorities. Grants paid in this spirit are usually referred to as block grants, or unconditional grants, to distinguish them from conditional grants. Conditional grants are different in that local governments may not only have to meet certain conditions to receive the grant, but might also have to use the grant in designated ways. For example, block grants usually cover basic costs like teachers' salaries for standard programs; conditional grants might be for building schools or for second-language programs.

Local initiative as a part of local autonomy means giving local school governments the authority to deviate from provincial norms with respect to raising revenue from local sources. To illustrate, most systems of school finance in Canada follow what is called a foundation program model. Under this model each school system uses a province-wide formula to calculate the revenue it would need to offer a basic, or "foundation," educational program to its students. The provincial government establishes a mandatory or a computational mill rate (to achieve equality of tax burden) that school boards levy to raise a part of the revenue required to pay for the foundation program. The provincial government then pays the balance of the money needed in the form of grants. If school finance statutes or regulations permit local leeway (and they usually do), then school boards that want to raise more money to finance a program at better than foundation level may do so by raising their mill rates above the level set by the provincial government.

There is a problem with local leeway that relates to the issue of financial inequality. Each extra mill of tax will raise more money per pupil in a rich school district than it will in a poor one. In this situation, local leeway threatens the principles of equality of opportunity and equalization of tax burden, since richer districts are able to finance superior programs with less effort. The principle of local autonomy conflicts with the equalization principle. However, local school governments in Canada believe so strongly in the value of local autonomy that all provinces with foundation programs permit some local leeway.

The full-state-funding provinces of Prince Edward Island and New Brunswick provide only limited local autonomy. Since all boards in these provinces receive all, or nearly all, of their revenue from the province, they do not have local leeway. They may, however, enjoy a high degree of local control if provincial monies are turned over to them as unconditional or block grants, which provide the boards with the freedom to expend the grants according to local needs and priorities.

PROVISION FOR CENTRAL CONTROL

The senior partner in financing education in all provinces is the provincial government. Regardless of the finance scheme adopted by a province, the senior level of government must retain some degree of control over the financing of education. This is a necessary principle, since the provincial government has constitutional authority (Constitution Act, 1867, section 93, Appendix A) to establish the goals of education and to determine priorities among these goals. It must provide the leadership and the incentive to ensure that adequate funding is available to achieve these goals, and that funding is implemented in accordance with adopted principles. Furthermore, the province has the broader responsibility of providing many other social programs. In discharging this broader responsibility, it must have the power to control allocations among competing and changing priorities and to control total appropriations so as to remain fiscally solvent.

PRINCIPLES IN CONFLICT

The principles that provincial governments use to govern their fiscal relationships with boards of education are more often than not in conflict with one another. For example, permitting local leeway violates both the principles of equal educational opportunity and equal tax burden; preserving local autonomy and yet exercising centralized control are contradictory objectives. This does not mean, however, that the principles are mutually exclusive; adherence to one does not necessarily mean ruling out the other. What it does mean is that governments must seek a balance among principles when setting public policy. The relationship is dynamic, moving according to time and circumstance along a continuum from more central control to more local control and back again.

TRENDS THAT MAY AFFECT ALLOCATION OF RESOURCES TO EDUCATION

Changing trends and shifting values and priorities affect the allocation of resources to education. This section contains a discussion of six trends in the Canadian social, economic, and political fabric that may affect educational funding in the future.

DEMOGRAPHIC TRENDS

Brown (1983) has studied the main demographic trends in Canada since 1959, chief among which are falling birth rates and a rapidly aging population. According to his calculations, the school-aged population as a percent of total population changed from 42 percent in 1961 to 32 percent in 1981, and is expected to drop to 27 percent by 2001. Meanwhile, the population that represents most of the workforce grew from 51 to 58 percent between 1961 and 1981 and will grow to 62 percent of total population by 2001. Furthermore, the older segment of the population, those 65 and over, will increase from 10 percent in 1981 to an estimated 12 percent in 2001.

Brown's calculations are based on dependency ratios (all persons under 20 and over 64 are assumed to be dependent, and all those between 20 and 64 are working age). These assumptions do not describe reality in many communities or for all families. The amount of public spending varies widely among educational programs but generally climbs to a peak in higher education. The dependency costs of several social programs (notably medical care) rise dramatically with age. Annual per person medical costs for the elderly considerably exceed the average per pupil costs of schooling. Nor will all the working-age population behave according to the theory, so there is some doubt that Brown's cheerful prospect will be realized:

> Increasing production by a maturing and highly skilled active population should provide the economic preconditions for adequate levels of financial support of education and other social services. (Brown, 1983, p. 4)

SHIFTING GOVERNMENT PRIORITIES

The Canadian Teachers' Federation claims that elementary and secondary education has been losing ground (and money) to other social programs in Canada as a whole and in most provinces. The percent of total provincial–local government spending allocated to elementary and secondary education in Canada declined from 17 percent in 1975 to 14.5 percent in 1988. Corresponding 1990 statistics show that the shares allocated to other social services (including higher education) increased slightly from 39 to 42.7 percent during the same period (Canadian Teachers' Federation, 1990b).

Whether or not these trends actually indicate shifting government priorities for education is difficult to say. The downward trend in education may be due simply to the fact that elementary–secondary enrollment has declined and therefore less money needs to be spent on education. Other statistics show that although educational shares of total spending have been declining, actual total dollar amounts spent on education and expenditures per pupil have increased (Brown, 1983, p. 9). Even when these increases are deflated using the Canadian Education Price Index, increases in real purchasing power have occurred.

There are other indications that adequate funding is still a high priority in Canadian education (Brown, 1983; Statistics Canada, 1985). Pupil–teacher ratios and class size have decreased. The teaching force is better qualified and more experienced; consequently, more teachers are at their maximum potential salary. Collective agreements have improved working conditions and employment benefits, although restraints and cutbacks have occurred in some provinces recently. These changes have all been high-cost items

Education appears to be holding its own in competition with other public services. Perhaps this is not as true in some provinces as in others, but the general picture for Canada appears positive. Priorities may change, however, as economic conditions fluctuate and other social needs become more pressing.

COMMITMENT TO EQUALITY

In 1981, Canada finalized the patriation of the Constitution and incorporated into it the Charter of Rights and Freedoms, which sets forth the principles on which the country is to be governed. The commitment to equality is paramount. Section 15 (1) states, "Every individual is equal before and under the law and has the right to the equal protection and equal benefit without discrimination." Further on, Section 36 (1) commits the federal and provincial governments to the following:

(a) promoting equal opportunities for the well-being of all Canadians;
(b) furthering economic development to reduce disparity in opportunities; and
(c) providing essential public services of reasonable quality to all Canadians.

Section 36 (2) addresses the problem of equalizing tax burdens that arise due to provincial disparities in ability-to-pay:

Parliament and the government of Canada are committed to the principle of making equalization payments to ensure that provincial governments have sufficient revenues to provide reasonably comparable levels of public services at reasonably comparable rates of taxation.

The commitment to equality is very clear in the Charter. For education, it means that future federal and provincial governments must continue to work together to achieve equalization of opportunity and tax burden. This goal is probably more critical at the elementary–secondary level than it is at the postsecondary level, because, as the Macdonald Commission (1985, vol. 2, p. 738) concluded, the payback to society for spending on elementary–secondary education is greater than for spending at higher levels.

TRENDS IN FEDERAL–PROVINCIAL RELATIONS

Brown (1983, 1985) has followed trends in federal–provincial fiscal relations and analyzed their impact on educational funding. He notes that in the 1960s and 1970s Canada experienced rapid economic growth and enjoyed near full employment with low levels of inflation (Brown, 1983). Resource allocation to education and other public services increased at rates exceeding historical averages, and resulted in high expectations that these trends would continue. Since the mid-1970s, however, there has been a reversal in the rate of economic growth and prosperity, and both governments and individuals have had to adjust accordingly. The result has been decreased growth rates in public spending—even cutbacks—and an expressed desire for greater control over government expenditures and deficits. The mid-1980s, more than any other recent period, has been characterized by restraints on spending at all levels and by changes to federal–provincial fiscal transfer arrangements that impose limits on payments to the provinces.

Slower economic growth, spending restraints, and limits on federal–provincial transfers have caused interprovincial disparities in ability-to-pay, which had been narrowing, to begin widening again. Both Brown (1985, p. 2) and the Macdonald Commission (1985, vol. 3, p. 193) speculate that the trend will continue as a result of the 1982–87 federal–provincial fiscal arrangements now in place. Brown (1985, p. 2) has looked specifically at differences among provinces in such educational matters as spending per pupil and provincial–local revenue allocations to education relative to total spending. He notes that interprovincial differences in these variables are increasing, and that the differences are related to ability-to-pay.

The drift to widening disparity must be a cause of concern to a country that has, in its Constitution, committed itself to equality. We may only hope that improved economic conditions and different federal–provincial fiscal arrangements in the future will reverse this trend.

DIVERSION OF RESOURCES FROM PUBLIC TO PRIVATE SCHOOLS

Another educational trend occurring in Canada in recent years has been the increasing enrollment in private schools. Concomitant with this has been the trend to greater support of private schools from public funds. Statistics Canada reported that private school enrollment as a percent of elementary–secondary school enrollment increased from 2.4 percent in 1971–72 to 4.94 percent in 1993–94. This trend has been interrupted statistically by the reclassification of the Catholic senior secondary schools of Ontario from private to public. This reduced the private enrollment in that province.

Meanwhile, other provinces have increased the level of financial assistance to private schooling, in effect encouraging their growth and reducing the expectations for the publicly financed systems. In 1985, five provinces (Manitoba, Saskatchewan, British Columbia, Alberta, and Quebec) provided grants for private schools (Shapiro, 1985, ch. 3). Between 1971–72 and 1979–80, this funding increased from 18.3 percent to 32.2 percent of total private school expenditures (Brown, 1983, p. 21).

Ontario may soon provide some public funding of private schools. A government commission investigating this matter in 1985 recommended a program of limited financial support for private schools, and a system for organizing "associated schools" whereby a private school could enter into an agreement with a public school for sharing services (Shapiro, 1985).

The extent to which resources may be reallocated from the funding of public schools to the funding of private schools in Canada is a matter of continuing debate and speculation, but the trend during the 1970s and early 1980s has been in the direction of a growing private schools movement with increased infusion of public monies. Opponents of this trend stress that Canada's heterogeneous society needs to provide the kind of socializing, acculturating experience possible through a common public school system. It is argued that private schools, which are often established to provide many diverse religious, philosophical, and cultural environments not found in the public schools, tend to perpetuate differences and divisiveness, and therefore should not be encouraged through public funding (Shapiro, 1985).

DECREASING RELIANCE ON THE PROPERTY TAX

Another important general trend in Canadian educational finance in the last fifteen to twenty years has been the decreasing reliance on the property tax and the increasing reliance on provincial funds to pay for education. The major reason for the shift is equity. The property tax is acknowledged to be a regressive tax in that it hurts low-income households. Provincial taxes, especially the income tax, are more equitable, distributing tax burdens more evenly among taxpayers according to ability-to-pay. Therefore, tax equity is promoted by shifting more of the burden of financing education to provincial tax sources. All provinces have moved in this direction, but economic circumstances have caused provincial–local sharing to fluctuate back and forth.

Provincial–local sharing arrangements of the the last fifteen to twenty years provide evidence that the trend of the province becoming the major supplier of funds for education seems to have become well established. However, there is now real concern that this trend may be reversed as Canada progresses toward the year 2000 because of the accumulation of mounting provincial and federal deficits. The growing public debt means that higher and higher percentages of both provincial and federal budgets go to paying interest, leaving less revenue for grants and transfer payments. This leads to a phenomenon called "down-loading": the federal government downloads its deficit to provincial governments by reducing transfer payments to the provinces. The ability-to-pay of provinces is thus diminished, forcing many of them to borrow more money to pay for existing public programs. The additional borrowing increases provincial public debt and interest payments, leaving less money for grants to school boards and local governments. As grants to school boards diminish, the boards must resort to increasing property taxes to make up for revenue shortfalls. Thus, the phenomenon of downloading progresses right through all levels of government—from federal to provincial to local—with the potential effect of reversing the trend of decreasing reliance on the local property tax that occurred in the last two decades.

CONCLUSIONS

Canadians allocate substantial resources to public education because they believe education to be a fundamental requirement for the maintenance and growth of a democratic society. Since education is a provincial responsibility, funds come from two main sources—provincial grants and local property taxes, with grants accounting for about 70 percent of the total. Indirectly, the federal government also contributes resources to education through the payment of equalization and other grants into the general revenues of each province.

Provinces and school systems within each province vary greatly in their ability-to-pay for education. If each were left to its own resources, great inequities would result both in educational opportunity and in tax burden. The federal government and the provinces have undertaken to redistribute funds to the governmental agencies responsible for education. The federal government uses its resources to equalize differences at the provincial level, and the provincial governments use their resources and federal transfers to equalize resources at the local level.

Certain principles have evolved in the theory and practice of educational finance that guide provincial governments in the design of their school funding programs. These principles include equalization of educational opportunity and tax burden, preservation of local autonomy, and provision for provincial control. Although the principles may conflict, they are balanced one against the other when implemented, resulting in a largely effective and efficient educational system.

At least six trends are evident in Canadian society that may influence the financing of education in the future. First, the structure of Canada's population is changing, so that the ratio of school-age population to working-age population is declining. Second, the rate of increase in funds allocated to education has slowed down relative to the rate of increase for other public services. Third, Canadians have firmly re-dedicated themselves to the principles of equality in the new Constitution. Fourth, economic hard times, growing needs in the public sector, and revised federal–provincial fiscal arrangements have halted and even reversed progress toward greater fiscal equality among provinces. Fifth, provincial governments are moving in the direction of diverting more funds from public schools to private schools, thus creating greater diversification in education. Finally, provinces are adopting policies to decrease reliance on the local property tax as a source of school revenue, although there are economic pressures now arising to halt and even reverse this trend.

DISCUSSION QUESTIONS

❑ The Canadian pattern of educational support is partly a consequence of internal disparity in conditions, but partly ideological. How can you explain the differences in provincial support for educational costs in such provinces as Ontario and Quebec, or Saskatchewan and New Brunswick?

❑ How can you explain the size of federal grants-in-aid to different provinces? How appropriate has it been to entrench such principles into the Constitution?

❑ If education is an investment, should the family, the community, the province, or the nation pay the costs of schooling?

NOTES

1. Education and finance statistics for this chapter were derived mainly from Statistics Canada (1992), Brown (1983), UNESCO (1992), and The Canadian Teachers' Federation (1986, 1990a, 1990b, 1990c).
2. Information regarding historical and present federal–provincial arrangements can be obtained from Lipsey et al. (1985, ch. 25), Carter (1985), and the MacDonald Commission (1985, ch. 22).

REFERENCES

Brown, W.J. (1983). The educational toll of the great recession. In B.D. Anderson, W.J. Brown, S.B. Lawton, P. Michaud, & E.W. Ricker. *The cost of controlling the costs of education in Canada.* (pp. 1–22). Toronto: Ontario Institute for Studies in Education.

Brown, W.J. (1985). Proposed reduction in federal transfers to provinces will harm education. *Link, 10*(1), 1–2.

Canadian Teachers' Federation. (1986). Elementary and secondary education losing ground to other social spending in Canada and in most provinces. *Link, 10*(2), 14.

Canadian Teachers' Federation. (1990a). Centralizing and decentralizing school funding. *Link, 14*(3), 18–19.

Canadian Teachers' Federation. (1990b). How are the public schools doing in the competition for scarce resources? *Link, 14*(3), 16–17.

Canadian Teachers' Federation. (1990c). Spending patterns for public schools. *Link, 14*(3), 22–25.

Carter, G.E. (1988). Taxation. In J.H. March (Ed.). *The Canadian encyclopedia.* (Vol. 4, pp. 2112–14). Edmonton: Hurtig.

Lipsey, R.G., Purvis, D.D., & Steiner, P.O. (1988). *Economics* (6th ed.). New York: Harper & Row.

Macdonald Commission. (1985). *Report of the Royal Commission on economic union and development prospects for Canada.* (Vols. 1–3). Ottawa: Supply and Services Canada.

Nwabuogu, M.N. (1984, Summer). On the meaning and application of equal educational opportunity: A review article. *Journal of Education Finance, 10*, 64–82.

Shapiro, B.J. (1985). *The report of the commission on private schools in Ontario.* Toronto: Ontario Ministry of Education.

Statistics Canada. (1985). *Advance statistics of education, 1985–86.* (Catalogue 81-220). Ottawa: Supply and Services Canada.

Statistics Canada. (1992). *Education in Canada 1990–1991.* (Catalogue 81-228). Ottawa: Supply and Services Canada.

UNESCO. (1992). *Statistical yearbook.* Paris: UNESCO.

FURTHER READINGS

Benson, C.S. (1978). *The economics of public education.* (3rd ed.). Boston: Houghton Mifflin.

Blaug, M. (Ed.). (1970). *An introduction to the economics of education.* London: Penguin.

Coombs, P.H. (1985). *The world crisis in education: The view from the eighties.* New York: Oxford.

Garms, W.I., Guthrie, J.W., & Pierce, L.C. (1978). *School finance: The economics and politics of financing education.* Englewood Cliffs, NJ: Prentice-Hall.

Jefferson, A.L. (1992, Summer). Financing education: A time for change. *Education Canada,* 23–25

Johns, R.E., Morphet, E.L., & Alexander, K. (1983). *The economics and financing of education* (4th ed.). Englewood Cliffs, NJ: Prentice-Hall.

Jones, T.H. (1985). *Introduction to school finance: Technique and social policy.* New York: Macmillan.

McCormick, C. (1990, Winter). The persistence of provincial and regional inequities in education finance in Canada. *Education in Canada,* 23–26.

Moffat, H.P., & Brown, W.J. (1973). *New goals new paths: The search for a rationale for the financing of education in Canada.* Ottawa: Canadian Teachers' Federation.

Ontario Institute for Studies in Education. (1991). The 8th OISE survey — Educational funding. *Orbit (Special Issue), 22*(2), 4–8.

Ray, D.W. (1986). Resources for education: Human rights and the Canadian system for redistribution of public funds. *Canadian Journal of Education, 11*(3), 353–63.

Richards, D.M., & Ratsoy, E.W. (1987). *Introduction to the economics of Canadian education.* Calgary: Detselig.

Schultz, T.W. (1963). *The economic value of education.* New York: Columbia University Press.

PART II

POLICIES

INTRODUCTION

Policies are formal means of implementing and directing change in society and its institutions. An analysis of educational policy is, therefore, an important consideration in understanding the relationship between educational and social change.

In Canada, both federal and provincial government policies have affected education over the years. Despite the fact that the federal government has no direct responsibility for what goes on in most classrooms, its impact is felt in funding and through the implementation of social programs. Such things as the federal policy of bilingualism (within a multicultural society) and the entrenchment of the Charter of Rights and Freedoms have made it necessary for provincial governments to develop educational policies in accord with federal legislation. Provincial responses have varied, both in terms of programs and structures, because of regional differences in the context of education. Differences in the sets of actors involved in the process of policy development, implementation, and action have also had a diversifying effect.

Suzanne Majhanovich discusses the policy of bilingualism, which makes English and French the official federal languages of Canada. However, among the provinces, only New Brunswick is officially bilingual; other provinces are officially unilingual but offer many services (including instruction) in both official languages. Typically, the provision of minority educational services in the minority official language has been contested by the provinces. In many cases, the right to instruction at all levels has been supported by court action. However, the population's support for official languages has transformed society. During a period of declining enrollments, French studies have expanded considerably in most provinces. Languages other than English and French have become increasingly important as languages of instruction, either as heritage language programs in most provinces or as other languages in Quebec.

Gloria Rong Zhang deals with the education required by those who have little experience in either of the official languages of Canada and whose education in other languages is undervalued and their learning in an official language truncated. The number of immigrants from such countries as East Asia and Latin America are growing rapidly—especially in metropolitan areas. There are successful programs for these people in the areas of greatest need, but where the numbers requiring English or French as a second language are small, schools are able to provide only limited help.

The impact of religion in moulding educational structures in Canada has been significant. Jud Purdy traces the development of a pragmatic working arrangement with the Christian church, which rejects both the legal establishment of the church, as in the British model, and the American way of separating church and state. After a decline in the importance of organized religion in Canadian society, the 1970s saw a resurgence in religion's role in society and education. By 1994 the debate regarding religion's place in education is beginning to force a reassessment of existing arrangements.

Walter Werner and Bill Knitter examine curriculum through different disciplines. Werner's chapter identifies the critical questions being debated in typical ministries of education and most school boards. These include which subjects should be offered in a time of declining revenues and enrollments; which languages should be taught, and for how many hours; which vocational considerations should be stressed; which citizenship objectives are important; and whether external examinations serve a useful purpose. Knitter examines the philosophical issues behind these typical debates.

Educational policy in Canada is the subject of Robert O'Reilly's chapter. He traces some steps in the policy process and points out that although public education in Canada has, until recently, been thought of by policy actors as being "apolitical," the federal government has influenced education in several ways. Perhaps the greatest impact has been felt in its role in the development of French-language instruction. O'Reilly also gives examples of policy at the provincial and local levels to illustrate how policy-making has become more political. Ultimately, the chapter concludes, policy actors at various levels will be the ones to create a new vision for Canadian education.

Marie McAndrew examines Canada's multicultural policy, which originally was aimed at resolving the conflicting claims of various groups by espousing unity in diversity. The implementation of this federal policy influenced a variety of multicultural policies in education at the provincial level. The author points out the ambiguity of the federal policy, which is evident in the different interpretations and emphases of multicultural education in the provinces, and particularly in Quebec. Multicultural policy has raised several important issues surrounding the content and context of education in Canada.

Claude Lessard explores the concept of equality in education and discusses data from recent literature on the relationship between educational opportunity and social class, language, ethnicity, and sex. These data indicate a reduction, but not the elimination, of inequalities in Canadian society.

Paul Olson looks at poverty in Canada and Canadian education. Beginning with a discussion of the implicit causes and reasons for poverty in a welfare state, the author identifies the poor and examines the structural, cyclical, social, and regional factors by which they are characterized. He demonstrates that because poverty continues to be intergenerational, education has not been a "cure" for poverty. Olson ends with some suggestions as to how schools should deal with poverty.

The final chapter in this section deals with adults, who are increasingly becoming a significant group in Canadian education. Deo Poonwassie focusses on the definition of adult education and points out its importance in a country with an "aging population." He distinguishes the *study* of adult education from the *practice* and ends by pointing to its significance in a rapidly changing and technologically advancing society.

6

OFFICIAL AND HERITAGE LANGUAGES IN CANADA: HOW POLICIES TRANSLATE INTO PRACTICES

Suzanne Majhanovich

Canada is internationally respected and sometimes envied for its language policies—although the most important of these is official bilingualism, heritage languages are also important to this assessment. However, there is little reason to be proud of our policies or practices regarding aboriginal languages (see Chapter 23).

The *constitutional* protection of languages is confined to official languages; there is also a rather vague protection of aboriginal languages and multiculturalism, and through the latter, of heritage languages. Most policies are based on ordinary legislation or regulations made by the ministries of education and are readily changed. The origins and implications of these various types of policies are the subjects of this chapter.

OFFICIAL LANGUAGES IN CANADA

English and French are official languages for federal purposes. New Brunswick is officially bilingual at all levels. Elsewhere, and for all other purposes, Canada is officially unilingual, although there are important concessions and constitutional guarantees for the two "official" language communities in places where they find themselves to be minorities. For example, Ontario and Quebec are not officially bilingual provinces, despite having large minority official-language populations, and despite their provision of many services in that minority language (including education, access to the courts, and government services in many communities). Community declarations of an official language policy (whether officially bilingual, monolingual, or multilingual) for municipal purposes are of dubious legal status and represent at best a political statement. The communities have no right to withhold a service (such as education in the minority official language) that has been authorized by provincial legislation, and by-laws can be overruled by the provinces, which control municipal government.

The existence and precise nature of language rights have been the source of much soul-searching, tensions, and wrangling. At times, real or perceived infringements upon the rights of significant linguistic communities (for example in the 1840s, 1890s, or 1960s) have brought Canada to the verge of being torn apart. It is unfortunate and ironic for a country in search of an identity to permit one of its main characteristics—bilingualism—to cause so much dissention.

Part of the problem may be that, despite the existence of two major European language groups in Canada since before its emergence as a collection of colonies, the notion of enshrining language *rights* in the Canadian Constitution is of relatively recent origin (Hébert, 1986). It must also be recognized that language, inextricably bound with identity, culture, and heritage, embodies the deepest personal values of individuals (Ashworth, 1988). Thus, issues touching upon language rights always have the potential to inflame. As has been noted in the *Annual Report 1988* of the Commissioner of Official Languages,

> If our linguistic tensions periodically resurface, it may in part be because we actively seek solutions to difficult problems that many other countries prefer to avoid. Our particular and necessary mixture of language rights, with its personal and territorial features, is the legacy of our history and of a desire for justice. (Fortier, 1989, p.iii)

Canada's historical legacy has not made it easy for Canadians and their governments to deal with language matters. French was attacked by the government of the day in Lord Durham's ill-informed attempt to rescind the promises of The Quebec Act. Heritage languages have been attacked regularly in various provinces, but never with more vehemence and effectiveness than by J.T.M. Anderson, once the minister of education and later the premier of Saskatchewan:

> There is an important duty to perform in seeing that the children of these newcomers are given every opportunity to receive proper training for intelligent citizenship. . . . It is essential to national unity and solidarity that the people of any country should be able to converse and conduct their business in a common tongue. . . . There must be one medium of communication from coast to coast, and that the English language. (Anderson, 1918, p. 93)

Native languages were similarly rooted out of the schools, in the experience of many persons still actively seeking a more just society (Cardinal, 1969). Indeed, many examples of legislation have been extremely ungenerous to the minorities, especially the French minorities outside of Quebec. But, at least since the establishment of the Commission on Bilingualism and Biculturalism in 1963, efforts have been made to redress injustices, and some very real progress has been made.

Before we turn to developments since 1963, language policies and especially official language rights regarding English and French will be reviewed. Heritage languages will be considered later. (Aboriginal rights are treated in Chapter 23.)

HISTORICAL OVERVIEW OF LANGUAGE POLICIES AND RIGHTS

Some find it difficult to understand why French-speaking people, unlike those of many other linguistic groups who came to the New World, could not simply be assimilated and accept English as the language of communication. This reasoning fails to appreciate the significance of being a member of a group that considers itself a founding people. The French colonists preceded English settlement and had already established their own traditions, culture, and religion by the time the French territory was ceded to the British in 1763. Several years later, Lord Dorchester assumed that they would always be the only significant immigrant population in Canada. Since the francophone population had been allowed to practise Roman Catholicism, and since education was available through church organizations, it was natural that the French language would continue to flourish. Dorchester urged that these practices be made more explicit, and they were in the Quebec Act of 1774. This legal foundation for French rights under Britain affirmed the right to use French and restored civil law legislation and customs of French origin. The British hoped that these moves would give power to the seigneurs and the Roman Catholic clergy, who would then support the British administration against the American rebels. Regardless of the success or failure of this policy, the Quebec Act certainly sustained the use of the French language.

When the Province of Quebec was divided into Upper Canada and Lower Canada in 1791, most of the elected assembly members from Lower Canada used French both in debates and in communications with their constituents. The Durham Report of 1839 responded to the 1837–38 Papineau Rebellion with a threat to rescind the right to use French, based on a faulty reading of the Rebellion's significance, but after some hesitation, the British Colonial Office rejected Durham's recommendation in the final terms of the Act of Union (1841), which maintained French as an official language in the legislature of the reconstituted and enlarged the Province of Canada, where almost half of the members used it in debate. The Act of Union essentially reaffirmed the promises to the French of the Quebec Act, safeguarding francophone rights and giving it official standing over language, religion, and civil law. The French were successful in securing recognition for their leaders: in 1848, under the tolerant administration of Governor General James Bruce, Earl of Elgin, responsible government was achieved with Louis-Hippolyte LaFontaine as First Minister. It remained uncertain whether French rights extended to all French communities or would apply only in Quebec. In the many appeals to the courts, minority religious rights were recognized more frequently than those of language.

The British North America Act (now known as the Constitution Act, 1867) entrenched the French language as a language of debate in the federal Parliament, in the Quebec legislature, and before federal and Quebec courts. However, the right to education in English or French was not specifically included, so sometimes it was argued that the existence of separate schools enabled parents to choose the language for their children's instruction. The equation of language and religion does not correspond precisely with the facts. Moreover, this argument has repeatedly been rejected by the courts.

However, a system of French schools was built in Ontario and the Prairie provinces before Confederation, and the rights to operate them preceded the Constitution Act (1867) or the provincial constitutions. It was possible for the francophone minorities in these provinces to use the de facto argument to reclaim rights that had been denied or eroded by the years of anglophone domination, a topic that will be discussed next.

Quebec, 1867–1967

Canada's "first century" was not always good to Quebec, and still less to the French of Quebec, for they fell steadily behind Ontario in income and government services. In their own province, a major gap developed between the educational rights available to the English and the French, for the English-speaking populations (whether Catholic, Protestant, or other) forged ahead on the basis of private initiatives in secondary schooling and higher education. The numerical minority (English) actually enjoyed a near monopoly of sophisticated educational services, largely through the operation of the private sector and partly due to the great wealth of certain English-speaking entrepreneurs.

This gap in school and university facilities and opportunities began to close when the Quebec government became actively involved in education in the 1960s, and disappeared within a generation (Quebec, 1975). The attempt to eliminate this gap was an initial stage of the democratization of educational, social, political, and economic opportunity. Expansion of secondary and higher education led eventually to better jobs for those who were proficient in French and who were technically qualified. The transformation was based on massively improving opportunities in French rather than stripping away the rights of the English, who continued to be served in their own language from the beginning of kindergarten through the Ph.D. level at some of the finest schools and universities in the world.

French Minority Education outside of Quebec

Soon after Confederation, the French minorities outside of Quebec were dealt some serious blows. Manitoba was one region where the French held a majority at Confederation, only to lose it through a flood of immigration, both from English settlers from Ontario and immigrants who were neither English nor French. Despite the fact that English- and French-language rights had been guaranteed when Manitoba entered Confederation in 1870, the right to *education* in either French or English was not so clear. The dispute was exacerbated by the existence of other groups, especially some Germans, who sought schools in their own languages. Fearing a Tower of Babel, the government tried to standardize with one language only: English. Thus, in 1890, when public funding to Catholic schools was abolished, access to French education was severely curtailed (Berger, 1981). The restoration of constitutionally protected rights to schooling in French had to wait for almost a century, and court action is still probable.

In Ontario, access to French-language education was almost cut off altogether in 1912 by Regulation 17, which restricted French as the language of instruction and communication to the first two years of elementary school. Later, Regulation 17 was amended to limit French study to one hour per day. This problem was partially remedied in 1927 when it was decided that the use of French in schools was permissible when approved by a departmental committee. Not until 1968 did the Ontario government fully authorize French as a language of instruction in public schools (Mougeon, 1984). Thus, in Ontario at least, French continued as an academic subject for anglophones in public secondary schools. France rather than Quebec was the typical context for discussing French culture, history, literature, or customs. In the early 1960s, a large and prestigious university in Ontario offered only one half-course on French-Canadian literature among the many literature courses of the French department.

New Brunswick serves as another example of francophones' educational and social disadvantage, despite the fact that the French (Acadians for the most part) made up about one-third of the population and lived in a relatively cohesive group. For the Acadians, primary education was conducted in French, but secondary and higher education were exclusively in English until Premier Louis Robichaud introduced the *Equalization of educational opportunity*. Because of their educational disadvantages, many Acadians were consigned to labouring jobs and low incomes.

Other provinces had smaller French populations, sometimes acquired not from migration from Quebec but from France or Belgium. In many provinces, these francophone minorities had little opportunity to be educated in the French language, especially beyond elementary schooling.

Meanwhile, the English minority in Quebec enjoyed educational privileges unsurpassed by other Quebeckers or even English-speaking populations elsewhere in Canada. When economic, cultural, political, and educational disadvantages were so evident, is it any wonder that by the 1960s, the flames of unrest were being fanned within Quebec?

The Royal Commission on Bilingualism and Biculturalism

Tensions between the two linguistic groups had reached a critical stage by the 1960s. Francophones in Quebec justifiably believed that they had received inferior opportunities to participate actively in the official life of Canada, especially in economic and political domains. Two distinguished prime ministers from Quebec (Laurier and St. Laurent) had been regarded as serving the interests of the rest of Canada above Quebec, and other francophone Quebeckers had little influence in cabinet. The average income of franco-phone Quebeckers was far below that of the English, unemployment was higher, and opportunities for advancement were bleak. The limited access to schooling in the French language contributed to the assimilation of francophones into the English population. Out-side Quebec, the French were in a foreign country.

In 1962, André Laurendeau, the editor of *Le Devoir*, called for an official inquiry into bilingualism. By the summer of 1963, the government of Lester Pearson had set up a Royal Commission with Laurendeau and Davidson Dunton as co-chairs; their mandate was to

> inquire into and report upon the existing state of bilingualism and biculturalism in Canada and to recommend what steps should be taken to develop the Canadian Con-federation on the basis of an equal partnership between the two founding races, taking into account the contribution made by the other ethnic groups to the cultural enrichment of Canada and the measures that should be taken to safeguard that contribution. (Privy Council, 1963, p. 1106)

After interviews with numerous Canadians during the regional consultations, the Com-mission's preliminary report in 1965 established the enormous linguistic inequality that existed in Canada. The educational implications of this inequality were summarized by Stuart Beaty:

- As languages of education in Canada, English and French have taken markedly dif-ferent paths both as majority and minority languages.
- Whereas English was able to establish and institutionalize itself as a powerful lan-guage of schooling in Quebec, efforts outside that province to afford French some reciprocal recognition as a medium of instruction were most often curbed, sometimes savagely, and might indeed have come to naught without the accidental shelter they found in the denominational school rights in Section 93 of the BNA Act.
- As a result, in the early sixties, there was a remarkably full and flourishing English school system in Quebec and a generally feeble and fragmentary pattern (one could not call it a system) of French language education almost everywhere in the other provinces and territories. (Beaty, 1987, p. 34)

From an elaborated but similar analysis of the situation, the Commission concluded that the language of instruction in schools was an important influence on language reten-tion. It recommended education in the minority language — even for small numbers of students. It also recommended that citizens in a country with two official languages should have access to the kind of education and training that would enable more people to become bilingual. Since most of those who were bilingual had French as their mother tongue, this meant that more anglophones should become functionally bilingual, at least in official capacities.

The challenge to the provinces was obvious: if Canada was to survive and to remain as a bilingual entity, improvements would have to be made to the education of the French minority groups outside of Quebec. An effort would have to be made to ensure that French Canadians could feel completely at home as francophones within Confederation (Laurendeau, 1987). And education for the rest of the population should attempt to increase proficiency in French.

Despite predictable opposition from some anglophone groups, jealousy from other language communities that failed to get a similar deal, and fear among anglophone politicians of a backlash, progress was made, and the Commission's recommendations began to be implemented to some extent. In 1969, the Official Languages Act was shepherded through Parliament by Gérard Pelletier. The act declared that English and French were official languages in Canada, thus requiring all federal institutions to provide services in both official languages in the federal bilingual districts and wherever there was sufficient demand for bilingual service. The Official Languages Act of 1969 was based on the principles of linguistic duality and the equality of the founding peoples outlined in the Commission. To oversee the implementation of the act, the Office of the Commissioner of Official Languages was established.

In 1970, further to the Commission's recommendation, the provincial and federal governments concluded bilateral agreements whereby the government of Canada would assist the provinces in meeting the costs of providing opportunities for their residents' children to be educated in one official language (English or French by choice) and to learn the other official language as a second language. Each province was guaranteed a minimum level of funding from the federal government. (Council of Ministers of Education, 1985).

Many of the objections to a bilingual Canada stem from a basic misunderstanding of the duality principle. Canada is *officially* bilingual. Thus, the federal institutions are committed to serving the public in the official language of the citizen's choice. The citizen is not required to be bilingual personally. Nor are provinces required to be officially bilingual: it is enough if they provide the stipulated services appropriately.

The federal government relied upon the provinces and the people to support and request the necessary bilingual services in the private sector and in provincial jurisdictions. Services in English in Quebec were adequate, but in the rest of Canada there were few services in French; the Official Languages Act sought to promote equal rights for both official languages. After its passing, some provinces (especially Ontario and New Brunswick) began to provide government services in both official languages and began to develop their own language policies regarding minority and second-language education.

With the lowest birthrate in Canada (13.0/1000 in 1986 — among the lowest in the world) and increasing emigration of its population to other provinces, Quebec anticipated an erosion of its share of the national population. Both the population balance and shift in the language of instruction would benefit the English unless something was done. In 1977, still concerned with the preservation of French within its own jurisdiction, the Quebec government introduced Bill 101, which declared Quebec to be a unilingual French province. Among the educational implications was the decree that unless immigrant children had already started school in English in Quebec or their older brothers or sisters had been educated in English in Quebec, they would have to be educated in French rather than enjoy freedom of choice for French, English, both, or one in combination with a heritage language. This part of the legislation was an attempt to stem the inordinate number of immigrants who had been opting for English-language education for their children. For the children of the English minority in Quebec, Bill 101 held no threat to their education, for their rights to schools under their control continued as before.

Bill 101 also restricted the right to education in English for children from other provinces—despite protections of section 23 of the Charter of Rights and Freedoms—unless a reciprocal agreement between the Quebec government and the other province existed (Kahn, 1992). The issue is still being debated and the language laws were reinforced with the introduction of Bill 178. It was up for review in 1993, and indications are that the current Quebec Liberal government may soften its requirements somewhat with regards to sections dealing with languages on signs.

THE CHARTER OF RIGHTS AND FREEDOMS

The next important breakthrough came with the Charter of Rights and Freedoms as part of the 1982 repatriation of the Constitution. Sections 16 to 23 enshrined English and French in the Constitution as official languages of Canada (s. 16(1)) and of New Brunswick (s. 16(2)). Minority language educational rights were dealt with in section 23, where good intentions have been marred by faulty implementation (see Beaty, 1987; Magnet, 1987; Lysons-Balcon, 1987).

Sections 23 (1) and (2) state that

> citizens of Canada (a) whose first language learned and still understood is of the English or French linguistic minority population of the province where they reside, or (b) who have received their primary education in Canada in English or French and reside in a province where the language in which they received that instruction is the language of the English or French linguistic minority population of the province or of whom any child has received or is receiving primary of secondary school instruction in English or French in Canada, have the right to have all their children receive primary and secondary school instruction in the same language.

Section 23 (3) seems to provide the loophole for denying those rights, for they apply where

> (a) the number of children of citizens who have such a right is sufficient to warrant the provision to them out of public funds of minority language instruction; and
> (b) includes, where the number of those children so warrants, the right to have them receive that instruction in minority language educational facilities provided out of public funds.

Because education is a provincial right, funding transferred from the federal government to encourage minority language education often disappears into the general budget of the receiving treasury. When decisions have had to be made regarding minority language education, as Professor Foucher of Moncton University discovered in his comparative study of provincial and territorial legislation on minority language education (see Beaty, 1987), the interpretations of the Charter clauses on this issue have not always been "full and generous." Important transgressions undermine the provision of education in the minority language, but even more so they withhold the right of the official language minority to education in a separate facility. For example, dual track schools with both French and English streams are places where

> Francophones watch their children being swept into the net of English in "mixed schools." Mixed schools are principal institutions of French education in Anglophone Canada. They are cauldrons of assimilation. (Magnet 1987, p. 31)

Since the Charter of Rights and Freedoms, with its attendant clauses on official languages, several events have undercut the spirit of the Charter with respect to language rights. In 1984, the Supreme Court of Canada ruled that "article 23 of the Charter of Rights and Freedoms limited Bill 101's power to regulate the language of instruction" (Hudon, 1988). A subsequent ruling of the Supreme Court (1988) declared part of Quebec's language laws unconstitutional, and detrimental to the rights of linguistic minorities. However, by using the Charter's "notwithstanding" clause, Quebec has persevered in enforcing legislation to protect the French language.

Although all provinces but New Brunswick have stopped short of declaring themselves bilingual, over the years they gradually recognized the linguistic rights of the francophone minority by legislation or orders-in-council providing, for example, trials in French and education in French under certain conditions. The loophole in section 23(c) of the Charter that made French-language education subject to the phrase "where numbers warrant" gave rise to heated disputes in several communities, especially in Ontario and the Western provinces. This difficulty was addressed in 1984 when the Ontario Court of Appeal ruled that every francophone in the province had a right to French-language education, and that linguistic minorities must be guaranteed representation on school boards and a say in minority-language instruction (Bothwell & Hillmer, 1988). In 1986, Bill 75 amended the Ontario Education Act to make it consistent with the Canadian Charter for the francophone minorities. By 1988, regulations on French-language instruction were fully incorporated as part XI of the Education Act. A similar progression has taken place in the Western provinces, where French communities had almost been assimilated.

It gradually became clear that the Official Languages Act of 1969 was not entirely consistent with the Charter of Rights and Freedoms. In 1988, the new Official Languages Act (Bill C-72) was passed, strengthening certain features of the former act. The Office of the Commissioner of Official Languages has undertaken several analyses comparing the two languages, notably in the *Annual Report 1987*, Appendix B, 226–30 (Fortier, 1988a, 1988b. See also Beaudoin, 1989; Federal and Provincial Linguistic Dates, 1989; Low, 1989; Pelletier, 1988).

Perhaps the most important feature of the 1988 act is that its preamble and certain other statements reaffirm the constitutional principle of Canada as a country with two official languages, both having equal status, and undertake "the commitment to support the development of the English-speaking and French-speaking minorities" (Fortier, 1989 p. 287).

Gérard Pelletier, the author of the 1969 Official Languages Act, was cautiously optimistic when comparing the 1969 and 1988 legislation, but still concerned with the many vaguely worded formulations of the "where numbers warrant" limitation of the right to minority language education and how various provinces have interpreted the clause (Pelletier, 1988, p. 6). Victor Goldbloom (1992) has confidently stated: "Canada's language policy is about freedom: the freedom to live one's life to the greatest extent possible in the language of one's choice."

The People Speak: For Bilingualism

Despite ongoing linguistic tensions throughout Canada—such as communities declaring themselves "English only" and new political movements promoting unilingualism, partly as a result of confusion and uncertainty over the failed Meech Lake Accord and, more recently, the failed referendum on the Charlottetown Accord—Victor Goldbloom, Commissioner of Official Languages, identifies several positive trends. For example, a *Globe and Mail*–CBC poll conducted in April 1991 reported that support for official bilingualism still remains strong (Goldbloom, 1993). Statistics for 1992 on second-language enrollments (including French immersion) show increases in both core and immersion French from the previous year's figures (Goldbloom, 1993, pp. 134–37). Numbers of students attending French immersion classes increased from 240 541 in 1988–89 to 291 650 in 1992–93. The elementary core French students increased from 1 360 896 in 1988–89 to 1 492 254 in 1992–93. Although students in secondary core French decreased from 942 043 in 1988–89 to 940 615 in 1989–90, the drop was caused by a decrease in total secondary population from 1 701 983 in 1988–89 to 1 696 910 in 1989–90. By 1992–93, 966 379 out of a total of 1 796 045 secondary students, or 53.8 percent, were in second-language (FSL) programs. Of greater significance is the long-term comparison. Between 1977–78 and 1992–93, despite a larger total school population in 1977-78 (5 178 753 compared with 4 977 960 in 1992–93), enrollment in French second-language programs has grown considerably, especially in immersion (from 37 835 to 291 650). The elementary core French enrollment as a percentage of the school population has also grown from 40.7 percent to 55.1 percent. In secondary schools there has been a slight decrease in the percentage of core French students (54.1 percent in 1977–78 to 53.8 percent in 1992–93). The number of schools offering French immersion increased to 2230 in 1992–93 from 2130 in 1991–92.

The Canadian government, through the Office of the Secretary of State and the Commissioner of Official Languages, and reflecting such legislation as the Official Languages Acts of 1969 and 1988, has provided incentives for French second-language education. But the real impetus for change has come from the Canadian people, through such nation-wide organizations as the Canadian Parents for French (CPF), whose activities focus on the enhancement of immersion education and core French. The CPF has successfully lobbied school boards across the country to provide and improve core and immersion French programs. They also organize and publicize extracurricular events fostering the development of the French language, such as the annual Festival national d'art oratoire, summer language camps, exchanges, and information conferences across the country. They keep parents and educators informed of the possibilities for learning and improving one's competence in French. Lately, CPF has allied itself with provincial francophone organizations to develop brochures outlining the differences between French first-language and immersion education. More important, they have also begun to lobby for better-quality French first-language education.

Language educators across the country have also been active in promoting improved second-language education. The Canadian Association of Second Language Teachers, funded by the Secretary of State, has just completed a massive three-year study of national core French. The project, which included six task forces on language; communicative/ experiential activities; culture, general language, professional development and teacher education; and research and evaluation, has conducted an intensive nation-wide examination of core French. The resulting data provide valuable guidelines on how to develop a multidimensional language curriculum combining the central components of language, communication, culture, and general language education.

Annotated bibliographies, such as the publication entitled *Professional development of core French teachers: Selective review of general literature in inservice education and specific literature on inservice education of second language teachers* (Lamarre, 1986), are also most useful for teacher educators in faculties of education.

French teachers continue to organize summer exchanges through the Secretary of State–funded SEVEC program (The Society for Educational Visits and Exchanges in Canada). The Official Languages Monitor and Summer Language Bursary Programs (funded by the same department) also provide ways for language educators to promote English or French second-language fluency. For example, francophone students studying at an English-language university anywhere in Canada may be assigned to a local school for eight hours per week to carry out a program of French-language activities developed by the language teacher with students in the school enrolled in French. Anglophone students in Quebec universities perform parallel services in English at local schools. Thousands of teachers have taken advantage of the Summer Languages Bursaries to improve their knowledge of the other official language through in-service or second-language courses. Unfortunately, because of financial restraints, the program terminated in 1993. Still, with the support of the Ontario and Quebec ministries of education, and organized by the Professional Modern Language Teachers Associations of Ontario and Quebec, the Ontario–Quebec Summer Seminar for Education continues to provide a venue where second-language educators can exchange views.

Without government assistance, these programs could not have taken place. But without the dedication and commitment of such groups as the Canadian Parents for French, French second-language teachers, teacher educators and researchers, and their professional organizations, the initiatives could not have been realized. It is largely the efforts of the latter groups that have changed attitudes of English-speaking Canadians over the past twenty years to come to accept and support language duality and equality.

At first glance, the picture for minority-language education programs would not seem to be as rosy (Fortier, 1990, pp. 260–61). After all, there were 444 942 children enrolled in these programs in 1970–71, a figure that fell to 255 800 by 1990–91 but increased slightly to 258 195 in 1992–93. The populations of students in minority-language schools fell mainly in Nova Scotia, Quebec (English-speaking minority), and Manitoba.

One possible reason for the decrease is the growth of immersion since the 1970s. Before immersion schools were available, anglophone parents who wanted to ensure that their children would learn French often sent them to the French-language schools. Once immersion became a possibility, naturally they switched their children over to that program—a move that was welcomed by francophone parents because anglophones in the French schools tended to dilute the quality of French-language instruction.

There are problems for the francophone minorities outside of Quebec. In 1985, the Churchill, Frenette, & Quazi report, *Éducation et besoins des Franco-Ontariens: Le diagnostic d'un système d'éducation*, addressed the issue in Ontario. The Ontario government responded to such reports and brought its policies into line with section 23 of the Charter of Rights and Freedoms, by giving more autonomy to francophone groups in decisions relating to the education of their children.

Francophones outside of Quebec struggle on, and can claim some victories (see Hébert, 1989). Across Canada, the Fédération des francophones hors Québec provides effective leadership for French-speaking minority communities. In spite of their concerns that "institutionalized bilingualism in the federal government and its courts, and the various forms of federal support for the minorities . . . are not enough to stop assimilation," they are pushing for further "protected institutionalized zones" in health and social and community services to help to assure their survival as a French-speaking minority in Canada (Fortier, 1990, p. 182).

The Supreme Court of Canada has interpreted section 23 of the Charter in a manner favourable to French- and English-speaking minorities, for example, in a case brought by some Edmonton parents, who are members of the Association de l'École Georges-et-Julia-Bugnet. In that decision, the Court guaranteed minority groups "not only the right to publicly-funded education in their own language where numbers warrant," but the power to "manage and control" their schools (*London Free Press*, 1990). This welcome decision would seem to contradict Alberta's position on the famous Mahé case, in which the Alberta authorities were required to establish a francophone school board (see also Chapter 16). Still, the Alberta government has yet to implement legislation to meet the ruling of the Supreme Court (Dubé, 1993; Julien, 1993).

After the failure of the Charlottetown Accord in 1992, Quebec felt that it had once again been rejected by the rest of Canada. Nevertheless, the prevailing view across the country seemed to reflect exhaustion over interminable constitutional wrangles, and concern to get on with measures that would address economic issues. Language tensions continue to simmer but have been pushed to the back burner because of fears about the economy and the future of the country under the North American Free Trade Agreement. From a historical perspective, enormous progress has been made to define and affirm Canada as a nation based on linguistic duality and equality. One can only hope that the good will of the majority of Canada's citizens of both official language groups will prevail.

MULTICULTURALISM AND HERITAGE LANGUAGES

The Royal Commission on Bilingualism and Biculturalism emphasized the investigation of the French and English languages in Canada, but Volume 4 of the *Report* (*The cultural contributions of other ethnic groups*) (1970) also dealt with multiculturalism. By the following year, the government had created a new cabinet post of Minister of State responsible for Multiculturalism and two advisory bodies: the Canadian Consultative Council on Multiculturalism and the Ethnic Studies Advisory Committee. Several provinces developed policies on multiculturalism. One particular area of interest was in teaching non-official (ancestral) languages.

The policy was initially criticized by some who saw it as a threat to the equality of the groups representing the two official languages, particularly for the French-speaking group (Rocher, 1973), and by others (Porter, 1969) who viewed multiculturalism as essentially perpetuating a lower status for the groups not belonging to the founding nations (English and French). The latter group called for a more vigorous language policy that would give greater recognition to ancestral languages and would better respond to ethnic aspirations (see Lupul, 1973). Still others have hinted at a cynical goal behind multiculturalism: namely, to preserve positions of power in Canadian society for the English-speaking elite (Porter, 1965). Jean Burnet argues that the real intent of the policy was

> to aid Canadian groups who wish to do so to set up or to maintain their ethnic organi-
> zations and their cultural symbols, because preserving one's ethnic identity is considered

to be consistent with acquiring a Canadian identity and taking part in Canadian society and culture. (Burnet, 1975, p. 209)

Holmes (1980) has spoken of the difficulty for governments in pluralistic societies: recognizing the aspirations of minority groups to preserve and promote their cultural identities while promoting valid nationalist policies. In Canada, government policy tries to support multiculturalism while remaining committed to promoting the official-languages duality. The problem is still a thorny one. When the Multiculturalism Bill, C-93, was proposed in 1987—"an act for the preservation and enhancement of multiculturalism in Canada"—the Commissioner of Official Languages cautioned that he supported the policy on multiculturalism, "provided that it respected Canada's official bilingualism and that newcomers were able to learn our official languages and the cultural values they convey" (Ohan, 1988, p. 9). Goldbloom (1992) has stated, "As long as Canada's multiculturalism policy is and remains a policy of convergence of building links rather than barriers, it is worth maintaining and defending" (p. 8).

It is not within the scope of this chapter to argue the merits of multiculturalism in an officially bilingual country. But multicultural policies are examined here with respect to the development of heritage language programs in each province.

ONTARIO

In 1977, the Ontario Ministry of Education announced through Memorandum 46 its intention to implement a Heritage Language Program *wherever requested by a group of interested parents*. In 1994, the Ontario Ministry of Education and Training changed the program's name to International Languages (Elementary). The continuing education programs of various boards were to administer the program, which would include two-and-one-half hours of language instruction per week at the elementary level. Classes were to be held outside of school hours: either on non-school days, after school, or through the extension of the regular five-hour school day. The individual boards would be responsible for staff, curriculum, and supervision of the classes. The instructors for the heritage language classes were not required to hold Ontario teaching certification, but would have to satisfy board and parent group requirements for individual qualifications. Although there is still no credit granted for international languages (elementary) in Ontario, many boards have collaborated with the different parent groups to develop a sequential curriculum for three years or more, and have introduced teacher training and development for the non-qualified language instructors.

After several years of the voluntary system, there were a total of 121 883 pupils enrolled in 63 different heritage international languages during the school year 1990–91 (Ontario Ministry of Education, 1992). The year the programs started (1977–78), 52 713 pupils were enrolled in 30 different languages. In 1986–87, the languages most heavily subscribed to included Italian with 31 889 pupils, followed by Portuguese (10 989), Cantonese and Mandarin (10 568), and Greek (6691). The only languages in which secondary teachers could receive certification in Ontario (besides English and French) were German, Italian, Russian, and Spanish—i.e., the languages traditionally associated with formal instruction as modern languages.

Many pupils who have taken heritage language programs wish to earn credit at the secondary level in their language, and indeed, some of the 58 heritage languages are now offered as credit courses at the secondary level. However, for all except the languages listed above there were no official guidelines, no approved texts, and the teachers could not gain certification in the subject. The latter problem has now been remedied with the implementation of the new International Languages Guideline, which recognizes 64 languages (not including aboriginal languages, which are covered under another guideline). Now faculties of education will have to consider providing certification for teachers of the various international languages, and texts for these courses will be evaluated for entry to the approved text lists, thus becoming eligible for grants.

QUEBEC

The case of Quebec with regard to heritage languages and cultural pluralism is treated in detail in a separate chapter. Suffice it to mention here that since the late 1970s Quebec has had a heritage language program called PELO (Programme d'enseignement des langues d'origines). At first, PELO was not well received by either the ethnic communities or the Quebec teachers' organizations. Community groups regarded PELO as interference in an area where they had previously held exclusive control and as a political concession to help offset protests against restricted access to education in English as per Bill 101. The teachers considered that the teaching of ancestral and heritage languages would hamper efforts to integrate allophone (those with a mother tongue other than French or English) children into the francophone milieu.

Nevertheless, PELO has slowly gained acceptance and currently enrols approximately 6000 children of various ethnic origins in classes where fourteen different languages are offered. All costs of the program are borne by the Quebec government. Courses of study on each language have been prepared either by the Ministry of Education or by school boards in consultation with various cultural communities. Another program, the Programme des langues ethniques (PLE), funded mainly by the ethnic communities, serves approximately 20 000 students from 35 language groups (Canadian Education Association, 1991).

THE PRAIRIE PROVINCES

In the Prairie provinces, the 1986 census reported that the population whose mother tongue was other than English or French ranged from 15.3 percent in Alberta to 21.8 percent in Manitoba. This diversity of ethnic origin and language explains why the Prairie governments are sensitive to the needs of heritage languages, even though it would be easy to provide adequately for the minority official-language communities, who reside in clearly defined rural areas or within cities large enough to permit some diversity.

Some Prairie linguistic groups have traditionally maintained language and cultural programs for their children (often with a religious connection, as is the case with the Mennonites, Hutterites, and Doukhobors), and at various times there has been government support (Mallea, 1989). For example, bilingual schools offering English and Ukrainian were operated in Manitoba and Saskatchewan from the nineteenth century until the First World War. Even after the Manitoba provincial government abolished provincial recognition for the Ukrainian schools in 1916, they continued as private vernacular schools. According to Frank Epp (1974, p. 358), because the Mennonites associated English with patriotism and militarism near the beginning of this century, they maintained that German in their schools was essential to maintain their religion, community boundaries, and pacifism. Language then had profound significance. It still has. In 1993, Manitoba tabled a

Policy for Heritage Language Instruction and currently has guidelines for Chinese, German, Filipino, Hebrew, Italian, Japanese, Portuguese, Spanish, and Ukrainian (Lazaruk, 1993).

Since 1974, Saskatchewan has allowed teaching in other languages at the request of the community. The Department of Education has curriculum documents for German and Ukrainian as second-language programs, and there are locally developed courses in Mandarin and Japanese. The Department of Culture, Multiculturalism and Recreation has funded non-credit after-school programs in an additional 25 heritage languages, but as of 1989 jurisdiction for these programs was transferred to the Education Department (Canadian Education Association, 1991).

Today, Alberta has a very well developed policy on schools offering languages in addition to English and French. The province supports Ukrainian, Jewish, and German bilingual schools, in which the regular programs are taught in English for about half of the teaching hours, and the remainder of the time is devoted to studies of the heritage culture, in the heritage language (Mallea, 1989). The Department of Education also develops curricular guidelines and materials in these languages as well as Italian, Japanese, and Spanish.

The heritage language programs of the Prairie provinces operate on the assumption that teachers will be qualified and that students will be given credits for their studies. In other words, there is no systematic preference for certain languages in the school programs, and courses will be offered wherever the community makes the request and qualifies under regulations.

These policies reflect a clear alternative to those of Ontario, where larger numbers of languages have been accommodated but where there has been some question concerning the effectiveness of the instruction. Teachers of heritage languages are qualified and the Prairie provinces give credit for these courses.

The costs of providing heritage language instruction are met in the usual ways, with funding from the Secretary of State's Cultural Enrichment Programme, the provinces, school boards or other community sources, churches, and families (Commissioner of Official Languages, 1986). For example, in 1985, Manitoba, Saskatchewan, and Alberta provided for 17 000 students in 1438 classes, with $700 000 in Cultural Enrichment Programme Grants; in Manitoba, 3112 elementary students were studying nine heritage languages. Heritage languages are taught in supplementary schools under programs operated by ethnocultural communities. Unlike in other provinces, these schools in the Prairie provinces are financed by both federal and provincial governments. In Manitoba alone, during the school year 1988–89, 30 000 students were studying heritage languages in these schools (Cummins, 1990).

BRITISH COLUMBIA

During the school year 1986–87, 140 supplementary schools received funding from the federal government to provide heritage language instruction to 14 590 students. The province does not provide funds for heritage language instruction but offers credit to students who have successfully completed approved heritage language courses at the secondary level, either in community-run or regular school programs. With the emerging economic significance of the Pacific Rim countries to the economy of British Columbia, the province has encouraged the establishment of heritage languages related to those areas. Currently, British Columbia has guidelines for Chinese (Mandarin), German, Japanese, and Spanish (Lazaruk, 1993).

THE ATLANTIC PROVINCES

During the school year 1986–87, approximately 1500 students in the Atlantic provinces were enrolled in supplementary language programs funded by the federal government. These programs do not receive provincial assistance and the classes are taught outside the regular school program. Arabic is the most commonly taught heritage language (Cummins & Danesi, 1990). Gaelic is also a dominant heritage language program.

CONCLUSIONS

Despite linguistic tensions that have erupted from time to time, real progress has been made in the protection and promotion of language rights over the past 30 years, notably in such federal initiatives as the Bilingualism and Biculturalism Commission, the Official Languages Acts of 1969 and 1988, the Charter of Rights and Freedoms (1982), and the Multiculturalism Act of 1988. Various provincial programs are administered by the ministries of education and sometimes other departments. School boards initiate many local programs. In addition to these official initiatives are the quiet efforts of individual Canadians (such as the approximately 100 000 patrons of the annual Edmonton multicultural festival), who implement and support the intent of the reports and legislation. Language educators are making concerted efforts to underline the importance of languages to Canadian society.

As Victor Goldbloom (1993) states, "Competence in languages can no longer be viewed as an educational or societal luxury." He points to the European Community, Australia, and New Zealand, where steps have been taken to ensure opportunities for citizens to gain proficiency in a number of international languages. If Canada wishes to compete in the global market, it can do no less.

Canada has chosen a difficult route in affirming and fostering linguistic duality while supporting the wishes of a pluralistic society to preserve its ethnic heritage. The Charter of Rights and Freedoms and the Official Languages Act provide the vehicles to make this uniquely Canadian concept work as long as Canadian citizens have the will to persevere.

DISCUSSION QUESTIONS

❏ Why have languages become such popular subjects for students while they are the subject of much debate among some adults?

❏ What are the four classes of languages provided in Canadian schools? What is the justification for each?

❏ What are the regional politics of language for your community? Do they differ from that of the province? the nation? How heavily do they rely upon culture for their success? Who are the most important trendsetters?

❏ Check the pertinent sections of the Canadian Charter of Rights and Freedoms (1982), the Official Languages Act (1988), and the Multiculturalism Bill C-93 and discuss how these policies promote linguistic duality while supporting cultural pluralism. In what ways have these policies translated into practices?

❏ What language innovations in the language of instruction are needed in the schools of your community?

REFERENCES

Anderson, J.T.M. (1918). *The education of the new Canadian.* Toronto: J.M. Dent.

Ashworth, M. (1988). *Blessed with bilingual brains—Education of immigrant children with English as a second language.* Vancouver: Pacific Educational Press.

Barber, M. (1988). Ontario schools question. In *The Canadian encyclopedia* (Vol. 3, p. 1578). Edmonton: Hurtig.

Beaty, S. (1987). What are we waiting for? *Language and Society, (19),* 17–20.

Beaudoin, G.A. (1989, Summer). The role of the judiciary in defining language rights in Canada. *Language and Society* (Special Report on the 25th Anniversary of the Bilingualism and Biculturalism Commission, and the 20th Anniversary of the Official Languages Act), 23–24.

Berger, T.R. (1981). *Fragile Freedoms: Human Rights and Dissent in Canada.* Toronto: Clarke Irwin.

Bothwell, R., & Hillmer, N. (1988). Ontario: Education. In *The Canadian encyclopedia* (Vol. 3, p. 1574). Edmonton: Hurtig.

Burnet, J. (1975). Multiculturalism in a bilingual framework. In A. Wolfgang (Ed.). *Education of immigrant students: Issues and answers* (pp. 202–15). Toronto: Ontario Institute for Studies in Education.

Canadian Education Association. (1991). *Heritage language programs in Canadian school boards.* Toronto: Canadian Education Association.

Cardinal, H. (1969). *The unjust society: The tragedy of Canada's Indians.* Edmonton: Hurtig.

Churchill, S., Frenette, N., & Quazi, S. (1985). *Éducation et besoins des Franco-Ontariens: Le diagnostic d'un système d'éducation* (Vols. 1, 2). Toronto: Le Conseil de l'éducation franco-ontarien.

Commissioner of Official Languages (1986). *Annual report, 1985* (Part V). Ottawa: Supply and Services.

Council of Ministers of Education. (1985).

Crunican, P.E. (1988). Manitoba schools question. In *The Canadian encyclopedia* (Vol. 2, p. 1299). Edmonton: Hurtig.

Cummins, J., & Danesi, M. (1990). *Heritage language: The development and denial of Canada's linguistic resources.* Toronto: Our Schools/Our Selves Education Foundation.

Dubé, P. (1993). Une étude de cas portant sur la genèse et les résultats de la judicalisation des droits scolaires: Le cas Bugnet en Alberta. *The Canadian Modern Language Review, 49*(4), 704–15.

Epp, F. (1974). *The Mennonites in Canada, 1786–1920: The history of a separate people.* Toronto: Macmillan.

Federal and Provincial Linguistic Dates (1989, Summer). *Language and Society* (Special Report on the 25th Anniversary of the Bilingualism and Biculturalism Commission, and the 20th Anniversary of the Official Languages Act), 31–32.

Fortier, I. (1988a). *Annual report 1987* (Appendix B, 226–30). Commissioner of Official Languages. Ottawa: Supply and Services.

Fortier, I. (1988b). A new commitment. *Language and Society, (22)*, 5.

Fortier, I. (1989). *Annual report 1988*. Commissioner of Official Languages. Ottawa: Supply and Services.

Fortier, I. (1990). *Annual report 1989*. Commissioner of Official Languages. Ottawa: Supply and Services.

Foulds, N.B. (1988). Québec. In *The Canadian encyclopedia* (Vol. 3, pp. 1793–1802). Edmonton: Hurtig.

Goldbloom, V. (1992). *Annual report 1991*. Commissioner of Official Languages. Ottawa: Supply and Services.

Goldbloom, V. (1993). *Annual report 1992*. Commissioner of Official Languages. Ottawa: Supply and Services.

Government of Ontario (1988, August). *Education Act*. Toronto: Queen's Printer.

Hébert, R.M. (1989, Summer). Francophone communities in the west: Setbacks and victories. *Language and Society* (Special Report), R-41–43.

Hébert, Y.M. (1986). Language rights in Canadian education. Presentation given at the American Education Studies Association Annual Convention, October 29–November 1.

Holmes, B. (Ed.). (1980). *Diversity and unity in education: A comparative analysis*. London: George Allen and Unwin.

Hudon, R. (1988). Bill 101. In *The Canadian encyclopedia* (Vol. 1, p. 217). Edmonton: Hurtig.

Julien, R. (1993). The evolution of francophone schools: The case of Alberta (1982–1993). *The Canadian Modern Language Review, 49*(4), 716–33.

Kahn, L. (1992). *Schooling, jobs, and cultural identity—Minority education in Quebec*. New York: Garland.

Lamarre, P. (1986). *Professional development of core French teachers: Selective review of general literature in inservice education and specific literature on inservice education of second language teachers* . (National Core French Study). Manitoba: The Canadian Association of Second Language Teachers.

Laurendeau, Y. (1987). Between hope and disenchantment. *Language and Society, 19*, 15–17.

Lazaruk, W. (1993). Heritage language curricular documents and contact persons at the provincial level. *Mosaic, 1*(1), 16–18.

London Free Press. (1990, March 16), p. A5.

Low, D.M. (1989, Summer). The roots of change: Legal sources of the 1988 Official Languages Act. *Language and Society* (Special Report on the 25th Anniversary of the Bilingualism and Biculturalism Commission, and the 20th Anniversary of the Official Languages Act), 25–26.

Lupul, M.R. (1973). Multiculturalism with a bilingual framework: An essay in definition. Cited in Burnet, J. (1975). Multiculturalism in a bilingual framework. In A. Wolfgang (Ed.). *Education of immigrant students: Issues and answers*. (pp. 205–15). Toronto: Ontario Institute for Studies in Education.

Lysons-Balcon, H. (1987). Minority language educational guarantees in the Canadian Charter. In R. Ghosh & D. Ray (Eds.). *Social change and education in Canada* (1st ed.). (pp. 155–66). Toronto: Harcourt Brace Jovanovich.

Magnet, J.E. (1987). The future of official language minorities in Canada. *Language and Society, 19*, 29–32.

Mallea, J.R. (1989). *Schooling in a plural Canada*. Clevedon, England: Multilingual Matters.

Monet, J. (1988a). Elgin, James Bruce, 8th Earl of. In *The Canadian encyclopedia* (Vol. 2, pp. 685–86). Edmonton: Hurtig.

Monet, J. (1988b). LaFontaine, Sir Louis-Hippolyte. In *The Canadian encyclopedia* (Vol. 2, p. 1164). Edmonton: Hurtig.

Mougeon, R. (1984). Retention of French among young Franco-Ontarians. *Language and Society, 13,* 17–20.

Ohan, S. (1988). An Act for the preservation and enhancement of multiculturalism in Canada. *Language and Society, 22,* 15–16.

Ontario Ministry of Education (1976–77). Memorandum 46.

Ontario Ministry of Education (1992). Education statistics. Toronto: Queen's Printer.

Pelletier, G. (1988). Who's afraid of C-72? *Language and Society, 22,* 6–7.

Porter, J. (1965). *The vertical mosaic.* Toronto: University of Toronto Press.

Porter, J. (1969). Bilingualism and the myths of culture. *Canadian Review of Sociology and Anthropology, 6,* 111–19.

Privy Council. (1963).

Rocher, G. (1973). *Le Québec en mutation.* Montréal: Hurtubise.

Quebec (1975). *Review of educational policies in Canada: Quebec report.* Quebec: Ministry of Education.

Royal Commission of Inquiry on Bilingualism and Biculturalism. (1965). *A preliminary report.* Ottawa: Queen's Printer.

Royal Commission of Inquiry on Bilingualism and Biculturalism. (1967). *Book 1: General introduction—The official languages.* Ottawa: Queen's Printer.

Royal Commission of Inquiry on Bilingualism and Biculturalism. (1969). *Book 4: The cultural contribution of the other ethnic groups.* Ottawa: Queen's Printer.

Swyripa, F.A. (1988). Ukrainians. In *The Canadian encyclopedia* (Vol. 4, pp. 2207–8). Edmonton: Hurtig.

FURTHER READINGS

Danesi, M., McLeod, K., & Morris, S. (Eds.). (1993). *Heritage languages and education: The Canadian experience.* Oakville: Mosaic Press.

Edwards, V., & Redfern, A. (1992). *The world in a classroom—Language in education in Britain and Canada.* Clevedon; Philadelphia: Multilingual Matters.

Fortier, I. (1989). *Annual report 1988* (Part 5, Second Language Instruction: Building Bridges). Ottawa: Supply and Services.

Fortier, I. (1990). *Annual report 1989* (Part 5, Second Language Instruction). Ottawa: Supply and Services.

Lamontagne, J. (1983). Minority official language education: Where can it be secure? In D. Ray & V. d'Orley (Eds.). *Human rights in Canadian education.* (pp. 176–97). Dubuque, IA: Kendall Hunt.

Language and Society. (1989, Summer). Special Report on the 25th Anniversary of the Bilingualism and Biculturalism Commission and the 20th Anniversary of the Official Languages Act.

Samuda, R.J., Berry, J.W., & Laferrière, M. (1984). *Multiculturalism in Canada: Social and educational perspectives.* Toronto: Allyn and Bacon.

7

TEACHING ENGLISH AS A SECOND LANGUAGE IN CANADA: A CRITICAL OVERVIEW

Gloria Rong Zhang

Canada has two official languages: English and French. Immigrants are expected to learn one or both of them. The use of French as a first language is in Canada restricted to Quebec and some parts of New Brunswick. Except in Quebec, English as a Second Language (ESL) is offered in the public system to children of non–English-speaking families or families where English is spoken in a vernacular radically different from that used in Canada. This group also includes children born in Canada but entering the school system speaking a parental language other than English or French. The objective of ESL instruction is scholastic and social integration into the mainstream of Canadian educational experience.

ESL is taught to adults in most parts of Canada, including to Native Indians and Inuit. These programs attempt to provide immigrants, especially recent arrivals, with the English-language facility necessary for the initial economic and social adjustment into the mainstream of society. Indeed, fluency in English or French is a basic prerequisite for the transition to full participation in Canadian life and true "citizenship" Traditional ESL education, as a vital service available to newcomers, has been a concern of federal and provincial governments and the educational system for over a century. Especially over the last two decades, the public concern over language education has greatly increased and ESL has become an important part of Canadian education.

This chapter reviews various approaches to teaching and learning English as a second language in English-speaking provinces. It deals with some current policy issues and perspectives and the provision of language programs. Pedagogy will not be discussed. The area of teaching ESL to Native people and to francophones will not be examined here, nor the teaching of French as a second official language.

IMMIGRATION: SOME STATISTICS AND PROJECTIONS

Within the last decade the composition of urban Canadian society has changed dramatically, with a majority of current immigrants coming from Third World countries. Major sources of immigrants have shifted from Europe to southern and eastern Asia, the Caribbean, Latin America, and Eastern Europe (Badets, 1993). In the period 1981 to 1991, over two-thirds of the newly arrived immigrants were born in developing countries. Only 25 percent came from Europe and 6 percent from the United States. Simultaneously, the proportion of immigrants with a low level of education in their mother tongue is continuously increasing.

According to the 1991 census, 4.3 million immigrants were living in Canada; 48 percent of all immigrants had arrived before 1971, while 24 percent came between 1971 and 1980 and 28 percent during the subsequent decade. According to Badets (1993), 94 percent lived in just four provinces: Ontario (55 percent), British Columbia (17 percent), Quebec (14 percent), and Alberta (9). The estimated annual total immigration rate for the period 1990 to 1995 is 250 000 (Canada Immigration and Employment Centre, 1990). Because current immigration policy emphasis is on the reunification of families, children will most likely become a larger component than in earlier periods. According to the official 1990–95 Immigration Plan (Canada Immigration and Employment, 1990) more than 300 000 children from diverse cultural and linguistic backgrounds can be expected. This is an increase from 160 000, the level experienced between 1984 and 1989. An estimated 55 percent of all immigrant children will settle in Ontario, 18 percent in Quebec, 12 percent in British Columbia, 8 percent in Alberta, 3 percent in Manitoba, and 2 percent in Saskatchewan and the Atlantic provinces respectively. The destination of approximately two-thirds of these children will be in the metropolitan centres of Toronto (40 percent), Montreal (16 percent), and Vancouver (10 percent) (Burke, 1992).

In keeping with the current immigration pattern, the distribution of school-age immigrant children by country of origin has changed substantially from before 1981 to 1991, as can be seen in Table 7.1.

Compared with earlier waves of predominantly European immigrants, the majority of present-day immigrants have racial, cultural, religious, and linguistic backgrounds substantially different from those of mainstream Canadian society. In spite of their diversity, these people share one common bond: the need for ESL instruction.

Recent immigration trends profoundly challenge education in urban Canada, particularly in the metropolitan centres of Toronto, Vancouver, and Montreal, which absorb the largest proportion of this ever-increasing influx of non–English-speaking immigrants. From 1987 through 1991 alone, nearly 270 000 school-aged children (up to 19 years of age) arrived in Canada. This student enrollment transformation created tremendous pressure on school

TABLE 7.1
Distribution of School-Age Immigrant Children by Country of Origin

	BEFORE 1981	1991
Europe	40	27
Asia	32	47
Caribbean/Central/South American countries	11	6
Africa	4	5
United States	7	4
Oceania	1	<1

board budgets and curricula. The affected boards must facilitate the new social and educational dynamics arising within the system as a result of this influx. Some of them have reached a crisis stage in their ability to accommodate the number of non–English-speaking children. Individual school boards have no control over the enrollment of immigrant students. The majority of immigrants are free to settle anywhere they wish. Metropolitan Toronto, the major recipient of immigrant population, has 1300 ESL teachers and almost 35 000 students learning English along with their other subjects (McInnes, 1993). The Metropolitan Separate School Board of Toronto, Canada's largest school district, with more than 100 000 students, has doubled its number of ESL classes in the last few years. Some other cities recorded a similar explosion. In Vancouver, roughly half of the students state that their mother tongue is not English; in 1989, 10 000 students attended ESL classes (*Vancouver Sun*, 1989).

IMMIGRANT CHILDREN AND ESL PROGRAMS

How does the school system adapt itself to immigrant students? Should the underlying philosophy be integration or segregation? When should students be moved to standard classes? How should they be taught other subjects while they are still struggling to understand English? How could the number of qualified ESL teachers be increased? How should teachers of other school subjects like literature, music, and mathematics be trained to be effective in teaching ESL students? These questions must be addressed by the Canadian educational system.

The Canadian School Trustees Association (CSTA, 1989) surveyed 27 school boards across Canada. The criterion for choosing most boards in the study sample was that there must be high numbers of immigrant/refugee students who could not speak English or French and/or indicated problems with respect to their ESL courses. Most boards complained about "incoming students [being] forced to accept lower standards of instruction, a lack of resource materials and insufficient staff attention—all the essentials of acquiring proficiency in one of the official languages and in achieving academic success" (CSTA, p. 62). The study isolated three main areas of concern: (1) a substantial, often unpredictable increase in the enrollment of immigrant/refugee children; (2) the inadequacy of various aspects of ESL programs in meeting the needs of some students, such as the amount of instruction time and support from teachers; and (3) the inadequacy of funding ESL programs, which prevented boards from providing the necessary programming and staff (CSTA, p. 43). A greater awareness of the needs of immigrant children for ESL was recommended by the Association. The report emphasizes in particular the dilemma of the federal government, which is committed to "higher levels of immigration and to its multicultural policy . . . [but] unwilling to accept responsibility for meeting the language training and other settlement needs of all immigrants and refugees, including school-age children" (p. 63). Indeed, in Canada, ESL instruction is considered part of the "prerogative" of the provinces for education under the Constitution. As a result, one of the most controversial and alarming issues is that of the official funding policy of programs that are uncoordinated, fragmented, and consequently confused.

There are no national statistics available on the number of ESL students or on the overall cost of various programs. ESL has been traditionally taught in quite different ways according to the perceived needs of the students and according to the facilities and means at the disposal of the relevant communities. Unfortunately, facilities and resources are inadequate for the needs, but they are frequently the major factors dictating the approach to teaching ESL. Even if the immigrant's national language, or one of their national languages, is English, as is the case with immigrants from the Caribbean and India, their English-language facility may be inadequate by Canadian standards. This may involve a question of judgement by the system. The lack of proper student assessment is demonstrated by the fact that shy lower-class children from the Caribbean, who speak Patois and English as a second language, may be considered a "problem," while outgoing children from Africa and India, who speak a "peculiar" version of English, are integrated into mainstream classes without question.

During the first half of this century assimilation was the objective in dealing with non–English-speaking students. English language and culture were to be adopted by the immigrants. It was assumed by the educational system that if only English were used for instruction, language learning would be more rapid and effective. The teaching of English was virtually imposed, using an immersion approach covering as many aspects of the child's life as possible, including classrooms and playgrounds. One of the principal exponents of this philosophy was the Hon. J.T.M. Anderson, a minister of education, and subsequently premier of Saskatchewan. His University of Toronto doctoral dissertation, "The education of the new Canadian," contended that, for scientific and technical reasons, English was the best language of instruction for new Canadians, and became a basis for this policy of assimilation (Anderson, 1918). A thinly veiled and academically dubious racism prevailed in public opinion at that time. Many Anglo-Canadians took for granted that people of other "races" were intellectually inferior.

During this period school authorities believed that few immigrant children were capable of mastering much more than the basics of education. This notion, combined with the belief in the supremacy of the English language, implied that English teachers were to be preferred (Lupul, 1974). Indeed, English teachers were given such strong preference that, in most Prairie provinces, teacher-training schools rarely admitted candidates who had "foreign" names. Another theory popular at that time was that learning two languages caused interference, or a type of educational "negative transfer," that could best be avoided by insisting on the use of English only. It should be noted here that these theories were also used to rationalize the effort to extinguish Native languages whenever Indian children were brought under relatively complete control in boarding schools (Cardinal, 1969).

The insistence on English finally disappeared with the advent of Canada's policy of multiculturalism. Giving status to every culture (Trudeau, 1971), this policy implied that an ancestral language, or a mother tongue, should be esteemed. Heritage language classes, which were introduced in the 1970s in several provinces, soon became popular. At the same time the notion of total assimilation became unpopular in sociological writing, politics, and in the public media. Learning several languages was encouraged, and "negative transfer" was no longer a major fear. Bilingual, heritage, and ESL teaching and research began to flourish in this new climate. Bilingual programs in which the mother tongue is utilized as an aid to learning are nowadays quite common.

It can be argued that, to this day, the spirit of Anderson's notion of "English first" still survives. ESL teachers who are fluently bilingual may find that they have a hard time keeping their jobs, facing supervisors who believe that native English speakers should be better teachers of ESL. Frequently, such decisions are masked by claims about lack of qualifications, since overt discrimination on the basis of ethnicity or national origin would violate provincial human rights codes.

The development of proficiency in English is a prerequisite in a school system in which English is used as its primary language of instruction. Usually ESL is taught for a limited period until students can master a basic level of English and participate in regular classes. In reaching this objective, however, other factors come into play, such as children's different educational backgrounds, level of literacy in their mother tongue, cultural differences, and personal value systems. Policy-makers agree that it is common sense to give special attention to non-mainstream children who are unable to converse in English so that they can be successful in school. There is disagreement, however, about whether special courses should be delivered in a differentiated program outside the mainstream system or become an integral part of the curriculum (Ashworth, 1988; Commission for Racial Equality, 1986). There is also no consensus as to what programs and services are required in order to effectively implement language skills within the school system. In other words, ESL instruction yes—but how?

Identifying school children who actually do need ESL also poses a problem. Ashworth (1988) discussed the absence of an accurate and comprehensive definition of "ESL students" and stressed the need for a common and inclusive definition of such students, one that would include all children who are learning standard Canadian English as their second language regardless of their performance. To meet this need, the Halifax District School Board defined their ESL students comprehensively:

> An ESL student is any student who may be unable to achieve academic success with the regular school program because of his or her language or dialect, and who can be included in one or more of the following categories: 1) Students who do not speak English; 2) Students who speak a language other than English as a first language in their homes and have not yet developed the English language skills necessary for success in their school programs; 3) Students who, because of limited educational opportunity prior to coming to Canada, require upgrading in basic skills; 4) Students recently arrived in Canada who require assistance in adjusting to the new environment, culture, and educational expectations. (Halifax District School Board, 1989, p. 3)

ESL for school children is delivered almost exclusively by school boards. In areas where there are few immigrants, their needs may be poorly served, but in regions of high immigration, children will be served reasonably well. In isolated cases a single child may be given little support by the teachers, and must rely on peer instruction and a few minutes of private attention from a teacher who has no special training and no materials. At the opposite extreme, however, some of the better-funded school boards of Toronto, Vancouver, and Montreal, with large numbers of children in need of ESL, have sophisticated materials, methods, and specially trained teachers to deliver effective programs.

Owing to the lack of institutional structured ESL teaching within each school board and each province, there are numerous types of ESL programs, each with its own format and objectives. School boards choose certain teaching formats to suit their philosophy, language facilities, funding, and student enrollment. Ashworth (1992) listed various ESL programs in those English-speaking provinces in which large numbers of immigrant children reside (such as Ontario, British Columbia, Alberta and Manitoba). This list again demonstrates the different philosophies, the lack of co-ordination and, last but not least, the scarcity of funding bedevilling ESL in the Canadian public school systems:

Teaching ESL in Canada: Administration and Teaching
1) self-contained programs
    a) full-day reception classes
    b) half-day reception classes
    c) bilingual classes
2) withdrawal or pull-out programs
    a) English language/learning centre
    b) itinerant ESL teachers
    c) tutorials
3) transitional programs
    a) subject matter transitional classes
    b) vocational/pre-employment programs
    c) academic booster programs
    d) special education and ESL programs
    e) pre-school programs
4) mainstreaming
    a) immersion programs
    b) mainstream support programs (Ashworth, 1992)

ESL FOR ADULT IMMIGRANTS: POLICIES, ORGANIZATION, AND FINANCE

Numerous writers have emphasized the importance of speaking an official language for employment in the mainstream labour force. Lack of English or French has been identified as one of the main reasons for immigrants' inability to move out of low-paying jobs in which they have been traditionally over-represented (Arnopolis, 1979, p. 33).

National, provincial, and local initiatives provide adult immigrant language training with the intent to prepare new settlers for economic survival, social participation, and integration (Magahay, 1991); in addition, numerous charitable and private organizations conduct language classes on a more or less formal basis. The divergence of aims that results from these varied sources of instruction stems partly from the different needs for ESL by adult immigrants of diverse cultural and educational backgrounds.

These various levels of provision cause ESL to fall victim to the usual contests over education in Canada: Whose responsibility is it? Is it a public or a private function? In the event that public authorities assume control, will it be federally, provincially, or locally directed and financed? How can these possibilities be combined? If they are combined, are the services organized to complement each other, or is competition and discrete planning more likely?

There is general agreement that privately initiated ESL exists in every situation and can frequently be quite effective. Private instruction may be provided without a user fee or it may consist of relatively expensive "professional tutoring." Informal coaching among peers, such as children helping their parents, co-workers, and friends, is probably one of the most effective methods. Private tuition may still meet the needs of some occupations requiring a high standard of professional performance and only a basic knowledge of technical English (for example, all airline pilots are required to learn technical terms in English for international use in flying). A large sector of immigrants initially depend either on charity or on friendship for ESL instruction. Some newcomers will make a desperate effort to learn English privately in the hope that this will help them secure permanent residency status from the immigration authorities.

ESL for adults was first organized by charitable institutions and churches on a local or community basis. Little information is available as to its conduct and organization. It can be assumed, however, that most programs were transitional and instruction was informal. Non-profit organizations serving immigrants still play an important role in providing language training and settlement services. Frontier College in Toronto is one of the most systematic and successful examples of these private voluntary agencies.

The changes that took place in ESL teaching in the public school system are paralleled in ESL teaching to adults. Within the last two decades ESL instruction became a public concern and a formalized learning process. Publicly controlled and financed ESL has become quite conspicuous and is typically of higher quality. School boards offer free part-time or full-time unilingual or bilingual ESL on their premises during the daytime and evenings. Classes are also offered through community agencies and workplaces, and instructors are provided by the boards. Those boards serving large numbers of immigrants have developed quite sophisticated approaches to issues of curriculum, program co-ordination, and teacher training.

Community colleges also deliver ESL programs. Here students usually pay a fee to attend part-time classes. In other cases, limited numbers of students are enrolled in ESL programs funded by the federal government and justified as a social investment leading to gainful employment. In recent years, their ESL programs have been extended to include co-operative arrangements with community agencies and the workplace. Short-term ESL courses are offered by universities to upgrade the English skills of immigrant students, either before or during degree programs. High fees are usually charged for these courses.

In summary, ESL is delivered by various authorities to thousands of immigrants, refugees, and even some illegal immigrants who are periodically given a chance to legalize their status before or at their final immigration hearings. It is also offered as a form of vocational training to adults who wish to secure advantages such as a better job, full-time work, a position with long-term prospects in the fields in which they are qualified, or a contract in a region that has a greater demand for their services.

Funding is at least partially provided by Employment and Immigration Canada, but the administration and staffing may be from local governments (especially school boards) or private agencies offering their services for profit. Employment Centres usually pay training allowances and income subsidies. Indeed, ESL training can literally be seen as an "investment" in vocational training. Unfortunately, recent demand has tended to outstrip available funding. As a result, many who are unable to enrol in ESL programs are likely to take jobs for which they are overqualified. The 1991–95 Immigration Plan admitted that language training traditionally focussed on the needs of immigrants entering the labour market, and thereby favoured certain immigrant groups over others. A high proportion of immigrant women will never join the labour force, yet twice as many women as men need ESL training, so it is an equity and justice issue as well as one concerning investment in human capital (Secretary of State, 1987).

Only recently have some agencies and private institutions providing ESL begun to co-ordinate what has been, apart from some highly effective and well-planned islands of professionalism, a confusing and amateurish provision of program delivery systems. Toronto has probably the best data, research, and planning. This relative success can be credited to a tradition of sharing among the Ministry of Education, the boards of education, and several private corporations (Ashworth, 1992, p. 47).

ESL approaches have traditionally been designed to provide language mastery. Only the most sophisticated and time-consuming programs try to assist the newcomer in the more demanding phases of adjustment and participation. Burnaby (1992, pp. 5–8) charged that the whole ESL system, apart from some exceptions, is neither well co-ordinated nor professionally delivered. Her criticisms covered funding variations and limitations imped-ing services, lack of social focus, and neglect of attention to environmental details that would attract or permit enrollment of those needing the services (see also Boyd, 1992, p. 141; Cumming & Gill, 1992, pp. 246–47).

At the close of the 1980s, the total annual expenditure for ESL by the federal govern-ment exceeded $100 million. Even this was not enough, and the 1991–95 Immigration Plan proposed an additional $200 million over the five years (Government of Canada, 1992). Financing ESL may include much more than the cost of tuition, since some students also require access to day care for their children if they are to study effectively, and transportation costs or even personal subsidies may sometimes be necessary. However, these additional costs are relatively small and are probably justified either as investments (short-term payments to prepare a person for employment and thereby to join the taxpaying base of society), as entitlements for parents of dependent children, or even as social secu-rity payments.

CONCLUSIONS

Programs in English as a Second Language are one of the most basic services the newly arrived immigrant needs to begin his or her new life in Canada. On a pragmatic level, ESL can be considered an investment that will increase the learner's productivity and income and, conversely, decrease the need for social assistance. English is needed to participate in the political and social life of the new country. It can be argued that immi-grants are entitled to the full development of their communicative potential, thus avoiding discrimination based on language and permitting participation through greater mastery.

Although ESL teaching in Canada in the 1990s is substantially different from the pseudo-academic approach of earlier years, ESL continues in the direction of mainstream-ing, regardless of political and/or sociological trends. Over time, there have been dramatic quantitative and qualitative changes. Multicultural issues have become important and have made policy-makers aware of the needs of ESL learners. Flexibility and sensitivity have become major policy objectives. Partly because of lobbying by a group of organizations involved with ESL, governments have established language and vocational referral services in the largest cities where most immigrants live. In these centres immigrants are linguis-tically assessed, and receive educational and vocational counselling and ESL benefits. Their progress is monitored over time, and the collected data are utilized in the planning and policy development of the provincial government.

Recently the trend has been toward co-operation between community agencies familiar with immigrant needs and traditional public educational institutions. This has greatly improved immigrant awareness of as well as accessibility to ESL. It virtually opened ESL to traumatized refugees, slow learners, and non-traditional immigrants who would not have approached a mainstream institutional setting of their own volition.

However, conditions remain poor in many regions and may deteriorate. Bilingual ESL classes are still not widely available outside the largest metropolitan centres. Another concern is the qualification and employment of teachers. Although standard qualifications for teachers were developed by the provincial authorities, it appears that the selection criteria frequently are traditionally and academically oriented and do not address the needs of an increasingly Third World immigrant population.

Almost no systematic research or means of evaluation have been developed to help teachers and instructors. How well do the methods work? How well do students learn? What methods are to be used for instruction? When should teaching be started? How long should it last? These are basic questions where instinct must still be a guide. The training of teachers and development of instructional materials should be directed by research, especially into the effectiveness of various kinds and levels of instruction. Little of this research has been attempted.

ESL finds itself in the middle of a key constitutional issue of Canada, namely the federal–provincial division of responsibilities for immigration and education. On the one hand, increasing immigration forces provinces to find additional funds to cope with the costs of ESL. On the other hand, the Constitution gives the federal government authority to refuse this necessary assistance. The increase of immigrants to this country will continue to make even greater demands on institutions that cater to the educational needs of the community, thereby increasing demand for public and private funding. Unless the whole ESL program is given greater exposure in the country at large, unless the providers are given more support, and unless overall program co-ordination is implemented, those who need the service will be impeded in their quest to become fully integrated members of Canadian society.

DISCUSSION QUESTIONS

❏ What are major competencies that each teacher or instructor should develop in order to satisfy the needs of current ESL learners?

❏ How are education for citizenship, political and social integration, and/or personal fulfilment involved in ESL?

❏ In what situations should the learner be expected to pay for ESL? Why?

❏ Should public funding of ESL be increased in the light of current demands? Explain.

REFERENCES

Anderson, J.T.M. (1918). *The education of the new Canadian.* Toronto: Dent.
Arnopolis, S.M. (1979). *Problems of immigration in the Canadian labour force.* A paper prepared for the Canadian Advisory Council on the Status of Women. Ottawa: Canadian Advisory Council on the Status of Women.
Ashworth, M. (1988). *Blessed with bilingual brains: Education of immigrant children with English as a second language.* Vancouver: Pacific Educational Press, University of British Columbia.
Ashworth, M. (1992). Views and visions. In B. Burnaby & A. Cumming (Eds.). *Sociopolitical aspects of ESL in Canada.* (pp. 35–49). Toronto: OISE Press.

Badets, J. (1993, Summer). Canada's immigrant: Recent trends. *Canadian Social Trends*, 8–11.

Boyd, M. (1992). Immigrant women: Language, socio-economic inequalities and policy issues. In B. Burnaby & A. Cumming (Eds.). *Socio-political aspects of ESL in Canada*. (pp. 141). Toronto: OISE Press.

Burke, M.A. (1992, Spring). Canada's immigrant children. *Canadian Social Trends*, 15–20.

Burnaby, B. (1992). Official language training for adult immigrants in Canada: Features and issues. In B. Burnaby & A. Cumming (Eds.). *Socio-political aspects of ESL in Canada*. (pp. 3–34). Toronto: OISE Press.

Canada Immigration and Employment Centre. (1990, October). Annual Report to Parliament. Immigration Plan for 1991–1995.

Canadian School Trustees Association (CSTA). (1989). *Scholastic adaptation and cost effectiveness of programs for immigrant/refugee children in Canadian schools: Report.* Ottawa: CSTA.

Cardinal, H. (1969). *The unjust society: The tragedy of Canada's Indians*. Edmonton: Hurtig.

Commission for Racial Equality. (1986). *Teaching English as a Second Language (Report of a formal investigation in Calderdale Local Education Authority)*. London: CRE.

Cumming, A., & Gill, J. (1992). Motivation or accessibility? Factors permitting Indo-Canadian women to pursue ESL literacy instruction. In B. Burnaby & A. Cumming (Eds.). *Socio-political aspects of ESL in Canada*. (pp. 246–47). Toronto: OISE Press.

Government of Canada. (1992). New immigrant language training policy. *IM 151/7/92*. Ottawa.

Halifax District School Board. (1989). *The English as a second language committee: Interim report*. Halifax.

Lupul, M.R. (1974). Some implications of bilingualism and multiculturalism for curriculum development. *TEMA, 6*, 12–17.

McInnes, C. (1993, May 3). First you have to learn English. *Globe and Mail*.

Magahay, W. (1991). Meeting the needs: A preliminary assessment of ESL program delivery to adult immigrants/refugees in Canada and a model towards language education for participation. *A TESL Canada Report*. Ottawa: Carleton University.

Secretary of State. (1987). *Profile of Canadians who speak neither French nor English*. Ottawa: Teega Research Consultants.

Trudeau, P.E. (1971, October 8). Statement by the Prime Minister in the House of Commons.

Vancouver Sun. (1989, May 30). ESL: Immigrant wave breaks on schools.

FURTHER READINGS

Benesch, S. (Ed.). 1991. *ESL in America: Myths and possibilities*. Portsmouth, NH: Boynton/Cook Publishers.

Burgess, D.A. (1993). Minority education rights: Some current issues. In L.L. Strewin & S.J.H. McCann (Eds.). *Contemporary educational issues*. Mississauga, ON: Copp Clark Pitman.

Celce-Murcia, M. (Ed.). (1991). *Teaching English as a second or foreign language*. Second edition. Boston, MA: Heinle & Heinle.

Coelho, E., et al. (1990). *Immigrant students in North York schools: Intermediate and senior division.* North York, ON: North York Schools, Curriculum and Instructional Services.

Gregor, A., & Jenkinson, D. (Eds). (1988). *Teaching English as a second language: Progress in diversity.* Winnipeg: University of Manitoba (Faculty of Education).

Mazurek, K., & Kach, N. (1990). Multiculturalism, society and education. In B. Titley (Ed.). *Canadian education: Historical themes and contemporary issues.* (pp. 133–60). Calgary: Detselig.

Mitter, W. (1992). Multicultural education: Basic consideration in an interdisciplinary approach. *Prospects, 22*(1), 81.

Nicholls S., & Hoadly-Maidment, E. (Eds.). (1988). *Current issues in teaching English as a second language to adults.* London: Edward Arnold.

8

RELIGION AND EDUCATION

Jud Purdy

"**I**nformation without religion is a positive evil," declared the Right Reverend John Strachan (1840), the Church of England's first bishop of Toronto. Most Christians in the Western world at that time would have agreed with the bishop's bald assertion. Education was not, in their opinion, simply the imparting of information. Religion was considered as important a part of every youth's education as mathematics and literature. Indeed, it was generally agreed that religious training was *more* significant, since it was seen as the cornerstone of character development: instilling moral values was viewed as essential to a child's development as a responsible citizen. During the period in which Canadian education was being institutionalized, religion was regarded as having a very important function.

Canadians have agreed, in large part, with the intent of Strachan's statement, but there have been continual differences over how to implement this view. A recurring question has been "How closely related should the schools be to a specific denomination?" Over the years, four responses to this query have emerged. First, the Roman Catholics, who have always been a substantial minority in most provinces outside Quebec, have constantly asserted that there is an intimate connection between education and religion; therefore, Catholics must have their own distinctive schools in which to train their children. Furthermore, the Church argued that it must have complete control of its schools. To share their direction with the state would tend to undermine the essentially religious nature of these institutions. During most of the nineteenth century, the Roman Catholic hierarchy waged a stout but unsuccessful campaign to maintain their independence from the state. With the exception of Quebec and Manitoba between 1870 and 1891, all provinces refused to grant such a broad concession to the Roman Catholics. But the Catholic community succeeded in having its position recognized and often received financial assistance for its school systems from provincial governments.

A second response, by the traditional Protestant churches and many non-Western religions, has generally been to eschew denominational schools. Instead, they have supported schemes to establish publicly controlled schools in which the essentials of Christian doctrine and ethics would be taught.

A third response has come from a small minority, including most Jewish and Islamic Canadians, some Sikhs, and various Protestant denominations. These groups have openly preferred religious schools and have been willing to finance their endeavours privately, although many provinces have begun to offer them limited financial aid.

Finally, there has been the response of the secular humanists, a very vocal faction, and certain other groups who argue that it is decidedly inappropriate to include religious instruction in a child's education.

These four approaches inform the debate concerning the respective roles of the church and the state in education.

The Church of England adopted a philosophy similar to its Catholic counterpart and played a large role in developing educational facilities throughout the British colonies in the nineteenth century. The Society for the Propagation of the Gospel, the leading Anglican missionary society, expended large sums of money building schools. The Scottish Presbyterians (the Church of Scotland), like members of comparable religions in Switzerland and the Netherlands, were also vigorous proponents of popular education.

These sectarian thrusts often disintegrated when confronted with the social, political, and demographic realities of the pioneer community. There emerged the practice of many Christian groups combining their resources to establish a single school for the entire community. A spirit of ecumenical co-operation in educational activities took shape early in the history of the Canadian colonies. Moreover, it was cheaper to have only one school in a community.

Organized Christianity played a leading role in the campaign for publicly supported schools that emerged in the middle decades of the nineteenth century throughout much of the Western world, including the colonies in British North America. No group of Christians displayed more enthusiasm for this cause than the Evangelical wing of Protestantism, which was, without question, the leading proponent of Protestant Christianity in the Victorian era. The aim of the Evangelicals was to redeem the individual and then, through these "new men," to regenerate society. Schools were a principal weapon in the Evangelicals' armoury. A Protestant was expected, at the very least, to be able to read the Bible, the primary source of individual salvation. Reading and interpreting the Scriptures demanded a high degree of literacy.

Yet Christianity's impact on the emergence of state education must not be overestimated. The demand for schools came from a number of equally significant forces (Gidney, 1972; Houston, 1972; Prentice, 1977). Scholars have formulated a number of interpretations about this movement. Although Christianity was a powerful ingredient, its role in creating a demand for a state-controlled and financed system of schools must be carefully balanced and integrated with other factors: the state of the economy, the social environment, the growing need for skilled workers, and the emergence of the national state.

Nevertheless, religion remained at the core of education for most Canadians. Resorting to the expediency of using the state to establish schools did not mean that they would be secular institutions. This idea was never seriously contemplated by the public. Rather, the schools would be non-denominational, teaching "Common Christianity." The Rev. E.R. Ryerson, the first superintendent of schools in Ontario and a leading Methodist minister, proposed

> By religion and morality I do not mean sectarianism in form, but the general system of truth and morals taught in Holy Scriptures ... To inculcate the peculiarities of a sect, and to teach the fundamental principles of religion and morality are equally different. (Hodgins, 1899, p. 147)

Thus, from the beginning of the debate about state control of education, it was assumed that an intimate relationship existed between education and Christianity. While Canada has never had an officially established state church, it has generally accepted the proposition that the churches have a role to play in the public sphere, and this fact of national life has been embodied in the preamble of the Canadian Charter of Rights and Freedoms. The concept of a secular state as practised in the United States has never been accepted as a model for church–state relations in Canada.

The conflicts arising between religious factions in Canada over the desire for a close connection between education and religion were addressed in a number of ways. One solution was devised in the colony of Upper Canada, later the province of Ontario. As in other Canadian colonies, a variety of schools had appeared in Upper Canada before 1840. Some had been opened by individual teachers, while others were formed by parents who banded together to build a community school. Naturally, the various denominations, including the Roman Catholic Church, also attempted to open schools for the children of their adherents. Often the government gave some financial assistance to these denominations, to help defray the costs and as a means of cementing their political loyalty (Gidney, 1973; Purdy, 1985).

PUBLIC AND SEPARATE SCHOOLS: ONTARIO

By the 1840s, many public officials in Upper Canada had begun, for a variety of reasons, to argue that the government should play a much larger role in the provision of educational facilities. Under the leadership of a new Chief Superintendent of Education, the Rev. Dr. Ryerson, a prominent Methodist minister, Upper Canada embarked on an ambitious program to provide common education in public schools for the entire population.

One of the primary reasons for promoting public schools was the desire to build a cohesive society, one in which all citizens would share a common set of values, attitudes, and institutions. The Roman Catholic community, on the other hand, was determined to have schools for its children under the direction of the Church. This demand was seen as a threat to the attempt to build a unified community and aroused the deep-seated anti-Catholicism of English Protestants.

The battle over denominational schools in Canada West lasted for a period of about twenty years, with each side offering and accepting compromises. Ultimately, a "final solution" was adopted in 1863, with the passing of the Scott Act. This legislation granted Roman Catholics the right to establish schools in any area of the province, and allowed them to receive a share of the provincial school grant and the local residential property tax. While this act gave Catholic officials much of what they had been seeking, it certainly did not give them a completely separate school system. The act enjoined their schools to accept the same textbooks, curriculum circulars, and teacher qualifications as the public system. It also stipulated that Roman Catholic schools be inspected by officials from the Department of Education. In other words, separate schools were to remain under the jurisdiction of the Department. This part of the settlement was a signal victory for Ryerson and the public-school advocates (Sissons, 1959, pp. 3–58; Walker, 1955, pp. 36–212; Wilson et al., 1970, pp. 231–39).

Significantly, no mention was made in this legislation about Roman Catholic interests in secondary education. Since few children in the nineteenth century attended any type of secondary school, it simply had not been a matter of debate. Many common schools taught what would now be regarded as high-school subjects. When the Ontario high-school system was established in 1871, the legislation contained absolutely no reference to Roman Catholic rights or privileges on this level. This omission laid the foundation for a continuous series of conflicts during the next century.

CATHOLIC AND PROTESTANT DISSENTIENT SCHOOLS: QUEBEC

While this raucous debate was proceeding in Upper Canada, a somewhat similar dispute emerged in Canada East (now Quebec). During the 1840s this colony created its own distinctive system of education. Owing to differences in demography, settlement patterns, and the religious composition of the population, a very different solution to the problem of religious education was devised. Although English Protestants were a minority in Quebec, they were economically and politically powerful. The Protestant and Catholic clerical leaders were equally determined to secure schools for their own adherents. As a result, it was easier to effect a solution, which was embodied in laws passed in 1845 and 1846 (Wilson et al., 1970, pp. 172–5) that gave the two principal Christian divisions their own schools, establishing what became known as the dual confessional system. While this conflict initially centred on religious differences between Catholics and Protestants, language was also a potentially divisive issue. To French Roman Catholics, religion and language were uniquely linked and this union could not be dissolved. In reality, it took about two decades to flesh out the complete structure, which allowed each group almost complete autonomy (Wilson et al., 1970, pp. 175–81). The Protestants immediately began to create a system similar to that of Ontario, except that from the outset they had the right to receive funding for both elementary and secondary schools. The Catholic system that emerged from this arrangement was comparable to that of continental France, which assumed that very few pupils attended high school. These two systems existed in virtual isolation from each other until the sweeping reforms of the 1960s.

ATLANTIC CANADA: COMMUNITY ACCOMMODATIONS

In the Atlantic colonies (Newfoundland, Prince Edward Island, New Brunswick, and Nova Scotia), a similar pattern of events, debates, and solutions emerged. Immigration to this area was not on the massive scale it was to the St. Lawrence basin. To the original settlements of United Empire Loyalists and Scots was added a smaller group of Irish Catholics, whose ecclesiastical leaders requested their own educational institutions. In this endeavour they were supported by the remnants of the Acadian population, who generally avoided overt political action. Except in Newfoundland, throughout the Maritimes a series of ad hoc arrangements were devised. However, the various debates on education consistently rejected the notion of a Roman Catholic separate school system similar to that established in Ontario.

The conflict and resultant settlement in New Brunswick characterized the way this issue was resolved in the Maritimes. Prior to Confederation, New Brunswick had established a non-sectarian public-school system and had not made any legal provisions for the establishment and funding of denominational schools. The only concession granted to the

Roman Catholics was permission to use the Douay version of the Bible in religious instruction for their children. In 1871, a new school act explicitly stated that all public schools in the province were to be non-sectarian. The Catholics claimed that this legislation contradicted the previous arrangement that, they argued, had given them the right to have publicly funded schools. They appealed to the Dominion Parliament and to the courts by invoking section 93 of the BNA Act, but failed to redress the grievance. After an episode of violence in an Acadian community, the provincial government arranged a compromise whereby Roman Catholic children attended one school in a district and the other children used a different building. Both types of schools were funded from the same sources and came under the jurisdiction of a single board of trustees (Wilson et al., 1970, pp. 271–73).

Prince Edward Island witnessed a very nasty debate over what was called the "Bible Question." Here it was primarily a dispute over the use of Holy Scriptures as a textbook. A settlement was reached that closely resembled the one in New Brunswick (Wilson at al., 1970, pp. 102–5). The Nova Scotia government totally rejected Roman Catholic attempts to obtain separate schools. The Roman hierarchy finally agreed to a scheme whereby local boards of trustees rented the already existing Catholic schools from the parish or a convent. In this unusual approach, Catholic schools received public aid but were accorded no legal status.

Newfoundland had a distinctive policy for the establishment of its public school system. Here a multi-confessional system evolved, wherein a number of denominations operated their own schools and received public funding. This solution was arrived at not only because of the usual sectarian disputes, but also because of the way schooling emerged in Newfoundland over the years (Wilson et al., 1970, pp. 136–40). After 30 years of continuous discussion and negotiation, funds were divided among a number of denominations. The original members of this multi-confessional scheme were the Church of England, the Methodists, the Congregationalists, the Church of Scotland, and the Roman Catholics. Later the Salvation Army, Seventh Day Adventists, and Pentecostals each had a few schools.

PROVINCIAL AUTONOMY: A POLITICAL NECESSITY

Most of the disputes mentioned above coincided with the movement toward the union of the British North American colonies. Given its emotional and political significance, education was a natural topic for discussion among the fathers of Confederation. While it was never one of the major issues, the problem of protecting existing religious minority rights raised the spectre of renewed denominational animosities (Creighton, 1964, pp. 399–401, 409–12). The outcome of this debate gave control of education to the provinces, as embodied in section 93 of the BNA Act (now the Constitution Act, 1867; see Appendix A). This section explicitly prohibits any province from interfering with the schools of any religious groups that had them "by Law in the Province at the Union." It is clear from the wording of section 93 that only the Roman Catholic separate schools in Ontario and the Protestant schools in Quebec were protected by this provision. Yet the wording of this entire section became very important in certain law cases, such as the Roman Catholic Separate High Schools Funding case of 1987 (see also Magnet, 1982). Section 93 also provided a mechanism for any group to appeal any attempted abridgement of its rights, but, as will be noted later, these appeals have been generally unsuccessful.

The entrance of Manitoba into Confederation in 1869 was fraught with many potential disputes about religion and language. The Red River/Assiniboine area had been settled by French Catholic Métis and English and Scottish immigrants. Provincial status was conferred on Manitoba as a result of Louis Riel's championing of the settlers' rights. The first educational legislation passed by the new legislature acknowledged the prior existence of both Catholic and Protestant schools, which the various denominations had been operating for decades. The new government adopted the Quebec dual confessional system as a suitable arrangement, and it was assumed, since the majority of the Roman Catholics were French, that the latter's language would be used in their schools, although this was never clearly stated in the act. For the next twenty years, this solution remained in effect. But as more English-speaking settlers arrived, anti-Catholic and anti-French sentiments developed. A campaign to abolish the dual confessional system and substitute non-sectarian schools emerged. In 1891, this was accomplished. This action led to the famous Manitoba School Question, an episode that has been thoroughly canvassed by Canadian historians (Crunican, 1974). In 1916, during the First World War, the legislature prohibited the use of French and other languages for instructional purposes. This right was restored by a 1981 decision of the Supreme Court of Canada, which held that the Act of 1891 was unconstitutional. For almost a century the French Catholic community in Manitoba had been denied their dual confessional and bilingual schools.

By the time British Columbia entered Confederation, in 1871, it had a distinctive school system. Even though missionaries from many denominations, especially Anglican and Roman Catholic, had opened their own schools, a demand emerged during the 1850s for public non-denominational schools. The proponents of this scheme were assured of victory when a law was enacted in 1865 setting up a highly centralized system in which all schools were to be non-sectarian. No concessions were granted to any Christian group, although clergy were permitted to offer religious instruction to children of their own faiths after school hours. This limited privilege was repeated in the Common School Ordinance of 1869, which applied to the newly united colony of Vancouver Island and mainland British Columbia. For over 100 years, British Columbia resisted all attempts to modify this arrangement. As a result, it possesses a school system that is strikingly different from its eastern counterparts (Johnson, 1964, pp. 25–43).

The first schools in the Northwest Territories were built by missionaries. In 1875, when the Territories were granted a limited degree of self-government, the federal authorities insisted on provisions that permitted the establishment of separate schools for either Roman Catholics or Protestants. Since the French were still the majority of the population, it was anticipated that the Territories, like Manitoba, would be bilingual and bicultural. Very rapidly, however, the French were outnumbered by English settlers who, once they achieved control of the local assembly, began to limit the rights of French Catholics. Finally, in 1901, the Territorial government enacted an educational ordinance that created a system of non-denominational schools but still permitted the minority to retain separate schools.

The phenomenal influx of settlers into Canada from Central and Eastern Europe at the end of the nineteenth century spurred the Protestant element to push for the extension of the public school system, which was now regarded as a vehicle to assimilate newcomers. The Protestants feared that their position would be overrun by these immigrants, with their different customs, languages, and religious traditions. The population of the West grew so rapidly that in 1905 the federal government decided to create two new provinces, Alberta and Saskatchewan. The enabling legislation originally included a clause that would have established a dual confessional school system, similar to that of Quebec. This proposal was regarded as regressive and dangerous by the English element. Once again, sectarianism divided the politicians in the federal cabinet. The West's leading government spokesman, Minister of the Interior Clifford Sifton, attacked his party's policy and had it significantly revised. To protect the rights of minority schools in the two new provinces, a clause similar in wording to section 93 of the BNA Act was inserted into their constitutions. This solution preserved the intention of the 1901 Territorial ordinance, since it permitted separate schools to exist within the public system but, as in Ontario, it compelled the minority schools to abide by the regulations and curriculum directives of the provincial departments of education (Lupul, 1974, chap. 9).

SECTARIANISM GIVES WAY TO SECULARISM

The arrangements devised to integrate religion into public education illustrate the Victorian Canadian belief that these two aspects of a child's development could not be separated. Religion was a central element of life. Personal identity and reputation were marked out as much by religious affiliation as by economic status or political association. The real problem was not whether schools should have a religious connection, however defined, but rather what role religion should play in the curriculum. For a number of reasons, most of Canada's Protestant leaders and their congregations were willing to adopt some compromise solutions that were unheard of in most of Europe. Still, denominational schools, apart from Roman Catholic schools, became anathema in Canada. By 1920, the concept of non-denominational public schools became the generally accepted approach throughout the nation.

In the early decades of the twentieth century Canadians turned their attention to other major problems. Industrialization, urbanization, the emergence of a consumer economy, the struggle for national independence, and the building of the welfare state overtook the ancient religious issues. The combined impact of these forces began to undermine the role religion played in the lives of Canadians. No longer was the church the sole arbiter of society's values. Gradually, in the years after World War I, church attendance began to decline, while people turned to new secular pursuits (Creighton, 1976, pp. 25–28).

By this time, Canada had acquired a remarkable religious diversity. While Protestants and Roman Catholics remained the predominant groups, with a sprinkling of Orthodox and other small Christian sects (such as the Mennonites, Hutterites, etc.) and Jewish congregations, recent decades have witnessed the arrival of Muslims, Buddhists, Hindus, Sikhs, and members of other Eastern religions. With the children of these faiths attending public schools, it has been very difficult to argue that schools are primarily Christian institutions. A few curriculum changes have occurred: World religions have been introduced and Christian holidays are now celebrated in the context of religious diversity. The spread of a humanistic philosophy rooted in science as a substitute for religion and the consequent emergence of agnosticism and atheism as acceptable public stances have also eroded the school's claim to instil Christian values (Stamp, 1982, p. 223). These forces, together with the rise of materialism and secularism, seemed to push religious disputes into the background while other pedagogical issues dominated the scene. The accepted decisions of the past were left to lie dormant. They would come to the fore once again during the most recent public debates over the role of religion in education.

DENOMINATIONALISM REVISITED IN ONTARIO

In Ontario the Roman Catholic separate schools question was revived in the 1960s with the increased enrollments of the "baby boom" generation sweeping into the schools. Also, there was a decline in the number of teaching nuns and brothers. These developments necessitated the extension of facilities and the hiring of many lay teachers. But the financial resources of the separate system were sorely taxed in the process. The bishops petitioned the government for more financial aid and the extension of funding to the Catholic system to the end of high school.

During the 1960s, Ontario's ruling Tories were deeply involved in revamping and expanding the province's educational structure (Fleming, 1972; Stamp, 1982). Although the government did grant some increased financial aid to the separate elementary schools, it feared a revival of the old religious animosities if it conceded the Roman Catholic demands for full funding of all Catholic schools to the end of secondary schools. This remained government policy until 1984 when, in a very dramatic and totally unexpected move, Premier William Davis announced that the government would begin to extend full funding to the separate system, which would now include all high-school grades. A new Liberal government elected within a year agreed to implement this policy. The legality of the government's actions was sustained by decisions of the Supreme Courts of Ontario and Canada.

While this legislation seemed to solve a century's-old dispute, it helped to spark debate on the old question of the role of religion in public schools. For several years spokespersons representing a variety of Christian and non-Christian groups had been pressing the Ministry of Education to include in the curriculum courses or programs in multi-faith education. The province had by this time acquired a sizable non-Christian population. By and large, Muslims, Sikhs, Buddhists, Hindus, and other non-Christian groups preferred to send their children to the pubic schools but, at the same time, they continued to adhere to the belief that religion and education were inseparable. The ministry established a Commission of Inquiry, chaired by G.A. Watson, on this issue (Report of the Ministerial Inquiry on Religious Education in Ontario, 1990), which recommended the introduction of compulsory courses in religious studies in Ontario public elementary schools. Instruction, not indoctrination was the thrust of this program. Students were to be taught to understand, appreciate, and respect the various beliefs and practices of a multitude of religious positions. Subsequently, the Ministry of Education announced that these courses would be introduced in September 1993. This innovative approach represents a significant departure for public education in this province.

At the same time that Ontario was seeking a way to extend more financial assistance to separate schools in the 1960s, the francophone population was requesting more use of their language in the instruction of their children. This coincided with the rise of Quebec nationalism and the efforts of the federal Liberal governments to enhance the status of the French language across Canada. Feeling that Ontario should take the lead in this matter, Premier John Robarts introduced legislation in 1968 giving the francophones more rights at both the elementary and secondary levels. However, these schools had to be a part of the public system and not the Roman Catholic system. Implementation of this legislation was left to the local school boards, which were dominated by anglophone trustees often reluctant to carry out these provisions. Again, a series of nasty emotional events occurred, forcing the government to intervene. The francophones, feeling that their interests were not adequately represented on school boards, pressed the provincial government either to give them control over their schools or to allow them to have seats on the boards. Finally, in 1987, legislation gave the francophones the right to elect trustees to boards where they had a sufficient population.

SECTARIANISM AS AN IMPEDIMENT TO OTHER GOALS: QUEBEC AND NEWFOUNDLAND

In Quebec, a Liberal government elected in 1960 decided to undertake an extensive series of reforms to that province's educational system. A Royal Commission (known as the Parent Commission) was established to tackle this problem. One of its chief recommendations was that Quebec should create a Ministry of Education, which would modernize schooling and bring it more under the control of the government, as was the practice in the other provinces. Such a policy was fraught with many difficulties, not the least being a potential clash with the powerful religious authorities, especially the Roman Catholic Church. When legislation was passed creating the new Ministry, it transferred control of the schools to the state. However, a link was maintained with the traditional religious powers by allowing Roman Catholic and Protestant representation on the new Superior Council, the Ministry's principal advisory board. In fact, no significant measures could be adopted without the Council's approval (Wilson et al., 1970, pp. 473–79). Clearly, the reforms initiated in the early 1960s had reduced the role and authority of religion in Quebec's educational system. Although the dual confessional system had been protected by the BNA Act, the reform measures went a long way to transforming it into a more secular one.

As the decade wore on, the emergence of the language issue began to supplant the religious one in public debates over education. With the reduction of the role of the Roman Catholic Church in Quebec society, the French language became the distinguishing characteristic of the Québécois. This development, coupled with the equally startling decline in the French birth rate and the rise of separatism, provoked successive provincial governments to seek ways of securing the role of the French language in the life of Quebec, including the educational system. The election of the separatist Parti Québécois government in 1976 heightened this trend. This government's policy was to make Quebec a unilingual province. Its educational legislation restricted the admission of pupils to English schools to those children whose parents had attended an English school in the province or whose siblings were already enrolled in one, or were temporary residents or Native Canadians. Now language, rather than religion, was becoming the principal factor in defining school divisions in Quebec (Magnuson, 1980, pp. 128–29).

Newfoundland also attempted to modernize its school system in the 1960s. One of the chief problems was to find a way of depriving the various denominations of the role they had been accorded in the multi-confessional system. A Royal Commission recommended a reduction of church power. Before the government decided to act on this suggestion, it actually enlarged the number of participating denominations by including the Pentecostals. However, subsequent legislation virtually eliminated the denominations from the educational system's policy-making process. The legislation created a new body, known as the

Denominational Policy Commission, that merely advised the Department of Education on the rights and roles of the various churches (Wilson et al., 1970, pp. 102–5).

INDEPENDENT RELIGIOUS SCHOOLS

A unique aspect of the religious issue in recent years has been the emergence of a number of private schools sponsored by religious groups. Some Jewish, Islamic, Sikh, and Anglican congregations have decided to build schools to educate their children, but it has been the Christian Reform Church and a number of Protestant fundamentalist groups that have led the way in this campaign.

The fundamentalist organizations generally decry the "progressive" philosophy of the public-school curriculum, the perceived lack of strict discipline, and the apparent relaxation of academic standards in the public schools. They feel that the public schools have betrayed their original purposes, especially by failing to include religious teaching. Moreover, they claim that the schools support and teach a philosophy of secular humanism that, in their opinion, makes science the measure of all things, denies the literal truth of the Bible, and substitutes a situational ethics for a code of moral absolutes. Their plea to operate their own schools is cloaked in the rhetoric of contemporary North American neoconservativism, a stance that espouses the right of parents to choose their children's education. Leaving education totally in the hands of the state, they maintain, has serious consequences of the type forecast in George Orwell's *1984*.

The fundamentalists also argue that parents who send their children to church-supported schools should be given some form of tax relief, since paying tuition fees places a heavy burden on parents who are already paying school taxes. Shapiro (1985) estimates that deductions of income for donations and fees to denominational schools in Ontario amount to a subsidy of perhaps 30 percent. In other provinces, it ranges as high as 80 percent.

Beginning in the 1950s, Roman Catholic and other religious and independent schools united in a campaign to secure public funding for their schools. While the success of this movement varied from province to province, perhaps the most spectacular victory for church-sponsored schools occurred in British Columbia, where the provincial government was persuaded to abandon a 100-year-old policy of not giving financial aid to denominational schools. The incumbent Social Credit government initially opposed this idea but relented over the next two decades and granted some concessions on such issues as free textbooks, busing, and health services. However, the failure to give larger grants played a part in the Social Credit's defeat in an election in 1972. When they returned to office three years later they had changed their minds and introduced the Independent Schools Support Act, which established two types of schools that could receive public assistance. Schools in the first category received aid equal to 30 percent of the public schools in their area if they provided a core curriculum and met other requirements. Schools that rejected a core curriculum and only met limited requirements were placed in the second division and received a grant of 9 percent.

Other provinces have formulated a variety of plans to try to satisfy these groups. Alberta has devised a complicated system with four different categories of independent schools, two of which can obtain public funding. The other Prairie provinces assist church-sponsored institutions. In the East, Quebec has the most generous policy, with a two-tiered scheme of non-public schools that can receive aid up to 80 percent of the average cost of educating a pupil in the public schools. The Maritime provinces and Ontario have continued to refuse to grant financial assistance to any private schools.

In late 1988 one of the most traditional aspects of the school day—reciting the Lord's Prayer before morning classes—was removed from Ontario schools. A group of non-Christian parents brought a suit against a local board, claiming that this practice—even though children could be excused from participating in it—contradicted the Canadian Charter of Rights and Freedoms. A lower court dismissed the case, but the Ontario Court of Appeal agreed with the parents' contention and held that the Ontario regulation infringed on the Charter's guarantees of freedom of religion and conscience. The ministry immediately ordered that the practice cease. Many boards now issue a set of readings and prayers drawn from a variety of religious and secular sources for use in their schools.

CONCLUSIONS

Throughout the course of Canadian history, religion has been one of the most significant forces moulding Canada's educational structures. Changes to society in the middle of the nineteenth century led the state to assume responsibility for providing educational facilities. Governments quickly realized they would have to make accommodations with organized Christianity, since so many voters wanted the retention of a religious presence in their schools. A number of compromises were effected that, with modifications, have endured to the present. Canadians have always accepted the idea that the churches should participate in public affairs, but Canada has rejected both the British model of a legally established church and the American method of separating church and state. Instead, this nation has developed a pragmatic working arrangement with organized religion. Not even the challenges posed by the forces of modernization have succeeded in undermining this relationship.

What the future holds is open to question. Certain fundamentalist groups have become a political force to be reckoned with in recent years, reopening the debate over the role of religion in education. Whether these groups will have any long-term impact on education in this country remains to be seen. Their presence is but one more manifestation of an issue that shows no sign of disappearing.

DISCUSSION QUESTIONS

❏ "Religion has no place in the public school curriculum. It is socially divisive." Is this a reasonable position?

❏ To what extent should governments fund private religious schools? If they undertake this responsibility, what kinds of controls, if any, should they exercise over the schools' curriculum and teachers' qualifications?

❏ Evaluate the pertinent reasons for the current controversy over the role of religion in public education.

❏ "Canadians have been too ready to accede to the demands of minority religious groups. The end result has been to fracture Canadian society." To what extent is this an accurate assessment of the current situation?

REFERENCES

Cameron, D. (1972). *Schools of Ontario*. Toronto: University of Toronto Press.

Creighton, D.G. (1964). *The road to Confederation*. Toronto: Macmillan.

Creighton, D.G. (1976). *The forked road: Canada 1939–1957*. Toronto: McClelland and Stewart.

Crunican, P. (1974). *Priests and politicians*. Toronto: University of Toronto Press.

Fleming, W.G. (1972). *Education: Ontario's preoccupation*. Toronto: University of Toronto Press.

Gidney, R.D. (1972). Public opinion and common school improvement in the 1830's. *Social History, 5*(9), 48–60.

Gidney, R.D. (1973). Elementary education in Upper Canada: A reassessment. *Ontario History, 65*(3), 167–85.

Hodgins, J.G. (1899). *Documentary history of education in Upper Canada* (Vol. 6). Toronto: Warwick Bros. & Rutter.

Houston, S. (1972). Politics, schools and social change in Upper Canada. *Canadian Historical Review, 53*(3), 249–71.

Johnson, F.H. (1964). *A history of public education in British Columbia*. University of British Columbia Publications Centre.

Lupul, M. (1974). *The Roman Catholic Church and the northwest school question*. Toronto: University of Toronto Press.

Magnet, J. (1982). Minority language educational rights. *Supreme Court Law Review* (4), 195–200.

Magnuson, R. (1980). *A brief history of Quebec education*. Montreal: Harvest House.

Prentice, A. (1977). *The school promoters*. Toronto: McClelland and Stewart.

Purdy, J.D. (1985). The development of education in Upper Canada. In *The shaping of Ontario*. Belleville, ON: Mika Press.

Report of the Ministerial Inquiry on Religious Education in Ontario Public Elementary Schools. (1990, January). Toronto.

Sacred Congregation for Catholic Education. (1977). The Catholic school. Rome.

Shapiro, B. (1985). The report of the commission on private schools in Ontario. Toronto.

Sissons, C.B. (1959). *Church and state in Canadian education*. Toronto: Ryerson Press.

Stamp, R.M. (1982). *The schools of Ontario*. Toronto: University of Toronto Press.

Strachan, J. (1940). *Letter book 1839–1843*. Toronto: Ontario Archives.

Walker, F. (1955). *Catholic education and politics in Upper Canada*. Toronto: Federation of Catholic Education Associations of Ontario.

Wilson, J.D., Stamp, R.M., & Audet, L.P. (Eds.). (1970). *Canadian education: A history*. Scarborough, ON: Prentice-Hall.

FURTHER READINGS

Curtis, B. (1988). *Building the educational state: Canada West, 1836–1871*. Barcombe Lewes, Sussex, England: The Falmer Press; and London, ON: The Althouse Press.

Houston, S.E., & Prentice, A. (1988). *Schooling and scholars in nineteenth century Ontario*. Toronto: University of Toronto Press.

Hoy, C. (1985). *Bill Davis: A biography*. Toronto: Methuen.

Lupul, M. (1974). *The Roman Catholic church and the northwest school question*. Toronto: University of Toronto Press.

Miller, J.R. (1985). Anti-Catholic thought in Victorian Canada. *Canadian Historical Review, 66*(4), 474–94.

Moir, J. (1967). *Church and state in Canada, 1627–1867: Basic documents.* Ottawa: Carleton University Press.

Prentice, A. (1977). *The school promoters.* Toronto: McClelland and Stewart.

Reference Re. Roman Catholic separate high school funding. (1987). 77 N.R. 241 (S.C.C.).

Stamp, R.M. (1982). *The schools of Ontario.* Toronto: University of Toronto Press.

Walker, F. (1976). *Catholic education and politics in Ontario.* Toronto: Federation of Catholic Education Associations of Ontario.

Wilson, J.D. (Ed.). (1984). *Canadian education in the 1980's.* Calgary: Detselig.

9

PERSISTENT CURRICULUM ISSUES

Walter Werner

The efficacy of schools is under question. Note how few journalists, politicians, business leaders, and special-interest groups express satisfaction with educational outcomes. At the root of these misgivings is the public perception that young people are not adequately prepared to deal with changing social, political, and economic realities. In response have come numerous proposals to "restructure" every aspect of school life, from its culture to teacher development (Newmann, 1993). In particular, the curriculum attracts critical attention because it outlines the agenda for teaching and learning. At issue for critics is the quality of its purposes and content. Although various criteria can be used to judge the quality of curriculum, the three that continue to have prominence across Canada are achievement, accessibility, and accountability (e.g., Dinning, 1991; Downey, 1992; Sullivan, 1988): Does the curriculum emphasize worthwhile student achievement? Is it accessible to all students? How should educators be accountable for its quality? (Robitaille et al., 1988) This chapter briefly examines some current proposals and persistent issues around these three values. Although there is little debate over the importance of these quality indicators, how to interpret or apply them in any given case often leads to disagreement.

ACHIEVEMENT

Promoting worthwhile student achievement is a major purpose of any curriculum. As a form of social policy, it identifies those dispositions, skills, and areas of knowledge that children should achieve. "What should be taught?" is the central question guiding all curriculum development. Selection has to be made out of a universe of potential achievements. Herein lies a source of controversy. Disagreement arises over how the question should be answered. Every curriculum is a response reflecting the beliefs of its sponsoring groups, or, where there is dispute among groups, compromise about what is important to learn. Even when there is agreement on general goals, the specifics may cause dispute. For example, although most Canadian curriculum documents claim that students should be taught to "think critically," there is less consensus among educators about what the slogan implies for teaching different subject areas to various age groups (Bailin et al., 1993). Debate arises over how critical thinking should be defined, and what it means for classroom practices such as using textbooks or assessing student learning. Public concern over achievement, however, is not focussed on the conceptual details or daily difficulties of classroom practice. Current criticism in the media is much more general and bold. It wonders whether academic standards are adequate to sustain Canada's economic health and global competitiveness throughout the 1990s. According to this argument, if schools are to do their part in fostering national excellence, the curriculum needs revision. Four proposals are advocated: curriculum organization, core curriculum, national curriculum, and differentiated curriculum.

CURRICULUM ORGANIZATION

One of the arguments is that curriculum organization should promote more systematic learning. The "spiral" curriculum gives students a smorgasbord of themes and concepts that are revisited each year. Within arithmetic texts, for instance, fractions are briefly reviewed at a number of grade levels. However, critics claim that jumping from topic to topic results in confusion and promotes superficial learning. As Andrew Nikiforuk complains, "a spiral design or 'low-intensity curriculum' repeats a mindless army of math topics, short and fast, year after year" (1992, A18). An alternative is to provide fewer topics at each grade level so they can be learned systematically and in greater depth before proceeding. Critics at times assume too much for curriculum organization. Scope and sequence are important issues, but no one structure is logically or psychologically necessary. Whether one form of organization is better than another depends upon a teacher's purposes, how a topic is taught, a student's level of understanding of the subject matter, and many other contextual considerations. This means that teachers have the responsibility and need flexibility to engage students in pedagogically sound ways. The quality of teaching becomes more important to children's learning than the particular format of a curriculum or textbook. Also, achieving challenging content requires teachers who have a depth of knowledge; a case in point is elementary science, where many teachers have a low commitment and a weak academic background.

CORE CURRICULUM

A second proposal is for a core curriculum that identifies the most important topics that deserve in-depth study. The argument is that unsatisfactory achievement—particularly in numeracy, literacy, Canadian history and geography—is exacerbated by the broad range of goals and subjects available within a curriculum. Focus on "the basics" is lost when everything appears to be equally important. Clear priorities are needed so that "fundamentals" don't have to compete with less important topics for time. The purpose of a core curriculum is to clearly prioritize subject areas and goals.

Dispute over a core curriculum is inevitable because it raises value questions: What subjects should be defined as "basic"? For whom? Who should decide? Disagreements result in negotiated compromises couched in general terms and often lacking coherence. Any core curriculum, if it is a product of political consensus, leaves many participating groups unsatisfied, and is in danger of becoming little more than a minimal list of concepts and skills to be transmitted to students. Although by the end of the 1980s all provinces had their own versions of a core curriculum, public perceptions continue to support the view that children are not adequately taught "the basics," particularly in reading and computation (Fennell, 1993). In some cases these perceptions are no doubt well founded, whereas other criticisms foster misunderstandings of what is actually prescribed in curriculum, simplistic assumptions about the diverse needs of children, or nostalgia about what should count as a "return to the basics."

NATIONAL CURRICULUM

A closely related proposal is for some form of a national curriculum. This is a core curriculum writ large because it is designed for the entire country. In England and Wales, for instance, the Education Reform Act of 1988 set in motion a national curriculum for students between the ages of 5 and 16 within state-supported schools; this means that all teachers are responsible for delivering similar core content (Ball & Bowe, 1992). But a national curriculum is not politically acceptable in the Canadian context because the vast majority of schools are under provincial or territorial control, and there is no federal office of education to co-ordinate such an effort. The Council of Ministers of Education provides a forum for discussing national goals for education, but there is little political will for a national curriculum. Despite variation in the types of achievement promoted across provinces, these differences are seen by politicians and educators as more of a nuisance than a hindrance to students moving across jurisdictions.

DIFFERENTIATED CURRICULUM

A fourth proposal for enhancing achievement, particularly at the high-school level, is through a differentiated curriculum in which students are streamed and challenged in ways appropriate to their abilities and aspirations. The argument is straightforward: bright students should not be bored by a curriculum designed for the mythical "average" child, and those less able should not be confused and discouraged. Curriculum should be sufficiently differentiated to allow students to be routed into one of two or three streams based upon grade-point averages, course sequences and prerequisites, and appropriate counselling.

Tracking in some form or other has deep roots. Low- and high-achieving students have commonly been separated into different courses, or pulled out of the regular curriculum and given special programs and teachers for some part of the week. Another form of streaming occurs on the basis of economic affluence or religious affiliation when parents choose private schools with modified curricula. The research consensus, however, indicates that many streaming practices are "neither equitable nor effective," especially for children placed in a lower track curriculum (Oakes, 1992, p. 12). Not only does the achievement gap between streams increase, but, unfortunately, expectations concerning students' academic potential are often subtly tied to their ethnicity and family income. Low- and average-ability children do better, whereas high achievers do not suffer, within a destreamed curriculum that promotes high expectations for all. Obviously achievement is a primary criterion for judging the quality of curriculum.

The intention behind the above proposals is for a more challenging curriculum that moves youth beyond the recall of information to a greater understanding and the ability to apply their knowledge to problems of various kinds. However, much of the debate trades in vague slogans about "back to basics" and "slipping standards" when it ought to raise questions about the range of achievements increasingly necessary for enlightened Canadian and global citizenship.

ACCESSIBILITY

Identifying what achievements are important, and how to maximize them, are issues that also need to be considered in the light of another value, that of accessibility. It is not enough for curriculum to promote excellence if all students are not encouraged to participate or benefit. Critics point out that 30 percent of high-school youth fail to graduate with their cohort group (Levin, 1992). Although many drop-outs do attain high-school equivalency at some later time, curriculum is not equally accessible and relevant to many young people across the spectrum of socioeconomic and cultural backgrounds, vocational aspirations, geographic locations, abilities, and interests. This is an issue of national concern, given the social status and economic importance that our society assigns to educational attainment. Underlying the criterion of accessibility is a recognition of the diversity that youth bring to the curriculum (Coombs, 1988). How is this diversity to be accommodated within the curriculum? At least three proposals have currency: a common curriculum, an integrated curriculum, and a more inclusive curriculum.

COMMON CURRICULUM

Accessibility is enhanced through some form of a common curriculum. This ensures that all students up to a certain age (e.g., Grade 10) have access to similar knowledge regardless of their ethnicity, gender, social class, learning style, geography, and even intelligence. No one is thereby denied citizenship preparation, nor are their options for further studies foreclosed too early. Because streaming is minimized—at least until senior high school—a child is not shunted off into subjects that are not challenging or that preclude future choices. This makes it less likely for a disproportionate number of minority groups to be represented in vocational and special education classes on the assumption that they would not succeed in academic programs. Fairness and the operation of a democratic society require that a quality common curriculum be open to all (Ontario Ministry of Education, 1992; Sullivan, 1988).

Problems with a common curriculum tend to be practical. High demands are placed on a teacher's instructional ingenuity (BC Ministry of Education, 1993a). Because one deals with large, heterogeneous classes, the organization of groups, as well as the pacing of lessons and levels of content difficulty, require ongoing modification to accommodate a range of student abilities and interests. Learning activities have to be developmentally and culturally appropriate. This need for a child-centred pedagogy also recognizes that achievement is not the receiving of inert knowledge and reproducing it on exams; learning is active as children create meaning by building on the understanding and experiences they already possess. Their preconceptions have to be made explicit, challenged, and extended through instructional methods that rely less on worksheets and more on critical discussion, group work, and hands-on experiments. Even with sophisticated pedagogy, though, subtle forms of streaming can occur in a classroom through expectations related to pupils' gender, ethnicity, or social class.

INTEGRATED CURRICULUM

A second proposal to enhance accessibility and relevance recommends an integrated curriculum (Jacobs, 1989; Case, 1991). The assumption is that students often see little connection between subjects within the curriculum and their everyday lives. Discrete topics are taught in lock-step fashion, unrelated to other courses or to what students already know. So teachers are encouraged, for example, to pursue interdisciplinary projects around important themes or controversial issues that are interesting and useful to pupils, or to integrate skills such as reading- and writing-across-the-curriculum, while constantly relating material in one course to what students are learning in other courses. All of this assumes a level of professional collaboration in planning curriculum across grades and subjects that is not now common in schools (Werner, 1991).

MORE INCLUSIVE CURRICULUM

A more inclusive curriculum is the third proposal. This goes beyond a concern for displaying the diverse faces of Canadian children in textbook illustrations. Rather, inclusiveness speaks to whether, and how, the experiences and achievements of a broad range of Canadians are represented in course content. Do science curricula give adequate attention to women's contributions and gender issues? Does Canadian history, for example, mythologize our French and British heritages to such an extent that the experiences of other groups are marginalized or even ignored? Whose cultural perspectives are subtly enshrined in the selection and treatment of course content? Some Canadians of African and Caribbean descent argue that schools offer little opportunity for their children to develop pride of heritage, and that courses should be offered in the history and culture of their peoples (Valpy, 1993). Greater cross-cultural understanding and self-esteem may be fostered as the history and views of minority Canadians are presented in a positive light, and as heritage languages continue to gain a place in the curriculum. There is little incentive for young people to engage the curriculum if they rarely see themselves included in what the school defines to be important.

Issues related to accessibility and relevance have resulted in an expanded role for the curriculum. Increasingly, schools are expected to deliver an array of community and social services. Teachers are now part of the front line for identifying and raising awareness about problems related to health, family violence, child abuse, racism, and poverty, and continue to be a liaison between children at risk and other professionals such as police, immigration officials, psychiatrists, social workers, and career counsellors. This expanding role makes demands on their time, energy, and focus, and impacts the academic curriculum. Some impacts are minor, but nevertheless can have a cumulative effect. For example, the curriculum taught during the half-hour before noon had to be modified in an elementary school that offered a hot lunch program because children were not concentrating as they anticipated their major meal of the day and wondered what was on the menu. Other impacts are far deeper. The trend toward mainstreaming students with special needs into regular classrooms, and the high proportion of students in larger Canadian cities who do not have English or French as their first language, require a curriculum suited to meet diverse needs. This diversity is not adequately accommodated by ensuring that all qualified students have equal access to the entire curriculum or that they are treated the same within courses. Fairness demands that at times the curriculum be modified or taught in ways that favour those who have been the least advantaged in the past without causing harm to others (Rawls, 1971, p. 302). To benefit equally from the curriculum, some students may have to be treated unequally. Take senior mathematics courses as an example. It is not enough that qualified students be given equal opportunity to enrol in such courses; we also want them to succeed, and this may require modifications to both curriculum and pedagogy to enhance accessibility and relevance for formerly disadvantaged groups.

Critics who decry the loss of the more narrow traditional curriculum are sometimes unfair. Teachers did not seek their expanded role, but responded to demands thrust upon them by larger social trends. Changes in other institutions, such as the family, meant that schools had little choice but to take on a larger role. Youth who are troubled, hungry, violent, or confused bring this baggage into the classroom, and their learning is affected. The result is a curriculum whose priorities serve a range of social purposes beyond traditional academic goals. However, this does raise questions: How elastic can the curriculum be before it loses coherence and focus? How can this expanded curriculum be effectively squeezed within the existing school day and year? Given the school's broader role, options such as cutting the curriculum down to size or extending the school year are not as realistic as organizing the curriculum more effectively through integration and better sequencing of subject matter.

ACCOUNTABILITY

Canadian governments spend more resources per capita on education than other Western countries (Advisory, 1991). Obviously the public has a right to know how these resources are used, why, and to what effect. This right, though, raises a number of contentious questions: Who should be held responsible for the quality and effectiveness of curriculum? To whom should they be accountable? What evidence would best show the extent to which the curriculum is fulfilling its purposes? How should that evidence be reported to the public? (Robitaille et al., 1988). On the surface the answers seem straightforward. In principle, politicians and educators are morally and legally responsible for their actions; they need to give evidence that allows the public to judge those actions. In practice, though, accountability is a tangled issue that elicits emotional charges and responses. This is because many factors account for the quality of a curriculum and its outcomes, and various groups are involved with specific interests to protect. Sorting out the responsibilities of each can be a difficult task. Usually, however, three groups—elected officials, curriculum committees, and school-based educators—are accountable for the curriculum, although in different ways.

ELECTED OFFICIALS

Elected officials—ministers of education and school trustees—have a legal right to prescribe, and are responsible for defending or censuring, what is taught in their jurisdictions. They are directly accountable to the public for ensuring that quality curriculum is developed and then used, and they provide the public with various kinds of documentary evidence. Sundry information is available concerning what is promoted and achieved through the curriculum: test scores and program evaluations for different subject areas; justifications for the nature and timing of new priorities; curriculum policy documents, and the principles and procedures for developing and implementing them. Further provincial reports are provided periodically by ministries of education, auditor generals, royal commissions, and various task forces. Elected officials are also morally accountable to provide teachers with the support they need to implement curriculum. With new policies come promises of realistic timelines, adequate funding for in-service training, and teaching materials to effect the desired changes.

CURRICULUM COMMITTEES

Curriculum committees are assigned the task of recommending policies and appropriate resources such as textbooks. Depending upon the particular curriculum, they are accountable not only to elected officials to address public concerns over what is taught, but also to members of the academic community to ensure consistency with new developments in pedagogical research and the disciplines, and to schools where the implications of the policies have to be worked out. Evidence that a quality curriculum is being produced are given in a number of ways. For example, committee memberships may include more than professional educators (e.g., teachers, administrators, civil servants), but also representatives of parents, university academics, and other groups. Rationales for curriculum changes and draft documents are made available for systematic public feedback and criticism from relevant experts. Although this actual process can be cumbersome, lengthy and politically complex, it is designed to demonstrate responsibility for producing quality curriculum.

TEACHERS AND SCHOOL ADMINISTRATORS

Teachers and school administrators have a contractual responsibility to follow a curriculum once it is endorsed by elected officials. In the past, school inspectors provided much of the evidence and incentive for compliance. More commonly today, ministries of education sponsor periodic program assessments, school audits, and student achievement testing in order to monitor the implementation and outcomes of curriculum. Schools also provide their communities with information about the curriculum through public meetings, parent liaison committees, and reports on pupil evaluation. Despite this, it is clear that many Canadians are not happy with current accountability procedures. There is a perception that they are little more than exercises in public relations carried out by educators and politicians. As in Britain, the most controversial issue to emerge in the first half of the 1990s is debate over the need to establish *national standards* and design *achievement tests* to see how well these standards are met. The call comes from business leaders, some provincial ministers of education, and especially the media, whereas teacher unions are generally opposed (Gilliss, 1993). At issue is the question as to whether Canada requires a set of standards against which student learning in various provinces can be compared and tracked over time. The role of such testing would not be to judge the individual performance of a student or school, but to provide more global information about levels of achievement and trends for certain subjects (e.g., numeracy, science) and populations (e.g., by gender, region, province). Proponents note that current provincial achievement data are not readily comparable because, as curriculum is a provincial matter, students do not always learn the same things to the same degree at the same time. They argue that a national testing program would impose some common focus across this diversity by regularly monitoring how well sample groups of students (at, for example, ages 7, 11, 14, and 16) are doing. The results for provinces and even school districts could then be compared, on the assumption that competition motivates improvement. Those jurisdictions that do not fare well have to face public pressure as an incentive to do better. Where scores are deemed by a province to be unacceptable, further research could clarify the reasons, and programs could be refocussed.

There are precedents. Some Canadian provinces have already participated with some twenty countries in testing programs to assess the performance of 9- and 13-year-olds in mathematics and science (BC Ministry of Education, 1993b). The results show differences across provinces, but do not explain the source of strengths and weaknesses. Nevertheless, the results have fuelled both enthusiasm for and resistance to national testing. There is no doubt that test scores allow educators and the public to judge how well some curriculum goals are achieved. An important accountability function, among others, can be served through such data, although there are serious shortcomings as well. Conventional multiple-choice and short-answer tests, easier to administer and cheaper to analyze than essay or portfolio formats, only measure a limited range of curricular goals. High scores in these areas cannot always be equated with broader achievements. Even more troublesome is the fact that if narrow achievement tests are the primary means for accountability, then those worthwhile attainments not easily measured by paper-and-pencil tests may be de-emphasized in classrooms. If tests are taken to define what learnings are important, this can seriously distort parts of a curriculum. McLaughlin notes that in parts of the United States, "tests have narrowed the curriculum to the specific topics they cover, and in some cases tests have turned the minimum curriculum, as expressed by test content, into the maximum (1991, p. 248).

There is also a fear, especially on the part of teachers' unions, that published test scores may be used by parents to compare schools, as is done in parts of Britain and the United States. Local schools are ranked according to student achievement, thereby giving parents a basis for school choice. Schools that perform well attract more students, thereby receiving greater government funding. On the other hand, schools not chosen by parents have an economic and professional incentive to save face and perform better. In other words, it is argued that competition for students helps schools focus on the curriculum more effectively. Advocates of choice also assume that competition allows some schools to offer a more specialized curriculum than is normally possible: they could advertise themselves as focussing on the fine arts or sciences, thereby attracting teachers and students who value that particular emphasis. In such cases, self-selection no doubt fosters a commitment to making the curriculum work. The downside of this scenario is that competition does not get played out on level ground for certain groups of parents or schools. Low-income families do not have the luxury of driving their children to schools out of the local community, whereas schools in more affluent neighbourhoods have easier access to greater resources: from volunteers to donated computers. Through competition, the curriculum offered in some schools could become richer or more impoverished.

An assumption underlying current accountability proposals is that low expectations are a cause of unacceptable student achievement. As standards are raised for curriculum and assessment, schools will live up to them. What is not recognized, though, is that standards are not improved merely because they are mandated and tested, but through quality teaching. As Eisner warns, "the problem is not one of correct policy formation. Policies are relatively easy to formulate and often easier to mandate. The problem is one of practice. Good teaching and substantive curricula cannot be mandated; they have to be grown" (1993, p. 224). Clear standards and valid testing may be important but not sufficient conditions for enhancing achievement and accountability.

CONCLUSIONS

Although there are many other issues, debate over achievement, accessibility, and accountability is persistent because these values are central to defining a quality curriculum.

Unfortunately, however, debate becomes polarized between those who support achievement and accountability, and those who emphasize accessibility. Obviously these values are compatible: without accessibility, for example, achievement suffers. Why then do individuals often argue for one or the other? The two sets of values can represent different social priorities to be promoted through the curriculum. Disagreement centres on what are assumed to be important problems facing Canadians. Note that those who stress achievement and accountability usually provide an economic rationale: Canada increasingly requires an educated workforce to successfully compete for global markets with countries such as Germany, Japan, Korea, and the United States. Education is a key ingredient for ensuring competitiveness. For instance, changes in the labour market are thought to require future employees with a strong grounding in "the basics"—science and mathematics—as well as good communication skills and a co-operative work ethic. Maximizing the potential of bright students is of particular concern because of what they could contribute to the workplace. Curriculum should therefore focus on clear goals and standards, to which schools can be held accountable because of the negative economic consequences of not doing so.

Those who emphasize accessibility more often appeal to social and moral arguments. Fairness demands that the curriculum, as an instrument for enhancing social unity and inclusiveness, serves the interests of all groups equitably. This means that those who are the least advantaged in our society—because of historical and current inequities due to their social class, gender, ethnicity, and region—should be given special consideration in the curriculum's goals, selection of content, and the ways in which it is taught and funded. Traditional Canadian values and educational practices that privileged certain groups should be questioned, and options considered in order to help make society more equitable. The curriculum can enhance social change and cohesion. Both of the above arguments assume that the curriculum is an appropriate instrument for shaping Canadian life; it is a tool in the service of some larger social or economic vision. This belief accounts in part for why special-interest groups try to influence what is taught, and why the media criticizes the curriculum. Although it represents an important form of social policy, questions can be raised concerning the extent to which it should be justified according to non-educational goals related to social trends, economic advantage, and political change. Learning is also for the sake of broadened perspectives and interests, the fostering of imagination and critical thought, and understanding for its own sake.

DISCUSSION QUESTIONS

❏ What other curricular issues do you see as currently important or emerging?

❏ What courses of action could resolve these issues in ways that are educationally defensible?

❏ Provide examples of how proposals to enhance achievement and accountability can be at odds with proposals to foster accessibility. Why do you think such proposals are at odds? What is a proper accommodation?

REFERENCES

Advisory body finds huge diseconomies in education. (1991). *CSSE News, 18*, 15–17.

Bailin, S., Case, R., Coombs, J., & Daniels, L. (1993). *A conception of critical thinking for curriculum. Instruction and assessment.* Victoria, BC: Ministry of Education.

Ball, S., & Bowe, R. (1992). Subject departments and the implementation of National Curriculum policy. *Journal of Curriculum Studies, 24*(2), 97–115.

BC Ministry of Education. (1993a). *The intermediate program: Policy.* Victoria, BC.

BC Ministry of Education. (1993b). *The second international assessment of educational progress.* Victoria, BC.

Case, R. (1991). The anatomy of curricular integration. *Canadian Journal of Education, 16*, 215–24.

Coombs, J. (1988). *Accessibility.* Paper presented to the Royal Commission on Education in British Columbia.

Dinning, J. (1991). *Vision for the nineties . . . A plan of action.* Edmonton: Alberta Education.

Downey, J. (1992). *Schools for a new century.* Fredericton: New Brunswick Commission on Excellence in Education.

Eisner, E. (1993). Reshaping assessment practice in education. *Journal of Curriculum Studies, 25*(3), 219–33.

Fennell, T. (1993, January 11). What's wrong at school? *Maclean's*, pp. 28–43.

Gilliss, G. (1993, January 12). Why national tests won't improve education. *The Globe and Mail*, p. A15 .

Jacobs, H. (Ed.). (1989). *Interdisciplinary curriculum: Design and implementation.* Alexandria, VA: Association for Supervision and Curriculum Development.

Levin, B. (1992). Dealing with dropouts in Canadian education. *Curriculum Inquiry, 22*, 257–70.

McLaughlin, M. (1991). Test-based accountability as a reform strategy. *Phi Delta Kappan, 73*(3), 248–51.

Newmann, F. (1993). Beyond common sense in educational restructuring. The issues of content and linkage. *Educational Researcher, 22*(2), 4–13.

Nikiforuk, A. (1992, February 28). Education. *The Globe and Mail*, p. A18.

Oakes, J. (1992). Can tracking research inform practice? Technical, normative, and political considerations. *Educational Researcher, 21*, 12–20.

Ontario Ministry of Education. (1992). *Everybody's schools: The common curriculum.* Toronto.

Rawls, J. (1971). *A theory of justice.* Cambridge, MA: Harvard University Press.

Robitaille, D., Oberg, A., Overgaard, V., & McBurney, J. (1988). *Curriculum in the schools of British Columbia: Commissioned Papers.* Victoria: British Columbia Royal Commission on Education.

Sullivan, B. (1988). *Royal commission on education.* Victoria, BC: Queen's Printer.

Valpy, M. (1993, May 4). Multiculturalism or cultural separatism? *The Globe and Mail*, p. A2.

Werner, W. (1991). *Curriculum integration and school cultures.* Burnaby, BC: Tri-University Integration Project, Occasional Paper Series No. 6.

FURTHER READINGS

Chapman, J., Wilkinson, V., & Aspin, D. (1993). *Quality schooling.* New York: Cassell.

Harnett, A., Carr, W., & Naish, M. (1993). *Understanding the national curriculum.* New York: Cassell.

Lewington, J., & Orpwood, G. (1993). *Overdue assignment: Taking responsibility for Canada's schools.* Toronto: John Wiley & Sons.

The quest for higher standards (Theme issue). (1991). *Educational Leadership, 48,* 3–69.

Resnick, D., & Resnick, L. (1985). Standards, curriculum, and performance: A historical and comparative perspective . *Educational Researcher, 14*(4), 5–21.

Schools of choice? (Theme issue). *Educational Leadership, 48,* 3–72.

Tomkins, G. (1986). *A common countenance. Stability and change in the Canadian curriculum.* Scarborough, ON: Prentice-Hall.

Untracking for equity (Theme issue). (1992). *Educational Leadership, 50,* 5–74.

Using performance assessment (Theme issue). (1992). *Educational Leadership, 49,* 8–78.

10

Policies and Policy Actors

Robert O'Reilly

Educational policies in Canada are not discussed to any great degree. Historically, educational practices have reflected our times and culture so harmoniously that discussion seemed unnecessary. Before and after World War II, educational issues in most provinces were seldom the topics of partisan debates. This period coincided with the rising professionalism of the teaching force and, in particular, of educational administrators. A common theme in those days was the "apolitical" nature of public education. For example, in 1937, the Ontario Department of Education assigned to two of its employees the task of defining the elementary curriculum. The resulting "Grey Book" remained in place until the 1950s. Also in Ontario, then premier and minister of education George Drew, in the spring of 1944, commissioned S.A. Watson, then principal of the Ottawa Normal School, to prepare a religious education curriculum that was introduced in the schools of the province that fall. The values underlying these decisions were never seriously debated. The decision-makers were very few and the policies were implemented with little comment.

With the growth of educational bureaucracies, the centre of policy-making for education shifted to a coalition of senior educational officials. Housego (1972) described the influence system that existed in most provinces through which senior provincial education officials and executives of provincial teachers' and trustees' associations developed and debated policy. Once consensus was achieved among these interest groups, their recommendations went to the cabinet and the legislature for ratification.

The "apolitical" nature of Canadian educational policy-making was described by the Organization for Economic Co-operation and Development (1976) in its review of Canadian education:

> Canadian education may be one of the least politicized in the world . . . Study of the rather meagre provincial Parliamentary debates on education reveals little evidence of political controversy in the realm of educational policies, except for some occasional debates on questions of financing separate and private schools. (p. 19)

In spite of the apolitical face that had been placed on public education in Canada, public education is by definition political. As with any activity funded by the public, the aims, resources, and processes of education are influenced by the policy and political processes of society at large. There is a trend today to return to the view that education is "good politics." As that view takes hold, the authority and influence of the educational profession is converted into a requirement to be accountable (Dale, 1989). Control over education is particularly affected by changes in the state and the political ideologies that are paramount in the state government. Two recent changes are that government expenditure is growing faster than the economy and that the national debt is growing rapidly. Dale suggests that these events shift the aims of education from individual development to national survival, to be achieved through a skilled and motivated workforce.

Policies are not only made by groups of formal policy-makers such as government ministers or members of a school board. They are, from the point of the raising of an issue to the implementation of programs, influenced by global and international events, the media, pressure groups, professionals, bureaucracies, and others. National educational policies are rooted in political, economic, and social theories affecting all aspects of national life. Allocation of resources to public education is influenced by the theories of state espoused by governments and by the perceived value of education to citizens, the economy, and the state.

POLICY DEFINED

The word "policy" has many meanings. At its most general, it refers to the conduct of public affairs or the activities of government. It also has meanings ranging from government intent through government decisions, laws, and regulations, and outcomes of these activities. The scholar B.L. Stringham (1974), after a lengthy study of the definitions of policy, suggested the following: "A public policy is defined as a major guideline for future discretionary action. It is generalized, philosophically based, and implies an intention and pattern for taking action." Others prefer to speak of a policy process, a dynamic activity dealing with problem identification, definition of issues, setting of priorities, analysis of options, enunciation of the policy, policy implementation, and outcomes of these activities.

More precisely for our purposes, a policy is associated with a public agency (government body, school board, or school) that makes one or more decisions or regulations, or carries out activities designed to attain some intention or goal. Since the regulations and activities are made by some competent public agency, policies usually involve some measure of influence or coercion to ensure compliance with them. To achieve their objectives, agencies use policy instruments that are often in the form of laws or regulations carrying penalties for non-compliance.

The foregoing definitions of policy are not precise. However, it is obvious that not all actions of an agency are derived from policy, not all "policies" are accurately defined or publicly stated, not all are successfully implemented, and, indeed, not all activities initiated in the name of a particular policy have outcomes conforming to the stated objective of the policy.

THE POLICY PROCESS

D.E. Mitchell points out that policy-making takes time: to sort out issues, to discover whose interests will be preferred or harmed, to guess how effective the policy will remedy an identified problem, to find out who will have interests in the policy and what their reactions will be, and to determine whether a proposed policy is worth the energy and resources needed to implement it (Mitchell, 1988).

According to Mitchell, the first stage in the policy process is *articulation*, or the identification of the interests involved and the definition of the policy problem. He suggests that the definition of an issue shapes the way decisions are made. The second stage is *aggregation* of interested parties into coalitions for support or opposition to the proposals, and the aggregation of different proposals into integrated programs capable of attracting sufficient support. The third stage is *allocation* of power and resources. At this point, power and resources begin to be allocated as competing proposals are ranked, maintained, or discarded. It is at this level that the question of values enters the decision-making process. Having decided what policies are to be supported, policy-makers must determine regulatory and budgetary details. Organizational structures in terms of who is given responsibility and resources are also involved. This stage is called *regulation. Implementation* is the fifth stage. Here policy turns into practice. The manner in which policies are implemented can mean the difference between the achievement of goals or the subversion of the political intent. The final stage is *evaluation.* Policy evaluations tend to be politically influenced and often have consequences for the continuation, modification, or demise of a political action. Mitchell further notes that each stage has its own set of key actors, required set of thinking skills, problem-solving skills, technical skills, and political skills.

INTERNATIONAL INFLUENCES ON CANADIAN EDUCATIONAL POLICIES

It is readily agreed that events in other countries influence government activity in Canada. The government of Canada in the late 1980s was not immune to the move toward privatization and the reduction of government involvement in a wide variety of economic and social affairs, a move made popular by the Thatcher government in the United Kingdom and by Reaganomics in the United States. Although this movement had little impact on educational policies in Canada, there were some related changes: the reduced level of support from the federal government for postsecondary education, by way of reduced transfer payments to the provinces; the tying of some research grant monies from the governments to the matching of grants from industry; and, at the local level, the growth of school and business partnerships. The disaster at Chernobyl made the world more conscious of the possible dangers of nuclear reactors, and media reports of the destruction of rain forests and the ozone layer made school curricula more sensitive to issues of conservation and to the importance of science in our lives. Reports of international comparisons of educational achievement that showed North American students lagging far behind their peers in standardized achievement tests helped to fuel the "effective schools" movement in Canada and the United States.

EDUCATION AND DISABILITIES: A CASE STUDY

By 1982, the Constitution Act, which included the Canadian Charter of Rights and Freedoms, was passed. Section 15 of the Charter states:

> Every individual is equal before and under the law and has the right to equal protection and equal benefit of the law without discrimination based on race, national or ethnic origin, colour, religion, sex, age or mental or physical disability.

The last words, "mental or physical disability," were not in the original draft of the Constitution, but were added only after strenuous lobbying by disabled rights advocacy groups and their supporters all across Canada. Section 15 gave great impetus to policy-makers to ensure that the educational rights of people with disabilities were protected and that programs were instituted to provide for them.

At the same time, one of the major American social trends of the 1970s and 1980s was the move to integrate people with disabilities into mainstream society. The movement, known as normalization or mainstreaming, greatly influenced American and Canadian educators in their treatment of exceptional pupils. The American Public Law 94-142, known as the Education of All Handicapped Children Act of 1975, provided for a free, public, and appropriate education for all children with disabilities from the ages of 3 to 21. This was the model for Ontario's Revision to the Education Act of 1980, which, beginning in 1985, provided for the education of all exceptional children in the province. By the end of the 1980s, all Canadian provinces and territories had revised their educational legislation to provide for the education of children with disabilities in the public school system. The actors who brought about these changes were, in large measure, groups of parents, educators, and disabled advocacy groups working with such organizations as the Council for Exceptional Children and the predecessor organizations of the Learning Disabilities Association of Canada, the Canadian Association for Community Living, and many others.

The case of special education is one example of the influence of international events on major changes in education. Following on the proclamation of the International Year of Disabled People in 1981, the Canadian government established the Special Committee on the Disabled and the Handicapped (Canada, 1981). The Committee's 1981 report, entitled *Obstacles*, was widely distributed and debated across Canada, and the changes that resulted from it gave a new and broader meaning to universal education. Following the American example, the movement also made the courts a participant in decisions concerning who is to be educated with public funds and, to some extent, how and where that education is to be provided. In some cases, the legislation emphasizes the role of parents as "educators" and as participants in the decision-making process regarding the education of their child. As a part of the policy process, provincial governments prohibited the exclusion of children from school on the basis of their disabilities, and altered their funding formulas to provide additional monies to school boards for special education. Educational programs for teachers were modified or added to so that they would be able to meet their new responsibilities to teach all children.

The case is by no means closed; there are still struggles to determine whether any child can be excluded from public education. Exclusions might be considered when disabilities are so severe that any educational program would be deemed of little or no value in improving the person's quality of life, or in cases of behaviour so extreme (such as severe psychiatric or behavioural disorders) that educators could not cope with that individual in a school setting. Finally, the manner in which schools and teachers implement the special-education legislation means that children with the same disabilities receive widely differing special-education services, depending on location, school or board practices, parental influence, and other related factors.

NATIONAL POLICIES AND ACTORS

In Canada, education is a provincial responsibility. Section 93 of the Constitution Act, 1982, which replaced the British North America Act of 1867 (Constitution Act, 1867), states that the provinces have exclusive authority to make laws relating to education.

However, the government of Canada has a number of responsibilities and powers that enable it to have a great deal of influence over education in Canada.

The federal government is responsible for a variety of educational services. Under the terms of the Indian Act (sections 114–23) and in accordance with treaties signed with Native groups, the government of Canada guarantees educational services to Native Canadians. The involvement of the government is becoming more indirect as the actual provision of services is in the hands of school boards organized by Indian bands, Native groups who have signed land settlement agreements (such as the James Bay Agreement), and the two territorial governments. However, many schools for Natives are still operated directly by the federal government.

Schools operating in federal prisons consist of academic upgrading courses, vocational training, and in some cases, university-level education. For the most part, the government purchases these educational services from nearby school boards, community colleges, or universities.

There is a major educational system in support of the Canadian Armed Forces. In addition to an extensive training program within each branch of the armed services and staff colleges for senior officers, the government operates three degree-granting universities: The Royal Military College at Kingston, Royal Rhodes at Victoria, and Collège Militaire Royal at St. Jean, Quebec.

The government also finances schools for the children of its personnel on military bases in Canada and in Europe. Although a provincial curriculum is followed and teachers hold provincial certification, school operations are supervised by boards composed of military-base personnel acting as civilians.

Among other training centres operated by the federal government is the Canadian Coast Guard College, which has a four-year program for prospective Coast Guard officers. There is also a major training centre for air traffic controllers in Cornwall, Ontario. Each department of government provides a range of educational services for their employees, including preliminary and in-service training, staff development, and preparation for retirement. The government also operates a centre for senior officers of the government located at Touraine, Quebec.

A major activity of the federal government is to support postsecondary education. One method of support is through the transfer of money to the provinces in the form of Established Programs Financing (EPF). However, the monies so received are placed in the general revenue fund of the province and there is no restriction on how they are spent. All provinces spend much more on postsecondary education than they receive for the purpose through the EPF. In recent years, there has been a relative decrease in the EPF transfer payments even though costs of all the programs involved have increased.

The federal government also supports postsecondary education through its funding of research, mainly by universities; the three research councils are the Medical Research Council, the Natural Science and Engineering Research Council, and the Social Sciences and Humanities Research Council. In addition, special-purpose research grants are offered by various departments of the government in support of their particular mandates. Canada Student Loans are available for students. The Department of Veteran Affairs offers some support for the children of disabled or dead veterans. Prospective military officers can obtain subsidies to obtain a university education.

Finally, many departments and agencies of the federal government offer large amounts of money to provinces, school boards, universities, or individuals in order to further their own aims. A major example is the Department of the Secretary of State, which has responsibilities for adult literacy, multiculturalism, and bilingualism. One case of the Secretary of State's involvement in furthering educational policy in Canada is described later in this chapter.

The federal government can also influence education by focussing its attention on a particular issue. An American example illustrates the possibilities. During the Reagan administration, Secretary for Education William Bennet was determined to improve the level of basic education in the nation without spending federal dollars. He sought to achieve his objective by creating a vast wall chart on which he plotted the annual relative achievement of school children on standardized tests by state. As state governors of the poorer-performing states became embarrassed, they began to place resources into their state educational programs to ensure that test scores increased. It is a moot point whether such activities actually improved education in the United States. One commentator observed that all states now report mean scores "above the national mean," which is a statistical impossibility. But at least many more governors have become actively involved in the public education program within their states.

A Canadian example is the use of education to prevent the spread of AIDS. Although public health and education are provincial responsibilities, federal officials mounted a major campaign to alert the public to the dangers of the spread of AIDS and called for programs to educate young people about the disease. With media support, the health profession took up the federal government's lead and pressured provincial education officials to make education concerning AIDS and other sexually transmitted diseases mandatory in schools. While such programs are valuable, it is unlikely that they would have become so widespread in the provincial curriculum without prompting from federal officials.

Tomkins (1986), in his definitive work on curriculum in Canada, describes the role of the federal government in education as confusing and ambiguous. In 1973, the Department of the Secretary of State was designated as the agency responsible for programs related to education. At first, this meant negotiating the federal government's contribution to postsecondary education. However, Ottawa used the department as a tool to promote its policies regarding vocational, bilingual, and literacy education and for Canadian Studies programs.

An earlier example of the federal government's influence was the passage of the Technical and Vocational Training Assistance (TVTA) Act of 1960. Technical and vocational curriculum had largely been ignored by all provinces until that time. The availability of federal funds meant a major national building program of vocational wings of high schools, vocational high schools, and postsecondary institutions devoted to vocational training. During the six-year term of federal–provincial agreements under the act, Ottawa supplied nearly half of $1.5 billion for capital projects. Such resources are believed to be partly responsible for the almost doubling of attendance among school-aged adolescents from 1961 to 1967. Hoey (1989) states that this initiative caused major curriculum changes not only in vocational education but in all secondary-school education.

This brief description of the major responsibilities of the federal government for education indicates the vast resources that the government allocates to educational functions within society. With its considerable resources, it can make significant funds available for educational programs in support of its economic, industrial, or social strategies. Its contributions in support of such initiatives are usually temporary, and the provinces are left to carry on. For instance, at the expiry of the TVTA agreements, local school boards had to maintain and operate schools built under the act with their own resources. The federal government has the expertise to exert considerable pressure on educators at all levels to examine alternatives, to respond to public needs, and — in the case of the teaching of second languages—to encourage them to adopt a particular method of teaching, as in the case of the French-immersion movement.

INFLUENCING NATIONAL EDUCATIONAL POLICY: FRENCH IMMERSION

Questions of curriculum are clearly within provincial jurisdiction, according to section 93 of the Constitution Act, 1867. However, curriculum policies can be influenced by activities of the federal government and parent pressure groups at the local, provincial, and national levels. For example, the combined efforts of government and parent groups influenced the quadrupling of elementary students studying French in British Columbia during the 1970s.

The most dramatic example of the spread of French-language instruction is the French immersion "movement." It can be said to have started in Canada in the early 1960s, when a group of parents of English-speaking Quebeckers, disappointed with traditional methods of teaching second languages, arranged to have small classes of English-speaking children taught in French.[1] The most famous case occurred in St. Lambert, Quebec, where researchers from McGill University assisted in the programs and conducted the evaluations. Considerable media attention was given to the apparent success of the program. The programs continued and grew modestly.

In 1968, the Report of the Royal Commission on Bilingualism and Biculturalism encouraged greater efforts on the part of Canadians to learn the "second language," whether French or English. As a result of the report, the Government of Canada created the Official Languages Act in 1969 and established an Office of the Commissioner of Official Languages. The first Commissioner, Keith Spicer, was anxious to garner support for the government's bilingualism policies and invited to a 1977 conference a small group of parents who were interested in discussing French-language learning opportunities. From this group of 30 parents was formed the Canadian Parents for French (CPF), a national pressure group with local and provincial organizations that encourages opportunities for learning French. With loose affiliations with such groups as teachers of French, academics, school trustees from areas where immersion classes were popular, and many others, the CPF lobbied school boards, provincial governments, the Canadian Council of Ministers of Education, the CBC, and the Secretary of State. In time, over 35 organizations would be involved in attempting to influence policy on this issue at the national level. Through programs of the Secretary of State, the contributions of the federal government to provinces for minority French-language instruction and French second-language instruction increased from $50 million in 1970 to $210 million in 1978. The 1988 agreement between the two levels of government was for $1.2 billion.

From 1979 to 1983 there was an impasse between the two levels of government on the signing of a new agreement. The federal government, seeing its costs escalating and dissatisfied with how its monies were being spent, suggested a "ceiling" on the amount it would contribute in the future.

The provinces reacted negatively to this. The impasse placed administrators in an uncertain position in planning for the increasing demand for French immersion and related programs. Moreover, it reminded provincial officials of other occasions when the federal government had initiated programs with rich grants and later pulled out, leaving the provinces to pay the total costs of operations.

Although the Secretary of State had the funds, it had little or no power to determine how those funds would be spent. The Council of Ministers of Education, which was negotiating on behalf of the provinces, became paralysed when dissenting provinces did not want to be bound by an agreement to which the majority had agreed. The Council can act only if it has 100 percent agreement of all the provinces. Both levels of government stood to lose if there were no agreements. The provinces would lose over $200 million; the federal government would lose a major plank in its bilingualism program.

The CPF, facing its first major lobbying effort, began to lobby with the provinces and the Secretary of State. It strengthened its lines of communication with the Office of the Commissioner of Official Languages. Soon it was apparent that federal funding decisions originated at a higher level. The CPF identified the Cabinet Committee on Social Development as the key federal decision-making body and began meetings with the senior staff of ministers who sat on that committee of cabinet, as well as other senior civil servants. As federal officials made known their problems, the CPF sought data and, after meeting with members of the Council of Ministers of Education, attempted to draft solutions to the impasse. In part, the CPF became a conduit of information between the two levels of government, applying their resources and their rights as citizens to obtain the information each side felt it needed to make reasonable decisions. In the meantime, other lobby groups—sometimes in concert with CPF—pressured the two levels of government to come to a compromise. An agreement that met the objectives of the provinces and the federal government was signed in 1983.

This case shows that the federal government can be a powerful agent in influencing what is taught in the provinces. By making available large sums of discretionary funds, new programs can be mounted and maintained. But the policy process is not a simple one, and there are many agents of influence. In this case, the staff of the Secretary of State, the Commissioner of Official Languages, the provincial ministries of education, the CPF, the media, and many other educational and cultural groups with interests in the matter, all played roles. Further, the issue was not without conflict and compromise, as each province was determined to obtain support to meet its own individual educational needs. The importance of bringing accurate information and indicators of strong social support to the attention of those who would make influential decisions (in this case, those federal ministers who sat on the Cabinet Committee for Social Development) could not be underestimated. As in many other areas of Canadian life, the final agreement was based on a partnership between two levels of government.

According to Mitchell's stages of policy development, the French immersion issue would represent elements of both the allocation and regulations stages. The process of negotiating on the basis of competing priorities among provincial and federal representatives illustrates the allocation stage; the fleshing out of the budgetary and regulatory details of who should be given funds, and under what conditions, is the heart of the regulation stage.

The decision in this case study is distributive in that funds and resources are moved from the federal level to the provincial (and eventually to the local jurisdiction). It is regulatory, as it specifies the conditions under which funds are to be transferred, used, and accounted for. There is also a symbolic element to the policy, as it confirms the federal government's commitment to bilingual policies in the country.

Finally, this case illustrates well the brokerage and consulting role that a well-organized lobby group can make in the policy process.

PROVINCIAL POLICY FORMULATION

RESTRUCTURING SCHOOL GOVERNANCE IN PRINCE EDWARD ISLAND

In 1990, the government of Prince Edward Island created a task force to review the organization of its school system. The task force was part of the government's broad reform initiative to examine how it delivered services in light of decreases in revenues and increases in government expenditures.

The task force consulted widely. One issue that arose was the division of responsibilities between the Department of Education and the five regional school boards, given the Island's population of 130 000 and approximately 24 000 pupils. The task force recommended the creation of an agency, with a governing board, that would assume some of the duties of the Department of Education and of the regional school boards.

In the spring session of 1992, the Minister of Education tabled the report of the task force. The minister adapted a key recommendation of the task force and announced the creation of a single Provincial School Board. The Board would replace the regional school boards and take on all but the basic policy-setting, financial management, and evaluation tasks of the Department of Education. Some local management of education would be assured by the creation of regional divisions within the Provincial School Board.

The minister also created a steering committee to oversee the process of provincial education reform and to make recommendations to the minister. The committee was chaired by the Deputy Minister of Education and included representatives of the Teachers' Federation, the Provincial Home and School Federation, and the Provincial Trustees' Association.

The steering committee established five work groups: (1) Structure and Accountability, (2) Age of Entry and Kindergarten, (3) Program and Human Resource Development, (4) French First Language Instruction, and (5) Junior and Senior High School. It is the first group, which was to recommend a division of responsibilities among the Department of Education and the proposed Provincial School Board and it proposed divisions, that will be reviewed.

The work group included representatives of government, trustees, parents, teachers, and local school administrators. For four months in 1992 it held hearings, received submissions, and prepared a working document.

The work group released a working paper outlining two alternatives. The first alternative was for a single elected provincial school board that would maintain both a central office and regional offices. The second alternative would provide for both centralization and regionalization: the creation of a provincial school board and the maintenance of existing regional school boards.

The reaction was immediate. All the provincial organizations with educational interests denounced the proposals. In particular, they rejected the idea of a provincial school board in favour of local school boards. Since almost all members of the work group were members of these provincial organizations, their work could not continue. The work group was disbanded, as was the steering committee. The province continued its educational reforms through other strategies.

Three of Mitchell's terms are illustrated in this case. The first is *articulation*. Political action seldom succeeds unless the key influential groups agree that there is a problem in the first place. Few groups in the Island agreed that the problems of their schools lay in their regional school boards or that the solution involved eliminating their regional school boards.

The second term is *aggregation*. In this case, most of the active players objected to centralization either on ideological grounds or on the grounds of self-interest. There did not seem to be any coalition of forces that would support the government's recommendation for the elimination of local school governance. This case illustrates the fact that for most educational issues at the provincial or territorial level, the key players tend to be educators and related groups such as associations of school trustees who are strongly committed to local school systems.

The third term is *allocation*. Most of the public who became involved in this issue appeared to value local self-government over centralization and its appearance of efficiency. Power then resided with those who opposed the creation of a provincial school board. Many provinces in Canada have gone through similar struggles of amalgamating local school boards.

This issue has arisen many times in the past. Many provinces have reduced the number of local school districts several times. The last major restructuring occurred in the 1960s and early 1970s. The issue of further reductions in the numbers of school boards is being raised again in such provinces as Saskatchewan and Alberta. What was different in the Prince Edward Island case was the attempt to eliminate all local boards in favour of one provincial school board.

The P.E.I. government revised its plans and introduced a new School Act (Chapter 35, 1993) in August 1993. In the act, local school boards were maintained but with a much reduced role. Many of their administrative functions were transferred to an Educational Services Commission and a provincial superintendent. The Commission, while not designated as a Provincial School Board, assumes such duties as staff development of educational personnel, payroll, collective bargaining, purchasing, school busing, property maintenance, and similar functions. Local boards, now freed of administrative matters, were to focus attention on educational matters, school improvement, and relationships with parents. Parents also received a stronger formal role through the creation of local school councils, which are advisory in nature.

Thus the government, while acknowledging a desire for local school boards, also responded to growing pressures for enhanced standards, greater centralization, and increased efficiency. The act provided a compromise. Within six days of the bill's introduction, it was passed after three readings.

ONTARIO'S BILL 109

Although Ontario has a French-speaking population of more than 460 000, it has not always met the educational needs of its French-speaking children. It was not until 1970 that public French secondary schools were authorized for full public funding, and then only if they were built by the (non-denominational) public school boards. In keeping with the spirit of the Canadian Charter of Rights and Freedoms, which guarantees both equality rights (section 15) and the rights to an education in the minority official language (section 23), in 1988 the province proposed Bill 109, in an effort to create a French-language school board for the area in and around the city of Ottawa.[2]

The bill announced the government's intention to create such a board, whereupon the government decided that the Standing Committee on Social Development would hold public hearings in Ottawa to shape the final form of the bill. Based on Mitchell's policy process framework (1988), the hearings represented the regulation process of policy formulation. The issue is one of educational governance.

The creation of a French-language board outside Quebec was a major event in Canadian politics. Under the terms of Confederation, citizens of Canada in most provinces had rights to denominational schools—that is, Catholic or Protestant schools. Over time, the Protestant schools became (with few exceptions) de facto non-denominational or public schools. There were no language rights prior to the Official Languages Act and the Canadian Charter of Rights and Freedoms. Even if Ontario created a French-language board, those religious rights would remain. The creation of a French-language board also had repercussions in the existing Ottawa and Carleton Catholic separate boards and public boards, which had many French-speaking students and schools they would lose if a French board were established. The questions of how local taxes would be apportioned and how existing schools, facilities, and staffs would be transferred from the four existing boards had yet to be decided. Teachers in the existing boards wondered how their rights would be protected if they had to transfer to the new board. In all, it was a touchy problem in which many groups had legitimate and somewhat competing interests.

The hearings would be the forum for airing the different views; the committee would make recommendations for regulatory and distributive decisions.

Forty-one groups or individuals participated, representing French-speaking and English-speaking groups, educators, parents, trustees, community groups, churches, and the Ontario government itself. Many organizations were provincial in scope: provincial associations of teachers, trustees, school boards. Interestingly enough, no ad hoc groups participated.

Mawhinney (1988) suggests that those who influenced the thinking of the committee (most of whose members had significant experience in public education) were mainly educators who either worked directly in the field (as employees of the Ministry of Education, for instance), members of well-established provincial educational groups, or representatives of the local school boards. The other significant party to the discussions was the Association canadienne-française de l'Ontario (ACFO), a well-organized lobby that works on behalf of the French-speaking population of Ontario and whose origins trace back to the infamous Regulation 17 of 1912, which forbade teaching in French beyond the first two grades in any Ontario school. (The repressive measures of Regulation 17 were lifted in 1927, although the regulation remained on the books until 1944.) As suggested by Mitchell (1988), the numbers who influenced the decisions were relatively small.

In this case, the decision to create a French-language school board originated outside of the educational domain. However, the decisions on how to implement the policy tended to rest with educators, often speaking for well-established provincial organizations. It was they who would try to satisfy the constitutional rights of religious groups and negotiate the legitimate interest of taxpayers—clients of the original school boards who would be diminished by the loss of French-speaking students and teachers and who would lose schools, facilities, and properties. These educators would also try to protect the job-related rights and careers of teachers involved in the changes; the procedures for establishing curriculum and teacher and administrator qualifications; the determination of who would be eligible to vote in the various school board elections and who would be eligible to sit as an elected trustee; and all the other related rights, obligations, and interests of those affected, directly or indirectly, by the legislation.

The outcome of the Bill 109 hearings was the law creating the French-language school board in Ottawa-Carleton. The result of the process was distributive in that it involved a distribution of powers and services; it was regulatory in that it regulated the behaviour of the new board; it was also symbolic in that it affirmed the rights of Franco-Ontarians in the Ottawa-Carleton region (and perhaps by implication elsewhere in Ontario and in other parts of Canada) to control of their own educational institutions.

PROVINCIAL CURRICULUM REFORM IN BRITISH COLUMBIA: EDUCATIONAL POLITICS

After two major studies of the provincial social studies curriculum, conducted during the 1970s, the British Columbia Ministry of Education launched a revision of social studies from grades 1 to 11. The intent of the ministry officials was that a logically sequential program would result.[3] The ministry was quite direct in its charge to the committee:

> The compulsory part of the Social Studies Curriculum will be based on the disciplines of history and geography, broadly defined, incorporating, where relevant, aspects of other social sciences.
>
> It is expected that a major part of the program will be devoted to the study of Canada.

A process model was developed, whereby the committee would draft materials and provide for public input through reaction and consulting groups.

The committee, selected by a ministry official, consisted of four practising teachers, one school trustee, and one professor of education. The ministry also provided the committee with some teacher-consultants. The high profile of teachers on the committee initially enhanced its credibility among teachers. However, it was decided not to include academic historians and geographers on the committee, but rather to invite them to react to proposals made by the committee. The belief was that to include academics on the committee would prolong matters by increasing the number and level of internal debates. The committee was also asked to work within tight time constraints.

The committee worked quickly, assigning the editorial work to a consultant and deciding early that an interdisciplinary approach would be preferable to the disciplinary approach that had been the mandate of the ministry. The roles of inquiry and values were to be important.

Early reactions were mixed. The committee did not pay much attention to the feedback, except to add Canadian material to the curriculum and shift some content from one grade to another.

Major criticisms began to emerge. Academic historians and geographers deplored the minor role assigned to their respective disciplines. The British Columbia Teachers' Federation (BCTF) also endorsed the opposition, more for reasons of ideology than of curriculum theory. The BCTF believed that it should have a stronger role in curriculum development, stating that the committee should have only teachers who were recommended by the BCTF and who supported the curriculum policies approved by the BCTF. By December 1981, the Federation directed its membership not to participate in the ministry's curriculum projects.

The new curriculum policy had been initiated by the ministry for several reasons. The old curriculum was outdated, and two major studies had pointed out its shortcomings. The ministry wanted its ideology to be reflected in the curriculum and gave clear directions to the curriculum committee to accomplish this. That ideology called for logical, sequential, discipline-based, Canadian-oriented curriculum. That ideology also included the belief that educational policy-making should include broadly based public input, but it should not be dominated by the BCTF. The ideology of the committee called for a curriculum based on inquiry methods and interdisciplinary content. The ministry officials saw curriculum development as the implementation of policy determined by government; to the BCTF, curriculum development was a professional matter. The various divisions meant that the making of crucial educational decisions by a small clique composed of senior education officials from government, teachers, and trustee organizations—a process described by Housego (1972)—was no longer operative in British Columbia. Perhaps it is not in any other part of Canada today.

In Mitchell's definition of the policy-making process, this case reflects the *aggregation* stage—that is, the aggregation of interested parties into coalitions for support. It is this that we generally think of when we speak of politics of education. The attempt by the ministry to limit the participation of academics and the BCTF, coupled with the failure to resolve ideological divisions between traditionalists and progressives, meant the failure of the attempted curriculum policy. This case also contains elements of the *allocation* stage, in which decisions are made to embrace some proposals and reject others.

LOCAL POLICY-MAKING: HERITAGE LANGUAGES IN TORONTO

The Toronto area has long been a magnet for immigrants and refugees to Canada. For example, one Toronto-area school board, North York, has a student population that is largely multicultural. By February 1988, there were 60 000 day students enrolled in the North York board. Of this number, two-thirds came from homes whose mothers were not born in Canada. One-third reported a language other than English as the primary language used at home (Handscombe, 1989). The board had large numbers of immigrant and refugee children for several decades. Since the 1960s, its policy was to assist these children through the provision of English as a Second Language (ESL) programs, which had been the typical response of urban boards across the country.

In the 1980s, there were questions about this relatively simple response to a complex problem (Cummins, 1989). For example, studies conducted in this period showed that children from immigrant families were not succeeding in schools as they should. One study pointed out that 70 percent of students in the technical and vocational schools in the Metropolitan Toronto area were from immigrant families. In the early 1970s, federal government policies on multiculturalism, the student population composition, and the results of studies showing the ineffectiveness of ESL led Toronto-area educators to re-examine the assumptions underlying school curricula and policies. Some of the research they studied indicated that children learn second languages better if they have a good command of their mother tongue.

The Toronto board set up a work group that proposed a variety of measures to promote children's knowledge of their mother tongue.[4] There was an immediate hostile reaction from groups who had not been privy to the efforts of the work group and from others who complained about the proposed costs of such an undertaking. Many suggested that maintenance of the home language would impede the students' learning of English and their integration into Canadian society. The work group had to withdraw many of its proposals.

In 1980, the issue flared up again when the Ukrainian and Armenian communities proposed that the Toronto Board of Education establish schools in which, in addition to the regular curriculum in English, instruction in Ukrainian or Armenian would be offered for one-half-hour in an extended school day. The first language of the students would also be used to make announcements and in the incidental and co-curricular activities of the school. Reactions from the community and the press again were antagonistic, with charges of "ghettoization" (Cummins, 1989).

The board referred the whole matter to another work group. This time, there were extensive consultations with community groups. The group recommended that the teaching of heritage languages be introduced into a regular extended school day whenever feasible. Further, the board should introduce bilingual and trilingual programs involving heritage languages. Another community debate ensued.

A major opponent to the recommendations were the teachers' federations. Teachers claimed that the curriculum was already overloaded and teachers overburdened. The Toronto Teachers' Federation submitted the matter to arbitration, organized a "work-to-rule" campaign, and threatened strike action. Teachers campaigned to inform parents that if the policies went forward, the education of their children would suffer.

Although the arbitration board agreed that the board could implement the recommendations, the elections of 1985 changed the balance of power on the board and the proposed heritage language programs were shelved.

According to Mitchell's model, this issue again was at the *aggregation* stage. The failure of the board to ensure that various competing groups be included in the policy-making process was the major cause of failure. Teachers and parents were not convinced that the educational merits of the plans outweighed the possible costs. In particular, teachers saw the programs as imposing a new burden on their already heavy workloads. Preparation time had been a key demand of the teachers in contract negotiations during this period.

This case also points out that board decisions are formally made by the elected trustees. Although the board members were originally in favour of these multicultural policies, the debates and the reaction of the press probably influenced the outcome of the school board elections. One can only speculate on the influence that the well-organized teachers' federations had on the election results. Again, the policies of the federal government, in its concern for immigration and immigrant populations, were a factor in the policy process. The growing multicultural nature of the province of Ontario had its effects on the policies of the government. Since these events, Bill 5 (1989) requires heritage language programs to be offered wherever 25 families request a particular program.

CONCLUSIONS

P olicy-making in Canadian education has become more visibly "political." The policies for the schools reflect the policies that the government of the day promotes for the governance of the state.

The particular policies chosen for discussion in this chapter have dealt primarily with attempts to make education more responsive to the needs of individuals, whether they be "exceptional" pupils or the children of immigrants and refugees. These are not the only policy trends in education. There are indications that as policies of state shift, there will be increased pressure to focus on national and provincial priorities, which are increasingly vocational and economic. Thus national priorities are for programs of adult literacy, vocational education, and education in the sciences. In the short term, educational administrators must cope with declining resources, the high retirement rate of senior educational officials, and the higher proportion of students who want to go on to postsecondary institutions and universities. Economic problems mean that the educational system will find it difficult to offer new services; the lack of funds means that educational buildings and facilities will continue to suffer from neglect; these problems also mean that policy-makers will be looking for increased returns for the expenditure of educational dollars.

The policy-makers in the educational domain will become a more diverse group. Government education officials, senior school board executives, and leaders of teachers' federations will continue to be key policy-makers, but they will be joined by other politicians and civil servants in related fields, including health, welfare, recreation, economics, and finance. Business people will likely take a more active role in education, especially now that they are asked to fund educational activities and join in school "partnerships."

Revolutions in practice follow revolutions in ideas. In the end, the key policy-makers will be those who can create and communicate new models and visions for educational institutions.

DISCUSSION QUESTIONS

❑ Canadian education places formal emphasis upon the provincial government, but how far does it actually determine what is taught the students?

❑ Pressure groups are anathema to some educators. How far can pressure groups influence the activities of schools? What means are there to absorb their impact?

❑ How political is the process by which educational decisions are made? Would the political process be more disciplined and more effective if it were always associated with political parties?

❑ Identify a current controversial educational issue and answer the following questions.

❑ How an issue is defined affects how it is treated. Identify at least two "definitions" of the issue that groups have used in an attempt to *articulate* the issue.

❑ Identify the groups in society that potentially can become involved in the issue (*aggregation*).

❑ Identify the basic values or interests and resources that each group brings to bear on the issue (*allocation*).

❑ Given your analysis, predict the resolution of the issue.

❑ Assume that a policy statement will emerge from the above discussions. How might the policy be implemented so as meet the demands of the various dominant groups without alienating the members of the less dominant groups (*implementation*)?

NOTES

1.   This section is based on an MA thesis by Janet Poyen, submitted to the University of Calgary in 1989 and entitled "Canadian Parents for French: A National Pressure Group in Canadian Education."
2.   This case is based on an MA thesis by Hanne Mawhinney, presented to the University of Ottawa in 1988 and entitled "A Political Systems Strategy to Analyze Policy Formulations."
3.   This case is based on an article by Fowler (1989).
4.   The material for this case is based on an article by Cummins (1989).

REFERENCES

Canada. (1981). Special committee on the disabled and the handicapped. *Report: Obstacles.* Ottawa: The Committee.

Cummins, J. (1989). Heritage language teaching and the ESL student: Fact and fiction. In J.H. Esling, *Multicultural education and policy: ESL in the 1990s.* (pp. 3–17). Toronto: OISE Press.

Dale, R. (1989). *The state and education policy.* Toronto: OISE Press.

Fowler, R.H. (1989). Curriculum reform in social studies: An analysis of Saskatchewan and British Columbia. *Canadian Journal of Education, 14*(3), 322–37.

Handscombe, J. (1989). Mainstreaming: Who needs it? In J.H. Esling, *Multicultural education and policy: ESL in the 1990s.* (pp. 18–35). Toronto: OISE Press.

Hoey, R.A. (1989). *Curriculum policy for the public and secondary schools in Ontario 1945–1965.* Doctoral dissertation presented to the University of Ottawa.

Housego, I. (1972). Pluralist politics and educational decision-making. In P.J. Cistone (Ed.). *School boards and the political fact.* (pp. 13–23). Toronto: OISE Press.

Mawhinney, H. (1988). A political systems strategy to analyze policy formulations. MA thesis. University of Ottawa.

Mitchell, D.E. (1988). Educational politics and policy: The state level. In N.J. Boyan (Ed.). *Handbook of research on educational administration: A project of the American Educational Research Association.* New York: Longman.

Organization for Economic Co-operation and Development. (1976). *Reviews of national policies for education: Canada.* Paris: OECD.

Stringham, B.L. (1974). *The School Act, 1970: A case study of public policy making in education.* Unpublished Ph.D. thesis. University of Alberta. National Library Microfiche Cat. No. 21986.

Tomkins, G.S. (1986). *A common countenance: Stability and change in the Canadian curriculum.* Scarborough, ON: Prentice-Hall.

FURTHER READINGS

Bezeau, L.M. (1989). *Educational administration for Canadian teachers.* Toronto: Copp Clark Pitman.

Dale, R. (1989). *The state and education policy.* Toronto: OISE Press.

Newton, E., & Knight, D. (Eds.). (1993). *Understanding change in education: Rural and remote regions of Canada.* Calgary: Detselig.

Tomkins, G.S. (1986). *A common countenance: Stability and change in the Canadian curriculum.* Scarborough, ON: Prentice-Hall.

11

REBUILDING THE CULTURAL CAPITAL OF VIRTUE TALK IN EDUCATION

William Knitter

Curricular arguments and activities reflect moral and epistemological points of view. This is necessarily so insofar as curricular arguments embody, or are informed by, views of the nature of persons and their development and views of the nature of knowledge. There are several reasons for exploring the philosophical foundations of our curricular approaches. One is simply that we should be informed about the approaches we use. We should understand the strengths and weaknesses of our views, and what is highlighted and what is left in relative darkness in them (see Schwab 1978). We should also be reflective about our beliefs in order to revise what is incoherent or contradictory in them. Isaiah Berlin (1978) makes the classic case for this function of philosophy in the following argument:

> The task of philosophy . . . is to extricate and bring to light the hidden categories and models in terms of which human beings think, to analyze clearly what is obscure or contradictory in them, to discern the conflicts between them that prevent the construction of more adequate ways of organizing and explaining experience . . . The goal of philosophy is always the same: to assist men to understand themselves and thus operate in the open and not wildly, in the dark. (pp. 10–11)

Finally, we need to understand not only our own practices, but also the intellectual and cultural climates of our schools and society; for it may be the case that in being novel or in being ancient or in simply marching to a distant drummer, our approaches may run counter to dominant themes in modern culture, thus making their reception more difficult. If the terms and assumptions of some approach are not part and parcel of school culture, miscommunication, misunderstanding, and rejection will be the likely result.

"VIRTUES" DEFINED

Reflecting the general theme outlined above, it was a particular and concrete occasion in my teaching that was the impetus for this chapter, the point of which is that for certain curricular approaches to be received with understanding, we need to rebuild the "cultural capital" of virtue talk in education. In reading Schwab's third Practical paper with a class of students, we came to the topic of the three faces of subject matter, one of which is the access disciplines. The access disciplines, according to Schwab, are constituted of skills, abilities, modes of questioning, and sensitivities essential to recovering the meanings of disciplined inquiry or creation. At the University of Chicago, for example, three texts in long use in the Humanities I course that focussed on access disciplines in the arts were *How to look*, *How to listen*, and *What to look for in literature*. The point of these texts and the Humanities course was to initiate students into the ways and traditions of recovering and making meaning out of literature, art, and music. The course was not so much about the facts and knowledge (the "knowing that's") of literature, art, and music (who wrote what when? what is the baroque era?), but rather about the acquisition of the arts and skills and sensitivities relevant to understanding works of art. That course, and in general curricular practices focussed on the access disciplines, are about the virtues necessary to engage in an activity or practice. Strangely, to me, the familiar truths of my own education, while eventually comprehensible to the class, were received as dark sayings; recognitions and examples came slowly, and the very framing of a face of subject matter in Schwab's terms seemed unfamiliar. As the idea of access disciplines became clearer, one student sharply rejected the whole notion. To paraphrase with licence, the student said that when she saw a movie, or read a poem, or listened to music, she just wanted to have her own reaction, without the interference of some intervening structure; for, after all, in the end, it's one's own taste or opinion that counts—there is no disputing taste.

In the case I have illustrated, curricular arguments involving notions of practices and the development of virtues run counter to emotivist themes in current culture. It is the equivalent of "emotivism's attempted reduction of morality to personal preference" (MacIntyre, 1981, p. 19) that characterizes my student's rejection of the access disciplines. Emotivist theory rests on the premise that value statements are expressions of emotion that "cannot literally be true or false" (Flew, 1984, pp. 103–4). This philosophical doctrine becomes a problem for virtues-oriented curricula in the sense that, as MacIntyre contends, "to a large degree people now think, talk, and act as if emotivism were true ... and this ... marks a degeneration, a grave cultural loss" (MacIntyre, 1981, p. 21). In order to develop the cultural capital and rhetorical power of virtue arguments, some of the concepts, terms, and distinctions in the tradition of virtue talk, particularly as explored by Alasdair MacIntyre in *After virtue*, will be reviewed in this chapter.

There are at least two more modern images of the virtues that stand in the way of a recovery of the Aristotelian moral tradition in which the virtues have such a central place. The first image is well captured in a story told by Hannah Arendt about the transmogrification of the meaning of virtue from ancient to Victorian times. The commonly understood referent of a person of virtue in classical Athens was a man who could do everything well; in Victorian times, the paradigm case of a person of virtue was a woman who hadn't done anything. One of the commonly inherited meanings of "virtue" is the absence of sin. The existence of this connotation of the term is one reason why William Frankena (1965) prefers to substitute the phrase "excellences of mind and body," a phrase also used by James D. Wallace (1978) in his attempt at recovering Aristotelian ethics in *Virtues and vices*.

The second and related modern image of the virtues is of a list of somewhat prissy personal attribute words, standing alone, out of relation to a function or activity. The reciting of scouts' and guides' mottos—the scout or guide is thrifty, brave, kind, loyal, and trustworthy—sometimes gives this impression. There is no special function or activity—no *telos*—that would give meaning or measure to the thriftiness, bravery, etc.; no addressing of such questions as how thrifty, or to what end, or what should we mean by "thrifty." These virtue words seem to be declared as simply good in themselves. (In an important sense, scouting and guiding do have a clear *telos*, namely, as the pledge goes, "to serve God, Queen, and country.")

MacIntyre's definition of the virtues directly counters these two modern images. Following his lead, and giving the second point priority, we can define the virtues as functional relative to practices. What MacIntyre means by a practice is

> any coherent and complex form of socially established cooperative human activity through which goods internal to that form of activity are realised in the course of trying to achieve those standards of excellence which are appropriate to, and partially definitive of, that form of activity, with the result that human powers to achieve excellence, and human conceptions of the ends and goods involved, are systematically extended. (MacIntyre, 1981, p. 175)

Denotatively, football, chess, farming, architecture, and the "enquiries of physics, chemistry and biology" are all practices. Including a wide range, as MacIntyre writes, "arts, sciences, games, politics in the Aristotelian sense, the making and sustaining of family life, all fall under the concept" (p. 175).

It is this concept of practices in terms of which MacIntyre tentatively defines virtue:

> A virtue is an acquired human quality the possession and exercise of which tends to enable us to achieve those goods which are internal to practices and the lack of which effectively prevents us from achieving any such goods. (p. 178)

Virtues are those qualities, then, that enable us to carry out the activities of practices. For sports, the virtues include not only physical skills, a trained eye for the developing situations of the game, courage, and stamina; they also include some measure of a respect for the rules and a sense of fair play that keep the game a game. Practices involving disciplined inquiry require as sustaining virtues appropriate habits and skills (knowing how to write grammatically, or how to do an analysis of variance); they also require what Scheffler (1991) calls the "rational passions," for example, feelings of unease and discomfort in not rewriting our incoherent sentences. In general, then, virtues are the means (defined in terms of skills, dispositions, propensities, and sensitivities) by which we are enabled to engage in valued activities.

Even on this limited explication of the relation of virtues to practices, one can see the contrast between the image of the virtues in the Aristotelian tradition and the two modern images of the virtues I cited above. Virtues do not stand alone; rather, they are always defined relative to a practice or tradition. It is by reference to the nature and point of the practice that one understands the nature and extent of the patience, courage, loyalty, etc., appropriate to the practice; a different courage is required to bear witness to an unpopular belief than that which is required of a soldier in battle, but a courage nonetheless.

The point that one can define personal traits and attributes as virtues *only by setting them in relationship to a practice or practices* was well caught in Robert Louis Stevenson's criticism of the character of Henry David Thoreau, namely, that Thoreau's asceticism resulted in some measure from nothing more than the fact that it was . . . much easier for Thoreau to say *no* than *yes*; and that is a characteristic which depicts the man. It is a useful accomplishment to be able to say no, but surely it is the essence of amiability to prefer to say *yes* where it is possible. (Stevenson, 1900, p. 80)

That is to say that living well involves a variety of activities and obligations, and virtues are understood to be those traits, dispositions, and abilities that enable us to live and do well. No trait, such as the disposition to say "no," can be considered a virtue except in relationship to the wider range of activities, duties, and obligations in which we are involved. Asceticism must be set in balance with amiability, among other things. Even dispositions like benevolence and generosity cannot be considered as true virtues in isolation; it is not always a kindness to give or to give in, which point is the insight at the heart of "tough love" therapies. As Aristotle argues, virtue involves practical wisdom: to be virtuous, one must be benevolent or courageous or thrifty in appropriate circumstances and in an appropriate manner (see Book VI, Chapter 13 of Aristotle's *Nicomachean ethics* [1947] for his treatment of the relationship between the virtues and practical wisdom).

The image of virtue as singular and as constituted of the absence of sin is also clearly challenged by the Aristotelian tradition. Virtues, as excellences of mind and body essential to engaging in worthwhile activities, are many and positive. To be virtuous is to live well and do well, not simply to be blameless.

On this latter point, it is interesting to contrast the Aristotelian and Victorian/modern interpretations of the phrase, "virtue is its own reward." The Victorian image of the reward of virtue is the goodness of not having sinned; psychologized in modern images, the reward of virtue is the feeling of satisfaction of being good, whether by doing something altruistic or by not having sinned. On the Aristotelian account, the central or primary reward of virtue is the good of being able to engage in practices. It's making the passing shot in tennis against a worthy opponent; it's the apt turning of a phrase that precisely expresses one's point; it's making the rhythmic bass run that carries the guitar player to the next melodic phrase; it is these that are the rewards of our virtues.

A crucial part of MacIntyre's concept of a practice is the distinction of goods internal to a practice from those that are external. The particular examples of virtues being their own reward in the previous paragraph are all examples of goods internal to practices. A means is internal, according to MacIntyre, "to a given end when the end cannot be adequately characterised independently of a characterization of the means" (MacIntyre, 1981, p. 172). The tactics and strategies of the chess player, the athletic prowess and sense of the game of the tennis player, and the sensibility to the evocative powers of language of the poet are internal means to the practices of chess, tennis, and poetry, respectively; the enterprises are not definable separate from such characterizations. External means, though in causal relation to ends, are not enmeshed in the very nature of the end itself. Where the only point to working is money, work is an external means; in such circumstances, you don't expect a person to keep the job after winning the lottery. Where work is also a source of enduring satisfaction and rewarding association with others, the lottery winner is more likely to be unsure about retiring. The exercise of the virtues, then, is essential to practices, and in this sense, a crucial component of living and doing well. And, beyond the "components" of the performance and products of a practice, what is discovered by practitioners in the course of participation in a practice is the good of a certain kind of life.

The corollary of this last point is that it is only from the inside that goods internal to practices can be recognized. As MacIntyre argues, one cannot be a competent judge of internal goods without the relevant "experience of participating in the practice in question"

(p. 176). This means that one is obliged to submit oneself to the authority of the standards of a practice. It does not mean that standards of practices do not change; indeed, a part of every living tradition involves reflection on, and criticism of, the point and character of the practice. What is ruled out is the denial of standards external to individual opinion. As MacIntyre concludes,

> In the realm of practices the authority of both goods and standards operates in such a way as to rule out all subjectivist and emotivist analyses of judgment. De gustibus *est* disputandum. (p. 177)

With this phrase we have come full circle back to the counterphrase in my student's argument that there is no disputing taste. To recapitulate the argument so far, my general point has been to show that curricular proposals reflect moral and epistemological points of view. In particular, curricular proposals focussing on access disciplines, as Schwab (1978) describes them, are grounded in a conception of human development informed by the Aristotelian tradition of making the virtues central to living and doing well. Where knowledge of the virtues tradition has fallen into cultural decline, where virtue talk has limited cultural capital, and particularly where such a tradition runs counter to dominant emotivist themes in current culture, then the point and character of curricular proposals grounded in the virtues tradition will be understood dimly, or even received with hostility, and rejected outright.

"VIRTUES" AND PRACTICES

Before I discuss potential objections to this account, I would like to raise an example of another area where the language and concepts of practices and virtues would be useful. An area subject to the distinction of goods into those internal and external to practice is that of faculty performance reviews and the motivation of faculty. At recent discussions of a performance review system tied to merit pay at my university, talk appeared to be strangely skewed by an apparent under-appreciation of this distinction. Arguing for merit pay differentials on the order of $300 per year, one economist put the rhetorical question, "If there is to be no difference in reward between the average performer and the high performer, why would the high performer continue to produce several publications every year?" Whatever the appropriate connection between internal and external goods, the pursuit of goods internal to practice should not be placed second to external rewards in appreciating the motivations and satisfactions of an academic way of life. We would all have suffered a grave cultural loss if the circumstances of our work became such that external goods are primary. Consider the story passed on by Ted Chamberlin (1991) from the poet Philip Levine, about working on the milling machines in the Chevrolet gear and axle plant in Detroit. A newcomer arrives to work beside him and after a while he asks what they're making, to which the poet answers

> I'm making
>   2.25 an hour,
> don't know what you're
>   making, and he had
> to correct me, gently, what was
>   we making out of
> this here metal, and I didn't know.

Chamberlin's point is that we should think about what it is that we are making at our universities. My point is that the point of our practice as academics, and the internal goods of this practice, ought to have a central place in discussions of faculty development and performance review.

Let me now turn to some difficulties to which this account is subject so far. One potential objection to curricular proposals informed by the virtues tradition is that we may have made a mistake in characterizing some practice, and thus a mistake in identifying certain attributes and skills as virtues. For example, the film *Dead Poets' Society* opens with a classroom scene in which the introduction to a poetry text is the topic of discussion. According to Dr. J. Evans Pritchard, the reputed author of the introduction, the significance of a poem may be appreciated as a function of the area covered in a graph the co-ordinates of which are artfulness of language and importance of the topic. Thus one may compare graphically poems that, for example, are artful in language but trivial in topic with those that are less artful treatments of important topics, and finally, with the truly great poems that are artful in expression on topics of great importance to the human condition. At this point, the most diligent students, the ones whose "virtues" as pupils are most developed, are neatly plotting the graphs of poems said to fit these descriptions. "Nonsense," cries the teacher, "tear those pages out of your text." And with this move, the teacher and students embark on a different practice of poetry, a practice in which the skills and dispositions called into existence by the tidy graphing of poems are no longer to be counted among the central virtues.

This objection brings to the fore an important characteristic of practices on MacIntyre's account. The moral of this story is not, as it might be for the relativist, that there is no disputing taste. Rather, the existence of argument and disputation about the character of the goods, which are the point of a practice or tradition, is an essential mark of a living tradition. "For all reasoning," argues MacIntyre,

> takes place within the context of some traditional mode of thought, transcending through criticism and invention the limitations of what had hitherto been reasoned in that tradition ... A living tradition then is an historically extended, socially embodied argument, and an argument precisely in part about the goods which constitute that tradition. (MacIntyre, 1981, p. 206–7)

This characteristic of living traditions makes requisite an additional virtue, namely, "the virtue of having an adequate sense of the traditions to which one belongs or which confront one" (p. 207). The point of such a virtue is not limited to its conservative function; rather, such a virtue is envisaged, by MacIntyre, to be progressive, since "an adequate sense of tradition manifests itself in a grasp of those future possibilities which the past has made available to the present" (pp. 206–8).

Returning to the possibility of being wrong about what we should consider to be virtues and what virtues are central, as a practice evolves, given the functional interrelationship of virtues to practices, so does what are taken to be the virtues. This is precisely the point to the example drawn for *Dead Poets' Society*. John Dewey (1908) makes much of this point in his *Theory of the moral life*, in emphasizing that "it is in the quality of becoming that virtue resides." Insofar as traditions are living and practices evolve, the notion of a completed or fixed moral self loses its normative appeal. In focussing on the quality of becoming, Dewey makes central the obligation to be responsive to the emergence of new goods and duties as practices are revised.

"VIRTUES" IN THE EDUCATION SYSTEM

This theme of revision and renewal and becoming, which is part and parcel of MacIntyre's and Dewey's visions of the development of moral persons, is reflected in or informs a number of curricular practices. One of the more important and interesting kinds of curricula involving this theme are those involving problem-solving. And, just as there are themes in current culture (e.g., strains of emotivism, modern images of the virtues) that stand in the way of the acceptance of curricula grounded in a virtues approach, so too are there images of problem-solving that run counter to giving problem-solving a reflective and deliberative turn. The following exploration of contrasting curricular approaches to problem-solving is meant to elucidate the revisionary possibilities in how problems can be treated in living traditions. It also provides an opportunity to explore the important distinction MacIntyre draws between virtues and narrowly proscribed skills.

In the first mode of teaching students to solve problems, a skill-training conception dominates (see Mary Kennedy's [1987] excellent characterization of contrasting approaches to the training of professional expertise, including the skills and deliberative approaches discussed here, in "Inexact sciences: Professional education and the development of expertise"). Where expertise is seen as technical skill, the problems presented to students are of clearly defined kinds—How do you calculate compound interest, the speed of a falling body, the strength of a concrete wall, or the time required to travel a set distance at a certain speed? The methods or procedures for solving such problems are known and meant to be followed precisely. Solutions to such problems are assessable as right or wrong, and the aim is to achieve certain knowledge. The standard teaching procedure is to model the skill, guide the practice, and finally to test the independent display of the skill. In William Reid's (1979) account, such problems are "procedural problems," problems to be addressed by known and set procedures coming to certain answers.

In contrast, what Reid calls "uncertain practical problems" have no precise definition or type, and the procedures for their solution are various and ill defined. In Reid's example, the problem of where to place a third London airport is of this type. It is not simply a problem of routing the flow of air traffic. Ground transportation, the effect on local residents, costs of different sites, general environmental impact, and so on, are all involved. Though there may be specific methods for calculating the values for specific parts of the problem, there is no procedural method for weighing the importance of different parts to the whole. As Schwab writes, there is

> a most marked and peculiar characteristic of the deliberative process: it must compare incommensurables. The task is not merely a technical one of forecasting consequences and costs. It is not adequately stated as merely determining *the* value or good of the forecast consequences. For "the" value is in fact a number of different values: a valued contribution to the maturity of the child; a valued effect on the present state of mind of the child; a valued effect on the community. These different values are the incommensurables which must be weighted against one another. There are no weighting factors which can be supplied to the deliberating group by which to simplify this process. (Schwab, 1978, p. 382)

Solutions to such problems admit of no certainty, no simple right or wrong, but rather are fallible judgements. Discussion and deliberation are central to teaching that makes broad practical problems its focus.

From the point of view of a skills approach, a deliberative approach may be seen as too concerned with words, opinions, and endless talk. The appeal of a skills approach is that something definite is learned, and one knows whether an answer to a problem is right or wrong. And, surely, in addressing broad practical problems, we usually need calculative skills of various kinds to assess the bearing of various factors on the whole of the situation. There is also the subjective appeal of feeling that one can be certain about an answer.

The appeal of a deliberative view of the nature of professional expertise and problem-solving, in contrast, comes from the sense that broad practical problems are complex, and admit of no simple solutions. The point is well put in Rustom Roy's phrase, citing "the inexorable logic that the real problems of society do not come in discipline-shaped blocks" (quoted in Klein, 1990, p. 35). More cynically, Stephen Toulmin quotes Walter Lippmann's quip that, "To every human problem ... there is a solution that is simple, neat, and wrong"; and that, writes Toulmin, "is true of intellectual as well as practical problems" (Toulmin, 1990, p. 201).

The kind of problem an educator considers to be the central business of teaching has clear implications for the mode of practice that constitutes the most effective learning situation. Joseph Schwab, for example, was very concerned with an education that engendered in students flexible habits of addressing broad problems. "The effective learning situation," he wrote,

> is not the one which leads by the quickest, most comfortable route to mastered habit and attitude, used precept and applied knowledge, but the one which is provocative of reflection, experiment, and revision. (Schwab, 1978, p. 173)

Mastered habit and applied knowledge are usually thought of as signs of success in teaching; but, where such terms indicate fixed and static routines for addressing set problems, and uncertain practical problems are the focus of study, such outcomes would miss the point of the curriculum.

At this point we are prepared to return to the general theme of this chapter, namely, that the kind of problem one takes to be central to one's practice or field also has clear implications for what counts as the virtues. A deliberative approach, whatever the field, implicates a different set of excellences or virtues than a procedural problem approach.

To make the issue more concrete, consider two Canadian university settings in which students must shift from courses emphasizing procedural problems to courses making central broad problem situations. The first setting is schools of engineering, where, for the most part, the procedural problem dominates course curricula. The problems may be complex—calculating attributes of various solids, gases, liquids, or electricity in various kinds of applications—but, by and large, the problems are presented as defined and students are taught set procedures for addressing such problems. In contrast, at least one kind of course emerging in Canadian universities over the past two decades makes central broad problems. Courses on the social aspects of engineering or on the assessment of environmental impact present students with a different sort of problem and require of students a shift in mind-set about the nature of the expertise to be acquired.

In a review of current trends in environmental literacy concerning the use of appropriate technology for sustainable development, David Pitt lists the following shifts of content and focus, among others: in technological objectives, from high mechanical end and efficiency to technology appropriate to local circumstances and needs; in philosophy, from Cartesian to holistic; from high energy consumption to conservation and renewable resources; from a remedial approach to environmental damage to a preventative or antic-ipatory mode; and, from a narrow professional focus to one that is both broad and inter-national, as well as grass-roots–oriented (think globally, act locally) (Pitt, 1993, pp. 12–14). Pitt also draws out some of the implications for a shift in pedagogic methods and models that should accompany the shift in focus to environmental literacy. Citing a number of important trends in engineering education, Pitt notes that

> teaching has become interdisciplinary, both in the sense of subject matter and having students part of a team and learning teamwork, with its concomitant communication skills. Teaching has shifted from top down to bottom up to learning where the student has much more independence and seeks out what information he or she needs. Learning has become continuous extending throughout the professional career. (Pitt, 1993, p. 33)

And, finally, he notes that these changes in the practice of environmental engineering will require a new ethics that emphasizes "the need to curb man's inhumanity to nature as well as man" (p. 35). The four virtues that will be central, "the cornerstone of the new environment profession," are conscience, competence, comprehensive awareness, and commitment (p. 35).

A second area of university curricula where the procedural is eschewed in favour of the broad problem is strategic management studies in management departments. In contrast to the more singularly focussed work in accounting, finance, marketing, or even organi-zational theory courses, policy courses confront students with cases to analyze in all their full complexity. The desirability of seeing broad problems from different angles and per-spectives, and for discussion with others of different viewpoints indicates why it is no accident that group projects and group work are a common feature of such courses.

The case method is a common pedagogic feature of policy courses, and the School of Business Administration at the University of Western Ontario (UWO) has been a leader in the development of case method teaching. In a UWO text, *Teaching with cases*, the authors explain why they use the case method:

> The case method is used "Because Wisdom Can't Be Told." The idea behind this title is that there are few truths or fixed rules that need to be learned in administration, since managerial situations and circumstances are usually unique and constantly modified. Learning to deal with new situations is, therefore, more profitable. Consequently, the case method involves the clinical approach of learning by doing. (Erskine et al., 1981, p. 17)

In addition to the skills and abilities involved in analyzing alternative courses of action, students also learn "to tolerate incompleteness of information and ambiguity of situations" and "to grapple with messy problems" (p. 19).

It is also clear that ethical considerations are central to environmental engineering and strategic management in a way they are not in curricula focussed on narrow problem-solving. Consequences for the environment as our natural home and consequences for workers and consumers would be taken into account in evaluating alternative courses of action. When General Dynamics billed the U.S. government inflated prices for ordinary products ($1000 toilet seats, $1500 hammers), perhaps it was just a consequence of the fact that a narrow cost-benefit analysis showed there was a profit to be made. Ethical considerations weren't a part of the picture. In environmental engineering and strategic management studies, values become a central focus of the curriculum.

In arguing that a practice (and the virtues relative to it) are "never just a set of technical skills," MacIntyre makes much of the open-endedness of practices, that is, of the possibility of revision and change:

> What is distinctive of a practice is in part the way in which conceptions of the relevant goods and ends which the technical skills serve—and every practice does require the exercise of technical skills — are transformed and enriched by these extensions of human powers and by that regard for its own internal goods which are partially definitive of each particular practice or type of practice. Practices never have a goal or goals fixed for all time—painting has no such goal nor has history—but the goals themselves are transmuted by the history of the activity. (MacIntyre, 1981, p. 180)

Thus, while any curriculum initiating students into a practice will have a history, traditions, internal standards, and conceptions of the goods of the practice, there needs as well to be some way of conveying the sense that the ongoing historical "argument" about the ends and goods of the practice continues.

In the shift to taking uncertain practical problems, rather than procedural ones, as central to a course curricula (or to a discipline or a practice, e.g., environmental engineering), there is a strong parallel with what Stephen Toulmin argues is involved in the humanizing of "modernity" by the recovery of practical philosophy. In the era of modernity, "philosophers ignored the concrete, timely, particular issues of practical philosophy, and pursued abstract, timeless, and universal (i.e., theoretical) issues" (Toulmin, 1990, p. 186). The three foundations of such thought were the ideals of certainty, formal rationality, and the idea of starting over with a clean slate. As we recover the values of the concrete, the timely, and the particular, Toulmin argues that we are shifting our underlying conception of rationality from a core image of formal logic to one of being reasonable. Where "reasonableness" is our image of what it is to be rational, a different order of virtues becomes central to our practices. Reasonableness requires, according to Toulmin, those sixteenth-century humanist ideals of, on the one hand, "developing modesty about one's capacities and self awareness in one's self-presentation" and, on the other, "toleration of social, cultural, and intellectual diversity" (p. 199).

CONCLUSIONS

In coming to a conclusion, let me recapitulate the general themes of this chapter. Concerning "virtue talk" (that is, the underlying terms, concepts, and presuppositions of curricula focussed on practices and virtues), the most general theme is that virtues are defined relative to practices. They are the arts and skills and sensitivities that enable us to engage in a practice. However, just as practices evolve, so do what are thought to be the central virtues. This is as true of curricular practices as it is of law and medicine and portrait painting. This is the point illustrated by the discussion of the shift in problem-solving curricula from a focus on procedural problem to one on uncertain practical problems. In environmental engineering, just as in strategic management, as the practice changes, different abilities and qualities of character are required of the students. Finally, because practices are subject to revision and change, the spirit of revision must be a part of any full account of the virtues of a practice as well. As MacIntyre argues,

> The virtues therefore are to be understood as those dispositions which will not only sustain practices and enable us to achieve the goods internal to practices, but which will also sustain us in the relevant kind of quest for the good, by enabling us to overcome the harms, dangers, temptations, and distractions which we encounter, and which will furnish us with increasing self-knowledge and increasing knowledge of the good. (MacIntyre, 1981, p. 204)

The obligation inherent in practices to continue to seek and refine their ends and goods has implications for some measure of tolerance, openmindedness, and, as Dewey (1908) wrote, "the will to know — the active desire to examine conduct in its bearing on the general good" (p. 143). We may be wrong about what we think are the virtues that are central to a practice, as the teacher in *Dead Poets' Society* thought of the text author, but we are still involved in a quest for the good of the practice, and our evolving understanding of that good bears directly on what virtues are central to our curricular practices.

DISCUSSION QUESTIONS

❏ Do you agree that virtue involves practical wisdom as argued by Aristotle? Support your answer with examples within your university's context.

❏ What constitutes "a person of virtues" in the present time?

❏ Do you think that the standards of excellence in our Canadian education system are adequate in preparing students for life in the modern era? If no, what changes would you propose? If yes, are there areas where you might improve the system?

❏ How would you define ethics, virtues, and success in the career you choose? In selecting a certain course of action, how would you reconcile conflicts that might arise between these three aspects?

❏ Make a list of a few subjects taught in schools, colleges, or universities, like English, mathematics, physical education, and so on. What are some of the standards of excellence in these subject areas? To what extent do these standards seem to you to be dependent upon the realization of goods internal to the practices that constitute these subject areas?

REFERENCES

Aristotle. (1947). *Nicomachean ethics. Introduction to Aristotle.* R. McKeon (Ed.). New York: The Modern Library, Random House.

Berlin, I. (1978). The purpose of philosophy. In *Concepts and categories: Philosophical essays.* (pp. 1–11). London: The Hogarth Press.

Chamberlin, T. (1991). Tradition and innovation. *International Education Magazine, 7,* 11–12, 22.

Dewey, J. (1908). *Theory of the moral life.* New York: Holt, Rinehart and Winston.

Erskine, J.A., Deenders, M.R., & Mauffette-Leenders, L.A. (1981). *Teaching with cases.* London, ON: School of Business Administration, University of Western Ontario.

Flew, A. (1984). *A dictionary of philosophy.* New York: St. Martin's Press.

Frankena, W. (1965). *Three historical philosophies of education.* Glenview, IL: Scott, Forseman.

Kennedy, M. (1987). Inexact sciences: Professional education and the development of expertise. *Review of Research in Education, 14*, 133–67.

Klein, J.T. (1990). *Interdisciplinarity: History, theory and practice.* Detroit: Wayne State University Press.

Knitter, W. (1988). The informing vision of the practical: The concepts of character, virtue, vice, and privation. *The Journal of Curriculum Studies, 20*, 483–92.

MacIntyre, A. (1981). *After virtue: A study in moral theory.* Notre Dame, IN: University of Notre Dame Press.

Pitt, D. (1993). Environmental literacy and appropriate technology: A review of Contemporary trends and future directions. Working paper. Geneva, Switzerland: International Academy of the Environment.

Reid, W.A. (1979). Practical reasoning and curriculum theory: In search of a new paradigm. *Curriculum Inquiry, 9*, 187–207.

Schwab, J.J. (1978). The practical: Translation into curriculum. In I. Westbury, & N.J. Wilkof (Eds.). *Science, curriculum, and liberal education.* Chicago: University of Chicago Press.

Scheffler, I. (1991). *In praise of the cognitive emotions.* New York: Routledge.

Stevenson, R.L. (1900). Henry David Thoreau: His character and opinions. In *Familiar studies of men and books.* New York: C. Scribner's Sons.

Toulmin, S. (1990). *Cosmopolis: The Hidden Agenda of Modernity.* Chicago: University of Chicago Press.

Veatch, H.B. (1961). *Rational man: A modern interpretation of Aristotelian ethics.* Bloomington, IN: Indiana University Press.

Wallace, J.D. (1978). *Virtues and vices.* Ithaca, NY: Cornell University Press.

FURTHER READINGS

Bellah, R.N., Madsen, R., Sullivan, W.M., Swidler, A., & Tipton, S.M. (1985). *Habits of the heart.* Berkeley: University of California Press.

Moline, J. (1982). Classical ideas about moral education. In E.A. Wynne (Ed.). *Character policy: An emerging issue.* Washington, DC: University Press of America.

12

ETHNICITY, MULTICULTURALISM, AND MULTICULTURAL EDUCATION IN CANADA

Marie McAndrew

UNITY, DIVERSITY, AND EQUALITY IN EDUCATION: SOME THEORETICAL CONSIDERATIONS

In most modern societies, the public school system represents an institution for socializing future citizens and influencing their social and political behaviour. In pluralistic societies, this crucial role for schools can become the focus of a group conflict about the definition of society itself. A majority or dominant group of the state may insist that the schools promote national unity (Schermerhorn, 1970), while minority groups (especially since the ethnic revival of the sixties [Smith, 1981]) may ask that the school system be responsive to their special ethnic needs and goals.

The pluralist dilemma in education can be summarized as follows:

> Few governments . . . can afford to ignore the claims of minority groups who wish to preserve and indeed to promote their cultural identities. Schooling is important if the language, religion and customs of the family are to receive public recognition. . . . In short, minority groups may demand the right to choose how their children are educated in schools.
>
> At the same time governments are aware that . . . schools are agents of nationalism. . . . A fine balance has thus to be drawn between policies which promote cultural diversity and those designed to mobilize national sentiment. The bases of the latter, religion or/and language, may well be in conflict with the aspirations of culturally different groups. (Holmes, 1980, pp. 3–4)

Since majority and minority groups may not agree about the national purpose of education, and may have divergent interests relative to the social or ethnic stratification in the society, there are conflicting visions of the role that school plays in either reproducing or transforming ethnic/religious/racial inequalities.

Indeed, in a society that defines itself as democratic and egalitarian, multicultural policies in education must also address the issue of equality of access and results for all groups in the schools and in society at large (Holmes, 1980). Moreover, in a context of diversification of immigration, special attention has to be given to racism and inter-racial relations.

Since the emergence of the democratic nation-state in the nineteenth century, the assimilationist position has traditionnaly been advocated in the name of equality.

> Equality of provision as an ideal influences the demands of minority groups and the
> response of government. It is not always compatible with the notion that parents should
> be free to choose the kind of education their children should receive. . . . Equality of
> provision is central . . . to most systems where educational policies are formulated,
> adopted and implemented to a considerable extent by the central government. (Holmes,
> 1980, p. 6)

According to various authors (Porter, 1975; Murphy & Dennis, 1979; Laferrière, 1981)
ethnic differences in education could even be misused to justify social inequalities, since
the ideology of pluralism in the school can be seen as a way of maintaining the "ethnic
hegemony" of the dominant groups in a society.

> The essence as well as the complexity of the pluralist dilemma may now be appreciated.
> From the point of view of adult members of ethnic groups within a pluralistic society,
> programs of "multicultural" education that cater to their lifestyles and cultural main-
> tenance have an obvious attraction, which might even be shared by some of their
> children. However, the components that make up these programs, their place in the
> school curriculum, and the way that curriculum is devised provide almost unlimited
> opportunity for the dominant knowledge managers . . . to exercise hegemony over the
> life chances of children from ethnic backgrounds. (Bullivant, 1981, p. 241)

That well-intentioned policies may foster greater social *in*equality or lead to increased
control by the state over minority groups is evident in the failure of uniformity in schooling
(which was promoted for over a century in most Western nations) to bring about a more
ethnically equalitarian society. The failure of the "traditional" assimilationist schools to
achieve equality of access and results for minority children has been well documented and
is the source of a new ideology of multiculturalism in the schools that considers pluralism
as a *sine qua non* condition for equality.

> Cultural pluralism . . . is a posture which maintains that there is more than one legiti-
> mate way of being human without paying the penalties of second class citizenship . . .
> social justice, alone, means a fair share of the pie; as a goal . . . it has usually meant
> an assimilative attitude. Cultural pluralism . . . demands the same fair share plus the
> right not to assimilate. (Hazard & Stent, 1973, p. 16)

Even if cultural pluralism is now a popular ideology in some modern pluralistic nations
(Bullivant, 1981), the debate around unity, diversity, and equality in education is far from
over. In Canada, there are numerous ambiguities surrounding the ideology of multiculturalism and its implementation in education. These ambiguities reflect the complexity of
political socialization in a pluralistic society.

ETHNICITY AND MULTICULTURALISM IN CANADA

Although many authors (Anderson & Frideres, 1981; Breton et al., 1980) have stressed
that Canada has always been a multicultural country (since the first Native peoples and

the subsequent French and English settlers constituted a variety of ethnic and cultural groups), it is generally considered that the importance of ethnic diversity in Canada is largely a phenomenon of late-nineteenth- and twentieth-century immigration. The proportion of non-Native, non-French, and non-English groups (which we will refer to as the "ethnic groups" even if this term is unsatisfactory — *all* groups in Canada are ethnic groups) in the overall population of Canada grew from less than 8 percent in 1871 (Breton et al., 1980) to almost 42 percent in 1991 (Statistics Canada, 1991a).

Nevertheless, it is important to stress that the persistence of current ethnic identity in Canada cannot be identified with ethnic origin. Over time, assimilation is important, especially in the area of linguistic behaviour: in 1991, only 16 percent of the Canadian population had an "ethnic" mother tongue and only 9.1 percent spoke that language at home (Statistics Canada, 1991b). Linguistically, Canada was anglophone (59.9 percent mother tongue, 67.5 percent home language) with an important francophone minority (24.1 percent mother tongue, 23.0 percent home language) and a definite multicultural component. As Breton et al. (1980) summarize it,

> In the last century, Canada was a country whose majority was anglophone *and* British. Immigration subsequently transformed its *demographic basis*. The newcomers, however, gave up their own languages and massively adopted English. If Canada is not henceforth a country with a British majority, it nevertheless has remained a country with an anglophone majority. (p. 24)

Even if linguistic assimilation has occurred, most observers stress that ethnicity is still an important factor in the social and political definition of citizens of ethnic origin. Obviously, cultural diversity is still prevalent in Canada and, particularly since the ethnic revival of North America in the 1960s, ethnicity is a focus for identification and mobilization (Breton, 1991). Some explanations proposed to elucidate the overall persistence of ethnic allegiance in Canadian society (Anderson & Frideres, 1981) are: the "visibility" of some minorities; inter-ethnic conflicts; a weak national Canadian identity or the institutional completeness of some minorities; the importance of survival for some unique groups; and ethnic inequalities in education and income. Porter (1965) characterized this persistence of ethnicity as a "vertical mosaic."

This ethnically and culturally diverse country is also becoming a multi-racial society, with the liberalization of discriminatory immigration policies in 1962 and the subsequent increase of immigrants from Third World countries, which, since the 1970s, have become the leading sources of immigrants (Breton, 1991).

In a country as large as Canada, regional variation is as important as it is inevitable. Driedger (1978) proposes a detailed regional analysis of the linguistic and cultural realities in Canada in which he distinguishes six main regions: the Northlands — multilingualism and multiculturalism (Native peoples); the West — anglophones and multiculturalism; Upper Canada — anglophones and multiculturalism; Lower Canada — francophones and multiculturalism; the Maritimes — anglophones and angloculturalism; and New Brunswick — bilingualism and biculturalism.

In 1971, Canada took a critical step with the adoption of a policy of multiculturalism within a bilingual framework, which was reinforced in 1988 by the more explicit Bill C-93 on the preservation and enhancement of multiculturalism in Canada. Former prime minister Pierre Trudeau (Palmer, 1975) stated:

> There cannot be one cultural policy for Canadians of British and French origin, another
> for the original peoples, and yet a third for all the others. For although there are two
> official languages there is no official culture, nor does any ethnic group take precedence
> over any other ... A policy of multiculturalism within a bilingual framework commends
> itself to the government as the most suitable means of assuring the cultural freedom of
> Canadians ... First, resources permitting, the government will seek to assist all Cana-
> dian cultural groups that have demonstrated a desire and effort to continue to develop
> a capacity to grow and contribute to Canada and a clear need to assistance, the small
> and weak groups no less than the strong and highly organized. Second, the government
> will assist members of all cultural groups to overcome cultural barriers to full partici-
> pation in Canadian society. Third, the government will promote creative encounters and
> interchange among all Canadian cultural groups in the interest of national unity. Fourth,
> the government will continue to assist immigrants to acquire at least one of Canada's
> official languages in order to become full participants in Canadian society. (p. 136)

This policy of not only tolerating but encouraging cultural diversity as a definition of
the Canadian identity represented a major shift from previous attitudes, as Jean Burnet
(1975) points out: "The policy of multiculturalism is new. Until the 1960s the mosaic,
which John Porter (1965) described as Canada's most cherished value, was regularly
lauded by prominent politicians ... However, no policy was inaugurated explicitly to
maintain and develop the mosaic" (p. 206).

Anderson and Frideres (1981) saw the Canadian government's new interest in the area
of inter-ethnic relations resulting from three factors: the growth of federal revenue and of
state intervention in society in general; the political development in Quebec; and the growing assertiveness of the more influential and powerful of the "other ethnic groups"
(p. 134).

Other observers have stressed the importance of group competition in a society already
struggling with the question of its national identity.

> In the United States it is often observed that the black liberation movement gave rise
> to cultural self-assertion of the many ethnocultural groups and other status groups ...
> In Canada, conflict over the cultural status of the "other" ethnic groups in the 1960s
> and 1970s has been greatly affected by the French-English conflict and the legitimacy
> given to new cultural claims of French Canadians ... increased French cultural and
> linguistic presence has raised the expectations of "other" ethnic groups for improved
> cultural status and recognition. (Berry et al., 1977, p. 379)

The Canadian policy of multiculturalism can therefore be seen as a response to the
major goals of political socialization in the turmoils that characterized Canadian society
in the 1970s. Its first aim is to foster national unity by giving ethnic groups a sense of
belonging to Canada, which is defined as a multicultural, tolerant, and equalitarian society.
"For groups which have a sense of being left out of Canadian Society, the multicultural
policy, by recognizing their contribution, can heighten their feeling that they belong to
Canada" (Palmer, 1975, p. 114).

At the same time, taking the politics out of ethnicity by defining it in purely "cultural"
terms made it possible to avoid the negative consequences of putting too much stress on
centrifugal forces on the society (Schermerhorn, 1970). Some observers (Porter, 1975)
have also questioned the basic postulate that culture per se fosters equality in society.
These critics have expressed concern that the multiculturalism policy could be "a strategy
of containment of the other ethnic groups" (Isajiw, 1981, p. 320). Even if the question is

still open, it is at least generally admitted that while multiculturalism may give more power to the ethnic groups in society, it also permits greater control of the state on the definition of goals, priorities, and even leadership in ethnic communities (Breton, 1991).

For the francophones (who have almost unanimously rejected it, especially in Quebec [Berry et al., 1977], since it defines French culture as only one of many cultures of Canada), the policy seemed to say that although Canada had two official languages, it did not have "two nations"—let alone, in the terms of reference for the Royal Commission on Bilingualism and Biculturalism (1967, p. 151), two societies. Rocher (1976) argues that by pretending that there is no official or dominant culture in Canada, the policy reinforces the dominance of the anglophone community while denying the francophone community its historic equivalent sociological and political status in Canada. Nevertheless, as we will see later in this chapter, Quebec has adopted in recent years its own brand of "multicultural policy" that, except for the status given to French as a common language, is very simular to the Canadian ideology and practices (Québec, 1990).

For the anglophone majority, the policy provided a lesson on the value of tolerance and pluralism in Canada. White Anglo-Saxon Protestants (WASPs) have not always been open to cultural diversity, and have often been less than tolerant of other races (Palmer, 1984). Even now, tolerance is generally restricted to white Europeans (Ministry of Multiculturalism and Citizenship, 1991a). The state thus felt obliged to foster a greater acceptance of all groups and a general awareness of the value and the importance of pluralism for all Canadians.

Although the policy of multiculturalism originally was intended to encourage cultural diversity in Canada, particularly in response to white European demands from Western Canada, attention is now more and more given to the problems of equality, as the different needs of a new immigrant population and racial discrimination have become major social issues (Breton, 1991).

As formal education is under provincial jurisdiction, the actions of the federal government in the area of multiculturalism have been generally limited to non-formal education and research. These endeavours have attempted first to support the maintenance of ethnic, linguistic, and cultural identity while fostering a better knowledge and appreciation of ethnic diversity in all Canadians. However, anti-racist policies and programs, as well as institutional change to foster better participation of minority groups and citizenship education stressing at the same time common national and respect for diversity, are now emerging as the main priorities (Ministry of Multiculturalism and Citizenship, 1991b; Senate of Canada, 1993).

This evolution is particularly noticeable in the content of the 1988 Act for the Preservation and Enhancement of Multiculturalism in Canada (Canada, 1988) in which, notwithstanding its title, out of nine principles, only one refers to multiculturalism in its narrow sense.

Although the policy of multiculturalism does not have a high visibility in the general public (Berry et al., 1977), a recent survey (Ministry of Multiculturalism and Citizenship, 1991a) has shown that it is generally well received and appreciated by Canadians.

MULTICULTURALISM AND MULTICULTURAL EDUCATION IN SELECTED CANADIAN PROVINCES

The following section discusses the policies on multiculturalism that exist in Ontario, the Prairie provinces, Nova Scotia, and Quebec. The discussion will concentrate on

Ontario, since this province constitutes the political, cultural, and economic core of English Canada and is the main destination of immigrants to Canada (Ontario Ministry of Citizenship and Culture, 1988).

ONTARIO

The emergence of multiculturalism as a major component of educational issues reflects the importance of ethnicity in Ontario, where, in 1991, 23.7 percent of the population were born outside the country (Statistics Canada, 1991c), 48.9 percent were of "ethnic origin" (Statistics Canada, 1991a), and 20.8 percent had a mother tongue that was neither French nor English (Statistics Canada, 1991b).

The major social and political consequences of this new demographic reality have made it necessary to promote multicultural education. First, the majority group, which had accepted the immigration of white Europeans in the 1950s, is now more hostile toward visible minorities, and a number of incidents of racism have been reported (Pitman, 1977). Moreover, the former acceptance of white European immigrant groups seems to have been related to a minimal tolerance of cultural and linguistic diversity, for the policy of publicly promoting minority languages and cultures is now meeting with opposition (Maseman, 1979).

The ethnic or racial groups are emerging now as a cohesive group, using ethnicity or race as a main factor of identification and mobilization (Breton, 1991; Isajiw, 1981) to achieve their goals—respect for pluralism and equality.

An awareness of the new trends led the Ontario government to adopt a policy of multiculturalism in 1977. The Ontario policy, which resembles the federal initiative, states that "multiculturalism is one of the essential characteristics of the Ontario Society and all policies in Ontario must reflect that reality" (Davis, 1977).

This conception of multiculturalism implies equality of persons and groups, universal access to and participation in government services and institutions, maintenance of heritage languages and cultures, and multicultural sharing between all groups (Davis, 1977). This "new pluralism," to quote former premier William Davis, was intended to be "unique, unifying, and stabilizing." It is interesting to note the emphasis put on unity and stability in this formulation of multiculturalism by a majority politician who tried to depoliticize ethnicity by giving an essentially cultural definition of "other" groups. More recently, responding to pressure from visible minorities, the Ontario government has adopted an anti-racist policy and set up an anti-racism secretariat responsible for providing equal participation of all Ontarians in institutions and all aspects of public life (Ontario Ministry of Civic Affairs, 1991).

The Ontario Ministry of Education has reacted to the new ethnic dynamic in the province by promoting an educational multicultural policy that tries, at the same time, to foster integration of the minority student *and* respect for pluralism in the school system. In order to provide equality of educational opportunity, the ministry encourages English as a Second Language (ESL) programs and other compensatory measures (at the discretion of the local school boards), advocates school sensitivity to cultural differences, and stresses the necessity of providing school curriculum and textbooks that are culturally and racially unbiased and relevant to students from a variety of ethnic backgrounds (Ontario Ministry of Education, 1975, 1980a). Although education in Ontario is largely decentralized, the ministry has published major curriculum guidelines in the areas of intercultural education: *Canada's multicultural heritage* (1977); *Multiculturalism in action* (1977); *People of native ancestry*

(1975, 1977, 1981); *Black studies* (1983); *The development of a policy on race and ethno-cultural equity* (1987); *Our cultural heritage* (1990); and *Unity and diversity* (1991). More recently, the government has announced its intention to make the elaboration and adoption of policies on racial and ethnocultural equity compulsory for all school boards of Ontario (Ontario, 1992).

Generally speaking, the measures stressing integration and equality of opportunities for minority students, or intercultural education for the school population as a whole, seem to have been well accepted by various school boards (Ontario Ministry of Education, 1979, 1980). Such measures are most developed in the metropolitan school boards like the Toronto Board of Education, which has generated numerous discussion papers and reports on ethnicity, multiculturalism, and race relations (Toronto Board of Education, 1974, 1976, 1979, 1980, 1982).

The Toronto Board has analyzed the situation of immigrant children in anglophone schools under the concept of "The Bias of Culture" and has advocated school adaptation to cultural pluralism in a variety of areas, including the reception, placement, and streaming of immigrant children, the hiring of teachers and liaison officers from a variety of backgrounds, the general sensitivity of the system to cultural differences, and school/community relations (Toronto Board of Education, 1976).

If compensatory programs and even school sensitivity to cultural and racial pluralism are now generally considered as the official policy in Ontario without much opposition, the issue of heritage language teaching has been much more controversial, as there is no general consensus in Ontario society on the appropriateness of involving the public school in an area that traditionally was considered the private responsibility of parents and the ethnic groups themselves (Shamai, 1985).

Reacting to ethnic pressure groups, left-wing trustees, educators advocating third-language instruction as a part of the regular classroom day (Toronto Board of Education, 1976), and polls showing that the majority of the Ontario population favoured a more "laissez-faire" approach to the heritage language issue (Livingstone, 1983), the Conservative government in 1977 adopted a political compromise. Memorandum 46 established a two-and-a-half-hour-per-week Heritage Language Program, funded by the Ministry of Education under the Continuing Education Program, that could be offered after school, on non-school days, or, where numbers justified, in an extended school day. The program was seen to be the responsibility of school boards, which were left free to establish it. Collaboration between schools and the ethnic community in the various aspects of the program, including curriculum and hiring of teachers, was considered essential for the effectiveness of the program (Ontario Ministry of Education, 1980b).

Heritage language programs had an enrollment totalling 121 883 students in 63 languages in 1990–91 (Ontario Ministry of Education, 1992), numbers that reflect the perceived importance of cultural and linguistic maintenance by ethnic groups. Despite this popularity, the program has also been the cause of political turmoil, because it fell short of the expectations of some ethnic communities and leaders for whom the issue of integration in the regular school curriculum was critical (Toronto Board of Education, 1982). When the Toronto Board of Education (then dominated by New Democratic Party trustees) decided to integrate the program in an extended school day (without prior consultation with the teachers' union) and to make it compulsory in any school where a majority of parents requested it, the non-ethnic community voiced its opposition to public schools assuming responsibility for the teaching of minority languages and cultures and to public funding of "cultural divisiveness" (Toronto Teachers' Federation, 1983). More recently, the reluctance of the Scarborough Board of Education to enter the program, despite its significant ethnic (mostly Chinese) population, has led the Ministry of Education to amend the Education Act (1989) obliging school boards to offer the program when such a request is made by 25 or more parents. The debates and conflicts around the Heritage Language Program indeed reflect how it has become a "symbolic issue" in the debate on unity and diversity in Ontario education (McAndrew, 1992).

ALBERTA, SASKATCHEWAN, MANITOBA

The three Prairie provinces have emphasized linguistic and cultural maintenance programs, a decision that reflects the deep-rooted European ethnic groups that constitute the majority of the population in some Prairie communities. Many ethnic groups are concerned about their very survival; indeed, until recently, some of these groups (Ukrainians and other Eastern Europeans) believed that their homeland was being threatened and that they had a "mission" to preserve their language and culture (*Edmonton Journal*, 1984).

In the Prairie provinces, legislative provisions and government policies provide for more than Canada's two official languages to be used as languages of instruction. A more linguistic view of multiculturalism prevails, although some element of intercultural and anti-racist education can be found in these provinces' respective policies on multiculturalism (Lessard & Crespo, 1992). This stress on linguistic and cultural maintenance has been especially remarkable in Alberta, where (in addition to English and French programs in all schools), seven contemporary languages are offered in high Schools (Cree, German, Hungarian, Italian, Polish, Russian, and Ukrainian). Moreover, Alberta has the most extensive bilingual schools program in the country (seven languages studied by 3004 students) and also supports "Saturday schools," attended by 10 806 students, representing 41 languages (Alberta Ministry of Education, 1992).

NOVA SCOTIA

Nova Scotia differs from the Western provinces in that it stresses intercultural education, reflecting the uniqueness of this province, which contains a deep-rooted black community (descendants of eighteenth- and nineteenth-century slaves and Loyalists) and where educational racial segregation existed until the 1950s in some areas (D'Oyley, 1978). According to McLeod (1981), "In Nova Scotia ... a broad cultural/intercultural thrust was adopted, based upon ethno-cultural awareness, equality of opportunity and equality of access, teacher sensitivity, curriculum reform, and the development of support services, program materials and resources" (p. 21). The province's Ministry of Education is currently in the process of adopting an official policy on these matters (Lessard & Crespo, 1992).

QUEBEC

Quebeckers of non-French and non-English origin, characterized as "cultural communities," constitute almost 17 percent of the population (Statistics Canada 1991a, 1991b). Since the 1970s, the Quebec government has implemented an assertive immigration policy in order to get its fair share of immigrants to Canada; this effort culminated in 1991 with the McDougall-Gagnon-Tremblay agreement, which gave important powers to the province in this matter (Québec, 1990).

After the period of the 1960s and early 1970s, when the province stressed the importance of the French language in all aspects of Quebec society, the Quebec government turned to the issue of cultural pluralism by the end of the seventies. While rejecting the Canadian policy of multiculturalism for reasons outlined earlier, in 1978 the Quebec government adopted a modified version of multiculturalism— "La politique Québécoise du développement culturel"—that stressed both the value of cultural diversity and the necessity of sharing cultural differences in a common society through a common medium: the French language (Ministère d'État au Développement Culturel, 1978). More recently, the province's policy statement on immigration and integration, *Let's build Quebec together*, clearly defined Quebec as a "pluralistic society open to diverse influences, within the limits set by the respect for democratic values and the need for inter-group exchange" (Québec, 1990). It also set forward three main orientations:

> increasing the accessibility and quality of French language instruction services and developing the use of French among immigrant and Quebeckers from the cultural communities; supporting the reception of newcomers and promoting full participation of immigrants and Quebeckers from the cultural communities in all aspects of social, economic, cultural and political life; developing harmonious intergroup relations among Quebeckers of all origins. (McAndrew, 1992b)

Generally speaking, although Quebec rejected the federal government's multicultural ideology, it committed itself to a series of similar interventions aimed at fostering unity and communication between groups, respect and support of cultural diversity, adaptation of the institutions to their pluralistic clientele, as well as equality and non-discrimination (Québec, 1990).

In the educational field, the Quebec Ministry of Education, since the 1960s, has established special programs fostering linguistic integration in the French schools (classes d'accueil) and supported the PELO (Programme d'Enseignement des Langues d'Origine, i.e., Heritage Language Program) now attended by over 6500 students in eleven languages (McAndrew, 1992a). The ministry has also encouraged the maintenance of heritage languages and cultures by unique subsidies of up to 80 percent of costs in ethnic private schools that meet the province's requirements for curriculum and language of instruction (McAndrew, 1993).

Until the passing of Bill 101 in 1977, more than 80 percent of Quebec's students of ethnic origin did not attend French schools (St. Germain, 1980), so the problem of communication between different groups in society and school has only recently been addressed. This neglect of intercultural education has created major challenges for the three communities (anglophones, francophones, and ethnic groups) that make up Quebec society—communities with a history of isolationism and prejudice. Intercultural communication and education is now emerging as one of the main issues in Quebec schools and society, and various government studies have stressed its importance (Québec, 1985, 1988; Conseil Supérieur de l'Éducation, 1983, 1987). This new awareness has led to the adoption of various measures regarding the elimination of stereotypes in textbooks, intercultural training for teachers, affirmative-action programs for the hiring of minority personnel, and the developement of school–community relations (McAndrew, 1993). Nevertheless, whether a Quebec society and school system defined as francophone *and* multicultural can offer a viable alternative to assimilation in the dominant anglophone culture of Canada and North America in general remains to be seen.

CONCLUSIONS

This chapter outlined the complexity of political socialization in multi-ethnic countries, especially when they define themselves as both pluralistic and egalitarian.

In Canada, we can see that the multiculturalism ideology grew from a political compromise aimed at appeasing the conflicting claims of various groups. In order to achieve this, the ideology stated that it is possible to resolve the "pluralistic dilemma" by favouring at the same time unity, diversity, and equality in Canadian society. Whether this can actually be achieved is not the subject of this chapter, but reinforcing national unity certainly has been the dominant goal of multicultural policy.

In the educational field, federal multiculturalism policy has influenced a variety of provincial "multicultural education policies." The ambiguity of the ideology of multiculturalism is reflected in the divergent stresses that each province places upon integration, maintenance, or intercultural measures in its definition of multicultural education and also in the extent to which cultural pluralism is considered as a priority over provincial cohesiveness. Indeed, provincial choices have reflected their regional traditions and values, and illustrated different interpretations of ethnicity among English-speaking provinces. These differences are still more evident in Quebec.

Ethnicity has emerged as an important component in educational issues in all parts of Canada. The definition of what constitutes legitimate curriculum and the debate around how far schools should adapt to ethnic diversity and ethnic needs have brought various groups into opposition, and neither definition nor debate are near to resolution.

As one of society's main institutions of socialization, Canadian schools will continue to be challenged by the necessity to educate future citizens to be able to live in a multicultural society even while they attempt to arrive at a viable definition of this "multicultural society." This often contradictory position is one from which schools cannot escape, given the changing face of Canadian society and the unique role of schools in finding viable accommodations to the pluralism question.

DISCUSSION QUESTIONS

❏   How do regional, economic, and political considerations affect the population mix of your community and province?

❏   Are multicultural programs necessary for all Canadian communities, or only those where there are significant minority populations?

❏   What kinds of innovations would improve the curriculum for your community or province? What factors inhibit the introduction of these changes? Who are the agents of change and how do they fit into the educational hierarchy?

❏   What do you forecast for the future of your community or province in connection with cultural differences and their impact upon school policy, including the curriculum?

REFERENCES

Alberta Ministry of Education (1992). *Current second language and bilingual (partial immersion) program activities in Alberta.* Language Services Branch.

Anderson, A.B., & Frideres, J.S. (1981). *Ethnicity in Canada: Theoretical perspectives.* Toronto: Butterworths.

Berry, J.W., Kalin, R., & Taylor, D.M. (1977). *Multiculturalism and ethnic attitudes in Canada.* Ottawa: Supply and Services Canada.

Breton, R., (1991). *The Governance of ethnic communities: Political structures and processes in Canada.* New York: Greenwood Press.

Breton, R., Reitz, J.G., & Valentine, V.F. (1980). *Cultural boundaries and the cohesion of Canada.* Montreal: Institute for Research on Public Policy.

Bullivant, B. (1981). *The pluralistic dilemma in education.* Australia: Allen & Unwin.

Burnet, J. (1975). The policy of multiculturalism within a bilingual framework: An interpretation. In A. Wolfgang (Ed.). *The education of immigrant students: Issues and answers.* Toronto: OISE.

Canada. (1988). *Bill 93: An Act for the Presentation and Enhancement of Multiculturalism in Canada.*

Conseil Supérieur de l'Éducation du Québec. (1983). *L'éducation interculturelle—Avis au Ministre de l'Éducation.* Quebec: Ministère de l'Éducation du Québec.

Conseil Supérieur de l'Éducation du Québec. (1987). *Les défis éducatifs de la pluralité.* Quebec: CSE.

Davis, W. (1977). Statement by the Premier of Ontario to a multicultural leadership luncheon. Toronto: Queen's Park.

D'Oyley, V. (1978). *Black presence in multi-ethnic Canada.* Vancouver: University of British Columbia, Centre for the Study of Curriculum and Instruction.

Driedger, L. (Ed.). (1978). *The Canadian ethnic mosaic: A quest for identity.* Toronto: McClelland and Stewart.

Edmonton Journal. (1984, October 18). Minority education amendment wanted.

Hazard, W.R., & Stent, M.D. (1973). Cultural pluralism and schooling. Some preliminary observations. In M.D. Stent, W.R. Hazard, & H.N. Rivlin (Eds.). *Cultural pluralism in education: A mandate for change.* New York: Appleton Century Co.

Holmes, B. (Ed.). (1980). *Diversity and unity in education: A comparative analysis.* London: Allen and Unwin.

Isajiw, W. (1981). *Ethnic identity retention.* Toronto: University of Toronto, Centre for Urban and Community Studies.

Laferrière, M. (1981). Éducation interculturelle et multiculturalisme: Ambiguïtés et occultation. *Canadian and International Education, 14*(1), 16–28.

Lessard, C., & Crespo, M. (1992). Éducation multiculturelle au Canada: Politiques et pratiques. Montreal: Université de Montréal. Repères, *Essais en éducation*, no. 14, 125.

Livingstone, D.W. (1983). *Public attitudes towards education in Ontario: 1982, Fourth OISE Survey.* Toronto: OISE Press.

McAndrew. (1991)

McAndrew, M. (1992a). *Relations ethniques et implication du système scolaire public dans l'enseignement des langues d'origine: Une analyse comparative du Heritage Language Program en Ontario et du Programme d'enseignement des langues d'origine au Québec*. Montreal: Les publications de la Faculté des sciences de l'éducation, Université de Montréal.

McAndrew, M. (1992b). *The Policy Statement on Immigration and Integration, "Let's build Quebec together," Towards a new intergroup consensus?* Paper presented at the CESA Conference, Winnipeg, October 25.

McAndrew, M. (1993). *The integration of ethnic minority students fifteen years after Bill 101: Some issues confronting the Montreal Island French language public schools.* Montreal: Direction des études et de la recherche, Ministère des Communautés Culturelles et de l'Immigration.

McLeod, K. (1981). Multiculturalism and multicultural policy and practice. In *Canadian Society for the Study of Education (CSSE) Yearbook.*

Maseman, V. (1979). Multicultural programs in Toronto schools. *Interchange*, 9(1), 29–44.

Mallea, J., & Young, J. (Eds.). (1984). *Cultural diversity and Canadian education.* Ottawa: Carleton University Press.

Ministry of Multiculturalism and Citizenship. (1991a). *Attitudes about multiculturalism and citizenship.* Ottawa: Supply and Services Canada.

Ministry of Multiculturalism and Citizenship. (1991b). *Le point sur le multiculturalisme.* Ottawa: Supply and Services Canada.

Murphy, R., & Dennis, A. (1979). Schools and the conservation of the vertical mosaic. In F. Juteau-Lee (Ed.). *Frontières ethniques en devenir.* Éditions de l'Université d'Ottawa.

Ontario. (1992). *Projet de Loi 21.* Loi modifiant la Loi sur l'éducation en ce qui concerne les commissions indiennes de l'éducation et les pouvoirs du Ministre. 2e session, 35e législature.

Ontario Ministry of Citizenship and Culture. (1988). *Immigrants to Canada and Ontario, 1925–1986.* Toronto.

Ontario Ministry of Civic Affairs (1991). *La stratégie anti-raciste pour l'Ontario.* Le Secrétariat ontarien de l'action anti-raciste (3 avril). Toronto.

Ontario Ministry of Education. (1975). *The formative years.* Toronto.

Ontario Ministry of Education. (1979, 1980). *Provincial review report, phase I and II.* Toronto.

Ontario Ministry of Education. (1980a). *Race, religion and culture in Ontario's school materials.* Toronto.

Ontario Ministry of Education. (1980b). *Heritage language fact sheet.* Toronto.

Ontario Ministry of Education. (1992). *Education statistics.* Toronto.

Palmer, H. (1975). *Immigration and the rise of multiculturalism.* Vancouver: Copp Clark.

Palmer, H. (1984). Reluctant host: Anglo-Canadian views of multiculturalism in the twentieth century. In J. Mallea & J.C. Young (Eds.). *Cultural diversity and Canadian Education.* Ottawa: Carleton University Press.

Pitman, W. (1977). *Now is not too late.* Council of Metropolitan Toronto.

Porter, J. (1965). *The vertical mosaic.* Toronto: University of Toronto Press.

Porter, J. (1975). Ethnic pluralism in the Canadian perspective. In N. Glazer & D. Moynihan (Eds.). *Ethnicity: Theory and experience.* Harvard: Harvard University Press.

Québec. (1978). *La politique du développement culturel.* Quebec: Ministère d'État au Développement Culturel.

Québec. (1985). *L'école québécoise et les communautés culturelles.* Rapport du Comité. Quebec: Ministère de l'Éducation du Québec.

Québec. (1988). *L'école québécoise et les communautés culturelles.* Rapport déposé au Bureau du sous-ministre par G. Latif, coordonnateur. Août. Quebec: Ministère de l'Éducation du Québec.

Québec. (1990). *Let's build Quebec together: Policy statement on immigration and integration.* Quebec: Ministère des Communautés Culturelles et de l'Immigration du Québec.

Rocher, G. (1976). *Le multiculturalisme comme politique d'état: Rapport de la conférence deuxième.* Conférence Canadienne sur le Multiculturalisme. Ottawa: Approvisionnements et Services Canada.

Royal Commission of Inquiry on Bilingualism and Biculturalism (1965). *A preliminary report.* Ottawa: Queen's Printer.

Royal Commission of Inquiry on Bilingualism and Biculturalism (1967). *Book 1: General introduction—The official languages.* Ottawa: Queen's Printer.

Shamai, S. (1985). *Ethnic relations in the Canadian context: The heritage language program conflict in Toronto.* Paper presented at the 8th Biennial Canadian Ethnic Studies Association Meeting, October 18.

Schermerhorn, R.A. (1970). *Comparative ethnic relations: A framework for theory and research.* Chicago: University of Chicago Press.

Senate of Canada. (1993, May). *Canadian citizenship: Sharing the responsibility.* Standing Senate Committee on Social Affairs, Science and Technology.

Smith, A. (1981). *The ethnic revival.* Cambridge University Press.

St. Germain, C. (1980). *La situation linguistique dans les écoles primaires et secondaires, 1971–72 à 1978–79.* Conseil de la langue française du Québec.

Statistics Canada. (1991a). *Population by selected origins, Canada, provinces and territories.* Ottawa: Statistics Canada.

Statistics Canada. (1991b). *Population by selected home languages, Canada, provinces and territories.* Ottawa: Statistics Canada.

Statistics Canada. (1991c). *Native and foreign-born population, Canada, provinces and territories.* Ottawa: Statistics Canada.

Toronto Board of Education. (1974). *The bias of culture.*

Toronto Board of Education. (1976). *Final report of the work group on multicultural programs.*

Toronto Board of Education. (1979). *The race relations report.*

Toronto Board of Education. (1980). *The challenge of languages.*

Toronto Board of Education. (1982). *Towards a comprehensive language policy.*

Toronto Teachers' Federation. (1983). *Role call: Special heritage language issue,* 6(1).

FURTHER READINGS

Anderson, A.B., & Frideres, J.S. (1981). *Ethnicity in Canada: Theoretical perspectives.* Toronto: Butterworths.

Holmes, B. (1980). *Diversity and unity in education: A comparative analysis.* London: Allen & Unwin.

Mallea, J., & Young, J. (Eds.). (1984). *Cultural diversity and Canadian education.* Ottawa: Carleton University Press.

13

EQUALITY AND INEQUALITY IN CANADIAN EDUCATION

Claude Lessard

The purpose of this chapter is to review the patterns of educational inequality in Canada. The chapter is roughly divided into two sections: first, an examination of the different meanings and conceptions of equal educational opportunity; second, an analysis of the data from a Canadian perspective (see also Carlton et al., 1977; Martin & Macdonell, 1982). The conclusion, building on the evidence presented and on some data pertaining to other countries, addresses some basic policy implications from a sociological standpoint.

EDUCATION AND EQUALITY: MEANINGS AND CONCEPTIONS

Following Lévesque (1979), we can identify three different meanings of "equal educational opportunity": equality of *access*, equality of *treatment*, and equality of *results*. Equality of access to formal educational structures and services means that all individuals, regardless of sex, race, religion, or social class, should have equal opportunity of access to education. Equality of educational treatment or equality within education requires that schools offer programs and use teaching procedures that respond to the expectations, needs, and cultures of diverse groups and be sufficiently flexible in structure to facilitate the learning of all individuals, regardless of their intellectual, social, or cultural heritage. Equality of educational treatment has generally been equated with uniformity of treatment for at least the initial stages in the curriculum, after which students would be "streamed" or "tracked" according to their educational performance. This differentiation of students was supposed to be determined solely by academic factors. The third meaning of equal educational opportunity focusses on equality of results or outcomes. This concept holds that school systems should compensate for the physical, intellectual, and sociocultural handicaps that individuals may bring to their schooling. Compensation would ensure that everyone in the system gets what is needed to function, contribute, and compete in the adult world.

As Husén (1979) and Lévesque (1979) indicate, the different meanings of equal educational opportunity reflect three different philosophies that have been prevalent since the industrialization of the Western world: the conservative, liberal, and critical traditions.

In most industrialized countries, the conservative conception prevailed throughout the nineteenth and early twentieth centuries. It considered that "aptitudes" and "gifts" were unequally distributed within the population, that this inequality was natural rather than cultural, and that it was up to individuals to develop to their fullest potential what nature had given them. This conception preceded the institutionalization of dual educational systems, with some form of public elementary schooling for all, and secondary and post-secondary education reserved for the elite. Problems arose when it was realized that the allegedly natural "aptitudes" and "gifts" were disproportionately found within the dominant social classes.

Although school structures have evolved along more unified and egalitarian lines, this conservative and elitist conception of schooling has not totally disappeared. Its contemporary version stresses that education fulfils its democratic responsibility to the extent that its doors are open to all, but that students who do not participate in schooling are either incapable or unmotivated. In other words, it is their problem, not that of the system or society. If some individuals do not obtain particular levels of schooling, the educational system should not be held responsible, since it is normal that schools should instead concentrate on giving gifted individuals the possibility of fully developing their "aptitudes." Others who are less "gifted" are expected, and often required, to have a shorter school career. This argument uses efficiency as a justification.

The liberal philosophical tradition holds that each individual possesses intellectual capacities and that economic, geographic, or other obstacles should not prevent that person from developing these capacities through formal schooling. Until the 1960s, schooling was conceived to be an instrument of social mobility (Horace Mann phrased it the "great equalizer" [Husén, 1979, p. 74]), represented by progressive, democratic institutions. It was also seen as contributing to the meritocratic organization of work and society in general. In most industrialized democratic countries, educational policies were designed and implemented to facilitate equal access to educational services. However, as major surveys indicated (Plowden, 1967, and Robbins, 1963, in Great Britain; Girard & Bastide, 1973, in France; Coleman, 1966, and the Organization for Economic Cooperation and Development [OECD], 1975, in the United States; and Forquin, 1979–80), the students who gained the most from the new school arrangements were already socially privileged. The democratization of school systems seemed to have little impact and influence on less-privileged social classes, both in terms of access to educational services and educational results. Within this context, the theory of reproduction (which views schools as agencies reproducing existing social classes and basic social hierarchies) was developed (Bourdieu & Passeron, 1970).

If equality of access to education and equality of treatment within education fare poorly with regards to educational inequality, and even worse with regards to social inequalities, then Husén (1979) questions "whether equality of results is more important than equality of initial opportunity. The practical implication of this is that extra resources should be provided for those who are socially and culturally disadvantaged" (p. 75). In other words, it is no longer sufficient to eliminate material and financial obstacles to schooling and to give to each individual the opportunity that fits best his or her aptitudes; equality of outcome implies unequal treatment favouring the less privileged. This unequal treatment has been called compensatory education. Its final objective is for children of low socioeconomic status to obtain educational performances comparable to children of other socioeconomic status. This reasoning applies also to other social categories (race, sex, ethnicity, geographical location). As Coleman (1966) wrote, "equality of educational opportunity implies not only 'equal' schools but equally effective schools, whose influence will over-come the differences in the starting point of children from different social groups" (in Husén, 1979, p. 72). Husén (1979) points out that

> the implication in terms of policy that ensues from the rethinking of the concept of equal opportunity is that it is rather pointless to put the final responsibility for scholastic success or failure on the individual. One has to shift the burden of responsibility to the system—to the educational system and/or to society at large. (p. 75)

In the liberal philosophical conception of equality, unequal educational results, even when they occur within a framework of equality of access to education and of equal treatment within education, are unfair to the individual who did not or could not profit from what society offered. From a critical standpoint, educational success or failure should be attributed not to the individual or milieu, but to the school. All children can succeed in school, and the best performances can be obtained by the majority of children *if the school system and its personnel respect their learning styles and pace.* Accordingly, schools should discard uniform structures for more differentiated and diversified patterns of educational practices.

The uneven success of compensatory educational programs has prompted further critical analysis of equality of educational opportunity, leading to the development of a global approach that stresses not only transformation of the educational system, but also of society—and its economy (Methe, 1983). The cause of educational inequality is here perceived to be social inequality. More precisely, educational inequality is seen as but one manifestation of social inequality that must be "attacked" or "treated" in a global or total perspective. Embedded in a matrix of relationships it helps reproduce, education cannot promote equal-ity within a basically unequal society.

Husén (1979) identifies two interrelated dilemmas concerning equality in education. The first is that the educational system imparts competencies and therefore necessarily creates differences. The school cannot at the same time serve as an equalizer and as an instrument that establishes, reinforces, and legitimizes distinctions. According to Husén, the only solution is to provide "multiple options based on different values that are not ranked along only one dimension" (p. 89). There must be more than one avenue to "the mainstream of dignity." Societies have to evolve along more pluralistic lines, with those aspects of culture that are incorporated within school curricula becoming less one-dimensional.

The second basic dilemma is between equality and meritocracy. According to Husén (1979),

> there is also a tendency for meritocratic prerogatives to be passed on from one gen-eration to the next. . . . The notion that the social classes will sort themselves out according to inborn capacity between generations is not supported by particularly con-vincing evidence. . . .
>
> There is an intrinsic element of meritocracy in the social fabric of advanced indus-trialization. It is connected with a strong demand for expertise, with advanced training in such fields as administration, technology, science, and communication (in a wide sense, including teaching). . . .
>
> Since economic growth so closely depends on efficient utilization of modern tech-nology and management techniques, a premium will be placed on competence that will guarantee successful incumbents an increasing number of key positions. The solution

to the equality problem is therefore intimately tied to how one resolves the problem of economic growth. (pp. 90–92)

The dilemma between equality and meritocracy does not simply refer to highly educated elites gaining more prestige, power, and influence within society. It is associated with the value attached to economic growth as a collective goal and to its perceived compatibility with one's conception of quality of life and social progress.

THE CANADIAN "FACTS"

This section reviews recent Canadian sociological literature on educational opportunity. It deals with research that addresses the effect that "background" variables (socioeconomic status, sex, geographical location, family size, birth order, etc.), school variables (type of program, teaching attitudes, ability grouping, etc.), and student variables (mental ability, achievement motivation, etc.) have on educational and occupational aspirations and expectations, educational achievement, and educational and occupational attainment. This field has been a major concern of Canadian sociological research.

Canadian data on educational opportunity must include John Porter's (1965) *The vertical mosaic*, a landmark book in Canadian sociology. Porter made significant contributions to the study of educational opportunity and achievement in Canada. Chapter 6 of *The vertical mosaic*, entitled "Social class and educational opportunity," used census data to show that the relative increase in the school population aged 10–24 from 1941 to 1961 was being best accommodated in Western provinces and certain cities. Elsewhere, drop-outs were common. When these figures were examined for the effects of socioeconomic class, using Blishen's occupational scale, it was found that class 1 (high socioeconomic status) fathers had 71 percent of their children (ages 14–24) at school, whereas class 7 (low socioeconomic status) fathers had only a little over one-third (34.8 percent) of their children in the same age group in school. Clearly, staying in school and going on to university was (and still is) associated with a father's occupational status. In Ontario, as Fleming's (in Porter, 1965) study of all Grade 13 students indicates, 39 percent of these students had fathers in professional, managerial, or executive occupations, while those occupations then made up only 16 percent of the labour force. At the other end of the occupational hierarchy, fathers in the semi-skilled, manual, and unskilled categories made up 31 percent of the labour force, but their children made up only 14 percent of Grade 13 students in Ontario. Bélanger's studies of drop-outs in Quebec in the early 1960s show that

> the most favoured children, from the point of view of staying in school, were those who lived in urban areas, who had a limited number of brothers and sisters, whose fathers were professionals drawing salaries which permitted them to have large well-furnished dwellings, and whose mothers were at home. The least favoured children of the province were the children of farmers of little education, in areas of low farm income, and with large families. (Porter, 1965, p. 182)

Porter's research also demonstrated the importance of social class position within the Canadian university student population. Indicators of family income, occupational level, Blishen's occupational scale, and the level of education of parents all point to the class bias of university students. Class was not random within faculties and professional schools:

law and medicine had a greater proportion of students whose fathers were professionals than did arts and science faculties. Fleming's major conclusion was that education to the university level was "to a considerable extent the privilege of a numerically small occupational class" (Porter, 1965, p. 188).

Porter's analysis of the Canadian census also revealed significant gender differences in school enrollment. In the 15–19 age group, 55.7 percent of females and 61.2 percent of males were in school. In the 20–24 age group, the gap increased: only 4.6 percent of females, as compared with 11.3 percent of males, were enrolled (Porter, 1965, p. 176).

The Carnegie Human Resources Data Bank, a five-year panel study of virtually the total population of students (90 719) who began high school (Grade 9) in the province of Ontario at the beginning of the 1959–60 academic year, has been drawn upon by three longitudinal studies.

A 1968 study done for the Royal Commission of Inquiry on Bilingualism and Biculturalism by A.J. King and C. Angi, entitled *Language and secondary school success*, provides data on the effects of language or ethnicity on educational attainment and the plans of Ontario students. The students in the Carnegie data bank were followed throughout their high-school years (until graduation or until they left school). Some results of that study were reported in the Bilingualism and Biculturalism Report (Bélanger, 1970, pp. 361–88).

The report stated that on the average, of 100 Grade 9 students from English-speaking families, 13 finished Grade 13 five years later; of 100 students from families other than those speaking French or English, 17 attained the same educational level. On the same basis, only three Franco-Ontarian students finished Grade 13.

Second, the drop-out rate of Franco-Ontarian students was both high and early: two years after the start of the Carnegie study, only 38 percent of the original Grade 9 Franco-Ontarian student population, compared with 52 percent of the original English-speaking students and 60 percent of students of other languages, were still in Grade 11.

Third, if geographical location (rural/urban), parental education, father's occupation, and number of children within the family explain part of the observed differences, one must also, according to the report of the Royal Commission on Bilingualism and Biculturalism (1968), look at school variables and how they affect Franco-Ontarian educational aspirations and achievement.

Clifton (1982) focussed on the academic achievement of German-speaking and French-speaking Ontario students. To explain the differences between ethnic groups in educational attainment by specific mediating variables, Clifton developed a theoretical model comprising ethnicity, socioeconomic status, intellectual ability, academic achievement (Grade 9), teachers' expectations, parental expectations, peer aspirations, student aspirations, and academic achievement (Grade 11). He too used the Carnegie data bank, from which he sampled French-speaking and German-speaking students. Path analytical techniques were used to verify the proposed model and to relate the questions raised to ethnicity. The results show that the "significant main effects of ethnicity as well as significant interactions between ethnicity and socioeconomic status and ethnicity and academic ability play important roles in the academic achievement process. In all comparisons, advantages accrue to the German students over the French students" (Clifton, 1982, p. 84). Clifton explains these results in structural terms as well as in terms of subcultural values. The German students usually started from more privileged socioeconomic positions. Their subcultural values reinforce aspirations that are congruent with success in education and work within a society that is mainly English-speaking. The French students usually came from homes of lower socioeconomic status; their subcultural values support the maintenance of their culture and institutions more than their integration and success within the larger societal context. Theirs is a "white siege culture" (p. 69).

The same data bank was used to analyze the influence of reference figures, including sexual difference, on educational aspirations in the adolescents' decision-making process regarding his/her educational future. Williams (1972) used a random sample of 5000 Grade 12 students from the Carnegie bank, with 3687 (1809 males and 1879 females) students enrolled in general academic programs forming the bases of the analysis. The theoretical model comprised the following variables: intellectual ability (Grade 9 [G9]), socioeconomic status (G9), academic achievement (G9), teachers' expectations (G10), parents' expectations (G10), peers' expectations (G10), peers' aspirations (G10), student's aspirations (G10), academic achievement (G11), teachers' expectations (G12), parents' expectations (G12), peers' aspirations (G12), and student's aspirations (G12). The complex path analysis (the model for males has 40 paths) can be summarized in the following propositions:

> The influence of adults as reference figures far exceeds that of student peers, a situation that offers support to the argument that the influence of reference groups cannot be generalized across all situations but, rather, is a function of the perceived expertise of the referent for the issue at hand. . . . The data seem to suggest that the educational decision to be made has (a) adult-world references (by virtue of its future occupational and socioeconomic implications) that establish adults as the appropriate reference figures, and (b) a greater saliency for males such that parental interests and influences are maximized, whereas for girls, where the decision is regarded of less import, the conduct of non-parental figures (peers and teachers) is allowed more importance. (Williams, 1972, p. 125)
>
> . . . the matter of a boy's educational future has a greater saliency for parents, who go beyond the visible evidence of his capabilities in forming their expectations of him. On the other hand, a lower valuation placed on educational attainments for girls would explain why demonstrations of ability have precedence for girls' parents in the development of their expectations. (p. 126)
>
> . . . teachers are influenced in the expectations they hold for boys in Grade 12 not so much by what the student does but by the educational expectations held for the ability group of which the student is a member . . . the particular structural arrangements schools make to deal with ability and/or performance may be crystallizing the expectations teachers have, tending to lock the student into an expected future. (p. 129)

Socioeconomic status plays a major role in the determination of parents' expectations for both boys and girls in Grade 10. In relation to academic achievement in Grade 10, socioeconomic background effects are relatively small and intellectual ability emerges as a major factor.

Breton's (1972) study gathered data on 145 817 students and 7884 teachers in all ten provinces. The first of its major findings, summarized in the concluding chapter of the report, states that the province, the size of locality of residence, and the presence/absence of postsecondary educational institutions are related to career indecision and educational plans. The more economically developed provinces seem to have higher proportions of students who intend to graduate from high school.

Second, there is a relationship between high-school students' aspirations and their social class position. Breton indicated that 14 percent more students from a high socioeconomic background intend to graduate from high school than those from a low socioeconomic background, and 12 percent more intend to go on to postsecondary education.

Third, the difference from low to high socioeconomic status of secondary-educational plans of boys varies from 8 to 21 percent (among the provinces). The difference from low to high socioeconomic status of *post*secondary educational plans for boys varies from 9 to 26 percent. The corresponding figures for girls are 3 to 24 percent (secondary plans) and 3 to 18 percent (postsecondary plans) (Breton, 1972, p. 156).

Fourth, there are no differences between English-speaking and French-speaking boys with regard to their intention of finishing high school. But, contrary to all expectations, more French-speaking students, boys and girls alike, intend to get a postsecondary education than their English-speaking counterparts. Breton interprets these results in terms of the expectations of the disadvantaged individual, who can set personal goals that are either very high or very low. Failure can be either stimulating or depressing. Minority group members may have low self-esteem because of their inferior status; the desire to raise their self-esteem often pushes them in the direction of "irrational" or "unrealistic" aspirations.

Finally, school variables are important determinants of educational aspirations. Foremost among these variables is the type of program of study (terminal or college/university preparatory). Breton's findings regarding French-speaking and English-speaking students' educational aspirations and his unexpected interpretations prompted a re-analysis and rein-terpretation of the data. Bélanger and Pedersen (1973) challenged Breton's data as well as his frame of reference. They showed that because of a higher drop-out rate among French-speaking students and the way the dependent variables were defined, Breton's study pro-duced artificially high educational aspirations for French-speaking students. Bélanger and Pedersen repeated Breton's analysis inside Quebec and obtained different results: French-speaking students had significantly *more* career indecision. And their educational aspira-tions differed from those of their English-speaking counterparts, who opted more frequently for professional sectors leading to high socioeconomic status (Bélanger & Ped-ersen, 1973, p. 102). The authors argue that national studies should systematically take into account important regional differences and that analyses of Canadian data, without proper consideration of regional differences, may be misleading. For them, Quebec appears to be an entity that is more sociologically significant than the country as a whole for the comparative analysis of the aspirations of young French and English Canadians. Lamon-tagne's comparative study (1983, pp. 176–97) of francophone education in Ontario and of anglophone education in Quebec is a good example of the type of study of minority education in Canada that Bélanger and Pedersen advocate.

During the 1970s, two major studies of this type were done in Ontario and one was done in Quebec. Porter et al. (1973) conducted a survey, *Ontario students' aspirations* (SOSA). It was partly co-ordinated with Bélanger et al.'s (1981) *Aspirations scolaires et orientations professionelles des étudiants* (ASOPE), done in Quebec. The SOSA study was reported in two publications: *Does money matter?* (Porter et al., 1973) and *Stations and callings: Making it through the school system* (Porter et al., 1982).

SOSA is a study of 9000 Ontario students and 3000 of their parents. The sample design was a stratified multi-stage cluster with language and grade (8, 10, 12) as the major strata. The study is not longitudinal; the authors call their group of students "synthetic." It is comprised of different students at different times.

The variables studied and their temporal ordering are presented in Figure 11.1. Cross-tabular analyses (Porter et al., 1973) revealed the following:

1. There is a close relationship between a student's social class position and his/her aspirations.

FIGURE 13.1

Temporal ordering of variables affecting educational aspirations.

Socio-cultural Climate Variables
—social class or socio-economic status
—degree of urbanization
—religion
—ethnicity
—cultural enrichment

Significant Other Variables
—influence of mother
—influence of father
—combined parental influence
—influence of teachers
—influence of friends (students' peers)

Demographic Variables
—sex
—age
—birth order
—size of family
—migration status of parents
—mental ability

All Other Variables

Occupational Variables
—occupational aspirations

Level of Educational Aspirations

Life Chance Perceptions Variables
—occupational expectations
—educational expectations

School Variables
—academic program
—school performance

Attitudinal Variables
—self-concept of ability
—attitudes of school work
—attitudes of teachers
—attitudes to the adult feminine role

Source: *Stations and callings: Making it through the school system* (Figure 3.2, p. 34) by Porter, Porter, & Blishen, 1982, Toronto: Methuen.

2. Family size is important to lower-class children.
3. A linear relationship exists between the birth order of a child and post–high-school expectations.
4. Self-concept of ability is related to social class.
5. Educational aspirations correlate with both urbanization and social class.
6. Regardless of social class, parents of Ontario high-school students hold positive values about education.
7. There is a relationship between mental ability and social class.
8. "Social class background has a greater impact than IQ in determining when a child leaves school" (p. 85).
9. The choice of program was related to both parental ability and socioeconomic status, and slightly more to mental ability.
10. "As much as class, sex determines a young person's expectations. For lower-class girls there is a double jeopardy" (p. 117).
11. French-speaking students have similar or slightly higher educational aspirations than English-speaking students.

To sort out the relative effects of these variables, and to determine how much of the variation in the educational aspirations might be attributed to each of them, Porter et al. (1982) utilized path analysis. But many variables that cross-tabular analysis had revealed relate to educational aspirations could not be incorporated into the path analytical model because of the model's assumptions and restrictions. Ethnicity, sex, urbanization, birth order, and size of family had to be dropped, but the path analytical model did contain socioeconomic status, mental ability, program of study, school performance, influence of significant others, self-concept of ability, and level of educational aspirations. This model was tested within each grade level and for boys and girls separately, with very similar results (Porter et al., 1982).

First, the model revealed that mental ability has a slightly greater influence than father's occupation on aspirations, through its greater influence on program. Program has a strong direct effect on aspirations, and also has an indirect effect through the influence of significant others and self-concept of ability. Second, school performance has a relatively insignificant effect on educational aspirations. Third, "the model might be described as one which is balanced between meritocratic and ascriptive qualities in that mental ability comes through as strongly as social origin, as measured by father's occupation" (p. 298).

Gilbert and McRoberts (1977), using the SOSA data and focussing on students' educational expectations (rather than aspirations), have tried to ascertain the relative importance of class background and the internal stratification system of schools. They oppose Breton's (1970) position that the internal stratification system of school (mainly the program of study) is more important than the class background of the student in determining the student's educational plans. Instead, they argue that one must not overemphasize the autonomy of educational structures, and that program of study is more appropriately conceived as an intervening variable than as an independent variable.

The authors tested with two models: a simplified one comprising socioeconomic status, mental ability, program, and level of educational expectations; and an extended one that also included mental ability, self-concept of ability, family influence, and academic achievement. The analyses reveal the importance of mental ability and show that socioeconomic status affects educational expectations through self-concept of ability and family influence, which both affect program and level of educational expectations. The study emphasizes not so much socioeconomic status itself as "the avenues through which it operates. . . . Our overall interpretive framework and one that appears to be supported by the data is that schools serve to perpetuate existing inequalities rather than to enhance equality of educational opportunity" (Gilbert & McRoberts, 1977, pp. 44–45).

In Quebec, a comparable, but longitudinal, study was undertaken by Bélanger et al. (1981). Twenty thousand students from secondary schools and CEGEPs, as well as parents, teachers, and principals, were observed. The first survey was conducted in the spring of 1972 among students who were at the time enrolled in secondary school: the first year (cohort 1), the third year (cohort 2), the fifth year (cohort 3), or the second year of CEGEP (cohort 4). Each year, from 1973 to 1977, subsamples of these cohorts were questioned. In addition, those students who dropped out of school and entered the labour market were also followed. The major findings of the study as they pertain both to educational aspirations and attainment are in Sylvain et al. (1985). They are as follows:

1. Access to higher education and more general equality of opportunity for education have improved during the period from 1972 to 1977, for both official language groups and both sexes.

2. If socioeconomic status does not have a greater effect among francophone students than among anglophone ones, it influences school careers up until the end of CEGEP.
3. At all decision points in education, students' choices progressively define and limit their future. This phenomenon is more pronounced in the francophone population than it is in the anglophone one.
4. Girls stay in secondary schools longer than boys. This is more true of anglophone girls. Francophone girls, on the other hand, tend to enrol more in CEGEP vocational courses.
5. In the first and fifth year of secondary school, the educational aspirations of English and other non–French-language students are comparable and higher than those of francophone students. Furthermore, when socioeconomic status is controlled, the educational aspirations of other non–French-language students appear significantly greater than those of anglophone students.
6. In general, students are aware of the limitations of their socioeconomic level, and their aspirations reflect them.
7. Sex has less impact on educational aspirations than academic achievement, socioeconomic status, and language.

In brief, the ASOPE data demonstrate that disparities in educational aspirations and attainments persist among Quebec's major linguistic groups — disparities that cannot be accounted for by the social composition of the linguistic groups, socioeconomic status, or the educational achievement of the students. It also shows clearly that educational inequalities persist within the francophone and the anglophone educational sector, a function of socioeconomic status, educational achievement, and sex.

In their conclusions, Sylvain et al. (1985) suggest two interpretations of the linguistic differences documented, by asking how value systems at various levels are related to culture, maternal language, and language instruction. However, the data do not answer this question; they only enable exploration of the hypothetical links between the "culture" and "school organization" of Quebec linguistic groups.

Other studies based on the ASOPE data bank have documented the importance of school variables (Ouellet, 1976) such as the public or private status of the school (Beland, 1978), the general/professional nature of program of study (Massot, 1979), ability groupings and time perspective (Mellouki, 1984), or socio-psychological variables like self-esteem. A systematic comparison of educational aspirations in Quebec and Ontario using the SOSA and ASOPE data banks has also been performed (Laforce, 1979).

A six-year longitudinal study of the educational achievements and work destinations of sampled Ontario high-school students by Anisef et al. (1980) gathered data in the spring of 1973 (Phase 1), November 1973 (Phase 2), October and November 1974 (Phase 3), and spring 1979 (Phase 4). The authors compare educational and work experiences of youths from different social backgrounds and different parts of the province. Many of their findings are congruent with those of previously presented studies, but those pertaining to the link between education and work are new and supportive of Marsden et al.'s (1975) study.

The following is a summary of the Anisef et al. (1980) study.

1. While socioeconomic status and other background factors are moderately related to the kinds of job and career beginnings of respondents, gender and educational achievement are stronger as determining factors. Postsecondary education amplifies, in a sense, socioeconomic status and other background differences. The choices of school and major or program aim a person toward a particular place in the occupational structure.

2. The segregation of the labour market on the basis of sex appears to have a profound impact on the kinds of jobs men and women obtain after completing their education. The majors and programs that men and women take in postsecondary institutions seem to feed into, and reinforce, the sex segregation of occupations (p. xxix).

3. With respect to current full-time jobs, 47.6 percent of men are found in white-collar occupations and 47.7 percent in blue-collar work, whereas 91.0 percent of women are in white-collar fields. In white-collar fields, men tend to concentrate in the categories of natural sciences, engineering, and mathematics; clerical and sales work; and managerial, administrative, and related occupations. Women tend to be found in the categories of medicine and health; the social sciences; teaching; and clerical and related jobs. Of women in the sample currently employed, 57.4 percent are in clerical work (p. xxx).

4. Women in the labour force are in white-collar fields, irrespective of educational achievement. Of women with university degrees, 42.4 percent are in clerical and sales work; 11.7 percent in teaching; 10.3 percent in natural sciences, engineering, and mathematics occupations; and 9.1 percent in medicine and health occupations. Of female College of Applied Arts and Technology (CAAT) graduates, 41.5 percent are in clerical and sales work, and 33.8 percent are in medicine and health areas. Of women with no postsecondary education, 84.6 percent are in clerical and sales occupations.

5. At the higher levels of educational attainment, men have an easier time obtaining the higher-prestige, upper-level, white-collar jobs. At the lower levels, women do better than men in terms of occupational prestige, shunning blue-collar work and opting for clerical and sales jobs.

6. High-school-only men whose current jobs date from 1978–79 earn, on average, $945 annually more than university graduates entering the job market in the same years; for high-school-only women, compared with university-degree women, the earning difference is $628, again in favour of the former group. University women earn, on average, 20 percent less than university men, whereas high-school-only women earn 30 percent less than high-school-only men (1978–79 current job beginnings) (p. xxxi).

7. A measure of underemployment, based on average General Educational Development (GED) scores by occupational unit group numbers, shows underemployment rates in current jobs of 42 percent and 56.1 percent for men and women university graduates respectively (p. xxxii).

Using the same data bank, Turrittin et al. (1983) explored the significance of gender role for educational attainment. Their analyses indicate that if good grades and high educational aspirations in high school lead boys to postsecondary education, academic programs, positive self-concept of ability, and high educational aspirations in high school lead girls to higher education. They conclude that "gender proves to be highly significant in the process of educational attainment ... schools play their role in the system of social inequality by allowing gender to be reflected in program selection and postsecondary educational aspirations, creating inequalities which are then amplified when women enter the segmented labour market" (Turrittin et al., 1983, pp. 415–16; see also Marsden et al., 1975).

Finally, on the importance and nature of teachers' expectations, Clifton (1981) and Clifton et al. (1986) have interesting results. According to their analysis of data obtained from a survey of junior-high-school students and teachers in Winnipeg, after controlling for the students' socioeconomic status, intellectual ability, academic performance, and expectations, it appears that teachers' normative and cognitive expectations of students from six ethnic backgrounds were affected by ethnicity and sex. Teachers seemed to base their expectations of students on both ascribed (sex, ethnicity) and achieved (academic performance) criteria. It is worth mentioning that these studies suggest that teachers have higher expectations, normative as well as cognitive, of female students than of male students.

STABILITY AND CHANGE

The question of the pattern of educational inequality in Canada has recently undergone empirical investigation. Guppy et al. (1984) have drawn data from the Canadian Mobility Study (1973) to chart the "educational attainment of Canadians from different social origins grouped into birth cohorts spanning a 40-year period, 1913–52" (Guppy et al., 1984, p. 321). Although historical trends were assessed by examining the educational attainments (elementary-secondary and postsecondary) of people from four birth cohorts: 1913–22, 1923–32, 1933–42, and 1943–52, neither ethnic nor regional differences were investigated.

The general patterns of the findings are consistent with the "diminishing effects" hypothesis (Guppy et al., 1984):

> High school completion rates have risen across the four cohorts from 37.1 to 67.5 percent. Furthermore, high school completion rates have increased for each socioeconomic category. Completion rates have remained the highest for the professional/man strata, increasing from 71.6 to 84.9 percent. For those from farming backgrounds, the rates have changed from 24.0 percent in the first cohort to 58.8 percent in the last cohort; the largest percentage increase over time for any occupational category. (p. 322)

According to the authors, the disparity in high-school completion rates by social origin, which was significant in the first decades of this century, has diminished, although it has not vanished. Using rates of completion instead of average years of education yields similar results.

Guppy et al. have not documented a gradual, uniform reduction in educational inequality, but one stemming particularly from the educational reforms introduced in the 1950s and 1960s. They note an ominous shift in the 1980s:

> Many of the reforms are now being withdrawn or sharply curtailed as governments react to the social and economic climate of the early 1980s. Should this process continue, the long term result of such retrenchment could be a return to the levels of educational inequality witnessed earlier in this century—a process which may enhance the importance of cultural capital as a vehicle to social reproduction. (Guppy et al., 1984, p. 329)

Recent data from Quebec indicate that the shift feared by Guppy et al. may be happening. Indeed, an Education Department study (1991) of secondary-school drop-out rates reveal their rise during the second half of the 1980s: a 20 percent drop from 1975–76 (probability of dropping out of secondary school, 47.9 percent) to 1985–86 (probability of 27.2 percent); the probability of dropping out rose to 35.7 percent in 1987–88. At the same time, the rates of passage from secondary to postsecondary education rose significantly: from 42 percent in 1979–80 to 63 percent in 1986–87 (CSE, 1988). This evolution points to an important split among Quebec's youth, separating those who do not complete secondary school from those who do and go on to postsecondary institutions (Lessard, 1994).

Dandurand and Fournier (1979, 1980), studying the evolution of Quebec's university student clientele, asked if Quebec's school reform of the 1960s presented real or fictional equality of educational opportunity. Their answer completes and refines the analysis of Canadian patterns of educational inequality begun by Guppy et al. Dandurand and Fournier's data not only document the socioeconomic status of the university population in 1961 and in 1978, but also the effects of sex and language on university enrollments and choice of faculty and discipline. If more students are from working-class origin (1961: 31 percent; 1978: 37.5 percent) or female (from 14 percent to 45 percent over the 1961–78 period), the socioeconomic status and sex distribution of students in the available faculties and disciplines indicates that they maintain their socioeconomic status. The ASOPE data bank contains information about the effect of language or ethnicity that supports the same conclusion. In other words, there may be more French-speaking, female, or low-socioeconomic-status students in Quebec universities than there were 25 years ago, but they tend to concentrate in the lower echelons of the hierarchy of university faculties and disciplines.

Dandurand (1990, 1991) and Cloutier (1990) provide information on postsecondary and university accessibility in the 1980s. Reflecting on existing statistics, Dandurand writes,

> While the postsecondary enrollment rate for the 18–24 age group was estimated at 3 to 5 percent during the 1940s and 1950s, it rose to 11 percent in 1960 and to 17.5 percent in 1970. It continued to rise until 1975–76 (23 percent) and then began to slow down from 1976 to 1980. Finally, at the beginning of the 1980s, in the midst of an economic crisis, the postsecondary enrollment rate once again rose, up to 37.8 percent in 1988. That year, 25 percent of the 18–21-year-olds were enrolled in the universities. (1991, p. 439)

Dandurand explains the progression of Quebec university attendance by the combined impact of social movements associated with feminism and Quebec nationalism. Indeed, the rise in enrollments is characteristic of female, francophone, and adult students. Female students now constitute the majority of the student population at the undergraduate level, and they have made significant breakthroughs in such important and prestigious fields as law, medicine, and administration. Dandurand notes:

> They form one of the social groups, if not the social group, that gained the most from the school reform. For reasons associated with the feminist movement, the greater integration of women within the labour force, transformations of marital and family life (Dandurand 1988), the educational aspirations and strategy of women have profoundly changed. Too often, we forget to underline that the rise of university enrollments, at least up to the early 1980s, was essentially a rise in [the number of] female students. In Canada, for example, the university enrollment rate of 18–24-year-old men was practically stable at 22 percent since the early 1970s (Fortin, 1987). (Dandurand, 1991, p. 441)

The greater access to Quebec's university also applies to adults, who now constitute the majority of the undergraduate population. Mainly of middle-class origin and/or status, these adults rely on the university for empowerment within the context of a professional mobility strategy or a career reorientation.

All these changes reveal, according to Cloutier (1990), an important change in the university student body. She ponders whether or not the "traditional" university student—young, male, middle-class, enrolled in a big-city university, full-time, with no interruption between pre-university and university studies—is being replaced by a "new" student clientele—adult (30+), female, working-class, part-time, enrolled in regional universities. Her analysis concludes that this indeed seems to be the trend and that the two types of students co-exist within a system of higher education undergoing a process of change.

Two final trends need to be mentioned. First is the professionalization of higher education; indeed, a majority of Quebec's university population is enrolled in some form of professional training (administration, applied sciences, health sciences, educational sciences, law). Second, two-thirds of today's university students hold a part-time job while studying. Dandurand (1991), who contends that the conditions of university students have deteriorated during the 1980s, postulates that young university students are claiming more and more autonomy and independence from adults and that there is a significant economic dimension to this claim.

WESTERN DEMOCRACIES

What about the prevailing educational situation in Western industrialized democracies? Using diverse sources of information (among them the OECD), Boudon (1973), while stressing the difficulty of international comparisons in this area, concludes that Europe has usually taken a middle path between the most egalitarian societies (the Scandinavian countries) and the less developed societies, such as Portugal (pp. 103–4).

The Canadian pattern of reduction, but not elimination, of inequalities seems to exist in different forms and degrees in other countries. Unfortunately, Boudon (1973) does not have data on Canada, so it is difficult to ascertain whether the Canadian situation is closer to that of the United States or Europe (for the United States, see Sewell, 1971). For a comparative analysis of American and European data, see Cherkaoui (1979).

CONCLUSIONS

Democratic societies have a long way to go in order to fully institutionalize the democratic ethos into their formal educational system. Equal educational opportunity may well be utopian or at odds with other basic societal characteristics. As Husén (1979) pointed out, it is a dynamic process, transformed over time through a collective will to reduce inequalities and transform society along more egalitarian lines. In the first section of this chapter, different meanings and conceptions of equal educational opportunity were discussed, emphasizing various definitions and showing how equality of educational opportunity is embedded within a broader matrix of social relationships. This process is by no means finished. All those committed to the development and success of equal opportunity should be wary of present socioeconomic conditions and governmental educational policies that seem to enhance inequality instead of significantly reducing or eliminating it. A global approach that stresses not only transformation of the educational system but also of the society—and the economy—in which the system operates is still very much needed today. As we now recognize, it is impossible to change society through education alone (Hurn,

1979; Jencks et al., 1972). Reforms in educational policy and practice must go together with reforms in other sectors of society if true egalitarianism is to be achieved within our democratic society.

DISCUSSION QUESTIONS

❏   What are the three meanings of equality of educational opportunity? How compatible are they with a meritocratic conception of society? What is your personal position on this issue?

❏   What are the major obstacles to equal educational opportunity? What are the best strategies to alleviate these obstacles? What should be the priorities of action in this area?

❏   Which sociological theory best describes your experience of the educational system? Explain.

REFERENCES

Anisef, P., Gottfried-Paaskhe, & Turrittin, A.H. (1980). *Is the die cast? Educational achievements and work destination of Ontario youth.* Toronto: Ministry of Colleges and Universities.

Beland, P.L. (1978). L'école privée et la democratisation: Sélection et procession. *Revue des services de l'éducation, 4* (2), 849–63.

Bélanger, P.W. (1970). L'école polyvalente: Ses incidences sociales. In P.W. Bélanger & G. Rocher (Eds.). *École et société au Québec, éléments d'une sociologie de l'éducation.* Montreal: HMH.

Bélanger, P.W., & Pedersen, E. (1973). Projets des étudiants québécois. *Sociologie et Sociétés, 5*(1), 91–110.

Bélanger, P.W., Rocher, G., Bedard, R., Beland, P., & Roberge, P. (1981). *Le projet ASOPE: Son orientation, sa méthodologie, sa portée sociale et ses réalisations.* Les cahiers d' ASOPE. (Vol.7). Université Laval et Université de Montréal.

Boudon, R. (1973). *L'inégalite des chances. La mobilité sociale dans les sociétés industrielles.* Paris: Armand Colin.

Bourdieu, P., & Passeron, J.C. (1970). *La reproduction.* Paris: Éditions de Minuit.

Breton, R. (1972). Academic stratification in secondary schools and the educational plans of students. *Canadian Review of Sociology and Anthropology, 7,* 17–34.

Breton, R., with the collaboration of MacDonald, J., & Richer, S. (1970). *Le rôle de l'école et de la société dans le choix d'une carrière chez la jeunesse canadienne.* Ottawa: Main-d'oeuvre et Immigration.

Carlton, R.A., Colley, L.A., & Mackinnon, N.J. (Eds.). (1977). *Education, change and society: A sociology of Canadian education.* Toronto: Gage.

Cherkaoui, M. (1979). *Les tendances de la réussite scolaire, sociologie comparée des systèmes d'enseignment.* Paris: P.U.F., coll. l'éducateur.

Clifton, R.A. (1981). The effects of students' ethnicity and sex on the expectations of teachers. *Interchange, 12,* 31–38.

Clifton, R.A. (1982). Ethnic differences in the academic achievement process in Canada. *Social Science Research*, 2, 67–87.

Clifton, R.A., Perry, R.P., Parsonson, D., & Hryniuk, S. (1986). Effects of ethnicity and sex on teachers' expectations of junior high school students. *Sociology of Education*, 59, 58–67.

Cloutier, R. (1990). *Les "nouvelles" clientèles universitaires québécoises: Différences et ressemblances avec le modèle de l'"étudiant traditionnel"*. Université Laval: Les cahiers du LABRAPS, série études et documents, vol. 7.

Coleman, J. (1966). *Report on equality of educational opportunity*. U.S. Government Printing Office for Department of Health, Education and Welfare.

CSE. (1988). *Le Rapport Parent, vingt-cinq ans après, Rapport annuel 1987–1988 sur l'État et les besoins de l'éducation*. Québec: Les publications du Québec et Conseil Supérieur de l'Éducation du Québec.

Dandurand, P. (1990). Démocratie et école au Québec: Bilan et défis, In F. Dumont & Y. Martin (Eds.). *L'Éducation 25 ans plus tard! et après?* (pp. 37–60). Quebec: IQRC.

Dandurand, P. (1991). Mouvements de la scolarisation, conditions de vie des étudiants et politiques d'accessibilité à l'université. *Revue des sciences de l'éducation*, 17(3), 437–63.

Dandurand, P., & Fournier, M. (1979). *Conditions de vie de la population étudiante universitaire québécoise*. Quebec: DGES.

Dandurand, P., & Fournier, M., with the collaboration of Bernier, L. (1980). Développement de l'enseignement supérieur, classes sociales et internationales au Québec. *Sociologie et Société*, 12(1), 101–32.

Forquin, J.C. (1979–80). La sociologie des inégalités l'éducation: Principales orientations et principaux resultats depuis 1965. *Revue française de pédagogie*, 48, 90–100; 49, 87–99; 51, 77–92.

Gilbert, S., & McRoberts, H.A. (1977). Academic stratification and educational plans: A reassessment. *Canadian Review of Sociology and Anthropology*, 14, 34–47.

Girard, A., & Bastide, H. (1973). De la fin des études élémentaires à l'entré dans la vie professionnelle ou à l'université. La marche d'une promotion de 1962 à 1972. *Population*, 3, 571–93.

Guppy, N., Mikicich, P.D., & Pendakur, R. (1984). Changing patterns of educational inequality in Canada. *Canadian Journal of Sociology*, 9(3), 319–21.

Hurn, C.J. (1979). *The limits and possibilities of schooling: An introduction to the sociology of education*. Boston: Allyn & Bacon.

Husén, T. (1979). *The school in question. A comparative study of the school and its future in western societies*. Oxford: Oxford University Press.

Jencks, C., et al. (1972). *Inequality: A reassessment of the effect of family and schooling in America*. New York: Basic Books.

King, A.J., & Angi, C. (1968). Language and secondary school success. In *Rapport de la Commission Royal d'Enquire sur la Bilinguisme et la Biculturalism. (Livre 2). Education*. Ottawa: Queen's Printer.

Laforce, L. (1979). *Les aspirations scolaires au Québec et en Ontario: Des observations des enguêtes ASOPE et SOSA*. Les cahiers d' ASOPE (Vol. 6). Université Laval et Université de Montréal.

Lamontagne, J. (1983). Minority official language education: Where can it be secure? In D. Ray and V. D'Oyley (Eds.). *Human rights in Canadian education*. Dubuque, IA: Kendall Hunt.

Lessard, C. (1994). La scolarisation, du déterminisme triomphant àl'utilitarisme straté-
gique. In F. Dumont, S. Langlois, & Y. Martin (Eds.). *Traité des problèmes sociaux.*
Quebec: IQRC.

Lévesque, M. (1979). *L'égalité des chances en éducation, considérations, théoriques et
approches empiriques.* Quebec: Conseil Superieur de l'Éducation.

Marsden, L., Harvey, E., & Charner, I. (1975). Female graduation: Their occupational
mobility and attainment. *Canadian Review of Sociology and Anthropology, 12*(4),
385–405.

Martin, W.B.W., & Macdonell, A.J. (1982). *Canadian education: A sociological analysis*
(2nd ed.). Scarborough: Prentice-Hall.

Massot, A. (1979). *Cheminements scolaires dans l'école québécoise après la réforme.
Structures décisionnelles dans le processus de qualification distribution du secondaire
V à l'université.* Cahiers d'ASOPE (Vol. 5). Université Laval et Université de
Montréal.

MEQ (1991). *La réussite scolaire et la question de l'abandon des études, un résumé des
plus récentes données disponibles.* Québec.

Mellouki, M. (1984). *Temps, temps d'apprendre et itineraires scolaires.* Les cahiers du
LABRAPS (Vol. 1, No. 2). Quebec: Université Laval, Faculté des Sciences de
l'Éducation.

Methe, L. (1983). Les stratégies face aux inégalités scolaires. In R. Cloutier et al. (Eds.).
Analyse sociale de l'éducation. (pp. 187–202). Montreal: Boreal Express.

Organization for Economic Cooperation and Development. (1975). *Education, inequality
and life chances* (Vol. 2). Paris: OECD.

Ouellet, R. (1976). *Influence de l'école sur les aspirations scolaires des jeunes de niveau
secondaire.* Quebec: Université Laval, Faculté des Sciences de l'Éducation.

Plowden Report. (1967). *Children and their primary schools.* London: Her Majesty's Sta-
tionery Office.

Porter, J. (1965). *The vertical mosaic: An analysis of social class and power in Canada.*
Toronto: University of Toronto Press.

Porter, J., Porter, M.R., & Blishen, B. (1973). *Does money matter? Prospects for higher
education.* Toronto: York University, Institute for Behavioural Research.

Porter, J., Porter, M.R., & Blishen, B.R. (1982). *Stations and callings: Making it through
the school system.* Toronto: Methuen.

Robbins Report. (1963). *Higher education.* London: HMSO.

Royal Commission on Bilingualism and Biculturalism. (1968). *Education.* Ottawa: Queen's
Printer.

Sewell, W.H. (1971). Inequality of opportunity for higher education. *A.S.R., 36* (5),
793–809.

Sylvain, L., Laforce, L., & Trottier, C., with the collaboration of Massot, A., & Georgeault,
P. (1985). *Les chemisements scolaires des francophones, des anglophones et des allophones du Québec au cours des années 70.* Quebec: Dossier 24 du Congrès de la
langue française.

Turrittin, A.H., Anisef, P., & MacKinnon, N.J. (1983). Gender differences in educational
achievement: A study of social inequality. *Canadian Journal of Sociology, 8*(4),
395–419.

Williams, T.H. (1972). Educational aspirations: Longitudinal evidence on their development in Canadian youth. *Sociology of Education, 45*(2), 107–32.

FURTHER READINGS

Baudelot, C., & Establet, R. (1989). *Le niveau monte*. Paris: Éditions du Seuil.

Boudon, R. (1973). *L'inégalité des chances. La mobilité sociale dans les sociétés industrielles*. Paris: Armand Colin, Collection U.

Breton, R., with the collaboration MacDonald, J., & Richer, S. (1970). *Le rôle de l'école et de la société dans le choix d'une carrière chez la jeunesse canadienne*. Ottawa: Main-d'oeuvre et immigration.

Cherkaoui, M. (1979). *Les tendances de la réussite scolaire, sociologie comparée des systèmes d'enseignement*. Paris: P.U.F., Coll. l'éducateur.

Dandurand, P. (1990). Démocratie et école au Québec: Bilan et defis. In F. Dumont & Y. Martin (Eds.). *L'Éducation: 25 ans plus tard! et après?* (pp. 37–60). Quebec: Institut québécois de recherche sur la culture.

Guppy, N., Mikicich, P.D., & Pendakur, R. (1981). Changing patterns of educational inequality in Canada. *Canadian Journal of Sociology, 9*(3), 319–21.

Husen, T. (1979). *The school in question. A comparative study of the school and its future in western societies*. Oxford: Oxford University Press.

Lévesque, M. (1979). *L'égalité de chances en éducation, considérations, théoriques et approches empiriques*. Quebec: Conseil Supérieur de l'Éducation.

Massot, A. (1979). *Cheminements scolaires dans l'école québécoise après la réforme. Structures décisionnelles dans le processus de qualification distribution du secondaire V à l'université*. Cahiers d'ASOPE (Vol. 5). Université Laval et Université de Montréal.

Porter, J., Porter, M.R., &. Blishen, B.R. (1982). *Stations and callings: Making it through the school system*. Toronto: Methuen.

Sylvain, L., Laforce, L., & Trottier, C., with the collaboration of Massot, A., & Georgeault, P. (1985). *Les cheminements scolaires des francophones, des anglophones et des allophones du Québec au cours des années 70*. Quebec: Dossier 24 du Congrès de la langue française.

Turrittin, A.H., Anisef, P., & MacKinnon, N.J. (1983). Gender differences in educational achievement: A study of social inequality. *Canadian Journal of Sociology, 8*(4), 395–419.

14

POVERTY AND EDUCATION IN CANADA

Paul Olson

UNDERSTANDING POVERTY IN CANADA

Poverty is a word most of us believe we understand. But do we? In Canada, poverty has historically been associated with happenings somewhere else—the Third World, ghettos, Native reserves, or the streets. Recently, many of us have seen the structural shifts in the economy and wonder if our futures will be poorer than in the past. Still, for many people, especially those in professions or the middle classes, poverty is a remote concern, one more for religious or humanitarian concern than for personal or professional worry. Yet is this the whole story? Encapsulated in a seemingly straightforward word—poverty —are sets of values and subjectivities, mores, and positions about other people in the world. Also involved are economic and social realities that are more than an abstraction to people who must live with poverty. These realities prefigure what one can do with those who are educated in conditions of poverty and how poverty itself can be influenced by education.

What is understood about poverty (and education) often influences outcomes. Poverty is therefore not a passively descriptive condition; it is socially constructed, and is mediated by how people understand, think, and act. It is a multilayered set of perceptions, relations, and actions toward people by people.

POVERTY, THE STATE, AND INDIVIDUAL AND COLLECTIVE INTEREST

Traditionally, people have had their own explanations for poverty. Many people see the poor as just lazy. Sociologically, however, we know that poverty tends to be neither random nor individual. Rather, it tends to be statistically associated with certain groups. Analyzing the make-up of these groups can help us shed light on the reasons why some groups are poorer than others. Often, we find that how rich or poor an individual is may depend on where (or even when) that individual lives. Most Canadians, for instance, have relative economic wealth because they live in an industrial country. In Canada, per capita family income in 1989 for a family of four was $51 342 (Statistics Canada, 1993a). By contrast, per capita income per person in much of the Third World is little more than several thousand per annum, if that high. The point is that material conditions are often beyond one's control, but can profoundly affect what is possible and what one experiences as "reality." One can be very industrious yet still be very poor. Collective or socioeconomic factors dramatically affect what can be accomplished in such contexts.

The relationship of wealth and poverty is also directly affected by government policies. Taxes, social programs, and schools are all forms of social policy. Such policies often create, as well as address, issues.

Pockets of poverty are found in every region in every province of Canada, with variations between northern and southern Canada, rural and urban. Generalizations are again dangerous since variations can occur both within communities as well as between them.

INDUSTRIALISM AND THE RISE OF THE WELFARE STATE

While Canada in the nineteenth century was still labouring under a variety of antiquated laws about poverty, gender, and the like, powerful new formulations associated with social and industrial relations were taking place. The Industrial Revolution was transforming Euro-American society and beginning to influence Canada. By the mid-1800s British liberals made a powerful variant on the theme of poverty as "just rewards." This was the rise of the welfare state spearheaded by the so-called "child-saving movement."

The child-savers (Platt, 1969) saw urbanization as destructive to the family. City slums were new "evils" that impacted especially on youth. Children in this new apocalypse were victims of the new social conditions and needed to be "saved." This new doctrine of child-saving, like today's "wars" on drugs, poverty, and social ills, had ardent support in the popular press, which (like today) alternatively portrayed the poor and youth as both villain and victim.

In asserting the incompetence of youth to fend off poverty, and therefore the need for the state to act as ward, the state also assigned to itself the right to intervene in poor children's affairs "for their own good." Curriculum theorist Madeleine Grumet (1985) has argued that curriculum is at its worst when the curriculum is "for other people's children." Grumet suggests that actions are taken on behalf of those who are supposed to be served by a governmental, educational, or service sector for their benefit; however, in fact, the aim of such action is to contain or limit those individuals so that they will not become a problem to society or the agencies that deal with them. Very often these actions take the form of policy decisions that those administering such programs would not allow to happen to their own children.

Helping the Children and the Poor or Controlling Them?

The idea of saving the poor was (and remains) very much a two-edged sword. On the one hand are the very real needs of the poor and the genuine efforts of many to help them. On the other hand, child-saving and programs for the poor may be seen as forms of containment of social programs.

In this latter thesis, the poor are problematic because of their potential to disrupt or limit a society. A traditional way of handling such problems was direct social control such as policing, prisons, and the like. In the nineteenth century, as Foucault (1979) and others have argued, the emphasis of social control shifted from regulation of the body by direct constraint (prisons, corporal punishment, expulsion) to control of the mind or of values held.

Socializing and regulating agencies became central to state operations. In this respect two independent theories put forward by American sociologist Amiti Etzioni (1961, 1964) may be useful to review. The first of these is Etzioni's hypothesis that one can tell the degree of social stability in a society by the types and amounts of social control it has to use. The most stable authority, in Etzioni's terms, is that based on normative regulations, wherein individuals conform to social values because they have been socialized to believe in them. Control is *internal*; that is, people believe in social values and therefore accept them. Most control in society, Etzioni reasons, is *utilitarian*. Utilitarian control is represented in the exchange of rewards. The most obvious example is that people work for money. If society offers the poor little opportunity, one way of making sure they are not driven to extreme measures is to establish some form of economic redistribution such as welfare. A cynical comment by a member of the British House of Lords in the era of Lloyd George is telling: Welfare, he reasoned, was the "ransom" the rich paid for peace. Etzioni's third form of social control is "direct coercion," or control through the legal system, the effect of which on society should not be underestimated.

WHO ARE THE POOR?

The poor in Canada are hardly a random group. Poverty has three general characteristics: it tends to be cyclical; it affects particular social and regional groups more than others; and it tends to be structural. Women and children make up 45 percent of all poor. Other groups are youth, the old, and marginalized groups, like Native Canadians.

Statistics Canada generates a series of reports detailing the income distributions in the country (Statistics Canada, 1993a, 1993b; see also Economic Council of Canada, 1992; Canadian Parliament, 1991). A brief review of these data is instructive. Statistics Canada determines that if an individual or household must spend 58.5 percent or more of total income on food, shelter, and clothing, they are considered poor (Statistics Canada, 1993a). Statistics Canada uses 1978 as its base year for constant-dollar comparisons of whether particular groups are "gaining" or "losing" in real dollars. Our comparisons in this section are based on these Statistics Canada criteria.

Let us examine our claims that poverty is cyclical, affects particular groups more than others, and is structural in light of the data.

THE CYCLICAL NATURE OF POVERTY

Statistics Canada estimated that in 1990, 13.2 percent of Canada's population was poor. This figure is 207 000 less than in 1987 and almost 800 000 less than in 1983 (Statistics Canada, 1988). The first half of the 1980s saw an actual decline in real wealth measured in constant dollars for most Canadians (Statistics Canada, 1989). The rate of real income growth for the 1980s as a whole was small: 0.05 percent, compared with 2.3 percent for the 1971–81 period or 3.9 percent for 1951–61. Within the 1980s there was a marked difference between the pre- and post-1985 periods. In the earlier period, incomes measured in constant or real dollars (dollars corrected for inflation) actually fell. The comparative rates of decline were greatest for men, although (as we will see) it was women who bore the disproportionate brunt of poverty.

The worst year of decline in the 1980s was 1982, when the country was in a recession. Poverty rates increased nationally and, to an even greater extent, regionally. Not surprisingly, the numbers of poor followed the economic trends and also increased. During the latter part of the 1980s, Canada was in a comparatively prosperous economic period, and levels of absolute poverty decreased. Boom times, however, do not account for all of the gains. As a group, Canadians were getting older, with the mean age reaching the thirties during the decade. Higher percentages of the population in the workforce also contributed to lessening levels of poverty. Thus poverty tends, in our current scheme, to mirror economic and demographic trends. With economic downturn, one can expect poverty to increase proportionally.

Much of the support for the poor in Canada has come in the form of social assistance programs devised by the federal government but implemented by the provinces. There was little change in the social support system of the "liberal welfare state" between the 1960s and 1980s. In fact, much of the state's handling of poverty was, until recently, characterized by indifference. Rodney Haddow observes:

> Despite the high public profile of poverty issues none of the national political parties gave poverty reform a major place in its program. In general they were not strongly motivated to reform policies what were mainly of interest to marginal citizens. (Haddow, 1993, p. 166)

Increasing pressures on federal transfer payments to the provinces are likely to mean that future poverty reform may depend on the extent to which Canadians can support programs already in place. Informally, various indices show that "social nets" are fraying. In the Christmas weekend of 1993, for instance, soup kitchens in Montreal fed almost 60 000, while in Toronto all shelters for displaced families were full and unable to accommodate everyone, including children.

HOW POVERTY AFFECTS DIFFERENT GROUPS

Gender, age, family arrangements, region, ethnicity, education, and geography are key determinants of who is poor. Single-parent families and the unattached elderly experience the highest levels of unemployment. Children accounted for one-quarter of all the poor in Canada (Canadian Parliament, 1991; Economic Council of Canada, 1992; Statistics Canada, 1993a, 1993b).

- *Age and gender.* One-income families had an average income of less than half that of double-income families. Young families have the lowest incomes of Canadians— 55.5 percent of young families have low incomes, compared with an average of 36.9 percent for all families. A lower proportion (46 percent) of those 70 years of age or more have low incomes (Information Canada, 1994; *Canada Yearbook*, 1994, p. 217). Low income is characteristic of certain categories of family status: 47.6 percent of lone-parent families headed by a female, compared with 16 percent for those headed by a male. Married couples with children or other relatives in the household have only 17 percent of the incidence of low incomes (Information Canada, 1994; *Canada Yearbook*, 1994, p. 218).
- *Marital status.* Single-parent families were virtually the only group that experienced no real growth in income. One-earner families had an average income of less than half.
- *Education.* The lowest poverty rates are found in families headed by holders of university degrees. The poverty rate was 6.8 percent for family heads with university degrees but 18.3 percent for family heads with eight years of school (National Council of Welfare, 1994).

- *Geography.* Percentages of persons living in poverty in 1990 varied from region to region. The lowest rates were in Prince Edward Island with 10.3 percent and Ontario with 10.9 percent, while Newfoundland with 15.8 percent and Quebec with 16.2 percent had the highest rates nationally. Differences within regions of various provinces were even greater, with noticeable disparities across the North. These areas are particularly susceptible to cyclical shift because of their dependence on single industries.
- *Ethnicity.* Canadians of European, and particularly Anglo-Saxon, backgrounds tended to earn several thousand dollars more than other groups. Many new Canadian immigrant groups, however, had incomes well above the mean.

POVERTY AND "STRUCTURAL ADJUSTMENT"

Our statistics illustrate that poverty is hardly random. In the 1990s Canada has experienced what many believe to be a global phenomenon; structural adjustment. Structural adjustment means that there are changes in where and how goods and services are made and produced. In general, the twin processes of technological replacement of labour and shifting of labour from comparatively high-cost areas (such as Canada) to low-cost areas (such as the Third World) are taking place.

The impacts of such shifts in developed countries like Canada in the early 1990s have been recessionary. This has had twin effects. First, the demands on social and educational programs have increased while resources have diminished. Government programs, such as transfer payments, have been reduced. Second, the "adjustments" do not hit everyone equally. Job losses in manufacturing, mining, and agriculture are borne by particular groups and social classes and sectors. People are either outright unemployed or transferred to where they are underemployed. This makes the so-called "high-risk" groups — youths, single mothers, the uneducated — more vulnerable. The process is not random (Gaskell, 1985).

THE FEMINIZATION OF POVERTY

In the last two decades, the feminization of poverty has become a focus of much research (Boyd, 1982; Connell, 1987; Connell, 1992; Eichler, 1986; Scott, 1984; Sidel, 1987). As family forms change, women are especially affected by poverty in a variety of quantitative and qualitative ways. The large number of single mothers with children under 18 (58.4 percent in 1992) means that many women are left to raise children on their own (National Council of Welfare, 1994). This not only leaves them with the expenses of child-rearing, but often limits their own ability to work. While female status in itself tends to be a factor in income distribution, other factors of social class (education levels, social prestige) further limit options to women. Women — particularly working-class women — are further burdened by a double standard: they are expected to carry out both paid work *and* domestic responsibilities.

Women are also burdened by a variety of other related economic factors. Particularly, there have been, and remain, income gaps between women and men. Jane Gaskell (1984, 1985) argues forcefully that these gaps are not attributable to "skill levels," but result instead from the ability of male-dominated trades to unionize, to restrict access to certification, and in general, to bargain for better conditions. Pat Connelly (1978) shows how, historically, women in Canada have also suffered by functioning as "reserve" labour, which Connelly typifies by the slogan "last hired, first fired." In the past decade, Canadian women have been entering the workforce in greater and greater numbers: today, 60 percent of women are in the workforce (Statistics Canada, 1993). In addition, women make up over one-half of those enrolled in postsecondary institutions: in 1992, women accounted for 54 percent of full-time college enrollments and 52 percent of university enrollments (Statistics Canada, 1993). However, women still tend to work in lower-paying jobs, just as they tend to be grouped into humanities, education, nursing, and other "traditional" areas in the postsecondary stream.

The second related consequence of the feminization of poverty is the increase in youth poverty: children of poor women cannot easily escape the cycle of poverty. Over half of Canada's youth living in independent circumstances qualify as living below the poverty line. (This statistic may, however, be a bit misleading, in that youth have the least access to jobs, are at the beginning of their careers, and are often in educational institutions or going through transitional phases in their lives.) Again, family situation plays no small part in this phenomenon. MacLeod and Horner's (1980) analysis suggests that families improve their economic chances if they remain united and both parents work. Double-income families are in fact a major stratifying variable on available income in Canada. The corollary is that single-income families undergo a decline in comparative income levels.

MacLeod and Horner also found that gains/losses in family income are influenced by the socioeconomic status of the parents. White-collar women benefit the most, in both percentages and absolute terms, from participation in the labour force, compared with their blue-collar counterparts. What all this means is that single, blue-collar women and their children bear a very heavy load in terms of poverty. The feminization of poverty is not only a "women's" issue, it is also very much an issue of marital status, occupational structures, pay rates, and social-class background. The biggest losers in this equation are the children of poor, single women.

SCHOOLING, SOCIAL CLASS, AND THE QUALITATIVE DATA: NEW EXPLANATIONS

The period since the 1960s saw a greater understanding of the relationship of schools, school curriculum, and education to socioeconomic status and poverty. A variety of studies (Apple, 1982; Bourdieu & Passeron, 1977; Connell et al., 1982; McLaren 1986) have illustrated that schools vary in the way they relate to children of different class backgrounds, and how they represent a systematic preference for middle-class values, language, and views of the world. Bernstein (1977) forcefully argues that the middle-class language/values of schooling represent a "code," or a way of mapping, that is accepted and sanctioned even by those members of society who are excluded by the coding. Bernstein documents how the working class and the poor vary in the form of their language (the working class tend to use nouns or "universal codes"). Despite formal differences in language, values, and world views between middle and working classes, the content of the two speech forms is equivalent. This was radically important, since it meant that in valuing one form as "correct" and the other as unacceptable, education was not measuring differences in "intelligence" or ability, but differences in cultural norms. This work also suggested that the curricular practices of schools actually drove a wedge between values practised in working-class homes and those practised in the school. Therefore it is on the basis of motivation (based partly on the co-operation of home and school) and access to varying degrees of difficulty of curricular material (based on evaluations of "ability" level) that schooling for working classes and middle classes varied.

This finding was noted in a variety of comparative empirical studies showing that forms of curriculum, testing, body regulation, level of material, and instructional techniques vary with the socioeconomic class being taught (Anyon, 1981; Connell et al., 1982). Working-class education tends to be rote learning, drill, and practice. Supervision is authoritarian and, as McLaren (1986) illustrates in his comprehensive study of under-class Portuguese youth in Toronto separate schools, the under-class face a rigid regime of both physical and mental control that contrasts dramatically with their outside lives.

HOW SCHOOLS FAIL THE POOR

We have noted that poverty tends to be structural and associated with various groups over time. Given the high expectation that schooling will attenuate poverty, it is reasonable to ask why education has not served the poor well.

Facile answers include variations on older moralist themes—i.e., viewing the poor as lazy, and the makers of their own destiny. Those who believe in genetic theories have their explanations, too (Hernstein, 1973; Jensen, 1973). But newer alternative explanations are evolving from empirical work within the micro level of schooling. Three notable examples of this newer work are studies by three Canadians: Jane Gaskell (1984, 1985), Alison Griffith (1984), and Ann Manicom (1981, 1984).

Manicom set out to examine how the teachers' work within classrooms related to the work of women, especially mothers within the home. Implicit was a second question: Why do teachers systematically report that they treat children equally when we know sociologically that outcomes of education are systematically skewed along class lines?

Manicom's empirical approach was to look at teachers' relations to students as "work processes" or material sets of practices. What she illustrated was that the work of teachers, especially in the elementary panels, was highly dependent on the implicit assumption that someone else (the mother at home) had already done some type of prior work. If a parent has done some prior work at home, such as instructing the child to draw or to "place paint brushes only in similar coloured paint jars," then one can proceed to other, more complex levels. If no one has given such instructions at home, the teacher must retard progress in order to reach this level. This is where the problem begins. Middle-class and better-educated parents tend to have the material circumstances and time to undertake such activities. Poorer and single-parent families often do not. The material practices of middle-class parents tend to complement the work of teachers, while the demands for child care, employment, and meeting basic needs of poorer mothers often conflict with the demands of the teachers.

In observing differences in "who can draw"—to continue the analogy—the teacher is really seeing differences in experience with drawing and not in innate talent or ability. Nonetheless, it is extremely easy for teachers (because of their own work demands) to view such differences not as experience differences (needing a few extra lessons), but as ability differences. What is insidious about such a judgement is that it quickly leads to tracking and stratification based on explicit or tacit labelling procedures. Children's access to knowledge therefore becomes limited.

Manicom's work complements Bernstein's early research on how the middle-class bias of language in schools effectively forced poorer and working-class children to operate in a foreign environment. Empirically, we know that poorer children are highly streamed in the school structure (Harris, 1989; Oakes, 1985). The result is that in 1985, one-third of children dropped out before finishing high school (Radwanski, 1987). In so-called general streams, where many of the poor are assigned, the dropout rate is two-thirds, and the real task of teaching is what might loosely be called "crowd control" (Jackson, 1968).

One significance of Manicom's work is that it illustrates that the evaluation and sifting taking place in tracking is not, as is often alleged, based on "natural" variation, but is instead based on a systematic reading of behaviour that has meaning according to the teacher's and the school's own special mandates. The processes and evaluations of schooling form, as well as mirror, results.

Manicom's work meshes nicely with the work of Griffith (1984), who empirically studied how the idea of "single parent" was treated by school systems in Vancouver and Toronto. In her study, educators claimed that the term "single parent" was used by schools only nominally. There were indications that no evaluation was placed on it, and that it was merely descriptive. When Griffith examined official records and files, a variety of patterns emerged that led her to question whether or not the use of such terms was strictly nominal. First, certain single parents were almost never referred to as such. Widows, for instance, were seldom classified as "single parents." More tellingly, "single parent" was used almost exclusively to describe possible causes for school failure or delinquency. By contrast, it was virtually never used to explain school achievement, even though numerous such instances could be cited. Sometimes the same parent would be listed in relation to a troublesome child as "single parent" and not so with a child doing academically well. Files often cited single parenthood as the "cause" of a child's problems; there were no testimonials of a child's doing well due to the excellent single parenting he or she was receiving at home.

Griffith found a further point of interest regarding this pattern. "Single parent" was most often used in official records to describe middle-class mothers. Her analysis of the reasons for this parallelled the notion of Bernstein's codes. "Code" in this instance means a set of implicit, institutionally understood terms of communication between formal agencies and workers, especially those described earlier as "para-professionals." "Single parent" as a key term was nested within a hierarchy of value-judgement labels that could supersede less powerful ones. In the official records, one did not need to use the term "single parent" as a tacit way of signalling to other professionals "this one is trouble" if one had other, even more powerful, coding labels such as "working class," "poor," "Native," "disadvantaged," "visible minority," "special," or the like. Gender, Griffith argued, was a layer of social convention that worked inside of class and racial hierarchies. If one was poor, or from an under-class ethnic group (Native, Portuguese, etc.), key institutional labelling had been done. "Single parent" only came to the fore as a "blame-the-victim" strategy when gender (and single parenting) were the only aberrations from the social ideal — in this case, the unspoken belief/role/code that children should live in traditional two-parent families like those of 1950s American television.

A third useful empirical analysis of class and gender difference in schooling comes from Gaskell's work in British Columbia (1984, 1987). Her findings were consistent with data discussed earlier: that the kinds of curriculum knowledge given in schools varies greatly in pedagogical style, context, rigour, and relevance, and is based on social class, economic background, and gender. In being taught to use computers, for instance, academic-stream learners (disproportionately boys) were taught math, logic, and programming. These are advanced skills with general applications. Girls in business streams, by contrast, were taught rote procedures, such as how to load punch cards on machines, even when these procedures were obsolete in actual applied business.

Gaskell also illustrated that few girls in such programs had romantic illusions that their own training would yield them rewarding careers. The reason, Gaskell showed, why girls stayed with such programs despite the fact that they recognized them to be poor, was that they judged the programs to be comparatively more relevant to their own life expectations than other school choices. One-half of all women employed in British Columbia are office workers. Among working-class women, 75 percent are office workers whose salary levels tend to peak ten years before those of their male counterparts.

POVERTY AND TEACHING

In teaching, the attitudes toward poverty that we have been discussing are often tacit, but powerful, factors in what the teacher is able to accomplish. This is because teaching itself is a work process dependent, as Manicom and others describe, on the norms, expectations, and resources children themselves bring to the classroom. There is a truism in teaching: teachers "teach to means but spend their time on extremes." In practice, this means that most teachers attempt to determine what the mean, or average, level of their class's ability may be. Teachers then attempt to teach according to this mean. Students who fall at the extremes of this curve—ironically, both the brightest and the most disruptive—are the ones on whom teachers spend the vast majority of their time. This phenomenon has two important consequences. First, if there are large numbers of "difficult" students, teaching automatically becomes more difficult. While poverty in itself is not a cause of or factor in "problems" at school, it is statistically associated with a variety of problems such as: higher rates of domestic violence, problems of self-esteem, higher incidence of health problems, differential rates of academic preparation, and so on. This suggests that teachers with higher rates of poor children also have lower expectations of what they may hope to accomplish because, in effect, their work load is increased.

A second consequence of this "loading" of student potentials is that many who are poor—because of poor family histories, experience with schooling, or a sense of being different—remain comparatively silent in the classroom. Teachers themselves may expect less or pay less attention to these students. Much of this type of analysis is embedded in the older idea that poverty is an intergenerational pattern.

Robert Connell and associates (1992) helped to illustrate that even intervention programs aimed at the poor (either official "inner-city" or "rural" poverty indices kept by many school boards across Canada) or individual actions of teachers to deal with poverty emphasize the "disadvantaged" or "deficient" factors, such as those cited above. What is invisible in these initiatives are class- and gender-based "differences." Many of the linguistic differences between the classes have historically resulted in a vocational/academic split wherein the poor were seen to be wedded to manual vocations. What we have seen in the past decade, as noted above, is that this dichotomy itself is linked to the increasing feminization of poverty, and that, consequently, state interventions such as social assistance become the tacit "father" in the relationship. What is important to recall here is that differences in class, family form, and economic situation as such are not good indices for intelligence, ability, or experience. Teaching itself should require an awareness of these differences and should not let implied means, supposed ability, or cultural differences determine how teachers view and act upon their students' abilities.

CONCLUSIONS

As we have seen, poverty tends to be structural, affecting women, children, and those in particular situations—such as the elderly, single parents, minorities, or inhabitants of specific regions. Moreover, poverty is often the result of constructed social policies and situations, and not of moral failings.

We have also seen that since the 1960s, numerous policy actions and programs pointed at ending poverty have been initiated, usually as remedies for "cultural deprivation" or to overcome "disadvantages." Since most of these have not worked, a key question is whether they *could* work and, if so, how?

Manicom, Griffith, and Gaskell suggest that at least part of why schools fail working-class children is that the labour practices of schools, the nature of the curriculum, the labelling and processing of children, and the differentiation of curriculum all make schooling less than relevant. Evaluations and differences are often not the result of "ability" or "cultural deprivation," but instead reflect differences in the amounts of time spent on particular tasks.

We know that programs for the disadvantaged (Connell et al., 1990, 1992) and headstart programs do help children. What they require is extensive labour and material commitment, which must attend to where the child comes from and not solely where the teacher or school would like to take "other people's children." Few would argue with the principle that each child should have access to needed resources; however, in reality, poor children seldom have that access. One reason is that such activity requires very real time and money. Teaching a child to read means someone must sit with that child—be it a parent, a teacher, a helper, or another child—and someone must organize and finance this undertaking. Will it be done?

If history is a guide, the most probable answer is no, because costs are real and those who are poor—women, children, and the marginal—are the least able to lobby for their own interests. Also, it is unlikely to happen because the reality of mass "people processing" is still too often undertaken for reasons of social control or in order to blame rather than to serve clients. What is needed is better support (day care, support teachers, programs to get people involved with others, alternative curricula, and new evaluation techniques). All of this is costly, and governments give it low priority.

But the cost of ignoring such programs grows. Costs of all social programs escalate when one program fails to address a specific social need. But the potential of moving even a portion of Canada's poor youth to the mean income level would result in literally billions of dollars in increased national wealth and competitiveness. At an individual level, the impact is also great: material rewards and enhanced dignity.

What must be emphasized is that poverty is not a given or natural phenomenon. It is constructed (and perpetuated) by things we do both socially and individually. It is easy to shift the blame for poverty. It is even easier (if it does not directly affect us) to ignore it. Yet to do so is to make us all less than we might be.

DISCUSSION QUESTIONS

❑ Canadian education is well supported financially by comparison with most other systems; in some ways schools represent an important step for the poor. In what ways could reforms ensure that education leads to a better, more financially rewarding life for the poor?

❑ Are schools isolated from the other institutions of society, so that the forces of poverty are less recognized there, and consequently not addressed? What reforms are appropriate?

❑ Some idealists have overcome the limitations of their time and place. Why do idealists have little impact upon society? Is idealism an advantage or a disadvantage?

REFERENCES

Anyon, J. (1981). Elementary schooling and distinctions of Class. *Interchange, 12*(2/3), 18–32.

Apple, M. (Ed.). (1982). *Cultural and economic reproduction in education.* Boston: Routledge and Kegan Paul.

Bernstein, B. (1972). *Class, codes and control.* (Vol. 3). London: Routledge and Kegan Paul.

Bernstein, B. (1977). Class and pedagogies: Visible and invisible. In J. Karabel & A.H. Halsey (Eds.). *Power and ideology in education.* New York: Oxford University Press.

Bernstein, B. (1982). Codes, modalities and the process of cultural reproduction. In M. Apple (Ed.). *Cultural and economic reproduction in education.* London: Routledge and Kegan Paul.

Bourdieu, P., & Passeron, J.P. (1977). *Reproduction in education, society and culture.* Beverly Hills: Sage.

Boyd, M. (1982). Sex differences in the Canadian occupational attainment process. *Canadian Review of Sociology and Anthropology, 19*(1), 1–28.

Canada Yearbook. (1994).

Canadian Parliament. (1991). *House of Commons Sub-committee on Poverty.* Ottawa: Queen's Printer.

Connell, R.W. (1987). *Gender and power.* Palo Alto: Stanford University Press.

Connell, R.W., Ashenden, D.J., Kessler, S., & Dowsett, G.W. (1982). *Making the difference: Schools, families, and social divisions.* Sydney: Allen and Unwin.

Connell, R.W., Ashenden, D.J., Kessler, S., & Dowsett, G.W. (1982). *Teachers' work.* Sydney: Allen and Unwin.

Connell, R.W., White, V., & Johnson, K. (1990). *Poverty, education and the disadvantaged schools program (D.S.P.).* Sydney: Department of Employment and Training at Macquarie University.

Connell, R.W., White, V., & Johnston, K. (1992). An experiment in justice: The disadvantaged schools program and the question of poverty, 1974–1990. *British Journal of Sociology of Education, 13*(4), 447–64.

Connelly, P. (1978). *Last hired, first fired: Women and the Canadian workforce.* Toronto: Women's Educational Press.

Economic Council of Canada. (1992). *The new face of poverty: Income security needs of Canadian families.* Ottawa: Ministry of Supply and Services Canada.

Eichler, M. (1986). *Families in Canada.* Toronto: OISE Press.

Etzioni, A. (1961). *Complex organizations: A sociological reader.* New York: Holt, Rinehart and Winston.

Etzioni, A. (1964). *Modern organizations.* Englewood Cliffs, NJ: Prentice-Hall.

Foucault, M. (1979). *Discipline and punishment.* New York: Vintage Books.

Gaskell, J. (1984). Gender and course choice: The orientations of male and female students. *Journal of Education, 166*(1), 89–102.

Gaskell, J. (1985). Course enrolment in the high school: The perspective of working class females. *Sociology of Education, 58*(1), 48–59.

Griffith, A.I. (1984). *Ideology, education and single-parent families: The normative ordering of families through schooling.* Ph.D. thesis. Toronto: OISE.

Grumet, M. (1985, March). *Other people's children.* Paper presented to OISE.

Haddow, R. (1993). *Poverty reform in Canada; State and class influences on policy making.* Kingston and Montreal: McGill–Queen's University Press.

Harris, P. (1989). *Child poverty, inequality, and social justice.* Melbourne: Brotherhood of St. Lawrence.

Hernstein, R. (1973). *IQ in the meritocracy.* Boston: Little, Brown.

Information Canada. (1994).

Jackson, P. (1968). *The practice of teaching.* New York: Teachers College Press.

Jencks, C., Bartlett, S., Corcoran, M., Crouse, J., Eaglesfield, D., Jackson, G., McClelland, K., Mueser, P., Olneck, M., Swartz, J., Ward, S., & Williams, J. (1979). *Who gets ahead?* New York: Basic Books.

Jencks, C., Smith, M., Acland, H., Bane, M.J., Cohen, D., Gintis, H., Heyns, G., & Stephan, M. (1972). *Inequality: A reassessment of the effect of family and schooling in America.* New York: Harper and Row.

Jensen, A. (1973). *Educability and group difference.* New York: Harper and Row.

McLaren, P. (1986). *Schooling as a ritual performance.* Boston: Routledge and Kegan Paul.

MacLeod, N., & Horner, K. (1980). *Analyzing post-war changes in the Canadian income distribution.* Winnipeg: Economic Council of Canada.

Manicom, A. (1981, October). *Reproduction of class: The relations between two work processes.* Paper presented to the Political Economy of Gender Relations in Education Symposium. Toronto: OISE.

Manicom, A. (1984). Feminist frameworks and teacher education. *Journal of Education, 166*(1), 77–87.

National Council of Welfare. (1994). *Poverty profile 1992.* Ottawa: National Council of Welfare.

Oakes, J. (1985). *Keeping track: How schools structure inequality.* New Haven: Yale University Press.

Platt, A. (1969). *The child savers.* Chicago: University of Chicago Press.

Porter, J. (1965). *The vertical mosaic: An analysis of social class and power in Canada.* Toronto: University of Toronto Press.

Porter, J., Porter, M., & Blishen, B.A. (1982). *Stations and callings: Making it through the school system.* Toronto: Methuen.

Radwanski, G. (1987). *Ontario study of the relevance of education and the issue of drop-outs*. Toronto: Ministry of Education.

Scott, H. (1984). *Working your way to the bottom: The feminization of poverty*. London: Pandora Press.

Sidel, R. (1987). *Women and children last: The plight of poor women in affluent America*. New York: Penguin.

Statistics Canada. (1988). *Family incomes, census families*. Ottawa: Government Printing Services.

Statistics Canada. (1989). *Total income: Individuals*. Ottawa: Ministry of Regional Industrial Expansion and the Ministry for Science and Technology, in co-operation with Canadian Government Publishing Centre and Statistics Canada.

Statistics Canada. (1993). *Selected income data*. Ottawa: Statistics Canada.

FURTHER READINGS

Eichler, M. (1979). *The double standard: A feminist critique of feminist social science*. New York: St. Martin's Press.

Love, R., & Wolfson, M. (1976). *Income inequality: Statistical methodology and Canadian illustrations*. Ottawa: Statistics Canada.

Sutherland, N. (1976). *Children in English-Canadian society: Framing the twentieth century consensus*. Toronto: University of Toronto Press.

Willis, P. (1977). *Learning to labour: How working class kids get working class jobs*. London: Collier Macmillan.

15

ADULT EDUCATION ISSUES IN CANADA

Deo H. Poonwassie

This chapter is an overview of selected topics that are crucial to the roles of adult education in the development of Canadian society. The controversy surrounding the definition, the study, and the practice of adult education will be examined. The question of adult education as an initiator of social change will be introduced in light of the changing dimensions of our nation; as well, ideas about the future of adult education will be discussed.

A PROBLEM OF DEFINITION

In our society, it is generally assumed that young people will attend school up to the age of 16 (at which age they can also receive a driver's licence). For some reason, we have identified this magic number as an age of responsibility for some things. Other responsible actions must wait for a few years; a minimum of 18 is required for voting and the consumption of alcohol in public places, but one can join the armed forces at the age of 17 and learn to kill! Thus, in our society, we arbitrarily make a connection between chronological age and expectations of responsible "adult" actions. Indeed, the genetic epistemologist Jean Piaget made various connections between chronological age and mental development in his studies on cognitive development (Piaget, 1968). However, society's expectations go one step further by assuming that levels of mental maturity translate into what is deemed responsible action (one of the criteria being what is acceptable according to law). How then do we explain the term "adult"?

There is no universally acceptable definition of adult; the term is culture bound and even within cultures and nations the criteria for separating adulthood from childhood are unclear and varied. However, certain criteria of adulthood are used in many industrialized countries such as Canada; these are: chronological age; social (civic) responsibility; ability to have a family (post-puberty), and the capacity to provide for oneself and/or family (independence through work). These are the most often generalizable, controversial, contradictory, but nonetheless utilized criteria for determining who is an adult. Furthermore, it is also clear that emphasis may be placed on different indicators according to what is under consideration: for example, the ability to have a family is not considered when deciding who can vote.

Another term that needs definition is "education." Many scholars (Freire, 1972; Peters, 1966; Scheffler, 1960; Soltis, 1968; Whitehead, 1929) have tried to clarify various meanings, proposing criteria that must be satisfied before one can speak of education. Three common terms in the writings of these scholars are the self, the environment, and learning —each of which can be described and expanded to include several volumes; hence these terms must be interpreted quite broadly. For example, the term "environment" includes social, political, and economic conditions, as well as the physical and intellectual surroundings in which a person is situated. Thus education may be defined as the critical awareness of one's environment through continuous learning.

A consideration of the terms "adult" and "education" exposes the complexities and ambiguities of meaning encountered in the literature. Combining these two words to produce "adult education" makes the problem of defining this term even more difficult as the sum of the parts does not equal the whole; in this case, adult education transcends the combined meaning of the two words. The term "adult education" is considered elsewhere, and an excellent summary on an international level is provided by Thomas (1981, 1988). However, it may be helpful for the reader to consider a definition provided by UNESCO (1980):

> the term "adult education" denotes the entire body of organized educational processes, whatever the content, level and method, whether formal or otherwise, whether they prolong or replace initial education in schools, colleges and universities as well as in apprenticeship, whereby persons regarded as adult by the society to which they belong develop their abilities, enrich their knowledge, improve their technical or professional qualifications or turn them in a new direction and bring about changes in their attitudes and behaviour in the twofold perspective of full personal development and participation in balanced and independent social, economic and cultural development. (p.3)

This definition is all inclusive, detailed, ambiguous, and contradictory. The problems of defining adult education will be considered again in some detail later in this chapter.

THE IMPORTANCE OF ADULT EDUCATION IN CANADA

Within the past two decades Canada has experienced a noticeable shift toward conservatism: the radical left of the 1960s and early 1970s has gone underground and the conservative right has taken over; the national economy has moved toward privatization, and social services have been reduced. Social action has been evident only when the individual has been affected financially, as in labour disputes (such as the closing of fish plants in Nova Scotia or the social contract policy in Ontario) or the introduction of the Goods and Services Tax. In spite of high unemployment, the national obsession has become deficit reduction.

Many projections have been made about Canada's population; the common finding indicates the growth of an aging population (Stone, 1983; Royal Bank, 1989). According to Thornton (1990, p. 384), "within thirty years, approximately 22%–25% of the Canadian population will be 65 years or over, and it is estimated that the proportion of those over 45 years of age will be approximately equal to those under the age of 45." If these projections about the Canadian population are accurate, it would be fair to assume that many of these people will require further education and training, both within and outside the established institutions, some for professional development and retraining and others for personal interest and growth. Further, it becomes clear that many will be returning to universities, colleges, and high schools (Campbell, 1984; Denton et al., 1990). The need for instructors who understand adults as learners will increase, and institutions of learning will be required to adjust to a more mature student population.

The majority of Canada's population is made up of immigrants or their immediate descendants. During the early waves of immigrants from Europe, several movements and organizations were developed to educate adults (Welton, 1987). In recent times, Canada has become a destination of choice for many immigrants from several countries, especially from the Third World. Both federal and provincial governments have recognized the need for skills training, retraining, and language acquisition. Most immigrants are adults, and, apart from cultural differences, their learning styles differ from those of their children who attend public schools. It is necessary for those involved in training these adult immigrants to have some training in adult education.

Increasingly sophisticated technology, coupled with the greater demands of our industrialized nation, requires a well-trained workforce. As the technology of the workplace becomes more complicated, many workers must be retrained to keep up with the new technology. Every established profession in Canada (law, engineering, dentistry, and teaching, to name a few) has a continuing education component, either through conferences and workshops or mandatory courses at a postsecondary institution. Opportunities for continuing education occur in other occupations, too. The learning adult is a primary asset of any profession—and eventually the nation. This need for continuous adult learning will increase as the country continues to grow.

Accessibility to education and training has become a major global issue. In recent times, we have seen the establishment of distance-education institutions in several parts of the world: the Indira Gandhi National Open University in India, the Radio and Television University in China, the Open University in Britain, Athabasca University and Téléuniversité du Québec in Canada, and, more recently, the Commonwealth of Learning (Commonwealth Secretariat) with headquarters in Vancouver. The major factors that have prompted the development of these educational facilities are sparsely distributed populations over large geographical areas (Canada, Australia), large concentrations of people in vast land areas (India, China), the great expense of on-campus full-time study, and the need to facilitate the global distribution of knowledge existing in the form of courses (at institutions such as the Commonwealth of Learning).

The part-time adult learner is becoming the major consumer of education and training (Campbell, 1984; Denton et al., 1990). The advent of distance education through new technologies in Canada (Mugridge and Kaufman, 1986; Stahmer, 1987) has increased adults' accessibility to education and training. The expansion of educational opportunities through the media of distance education (television, interactive radio, teleconferencing, satellite, and correspondence through print and audio materials) appears to present a viable means for adults to pursue education in a land as large as Canada.

Canada is not only large in land mass, but also diverse in its ethnic composition. This ethnic diversity calls for an understanding of the needs of various groups. One aspect of the Canadian state is its official policy of bilingualism in a multicultural society; another involves the concept of founding nations—English and French; the terms "mosaic" and "tapestry" are also widely used. The Meech Lake controversy (1987–90) made it clear that Canada is in search of its identity. In June 1990, in the Manitoba legislature, Native MLA Elijah Harper delayed debate on the Accord to underscore the importance of Native concerns and that fact that the aboriginal peoples had not been consulted on the issue of entrenching Native rights in the Constitution. All Manitoba Indian chiefs and the Assembly of First Nations supported Mr. Harper's stand, and many Natives demonstrated in front of the legislative building. Native people are critically aware of their plight, but there appears to be little political will on the part of the public or of provincial and federal governments to give them the necessary conditions and opportunities to participate meaningfully in Canadian society. One fundamental condition is education for both children and adults. As François Mitterand (1983) observed:

> Cultural inequality breeds all the other injustices—oppression, discrimination, violence —and even hunger and poverty. The control of the means of transmitting knowledge is still the privilege of a few who are all the more intent on maintaining this advantage because it is one of the bases of their power. (p. 21)

Instead of re-emphasizing the notion of two founding peoples, future attention will probably be directed to the concerns of Native and ethnic groups, who must forge ahead toward viable forms of self-reliance. Adult education can be an instrument through which knowledge—and hence power—can be fairly distributed in our society.

Women have traditionally suffered inequality in opportunities for education, employment, and power (Gaskell, 1981) According to Angela Miles (1989, p.1), "a creative response to the presence of increasing numbers of women in adult education would strengthen the important and currently embattled social purpose tradition in the field." In a recent research article Denton et al. (1990, p. 74), found that "women participate more frequently than men in most kinds of continuing education, and this is true for almost all age groups." Why, then, are women not equally represented at various levels of employment in professional jobs, but over-represented in non-technical, low-paying careers? Why do women still not receive equal pay for equal work? In most cases, the answers to these questions may be found by exploring traditions in Canadian society that are sometimes unequal and unjust. Adult education can be organized so that women may empower themselves to create changes in society toward the achievement and maintenance of sexual equality.

THE STUDY OF ADULT EDUCATION

Three institutions in Canada offer doctoral studies in adult education: the University of British Columbia, the Ontario Institute for Studies in Education (OISE), and the University of Montreal (Department of Andragogie). In 1987, Alan Thomas sounded the alarm that "the academic arms of adult education are in trouble" (1987a, pp. 51–58); by the "academic arms," Thomas was referring to the study of adult education at the graduate level, which involves the professional responsibilities of research, publication, and teaching. Since there were attempts to close departments in some universities (and the actual loss of the Ph.D. program at OISE), it was timely for Thomas to raise the question of directions for the study of adult education in a university setting.

Perhaps the most celebrated Canadian adult educator in recent times was the late J. Roby Kidd. Born in Saskatchewan in 1915, he studied in Canada and the United States and worked with the YMCA before joining the staff of the Canadian Association for Adult Education (CAAE), becoming its director in 1951. He travelled extensively throughout

Canada and later became involved in many international organizations (such as UNESCO), assisting several countries (e.g., India, Trinidad, and Tobago) in developing programs in adult education. Kidd launched the International Council for Adult Education (ICAE) in 1972, believing that a non-governmental organization such as ICAE was important in countering the influences of some governments. The council represented "an alternative world vehicle for the nourishment and protection of the principles of life-long learning" (Thomas, 1987b, p. 196). Kidd was not only heavily involved in the practice and promotion of adult education, but he was also deeply involved in the study of adult education. He became the first chairman of the Department of Adult Education at OISE in 1966 and worked "strenuously for the increase in opportunities for the systematic preparation of practitioners of adult education" (Thomas, 1987b, p. 195).

The study of adult education at Canadian universities is in search of itself; there are many problems dealing with the very concept and definition of the term. In many cases such terms as "life-long learning," "andragogy," "extension education," and "continuing education" are all used interchangeably with "adult education" (see Darkenwald & Merriam, 1982, chap. 1; Ironside, 1989; Thomas, 1988). Adult education is regarded as a field of study, not an academic discipline, with a great need to develop theory and increase research (Cross, 1981). Indeed, the false question of whether adult education is an academic pursuit or a field of practice plagues the discipline. Adult education began in Canada (and elsewhere) as social movements seeking sometimes radical changes (Welton, 1987); the history, nature, and purposes of some of these movements have become more sophisticated and complex (see Selman, 1989). It is increasingly urgent for society to face the challenges of educating adults as they return for further and higher education. This involves the study of adult education for the purpose of improving practice in many fields. The study and practice of adult education should not be separated by spurious and untenable arguments; one cannot grow without the other.

Degree studies in adult education at the graduate level have become important for several reasons. First, the population has become more sophisticated in its demands for better and more-informed instructors/facilitators; many people who are participating in adult education activities have already achieved diplomas from postsecondary institutions. Second, graduate students assist in the process of research and theory building. Third, the demographic configuration is changing to include more adults in institutions of learning; our society will need more qualified people with graduate degrees to plan and execute innovative and creative programs.

Except for certificate programs, which are often provided by university extension units and community colleges, most studies are undertaken in units attached to faculties of education. Any fledgling field such as adult education competing for scarce resources on university campuses is relegated to the margins of academia; so the problem becomes less one of need for the study of adult education in society than one of who has power to control the allocation of resources in our changing society and whose purpose is served best within the institution.

In most universities, the professional faculties (such as social work and nursing) face similar kinds of questions with regards to financing and the emphasis on theory/research and practice. In graduate programs involving adult education, both sets of needs must be met through flexible programming. These are the general patterns at the University of Montreal, OISE , and the University of British Columbia. The study of adult education is important for the growth of the field, the development of a vision, and common understandings that will better inform practice.

THE PRACTICE OF ADULT EDUCATION

Adult education in Canada evolved through sociopolitical movements like the National Farm Radio Forum, the Antigonish Movement, Frontier College, Women's Institutes, and the Montreal Mechanics' Institute. These organizations were concerned with developing the potential of ordinary people and training them for their proper roles as citizens. In 1946 the CAAE conference declared the basis of the adult education movement to be the "belief that quite ordinary men and women have within themselves and their communities the spiritual and intellectual resources adequate to the solution of their problems" (Selman, 1987, p. 37).

While early movements in adult education were oriented toward the development of community, the initiation of social change, and the shaping (and control) of citizens, the practice has changed considerably over the past 40 years—from an emphasis on the community and social change to institutionalization and entrepreneurship. Possible explanations for this shift may be found by examining such factors as demographic shifts, the expansion of training institutions (such as universities and community colleges), the affluence of the 1960s and early 1970s, the exponential growth of technology (especially in communications), and the strong push for academic legitimation.

The practice of adult education runs the full gamut of human activity, from prenatal classes to mature university programs (elderhostel), and from volunteer social activities to mandatory continuing professional education. Community organizations, such as church volunteer groups and the YW/MCA , have a history of working with adults to bring about co-operation in community development. The goal of these and other similar groups is still the motivating factor in keeping the spirit of advancement alive. However, volunteer groups are not without their ideological convictions, and a close examination of their activities may reveal deliberate efforts toward social control and influence (for example, volunteer groups in the days of prohibition).

Native groups and ethnic organizations employ large numbers of people in the practice of adult education. Every Native reserve in Canada has some form of training or programming for adults. For example, northern Manitoba reserves have community-based training programs for band staff, counsellors, and alcohol- and drug-abuse workers; most of the trainees have not completed high school and have either been unemployed or never employed. Ethnic organizations employ adult educators as culture brokers, as well as language and literacy trainers.

The practice of adult education is becoming increasingly evident in business, government, and professional organizations. With the expanded use of complicated technology, businesses have increased their budgets for training and retraining of staff; these efforts are evident in the profusion of workshops and seminars held by advertising firms, financial institutions, and chambers of commerce. Many provincial governments have created departments of adult and continuing education because they have recognized the need for training their own staff and, further, for training citizens for the workforce. Several training institutions have been created by governments to provide accessibility to adults who are unable to take advantage of the traditional on-campus delivery system—notably the Open Learning Institute in British Columbia, Athabasca University in Alberta, and Télé-université in Quebec. Provincial governments have also been involved in training programs for prisoners, inner-city residents, and illiterate adults.

The professions are major participants in adult education activities through continuing professional training. In engineering, for example, it is estimated that practising engineers update their knowledge every five years; this calls for the organization and delivery of a considerable number of seminars and workshops. In many cases, professional organizations look after the retraining of their own members. Other professions, such as medicine, dentistry, and law, are similarly involved in keeping their members well informed and up-to-date on new knowledge and techniques.

The practice of adult education in universities is seen in the activities of the continuing education units (also known as extension units, divisions, or departments). The organization of these units in the university setting varies from institution to institution. Some staffs are academics with professional rank and eligibility for tenure, while others have no academic rank and sign year-to-year contracts. Several university continuing education units fall somewhere in between these extremes. Some units are expected to be fully self-supporting, whereas others receive varying amounts of subsidies. (Apparently, there is no unit in Canada that receives 100 percent financial support from its central administration.)

It appears that continuing education units are seen as tenuous and marginal to mainstream university activity (research and teaching); they are viewed as the service and public relations arm of the university. The practice of adult education through university continuing education units is dealing with several major questions. The first of these is: should there be a strong push for academic legitimacy? Second, should the mission of adult education be research and teaching, or should it continue to be service and accessibility? Third, to what extent should adult education units be pursuing financial profits? Should they be concerned about equality of access for those who cannot pay tuition? Finally, should continuing education units remain at the "bleeding edge" of the university where there is flexibility and the possibility of quick response to urgent community requests or should they become ossified in the bureaucratic entanglements of senate committees and university funding commissions?

Many of these issues have been separated in the establishment of two national organizations: the Canadian Association for the Study of Adult Education (CASAE) and the Canadian Association for University Continuing Education (CAUCE). Both of these organizations are university-based and involved with adult education; both hold annual general meetings and produce refereed journals. But there are differences: those involved in the practice (extension departments) and the study (academic departments) of adult education may not be informed of each other's activities at the same university. Members of CASAE regard themselves as academics who have connections with the Learned Societies, whereas CAUCE members are prone to view practice as their main objective (although some would prefer to be academics). The fight for hegemonic advantage will probably keep the professors of adult education on the margins of the professoriate and confirm the practising adult educators in continuing education units as the service people of the academic faculties. This may constitute a fatal blow for both the study and practice of adult education in universities and should be avoided because the contributions of both groups are essential to the growth of adult education.

SOCIAL CHANGE AND ADULT EDUCATION

One ideal of adult education in Canada is to influence social change. Adult education is practised in many settings with different objectives; in professional organizations, for example, the objective is to train or retrain members to be more competent, efficient, and effective. This desire to be equipped with state-of-the-art technology is derived from a social responsibility to clients, which in turn makes clients demand more and better service; thus the threshold of acceptable services increases, causing change within society in a very directed way.

It is a truism to state that no society is static and that change itself is a constant; however, what has become clear is that the rate of change is increasing. Another role of adult education therefore is to assist people in their adjustment to these changes in society. Changes in society create needs, and one of the purposes of adult education is to respond adequately and creatively to these needs. A cursory look at Canadian society reveals several changes that evolved from a heightened consciousness of social issues. For example, in recent times the women's movement has used all forms of adult education techniques to analyze, criticize, and publicize the inequality that women have suffered in employment, education, and status. The vigils, marches, symposia, and effective use of the media by the movement have all helped to raise the consciousness of citizens about the plight of women. This politicization and awakening of social consciousness has led to policy formation, government legislation, and action on the part of employers. Similar action and consequent social policy formation have been developed in areas like multiculturalism, peace education, human rights, various aspects of health, and abortion.

The principles of democracy assume informed choice based on social values; the bureaucratization of our educational and political institutions has resulted in technical language and hidden ideologies that are often not understood by many adults. However, because adults are the decision-makers who shape both the present and future of our society, adult education has a critical role to play in assisting citizens to examine political choices in order to shape the quality of social change.

TOWARD THE TWENTY-FIRST CENTURY

The curriculum of education and training will continue to change because of new demands in the workplace created by such forces as technology, unemployment, the world economy, and the formation of international regional trading blocs. The politics of control will have its effects globally and nationally, and this will affect schooling even at the local levels. In Canada, the federal government will influence education despite provincial jurisdiction in this area; such terms as training, learning, human resource development, and maintaining the competitive edge will be used if only to avoid open conflict with the provinces on this issue. Indeed, we have evidence of this type of federal activity through the many national training schemes implemented by Ottawa.

The predictions by the Conference Board of Canada and other economic organizations reveal that economic recovery in our country will be slow over the next five to ten years. Unemployment is expected to remain relatively high for some years to come. The emphasis is now on retraining for new jobs that are not yet available. Concrete incentives for adults to return to school for further training are difficult to find. The federal government has launched a "stay-in-school" campaign, the underlying theme being that the more schooling you have the better your chances of enjoying "the good life." One of the government's pamphlets, entitled *Straight talk about staying in school* provides three "Facts": (1) more education = more job choices; (2) more education = more money; (3) more education = more freedom (Canada, 1991, pp. 5–7). The oversimplification of complex relationships, as expressed in the above three equations, is at best misleading. In the late 1960s and early 1970s, a similar type of propaganda was attempted, and for the same reasons: to keep young people in school so that they do not increase the numbers of the unemployed, and so that jobs could be maintained by those already employed.

There are many adults returning to public schools; the high-school diploma is seen as an important credential to pursuing further training. In Ontario, for example, in 1988 there were about 153 000 persons 19 years or older taking credit courses in secondary schools (Thomas, 1993, p. 6.), which was approximately 20 percent of the total number of credit students in secondary schools; in 1986 the number was 132 870, or 19 percent of the total (Draper, 1991, p. 190). In Manitoba, school boards have organized extension divisions to accommodate adults returning to take both credit and non-credit courses. Indeed, there are many adults returning to full-time day studies in secondary schools across the country. It appears that this trend will continue as the drop-outs of today seek a high-school diploma at a later date; indeed, the level of sophisticated training required in the job market today and in the future will demand a high-school diploma as a bare minimum for any type of employment or further education.

This phenomenon of adults returning to secondary schools raises several questions about teaching in these situations: how would adults in regular high-school classrooms affect learning, curriculum, and classroom control? Are teachers trained to deal with adult needs in these environments? Are teacher training institutions changing to meet these new challenges? (Quebec is the only province that has recognized this need to train teachers to deal with adults in the secondary-school classroom.) It is becoming clear that the old model of initial training for life must be re-examined in light of *lifelong education*.

As survival becomes more complicated and demanding, and knowledge is constantly reassessed, learning throughout one's life span becomes a necessity. Learning can take place anywhere and under conditions that become particular to the individual learner; facts are learned, remembered, and forgotten as new information is constantly being produced. "Maintenance" learning becomes obsolete; what is needed is "anticipatory" learning and "participatory" learning that lead to co-operation and creativity throughout one's lifetime. (Bhola, 1988. p. 175.)

While lifelong education has often been treated as a synonym for adult education, it must be made clear that this is not the case here. Whereas adult education deals with the education of whomever a society deems to be an adult, lifelong learning encompasses all learning throughout the life span. Indeed the sum total of pre-school, elementary, secondary, tertiary, and adult education does not add up to lifelong education. The concept of lifelong education includes knowledge about communication, expression, concentration, observation, and where and how to find information. Each part of a person's life must be seen as a unique experience in itself and also as a basis for future development; in this sense education becomes a way of life, possibly different in content and approach as one grows older (Lengrand, 1989, pp. 5–9).

Adult education in Canada will deserve and demand greater attention. The indicators are numerous:

- Nationally only about 65 percent of our students complete high school; the non-completers will return as adults for basic training.
- Changes in technology will require retraining for many of those employed.
- Continuing professional education will become an essential part of the business agenda.
- Aboriginal peoples and recent immigrants will demand further adult training in such areas as language and job skills.

Governments and institutions will have to find more resources to provide services for adults to continue purposeful learning; users of these services will have to exercise better judgement in accessing these resources so as to avoid waste.

CONCLUSIONS

The proper management and use of Canada's abundant resources can provide us with a continuing high quality of life. However, we are plagued with problems arising from issues of national unity, multiculturalism, equality, and regionalism. Many social institutions have been created to assist us in solving these problems; among these are universities, colleges, and public schools. Considering the changes in the demographic, social, and economic character of the country, efforts must be made to include adult education in the form of viable programs of choice in relevant areas at all levels.

This chapter attempted to expose the reader to some of the major issues in adult education in this country. The importance of adult education in our aging society (Ray et al., 1983) cannot be overemphasized, and the time to consider this issue is now, not at the eleventh hour.

Considering its high number of immigrants, rapidly changing technology, need for literacy training, and formation of regional trading blocs, Canada must increase the possibilities for debate of critical issues, so that its citizens can make informed choices. The practice of adult education in community settings (non-formal education) can enhance this process.

Finally, the study of adult education must be taken seriously by universities and governments. Adult educators must be provided with the opportunity to develop both skills in and a vision of adult education. The development of research and theory needs immediate attention if this field is to develop adequately to cope with and create a suitable climate for social change. These challenges are not confined to any one constituency, but require joint action from concerned citizens, practitioners, academics, and political decision-makers.

DISCUSSION QUESTIONS

❑ Define adult education. Show how you arrived at this definition and state some of the difficulties you encountered in the process.

❑ Why is adult education important in the development of the Canadian nation?

❑ What are some of the problems in the study of adult education?

❑ Is the practice of adult education a marginal activity in a university setting? Why?

❑ Describe your understanding of social change. How can adult education enhance this process?

❑ Discuss factors that will affect the future development of adult education.

REFERENCES

Bhola, H.S. (1988). *World trends and issues in adult education.* London: Jessica Kingsley Publishers.

Campbell, D.C. (1984). *The new majority: Adult learners in the university.* Edmonton: University of Alberta Press.

Canada. (1991). *Straight talk about staying in school.* Ottawa.

Cross, P.K. (1981). *Adults as learners.* San Francisco: Jossey-Bass.

Darkenwald, G.G., & Merriam, S.B. (1982). *Adult education: Foundations of practice.* San Francisco: Harper & Row.

Denton, F.T., Pineo, P.C., & Spencer, B.G. (1990). The constituencies of adult education programs: Similarities and differences among age groups and other components of the population. *Canadian Journal of Education, 15*(1).

Draper, J. (1991). Adults as an important learning group. In R. Ghosh & D. Ray (Eds.). *Social change and education in Canada.* (Second edition). Toronto: Harcourt Brace Jovanovich.

Freire, P. (1972). *Pedagogy of the oppressed.* New York: Herder & Herder.

Gaskell, J.S. (1981). Equal educational opportunity for women. In J.D. Wilson, *Canadian education in the 1980's.* Calgary: Detselig.

Himmelstrup, P., Robinson, J., & Fielden, D. (1981). *Strategies for lifelong learning.* Denmark: University Centre of South Jutland.

Ironside, D.J. (1989). Concepts and definitions. In C.J. Titmus (Ed.). *Lifelong education for adults: An international handbook.* Oxford: Pergamon Press.

Lengrand, P. (1989). Lifelong education: Growth of the concept. In C.J. Titmus (Ed.). *Lifelong education for adults: An international handbook.* Oxford: Pergamon Press.

Miles, A. (1989). Women's challenge to adult education. *Canadian Journal for the Study of Adult Education, 3*(1).

Mitterand, F. (1983). The joining of forces for an authentic development. *Convergence, 16*(1).

Mugridge, I., & Kaufman, D. (Eds.). (1986). *Distance education in Canada.* London: Croom Helm.

Peters, R.S. (1966). *Ethnics and Education.* London: George Allen & Unwin.

Piaget, J. (1968). *Six psychological studies.* New York: Vintage Books.

Ray, D., Harley, A., Bayles, M. (1983). *Values, life-long education and an aging Canadian population.* London, ON: Third Eye.

Royal Bank of Canada (1989, Fall). *Reporter.*

Scheffler, I. (1960). *The language of education.* Springfield, IL: Charles C. Thomas.

Selman, G. (1987). Adult education and citizenship. In F. Cassidy & R. Faris (Eds.). *Choosing our future: Adult education and public policy in Canada.* Toronto: OISE Press.

Selman, G. (1989). 1972—Year of affirmation for adult education. *Canadian Journal for the Study of Adult Education, 3*(1).

Soltis, J.F. (1968). *An introduction to the analysis of educational concepts.* Don Mills, ON: Addison-Wesley.

Stahmer, A. (1987). *Communications technology and distance learning in Canada: A survey of Canadian activities.* Ottawa: Government of Canada, Social Policy Directorate, Dept. of Communications.

Stone, L. (1983). Canadian population aging, with projections. In D. Ray, A. Harley, & M. Bayles (Eds.). *Values, lifelong education and an aging Canadian population.* (pp.16–29). London: Third Eye.

Thomas, A.M. (1987a). Academic adult education. *Canadian Journal for the Study of Adult Education, 1*(1).

Thomas, A.M. (1987b). Roby Kidd—Intellectual voyageur. In P. Jarvis, *Twentieth century thinkers in adult education.* London: Croom Helm.

Thomas, A. M. (1988). The new world of continuing education. In T. Barerstein & J.A. Draper (Eds.). *The craft of teaching adults.* Toronto: OISE Press.

Thomas, A.M. (1993). The new world of adult learning. *Learning Magazine, 6*(2), 5–8.

Thompson, A. (1981). Education: Reformation and renewal in the "80's"? In J.D. Wilson, *Canadian Education in the 1980's.* Calgary: Detselig.

Thornton, J.E. (1990). Adult education in an aging society: Introduction. In *Proceedings of the 9th annual conference of Canadian association for the study of adult education.* Victoria, BC: University of Victoria.

UNESCO, Canadian Commission for. (1980). Recommendation on the development of adult education. Occasional Paper 34. Ottawa.

Welton, M.R. (Ed.). (1987). *Knowledge for the people: The struggle for adult learning in English-speaking Canada, 1825–1973.* Toronto: OISE Press.

Whitehead, A.N. (1929). *The aims of education and other essays.* New York: Free Press.

FURTHER READINGS

Campbell, D.C. (1984). *The new majority: Adult learners in the university.* Edmonton: University of Alberta Press.

Cassidy, F., & Faris, R. (Eds.). (1987) *Choosing our future: Adult education and public policy in Canada.* Toronto: OISE Press.

Griffith, W.S. (1980). Personnel preparation, Is there a continuing education profession? In P.E. Frandson, *Power and conflict in continuing education.* Belmont, CA: Wadsworth.

Selman, G., & Dampier, P. (1991). *The foundations of adult education in Canada.* Toronto: Thompson Educational Publishing.

Thomas, A.M. (1987). Academic adult education. *Canadian Journal for the Study of Adult Education, 1*(1).

Welton, M.R. (Ed.). (1987). *Knowledge for the people: The struggle for adult learning in English-speaking Canada, 1825-1973.* Toronto: OISE Press.

PART III

RIGHTS

INTRODUCTION

The Canadian Charter of Rights and Freedoms provides people in Canada with several fundamental freedoms and rights, such as the freedom of speech, expression, religion, and conscience (section 15). These freedoms and rights are entrenched in the Constitution Act, 1982, meaning that they cannot be removed or abridged by government except through the notwithstanding clause (section 33) or the reasonable limits clause (section 1). Some Charter sections have been judicially considered and applied in the educational context, especially section 23, which guarantees minority language education rights. In addition, section 2 (freedom of religion and conscience) has been successfully invoked to strike down religious exercises and curricula in Ontario schools. The Charter's equality rights provision (section 15) did not come into force until 1985, and its possible effect on education is only gradually becoming known. Possible applications of section 15 to educational policy and practice exist in the areas of employment equity and equality of educational opportunity for students with disabilities, Native Canadians, and students from various ethnic groups.

A. Wayne Mackay discusses the concept of rights and the rights paradigm, and their relationship to educational policy. He points out that policies may not be effective without the provision of rights, as in the case of multiculturalism policy, which has not been effectively implemented in education because it has had neither legal nor political weight, and does not even now have a substantive rights guarantee in the Constitution. MacKay illustrates how the legalizing of education through the Charter has the potential to enhance the development of Canadian education, although the rights guaranteed are not absolute, and, in the case of education, the burden is clearly on the provinces.

Aniko Varpalotai deals with changes in educational practice that might contribute to a lessening of inequalities. She addresses some of the hard issues that face policy-makers: sexual orientation, family status, and racism. Varpalotai points out how the policy decisions that might bring more equal opportunity in these areas have been officially ignored in many cases.

Teachers have traditionally been vested with custodial responsibilities for pupils during school time. Greg Dickinson focusses on the responsibilities and authority given to teachers as surrogate parents. As schools have evolved into more complex institutions, the legal role of the teacher has been redefined. Teachers are now recognized as professionals and state agents, although their *in loco parentis* function has been retained. The author looks at the teacher's position with regard to liability for negligence and responsibility for enforcing discipline.

Steen Esbensen examines the rights of young people as a special class of citizen in the context of the political and sociocultural environment. In a paternalistic system, he points out, there is bound to be confusion over what constitutes students' rights. Basic questions are analyzed, such as: when are students old enough to participate in the decisions that affect their own education? and what constitutes fair treatment in grievances that may involve them?

Perceptions of parental authority over children have changed in Canada, partly because of changes in federal legislation (e.g., the Criminal Code, the Young Offenders Act). Romulo Magsino traces the history of the gradual dilution of parental rights, both in the provinces where common law is the basis of the legal system, and in Quebec, whose civil system has its roots in French and Roman legal codes. In both areas, the rights of the parents and the primacy of their rights were well established, and parents were penalized only when harm to the child could be proven. Parents' rights are discussed within the context of family rights, children's rights, and state authority. Court cases suggesting a variety of educational issues provide examples of the new emerging rights of parents and the family in Canada.

Léonard Goguen and Donald Poirier look at the rights of exceptional children in Canada— gifted students and those with disabilities. The authors discuss the special educational needs of these students in terms of specific resources and procedures in education, and the shift in Canada from the concept of need to that of right. They focus on the legal protection of provincial and territorial educational legislations, the Canadian Charter, and court cases.

Nancy Sheehan's chapter discusses sexism in education. She analyzes this problem in Canadian education over the past century in terms of power differentials between women and men and the influence of curriculum in defining women's position in society. She points out the conflict between the rhetoric of equality and the reality of women's unequal position despite several gains that have been made.

Perhaps the greatest discrimination, in society generally and in education, has been faced by Canada's Native peoples. Jo-Ann Archibald examines recent developments in education for the Indian, Inuit, and Métis. She focusses on developments in British Columbia, one of the regions where Native land claims are strongest in law. She examines the literature of aspirations and achievements and points out the difficulties still to be overcome. Archibald makes a strong case for aboriginal peoples to control their own education, both in decision-making and in delivery, and in this way to become equal participants in future Canadian society.

16

THE RIGHTS PARADIGM IN THE AGE OF THE CHARTER

A. Wayne MacKay

Canadians might be forgiven for concluding that the concept of rights burst upon the scene in 1982 with the arrival of the Canadian Charter of Rights and Freedoms (hereafter the Charter). This is, of course, not true. Legal rights in the form of statutory guarantees and judge-made common law rules are part of the British heritage that Canada carried into Confederation in 1867. Even constitutional rights were around before 1982, including guarantees of collective rights to denominational schools and Canada's two official language groups in the Constitution Act, 1867 (sections 93 and 133 respectively). We also had human rights codes since the late 1940s and a statutory guarantee of individual rights in the Canadian Bill of Rights (1960). However, it was not until the Charter's arrival in the 1980s that rights discourse became a regular part of Canadian life.

The rights paradigm has also invaded the discretion-laden area of educational policy-making. One of the elements that distinguishes rights from policies is that the latter allow for considerable flexibility and discretionary judgements on the part of the front-line actors. While rights are certainly open to interpretation and debate, there are elements of hierarchy and rigidity that give educators less room to manoeuvre. Even more disconcerting for educational administrators is the fact that the final arbiters of the meaning of rights are lawyers and judges. Policies are, in general terms, interpreted and applied by the same group who make them; rights will be interpreted and applied by outsiders. This growth of rights discourse within educational policy-making has brought with it both benefits and burdens (MacKay, 1988).

Rights and policies are not completely separate, but rather are different species within a single genus. Indeed, policies can be the source of rights—albeit ones that are lower in the legal hierarchy. This hierarchical ordering of rights is a vital aspect of the rights paradigm. In legal terms, the hierarchy of rules is quite clear. As section 52 of the Constitution Act, 1982, states, "the Constitution of Canada is the supreme law of Canada" and any laws inconsistent with it are "of no force or effect." This statement applies to both the original Constitution Act, 1867, and to newer aspects of the Canadian Constitution, such as the Charter. Thus the card that trumps all others in the rights game is the constitutional card. That is why interest groups were so eager to have their rights included in the 1982 Charter. For example, women's groups were effective and successful in having gender equality enshrined in the Charter in section 28, which reads "Notwithstanding anything in this Charter, the rights and freedoms referred to in it are guaranteed equally to male and female persons."[1]

Next to constitutional documents in the hierarchy of legal rules are regular statutes, passed by either provincial legislatures, territorial governments, or the Parliament of Canada. As expressions of the will of the elected representatives, statutes are given great weight by judges, who must interpret the legislative language but may not disregard it. Human rights codes and education statutes are examples of this form of legal rules, and they have a significant impact on educational policy-making. Judge-made common law, in the form of cases, is another source of legal rights, but one that is secondary to statute law. If there is a conflict between a statute and a common-law rule arising from a judge's ruling, it is the clearly worded statutory provision that will prevail. Common-law rules that allowed landlords to discriminate on the basis of race or gender have been reversed by anti-discrimination statutes. This primacy of statutory law is the hallmark of British parliamentary government—often referred to as the principle of parliamentary supremacy. In a country with a written constitution, such as Canada, this principle is modified to the extent that the statute law must conform to the written constitution. This means, among other things, that statutes must not violate the rights guaranteed in the Charter.

At the bottom of the hierarchy of legal rules is delegated legislation. The authority to make these rules arises from statute law and is delegated from the elected representatives of the people. Regulations, which are normally given the same legal force as statutes, are one of the most high-profile versions of delegated legislation. Unlike statutes, which must receive majority approval in the legislature, regulations are made by the executive branch of government — either by the Cabinet as a whole or by an individual minister of the Crown. Other versions of delegated rules include policy statements or directives, school board by-laws, and municipal ordinances, to name but a few. The legal weight that these rules carry depends upon their statutory source, but in general they carry little or no legal force. While these lower-level rules and policies are low cards in the game of rights, they are often vital to the daily operation of the government enterprise. In practical application, the legal hierarchy of rules may be inverted, with policies being more important than statutory or constitutional guarantees of rights.[2] Thus the line between policy issues and rights issues is blurred.

Canada's policy on multiculturalism provides a good example of the difficulty in drawing a clear line between policies and rights. Multiculturalism has been a matter of federal government policy in Canada for many decades, but because it has not been backed by either legal or political weight, it has not been effectively implemented. This is certainly true in the field of public education (Schmeiser, 1987). In the 1980s, some of the principles of multiculturalism have been put into statutory form, but these enactments have no real teeth (Canadian Multiculturalism Act, 1988). The principle has also been constitutionalized in the form of section 27 of the Charter, which reads: "This Charter shall be interpreted in a manner consistent with the preservation and enhancement of the multicultural heritage of Canadians."

Section 27 of the Charter is not a substantive rights guarantee, but rather a principle of constitutional interpretation. This devalues its currency within the rights paradigm. That is not to say that interpretation doctrines are of no value. The "distinct society" clause, recognizing the unique nature of Quebec in Canada, was at the heart of the failed Meech Lake Constitutional Accord of 1987. Yet this clause was an interpretive one, rather than a substantive rights guarantee . When used in conjunction with other sections of the Charter, section 27 can augment the rights of ethnic groups in Canada (MacKay, 1983). This has already happened with respect to the section 2 guarantees of freedom of religion (*Big M. Drug Mart*, 1985). Thus multiculturalism has become a policy with greater clout, but may still fall short of the status of a guaranteed right.[3]

This brings us to the crucial question of defining the term "rights." There is much jurisprudence exploring the links between moral and legal claims and the fine distinctions between policies and principles. Some argue that rights enshrine principles in legal form and that these principles are clearly distinguishable from policies (Dworkin, 1977). However, a less grandiose approach to rights recognizes the political content of legal guarantees and demystifies the nature of rights in a legal system (Samek, 1982). Rather than discuss rights in absolutist terms, we will adopt the following definition:

> In simple terms, "rights" is the label that has been used to refer to those interests that have acquired sufficient societal acceptance to be protected by the Canadian legal structure. Because a right is an interest recognized by the courts they are usually willing to provide some kind of remedy when a right has been violated. (MacKay, 1984)

Rights are rarely absolute moral claims, but frequently arise from conflicting claims for the attention of the state. The assertion of one person's rights may restrict the rights of another. The controversy surrounding abortion is a case in point. Claims made on behalf of the fetus and its right to life restrict the right of the mother to choose whether or not to abort. Similarly, claims to the right to choose between abortion and carrying the fetus to term can deny totally the claimed fetal right to life. In a school context, a teacher's right to freedom of expression in the classroom can interfere with a student's right not to be discriminated against by the state (*Keegstra*, 1983).[4] What is at issue in most of these rights disputes are conflicting values. Canadian courts offer an adversarial structure within which to resolve such conflicts. This approach runs counter to the school's bureaucratic tendencies to compromise and work things out on an informal basis, and produces a clash of educators' and lawyers' values (MacKay, 1988). When we speak the language of rights, we make many assumptions and move toward a different value system. This rights discourse has become fashionable since the end of World War II and the adoption of the Universal Declaration of Human Rights in 1948.[5] This trend has been greatly accelerated in Canada by the 1982 arrival of the Charter.

THE NATURE OF THE CHARTER

In spite of the prevalence of human rights codes at the provincial and federal levels and the 1960 statutory Canadian Bill of Rights, it was not until the Charter arrived in 1982 that rights discourse permeated the policy-making process. It is now rare that one can read a newspaper or watch a television newscast that does not include some discussion of legal rights. Whether this change in language reflects a significant change in thinking is not yet clear. Equally unclear is whether the move toward the rights paradigm will advance or impede social change. Later in this chapter, some assessment will be made of the Charter's impact in the field of education, but first we should consider the origins and nature of the Canadian Charter.

The Charter was crafted in the context of the strengths and weaknesses of the United States rights jurisprudence, the disappointing Canadian experience with the Canadian Bill of Rights (1960), and from the political compromises leading up to the Charter's passage in 1982. The Charter allows for judicial intervention into governmental action, including educational decision-making, where traditionally only experts held sway. This alarms many educators. It certainly means changes in the ways that things have been done. Those on the outside of the decision-making circle will be encouraged, and those on the inside threatened.

In the United States, the courts have been viewed as the logical forum for enforcing rights—educational and otherwise. Some academic commentators feel that Canadian society is now heading in the same direction (Sussel & Manley-Casimir, 1986). Canadian tradition has been to resolve education issues in the political rather than the judicial arena. Courts, as part of their deference to the parliamentary process, have taken a hands-off approach to the decisions of school boards and school administrators. It is unlikely that lawyers and judges will quickly assume a new intentionist role. However, educational decisions that clearly violate the Charter have forced the resolution of these decisions through legal channels. The Charter also has the potential to enhance the development of Canadian education. This legalizing of education presents an opportunity to be seized as well as an obstacle to be surmounted.

With the arrival of the Charter, we have seen disgruntled parents who have become frustrated by the "quiet diplomacy" approach prepare themselves to go to court. As Anderson (1985) and others predict, "legal work will surely multiply in the next decades in the area of schoolhouse law." However, it will not be to the same extent or with the same frequency as we see in the United States. This is due to our historical differences. The United States grew out of political and social revolutionary fervour and favours individual rights, whereas the Canadian experience has been quintessentially British, with emphasis on the preservation of social order. It is commonly accepted that Canadians are a more deferential people and consequently not as litigious. Whether this is really a matter of deference or not, the courts have not been a major policy forum. The early Charter cases in the field of education do not suggest that the Supreme Court of Canada, or other judges in the system, want to be a "national school board."

The Charter has already caused many school administrators to modify institutional procedures and requirements so as to avoid future legal problems. Educators may be more progressive in anticipating Charter challenges than judges would require them to be. As Cruickshank (1986) remarks, educators, like policemen, prison guards, tax collectors, and Crown prosecutors, will learn to accommodate, if not embrace, the Charter and to live with the inevitability of litigation. Those who accommodate it best will be those who appreciate that individual rights cases can improve the education system for generations to come. They will also recognize that courts will continue to give deference to the educational experts on matters of substantive policy.

The Charter is part of Canada's patriated Constitution. In 1982, Canada adopted an entrenched package of rights that can only be changed by constitutional amendment or the proper use of the legislative override in section 33 of the Charter itself. This section allows Parliament or a provincial legislature to opt out of specific Charter rights, including equality. In other words, if a legislature wants to preserve certain inequalities or to undo the effect of a court decision, it must simply pass a law declaring that its education statute operates "notwithstanding" the Charter. This section will not be used often, but it does give an elected government control over any excesses it perceives in the decisions of judges. When the Quebec government used section 33 to reverse the Supreme Court ruling on bilingual commercial advertising, it caused a major political controversy (*Ford*, 1988).

It must be emphasized that the rights guaranteed in the Charter are not absolute. Courts are invited by section 1 to consider what are the "reasonable limits prescribed by law as can be demonstrably justified in a free and democratic society." It may be hard to justify different levels of services between provinces, as they are surely examples of "free and democratic" societies. It may be a reasonable limit for a school board to supply only the kind of special services that it can afford in times of financial restraint (*Andrews*, 1989; *Turpin*, 1989).[6]

The burden is clearly on the province (in the field of education, the departments of education, school boards, administrators, and teachers) to demonstrate that any limitations on rights are reasonable. This is the mechanism that will be used in order to balance the competing rights of individuals and society. The traditional hands-off approach to the courts in matters of education will incline them to listen carefully to governmental objectives. The Supreme Court of Canada ruling in *R. v. Oakes* (1986) suggests a sparing application of section 1 and a broad reading of rights. There has been some retreat from this position in more recent cases, such as *Ford* (1988) and *McKinney* (1990), but the burden is still squarely on the state agents to justify the limitation of rights.

What are "reasonable limits" in a "free and democratic" society? This will pose a difficult problem for judges and will require the examination of evidence from experts in the field. The judge in *Bales v. Board of School Trustees* (1984) did not rely exclusively on statute analysis to resolve the legal issues. Educational experts presented evidence on the desirability of "mainstreaming" students with disabilities and the importance of putting them in the "least restrictive environment." These experts were drawn from both Canada and the United States. In the end, the judge in *Bales* decided in the school board's favour, but it was decided before the section 15 equality guarantees came into effect in 1985.[7] The judge also put the burden on the parents to show that the school authorities were acting unreasonably. Once a Charter violation is shown, it is the educators who would have the burden of proving that any limitations on rights were reasonable (MacKay, 1985).

All of the Charter rights (with the possible exception of gender equality in section 28) are subject to the section 1 "reasonable limits" clause. The Supreme Court of Canada in *R. v. Oakes* (1986) stressed that section 1 must be applied cautiously. There must be a proportionality between the governmental objective and the means employed. The objective must be a pressing and substantial one and the means adopted must limit rights to the smallest extent possible. Chief Justice Dickson in *R. v. Oakes* (1986) emphasized that giving effect to rights will be the norm and limitations on them the exception.

Can the school boards plead financial restraint or administrative inconvenience as "reasonable limits" under section 1 of the Charter for failing to provide equality to students with disabilities? Lack of funds is no answer to inequality of educational opportunity. Section 1 cannot be an absolute defence, but may form a limited defence, and is one of the factors to be considered by the courts (*Singh v. M.E.I.*,[1985]). The school board would have to present a reasonable and feasible plan for bringing itself into conformity with section 15 within a reasonable time period. This approach would allow costs to be spread out and absorbed without undue disruption to government services. There is no doubt that the Charter will force educators to justify their actions when they limit the rights of students, parents, or teachers. This kind of accountability should work to the benefit of the ultimate consumers of education—the students.

Apart from the political limits of section 33 (the override provision) and the judicial limits of section 1 (reasonable limits), the application of the Charter itself is constrained by section 32. This section indicates that the Charter applies to the legislative and executive branches of governments. There is no mention of the private sector, and the Supreme Court has ruled that the Charter does not apply to the private sphere (*R.W.D.S.U. v. Dolphin Delivery*, 1986). This may mean that a private school would not be subject to the Charter. While there might be some argument that teachers perform their duties *in loco parentis*, it is clear that educators derive their real authority from statute and are thus part of the public sphere to which the Charter applies (MacKay, 1987). Parents, as private citizens, are not subject to the Charter, but teachers, school officials, and school boards are.

Finally, we turn to the important matter of remedies under the Charter and the new role for courts implicit in these provisions. The Canadian tradition is not one of judicial activism in school matters, but rather one of deference to the educational experts. While the potential for innovative remedies is broad, the reality is likely to be more conservative. This observation has partly been validated by the early Charter cases in the educational domain. The judicial role has been expanded by the Charter but the judges will not revolutionize the educational system.

Under section 24 of the Charter, courts have a broad power to give a remedy to people denied a right protected by the Charter. They could order compensation or force a school board to take corrective action. Where the language of the law itself produces inequality, the courts can, under section 52 of the Constitution Act, 1982, declare the law to be of "no force or effect." The combined effect of these remedial provisions is to give courts a potentially expansive role in shaping Canadian society. When these board remedial powers are combined with section 15 and the other expansive Charter guarantees, the possible results are staggering. The net effect is that judges can give any remedy that is "just and appropriate."

Although the potential is great, in fact the remedies will sometimes be conservative. This point can best be highlighted by quoting two passages from *Mahe v. R.* (1985), which read: "Compliance with the Charter cannot be achieved instantaneously and as long as *reasonable* progress is being made, the courts should not interfere. . . . Courts must *not* interfere by decreeing methods or becoming involved in ongoing supervision or administration." When the *Mahe* case was decided by the Supreme Court of Canada in 1990, it was more adventurous on the remedies question than the Alberta trial court (*Mahe*, 1990). The effect of the Supreme Court ruling was to require the Alberta authorities to establish a francophone school board, as a way of ensuring that parents would have control over the minority language education of their children. This kind of judicial intervention in the operation of local school boards would have been unheard of before the Charter.

Remedies such as the U.S. racial busing model for constitutional violations have been both complex and controversial and should be avoided. The U.S. Supreme Court has not hesitated to override the policy-making and spending functions of school boards. Cruickshank (1986) rightly predicts that Canadian courts, being more comfortable with exclusively legislative controls over policy and expenditures, will probably be slow to advance such remedies. This is indeed the message from the decision in *Dolmage v. Muskoka Board of Education* (1985). The Court held it should not get into the details of enforcement of the "appropriate" placement of a student under the Ontario statutory structure. With the exception of the clear judicial mandate with respect to minority-language educational rights under section 23 of the Charter, the early signs are that Courts will move cautiously in using their remedial powers to reshape the direction of Canadian education.

INDIVIDUAL AND COLLECTIVE RIGHTS IN THE CHARTER

Many have suggested that the Charter moves Canada away from its British parliamentary roots toward the American individual-rights model. This shift has encouraged some (Tarnopolsky, 1983) and alarmed others (Fulford, 1986). While many of the rights enshrined in the Charter are individualistic in nature, that is not its exclusive character. There are also collective or group rights that better reflect Canada's pre-Charter tradition. The fact that section 1 of the Charter calls for "reasonable limits" on rights as can be justified in a "free and democratic society" emphasizes the need to balance individual rights against the claims of the larger society. Indeed, this is the kind of interest balancing that occurs in the United States as well. However, the express statement of this balancing principle in the Charter sets it apart from its American counterpart. The existence of the section 33 legislative override is a further indication that the Canadian constitution makers did not totally abandon their parliamentary roots.[8]

In the Constitution Act, 1867, there were only two provisions that could be classified as granting rights. Section 93, by way of an exception to the exclusive power of the provinces to legislate with respect to education, guarantees the continued operation of denominational schools for those provinces that had such structures at the time of Confederation. The main beneficiaries of this protection are the Protestant and Catholic denominations who acquired the right to operate their own publicly funded school systems. The other rights provision is section 133, which guarantees certain minimal language rights, in relation to the government, for francophones in Canada and anglophones in Quebec. What is noteworthy about both these guarantees is that they are group rights rather than individual ones.

In the Charter itself, the rights of both denominational schools and the official linguistic minorities were reaffirmed and extended. Section 29 of the Charter guarantees that nothing in the Charter detracts from the rights of the denominational schools. Sections 16–23 of the Charter extend the traditional language rights vis-à-vis the government and add a new affirmative right to minority language instruction "where numbers warrant." This latter provision has sparked the most education litigation to date. Other Charter provisions that have a collective rather than individual character are the section 15 equality guarantees, aboriginal guarantees in sections 25 and 35, multicultural rights in section 27, and the affirmation of gender equality in section 28. Thus the Charter addresses collective as well as individual rights, and in that respect is distinct from the American tradition. Even in respect to the individual rights provisions, the language of the Canadian Charter is often closer to the wording of European or international documents than to the text of the equivalent American provisions.

Another sense in which the Charter has a collective aspect is in the litigation of issues. Because of the high cost of litigation, many of the early Charter claims have been made by corporations or groups, rather than by private individuals. Even when a case proceeds in the name of a particular individual, he or she is often supported by a public interest group. Claims for minority language education are usually funded by the federal government and orchestrated by parents' groups. Women have formed an effective litigation arm called the Women's Legal Education and Action Fund (LEAF) that supports many equality cases. Parents, pursuing Charter rights for children with disabilities, are frequently supported by organizations such as the Canadian Association for Community Living (CACL). Finally, teachers rarely pursue litigation on their own, but are supported by their unions and professional organizations. The Charter has provided a focus for a new form of pressure-group politics.

Turpel (1989–90) argues that discussions of individual and collective rights produce a false dichotomy. She argues that the whole rights discourse fails to take into account the cultural differences between aboriginal people and other Canadians. It is, in her view, the property-based concept of rights that has added to the oppression of aboriginal people.

Rights discourse, whether in the form of collective or individual rights, is seen as a further device to assimilate aboriginal people into the western European definition of the norm. There is considerable merit in Professor Turpel's views, which point out that the Charter and rights talk can be used for bad as well as good ends. Rights have often been claimed to prop up the status quo rather than to promote social justice. The Charter will only be as good as the vision of those who apply it. We should bear this in mind as we turn to the early Charter litigation.

THE EARLY CHARTER LITIGATION

Limits of space and time dictate that the treatment of these early Charter cases will be cursory in nature. We therefore limit the discussion to cases arising in the education context and only scratch the surface of the numerous complex Charter issues that have arisen in the public school setting. Dickinson and MacKay (1989) provide a comprehensive review of the intersection between the Charter and education. A more detailed analysis of some of these cases appears in the other chapters of this section. Rather than organize these cases on the basis of the litigants—students, parents, and teachers—we have focussed on the nature of the rights claimed.

COLLECTIVE RIGHTS CLAIMS

In the eight years since the Charter arrived in Canada, its major impact in the field of education has been with respect to minority language educational rights. In *A.G. Quebec v. Quebec Association of Protestant School Boards* (1984), the Supreme Court ruled that the Quebec government could not restrict the rights of the anglophone minority in the province by enacting laws that did not conform with the guarantees in section 23 of the Charter. Since that ruling, most of the cases have concerned the rights of francophones elsewhere in Canada to have their children receive minority language instruction. The crucial limitation is that instruction, and in some cases a facility, will only be provided "where numbers warrant" such provision. Some provinces have passed laws indicating what numbers warrant instruction in the minority language, but the ultimate determination of this numbers question rests with the courts.

An important Ontario case established that the provision of minority language education is a provincial responsibility and that numbers cannot be arbitrarily limited by a particular school board (*Reference Re Education Act of Ontario and Minority Language Education Rights*, 1984). This case also established that there was implicit in section 23 of the Charter a right of control by the minority language community. The Supreme Court of Canada agreed that parental control was a vital part of the section 23 guarantee and instructed the Alberta government in *Mahe* (1990) to make that control meaningful by school board representation. In less populated provinces, such as Nova Scotia, the issue was what numbers would warrant the provision of instruction or a separate minority language facility.

As the culmination of a hotly contested struggle between a francophone parents' group and a resistant Cape Breton School Board and Nova Scotia Attorney General, the court in *Lavoie v. A.G. Nova Scotia* (1989) ordered the provision of minority language instruction for 50 qualified students. In an earlier ruling in this case (*Lavoie*, 1988), the trial judge outlined the role of the courts in giving effect to these section 23 rights:

> It is not sufficient for a School Board to simply decide that if it is not too inconvenient to its other plans, it will provide a facility to comply with section 23 Charter rights. The minorities have education rights that are not dependent on the will of the elected representatives of the people but are guaranteed by the Constitution and should be enforced by the Court if these rights have been infringed or denied. (p. 401)

Another area where parents and school authorities clash is with respect to education for children with disabilities. As with the court battles surrounding minority language educational rights, the heart of the dispute is control over the education of the child. Who should have the final say about what placement and program best suits the needs of children with physical or mental disabilities? Parents have begun to use the Charter to challenge the broad discretion exercised by provincial education officials to exclude disabled children from the school altogether or segregate them in special classes. Unlike the minority language area, there have been few court cases to shed light on these conflicting claims of parents and educators.

There has yet to be a clear court ruling on whether the Charter mandates the integration of disabled students into mainstream classes. In *Elwood v. Halifax County-Bedford District School Board* (1986), Chief Justice Glube granted a temporary injunction that effectively integrated the mentally disabled Luke Elwood for one year, pending a trial on the merits. In fact, the case did not go to trial, but settled at the last minute. The settlement was clearly reached in the shadow of Charter litigation, and the original injunction was obtained on the basis of Charter arguments. The result of the agreement is that Luke Elwood is to be integrated until at least senior high school and his parents are to be fully involved in his program as well as placement. Prior to the court case, the parents were given little input or opportunity to be heard, and these omissions provided additional grounds for legal challenge.

School board officials must now face the prospect of courts reviewing their placement and/or program decisions on the basis of both procedural irregularities and conformity with the equality guarantees of the Charter. It is not yet clear what approach the courts will take, because of the lack of decided cases. What does appear clear is that legislators and school board members will be required to take greater care in formulating their educational policies and practices. As has been the case with minority language educational rights, parents will use the courts as a way to make educational officials accountable for their actions.

One of the last acts of the government of Premier William Davis of Ontario was to extend public funding of Roman Catholic separate schools to the end of high school. This sparked a controversy not between the government and parents, but rather between groups supporting and opposing the full funding of Catholic schools in Ontario. Supporters argued that they were entitled to this funding as part of the section 93 guarantee of the Constitution Act, 1867. Opponents argued that to fund Catholic education and not other denominational education was a violation of both freedom of religion and equality as guaranteed in the Charter. This hot political controversy went to the courts in *Reference Re Roman Catholic Separate High School Funding* (1987). The Supreme Court upheld the funding of Catholic schools, relying upon the constitutional guarantees for the original denominational schools. It would appear that non-traditional claims to denominational education will have no more success than claims to be educated in a heritage rather than official language.[9]

Another challenge to denominational schools based on the human rights code, rather than the Charter, was mounted by a British Columbia teacher. In *Re Caldwell and Stuart*

(1984) the Supreme Court upheld the right of a Catholic school to dismiss a teacher for marrying outside the faith. There is no complete immunity from human rights codes and the Charter, but denominational schools are given broad discretion on matters vital to the character of the schools and their goals. It is not easy to determine what is vital to the denominational character of a school system. The Supreme Court ruled in *Greater Montreal Protestant School Board v. A.G. Quebec* (1989) that only the denominational aspects of the school curriculum, in the narrow sense, were immune from provincial powers to alter the curriculum. In general, the powers of denominational schools have not been reduced in the early days of the Charter.

SUBSTANTIVE INDIVIDUAL RIGHTS

One of the first questions to emerge when individual rights are concerned is whose rights are in issue. This is complicated in the education field, because parents usually act on behalf of their children. When it comes to education, the primary right should be that of the child (MacKay, 1984). It should also be noted that teachers who can be the target of a Charter challenge also have rights to litigate under the Charter. Thus individual teachers, parents, and students are the main litigants.

Religion appears to be the major concern of parents in early Charter cases. Section 2(a) of the Charter guarantees freedom of "religion and conscience," and this was the basis of a challenge to compulsory school attendance in *R. v. Jones* (1986). Alberta, like most provinces, made school attendance compulsory unless an individual fit a recognized exception. Reverend Jones kept his children out of school and educated them in his church basement. He would not ask the state authorities to certify his school because that would also have been contrary to his religion. The Supreme Court rejected his challenges to the provisions of the Alberta education statute. Some judges found that there was no violation of freedom of religion and others that the limitations of the Alberta statute were reasonable.

In *Zylberberg v. Sudbury Board of Education* (1988) the Ontario Appeal Court invalidated the school prayer at the beginning of the day as violating freedom of religion under the Charter. At the trial level, the prayer was upheld as promoting moral values in a predominantly Christian country. Finally a Sikh student won the right to take his kirpan (a ceremonial dagger) into the classroom, so long as it was blunted and remained in its sheath (*Tuli v. St. Albert Protestant Board of Education,* 1985). A later human rights board of inquiry found that there was no religious discrimination against Mr. Tuli, but by then he had already graduated from school.

Freedom of expression in the schools has not attracted as much attention as religion. In *Cromer v. British Columbia Teachers' Federation* (1986), a teacher was disciplined for criticizing a fellow teacher in a public meeting. In her defence, she relied upon freedom of expression under section 2(b) of the Charter. The court held that the limitations of the teachers' Code of Ethics were reasonable and Ms. Cromer's challenge failed. Freedom of association claims by parents and teachers have also met with little success under the Charter.[10]

The major equality challenge to the educational system has been with respect to mandatory retirement. A conflicting case in this issue was resolved by the Supreme Court in *McKinney v. University of Guelph* (1990). The majority of the Court held that universities in this case were legally autonomous and hence that the Charter did not apply. It did not preclude the possibility that the Charter might apply to other universities, or that other university functions might come under Charter scrunity. The majority also argued that, even if the Charter did apply, the universities' policies would be saved under section 1 as being reasonable and justifiable limits. In *Nevio Rossi v. School District No. 57* (1985) a male physical education teacher was awarded damages for being denied a job teaching female students. This was a human rights case, but the same principles would likely apply to the Charter.

PROCEDURAL INDIVIDUAL RIGHTS

Canadians have the right to a fair hearing before an unbiased decision-maker when the state adjudicates their interests. These procedural rights predate the Charter in the forms of statutory guarantees and the common-law rules of natural justice and fairness. In spite of these protections, educators have not always respected these rights. In the placement of children with disabilities, the parents are sometimes not involved in the process. The failure to include the parents in the assessment of Luke Elwood and the inadequate opportunity for the parents to present their own case before the school board were the grounds of legal challenge in the 1986 *Elwood* case (Batten, 1988, chap. 2). Teachers' procedural rights have generally been better protected in the form of both legislative provisions and the terms of collective agreements. Students, who tend to be at the bottom of the school hierarchy, have had few procedural protections in the school discipline process, but in recent years, notice to parents and hearing rights have been introduced by statutory amendments. Procedural issues have become more central in the enforcing of school rules (Dickinson & MacKay, 1989, chaps. 4, 5).

The key Charter provision with respect to procedural rights is section 7, which states that "Everyone has the right to life, liberty and security of the person and the right not to be deprived thereof except in accordance with the principles of fundamental justice." The principles of fundamental justice are a constitutional form of the fair-hearing rights discussed above, but the thorny issue is just what constitutes the "life, liberty and security of the person" interests that trigger this section.

Does the protection of section 7 apply when a decision is made affecting the livelihood of a teacher? In *Noyes v. South Cariboo School District No. 30* (1985), the court held that it did not apply to the employment interest. A later conflicting case concerning doctors practising their profession held that section 7 did apply to the livelihood interest (*Wilson v. Medical Services Comm.*, 1989). The impact of section 7 on teachers remains unclear. With respect to students and parents, the key question is whether section 7 embraces a right to education. Elsewhere it has been argued that there is such a constitutional right to education in Canada (MacKay & Krinke, 1987). A Newfoundland court concluded that section 7 interests did extend to education in *R. v. Kind* (1984). That section 7 extends to education was also assumed but not decided by the Supreme Court of Canada in *R. v. Jones* (1986). Such an extension of section 7 would enhance the rights of parents and students in both academic and disciplinary matters.

The applicability of the Charter's legal rights (sections 7–14) to the school setting has received little attention to date. These sections have generally been applied in the criminal context. Their implications for schools were addressed in *R. v. G. (J.M.)* (1986). A school principal searched a student's socks after being informed by another student that J.M.G. possessed narcotics. The principal found marijuana and the student was later charged with possession. This was held to be a reasonable search and thus not in violation of the student's section 8 Charter rights. There was also found to be no need to read the student his rights in accordance with section 10 of the Charter, because the student was not detained by the principal. Teachers and parents fare better on procedural rights than students, who have the least protection both before and after the Charter.

CONCLUSIONS

Rights discourse in the school has probably made the educational environment more adversarial than it has been in the past. This has some negative effects, as conflict can hinder the learning process. It also has some positive aspects. Gone are the days when teachers and principals could be self-appointed gods, exercising their discretionary powers as they felt appropriate. School officials must be more clearly accountable to parents, students, and fellow teachers for their decisions and actions. The Charter has also forced a re-examination of rules, which is a good educational and legal exercise.

Whether the Charter is used for good or bad depends to a great degree upon the vision of the judges who will put the flesh on the bare bones of the document. At the level of the Supreme Court of Canada, the vision has been a positive one, which offers some hope that the Charter can be a vehicle for social change. The highest Court has repeatedly called for a broad reading of the Charter, so as to advance the powerless and the dispossessed in Canada. In the school environment, this would be the students and, to a lesser extent, the parents.

There is no doubt that the high cost of litigating Charter rights impedes the use of the courts to promote social change. This factor explains why few cases have been instigated by students. It is not surprising that minority language educational claims have been most frequent, as the parents pursuing these claims usually have federal funding to assist them. However, the threat of Charter litigation and the educative value of this rights discourse will help to raise people's consciousness. While we should not expect rapid change, the Charter may assist schools in becoming fair and just. Students would be able to learn good citizenship by the deeds of education officials as well as by their words. Rights discourse is not a cure for society's ills, and there are some negative side effects, but it does offer some promise.

DISCUSSION QUESTIONS

❏ What are the advantages and disadvantages of adopting the rights paradigm in the field of education?

❏ Which major educational issues do you think should be resolved in the courts? Who do you think would be the major beneficiaries of such judicial resolution?

❏ Is it accurate to suggest that the Canadian Charter of Rights and Freedoms moves Canadian educators away from their traditional focus on "collective rights" and toward the American-style focus on "individual rights"? Support your answer by referring to early Charter cases dealing with educational issues.

❏ What distinguishes rights from policies or privileges? In legal terms, there is a hierarchy of rights. In practical terms, what does that mean?

❏   In what respects might lawyers and educators be described as having different values? How might these differing value systems be accommodated within a modern school system?

NOTES

1.   Not only does this provision trump other forms of law that are lower on the hierarchy, but it also claims to trump the other rights guaranteed in the Charter. Ironically, the section has been most successfully used by males to date, rather than to enhance the equality of women, as it was intended to do. This is a sobering reminder of the limits of rights talk as a means to real social change.

2.   Schools provide a good example of the hierarchy of legal rules being inverted. It is the low-level policies of school boards, principals, and individual classroom teachers that dictate how a school runs, rather than the vaguely worded provisions of the education statutes or the Charter. This is starting to change as the courts give concrete meaning to the Charter and thereby limit discretionary policy-making. Nonetheless, one should not underestimate the value of a policy in applied terms, even if it has little legal currency.

3.   Because other provisions of the Charter give credence to the bicultural vision of Canada by guaranteeing language rights for the official English and French groups, the real constitutional commitment to multiculturalism is not clear. Sections 16–23 of the Charter give special status to Canada's two official language groups. In the realm of religion, section 29 of the Charter still gives preference to certain well-established denominations and protects their school systems. The Charter reflects the conflicting principles that animate Canadian society.

4.   While neither the civil nor the criminal cases involving James Keegstra have directly identified the right to be free of discrimination as a student's right, that is the logic of extending the hate propaganda laws to the classroom context. The majority of the Supreme Court in *R. v. Keegstra* (1990) found that the law that prohibits willful promotion of hatred is a justifiable limit under section 1 to the freedom of expression guaranteed by section 2(b).

5.   After the world became aware of the atrocities committed during the Second World War, and in particular the treatment of Jewish people, the nations of the world recognized the importance of human rights. These rights were not only enshrined at the international level, but also many countries (including Canada) enacted human rights codes to provide legal protection for the victims of discrimination. This increased rights consciousness has been reflected not just in the legal system but throughout Western society.

6.   Since the rulings of the Supreme Court of Canada in *Andrews v. Law Society of British Columbia* (1989) and *R. v. Turpin* (1989) the potential scope of equality rights in section 15 of the Charter has been narrowed. First, the Court insists that the unlisted grounds of discrimination in section 15 of the Charter must be analogous to the listed grounds. Second, the Court sends a clear signal that it will be reluctant to use section 15 in the economic sphere. Thus it is less likely that the Court would use section 15 to ensure equality of educational services in all provinces, since the *Andrews* and *Turpin* cases have been decided.

7.   Section 15 of the Charter was delayed until 1985 so that the various governments would have time to put their legislative houses in order. This important equality provision reads as follows:

(1) Every individual is equal before and under the law and has the right to the equal protection and equal benefit of the law without discrimination and, in particular, without discrimination based on race, national or ethnic origin, colour, religion, sex, age or mental or physical disability.

(2) Subsection (1) does not preclude any law, program or activity that has as its object the amelioration of conditions of disadvantaged individuals or groups including those

that are disadvantaged because of race, national or ethnic origin, colour, religion, sex, age or mental or physical disability.

8. The overall provision was the price exacted by the provinces in return for supporting Prime Minister Trudeau's Charter. These provinces were not comfortable in giving the final word to judges in policy areas where legislators normally have the final say. This override provision does not apply to democratic, mobility, or language rights, but does apply to the rest of the Charter. It is the classic Canadian compromise between parliamentary sovereignty and an entrenched bill of rights. Since the introduction of the Charter, the override clause has been invoked only three times.

9. Denominational rights are held by those who operated separate schools at the time the province entered Confederation. This means that some religions are more equal than others under the Canadian Constitution—a principle that flies in the face of freedom of religion. Similarly, in the field of language rights, the official languages of Canada are given protections not available to heritage languages or, for that matter, aboriginal languages. This would appear to violate equality under the Charter, but the point has not yet been litigated.

10. Freedom of association in the economic sense of the right to bargain and to strike has been regarded as a private matter outside the reach of the Charter. In any event, these rights are protected for teachers by statutes and collective agreements.

REFERENCES

A.G. Quebec v. Quebec Association of Protestant School Boards, [1984] 2 Supreme Court Reports 66.

Anderson, J. (1985). Will Charter usher in a "new school law?" *Ontario Lawyers' Weekly*, 5, 25.

Andrews v. Law Society of British Columbia (1989), 1 Supreme Court Reports 143.

Bales v. Board of School Trustees (1984), 8 Administrative Law Reports 202 (B.C.S.C.).

Batten, J. (1988). *On trial*. Toronto: Macmillan.

Big M. Drug Mart v. R (1985), 18 Dominion Law Reports (4th) 321 (S.C.C.).

Canadian Bill of Rights. (1960). Revised Statutes of Canada. (1970). Appendix 3.

Canadian Multiculturalism Act. (1988). Statutes of Canada. c.31.

Constitution Act, 1867. (U.K. 30 & 31 Vict., c.3). Formerly the British North America Act (BNA).

Constitution Act, 1982. (Enacted by the Canada Act, 1982 (U.K.), c. 11—Schedule B, Part 1 being the Canadian Charter of Rights and Freedoms).

Cromer v. British Columbia Teachers' Federation (1986), 4 British Columbia Law Reports (2d) 273 (C.A.).

Cruickshank, D. (1986). Charter equality rights: The challenge to education law and policy. In M.E. Manley-Casimir & T.A. Sussel (Eds.). *The Courts in the classroom: The Charter and educational change*. Calgary: Detselig.

Dickinson, G.M., & MacKay, W. (Eds.). (1989). *Rights freedoms and the education system in Canada*. Toronto: Emond Montgomery.

Dolmage v. Muskoka Board of Education (1985), 49 Ontario Reports (2d) 546 (Div. Ct.).

Dworkin, R. (1977). *Taking rights seriously*. London: Duckworth.

Elwood v. Halifax County-Bedford District School Board (1986), An unreported decision of October, 1986 (N.S.T.D.).

Ford v. A.G. Quebec (1988), 90 National Reporter 84 (S.C.C.).

Fulford, R. (1986, December). *Saturday Night*.

Greater Montreal Protestant School Board v. A.G. Quebec, [1989] 1 Supreme Court Reports 377.

Lavoie v. A.G. Nova Scotia (1988), 54 Nova Scotia Reports (2d) 387 (N.S.T.D.).

Lavoie v. A.G. Nova Scotia (1989), 58 Dominion Law Reports (4th) 293 (N.S.C.A.).

MacKay, W. (1983). Protecting ethnic rights under the Canadian Charter of Rights and Freedoms. *Multiculturalism, 6*(23).

MacKay, W. (1984). *Education law in Canada.* Toronto: Emond Montgomery.

MacKay, W. (1985). Case comment: Bales v. Board of School Trustees: Parents, school boards and reasonable special education. *Administrative Law Reports, 8*, 225.

MacKay, W. (1987). Students as second class citizens under the Charter. *Criminal Reports, 54*, 390.

MacKay, W. (1988). The judicial role in educational policy-making: Promise or threat? *Education Law Journal, 1*, 127.

MacKay, W., & Krinke, G. (1987). Education as a basic human right: A response to special education and the Charter. *Canadian Journal of Law and Society, 2*, 73.

Mahe v. R. in Right of Alberta (1985), 22 Dominion Law Reports (4th) 24 (Alta. Q.B.).

Mahe v. R. in Right of Alberta, (1990) 1 Supreme Court Reports 342.

McKinney v. University of Guelph [1990], 3 Supreme Court Reports 229.

Nevio Rossi v. School District No.57 (1985),7 Canadian Human Rights Reporter Sll (B.C.).

Noyes v. South Cariboo School District No. 30 (1985), 64 British Columbia Law Reports 287 (S.C.).

R. v. G. (J.M.) (1986), 54 Criminal Reports (3d) 380 (Ont. C.A.).

R. v. Jones (1986), 2 Supreme Court Reports 284.

R. v. Keegstra (1990), 1 C.R. (4th) 129 (SCC).

R. v. Kind (1984), 149 Atlantic Provinces Reports 332 (Nfld. D.C.).

R. v. Oakes (1986), 65 National Reporter 87 (S.C.C.).

R. v. Turpin (1989), 1 Supreme Court Reports 1296.

R.W.D.S.U. v. Dolphin Delivery, [1986] 2 Supreme Court Reports 573.

Re Caldwell and Stuart (1984), 15 Dominion Law Reports (4th) 1 (S.C.C.).

Reference re Education Act of Ontario and Minority Language Education Rights. (1984). 47 Ontario Reports (2d) 1 (C.A.).

Reference re Roman Catholic Separate High School Funding. (1987). 40 Dominion Law Reports (4th) 18 (S.C.C.).

Samek, R.A. (1982). Untrenching fundamental freedoms. *McGill Law Journal, 27*, 757.

Schmeiser, D.A. (1987). Multiculturalism in Canadian education. In Canadian Human Rights Foundation (Ed.). *Multiculturalism and the Charter: A legal perspective.* Toronto: Carswell.

Singh v. Minister of Employment and Immigration (1985), 1 Supreme Court Reports 177.

Sussel, T.A., & Manley-Casimir, M.E. (1986). The Supreme Court of Canada as a national school board: The Charter and educational change. *Canadian Journal of Education, 11*, 313.

Tarnopolsky, W.S. (1983). Canada's new Charter of Rights and Freedoms. *Multiculturalism, 6*, 11.

Tuli v. St. Albert Protestant Board of Education (1985), An unreported decision of April, 1985 (Alta. Q.B.).

Turpel, M.E. (1989-90). Aboriginal peoples and the Canadian Charter: Interpretive monopolies, cultural differences. *Canadian Human Rights YearBook, 6*, 3.

Wilson v. Medical Services Commission of British Columbia, [1989] 2 Western Weekly
Reports 1 (B.C.C.A.).

Zylberberg v. Sudbury Board of Education (1988), 65 Ontario Reports (2d) 641 (Ont.
C.A.).

FURTHER READINGS

Bayefsky, A., & Eberts, M. (Eds.). (1985). *Equality rights and the Canadian Charter of Rights and Freedoms*. Toronto: Carswell.

Birch, I., & Richter, I. (1990). *Comparative school law*. London: Pergamon Press.

Csapo, M., & Goguen, L. (Eds.). (1990). *Special education across Canada: Issues and concerns for the 90s*. Vancouver: Centre for Human Development and Research.

Dickinson, G.M., & MacKay, A.W. (Eds.). (1989). *Rights freedoms and the education system in Canada*. Toronto: Emond Montgomery.

Foucher, P. (1985). *Constitutional language rights of official language minorities in Canada*. Ottawa: Department of Secretary of State.

Giles, W.H. (1988). *Schools and students*. Toronto: Carswell.

Hurlbert, E.L., & Hurlbert, M.A. (1989). *School law under the Charter of Rights and Freedoms*. Calgary: University of Calgary Press.

Lam, Y.L.J. (Ed.). (1990). *Canadian public education system: Issues and prospects*. Calgary: Detselig.

MacKay, A.W. (1984). *Education law in Canada*. Toronto: Emond Montgomery.

Manley-Casimir, M., & Sussel, T.A. (Eds.). (1986). *Courts in the classroom: Education and the Charter of Rights and Freedoms*. Calgary: Detselig.

Nichols, A., & Wuester, T. (Eds.). (1985). *The Canadian Charter of Rights and Freedoms and education law in British Columbia*. Vancouver: British Columbia School Trustees Association.

Poirier, D., Goguen, L., & Leslie, P. (1988). *Education rights of exceptional children in Canada*. Toronto: Carswell.

17

AFFIRMATIVE ACTION[1] FOR A JUST AND EQUITABLE SOCIETY

Aniko Varpalotai

> Equality is, at the very least, freedom from adverse discrimination. But what constitutes adverse discrimination changes with time, with information, with experience, and with insight. What we tolerated as a society 100, 50, or even 10 years ago is no longer necessarily tolerable. Equality is thus a process—a process of constant and flexible examination, of vigilant introspection, and of aggressive open-mindedness. (Abella, 1984, p. 1)

EDUCATION AND EQUITY

Justice Rosalie Silberman Abella's findings in the Report of the Commission on Equality in Employment are as relevant to education as they are to the work world. In fact, it can be argued that unless there is equity in education, there cannot be equity in employment or other aspects of our society. Equity issues are currently among the most central and contentious concerns in Canada—not only in education, but throughout our society. Equality is now enshrined in Canadian law—in the Charter of Rights and Freedoms, as well as in federal and provincial human rights codes. Despite the fact that equity is not only law but also policy in many jurisdictions, including education, the debate continues over its interpretation and application in practice.

Equity is a social issue, an economic issue, a legal issue (see Chapter 16); in short, the presence or absence of equity touches all aspects of our lives. Because of these far-reaching consequences, there has been a great deal of resistance, hype, misinformation, and emotional reaction in response to efforts to create a more just and equitable society in Canada, particularly as these efforts become more formalized and implemented. One of the key issues in Canada today is the gap between formal and real or substantive equality (Ayim, 1991).

Increasingly the principles of equality are enshrined in law and policy; even young children know the rhetoric of equity as they increasingly name unfair practices as sexist or racist. Although some progress in this regard is becoming evident, particularly in awareness levels, real change in the power relations between historically dominant and subordinate groups has yet to happen in any significant way. For this reason groups, including

educators, are increasingly calling for legislated affirmative action to replace largely inef-
fective voluntary programs (FWTAO, 1993).

The inclusion of equity issues in educational policies is said by some to have "politi-
cized" education (see D'Souza, 1991). One only has to recall the earliest principles of
public education in this country to realize that not only has education always been a
political enterprise, but also that "equality of opportunity" has long been one of the fundamental premises of a publicly funded educational system. Educators today are being
asked to be accountable like never before, and equity in principle only is no longer acceptable. Just as teachers are being asked to use "benchmarks" and standardized tests to
provide evidence of learning outcomes in their classrooms, so too are they being asked to
ensure that equity policies and laws are translated into day-to-day practices within their
schools.

What are some of the issues that need to be addressed in this regard? And what exactly
is meant by equity? affirmative action? equal opportunity? Does educational equity mean
sacrificing excellence? Does it mean teaching to the lowest common denominator? Educational and employment equity have raised fears that unqualified people will get hired
for jobs simply because of their sex or race. Others fear "reverse discrimination" for
previously advantaged groups. Will it cost a lot of money? How are we going to teach
math and reading if, on top of everything else, we now have to worry about equity too?
These are some of the common concerns and reactions to the issue of equity, most, if not
all, of which are based on misunderstandings. One must also consider the source of "anti-
equity" rhetoric, and the fuelling of the "politically correct" vs. "academic freedom"
debates (D'Souza, 1991). Nonetheless, it is true that the journey toward greater equity will
be felt by everyone as the "playing field" is levelled and organizations take on a more
diverse appearance and culture at every level.

HISTORICAL AND SOCIAL OVERVIEW

The struggle for equality by various groups is not a new and passing fad, as some would
argue. Equality among groups has been and continues to be used as the measure to judge
the fairness and justness of any given society. One of the United Nations' measures for
standard of living in any given country is the status of women and children; both groups
have historically suffered from a lack of power and status in most societies. A brief historical and social overview of some of the key struggles for equality in Canada sets the
stage for a discussion of these issues as they pertain to education. An introduction to some
of the definitions of equality that are currently in use, and the educational implications of
these terms, will also be discussed.

Previous chapters have provided some data on the changing nature of Canadian society
(see the chapters by Young, Purdy, Zhang, McAndrew, and Olson). Over the years the
demographics of our population have shifted as a result of fluctuating birth rates and waves
of immigration from different parts of the world, resulting in what we now call a "multicultural society" (see Chapter 12). Despite these major shifts in our population, we know
relatively little about the ways in which some groups benefit more than others from their
schooling experiences. Although it is assumed that equal opportunity exists for all, sociological studies tell us that many groups are disadvantaged in society in general (see Porter,
1965; Porter et al., 1982; Connell, 1993), and education in particular. There have, however,

been few data available to enable educators to attempt to identify and resolve differences in access or opportunity. Nonetheless, education policies throughout Canada have at least paid lip-service to the need to provide equality of opportunity to each student eligible for schooling. For example, a recent Ontario Ministry of Education curriculum document states:

> A commitment to equity means a commitment to social justice. This includes a commitment to removing established barriers and biases in school policies, programs, and practices so that the intended learning outcomes may be achieved by students of all societal groups, including those that have been traditionally disadvantaged. (1993, p. 2)

Moreover, inside and outside of education, many groups have organized themselves and raised questions about the nature and structure of a society that permits ongoing, systemic inequalities. Much of the questioning has focussed on the role of schooling as the major social institution for the young. It is argued that equality of opportunities and a change in attitudes must begin with the education of our youth.

Throughout the 1980s, the demands intensified for schools to respond to social needs; therefore the government, ministries of education, local school boards, and teachers' federations and associations have begun to address issues of equity in terms of educational policy, curriculum, and teacher education. For example, the Ontario Teachers' Federation includes a statement on discrimination in their policy handbook, stating that "a society in which all people may participate equally with equal access to opportunity is a basic tenet" (1993–94, pp. 24–25). The policy goes on to say that teachers must assume a leadership role "in the development of attitudes which foster a society in which all people may participate equally with equal access to opportunity . . . vigorously oppose any discrimination against any person . . . eliminate all forms of discrimination in their workplace . . . and that every person . . . has a right to equal treatment without discrimination because of race, creed, colour, national origin, political or religious affiliation, sex, sexual orientation, age, marital status, family relationship and disability" (pp. 24–25). Elsewhere, curriculum transformation projects seek to develop an "inclusive curriculum," wherein race, class, and gender issues are integrated into the curriculum to resist the marginalization of these issues, as well as to challenge the mainstream, exclusionary disciplines (Smith et al., 1990). For the most part these are not new issues, although some, like sexual orientation, have only recently begun to be recognized in official policies, amidst much controversy, and still with little support for gay and lesbian students in public schools (Eaton, 1993).

Many social movements formally organized themselves in North America during the activist 1960s, but there is evidence of collective action toward similar ends over centuries of struggle, by workers, women, and other disenfranchised groups. However, the 1960s popularized the notion of "consciousness raising" — in other words, the creation of an awareness of the inequalities faced by members of particular social groups—for example, blacks and the civil rights movement, the women's liberation or feminist movement, workers and the labour movement, Native peoples' struggle for self-determination, people with disabilities, and the gay and lesbian rights movement. Other social change agents, such as peace and environmental activists, have given rise to global efforts.

These grass-roots movements provided a voice for previously powerless groups and greater visibility to existing inequities, leading to pressures for change on the powerful and dominant mainstream institutions and decision-makers, including those involved in education. More recently, coalitions have developed between some groups as links and commonalities were recognized. For example, the women's movement in North America has been criticized for being primarily white, middle class, and out of touch with the concerns of poor and working-class women, as well as immigrant and minority women. The 1980s and 1990s has seen the development of a more inclusive women's movement, along with alliances forming with labour groups, immigrant women, Native women, women with disabilities, anti-poverty coalitions, gay and lesbian rights activists, and others. These changes reflected struggle within and among equality-seeking groups themselves. With increased political experience and analysis, activist groups have begun to create an awareness of *systemic inequalities*, that is inequalities that are reflected in and reproduced by the major social institutions, including education, within their very structures and organization. This concept will be discussed in greater detail below.

WHERE DO I BELONG AND HOW DOES EQUITY AFFECT ME?

W hen studying specific equity issues, be they related to race, ancestry, colour, ethnic origin, citizenship, creed, sex, sexual orientation, age, marital status, family status, or disability, it is important to keep in mind the interconnections and the social complexity of equality—in other words, its systemic nature. Equality in this context has to do with social equality rather than individual equality. It is clear, however, that all forms of inequality will have personal, individual ramifications. Within any group there will be differences in intelligence, skill, aptitude, and ambition. These individual differences are to be expected both within and between groups. Social and structural inequalities, on the other hand, are those in which entire groups are disadvantaged in some respects with regard to education, employment, social status, or quality of life, not due to their individual characteristics, but rather because of discrimination against their entire group, whatever its social label might be. By the simple fact that they were born into that group they are perceived by society to fit particular social and cultural roles, which are differently valued in society relative to others. These are the socially prescribed inequalities that social *policies* are intended to address. These are what are referred to as systemic inequalities— based on deeply rooted prejudice, bigotry and adverse discrimination, and irrational fears of difference and diversity. These attitudes and beliefs rarely have any sound basis in fact but lead to attitudes such as sexism, homophobia, and racism with their subsequent negative behaviours and consequences. On average, regardless of race, gender, or creed, people are more alike than they are different. But by labelling and treating groups of people differently, including educating them based on perceived differences in ability and potential, disparities are created and exacerbated. Several typical examples follow.

A girl who has not been exposed to sports since early childhood will inevitably have fewer associated skills and interests than a boy who has been socialized into sports activities since early childhood. While our society continues to encourage boys to participate in sports more than girls, the disparity in participation rates is often linked to seemingly inherent biological factors ("girls are physically weaker than boys") than to the cultural milieu in which the two genders are differently educated. Girls who are not exposed to sports, or are actively discouraged from participating, will inevitably show less interest in these activities as they get older, which then justifies the unequal allocation of resources for girls' sport ("they're not interested anyway"), and which makes it difficult for girls who *are* interested to pursue these activities. With so few girls encouraged and supported to participate, even fewer adult women become professional or world-class athletes; this lack of visibility of female role models further reinforces the notion that sports are not for females, and the cycle continues: it becomes a self-fulfilling prophecy.

This is just one area where sex-role stereotypes have been created and fostered. Yet we know that many girls and women are interested in sports and have become successful athletes when they were encouraged and provided with the necessary resources. Still, the attitude prevails and is reproduced generation after generation and reflected in our school sports and physical education programs. In a similar process, black or working-class children are assumed to be uninterested in attending university. The resulting inequities from stereotypes such as these, entrenched in early childhood, are reflected in all of our major social institutions: our governments, boards of directors, school curriculum, and so on. These ultimately lead to differential relations of power and dominance between designated groups in a particular society, with major social repercussions not only for the individuals affected but for all of society. While a dominant group appears to gain from their power within this socially constructed hierarchy of privilege, many more lose out in a variety of ways. The only way to interrupt these repetitive cycles of systemic inequalities is through some form of affirmative action.

To get a sense of these interconnections and relations of power and dominance as they affect your own life, consider the following and situate yourself within the current Canadian framework of dominant and subordinate groups. Think about the ways in which you were socialized, encouraged (or discouraged) to pursue certain interests or activities, based on your gender, race/ethnicity, religion, abilities/disabilities, socioeconomic status, sexual orientation, skin colour. How might your life have been different if you were a member of a different sex, race, socioeconomic class, religion, sexual orientation, and so forth? Consider the ways these might have affected your range of choices.

It is important to remember that perceptions will differ based on one's relation to the dominant group(s). You may recall that the "Montreal massacre," in which fourteen women were murdered by a gunman at the engineering school of the University of Montreal in 1989, was interpreted quite differently by women and men. For women it was representative of the violent resistance still present in our society against women entering non-traditional fields, in this case a school of engineering. For some men, the act was viewed not as another example of systemic violence against women, but simply the act of a solitary "madman." Women were told they were politicizing an isolated incident, despite the fact that the gunman's suicide note stated explicitly that he hated "feminists" and he had a list targeting prominent Canadian women (Malette & Chalouh, 1991). Regardless of one's interpretation of this horrible tragedy, the fact that it occurred within an educational institution galvanized both men and women to make changes with regard to educational equity, particularly in the encouragement of more women entering science and technology programs.

There are many other examples to illustrate the impact of systemic inequities on educational performance and achievement. Still, some will argue that their success is due to their own hard work and persistence, and that it has nothing to do with their gender, race, or social class. While individual perseverance certainly counts, it doesn't explain the great disparities between groups of people. This attitude also leads to a "blame the victim" mentality and discounts all of the social advantages or disadvantages that contribute to an individual's relative "success" or "failure" in our society. While a relatively small group of individuals, notably those who also identify with the dominant group(s) in our society, are prepared to argue that white, able-bodied, heterosexual males are inherently superior to all others, and therefore are entitled to the greatest proportion of power and wealth in our society, most would concede that this belief does not make sense given the fact that there is no biological, social, cultural, or scientific evidence of their superiority. It is helpful to occasionally imagine ourselves in someone else's shoes—the struggle toward equality entails a certain amount of understanding and empathy.

In addition to recognizing existing power differentials, this exercise also illustrates the complexities of social structure and identification. We are not easily categorized as members of one group or another—each of us may in fact belong to more than one group, and therefore it is artificial in some ways to treat these issues as separate, isolated entities. For this reason, those working to make the curriculum more inclusive talk about the integration of issues, rather than the separation and segregation of issues in which equity concerns are frequently marginalized and considered to be of interest only to those who are directly affected. An example of this is women's studies or black studies. While an argument can be made to retain these as distinct entities for those interested in developing and studying in an area that has had little institutional support in the past, it is imperative that we all become introduced to these issues of concern if we are to understand the need for greater equality. All history or social studies curriculum, for example, should address the diverse make-up of our country. An inclusive, integrated curriculum would make it clear that we are all affected by the contributions of diverse cultures, and by the inequalities that continue to impede our society.

The complexity of these issues is such that while white males, for example, may appear to be the most privileged group among us, there are many poor white men, as well as gay white men who would argue that they are also left out of the dominant group—and so they are. These complexities reinforce once again the systemic nature of inequality and the ways in which the presence or absence of equity impacts on each of our lives. The objective is not to establish a hierarchy of oppression, but simply to point out that equity is relevant to everyone, one way or another, and that it is exceedingly complex, as is anything social or cultural—there are no easy answers or solutions.

Equity policies are intended to address group concerns. Despite the fact that some members of certain groups appear to have enjoyed greater social mobility in recent years —women have become prime ministers, black men have become federal court judges, gay and lesbian politicians and entertainers have become more visible—the true measure of equity is a cross-group comparison. We need to move beyond tokenism to systemic change; assimilation of members of previously subordinate groups into unchanged structures constructed by members of a dominant group does not alter fundamental social relations leading to a more equitable society. Relatively speaking, how many women have attained political office? How many black people have been promoted to significant and powerful positions, and how many gays or lesbians have dared to publicly identify themselves as such? Individual examples may be signs of social change, but we need to look at the bigger picture to get a true sense of a society's commitment to equity. Have these individuals had an impact on social policy? Have they been able to pave the way for more diversity in the workforce or for greater tolerance for alternative views? Despite some apparent progress, we continue to hear about women being forced to quit their jobs because of sexual harassment, blacks experiencing disproportionate police brutality, and violence against homosexuals. Viewed within this context, we get a sense of the ongoing systemic inequalities in our society—and this is where the education system begins to play a part.

EDUCATIONAL IMPLICATIONS

Education is not immune to the inequalities cited above. Educational equity encompasses teachers as well as students, and includes the right to an education, as well as rights *within* education. Educational equity is also intended to prepare children and youth to live their lives in a more just and equitable society.

Even before children begin their formal education they have already learned a variety of social lessons; very young children will solemnly declare the "rules" of sex roles, including the kinds of toys and games that are appropriate for girls and boys (Bailey, 1993). The educational workforce is also skewed in terms of its diversity throughout the ranks, including small proportions of men teaching primary grades, few women in administration, and little cultural diversity in the teaching force.

Changes are needed both within the education system and in the curriculum if educators are to contribute to the creation of a more just and equitable society. Many educators are becoming overwhelmed by reports of schoolyard violence motivated by race, gender, or sexual orientation. More subtle forms of discrimination occur daily in classrooms through the "hidden curriculum," in some cases through the words and actions of well-meaning teachers. The differential treatment of boys and girls, members of ethnic minority groups, and children from varied socioeconomic backgrounds is now well-documented. Teacher education programs, in-service professional development workshops, and teachers' associations are in varying degrees researching and responding to concerns that schools in fact reproduce the inequalities of the larger society.

Many of the social movements mentioned earlier have focussed on the educational system as both part of the problem and part of the solution to the systemic inequalities identified in society. For example, the civil rights movement challenged systemic racism and raised central questions about the meaning of equality and the ways in which some groups were excluded from full participation in society. Integration of the schools and the right to equal educational opportunities were key demands.

Similarly, the women's movement was organized to challenge economic and social inequalities stemming from gender discrimination, and the educational system was criticized for its sexism in school texts, the absence of women in positions of educational leadership, the sex stereotyping of some subjects, and the career guidance given to both girls and boys based on their sex rather than their interests or abilities (see Chapter 22).

Native people continue to challenge the structural inequities that face them. Here, too, education has been identified as part of the problem: both the curriculum and the predominantly white teachers are often racist and deemed irrelevant to the Native culture (see Chapter 23).

Our educational system has also been criticized for both reflecting and reproducing unequal social relations between socioeconomic classes. It has been shown that working-class kids are streamed in such a way that they end up with less and inferior education and fewer job opportunities. A survey of the vocational and academic programs of any secondary school will bear this out (see Curtis et al., 1992).

Interestingly, despite the fact that all of these groups have heavily criticized the education system for perpetuating all of these inequalities, education is rarely rejected outright. Instead, education is seen as a key to social change. The vast majority of people continue to want the benefits of education for their children. Some people will argue that education should not be involved in the business of "social engineering," but recall once more the original ideas behind public education—when has education *not* been engaged in so-called social engineering? Is it not the ultimate purpose of public education to create a better society for all? Are individuals not drawn to the teaching profession because they have visions of creating a better world through their teaching and influence on the young?

DEFINITIONS OF EQUALITY

Despite years of struggle for equality there is still a lack of consistency in the meaning, application, and measure of the varieties of definitions of equality, and their subsequent applications to education. Nonetheless, social activists continue to see education as a means to social change and equity, and educational policy-makers continue to introduce various programs and plans designed to achieve this goal. Why do these groups persist when education has been slow to respond to these demands in the past? How is equality defined by these groups, and what do they hope to achieve through the schools? Finally, what is the role of the education system in relation to social justice and equality objectives?

It should be understood that these groups vary in their objectives. Some have very specific objectives, such as access to the schools for the teaching of heritage languages, which may or may not be connected to deeper equality goals for ethnic minorities (Cummins & Danesi, 1990). Others, such as the women's movement, have more radical objectives, and the school system is only one of the major social agencies considered as an instrument for achieving broad political and systemic changes (Gaskell et al., 1989).

Equality itself is understood in a variety of ways. People are often unclear about what they mean by equality. There are several possible frameworks within which equality can be analyzed. Claude Lessard, in Chapter 13, discusses the distinctions between equality of access, equality of treatment, and equality of results. These definitions will be revisited here as they apply to some of the more controversial areas of equity in education. Equality of opportunity and equality of outcome are the two key ways of understanding educational equity; one is based on the entry point (access and treatment), the other is a measure of educational results upon completion or exiting from the schooling system. Abella's remarks with regard to employment equity are equally relevant in education:

> To create equality of opportunity, we have to do different things for different people. We have to systematically eradicate the impediments to these options according to the actual needs of different groups, not according to what we think their needs should be. And we have to give individuals an opportunity to use their abilities according to their potential and not according to what we think their potential should be. The process is an exercise in redistributive justice. Its object is to prevent the denial of access to society's benefits because of distinctions that are invalid. (1984, p. 4)

The various approaches and definitions of equality are not necessarily mutually exclusive. They may in fact be steps along the way to achieving fundamental social change. They differ in degree of impact, and the extent of structural, systemic change involved.

EQUALITY OF ACCESS

Equality of access implies that all individuals, regardless of their social group affiliations, are entitled to a basic level of education. It rests on an earlier assumption that education is the gateway to social mobility—in other words, the merit system. The school doors are theoretically open to all (by law in Canada), and it is up to each individual to come in and take part in the schooling process, and thus take advantage of the opportunities that education affords. In the end, each individual reaps educational and occupational rewards based on their ability and hard work—in other words, everyone gets what they deserve. Compulsory and free public education, subsidized postsecondary tuition fees, student loans for needy students, wheelchair ramps and elevators, co-educational classes, are all based on this notion of equality of access. In principle, no one of school age is barred from schooling because of financial hardship or physical barriers; in fact, everyone must receive a minimal amount of education up to the age of 16 because of compulsory-attendance laws.

It could be argued that this is the most any society can be expected to do for its citizens in terms of educational equality of opportunity. However, this assumes that everyone starts on an equal footing when they enter the public school system, and that everyone has equal resources to benefit from their schooling. Marxist sociologists have argued that some children come to school with more "cultural capital" than others. A child from a wealthier home will most likely come to school with cultural advantages outweighing those of a child from a poor home; simple things like books at home, travel, educational toys, computers, and so on, and the more basic provisions of proper nutrition, warm clothes, a peaceful and loving home, and good health. Meanwhile, feminists and other groups have argued that access to an educational system that has been created primarily by and for a dominant group and that negates the experience of women and minorities, does not constitute access to an equitable education at all. Access, in this expanded definition, includes access to equitable curriculum content as well as decision-making and leadership roles. Simply granting access to education does not take into account the effect of these advantages and disadvantages inherent in the traditional school system and curriculum. There is the further issue of what kind of education one is given access to. While equality of access is a step in the right direction, access alone does not address the deeper issues of inequities within the educational system itself.

EQUALITY OF TREATMENT

Equality of treatment means that beyond simple access to education, schools should treat all students alike—they should not discriminate. But discrimination is not always a bad thing if one student's needs are greater than another's. Affirmative action, in fact, means positive discrimination—helping those who have been traditionally disadvantaged in our society to overcome societal and systemic barriers so they will in fact have equal opportunities. Feminists and those fighting racial discrimination have distinguished between equality of treatment, which may be the equivalent of non-sexist (or gender-neutral) or non-racist treatment, with the more active form of anti-sexist (gender-sensitive) or anti-racist approaches. A teacher does not provide equal opportunities for his or her students if he or she ignores the gendered socialization that both the boys and the girls have experienced throughout their young lives. By taking these factors into account, and encouraging activities and experiences that a girl or a boy may have been steered away from despite their interest or aptitude, the teacher is practising gender-sensitive education, and is promoting social change rather than an acceptance of the inequitable status quo. This approach will in fact achieve what most educational policies claim to promote—that is, the full potential of each student regardless of their sex, race, and so forth—while recognizing and challenging the barriers society has put in their way based on these factors. Canadian schools have already gone beyond the pure equality-of-treatment approach by offering a variety of compensatory programs, and providing resources for disadvantaged or "exceptional" students. In some instances this has led to segregation, which may or may not be based on prior social factors (gender, race, class), or they have been provided a common curriculum in mixed-ability classrooms to overcome social barriers (Ayim, 1991).

There have been mixed interpretations of what equality of treatment entails—does it mean treating all children the same, or does it mean treating children according to need? Both interpretations are problematic in one way or another, and both are individualistic in nature, devoid of social context. Compensatory programs are often interpreted to mean that the problem lies with those who are less equal and that therefore they must be helped to do better within the mainstream. Fundamental assumptions are not questioned, such as: does the curriculum address the interests of girls? do Native children see themselves in a positive light in the resource materials? are the children the problem or is it a deeper issue of an exclusionary, inappropriate curriculum? In comparison with the earlier notion of equality of access, which simply advocates the provision of education for all, equality of treatment intends to tailor the educational program to meet individual students' needs. The critical point is that students are treated as unique individuals, without social qualifiers or context. Thus, a student is either more or less intelligent or capable than others as determined by tests and other evaluation techniques, and these results are considered as innate abilities rather than socially derived or influenced.

Once again, this definition of equality of opportunity is based on an individualistic, competitive, meritocratic system, wherein students are "sifted and sorted" by the education system for future occupational roles. There is no overt discrimination; educators working within this system sincerely believe that they are offering all children an equal educational opportunity, suited to their levels of ability and potential—some students simply have more ability and potential than others. This perspective leaves the mainstream educational system and curriculum unexamined; it simply "treats" the symptoms, and tries to make students fit into the mainstream educational model.

Viewed from the perspective of systemic inequality, however, clear patterns begin to emerge. According to current streaming and drop-out patterns, it would seem that ability and potential are not randomly distributed. Poor, black, and Native students appear in the so-called lower ability groups more often than others. Girls and boys are disproportionately distributed in certain subject areas. There seems to be more than academic ability and individual potential at work in the educational decisions made for and by students. Equality of treatment does not produce equality of results.

EQUALITY OF RESULTS

The idea of *equality of results or condition* has been the most controversial of all approaches, because it is the most interventionist, and because it requires fundamental changes in the ways we educate. This is the *affirmative-action* or "positive-discrimination" approach within education, which, as in other contexts, has been misunderstood, inconsistently practised, and actively resisted. This is the point at which detractors argue that striving for equality will compromise excellence. The "tyranny of political correctness" is invoked, as those standing to gain from the status quo resist any significant changes to the way schooling functions. There are fears that the "average student" will be overlooked in favour of attending to special needs or exceptional students. It is true that there have been instances of misapplication and abuse, which is all the more reason for better teacher preparation and resource materials to prevent these from happening in the future.

The equality of results approach shifts the responsibility for scholastic success and academic achievement away from the individual (though not completely) and lays it at the feet of the educational system itself. Rather than slotting students into convenient ability groupings, with lower or higher expectations, this perspective maintains that the system must change in order to meet the needs of the client group, to ensure that all students leave school with the same high-quality education. This means that some students will have considerably more resources directed their way than others in order to help them attain the highest possible results. In effect, this establishes a form of affirmative action, or positive discrimination, in favour of those most in need. Furthermore, the educational system is re-evaluated both in terms of structure and content to determine why some groups appear to be less successful in attaining positive results. For example: Why do girls reject maths and sciences in secondary schools (Walkerdine, 1989)? Why are basic-level courses filled with predominantly poor and visible-minority students? Why are there more boys than girls identified for special education or enriched programs? Why are gay and lesbian youth alienated by the school climate and the apparent indifference to their concerns (Eaton, 1993)? Who are the drop-outs and why do they leave school prematurely (Fine, 1991; Radwanski, 1987)?

If the education system, and educators, are truly committed to equitable outcomes, benchmarks need to be established not just in the academic sense but with a view to "affirmative action" — that is, a clear social agenda toward equity. In order to achieve this, curricular and teaching methods will have to change. Schools may need to work more closely with other social agencies, rather than in isolation, to ensure and advocate the well-being of children and youth in our communities. The basic needs must be met if children are to learn to the best of their abilities. Some schools already provide a variety of compensatory programs such as "head-start" programs for disadvantaged pre-schoolers, breakfast and lunch programs for the poor, single-sex math and science classes to overcome gender stereotypes, lower student–teacher ratios for children with special needs, and translated school newsletters for immigrant parents. These are important but relatively superficial programs to accommodate visible needs. More fundamental are those efforts that encourage an inclusive, non-racist and non-sexist curriculum, that value each member of the class for the diversity they contribute, and that foster co-operative and collaborative learning so all can succeed. Briskin (1990) talks about the need to advance beyond merely a gender- and race-neutral classroom that claims to offer equal opportunity to all, to an anti-sexist and anti-racist classroom that openly challenges the daily instances of discrimination and socialization leading to inequities.

The above examples reflect the continuum of definitions of equality and inequality ranging from piecemeal efforts of "compensatory education" that attempt to make up for individual disadvantages, to fundamental changes to the education system itself in which everyone plays a part.

Efforts to create a truly equitable society are slow and frustrating—the resistance is strong. It has been argued that sound, committed efforts are needed in order to make a true difference, given that rhetoric and "gentle persuasion" have not worked in the past. Teachers, too, must be educated about what is at stake. Teachers must be able to distinguish between formal and substantive equity if their work is to be meaningful in this regard. While recent laws, policies, and increased talk are all indications of our society's commitment to equality for all groups in Canada, and particularly within the educational system, we must search for evidence of results. How effective are these laws and policies? What do we do in our curriculum and day-to-day classroom interactions to ensure that equality principles are translated into practice? We must learn to identify issues of injustice, and determine when and how we might best deal with them. Schoolyard taunts and discriminatory hiring practices will warrant quite different strategies. While it is true that schools and teachers can't make fundamental social changes happen on their own, educators must ask themselves what is the particular role of the school in this regard? What can each individual teacher and school administrator do to create a more equitable learning environment and ultimately contribute to a more just and fair society for all?

CONCLUSIONS

Abella's call for affirmative action applies to education as it does to any other social institution:

> If we do not act positively to remove barriers, we wait indefinitely for them to be removed. This would mean that we are prepared in the interim to tolerate prejudice and discrimination. By not acting, we unfairly ignore how inherently invalid these exclusionary distinctions are, and we signal our acceptance as a society that stereotypical attributes assigned to these groups are appropriate justifications for their disproportionate disadvantages. (1984, p. 5)

The Charter of Rights and Freedoms (1982) also enshrined equality provisions (which took effect in 1985) to complement and enhance other human rights provisions and laws. It specifically endorsed *affirmative action* as a necessary means to attaining equality:

> Subsection (l) [Equality Rights] does not preclude any law, program or activity that has as its object the amelioration of conditions of disadvantaged individuals or groups including those that are disadvantaged because of race, national or ethnic origin, colour, religion, sex, age or mental or physical disability. (Canada, 1982, p. 15)

Clearly, there is an onus on Canadians to strive, collectively, for a more just and fair society. It has been recognized by the government, and the courts, that in some instances this will take measures beyond the slow, incremental changes with which we are all more comfortable, but that result in little, if any, systemic change. Teachers, too, are expected to make a commitment, especially because of their pivotal role in the education and socialization of the young. While there is no easy prescription for how to achieve a just and equitable society, there are now model programs available to those willing to try. Educators working in collaboration with one another, and with other social organizations, are the key to a more equitable future.

DISCUSSION QUESTIONS

❏ What is the relationship between education and equity, between schooling and social justice?

❏ Why are schools seen as crucial to the development of an equitable society?

❏ How have schools responded to the demands that education must promote equality? Can you think of any examples of innovative programs in your community?

❏ How might we begin to "measure" equality within our educational system? within your own classroom?

NOTE

1. The language that has collected around the issue of equality often produces overwhelmingly emotional responses. Positions are frequently taken that have not been thought through either to their logical origins or conclusions, and this is true regardless of which side of the argument is being presented; yet they are so strongly held that they leave little room for the introduction of information or contrary judgements. ... People generally have a sense that "affirmative action" refers to interventionist government policies, and that is enough to prompt a negative reaction from many. For others, however, much depends on the degree and quality of the intervention ... there may be a willingness to discuss eliminating discriminatory employment barriers but not to debate "affirmative action" as it is currently misunderstood ... Efforts to overcome barriers in employment [or elsewhere] are what have generally been called in North America affirmative action measures. (Abella, 1984, pp. 6–7)

    While terms such as employment or educational equity have been substituted for affirmative action in some instances (including Abella's report), most people concerned with these issues continue to promote or react to what in fact are active remedies to societal injustices. Therefore, while recognizing the controversies surrounding this debate, regardless of language used, this chapter will use the term affirmative action interchangeably with educational equity to mean pro-active strategies for social justice through education.

REFERENCES

Abella, R.S. (Judge). (1984). *Report on the Commission on Equality in Employment.* Ottawa. Minister of Supply and Services.

Ayim, M. (1991). Equity in educational reform: A feminist perspective on the Radwanski Report. In D.J. Allison & J. Paquette (Eds.). *Reform and relevance in schooling: Drop-outs, destreaming, and the common curriculum.* (pp. 61–71). Toronto. OISE Press.

Bailey, K.R. (1993). *The girls are the ones with the pointy nails: An exploration of children's conceptions of gender.* London, ON: The Althouse Press.

Briskin, L. (1990). *Feminist pedagogy: Teaching and learning liberation.* Ottawa: Canadian Research Institute for the Advancement of Women.

Canada. (1982). *The Charter of Rights and Freedoms: A guide for Canadians.* Ottawa: Ministry of Supply and Services.

Connell, R.W. (1993, March/April). Schools and social justice. *Our Schools/Our Selves.* Toronto: Education Foundation.

Cummins, J., & Danesi, M. (1990). *Heritage languages: The development and denial of Canada's linguistic resources.* Toronto: Our Schools/Our Selves Education Foundation.

Curtis, B., Livingstone, D.W., & Smaller, H. (1992). *Stacking the deck: The streaming of working-class kids in Ontario schools.* Toronto: Our Schools/Our Selves Educational Foundation.

D'Souza, D. (1991). *Illiberal education: The politics of race and sex on Campus.* Toronto: Collier Macmillan Canada.

Eaton, S. (1993, July/August). Gay students find little support in most schools. *The Harvard Education Letter, 9*(4), 6–8.

Federation of Women Teachers' Associations of Ontario (FWTAO). (1993). *Affirmative action, Employment equity.* Toronto.

Fine, M. (1991). *Framing dropouts: Notes on the politics of an urban public high school.* Albany: State University of New York Press.

Gaskell, J., McLaren, A., & Novogrodsky, M. (1989). *Claiming an education: Feminism and Canadian schools.* Toronto: Our Schools/Our Selves Education Foundation.

Lee, E. (1990). *Letters to Marcia: A teacher's guide to antiracist education.* Toronto: Cross Cultural Communications Centre.

Malette, L., & Chalouh, M. (Eds.). (1991). *The Montreal massacre.* Charlottetown, PE: Gynergy Books.

Ontario Ministry of Education and Training. (1993, Feb.). *The common curriculum— Working document (Grades 1–9).* Toronto.

Ontario Teachers' Federation. (1993–94). *We the teachers of Ontario.* Toronto.

Porter, J. (1965). *The vertical mosaic: An analysis of social class and power in Canada.* Toronto: University of Toronto Press.

Porter, J., Porter, M.R., & Blishen, B.R. (1982). *Stations and callings: Making it through the school system.* Toronto: Methuen.

Radwanski, G. (1987). *Ontario study of the relevance of education, and the issue of dropouts.* Toronto: Ontario Ministry of Education.

Smith, C.H., Olin, F., & Kolmar, W. (1990). *The New Jersey Project: Integrating the scholarship on gender, 1986–1990.* Rutgers. Institute for Research on Women Rutgers, The State University of New Jersey.

Walkerdine, V. (1989). *Counting girls out.* London: Virago Press.

FURTHER READINGS

Case Comment. (1992–93) Sexual harassment. *Education and Law Journal, 4*, 309–40.

Gaskell, J. (1993). Feminism and its impact on educational scholarship in Canada. In L.L. Stewin & S.J.H. McCann (Eds.). *Contemporary educational issues.* (pp. 145–60). Toronto: Copp Clark Pitman.

Manley-Casimir, M.E., & Sussel, T.A. (1986). *Courts in the classroom.* Calgary, AB: Detselig.

Quandt, T. (1992–93). Learning exclusion: A feminist critique of the law school experience. *Education and Law Journal, 4*, 279–308.

Shorten, A. (1989–90). Equality of educational opportunity in Australia: Some thoughts on the policy implications of the decision in *Leves v. Haines* (1986) and in *Haines v. Leves* (1987). *Education and Law Journal, 2*, 265–97.

18

THE LEGAL DIMENSIONS OF TEACHERS' DUTIES AND AUTHORITY

Greg Dickinson

A century ago in England, some mischievous adolescent schoolboys got into a cupboard at school where phosphorus had been stored by their schoolmaster. One of the boys was burned when the chemical ignited. His subsequent lawsuit against the schoolmaster for damages for the injury he suffered resulted in a precedent that still provides an important legal rationale for holding educators responsible for guarding the physical safety of their students. In holding the schoolmaster liable for damages, Lord Esher developed what has become known as the "careful parent" test: "the schoolmaster was bound to take such care of his boys as a careful father would take of his boys, and there could not be a better definition of the duty of a schoolmaster" (*Williams v. Eady,* 1894, p. 42).

In other words, the teacher was invested with the important parental responsibility of keeping the children in his charge safe from physical harm. Since teachers stand *in loco parentis* (in the place of a parent), they are invested with the parents' custodial responsibilities. This doctrine can also be applied to invest the teacher with parental authority. The focus in this chapter, therefore, is upon teachers as surrogate parents and upon the responsibilities and authority that devolve to them as a result of that status.

The incidents of the *in loco parentis* standing, however, have not remained constant over the years. In fact, the legal relationship among parents, their children, and the state has changed significantly in the last hundred years or so. As MacKay (1984a) points out, one legacy of the English common-law heritage has been the almost absolute legal control exercised by parents over their children:

> In the past children have been viewed as the property of their parents, and in particular of their father. . . . The justice of a master or a father is a different thing from that of a citizen, for a son or slave is property, and there can be no injustice to one's own property. (MacKay, 1984a, p. 173)

Gradually, however, the notion of children as chattels of their father has been supplanted by a recognition that not all parental decisions are in the best interests of their children. The reduction in parental authority has necessarily affected teachers' *in loco parentis* standing.

Leon (1978, p. 37) argues that state concern about the welfare of children was illustrated as early as the eighteenth century, by legislation in favour of children with no (and later inadequate) parents. State encroachment on the domain of parental authority over children gathered momentum under the impetus of a strong children's law reform movement in the late nineteenth century. Moreover, in English law, the Court of Chancery had for some time maintained a *parens patriae* jurisdiction, thus reserving to itself the right to act as the guardian of the interests of those who could not take care of themselves (Leon, 1978, p. 36). Canadian superior courts have clearly inherited this *parens patriae* jurisdiction. Now legal obligations to and authority over children involve the authority of the state to enact and enforce child welfare legislation; parents' duties, rights, and authority; and rights of children as individuals before the law, which can be legally exercised both against their parents and the state.

The courts must ultimately weigh and balance the competing interests and rights that comprise this matrix of obligations and authority concerning children. The duties and authority of teachers are circumscribed by this changing and diluted concept of *in loco parentis*. Teachers must now look beyond delegated parental powers and duties in order to define their authority and responsibilities. Indeed, child welfare legislation has imposed responsibilities on educators that may place parents and educators in an adversarial relationship. Moreover, educators must recognize the potential of the Canadian Charter of Rights and Freedoms to redefine the relationships of authority and responsibility between teachers and pupils.

It is within this context that this chapter will examine the legal expectations placed on teachers by society, the legal means that society gives them to meet those expectations, and the sanctions that may be imposed when such expectations are not met. The discussion of teachers' duties and authority will focus upon three areas of concern: the physical health and safety of pupils, the academic welfare of pupils, and the enforcement of discipline within the school.

THE PHYSICAL HEALTH AND SAFETY OF STUDENTS

Schools are dangerous places. This should not be surprising, given the exposure of school children to equipment and activities that bear potential for injury. Moreover, active involvement by the learner is a major underpinning of educational theory, and, regardless of disability, learners are encouraged to participate as fully as possible in the mainstream of activity. While the learning environment has changed dramatically in a hundred years, it is unlikely that the nature of the learner has. If anything, today's children are *more* mischievous and have a greater sense of individuality and curiosity than their nineteenth-century counterparts!

Certainly, in the eyes of the court, children's proclivity for mischief has remained at least constant. There is a remarkable similarity in the reasons for the judgement of Mr. Justice McIntyre in a 1981 Supreme Court of Canada decision and those of Lord Esher almost a century before. In holding a teacher negligent for having allowed a 17-year-old boy to go unsupervised to practise on the flying rings, Justice McIntyre said:

> The respondent [teacher] should have anticipated reckless behaviour from at least some of the young boys sent off by themselves to work on gymnastics equipment . . . and the proclivity of young boys of high school age to act recklessly in disregard, if not in actual defiance, of authority is . . . well known. (*Myers v. Peel County Board of Education*, 1981, p. 238)

Apparently, Lord Esher was of like mind when he stated in 1893 that the teacher who had left phosphorus in an unlocked cupboard was "bound to take notice of the ordinary nature of young boys, their tendency to do mischievous acts, and their propensity to meddle with anything that came in their way" (*Williams v. Eady*, 1894, p. 42).

The proclivity of children for accidents remains constant, but today's educational environment and modern life provide more opportunities for these accidents to occur. A recent Canadian study (Feldman et al., 1983) has shown that in 212 schools in the 1981–82 school year, there were 5.8 injuries per 100 elementary school children, about 25 percent of which were serious. The investigators concluded that even this reported rate appeared to be an understatement of the actual rate.

Coupled with these statistics is a readiness among students and their parents to enforce accountability for these accidents and injuries through civil suits for damages. Because of a traditional deference for authority, Canadians may have been slower in the past than Americans to invoke litigation to protest what were perceived to be infringements of constitutionally protected rights and freedoms (Manley-Casimir, 1983). However, there can be little doubt that Canadians are becoming increasingly ready to sue state authorities for damages for what they perceive to be wrongful acts by the state and its agents.

Given a modern school environment fraught with potential danger, a readiness among pupils and their parents to sue, and the undiminished proclivity of children to fall prey to accidents, a preoccupation by educators with their potential liability for negligence is not surprising.

WHO IS LIABLE?

A teacher pondering personal vulnerability to a lawsuit for negligence might reasonably ask, "If I am sued and lose the case and the court awards to the plaintiff, will I have to pay that money personally?" The answer involves two general types of civil liability: personal liability and vicarious liability. What the teacher is really asking is, "Will I be personally liable?" The law provides that employers (school boards) are responsible for the torts (civil wrongdoings such as assault or negligence) of their employees (teachers) that are committed during the ordinary course of their employment (Fleming, 1983). This is the doctrine of vicarious liability.

Vicarious liability arises by "operation of law" and represents somewhat of a fiction; that is, certain people are found to be liable not because they personally committed a wrongful act, but rather because the law imposes upon them legal responsibility for the acts of people who are in a particular legal relationship with them, such as employment. This doctrine does not completely absolve teachers from legal liability; it simply means that their employers will *also* be legally responsible for the payment of any damages awarded. In practical terms, however, it *does* mean that the teacher is insulated from the monetary shock of the awarded damages. Regardless of the number of defendants found to be liable, plaintiffs are only entitled to be compensated once for the full amount of the damages awarded, so it will be the boards' insurers who will usually pay the damages. In law, the insurance company would probably be entitled to seek indemnity from the defendant teacher, but this seems to have been done rarely, if ever, in Canada (MacKay, 1984a). The possibility, however, of a successful claim for indemnity suggests that teachers ought to seek provisions in their collective agreements with boards that would preclude such claims, or, alternatively, that they should investigate the possibility of obtaining their own insurance, personally or through their federations.

If a teacher's negligent act occurred "outside the scope of his or her employment," then the board would be entitled to deny its vicarious liability. Boards (in reality their insurers, who have the right to defend the lawsuit on behalf of boards) may make such denials in certain circumstances. For example, in *Beauparlant v. Board of Trustees of . . . Appleby* (1955), two teachers had arranged for students to attend a concert in a nearby town and had obtained a truck to transport the children. After some of the children tumbled out of the overloaded and unsafe truck and were injured, a lawsuit for negligence was brought against the teachers' school board. The court found that the teachers had been negligent in failing to ensure that the method of transportation was safe, but upheld the board's denial of liability on the basis that there was not "any express or implied authority" from the board for this outing and that the accident, therefore, had occurred outside the scope of the ordinary course of the teachers' employment. Had the teachers been sued, they would have been left to their own personal financial resources to satisfy the judgement that would have been rendered against them. This case warns teachers that if they expect to be sheltered by their boards' insurance, they ought to be certain that any extraordinary activities that they plan, especially those occurring off school property or outside school hours, have been authorized by the board.

The Legal Bases of Liability: The Concept of Negligence

The duty of teachers to protect the health and safety of their pupils obliges them to neither intentionally nor unintentionally commit acts or omissions that result in physical harm to their pupils. Intentional acts, such as assaults and batteries, will be discussed later in the chapter, under the heading "The Enforcement of Discipline." The present concern is with teachers' responsibility not to carelessly cause injury to their pupils — or, put in more legalistic terms, not to be negligent in their care of their pupils. "Negligence" in law means the breach of a recognized legal "duty of care" toward another person, measured against a standard of care, that causes injury to that person and gives rise to damages.

Many legal duties of care exist in society. While one can correctly say that there is a general legal duty not to be negligent toward one's neighbour (in the broad sense of the word), more exacting legal duties of care derive from a proximate relationship between two parties, often a professional and a client. Thus legally recognized duties of care exist between doctor and patient, solicitor and client, accountant and client, and so on. Similarly, the proximity of teacher and pupil has been seen as justifying the existence of a legal duty of care. Ever since Lord Esher's 1894 judgement, there has never been doubt that teachers have a common-law duty of care to safeguard their pupils from physical injury. Moreover, various legislative provisions have reinforced this common-law duty. Provincial education statutes and regulations commonly provide that teachers' duties include seeing to the safety of their pupils (see, for example, the Education Act of Ontario, s. 265[j] and Ontario Regulation 298, s. 20[g]).

Is such a duty of care absolute? In other words, are teachers legally responsible for all injuries that befall students under their supervision? The answer is clearly "no," because of the nature of the concept of negligence. People under a legal duty of care are not expected to be perfect and act as virtual guarantors of the safety of their charges; rather, their duty is to act reasonably under the circumstances. In the case of teachers, the standard of care is derived from the concept of *in loco parentis*. The "careful parent" test derived from *Williams v. Eady* (1894) is routinely (though not exclusively) applied by courts in determining whether teachers have been negligent. Put simply, in a given case, negligent teachers are those who *did not* act as a careful parent would.

This test may not always be appropriate for determining teachers' liability for negligence. For example, is it fair to judge a teacher's conduct in the supervision of 30 students against that of a parent who would normally have only two or three to oversee? This would suggest that the application of the careful-parent test is too harsh. Conversely, is it sensible to utilize a standard of care based on what a parent would have done in circumstances that include the use of technical equipment, complicated activities, or particular expertise normally viewed as inconsistent with most parents' knowledge, training, and experience? This suggests that the test is sometimes too lenient, thus exposing children to substantial risk.

The solution to this apparent dilemma depends on a court's consideration of the particular circumstances in a given case. Some courts have attempted to modify the "careful parent" test, while others have rejected it outright and substituted an alternative test. For example, in both *McKay v. Board of Govan* (1968), and *Thornton v. Board of School Trustees* (1975), the problem of disparity in the number of children normally supervised by teachers as opposed to parents was recognized by the courts. An attempt was made to resolve the problem by modifying the test so that the standard of conduct expected became that of a careful parent of a *large* family. Such a cosmetic change hardly advances the cause of sensible determination of teachers' responsibility.

A more reasonable approach is taken when the courts recognize that certain activities undertaken by school children, and certain expertise and training possessed by teachers, render the teacher–parent analogy inappropriate. Accordingly, the courts in *McKay* (1968) and *Thorton* (1975) both refer to a possible second test that is based on the teacher's status as a trained, skilled, and knowledgeable professional. This second test requires one to consider not what a "careful parent" would have done under the circumstances, but instead, what an "ordinarily competent instructor in the field" would have done (*McKay*, 1968, p. 523; *Thornton*, 1975, pp. 632–34). In both *McKay* and *Thornton*, which involved injuries suffered during gymnastic classes, the courts ultimately found that the "careful parent" test was adequate for judging the teachers' conduct.

Courts are reluctant to dispense with the "careful parent" test, and the exclusive application of the "competent instructor" test appears to be restricted usually to cases where the activity surrounding an accident includes the use of complicated machinery or equipment or dangerous chemicals — those sorts of activities that by their nature obviously require trained and expert supervisors. In *Myers v. Peel County Board of Education* (1981), the Supreme Court of Canada noted the varying circumstances of cases that courts must consider when determining the applicable standard of care:

> The standard of care to be exercised by school authorities in providing for the supervision and protection of students for whom they are responsible is that of the careful or prudent parent. ... It has, no doubt, become somewhat qualified in modern times because of the greater variety of activities conducted in schools, with probably larger groups of students using more complicated and more dangerous equipment than formerly. ... It is not, however, a standard which can be applied in the same manner and to the same extent in every case. Its application will vary from case to case and will depend upon the number of students being supervised at any given time, the nature of the exercise or activity in progress, the age and degree of skill and training which the students may have received in connection with such activity, the nature and condition of the equipment in use at the time, the competency and capacity of the students involved, and a host of other matters which may be widely varied but which, in a given

case, may affect the application of the prudent parent standard to the conduct of the school authority in the circumstances. (pp. 235–36)

The essential question is not which test the court will invoke to establish a standard of care, but how the standard is applied in a given case. What criteria do courts use to determine whether a teacher's actions measure up to the chosen standard—be it that of the careful parent or competent instructor? Some criteria are suggested in the *Myers* (1981) judgement. It is always dangerous to generalize about how courts arrive at their decisions, for the administration of justice is a human activity subject to the biases, predilections, and emotional and intellectual frailties of its human participants. For this reason, law does not qualify very well as a predictive science. Nevertheless, there is some common ground in the criteria courts have traditionally used to rationalize their decision that teachers did or did not meet the expected standard of care.

While teachers have a duty to supervise their students, this duty does not mean constant supervision (*Board of Education v. Higgs*, 1959). Whether a teacher breached his or her duty of care will depend upon a consideration of whether the teacher's conduct was reasonable under the circumstances, and this consideration almost invariably takes into account a number of factors. These include the nature of the accident, approved general practice, and the foreseeability of the accident.

A distinction is often drawn between those activities that are "inherently" dangerous and those that are merely "potentially" dangerous. For example, courts have held that grass hockey (*Gard v. Board of School Trustees of Duncan*, 1946) and wrestling (*Hall v. Thompson*, 1952) are merely potentially dangerous. The mere possibility of accident is not sufficient to classify an activity as inherently dangerous, nor is the mere possibility of injury sufficient to establish breach of duty. As the activity becomes more dangerous, however, the degree of care to be exercised by a supervisor rises accordingly. One would therefore expect teachers to exercise a high degree of care, for example, in laboratory experiments involving caustic chemicals (*James v. East River School Division No. 9*, 1976), or in shop classes utilizing dangerous equipment (*Dziwenka v. The Queen*, 1972).

Similarly, the degree of care owed by teachers to their pupils may be seen to depend also on the varying attributes of the pupils. Considerations of such things as pupils' age, experience, strength, and intelligence commonly determine whether a teacher's conduct in supervising students meets the expected standard of care. Thus the youngest, weakest, least experienced, least trained or instructed, least aware, and least intelligent pupils usually merit the greatest degree of care. With the recent introduction of increased numbers of children with disabilities into regular classrooms as a result of special-education reform, teachers must now realize that the degree of care that they customarily exercise over their "normal" students may not be sufficient for "exceptional" students.

The old adage "once bitten, twice shy" may determine whether a teacher has been negligent. The teacher who neglects to investigate thoroughly the cause of a prior mishap and take reasonable steps to preclude its recurrence, will appear all the more negligent in the eyes of a court determining his or her liability for the subsequent accident. As the court in *Thornton* (1975) observed, "once one youngster had become hurt would not a prudent father want to know how and why his child had become hurt in order to avoid the same kind of risk to another child? I think he would have" (p. 633).

How important is it for a teacher to follow the normal operating procedures laid down for an activity by conventional practice, school or board policy, or trade safety guidelines?

For example, in *Myers* (1981) a teacher was found liable for an injury to a student who had fallen from the "flying rings." His liability was based partially on the finding that the mats placed under the rings were not the type normally used for such an activity. Adherence to alleged approved general practice, however, is no guarantee of exoneration, because the word "general" suggests the "practice" may not apply to all cases, especially given the possible variants in the activity itself and its participants. Approved general practice may be a satisfactory measure of required safety for an experienced lathe operator, but not for an inexperienced and handicapped shop student (*Dziwenka*, 1972). A second objection is that if approved general practice constituted automatic vindication of a teacher and thus determined in advance the issue of teacher liability, the court's role of arbiter of the question of negligence in each case would effectively be obviated.

An overriding consideration that generally encompasses the previously mentioned criteria is the foreseeability of accident and injury. Generally speaking, the greater the foreseeability of an accident occurring, the greater the degree of care owed by the teacher. Thus if a court finds that an accident was reasonably foreseeable by a careful parent (or competent instructor, as the case may be), and that a teacher failed to adopt reasonable precautions (again those that a careful parent or competent instructor would have taken) to avoid the accident, the teacher will normally be found negligent. In order to hold a teacher negligent, it is not necessary that the teacher actually foresaw the danger, but only that he or she simply failed to foresee what ought to have been foreseen. In other words, it is an objective, rather than subjective, determination. Indeed, if a teacher were to foresee danger and take no steps to reduce it, he or she might come perilously close to criminal liability. Thus, if a teacher disregards a dangerous situation so that a court could subsequently determine that he or she "showed wanton or reckless disregard for the lives or safety" (Criminal Code, 1985, s. 219) of the students, he or she could be found criminally liable. Sanctions such as fines and imprisonment could be imposed if a student were killed or injured as a result of a teacher's criminal negligence. Prosecution of teachers for criminal negligence is uncommon, however, as teachers rarely advertently cause injury to their pupils.

Matters of Defence

Even if a teacher is found by a court to have been negligent and thereby to have caused injury to a pupil, it cannot be assumed that there will be a finding of complete liability, or, in some cases, liability at all. It has already been seen that the doctrine of vicarious liability relieves the teacher, in most cases, from the financial implications of an award of damages. Two other important matters must also be considered: the doctrine of voluntary assumption of risk and contributory negligence.

Just because a person happens to be a pupil, the law does not permit that person to travel through life turning a blind eye to danger. The law recognizes that some children have the capacity to willingly assume risks and, in fact, do so. Moreover, the law also expects children to exercise a degree of care for their own safety commensurate with their age and intelligence. If a court finds that a pupil voluntarily assumed the risk inherent in an activity in which he or she was injured, that finding could result in the complete absolution of the teacher from legal responsibility for the injury. Findings that children voluntarily assumed risks are rarely made, however, due to their limited life experience and sophistication. Except where the victim was an older, rather mature, and intelligent student who demonstrably understood and assumed all dimensions of the risks involved in an activity, it is unlikely that a court would apply the doctrine of voluntary assumption of risk to school accident cases. In a recent case where a 16-year-old Grade 11 student was injured playing "rag ball" during a physical education class, the Supreme Court of British Columbia rejected a defence based on voluntary assumption of risk. The court refused to apply this general tort defence to school classes since it is the teacher, not the students who should be expected to understand the attendant risks in an activity and the ways of avoiding them. (*Petersen v. Board of School Trustees*, 1991). Moreover, there are few activities at school in which students have a real or perceived choice as to whether they participate. Even permission slips, signed by parents and purporting to relieve teachers and boards from liability for accidents to pupils during certain activities, are not effective ways of precluding lawsuits for negligence. This is so because the law does not permit parents to waive their children's independent legal right to sue (MacKay, 1984a)—an example of the recognition of a legal identity for children that is separate and distinct from that of their parents.

While courts are loath to apply the doctrine of voluntary assumption of risk, they will place some degree of responsibility on children to safeguard their own interests through the application of the doctrine of contributory negligence, whereby blame for an injury can be apportioned between the teacher and the victim-pupil. For instance, a pupil who was old enough, experienced enough, and intelligent enough to realize that he ought not to attempt a certain gymnastic manoeuvre without a spotter, and who was told by the teacher not to do so, was found to be partially responsible for the injury he suffered from a fall during the manoeuvre (*Myers*, 1981). The damages that he would otherwise have been awarded (since the teacher was also found negligent in allowing him to practise gymnastics out of the teacher's sight) were consequently reduced in proportion to his degree of fault. Criteria similar to those used to determine whether a teacher's conduct met the standard of care will be applied to determine whether a pupil was contributorily negligent. The question then becomes whether, given the nature of the activity involved, the victim exercised that degree of care expected of a child of like age, intelligence, and experience (*McEllistrum v. Etches*, 1956).

The Duty to Report Child Abuse: A Special Case

We have seen that teachers have a common-law duty to protect their pupils from physical harm and that this duty originates from the doctrine of *in loco parentis*. This duty of care is usually defined by the "careful parent" test, which reinforces the notion of the teacher as a surrogate parent. Legislation in most provinces places on teachers an additional and rather specific onus concerning their pupils' physical, and in some cases mental, welfare. Ironically, far from being a reflection of parental authority and control, this onus often places teachers in a role where they must protect pupils from their parents or guardians.

Provincial child welfare legislation typically provides that every person who has reason to suspect that a child is suffering physical or mental abuse has a legal obligation to notify a child welfare agency. Some provincial legislation specifies that because of their frequent and close contact with children, child-care professionals, such as teachers, have a special duty to report child abuse (see, for example, New Brunswick's Child and Family Services and Family Relations Act, s. 30[3], and Ontario's Child and Family Services Act, s. 72[3]). In Ontario, there is no penalty prescribed for an ordinary citizen who refuses or neglects to report child abuse; teachers, however, are liable to a fine of up to $1000 for breach of their statutory duty (Child and Family Services Act, s. 85). Whether through their duty to report child abuse as an ordinary citizen or as a child-care professional, teachers are important players in the reinforcement of the state's superordinate role as protector of children.

THE ACADEMIC WELFARE OF STUDENTS

Teachers' supervision duties may seem somewhat ancillary to their perceived central role—that of academic mentor and guide. If teachers can be held accountable for their ancillary duties, must they likewise be accountable for the duties that form the very essence of their professional role? To examine this question, we will consider the dimensions of teachers' accountability for what they teach, and for what they fail to teach—or, put more fairly, for what their pupils fail to learn.

While provincial educational legislation provides for a good deal of central control of curriculum content and materials, substantial scope still exists for local educators to determine content and material, pedagogical methods, and assessment of students' progress. How far are educators legally accountable for their acts and omissions in the delivery of the academic or intellectual portion of educational services? Two particular aspects of this general issue will be considered: first, the viability of civil lawsuits by pupils and their parents against educators for failure to educate, and second, indoctrination of students by an individual teacher with notions that offend widely held societal values.

EDUCATIONAL MALPRACTICE: NEGLIGENT PROVISION OF ACADEMIC SERVICES

The concept of educational malpractice is an amorphous one. Legal actions for educational malpractice have typically claimed that one or more teachers and their school boards were responsible for failure to instil certain attributes (for example, wisdom) or teach certain competencies (such as reading), for incompetent pedagogical methods or inappropriate curricula, for failure to diagnose a particular learning handicap of a student, for incorrect diagnoses of handicaps, or for inappropriate placement of a disabled student (see, for example, *Trustees of Columbia University v. Jacobsen,* 1959; *Peter W. v. San Francisco Unified School District,* 1976; *Donohue v. Copiague Union Free School District,* 1978; *Pierce v. The Board of Education of the City of Chicago,* 1977; *Hoffman v. Board of Education of City of New York,* 1979). Common to all these claims is the presupposition that as a result of the alleged acts or omissions by the educators, the student suffered some psychic injury and consequent economic loss. The two best-known American educational malpractice cases are the *Peter W.* (1976) and *Donohue* (1978) cases. Both of these lawsuits ultimately failed because the courts refused to recognize a legal duty of care due to problems with establishing a standard of care and legal causation. The courts also relied on several public policy rationales.

The finding that there should exist no actionable duty of care concerning the provision of academic services is an aberration, for professionals are usually seen in law as owing a legal duty of care to their clients. Moreover, the courts have generally been willing to expand the list of professionals owing legal duties of care to their clients. Is teaching somehow essentially different from law, medicine, nursing, and other professions?

Funston (1981) argues that the analogy between teachers and other professionals who do owe a legal duty of care is not a compelling one. Suggesting that teachers are "at best, aspiring semi-professionals" (p. 775), he argues that self-characterization as a professional is not sufficient to found a legal duty. Moreover, he suggests that sociological studies on the professions normally exclude teachers, as they fail to meet certain criteria used to define professionals. For example, teachers possess "no well-defined technical knowledge comparable to that of a legal or medical professional" (pp. 774–75) and if they possess any special skills or knowledge at all, they relate to a particular substantive area such as biology or history, rather than to the process of education itself. Funston's thesis is not wholly valid; some teachers *do* possess pedagogical knowledge and skill derived from educational theory, especially in the field of special education, that would not be common to laypersons. Moreover, there are other criteria of professionalism that might apply to the role of educators—namely, the essential nature of the services delivered, the existence of a code of ethics and disciplinary machinery to enforce it, a traditional sense of devotion to one's clients, legally prescribed requirements for admission to the profession, and an inherently intellectual rather than physical quality of the occupational activity.

Accordingly, the analogy of professionalism would seem to afford a better rationale for a duty of care than some would admit. In fact, in a strong dissenting judgement in *Donohue* (1978), one judge made it clear that he believed the case before the court to be "no different from [an] analogous cause of action for medical malpractice" (p. 38). It seems that educators may be caught on the horns of a dilemma concerning their professional status. The more they argue that their particular knowledge and skills transcend mere expertise in a particular substantive area, the more vulnerable they are to the application of a professional duty of care; however, the less they argue that their expertise includes process-oriented abilities—knowledge and application of educational theory—the less enhanced is their occupational self-image.

An important argument that the American courts have utilized to reject educational malpractice lawsuits relates to problems of proof. In the courts' view, it is virtually impossible both to establish sufficient unanimity concerning an appropriate standard of care and to prove that certain acts or omissions caused the injury alleged by the student. If there is neither a commonly accepted proper way to teach nor a commonly accepted theory of how children learn, it follows that there can be no fair standard to which teachers can be held, or reliable methodology for linking teachers' conduct of students' failure to learn. These problems of proof should not be viewed, however, as immutable obstructions to recovery of damages for educational malpractice, particularly as the relationship between teaching and learning becomes grounded on commonly accepted empirical bases. Thus a renewed emphasis on the teaching of fundamental skills and competencies (competency-based education) and the accompanying methodologies of testing whether pupils have acquired the competencies (standardized minimum competency tests), may advance the cause of those who would seek to hold educators responsible for their pupils' failure to learn (Pabian, 1979).

American courts have found that a number of public policy reasons also militate against allowing such lawsuits. The courts have examined the issue against a backdrop of several social factors that have three primary focuses. First, it is feared that entertaining lawsuits for educational malpractice would result in a flood of claims, many of them spurious, thus placing a tremendous burden on financial and human resources (*Peter W.*, 1976, p. 825). Second, the courts foresee such lawsuits having a stifling effect on educational innovation (Funston, 1981; *Hunter v. Board of Education of Montgomery County*, 1982). Instead of deterring incompetent teaching and administration, litigation would conceivably stultify and perhaps have a retrogressive effect on the quality of education. Educators might be loath to adopt any innovative practices for fear of their failure, preferring instead to stay with "safe" practices, the educational benefits of which—even if minimal—could be demonstrated. Finally, the courts fear that allowing lawsuits for educational malpractice would inevitably cast them in the role of educational policy-maker, a role for which they feel ill-equipped (*Donohue*, 1978, pp. 33–34; *Hunter*, p. 586). The courts would rather not be placed in a position whereby their rulings would seem to vilify one particular educational approach or lend credence to another.

Such public policy rationales have determined the American cases. They represent the classic struggle between the rights of an individual to compensation and the cost to society of the recognition of that right. The policy question is thus reduced to who should bear the burden of the injuries that occur as the result of educators' negligent conduct. In the matter of physical injury, the pupil-victim is clearly entitled to compensation from the public purse through litigation against the school board. Where the injuries are less tangible, however, and amount to deficiencies in the delivery of the academic side of educational services, pupils and their parents may find themselves foreclosed from even bringing a lawsuit. Inasmuch as our society mandates universal compulsory education— which for most pupils means public education— should society not assume the ultimate responsibility for the economic and social costs that occur when that education is carried out in a negligent and injurious fashion?

The viability of educational malpractice suits has been tested rarely in Canada. In *Bales v. School District 23 (Central Okanagan)*, 1984, the parents of a child with a mental disability sued a school board for, among other things, negligence in placing him in a segregated school for children with disabilities. The Supreme Court of British Columbia implied from the British Columbia School Act a legal entitlement to an education "which meets some basic educational standard." While the Court ultimately dismissed the plaintiffs' claim in negligence, in doing so it inferentially recognized the potential viability of such suits. That is, the claim was dismissed not because of a lack of a duty of care but rather because the evidence in the case fell short of demonstrating injury in the tort sense. As the court put it, the law of negligence enforces a duty to try to avoid what seems to be harmful, but not a duty that the greatest benefit will result.

However, in a more recent Ontario case, *Hicks et al. v. Board of Education for the City of Etobicoke et al.*, 1988, the court adopted the American courts' habit of refusing to recognize even a duty of care in such cases. In *Hicks*, a parent sued the school board for the improper identification and placement of her child as an exceptional pupil. The parent also alleged that the board's actions were contrary to its obligation under the Ontario Education Act to provide the child with proper instruction. The suit claimed damages for developmental harm, mental anguish, and embarrassment. Though not bound by the American cases, District Court Judge O'Connell was clearly persuaded by their reasoning in his decision to reject the plaintiff's claim. In refusing to recognize the Court's jurisdiction over such cases, he stated:

> There are no authorities in Canada which recognize educational malpractice as a tort. All of the American authorities have consistently held that the cause of action for damages for acts of negligence in the educational process are precluded by major considerations of public policy. (*Hicks*, 1988)

While educational malpractice suits based on negligence would appear to be ill fated, a resourceful plaintiff might attempt to invoke section 7 of the Canadian Charter of Rights and Freedoms in aid of such a lawsuit. Section 7 provides that "[e]veryone has the right to life, liberty and security of the person and the right not to be deprived thereof except in accordance with the principles of fundamental justice." Inasmuch as compulsory attendance laws affect a child's right to liberty, one could conceivably argue that this infringement of liberty ought not to occur except in accordance with the principles of fundamental justice. Fundamental justice, it could further be argued, must surely include the right to be compensated when the purposes for which one's liberty was infringed were carried out negligently (MacKay, 1984a). It should be noted, however, that the court in *Bales* tersely but firmly rejected the claim that the child's segregated placement represented a deprivation of liberty or security of the person under section 7 of the Charter.

Moreover, a further potential roadblock to such an argument is section 1 of the Charter, whereby all rights and freedoms provided in the Charter are subject to "such reasonable limits prescribed by law as can be demonstrably justified in a free and democratic society." This "reasonable limits" qualification would seem to raise squarely for a Canadian court the public policy issue addressed above. Canadian courts might well reason, on public policy grounds similar to those advanced by their American counterparts, that this sort of limitation on students' liberty is "demonstrably justified in a free and democratic society" and that the Charter offers no avail to a plaintiff who would sue a school board for educational malpractice. However, it is doubtful that a court that found a limitation on rights to be contrary to fundamental justice under section 7 would turn around and find it to be "demonstrably justified" under section 1.

EDUCATIONAL INDOCTRINATION AND THE LAW

While the law may not hold educators accountable in damages to pupils and their parents for what is not taught, it clearly will hold educators accountable for teaching subject matter that offends certain widely held societal norms. This type of accountability is well illustrated in the case of James Keegstra, who was accused of indoctrinating his students with information and ideas about the Holocaust that offended community standards, violated Ministry of Education curriculum guidelines, and were maintained despite cautions from his board (Mertl & Ward, 1985).

For more than ten years, James Keegstra taught his Alberta high-school history classes that the Jewish Holocaust had been portrayed inaccurately by most historical accounts. According to Mr. Keegstra's interpretation of history, the mass destruction of Jews described in most histories of World War II had not occurred. The myth of the Holocaust, he claimed, was part of an international conspiracy of lies by influential Jews who were also responsible for many of the world's major problems.

The Keegstra case raises a number of interesting and important issues concerning accountability for the content of what is taught. A teacher whose interpretation of his subject is biased and contrary to sound scholarship may be criticized for providing an unacceptable model. Incompetence in the substantive area of one's teaching is potential cause for a board to dismiss a teacher, thereby controlling the quality of the academic experience of students. Although it is difficult for boards to dismiss incompetent teachers who are often protected by an unduly powerful system of teacher tenure (Czuboka, 1985), Keegstra was eventually both fired and decertified with due consideration given to his rights to counsel and appeal (*Keegstra v. Board of Education*, 1983).

But Keegstra's case goes beyond alleged academic malpractice. He had also allegedly promoted hatred toward an identifiable group—Jews—in violation of the Criminal Code. Such conduct is said to injure society as a whole, so accountability is enforced through state prosecution for the breach of the criminal law instead of lawsuits by individual students or parents for damages. This case became a classic confrontation, because it involved the conscious indoctrination of students with views that, while fervently held by the teacher, flew squarely in the face of widely held societal values. It thus raised issues of freedom of thought, belief, opinion, and expression, which in the school context are often discussed as academic freedom. Do teachers of high-school history enjoy academic freedom in the usual sense of that phrase? Any sensible consideration of this question would suggest that they do not. There is no convention of academic freedom in the first two levels of public education as there is in higher education; in fact, Canadian practice suggests central control over curriculum. Freedom of speech exercised at a soapbox in the park or a university lecture hall is quite different from that at the front of a class full of young and impressionable minds. Obviously, the younger and less sophisticated the audience, the less compelling will be any claim of academic freedom.

Keegstra's dismissal from his job, decertification, and conviction for promoting hatred all clearly were inconsistent with and violated his rights to freedom of thought, belief, opinion, and expression under the Canadian Charter of Rights and Freedoms—insofar as those rights are viewed as absolute. But no right is absolute. It is necessary to limit the exercise of an individual's rights when they trammel the rights of others in society. Thus it might well be argued that the actions taken against Keegstra represent a reasonable limitation on his freedoms, in the interest of protecting the rights of his students and the Jewish community, and preserving social harmony. While the Alberta Court of Appeal ruled in 1988 that the Criminal Code section under which Keegstra was convicted was of no force or effect because it violated freedom of expression under the Charter (*R. v. Keegtsra*, 1988; Dickinson, 1988–89), on further appeal, the Supreme Court of Canada upheld the section's constitutionality as a reasonable and justifiable limit on free expression (*R. v. Keegtsra*, 1990).

A variation on the issues raised by the Keegstra affair occurred in the later case of Malcolm Ross in New Brunswick. Ross, a secondary-school teacher, allegedly published racist and discriminatory statements regarding Jews. Like Keegstra, Ross's publications involved a denial of the Holocaust and claims about an international Jewish conspiracy. Unlike Keegstra's case, however, Ross's controversial behaviour occurred largely outside the classroom. Offended Jewish parents lodged a complaint against Ross and his school board under the New Brunswick Human Rights Act (1973), claiming that Ross's conduct, and the school board's failure to prohibit it, were discriminatory (*Attis v. Board of School Trustees, District 15*, 1991).

The Board of Inquiry set up to hear the complaint easily concluded that Ross's behaviour had impaired his ability to teach because it had poisoned the environment, and this interfered with his teaching. The Board also found that the school board had directly violated the Human Rights Act by failing to address the problem of Ross's conduct. Moreover, the school board was found vicariously responsible for its employee's actions. Hence, the Board of Inquiry ordered the school board to place Ross on a leave of absence without pay for eighteen months and to appoint him to a non-teaching position should one come up during that period. If no such position were available, the Board would be free to dismiss him. The order further provided that Ross was to be fired immediately should he continue his offensive writings during the eighteen-month period.

Upon appeal to the New Brunswick Supreme Court, the Board's order was essentially upheld (*Ross v. Moncton Board of School Trustees, District No. 15*, 1991). Ross's complaint that the order violated his Charter rights was rejected by the court, which, while agreeing that his freedoms of thought, belief, opinion, and expression had been infringed, ruled the infringement to be a reasonable and justified limitation under section 1 of the Charter. However, when Ross appealed again to the New Brunswick Court of Appeal, the Court accepted his contention that the Board of Inquiry order was not a reasonable limit on his constitutional right of free expression (*Ross v. Board of School Trustees, District No. 15*, 1993). Relying on the Supreme Court of Canada's decision in *R. v. Zundel* (1992), the Court of Appeal noted that there must be a "specific purpose so pressing and substantial as to be capable of overriding the Charter's guarantee." It was the court's view that the evidence in the Ross case did not disclose a connection between the out-of-class opinions expressed by Ross and any offensive remarks made against Jewish students by other students at school. The court was therefore not prepared to uphold an order restricting a teacher's employment unless it could be proven that his conduct had actually sparked acts of racism among the school's population.

The Keegstra and Ross cases demonstrate another mode of accountability of educators for their conduct both inside and outside the classroom. This accountability is enforceable through discipline by the employer, decertification by the provincial government, human rights complaints, and, in extreme cases, by criminal prosecution. It also illustrates the visibility of schoolroom activity and teachers. When the school child is asked, "What did you learn in school today?", all of society may well be interested in the answer.

THE ENFORCEMENT OF DISCIPLINE

The responsibility of educators to provide a learning environment that is both physically safe and academically sound carries a necessary corollary—the responsibility to enforce rules of discipline within the school. It has been said that without discipline there can be little assurance of learning (*R. v. Dimmell*, 1980). Discipline within schools is undoubtedly a high societal priority (see, for example, Livingstone & Hart, 1980; Ontario Ministry of Education, 1979). Despite many ebbs and flows in the importance attached to discipline and in the methods of enforcing it, the maintenance of order and discipline in the school environment remains a primary duty of educators.

LEGAL BASES OF TEACHERS' AUTHORITY TO DISCIPLINE

The legal sources of teachers' authority over students' conduct are based both in statues and the common law (judges' decisions). Most provincial education legislation determined the general responsibilities and powers of educators concerning the maintenance of order and discipline within schools. For example, the Education Act (1990) of Ontario requires principals "to maintain proper order and discipline in the school" (s.265[a]) and teachers "to maintain under the direction of the principal, proper order and discipline in his classroom and while on duty in the school and on the school ground" (s.264[1][e]). A clue to what might be considered "proper" order and discipline is provided in an Ontario regulation stating that it is the duty of a student to "accept such discipline as would be exercised by a kind, firm and judicious parent" (Reg. 298, s.23[1][c]).

This regulation suggests that the fundamental traditional legal basis of teachers' authority in matters of discipline depends upon the doctrine of *in loco parentis*; that is, the teacher's authority derives from an implied delegation of parental authority. Can it fairly be said that a teacher is entitled and indeed obliged to discipline a pupil in the same way that pupil's parent would? While the answer may have been an unqualified "yes" in the nineteenth century (*Hutt v. The Governors of Haileybury College*, 1888), it is clearly a hesitant "yes" today, because of changing social attitudes about disciplinary practice toward children and the growth of children's independent legal rights.

Any legal theory of discipline over school children that rests exclusively upon an implied delegation of parental authority will be vulnerable when parents begin to withdraw their delegated authority. Thus some parents spank their children and are content to delegate authority to teachers to do likewise, while others would reserve only to themselves the "right" to corporally punish their children. Still others would not tolerate physical punishment of children by anyone. Because of potential administrative chaos that would ensue if school authority and discipline depended solely on authority delegated from parents, Canadian courts have preferred to ground educators' disciplinary authority in the social utilitarian need to maintain order and discipline in the schools in order to foster an environment where learning can take place (*Murdock v. Richards*, 1954). Teachers may therefore discipline pupils without the permission of their parents. This dilution of the *in loco parentis* doctrine is quite consistent with the overall development of the state and ultimately the courts, as the supreme arbiters of the best interests of children. Moreover, the Supreme Court of Canada's ruling in *Ogg-Moss v. R.* (1984) cast substantial doubt on the viability of the doctrine of *in loco parentis*, per se, as a legal rationale for teachers' disciplinary authority.

LIMITS ON TEACHERS' DISCIPLINARY AUTHORITY

It is clear that the exercise of discipline in schools is limited by federal legislation and by judicial policy expressed in court decisions, rather than by subjective parental delegation of authority. Currently, the most common limitation is the law of assault. A teacher who uses physical force to discipline a pupil may find that his or her conduct results in a charge of criminal assault. Parents may also institute civil actions for assault in which they claim damages on their child's behalf. While liability for criminal and civil assaults has provided a traditional legal limitation on the exercise or discipline within the school, the Canadian Charter of Rights and Freedoms has given additional scope for the courts to intervene in school authority relationships.

Section 43 of the Criminal Code and "Reasonable" Force

The Parliament of Canada has legislated limits on the use of physical punishment by parents, teachers, and others acting *in loco parentis*. These limits are set out in section 43 of the Criminal Code of Canada:

> Every schoolteacher, parent or person standing in the place of a parent is justified in using force by way of correction toward a pupil or child, as the case may be, who is under his care, if the force does not exceed what is reasonable under the circumstances.

This statutory defence available to teachers charged with assault is based upon the imprecise test of whether the force applied was "reasonable under the circumstances." Reasonableness must be decided on a case-by-case basis in light of each case's particular facts (*R. v. Haberstock*, 1970). While this decision depends substantially upon a particular judge's and/or jury's general philosophy of punishment, courts tend to take into consideration several factors in deciding that punishment is reasonable:

> a. It is for the purpose of correction and without malice.
> b. There is sufficient cause for punishment.
> c. It is not cruel or excessive and leaves no permanent mark or injury.

d. It is suited to the age and sex of the pupil.

e. It is not protracted beyond the child's power of endurance.

f. The instrument used for punishment is suitable.

g. It does not endanger life, limbs, or health, or disfigure the child.

h. It is administered to an appropriate part of the pupil's anatomy. (Bargen, 1961, p. 129)

Most cases of allegedly excessive force reflect a confrontation of wills in which emotions exacerbate or even precipitate the violent conduct (see, e.g., *R. v. Lauzon*, 1991). Rarely is the punishment administered in a detached, cooled-out environment where excesses or undeserved punishment through misperceptions or misunderstandings are less likely to occur. A good requirement for corporal punishment procedures is a prior review of the situation, preferably by a third party. Even though the criminal law will excuse a teacher who uses force in error (for example, on a child who is innocent of wrongdoing), so long as his mistake is an honest one (*R. v. Haberstock*, 1970), teachers should recognize that such mistakes undermine the attempt to inculcate an appropriate sense of justice among students.

Implications of the Canadian Charter of Rights and Freedoms

The Canadian Charter of Rights and Freedoms can be viewed as a tree that was planted as part of the 1982 repatriation of the Canadian Constitution. This tree will continue to grow and extend itself into more and more aspects of Canadian society. How far its branches will reach into Canada's educational systems is currently a matter of speculation. The Charter provides a potential tool for the courts to shape disciplinary rules and practices. Whereas, in the past, educators enjoyed rather broad discretionary powers over the exercise of discipline, with little fear of challenge to their authority, they must now consider the Charter's provisions as they make and enforce school rules and impose penalties on pupils who break them.

Rules of conduct made at the board and school levels are probably subject to scrutiny under the Charter. These rules must not infringe rights or freedoms guaranteed under the Charter. For example, a rule that required only female students to conform to a dress code might be struck down by the courts as an infringement of the equality provisions of section 15 of the Charter (see Appendix B). Such a rule would treat people in the school differently on the basis of their sex. This sort of rule might also be repugnant to provincial human rights legislation. However, a rule that treats two people or groups differently will not necessarily be struck down by the courts as discriminatory. The Supreme Court of Canada has ruled that discrimination, in the legal sense, means:

a. a *distinction*, intentional or unintentional;

b. based on grounds related to *personal characteristics* (e.g. sex, race, handicap);

c. having the effect of *imposing burdens*, obligations or disadvantages on an individual or group not imposed on others, or *withholding or limiting access to opportunities, benefits and advantages* available to other members of society. [*Andrews v. Law Society (B.C.)*, 1989; emphasis added]

There are often sound reasons for rules treating people differently. For example, while a rule that allowed only senior students access to certain facilities in the school might be discriminatory on its face, there might be bona fide administrative reasons (such as safety) that justify it. The generally recognized higher degree of responsibility residing in older students might be seen as an appropriate reason for discriminating between the two groups of students and limiting the equality of treatment afforded the younger students. The court's power to recognize "reasonable limits" on rights is provided for in section 1 of the Charter. Hence the fairness of differential treatment would be determined by the application of the "reasonable limits" doctrine in section 1.

Rules might not be discriminatory, but they might interfere with other substantive rights and freedoms claimed by students under the Charter. MacKay (1985) points out that banning slogans on T-shirts or buttons, prohibiting gay-rights meetings, and censoring school library materials are just a few examples of rules that could be viewed as contravening the freedoms set out in section 2 of the Charter (see Appendix B). These freedoms are not absolute, however, and again it would be open to the court to determine whether a board rule that infringed upon students' freedom of symbolic expression by banning the wearing of T-shirts with slogans was a reasonable and justified limit insofar as it sought to ensure that students' attire did not disrupt the learning environment. In applying American constitutional guarantees of freedom of expression to school situations, American courts have routinely utilized a test of whether the student's conduct caused "substantial disruption" in the school (MacKay, 1984b). The rather substantial onus, however, of showing that the rule was a "reasonable limit" that was "demonstrably justified in a free and democratic society" (Charter, section 1) would fall on the party seeking to impose it—in this case, the school board.

While few cases have arisen in Canada to test the applicability of section 2 Charter rights to students' dress and appearance choices, a student in Stratford, Ontario, in 1993 invoked section 2 to challenge his suspension for wearing his baseball cap to class contrary to a school rule. While the school board upheld the suspension on appeal, the rule was subsequently repealed. In the course of a civil action begun by the student and his parents against the school board, the Ontario Court of Justice granted an injunction staying the suspension pending determination of the Charter issues in a trial that has yet to occur (*London Free Press*, 1993b). While this case might strike many as a frivolous use of the Charter (*London Free Press*, 1993a), it nevertheless demonstrates the power of the Charter to challenge and alter traditional authority relationships and assumptions in schools (see, e.g., *Re Ward*, 1971). As the student's lawyer put it, "if administration is seeking to impose rules on a student, they have to be prepared to demonstrably justify those [rules] as being required for educational purposes" (Kelly, 1993, p. B10).

A more difficult situation arises where a pupil's dress involves religious implications. Cases have occurred in both Alberta (*Suneet Singh Tuli*, 1987) and Ontario (*Ontario Human Rights Commission v. Peel Board of Education*, 1990, 1991) involving Sikh students who wore to school their ceremonial daggers, known as kirpans, in violation of board rules against bringing weapons onto school property. Complaints were brought under provincial human rights legislation, rather than the Charter, although the issue still centred around the legal concept of discrimination. In the Ontario case, a Board of Inquiry found that the Peel Board of Education's ban on the carrying of weapons indirectly discriminated against Sikhs, a religious minority protected by the Ontario Human Rights Code, 1981. The school board appealed this decision to the Ontario Divisional Court, which upheld the Board of Inquiry's conclusion that the rule was unreasonable. The Court noted that the Board of Inquiry had not ignored the issue of safety in schools:

> That the Board of Inquiry was alive to the genuine concerns of the board about safety and the reasons for its policy, is reflected in the many safeguards the chair built into

his order to meet the concerns of the board, including the power of the school authorities to intervene in the case of actual or threatened misuse of kirpans and the power
of the school authorities to add restrictions if a climate of increasing violence should
develop. (*Ontario Human Rights Commission v. Peel Board of Education*, 1991, p. 535)

In fact, the Board of Inquiry had ordered that students, staff, or teachers be allowed to
wear kirpans to school subject to the condition that they be of reasonable size, not worn
visibly, and secured to make removal difficult.

Hence, school boards will need to show that seemingly "neutral" rules that have a
differential and detrimental impact on groups protected by human rights legislation are
reasonable and that the particular needs of the group in question cannot be accommodated
without undue hardship.

The process of enforcing school rules may be affected by section 7 of the Charter,
which guarantees individuals the right to "life, liberty and security of the person." The
section further provides that one may only be deprived of these rights "in accordance with
the principles of fundamental justice." Before being deprived of liberty or security of the
person, one must be accorded a degree of due process, which would likely include at least
notice of the reasons for the deprivation and a reasonable opportunity to be heard. If school
attendance is a matter covered by section 7, then a pupil may be entitled to be heard before
being suspended from school. The U.S. Supreme Court has recognized such a right to due
process for school suspension (*Goss v. Lopez*, 1975).

Suspension procedures are merely one example of a host of possible applications of
the due process requirements of section 7 to the enforcement of school rules. Whenever
a pupil's liberty or security is infringed—for example, through the assignment of detention
or the infliction of corporal punishment—the student must be fully apprised of the reasons
for the disciplinary action and given an opportunity to explain his or her side of the matter.
Obviously, students' freedom is infringed upon daily in the schools in a variety of ways.
It is unlikely that the Charter will be applied in every instance where a student is required
to do something or submit to something against his or her will. Until the courts provide
more interpretation of the words "liberty" and "security of the person" in the school
context, one can only surmise that it will be those disciplinary actions that have reasonably
serious implications—such as suspension, expulsion, and corporal punishment—that are
likely to attract the due process requirements of section 7.

From time to time, educators must conduct investigations to determine whether students
have broken board or school rules or, in more serious cases, the criminal law. This role
raises the question of the extent of teachers' authority to search students and, conversely,
the extent of their responsibility to respect students' rights under the Charter and the Young
Offenders Act. The few cases dealing with these questions provide only limited definition
to the legal dimensions of educators' investigatory role.

In a 1986 ruling, the Ontario Court of Appeal held that school principals had lawful
authority to search students as a result of their duty in section 265(a) of the Education Act
to maintain "proper order and discipline" (*R. v. J.M.G.*, 1986). The court assumed, however, that students were protected against unreasonable searches by section 8 of the Charter.
Adopting the reasoning of the United States Supreme Court in a similar case, the Court
of Appeal ruled that a school-based search of a pupil by a principal had to be reasonable
in two ways: at its inception and in its scope. To be reasonable at its inception, a search
must be based on reasonable suspicion by the principal that the search would turn up
evidence of a breach of the criminal law or a school rule. Even if justified at its outset,

the search must not be overly invasive in light of the nature of the suspected offence and the sex and age of the student (*R. v. J.M.G.*, 1986). In this case, a principal had reached into a student's pant cuff and retrieved a small amount of marijuana, after having been told that the student was in possession of drugs and after having seen him swallow what looked like a marijuana cigarette. The Court of Appeal held that the search was both justified by a reasonable suspicion and not overtly invasive.

It is worth noting that the court's ruling in this case is, as in all cases, limited by its facts. That is, strictly speaking, the case stands only for the proposition that a principal has authority to search a student, and it may be dangerous to conclude that a teacher enjoys the same right. Given, however, that principals' and teachers' duties regarding discipline derive from almost identically worded sections (265[a] and 264[1][e]) of the Education Act, it would be logical to so conclude.

The educator who becomes involved in the investigation of suspected criminal activity of students has the responsibility, under some circumstances, to ensure that student-suspect's rights under the Charter and the Young Offenders Act are not violated. This responsibility may include providing the student with an opportunity to consult legal counsel (and advising him or her of this right under section 10 of the Charter) and warning the student about his or her right to remain silent under section 56 of the Young Offenders Act.

The necessity for a principal to conform to section 10 of the Charter and to provide a detained student with the opportunity to consult a lawyer was considered in *R. v. J.M.G.* (1986). The Court of Appeal, however, rejected such a requirement, holding that section 10 of the Charter did not apply to school-based detention, which simply enabled principals to obtain the information they required to decide how to deal with student misconduct. Only in cases involving "heinous crimes," where "significant legal consequences" seemed inevitable and where the principal intended to turn the student over to the police, might section 10 rights arise (*R. v. J.M.G.*, 1986). It thus appears that the courts recognize that in matters of discipline, principals usually act as state agents for *educational* purposes, but that occasionally they act as agents of the *criminal justice system*.

A principal has also been held to be a "person in authority" within the meaning of section 56 of the Young Offenders Act. Under that section, a "person in authority" has certain obligations *prior to* receiving a confession to a criminal offence from a "young person" (aged 12 to 17 inclusive). Specifically, the young person must be told that there is no obligation to make a statement and that any such statement could be used as evidence in court. The young person must also be given the opportunity to consult a lawyer, a parent, or other adult of his or her choice. In *R. v. H.* (1986), where a principal failed to advise a student of his rights under section 56 prior to getting him to confess to a theft, the student's statement was ruled inadmissible and the charges against him were dismissed.

In addition to affecting the making and enforcement of rules of discipline in schools, the Charter may redefine the scope of penalties that may be imposed on students who break school rules. For example, the lawfulness of corporal punishment of school children must now be considered in the light of sections 12 and 15 of the Charter, rather than merely under section 43 of the Criminal Code. Section 12 of the Charter provides that "[e]veryone has the right not to be subjected to any cruel and unusual treatment or punishment." Canadian courts may not apply this section to school discipline since the Supreme Court of the United States held in 1977 in *Ingraham v. Wright* that the 8th Amendment to the U.S. Bill of Rights—which is similar in wording to section 12 of the Charter—applied only to the criminal justice system and not to schools. However, section

12 includes the word "treatment," while the 8th Amendment does not—which may be an important point of distinction.

Corporal punishment of school children might also be viewed as inconsistent with section 15 of the Charter, which guarantees equality before and under the law and equal protection of the law without discrimination based, among other things, on "age." Since both section 43 of the Criminal Code and the common law seem to discriminate against children by permitting what would be assault if inflicted on an adult, they may not stand the test of section 15 of the Charter. Ultimately, both the practice of corporal punishment and its statutory and common-law bases of legitimation may be struck down by the courts. However, all Charter rights are subject to "reasonable limits" (section 1), so the courts may declare that corporal punishment of children is "demonstrably justified" in our society (section 1).

Whether corporal punishment will be struck down as unconstitutional will likely depend on a consideration by the Supreme Court of Canada of both the substantial body of scholarly literature, which tends to condemn corporal punishment as a disciplinary technique, and public opinion, which tends to be more divided. A survey conducted by the Ontario Ministry of Eduction in 1981 demonstrated that approximately 50 percent of parents and teachers surveyed approved of the use of the strap as a last resort in cases of persistent misbehaviour (Ontario Ministry of Education, 1981). Given this controversy, the court may have difficulty in concluding that corporal punishment should not be tolerated under *any* circumstances in the schools. The courts may therefore reject a constitutional prohibition of the practice and reaffirm their traditional role of monitoring the exercise of corporal punishment on a case-by-case basis according to whether the force used was "reasonable under the circumstances."

While there is no lack of pressure to eliminate corporal punishment in the schools, a 1981 survey found that only one province (British Columbia) had banned corporal punishment (Ontario Ministry of Education, 1981). However, in a report released in 1984, the Law Reform Commission of Canada condemned the institutionalization of force within schools and called for the repeal of the federal law legitimizing reasonable corporal punishment of school children. It should be noted, however, that the Law Reform Commission carefully distinguished between *punitive* force and *restraining or coercive* force. While, in their view, the former was rarely justified, the latter often was—in order to protect oneself, other pupils, and school property, or to enforce compliance with teachers' lawful orders. In the revised Criminal Code proposed by the Commission to the Government of Canada in 1989, section 43 of the current Criminal Code was replaced by a provision that would permit corporal punishment by teachers only with the prior approval of the student's parent(s). Although the government has not acted on the proposal, the Law Reform Commission's philosophy appears to be consistent with the situation in Europe, where corporal punishment contrary to parents' wishes has been ruled by the European Court of Human Rights to be a violation of the parents' rights under the European Convention on Human Rights (Dickinson & MacKay, 1989, pp. 363–65). Under the influence of this ruling the United Kingdom abolished corporal punishment of pupils in 1987 (Parker-Jenkins, 1990–91).

If a Canadian court rules that sections 12 and 15 of the Charter apply to disciplinary practices in the schools, the implications would transcend the matter of corporal discipline to other school disciplinary practices that might be oppressive, degrading, or discriminatory, including unduly long detention, derision, and some other non-physical behaviour-modification techniques that make use of isolation.

In summary, educators derive their disciplinary authority over pupils from a number of sources: implied delegated parental authority via the doctrine of *in loco parentis*, legislation, and the common law. Emphasis on delegated parental authority has waned considerably in recent years as educators' authority is viewed more in the context of their role as agents of the state. As agents of the state, their authority is subordinate to the constitutionally entrenched Canadian Charter of Rights and Freedoms, which means that educators must now pay attention to whether their rules interfere with any substantive rights and freedoms that students enjoy under the Charter. In enforcing their rules and investigating student conduct generally, they must recognize that students may be entitled to due process. In cases where the criminal law is involved, educators may have a positive onus to read students their rights. Finally, they must be prepared for possible challenges to certain disciplinary practices and penalties that might be claimed to be either discriminatory or "cruel and unusual treatment or punishment."

CONCLUSIONS

Historically, the legal relationship of teachers with their pupils has been defined in a number of ways. Early schooling methods, such as boarding schools and one-room schoolhouses, meant that for many purposes teachers served as surrogate parents. Much of their legal authority and responsibility was derived then from the legal concept of *in loco parentis*. As schooling became a larger, more complex, and more public enterprise, teachers began to act as agents of the state.

The doctrine of *in loco parentis* has traditionally provided a basis both for teachers' authority to discipline students and their responsibility for students' safety and welfare. Thus the discipline exercised over students by teachers has historically been that of the kind, firm, and judicious parent. Section 43 of the Criminal Code codifies this common-law concept, as it recognizes that teachers and parents stand on the same footing concerning the extent of their lawful authority to use force to correct a child. Teachers' roles as surrogate parents also meant that parental responsibilities for children's physical safety became a significant part of their professional duties. In fact, the law requires teachers to exercise such care for their pupils as would a "careful parent."

As schools have evolved into more complex and public institutions, teachers' roles have likewise undergone legal redefinition. While the "careful parent" remains an important concept in determining teachers' liability for negligence, it is no longer the sole criterion. The complexity of tasks and activities for which teachers are responsible, and the nature and degree of their training and expertise, have resulted in teachers' conduct being measured against criteria of professional competence. In response to this need, the courts have developed another standard of care owed by teachers, which they have referred to as the "ordinarily competent instructor" test.

Regardless of how teachers are viewed — as surrogate parents or trained professionals — an abundance of court decisions has made it clear that they are under a heavy legal onus to protect their students from physical harm. To date, this legal duty of care has not been transposed into the sphere of academic services. Lawsuits for failure to educate have failed in the United States and Canada. As MacKay (1984a) puts it, while teachers have potential liability for "broken bones," it would appear that they are not legally responsible for "broken minds."

The increasingly public nature of the teacher's role has served to redefine the relationship between teachers and their pupils in several ways. The common-law rule that teachers may lawfully exercise disciplinary authority in the absence of parental permission recognizes the public interest in order and discipline in schools. Moreover, inasmuch as educators are seen to be agents of the state rather than merely substitute parents, the prescriptions of the Canadian Charter of Rights and of Freedoms and the Young Offenders Act, which constrain the activities of state, may have a substantial impact upon the establishment and enforcement of school rules. While the Charter's implications for school discipline are uncertain (due to the lack of Charter cases applicable to schools), the few judicial decisions that do exist suggest that when educators act in aid of the criminal justice system by investigating students' criminal conduct, their role approaches that of state law-enforcement agents. This role attracts legal requirements concerning the protection of the rights of individuals suspected of criminal offences. Before questioning students about suspected criminal activity, educators have a legal obligation to warn them that they are not obliged to make a statement, that if they do it could be used against them in court, and that they have a right to retain and consult a lawyer without delay. Educators will need to give serious consideration to how these prescriptions might alter the school climate. Should schools be transformed into a microcosm of the criminal justice system, or should the interrogation and search of student criminal suspects be left to the police?

In summary, the legal identity of teachers can be viewed as a rather complex hybrid of surrogate parent, professional, and state agent. All of these descriptors are important determinants of the boundaries of teachers' legal duties and authority.

DISCUSSION QUESTIONS

❑ How have the Canadian Charter of Rights and of Freedoms and the Young Offenders Act affected the authority and duties of educators? Do you view the effects as beneficial? Why or why not?

❑ "It no longer makes sense to legally characterize teachers as persons acting *in loco parentis*." Discuss why you agree or disagree with this statement.

❑ To what extent should the courts be involved in resolving disputes where parents claim their children have suffered as the result of incompetent teaching and assessment? In your answer, discuss American and Canadian courts' current policy toward these so-called educational malpractice cases.

REFERENCES

Andrews v. Law Society (B.C.), [1988] 1 S.C.R. 143.

Attis v. Board of School Trustees, District 15 (1991), 15 C.H.R.R. D/339 (N.B.Bd.Inq.).

Bales v. School District 23 (Central Okanagan) Board of School Trustees (1984), 54 B.C.L.R. 203 (S.C.).

Bargen, P.F. (1961). *The legal status of the Canadian public school pupil.* Toronto: Macmillan Canada.

Beauparlant v. Board of Trustees of Appleby, [1955] 4 D.L.R. 558 (Ont. HC).

Board of Education for City of Toronto and Hunt v. Higgs (1959), 22 D.L.R. (2d) 46 (SCC).

Child and Family Services and Family Relations Act, S.N.B. 1980, c. C-2.1.

Child and Family Services Act, R.S.O. 1990, c. C-11.

Constitution Act, 1982 (en. by the Canada Act, 1982 [U.K.] c. 11, Sched. B.) (Charter of Rights and Freedoms, ss. 1-34).

Criminal Code, R.S.C. 1985, c. C-46.

Czuboka, M. (1985). *Why it's hard to fire Johnny's teacher*. Winnipeg: Communigraphics/ Printers Aid Group.

Dickinson, G.M., & MacKay, A.W. (Eds.). (1989). *Rights, freedoms and the education system in Canada*. Toronto: Emond Montgomery.

Dickinson, G.M. (1988–89). Case comment: R. v. Keegstra. *Education and Law Journal, 1*, 199–207.

Donohue v. Copiague Union Free School District, 64 A.D. 2d 29 (1978) affirmed 47 N.Y. 2d 440 (1979).

Dziwenka v. Regina, [1972] S.C.R. 419 (SCC).

Education Act, R.S.O. 1990, c. E. 2.

Feldman, W., Woodward, C.A., Hodgson, C., Harsanyi, Z., Milner, R., & Feldman, E. (1983). Prospective study of school injuries: Incidence, types, related factors and initial management. *Canadian Medical Association Journal, 129*, 1279–83.

Fleming, J.G. (1983). *The law of torts* (6th ed.). Toronto: Carswell.

Funston, R. (1981). Educational malpractice. *San Diego Law Review, 18*, 743–812.

Gard v. Board of School Trustees of Duncan (1946), 2 D.L.R. 441 (BCCA).

Goss v. Lopez, 419 U.S. 565 (1975).

Hall v. Thompson, [1952] O.W.N. 133 (HC).

Hicks et al. v. Board of Education for the City of Etobicoke et al. (1988), School Law Commentary 3-8-3.

Hoffman v. Board of Education of City of New York, 64 A.D. 2d 369 (1978) reversed 49 N.Y. 2d 121 (1979).

Human Rights Act, R.S.N.B. 1973, c. H-11.

Human Rights Code, 1981, S.O. 1981 c.53 [now Human Rights Code, R.S.O. 1990, c.H. 19].

Hunter v. Board of Education of Montgomery County, 50 USLW 2430 (1982).

Hutt and Another v. The Governors of Haileybury College and Others (1888), 4 T.L.R. 623 (Q.B. Div.).

Ingraham v. Wright, 430 U.S. 651 (1977).

James v. East River School Division No. 9, [1976] 2 W.W.R. 577 (Man. CA).

Keegstra v. Board of Education of Lacombe No. 14 (1983), 25 Alta. L.R. (2d) 270.

Kelly, A. (1993, June 31). Both sides still at odds over student's cap caper. *London Free Press*, p. B10.

Law Reform Commission of Canada. (1984). *Assault*. (Working Paper 38). Ottawa: Law Reform Commission of Canada.

Law Reform Commission of Canada. (1988). *A new criminal code for Canada?* Ottawa: Law Reform Commission of Canada.

Leon, J.S. (1978). New and old themes in Canadian juvenile justice: The origins of delinquency legislation and the prospects for recognition of children's rights. In H. Berkeley, C. Gaffield, & W.G. West (Eds.). *Children's rights*. (pp. 35–58), Toronto: OISE Press.

Livingstone, D.W., & Hart, D.J. (1980). *Public attitudes toward education in Ontario 1980* (3rd OISE Survey) Toronto: OISE Press.

London Free Press. (1993a, June 4). A frivolous use, p. B8.

London Free Press. (1993b, June 10). Student 1, school 0, p. B8.

McEllistrum v. Etches, [1956] S.C.R. 787 (SCC).

MacKay, A.W. (1984a). *Education law in Canada.* Toronto: Edmont Montgomery

MacKay, A.W. (1984b). The Canadian Charter of Rights and Freedoms: A springboard to students' rights. *Windsor Yearbook of Access to Justice, 4,* 174–228.

MacKay, A.W. (1985, November). *Making and enforcing school rules in the wake of the Charter of Rights.* Paper presented at a meeting of the British Columbia School Trustees Association, Vancouver, B.C. To be published in A. Nicholls & T. Wuester, (Eds.). *The Canadian Charter of Rights and Freedoms and education law in British Columbia.* Vancouver: British Columbia School Trustees Association.

McKay v. Board of Govan School Unit No 29 (1968), 68 D.L.R. (2d) 519 (SCC).

Manley-Casimir, M. (1983). Canadian and U.S. legal traditions—Implications for administrative practice. In J. Balderson & J. Kolmes, (Eds.). *Legal issues in Canadian education/Proceedings of the 1982 Canadian School Executive Conference.* Edmonton: The Canadian School Executive.

Mertl, S., & Ward, J. (1985). *Keegstra/the issues, the trial, the consequences.* Saskatoon: Western Producer Prairie Books.

Murdock v. Richards, [1954] 1 D.L.R. 766 (NSSC).

Myers v. Peel County Board of Education (1981), 37 N.R. 227 (SCC).

Ogg-Moss v. R. (1984), 11 D.L.R. (4th) 549 (S.C.C.).

Ontario Human Rights Commission v. Peel Board of Education (1990), 12 C.H.R.R. D/364.

Ontario Human Rights Commission v. Peel Board of Education (1991), 3 O.R. (3rd) 531 (Div. Ct.) leave to appeal to Ont. C.A. refused (1991), 3 O.R. (3rd) 531n (C.A.).

Ontario Ministry of Education. (1979). *Attitudes of the public towards schools in Ontario.* Toronto: Canadian Gallup Poll.

Ontario Ministry of Education. (1981). *Corporal punishment in the schools* (Review and Evaluation Bulletins. Vol.2, No.1). Toronto: Ontario Ministry of Education.

Pabian, J.M. (1979). Educational malpractice and minimal competency testing: Is there a legal remedy at last? *New England Law Review, 15,* 101–27.

Parker-Jenkins, M. (1990-91). No more stick: An examination of the legal background to Britain's abolition of corporal punishment. *Education & Law Journal, 3,* 149–66.

Peter W. v. San Francisco Unified School District, 60 C.A. 3d 814 (1976).

Petersen v. Board of School Trustees (1991), *School Law Commentary* 7-1-5.

Pierce v. The Board of Education of the City of Chicago, 69 Ill. 2d 89 (1977).

R. v. Dimmell (1980), 55 C.C.C. (2d) 239 (Ont. Dist. Ct.).

R. v. H. (1986), Alberta Court of Queen's Bench, Judicial District of Edmonton, No.8503-0478-S2.

R. v. Haberstock (1970), 1 C.C.C. (2d) 433 (Sask. CA)

R. v. J.M.G. (1986), 56 O.R. (2d) 705 (CA).

R. v. Keegstra (1988), 60 Alta. L.R. (2d) 1 (CA).

R. v. Keegstra (1990), 1 C.R. (4th) 129 (SCC).

R. v. Lauzon (23 May 1991). (Ont. Prov. Div.). Merredew Prov. J. [unreported]

R. v. Zundel (1992), 1 S.C.R. 731 (SCC).

Re Ward and Board of Blaine Lake School Unit No. 57 (1971), 20 D.L.R. (3d) 651 (Sask. Q.B.).

Ross v. Moncton Board of School Trustees, District No. 15 (1991), 86 D.L.R. (4th) 749 (N.B.Q.B.).

Ross v. Moncton Board of School Trustees, District No. 15, (20 December 1993), N.B.J. no. 547 (CA).

Suneet Singh Tuli v. St. Albert Protestant Board of Education (1987), *School Law Commentary* 1-6-3.

Thornton v. Board of School Trustees of School District No. 57, [1975] 3 W.W.R. 622 (BCCA).2

Trustees of Columbia University v. Jacobsen, 31 N.J. 221, 156A. 2d 251 (1959).

Williams v. Eady (1894), 10 T.L.R. 41 (CA).

Young Offenders Act, R.S.C. 1985, c. Y-1.

FURTHER READINGS

Berkeley, H., Gaffield, C., & West, G.W. (Eds.). (1978). *Children's rights—Legal and educational issues* (Symposium series 9). Toronto: OISE Press.

Dickinson, G.M. (1989). Principals and criminal investigations of students: Recent developments. *Canadian Journal of Education, 14*(2), 203–19.

Dickinson, G.M. (1992–93). Exploding the myth . . . one more time. *Education & Law Journal, 4*, 226–30.

Dickinson, G.M., & MacKay, A.W. (Eds.). (1989). *Rights, freedoms and the education system in Canada*. Toronto: Emond Montgomery.

Foster, W.F. (1985). Educational malpractice: A tort for the untaught? *University of British Columbia Law Review, 19*, 161–244.

Hoyano, L.C. (1984). The prudent parent: The elusive standard of care. *University of British Columbia Law Review, 18*(1).

Hurlbert, E.L., & Hurlbert, M.A. (1992). *School law under the Charter of Rights & Freedoms* (2nd ed.). Calgary: University of Calgary Press.

MacKay, A.W. (1984). *Education law in Canada*. Toronto: Emond Montgomery.

MacKay, A.W. (1985). The Canadian Charter of Rights and Freedoms: A springboard to students' rights. *Windsor Yearbook of Access to Justice, 4*, 174–228.

Proudfoot, A.J., & Hutchings, L. (1988). *Teacher beware*. Calgary: Detselig.

Sussel, T.A., & Manley-Casimir, M.E. (1986). The Supreme Court of Canada as a "national school board": The Charter and educational change. *Canadian Journal of Education, 11*(3), 313–37.

19

STUDENT RIGHTS IN CANADA: BEYOND EQUALITY ISSUES

Steen Esbensen

Student rights is a complex issue encompassing such concepts as human rights, liberty and freedom, equality, and opportunities common to a democratic society. The issue is also complicated by the political, cultural, economic, and ecological conditions prevalent in the society in which the schools are located (Aberle, 1961; Inkeles, 1968, 1969). Student rights are discussed at many levels in the educational system. Most recently, an abundance of literature on student rights has related the issue of rights to integration and access to education for all children. Others associate the issue with concepts of classroom management, student discipline, and rights to expression of opinions. In this essay we associate student rights with articles from the U.N. Convention on the Rights of the Child as well as specific sections of the Canadian Charter of Rights and Freedoms to support our arguments for changing attitudes and behaviours of adults and children. The extent to which students are perceived to have rights varies not only between societies such as the United States and Canada, but also between schools in the same geographic and political community. The degree to which students' claims can be realized at their option makes the label "rights" dubious in some instances.

Schools have traditionally been recognized as a nation's primary vehicle for socialization. For some time schools have also been the initial bureaucratic organization with which children have gained first-hand experience (Nelson, 1985). However, with the rapid growth of day-care centres and other early childhood programs, children are being exposed to bureaucratic structures at increasingly earlier ages.

This paper analyzes and discusses the issue of student rights within two dimensions: the political and the sociocultural. The political dimension refers to the decision-making, participation, custodial, instructional, ideological, and governance issues of the school. The sociocultural dimension consists of the responsiveness of the schools to such issues as physical space, climate, and temporal environment. This framework will serve to elaborate the theme of students' rights in schools beyond the legal and familial analyses explored in chapters 18 and 20 respectively.

In this chapter we have chosen to define "student" as any young individual involved in the learning process within an educational institution—from early childhood education programs through the compulsory secondary level. This definition does not include adults who voluntarily take advantage of educational opportunities. This definition is established to help us deal with two major questions that have an impact on the issue of rights for students. The first is whether or not the child in Canada is a "person" for constitutional purposes or, more explicitly, how the child is viewed in federal statutes. The second is how young Canadians are educated.

Compulsory schooling begins at age 6 for children in all provinces in Canada. Most provinces and territories provide Kindergarten to the majority of 5-year-old children, and increasingly school boards in urban centres are offering Kindergarten to 4-year-olds. Furthermore, we know that there were 333 082 full-time day-care spaces in Canada in 1991 in centre-based programs and family day-care programs. These facts illustrate in part the change in the sociocultural, child-rearing, and education systems that have occurred in Canada over the past twenty years.

Before examining student rights in schools in Canada, let us establish the constitutional position on age discrimination. Section 15 of the Canadian Charter of Rights and Freedoms prohibits discrimination on the basis of age, but some discrimination may be found justifiable in a free and democratic society (section 1). For example, the age of majority is established as 18 years for voting purposes, this being the point when the federal government recognizes a person's ability to participate actively in the democratic process. The age of majority is also used to distinguish most young offenders from adult criminals who are charged with deviant, anti-social, and criminal acts. For example, the Young Offender's Act provides anonymity to persons involved in and charged with criminal behaviour if they are under the age of majority. It is argued by some that this special consideration is for the "child's" own protection. Others postulate that the age of majority serves to protect both young people and society, on the assumption that when a person is granted the right to vote, the responsibilities inherent in such a right preclude special distinctions and make all federal statutes applicable to the person. By thus identifying the age of majority, federal statutes have established an age beyond which parents are no longer required to support their children.

Section 15 of the Canadian Charter of Rights and Freedoms (see Appendix B) is significant for students in several other ways. Equality of rights requires all governments (including school boards, which are established by provincial authority) to have a rational and fair basis for any distinctions they make among persons or classes of persons, particularly on the grounds of race, national or ethnic origin, colour, religion, sex, age, and mental or physical disability. Section 15 is part of the Constitution of Canada. As such it has precedence over any other law that may conflict with it. Only the Charter's notwithstanding clause can be invoked against it, but that can only be temporary. Section 15 is binding at both the federal and provincial levels. The human rights of children and young people imply a special status.

Students have the right to be nurtured and cared for by their parents and teachers. They are also protected from the legal consequences of any anti-social behaviour they might display. They are not treated equally under the law, and many of their rights are those that their parents grant them. These privileges are recognized by society as reasonable until they encroach on the rights of other children or adults in society. One important statement of this is found in Article 14 of the U.N. Convention on the Rights of the Child (1989), which affirms the right of the child to freedom of thought, conscience, and religion, subject to appropriate parental guidance and national law.

POLITICAL DIMENSIONS

The federal government is only partly involved with the issue of children's rights as they apply to students in schools. The education of children is a provincial responsibility.

Article 93 of the Constitution Act, 1867 (formerly the British North America Act), reads: "In and for each Province the Legislature may exclusively make Laws in relation to Education." Since the provincial educational systems operate independently of one another, they are characterized by different administrative rules and political conditions. Each province in Canada has passed school acts creating school boards and granting them the power to control the operation of schools, including the conduct of the students. In effect, the school boards act as administrative agents for the provincial ministries of education. Insofar as they act within the framework of the delegated authority, their formulated policies have the force of law and constitute part of the legal framework within which the schools operate.

The political dimensions in each province influence the objectives of the schools, as well as the values placed upon education and the role of the parents, teachers, and students. Through the school boards, the provinces encourage community participation in the running of the schools. To a great extent, school boards determine the quality of life of students and teachers through the rules and regulations they establish for their schools. The boards are also responsible for the administration of budgets and for ensuring that the broader objectives of provincial education policies are implemented at the local level.

AUTHORITARIANISM

The relationship between the province and the local boards is designed to provide a provincial check and balance on locally defined needs. Consequently, the relationship between these two administrative bodies can be contentious and authoritarian. In April 1985, for example, the government of British Columbia fired the members of the Vancouver Board of Education and assumed responsibility for the administration of the schools in Vancouver. The action initially met with a great public outcry and even an unsuccessful legal challenge from former Board members. It was not until new school board elections, held in February 1986, that elected representatives of the Vancouver Board reassumed their responsibilities. All the members of the original Board in Vancouver were re-elected, except for those aligned with the government.

In 1993, the Newfoundland government called a provincial election primarily to determine whether the citizens supported the teachers or the provincial government in setting an agenda for fiscal restraint. The government won and has embarked on a cost-cutting program that will affect teachers' salaries and working conditions.

In the spring of 1990, teachers of the Ottawa Board of Education went on strike for five weeks prior to the end of the school year. Upon returning to school, Grade 8 students in several schools were informed by their principals that some of the end-of-year graduation celebrations would have to be eliminated. Students in one Ottawa school responded with a walk-out and strike. The response of the administration was to threaten them with expulsion if they didn't return to their classes. Students responded by calling the media, and several parents met with the school administration. Subsequent to much discussion, all graduation celebrations continued.

Many provinces have experienced similar demonstrations of ministerial authority, and not all were followed by a rebuke from voters. Nevertheless, the strength of the paternalistic system should be of some concern to citizens living in a democratic society. In the British Columbia incident, parents, students, and teachers became aware of the power of the provincial government relative to the local school boards. The hierarchy of power demonstrated in this political context reinforces the concept of responsibility—in this case, learning to live with and respect authority and the paternalistic system. The political context in which students attend school provides valuable lessons in understanding bureaucracy and the social context of their lives. As Faber (1970) stated, "it is not what you're taught that does harm, but how you are taught. ... The real lesson is the method. The medium in school is the message. And the message is, above all, coercive" (pp. 19–20).

What do students learn about their own rights when surrounded by such a variety of turbulent political influences? When can students begin to participate in the decision-making process in school? These questions should be addressed in view of the education system's ostensible objective to foster the acquisition of democratic skills, analytical thought, views of justice and morality, and knowledge to compete in society. However, Nelson (1985), postulates that students on the path to their diplomas and degrees

> have learned how to take direction (to co-operate) without worrying too much about whether or not the directions make sense to them; the best part, from the prospective employer's point of view, is that they do so in an uncomplaining (unemotional) way. It is the perfect training for potential employees required to function in a bureaucracy where a specialized administrative hierarchy governs authority relations among career-oriented (time-serving) and impersonally detached officials attempting to maintain an efficient social distance from clients by the neutral application of explicit rules and regulations. (pp. 142-43)

If Nelson's theory is correct, schools that turn out students who always conform and comply are preparing them to participate in a totalitarian rather than a democratic society. When does the education of the democratic citizen commence, and what means do the schools use to produce such individuals? These questions are particularly relevant for a paternalistic system that proposes to educate competent, free-thinking, analytical citizens.

DEMOCRATIC SCHOOLING PHILOSOPHY

Several questions pertinent to the political dimensions of student rights have been raised: When does the education of the democratic citizen commence? When can students participate in the decision-making process in schools? What do students learn about their own rights when surrounded by political turmoil? Fenstermacher (1986) suggests that teaching is a moral, purposeful activity through which a teacher's performance emerges from decisions and judgements grounded in assumptions about teaching, learning, and classrooms. Ayers (1986) furthermore suggests that by involving students in classroom activity, and by helping them take active control of their learning, the purpose of teaching is enhanced. We would argue that the acquisition of knowledge is based both on the biological process of maturation and on the experiences of an active subject who gains knowledge through those experiences. The learner is thereby able to construct increasingly useful and more complex hypotheses about reality. Magsino (1980) argues that

> the crucial element in preparing children for democracy is not that of giving them every opportunity to go through the motion of exercising political and civil rights. Such motions are easy enough to learn. The more urgent, indispensable task is to have students initiated and developed along the lines of understanding and dispositions required of a Millian democrat: that is, an individual concerned not only with pursuing his welfare rationally, but also with avoiding harm to others. The problem in a blanket affirmation of the constitutional personhood of the young is that it would allow the

young to go through the motions of exercising political and civil rights even without necessitating the internalization of those skills and dispositions that would result in the elaborate responsible discharge of those rights. (p. 99)

CHILD DEVELOPMENT AND EDUCATION

Children begin compulsory schooling in Canada at the age of 6 years. Most children attend public school for at least one year before entering the compulsory system. In addition, more than ever before, children between 2 and 5 years of age are enrolled in some form of preschool program. This increased enrollment in day-care settings, nursery schools, and junior kindergartens has caused us to consider children as students at a much earlier age than in the past and to reconsider our notion of when student rights actually begin. Although preschool youngsters are not enrolled in the compulsory system, they are enrolled in formal institutional settings. The early childhood program is a formal organizational structure with official policies on a wide variety of issues: admissions, parent participation, grouping, dress, attendance, daily schedules, and assessment. These early childhood centres also relate to the community as a social system. Increasingly the day-care centre is located within a school building, and children may divide their day between junior Kindergarten and day care or primary grades and after-school day care. In some cases this sharing of facilities has contributed to bringing about a change in the teaching style in the early primary grades, but, interestingly enough, there has also been a tendency for the day-care centres to adopt some of the traditional primary school bureaucracy.

The preschool child has developed the mental ability to represent and direct his or her actions and experiences, and to communicate thoughts verbally to others (Hohmann et al., 1979). At this age, the child becomes increasingly able to reflect on his or her own actions, to recall previous experiences, to predict the consequences of familiar cause-and-effect sequences, and to solve everyday kinds of problems mentally without relying on physical trial and error.

The young child enrolled in a social system is a dynamic individual capable of learning to distinguish symbols or representations from the things they stand for, and thus can be recognized as a student. Therefore the age spectrum for considering student rights begins much earlier than compulsory attendance. Consequently, questions that ask when education for democratic citizenship begins, and when students can participate, are relevant to children before the age of compulsory attendance. The additional question—what do children learn about their rights?—is more appropriately geared to older, more politically aware children at the intermediate and secondary-school levels. The importance of teaching rights at this level is implied by the U.N. Convention on the Rights of the Child (1989). As Article 12 of the Convention states, "parties shall assure to the child who is capable of forming his or her own views the right to express those views freely in all matters affecting the child, the views of the child being given due weight in accordance with the age and maturity of the child."

Aidarova (1982) emphasizes that the individual child is socially and culturally conditioned by the responsible adults in the social system (p. 8). Indeed, before commencing the public school, many Canadian children will have spent up to 12 000 hours in an early childhood centre. The curriculum in these early childhood centres will play a critical role in determining the type of social and cultural conditionning they receive. Time to concentrate on activities of their choice as well as time to pursue non-directive activities is critical to their development. Delamont (1976) contends that while all schools have established rules and policies concerning pupils' conduct, "the extent and nature of the institutional control system varies from school to school, as does the extent to which the school regime penetrates into the classroom" (p. 36).

The individual teacher is in a pivotal position not only for determining the outcome of the content to be taught, but also in dealing with the custodial and bureaucratic aspects of the system. While the individual teacher operates relatively freely within the classroom, the peer pressures for maintaining order, silence, and imparting the bureaucratic authority of the school to the students are immense. The social fabric of the educational system in Canada, like most other school systems, is plagued by pressures for teachers and students to conform to institutional rules. These rules are rarely made by the students, and are often left over from previous administrations.

In 1980, Magsino found that only 14 percent of the superintendents in Newfoundland responded positively to having students provide significant input into the development of codes of personal appearance and conduct. The apparent lack of student participation in the decision-making process in elementary and secondary schools was confirmed through interviews and observations in schools in Ottawa and Gatineau in 1986 and 1992–93. Furthermore, Wolfson and Nash (1968) and Lee et al. (1983) found that children in elementary schools see themselves as relatively inactive decision-makers, while teachers appear to be making the majority of decisions; students view themselves as having fewer decision-making opportunities than they are perceived to have by teachers. Within the political context of Canadian society and the political dimensions of the school, student rights are clearly privileges granted to the students by the adults responsible for the institution.

SOCIOCULTURAL DIMENSIONS: SPACE AND TIME

The sociocultural dimensions of the school environment serve to indicate the extent to which students have input in affecting their learning environment. Research has suggested that physical arrangement, authoritarian climate, and time control significantly affect the students' perceptions as well as their behaviour in school. Schools must pay much more attention to the subtle messages transmitted to students through the dimensions of time and space, for they undermine students' educational rights. In particular, rigid time schedules, formal spatial arrangements, and non-mobility of classroom furniture instil rigidity and dependency upon routine, which may lull students into a state of complacency.

The physical aspect of school life has received limited attention in research literature. Space and time arrangements affect students' rights because they influence and relate to their classroom participation and behaviour. Although teachers consider classroom layout as relatively unimportant compared with the educational program and the student–teacher relationship (Esbensen, 1990; Sommer, 1977; Weikart, 1986), the way a teacher organizes the desks in a first-grade, nursery, or day-care classroom reveals how the teacher perceives his or her role vis-à-vis the student. A classroom with fixed desks in a rectangular arrangement with the teacher's desk in front implies a perception of the student as an empty vessel to be filled with knowledge; a circular arrangement implies a perception of the pupil as a social learner; and an open classroom indicates an active problem-solving environment (Getzels, 1974).

Research into the fit between person and environment has become an invaluable aid to educators. For instance, when a small climbing frame was placed at the front of a nursery school classroom, several children played almost exclusively on or around this frame for several weeks. The teaching staff was unable to redirect their interest. Finally, the teachers decided to change the room arrangement. The climbing frame was relocated in a corner of the classroom, away from the quieter activities. This resulted in a dramatic change in the noise level of the classroom, and the climbers changed their play patterns by taking more time to interact with other children in other areas of the room.

Rosenfield et al. (1985) found that "desk arrangement, and not student ability, student interest, observer bias, or other architectural features, significantly affected pupil behaviour" (p. 106). In another study on person–environment fit in the elementary school, Fraser and Fisher (1983) found that classroom achievement might be enhanced by changing the actual classroom environment in ways that make it more congruent with that preferred by the class" (p. 311). The physical environment provides cues to children, and their reactions to these settings can either facilitate or hinder their desire to learn. Whereas desks in rows produce more withdrawal and off-task behaviours, desks arranged in circles can facilitate classroom discussion as well as reduce unwanted behaviours (Rosenfield et al., 1985). The results of these recent studies support the proposition that room layout, especially the arrangement of desks, will influence student participation, thinking, and behaviour, all of which have obvious effects on learning.

The time teachers give to students is an equally important factor in determining how teachers perceive students. That individuals learn at different speeds remains a common generalization within the educational community. In a learning environment where the time allotted to subjects remains constant, achievement among individual learners varies markedly. Notwithstanding this generalization, it is important to note Gettinger's (1985) comments that

> the relation between time allocated or time spent in learning and achievement appears to be intricately tied to the amount of time actually needed for learning . . . how much time should be allocated for learning depends, in part, on how much the learner needs to attain the intended learning goal. (p. 5)

The opportunity for students to communicate their need for more time to complete their work is therefore a critical dimension of the climate in the school. Do students feel free to ask the teacher for more time, or does the teacher make the decision that they have been given enough time? If the latter, then how has such a decision taken into account the students' different rates of learning? The extent to which students feel that they are free to ask about, comment on, or criticize the events in the classroom further indicates the degree to which the social system encourages the development of critical and analytical thought, inquiry, and the ability to discuss issues rationally.

The time allocated to students to accomplish their work not only affects their academic achievement, but also serves to inculcate time-use behaviours. Students rapidly acquire a sensitivity to the amount of time available to them to undertake an activity and will in some cases refuse to start or continue a project for fear of lack of time. It is also quite common for students to withdraw from activities when the stress of time constraints is present. For example, Kindergarten children involved in building skyscrapers with wooden blocks in their classroom's construction area were observed to destroy their construction when the teacher announced clean-up time. The look of frustration on their faces explained in part their overt behaviour, which the teacher in this case failed to understand—they needed more time to complete their construction. Another method could have been used to provide the builders with a sense of importance, and thereby their achievements could have been extended. The temporal component of the physical environment also affects the way students are afforded rights in schools. Strictly regimented time may have less than the desired effect on children's behaviour and achievement.

STUDENT ATTITUDES

Although schools are paternalistic and authoritarian, students nevertheless accept the sociocultural restrictions imposed on them. As Lee et al. (1983) state, "Older children continue to view the school as supportive of important values and report themselves as liking school even more than their younger schoolmates" (p. 847). This same study concludes that

> The school communicates support and sympathy for the child's values even as, from the child's view, it constrains opportunities for the expression of social competence. Children do not seem to judge these constraints as unduly oppressive, nor do they invoke them as criteria for evaluating the school. (p. 846)

These findings are undoubtedly most reassuring for the paternalistic proponents among us; however, student acceptance of the social framework in the elementary school should not be construed as relieving the school of responsibility for dealing with the issue of student rights and freedoms. In fact, it may be that sixth-graders have become "streetwise" to the ways of the school and thus tolerate the way it functions. However, as children grow and "tip over into adolescence, continued circumvention of their competence aspirations may partially determine the manifest tension and alienation at the secondary level" (Lee et al., 1983, p. 846). If the discrepancy between the social competence of the students and the paternalism of the school system continues, students' perceptions of their school may change dramatically. It may well be that such discrepancy can be "associated with the violence, vandalism, and apathy common at the high school level" (p. 846).

Students' attitudes toward the school, their teachers, and society are not immutable. As children grow and experience the world, their sense of justice continues to evolve. The extent to which the school system recognizes and facilitates the development of its students as democratic citizens is contingent upon the dynamic interaction of dimensions discussed in this chapter. The political and cultural (including ecological) dimensions of the school system combine to create a school environment. Therefore, a number of interrelated variables impact upon students' rights and freedoms.

CONCLUSIONS

The debate about student rights in the context of the educational system in Canada is ongoing. Clearly, the federal and provincial governments recognize that students have rights as persons. In addition to the basic right to be cared for and to be provided with the opportunity for an education, procedural rights and due process policies are being established to ensure fair treatment of students in the schools. These measures are greatly influenced by litigation and the children's-rights movement in the United States and Canada. However, the granting of rights within what is essentially a paternalistic system is bound to be difficult: students, parents, teachers, principals, and school board members all approach the issue from different philosophical perspectives. Such divergent views are bound to cause confusion over what ought to constitute student rights. "A slogan in search of a definition" (Rodham, 1973) is certainly one way to summarize the confusion that is generated when the issue of student rights is raised. The issue is much more than a debate between proponents of the children's liberation camp ("kiddy libbers") and the child welfare ("child savers") movement (King, 1982). It is a fundamental element in the determination of the role of schools and the goals envisioned for an educational system in a democratic society.

If prescriptive socialization techniques such as indoctrination are disdained as a means of socializing children and young people, then the issues become much more pragmatic than the more theoretical analysis often accorded this debate. Specific discussion should focus on the relationships that teachers encourage with students at all levels of the system, since autocratic postures are perhaps less efficient in developing analytical and free-thinking citizens than are participatory interactive teaching techniques (Schweinhart et al., 1986). Likewise, allowing children to participate in the development of classroom roles and codes of behaviour serves not only to fulfil the ultimate goal of establishing acceptable rules of conduct, but also enables children to participate in the development of what is considered socially tolerable behaviour (Ayers, 1986). Such small measures of democratic participation in the daily routines of the school may take time away from the actual subject matter to be taught, but in the process they serve to enhance the students' abilities to manage their individual and collective rights, responsibilities, and freedoms.

Schools must continue to provide the means for generating and sustaining the commitment of young people to the educational system, by giving them opportunities for active involvement in the classroom and throughout the school. The issue of student rights in the Canadian educational context is a fundamental matter that warrants considerably more attention than it has been given to date.

DISCUSSION QUESTIONS

❏ Discuss the potential implications of the Canadian Charter of Rights and Freedoms for such aspects of school discipline as rules and codes of behaviour.

❏ Discuss the impact of the freedom of speech declarations of the U.N. Convention on the Rights of the Child (1989) on the traditional relationships between teachers and students.

❏ At what age level would you deem it appropriate for children to participate in the setting of school codes of behaviour? Explain.

❏ Discuss the link between prescriptive socialization techniques and autocratic behaviours in schools. Draw upon personal and popular examples to generate ideas on how to change such behaviours.

REFERENCES

Aberle, D.F. (1961). Culture and socialization. In F.L.K. Hsu (Ed.). *Psychological anthropology*. Homewood, IL: Dorsey Press.

Aidarova, L. (1982). *Child development and education*. Moscow: Progress Publishers.

Ayers, W. (1986). Thinking about teachers and the curriculum. *Harvard Educational Review, 56*, 49–51.

CCCY. (1978). *Admittance restricted*. Ottawa: Canadian Council on Children and Youth.

Delamont, S. (1976). *Interaction in the classroom*. London: Methuen.

Esbensen, S. (1990). Designing the setting for the early childhood education program. In I. Doxey (Ed.). *Child care and education: Canadian dimensions*. (pp. 178–192). Toronto: Nelson.

Faber, J. (1970). *The student as nigger*. Richmond Hill, ON: Simon and Schuster.

Fenstermacher, G.D. (1986). Philosophy of research on teaching: Three aspects. In M.C. Wittrock (Ed.) *Handbook of research on teaching* (3rd ed., pp. 37–49). New York: Macmillan.

Fraser, B.J., & Fisher, D.L. (1983). Use of actual and preferred classroom environment scales in person–environment fit research. *Journal of Educational Psychology, 75* (2), 303-13.

Gettinger, M. (1985). Time allocated and time spent relative to time needed for learning as determinants of achievement. *Journal of Educational Psychology, 77* (1), 3–11.

Getzels, J.W. (1974). Images of the classroom and visions of the learner. *School Review, 82*, 527-40.

Health and Welfare. (1993). *Status of day care in Canada 1991*. Ottawa: Minister of National Health and Welfare.

Hohmann, M., Banet, B., & Weikart, D.P. (1979). *Young children in action*. Ypsilanti, MI: High/Scope Press.

Inkeles, A. (1968). Society, social structure and child socialization. In J.A. Clausen (Ed.). *Socialization and society*. Boston: Little, Brown.

Inkeles, A. (1969). Social structure and socialization. In D. Goslin (Ed.). *Handbook of socialization theory and research*. Chicago: Rand McNally.

King, M. (1982). Children's rights in education: More than a slogan? *Educational Studies, 8*(3), 227–38.

Lee, P.C., Statuto, C.M., & Kedar-Voivodas, G. (1983). Elementary school children's perception of their actual and ideal school experience: A developmental study. *Journal of Educational Psychology, 75*(6), 838–47.

Magsino, R.F. (1980). *Student rights in Newfoundland and the United States: A comparative study*. St. John's, NF: Memorial University.

Nelson, R. (1985). Books, boredom, and behind bars: An explanation of apathy and hostility in our schools. *Canadian Journal of Education, 10*(2), 136–60.

Rodham, H. (1973). Children under the law. *Harvard Educational Review 43*(4), 487–514.

Rosenfield, P., Lambert, N.M., & Black, A. (1985). Desk arrangement effects on pupil classroom behavior. *Journal of Educational Psychology, 77*(1), 101–8.

Schweinhart, L.J., Weikart, D.P., & Larner, M.B. (1986). *Consequences of three preschool curriculum models through age 15*. Ypsilanti, MI: High/Scope Press.

Sommer, R. (1977). Classroom layout. *Theory into Practice, 16*, 174–75.

United Nations. (1989). *The Convention on the Rights of the Child*.

Weikart, D.P. (1986, April 10). Evaluation of preschool programs. Seminar at the Institute of Psychology, University of Aarhus.

Wolfson, B.J., & Nash, S. (1968). Perceptions of decision making in elementary school classrooms. *Elementary School Journal 69*(2), 89–93.

FURTHER READINGS

Bauer, A.M. and R.H Sapona. (1991). *Managing classrooms to facilitate learning.* Englewood Cliffs, NJ: Prentice-Hall.

Bowers, C.A., & D.J. Flinders. (1990). *Responsive teaching: An ecological approach to classroom patterns of language, culture and thought.* New York: Teachers College Press.

Elkind, D. (1984). *The hurried child.* Don Mills: Addison-Wesley.

King, M. (1982). Children's rights in education: More than a slogan? *Educational Studies,* *8*(3), 227–38.

Lawrence, R. (1985). School performance, containment theory, and delinquent behaviour. *Youth and Society,* *17*(1), 69–95.

Le Shan, E.J. (1971). *The conspiracy against childhood.* New York: Atheneum.

Magsino, R.F. (1980). *Student rights in Newfoundland and the United States: A comparative study.* St. John's, NF: Memorial University.

Nelson, R. (1985). Books, boredom, and behind bars: An explanation of apathy and hostility in our schools. *Canadian Journal of Education,* *10*(2), 136–60.

Wolfson, B.J., & Nash, S. (1968). Perceptions of decision making in elementary school classrooms. *Elementary School Journal,* *69*(2), 89–93.

20

THE FAMILY: PARENTS' AND CHILDREN'S RIGHTS

Romulo Magsino

Margaret Mead once claimed that the family is the toughest institution we have. Although it has recently been predicted to be headed toward disintegration, more cautious analyses indicate that the strains and changes being experienced within contemporary family life are signs of evolution rather than dissolution. Moreover, as Kain (1990) points out, the notion of family decline is largely a myth drawn from misconceptions about realities of family life in the past and from preconceived expectations about it in the present and the future.

In Canada, considerable changes in the family have elicited calls for a systematic examination of existing policies. In suggesting such an examination, Armitage (1977) points out that Canadian policy-makers have not formulated any deliberate family policy that addresses family changes and stresses. So far, whatever policy exists "is often scattered between different programs, is often internally contradictory, and is rarely conceptualized as part of a whole" (p. 26). Particularly in relation to child welfare, Wharf concludes that current child welfare policy represents an extreme cultural lag. It has failed to recognize women's roles, the impact of poverty, the importance of cultural values and traditions, and the fundamental features in Canadian families including high divorce rates, women's unemployment, and violence against women and children (Wharf, 1993, pp. 210–11).

Armitage's criticism of the situation in Canada applies directly to parent–child relationships. Although the Divorce Act of 1968 set the stage for re-evaluation of the family and new laws reflecting a changed social reality, clear-cut statements on parents' and children's rights are still not available. Mohr (1984) notes that differences in the legal definition of children still exist, with some protagonists advocating independence for children so that they will fit into the legal conception of persons. Mohr sees the problem this way:

> At the same time as the law tries to increase children's autonomy, it increases parental responsibility . . . to the breaking point. When the break is achieved, the State steps into the breach. The age old covenant has become a contract with many specific performance claims. (p. 263).

The question of which "specific performance claims" or rights can be claimed against one another by parents, children, and the state (that is, government) has become problematic in the confused contemporary context. In addressing this contentious issue, this chapter presents an historical overview of the family as the setting of parental exercise of their rights, traces the development of the conflict of rights within the Canadian family, illustrates the extent of the problem in the present, looks at the question of parental rights in education, and examines what parental rights should receive continued societal support and legal sanction. In so doing, it is hoped that a justifiable perspective on family policy in Canada will emerge.

THE EVOLVING FAMILY AND THE DEVELOPMENT OF PARENTAL RIGHTS

Understanding the conflict between the rights of parents and those of the child and/or the state requires a familiarity with the development of the family insofar as rights involve relationships imbedded within that institution.

The prevailing view of the family today has been fashioned by "sentiments writers," including Aries (1962), Flandrin (1979), Shorter (1975), and Stone (1977), who focus on the character of the emotional and personal links among family members, as well as on the factors influencing them. While not agreeing on every issue, they conclude that the family as we perceive it—an independent nuclear unit made up of husband, wife, and children with close personal ties—is a comparatively recent phenomenon (Aries, 1962, pp. 405–7; Flandrin, 1979, pp. 9–10). The early modern family was characterized by little genuine affection, either between husband and wife or between parents and children, and by authoritarian relationships dominated by the husband who, during the age of reformation, almost completely stifled both wife and children. The family was markedly patriarchal: the father controlled economic and moral matters; the wife and children were expected to defer to the father, who was expected, and who regarded it his duty, to use physical force to maintain discipline. In all of its aspects, the family was to a large degree an extension of the community. As Flandrin (1979) contended, "traditional society gave the husband the means to impose his will, but also demanded that he did impose it" (p. 123).

During the last few centuries, however, population growth and increased migration, diminished community control over individuals, the appreciation of privacy, the religiously motivated concern for the consequences of so-called promiscuous living arrangements, and the emphasis on the separation of domestic life from the pressure-filled world of work have all contributed to the emergence of the autonomous conjugal family unit. These factors and others, including the emerging emphasis on schooling, altered interest in traditional interpersonal family relationships, the criteria for spouse selection, the perceived functions of marriage, and attitudes about sex (Anderson, 1980, pp. 45–64). By the seventeenth century, the modern family was already identifiable.

The concept of childhood developed with the emergence of the modern family. Aries (1962) asserts that just like the concept of the family, the concept of childhood did not exist in medieval society. This is not to say, he warns, that children were neglected, forsaken, or despised. Rather, they were regarded as adults as soon as they could live without the constant care of their mothers, nannies, or cradle-rockers (p. 128). In the seventeenth century, however, moralists and pedagogues were already showing concern for the special nature of childhood through their interest in and pronouncements on children's psychology and morals. Children had become "fragile creatures" who needed to be both safeguarded and reformed (p. 133). Childhood would be the stage for adult intervention to ensure disciplined, rational behaviour in the younger generation.

Sentiments writers have been criticized, particularly by Anderson (1980), Ozment (1983), and Pollock (1983), not only for their approach but also for their substantive claims and conclusions. Whatever the outcome of this disagreement, one thing is clear: parental authority, with its power of coercion, increased from the sixteenth century onward. In France, although the Church diminished paternal authority by recognizing the validity of marriages without the father's consent, fathers still preserved most of the rights granted them by the ancient Roman laws (Flandrin, 1979, pp. 130–31). Similarly, in England, there was an increased emphasis on discipline (as opposed to punishment) beginning in the seventeenth century. Thereafter, parents became more concerned with training their children to ensure the absorption of the values and beliefs required by a responsible citizenry. Early in the 1800s, adult demands for obedience and conformity intensified. Socialization and control of children became customary parental prerogatives (Pollock, 1983, pp. 268–71).

THEORETICAL CONSIDERATIONS

Both historical and sociological accounts of the family reveal changing and contradictory perceptions of the entitlements of its members. One possible approach toward a viable perspective that could shed light on parental and children's rights requires an exploration of the ideal conception of the human family. This approach calls for no less than a theory of the family that does justice to our understanding of the nature of and possibilities for human beings within the context of society and its institutions.

One pervasive theory of the family that has been used to support modern advocacy of rights for certain family members, particularly children, needs to be disposed of immediately. This theory, which we will call the "functionalist theory," depicts the family as a social group characterized by bonds created largely for economic and reproductive purposes (Bates, 1978, pp. 454–61). This view sees the family as a functional unit intended to further the interests of individual family members. Where the unit no longer serves such a purpose, it is not only dispensable but also should be disbanded. In broader terms, if it is shown that the family as an institution is no longer functional in terms of economic and reproductive purposes, it should be superseded or replaced by another institution.

Geared toward members' individual good, rather than that of the family as a whole, this theory provides a natural habitat for conflicting demands. Where one family member is able to exert himself/herself with the support of the wider society, the well-being of the other members is correspondingly compromised. The traditional family, marked by unbridled paternal control, clearly hampered the interests of the wife and the children, yet remained functional because the father/husband was the unit's economic provider. Fortunately, increasing societal acceptance of the ideals of justice for the young and equality for the wife has introduced new elements into the equation. Apart from matrimonial equality, paternal rights have been diminished through the implementation of the principle of the best interests of the child. The conflict goes on nevertheless. Under the neoconservative banner, Goldstein et al. (1979) have argued, with a great deal of authority and influence, against governmental and judicial interference in family autonomy and parental rights unless family members are clearly endangered. Unfortunately, as Dickens (1981) points out, such a position, no matter how attractive, fails "to address parents whose well-meaning and conscientious initiatives are misguided or insensitive in ways denying children (their) future rights" (p. 474). Yet his own view that the modern function of parental rights is nothing but "to prepare children and adolescents for maturity" (p. 485) does not do justice to the complex relationships between parents and children. Unless the reciprocity of the relationships within the family is fully recognized and respected, the tendency toward confrontation in our society will remain and increase. Naturally, this tendency will require even more action on the part of the state—whether through its legislatures or its courts. Confrontations need to be mediated by a third party.

A second theory suggested for consideration recognizes that just like any other institution, the family arises from human needs and purposes. It does not deny economic or any other materialistic purpose behind marriage or reproduction. It insists, however, that the family's distinctiveness lies in its capacity to respond to the human need for stable and intimate emotional relationships among individuals. The family consists of a web of interrelationships between people who find their bonds mutually satisfying. Naturally, carrying on such relationships will promote certain instrumental benefits, such as economic security and the development of mature, responsible social members and citizens. However, the unique value of the family lies in the desirability of the intrinsically satisfying bonds among its members. It is important enough that the family is, as Blustein (1979) puts it, a "community characterized by the mutual love and the harmonious development of personalities" (p. 118).

For want of a better, more established expression, we will refer to this view as the "personalist theory." It is personalist because it highlights the normative idea that a family is made up of people, not individual atoms bumping against one another, "whose individualities interact and communicate with each other in the quite concrete circumstances of human life" (Melden, 1977, p. 120). Within this natural unit, people carry on "their multifarious affairs with one another, in the course of which, as the quite particular agents they are, they bring their lives together and support each other's agency" (p. 120). Thus the theory involves socialization—that is, efforts on the part of full agents, namely parents, to develop capacities needed by children to assume full agency or decision-making powers of their own. At the same time, however, it recognizes the right of parents not only to enjoy continued interaction with their children but also to determine the means by which the interaction can be promoted and enriched.

Unhappy with theories as applied to child welfare policy, Wharf (1993), Armitage (1993), and others espouse a third theory, which they call the "social development view." Similar to Dizard and Gadlin's (1990) notion of "public familism," this view or theory not only accepts that "social services are a necessary social provision that should be available to families"; it also calls for changes in the "grand issues of social policy by interfering in present economic arrangements and by increasing the numbers of people who participate in governing" to promote the goals and the viability of societal institutions like the family (Wharf, 1993, pp. 211–12). Concerned about the plight of the family, the social development theory or public familism sees increased family autonomy and choices through widened public participation in institutional decisions and through responsive public support services. Further, it acknowledges that, under present circumstances, neither unassisted family efforts nor active professional services will provide adequately for family objectives.

PARENTS, CHILDREN, AND THE STATE IN CANADA: FROM LEGACY TO CHANGE

The caution needed in reaching conclusions about the family as a concept clearly applies to the Canadian family. The solicitous parental child rearing by fathers in the fur trade society near Hudson Bay and the absentee child rearing by fathers in the Northwest presented at least two "different kinds of families and experiences of parenthood . . . in the same territory at the same time and among men engaged in the same economic activity" (Parr, 1982, pp. 11–12). Still, by the 1870s, a view of the parental role was already prevalent, at least in English-speaking Canada. There, parents were to "fashion hardworking, productive adults" out of resistive and refractory, though basically plastic, raw material (Sutherland, 1976, p. 11).

By the 1880s, increased industrialization, together with associated forces, had ushered in new ideas about child rearing. Such ideas included the view that children had seeds of divine life within them to be nurtured rather than moulded and that parents had to tackle their nurturing duties diligently and systematically. Consequently, they had to provide an appropriate home environment and suitable models of behaviour. As well, parents were expected to oversee and control activities and conditions outside the home that could corrupt the young's morally fragile nature. They were to be watchful of entertainment, drinking, smoking, "dangerous" literature, and the like. Corporal punishment, although questioned as a parental prerogative, was generally accepted for use as a last resort (Sutherland, 1976, pp. 12–21).

The period from the 1880s to the 1920s represented, through the efforts of a small band of Canadian reformers, the stage of transformation of social consensus on child rearing and the family. The family was taken increasingly not as "a sentimental end in itself, but as a means: it was the social agency that had the prime responsibility for ensuring that the whole of the next generation represented the best that Canadian society could produce" (Sutherland, 1976, p. 20). In this light, mothers assumed a central importance in giving children stable and ever-present loving care. Where the father and the mother could not provide this, and where rehabilitation of a damaged family situation was unattainable, resort to state action was deemed justifiable. The late 1880s marked the beginning of government incursion into family life to protect or ensure the welfare of the young.

Having made education compulsory in 1874, the Ontario government led the country in enacting child welfare legislation by passing the Ontario Factories Act in 1884 to regulate child labour. This government was also first to pass a child protection act in 1893. Subsequently, other provinces adopted similar statutes, which conferred on the government or its agencies the right to assume guardianship over children whose parents had failed or neglected to comply with a legislated minimal standard of care and protection (White, 1980). Today, under most provincial laws on child welfare, nearly every person who has information on abandonment, desertion, and child abuse is required to report it to an appropriate authority.

The legacy of the reform movement of 1880–1920 is also clearly evident in the provisions of federal legislation relating to children. The Canadian Criminal Code penalizes parents or guardians for assault causing bodily harm to their children, incest, procurement, sexual immorality affecting the young, abandonment, and neglect in providing the necessities of life required by children under 16 years of age. And even as the Code justifies parents' use of force to discipline their children, it stipulates that such force should not exceed what is reasonable under the circumstances. Interestingly, the Young Offenders Act (1982 and proclaimed in 1984) retains its predecessor's protectionist intent. While it recognizes that young people have rights, freedoms, and responsibilities equal to those of adults, it admits that young people require supervision, discipline, and control. Moreover, because of their state of dependency and lack of maturity, children have special needs and require guidance and assistance (Wilson, 1978, 1980; Young Offenders Act, 1982, p. 4).

State intervention, however, has had implications for the exercise of traditional parental rights. Such rights have been particularly extensive in the province of Quebec, where the legal system is based on Roman civil law rather than the common law found in English-speaking provinces.[1] The doctrine of *patriae potestas*, which conferred rights and powers on the head (father) of the family to ensure its union and preservation, once gave the father the power of life and death over his children (and similarly over his slaves). From this doctrine derived the notion of "puissance paternelle," which was incorporated into Quebec's 1866 Civil Code and which entrenched not only paternal authority over children but also the denial of rights to the wife-mother. Fundamental changes in the law came about only in 1977, when amendments to the Code established parental (versus paternal) authority and recognized equality between father and mother in exercising rights and duties (Civil Code of Quebec, 1980, Articles 441–47). These rights are explicitly laid down and include entitlements to respect from the child (regardless of age); authority over him/her until the age of majority or emancipation; custody, supervision, and education; control over the children's residence; correction of the child with moderation and within reason; and restoration of rights withdrawn by the courts, provided that parents can fully show changed circumstances (Articles 645–58). Significantly, however, the Code also opened the way for the courts, in the interests of the child, to arbitrate on family matters when parents disagree in the exercise of parental authority (Article 653). It also gave the courts the power to deprive parents of their authority, partially or fully, and to designate guardians for their children (Articles 654–55).

The dilution of parental rights in English-speaking provinces has been evident for about a century, beginning with the reform movement in the 1880s. Under common law, there is neither a statutory definition of parental rights nor any judicial attempt to formulate one (Godfrey, 1976). The relationship between parent and child has been largely a matter of ethical or moral standards and custom, rather than being governed by any legally enforceable measure (McKnight, 1976). However, compared with civil law, common law has developed a milder philosophy of parental rights. Initially, common law did not require any parental obligations toward children; in fact, as in civil law, it supported the near absolute right of the father to custody of his child (Hall, 1972). But in the 1760s, the great English jurist William Blackstone indicated in his commentary on English law that the law had incorporated the notion that parents not only had rights but also owed positive duties to their children (White, 1980). Thus Eekelaar (1973) writes that "the expression 'parental rights' is clearly a loose way of describing the conglomeration of rights, powers, liberties *and (perhaps) duties* which a parent has with respect to his child" (p. 212; emphasis in original). However inappropriate the inclusion of "duties" within the notion of rights might appear, the reality is that modern federal and provincial laws do impose on parents obligations to maintain, protect, educate, discipline, and punish (where appropriate) their children (White, 1980, pp. 231–43). Throughout Canada, state power with respect to child rearing is an established fact.

Nonetheless, parental rights as powers or liberties that are enforceable against children and the state continue to receive support from the courts. An 1895 case, *Re Hatfield*, held that denial of a father's entitlement to custody of his child required the gravest objection to his habits and character. Earlier, it was held in the custody case of *Farrell v. Wilton* (1893) that the father had the right to take back his child at any time. Later, in *Re Mackay* (1923), the court held that the natural parents had a *prima facie* right to custody and that parental deprivation of that right required definite and clear reason why continued parental custody would be contrary to the child's welfare. A similar holding was rendered in *Re Thompson* (1935). The parental right to discipline the child, even with the use of stern physical punishment, was confirmed by the court in *In re O* (1978), where it was found that parental conduct fell within reasonable limits.

PARENTAL RIGHTS: PRESENT CHALLENGES

In Canada, the family as a basic societal unit has been left to function with minimum interference. The right of parents to full custody of their children has been a deeply ingrained value. Child protection laws have allowed removal of children from their homes only as a last resort. Government intrusion is presumed justifiable on the basis of significant parental fault alone. As the Canadian Council on Children and Youth (CCCY, 1979) put it, "child welfare legislation in Canada expresses a standard of negative behaviour" (p. 61–62). Parents are penalized only when their negative behaviour can be proven—that is, in cases of physical harm to the young.

The Supreme Court of Canada established the primacy of parental rights in its rulings on *Re Duffell* (1950) and on *Hepton v. Maat* (1957). In the latter, Mr. Justice Rand stated

> Prima facie the natural parents are entitled to custody unless by reason of some act, condition or circumstances affecting them it is evident that the welfare of the child requires that fundamental relation be severed.
>   . . . the welfare of the child can never be determined as an isolated fact, that is, as if the child were free from natural parental bonds entailing moral responsibility. . . .
>   The view of the child's welfare conceived it to lie, first, within the warmth and security of the home provided by his parents. (p. 607)

Clearly, from the perspective of the highest court in the land, there is a presumption in favour of parental rights. Lower court decisions would have been expected to reflect such a presumption.

The Ontario Court of Appeal, however, chose to depart from the Supreme Court's precedent when it handed down *Re Moores and Feldstein* in 1973. Speaking for the court, Justice Dubin questioned the appropriateness of assuming that blood relationship would bring about benefit to a child. Insisting that this was a question that must be ascertained in every case, he concluded as follows:

> It is the duty of the court to view all the circumstances relevant to what is in the interest of the child, including a consideration as to whether the evidence disclosed that the child would benefit from the tie of a child to its mother. (p. 287)

Five years later, the court in *Children's Aid Society of Ottawa v. G.M.* (1978) balanced the claims of parental right with the best interests of the child by avoiding the presumption in favour of the parent and instead by considering whether, in fact, the parents' situation justified returning the child to them. Nonetheless, parental rights remain alive in different Canadian jurisdictions. Thus the BC Court of Appeal, in delivering to the father his child placed on adoption by the mother, declared that denial of custody by the father was to ignore wrongly the blood ties between the parent and his child (*M. (C.G.) v. W. (C)*, 1989). Clearly, this is a parental rights case that acknowledges the doctrine that a natural parent has a *prima facie* right to custody, subject only to proof of abandonment, misconduct, or detriment of the child.

Still, the principle of the best interests of the child has gained adherence not only in the courts but also in legislatures. The idea that the first and paramount consideration to be employed in decisions affecting the child should be the good or well-being of the child, rather than the wishes or interests of the parent, has found its way into the legislation of various provinces. Thus, as Bala (1991, pp. 7–10) and Barnhorst and Walter (1991) note, child protection agencies under such legislation are given extensive powers to search for children who may need protection and to force parents to surrender custody when necessary. To ensure the best interests of the child, such agencies are charged with providing for child protection or family services and child care. In so doing, they are involved with the court system, have access to adequate legal services, and work in conjunction with other agencies and professionals in the field. Moreover, as Cruickshank (1991) observes, the child's well-being is provided for by child protection workers and supervisors authorized to make place-ment and access decisions, when a decision is reached to terminate parental custody.

While developments related to child protection and care have generally been greeted positively, advocates of parental rights have viewed them with great concern. An issue frequently raised is that the flagrant and unjustified state intrusion into family life has undermined not only parents' attempts to preserve family autonomy, but also their efforts to discharge their responsibilities toward their children in ways consistent with parental prerogatives. Undoubtedly, the conflict of rights claims between parents, the state, and children has escalated into a disturbing reality. Such escalation is likely to increase now that the Canadian Charter of Rights and Freedoms is in full operation. As a result, a closer examination of the dimensions of the conflict is imperative.

PARENTAL RIGHTS VERSUS CHILDREN'S RIGHTS

The incidence of various forms of child abuse and child neglect, combined with changing perspectives on the nature of children and society, has elicited claims that the parental rights doctrine is now an anachronism that should be discarded. Although a conservative tide is trying to restore parental responsibility, protection of the child often justifies sep-aration of children from their parent when they live with him or her in an unfit or improper place, when they are neglected, or when the parent endangers their emotional and mental development. What makes for an "unfit" or "improper" place, "negligence," or for "endangered emotional and mental development" is left to be determined by agencies of the government. And when cases reach the courts of law, such notions provide occasions for judges to rule in favour of children, based on their subjective and valuative understand-ing of these notions and of the principle of the best interests of the child (Barnhorst and Walter, 1991; Fraser and Kirk, 1984; Levy, 1976). Similar provisions for legal represen-tation are included in the statutes of Alberta, Manitoba, Ontario, Quebec, and New Bruns-wick (Himel, 1991, pp. 196–207).

The decline in parental rights has occurred not only under the banner of "the interests of the child" principle. Attacks against parental rights have sprung from more radical advocates of children's rights. Some Canadian thinkers (for example, McMurtry, 1979–80) have argued the case for the elimination of legal and personal restrictions against children, echoing similar demands for children's liberation in the United States. There, Holt (1974) has proposed that "the rights, privileges, duties and responsibilities of adult citizens be made available to any young person, of whatever age, who wants to make use of them" (p. 1). Holt would give children extensive rights: to vote, travel, live away from home, choose one's own home or guardian, and receive from the state whatever minimum income it may guarantee adult citizens—to do, in general, what any adult may legally do. To this list may be added Farson's (1974) suggestions: the right to sexual freedom, to information, to self-education, to freedom from physical punishment, and to economic power.

In Canada, gradual change has occurred in the area of legal representation for children in cases before the courts. In 1978, British Columbia passed the Family Relations Act, which provided for the appointment of a family advocate who, in cases reaching the courts, may intervene at any stage of any proceeding (for example, adoption, guardianship, custody, and determination of offence) and act as counsel to represent the welfare and interests of the child.

Children's rights are now partly determined relative to the Canadian Charter of Rights and Freedoms (1982). Since its equality rights provision (section 15) guarantees equal enjoyment of rights without discrimination based on age,[2] young people could argue that they are equally entitled to the other guaranteed rights and freedoms in the Charter. For example, they could claim the liberty to make certain vital personal decisions in their lives based on section 7.[3] Thus in Re R.A.M. (1983), a 13-year-old child was declared to be within the ambit of section 7 of the Charter; his right to be present at a wardship hearing and to be represented by legal counsel was confirmed. Also, a pregnant adolescent's right to a therapeutic abortion suggests itself as a possible test case. At present, legislation and hospital practice require the consent of a parent or guardian before any girl under a certain age (varying with the province) can have an abortion. A pregnant adolescent might, under the Charter, claim that hospitals should not require parental consent. Conversely, she may be legally able to resist her parents' command that she undergo an abortion, if she wants to have her baby. At present, a number of provinces allow only children who are 16 years of age or older to give a valid consent for diagnostic and surgical procedures that take place in a public hospital (Landau, 1979). Under the Charter, which makes no age quali-fication, a 14- to 15-year-old child may be able to override the common law and statutory right and responsibility of parents to determine his or her health care. Should a public agency provide contraceptive pills to adolescent girls, at their own request or in conjunction with some government-funded programs, despite parental objection to the dispensation of the pills?

Generally, children lack the cognitive and emotional capacities, at certain ages and under certain circumstances, to make important decisions. However, many children are quite capable of making their own reasonable and mature decisions. Under what circum-stances and to what extent the Charter entitles the young to the rights fully enjoyed by adults are questions that the Canadian Supreme Court will eventually have to decide upon. Interestingly, the lower courts in the country have started to recognize children's rights under the Charter. In Re L.D.K. (1985), the Ontario provincial court had to deal with a leukemia-stricken 12-year-old Jehovah's Witness who refused chemotherapy and blood transfusion. In its ruling, the court declared that her rights under section 15(l) of the Charter had been violated. By giving her a blood transfusion without her consent, the hospital had, in the court's opinion, discriminated against her on the basis of age and religion. Further, "upon being given a blood transfusion, her right to the security of her person pursuant to section 7 was infringed" (p.171). In *Re J. and C.* (1985), the court was asked by a Toronto Children's Aid Society to terminate the natural parent's access to her child under adoption by a foster parent. In refusing the request, the court stated that children are entitled to associate with family members (as guaranteed in section 2d) and that any legislation that restricts their right to see their birth parents profoundly violates section 7 (pp. 385–89). In these two cases, parents and children ranged themselves against the state. It may not be very long before the rights of children as they relate to parents under the Charter are litigated extensively in the courts.

In any case, the independent rights claims of children against their parents—and against the state, for that matter—have received strong impetus not only nationally (Task Force on the Child as a Citizen, 1978) but also internationally. The first international instrument recognizing that children are entitled to special care and attention, the Declaration of Geneva, drafted in 1924, was supplemented by the ten-principle 1959 document, the *Declaration of the Rights of the Child* (Cohen, 1989). The latter, in turn, has been reinforced by the *Convention on the Rights of the Child* (United Nations, 1989). This document, as Cohen notes (p. 1448), is a unique human rights document in that it not only protects children's civil and political rights but also extends protection to their economic, social and cultural, and humanitarian rights. Thus Articles 13, 14, 15, and 16 of the Convention declare rights to freedom of expression; freedom of thought, conscience, and religion; freedom of association and assembly; and freedom of privacy respectively. The Convention also mandates that States Parties (states agreeing to the convention) ensure the discharge of parental responsibility (Article 18); protect children against all forms of physical or mental violence, injury or abuse, neglect or negligent treatment, and maltreatment or exploitation (Article 19); provide for the highest standard of health care (Article 24) and for the child's social security (Article 26); and the like. These and other provisions will have at least persuasive influence on Canada and its provinces when the Convention goes into force after the twentieth instrument of ratification is deposited with the Secretary-General of the United Nations (Cohen, 1989).

Nonetheless, the document exhibits the ambiguity shown by different Canadian institutions having to do with children. In Article 2, it enjoins States Parties to ensure the child's protection against *all* forms of discrimination or punishment on the basis of the expressed opinion or beliefs of the child's parents; Article 3 mandates the use of the principle of the best interests of the child in all actions affecting him/her. Yet it also takes into account the rights of parents (Article 3), and requires States Parties to respect the rights and duties of the parents in providing for the direction of the child in the exercise of his/her rights in a manner consistent with his/her evolving capacities (Article 14). Still, the Convention will exercise salutary effects in terms of governmental re-examination of laws and regulations affecting children. To date, for example, provincial and territorial reporting laws do not unambiguously impose on educators an obligation to report to appropriate authorities *all* incidents of abuse, actual or suspected, inflicted on students under their authority (Foster, 1990). The Convention could plug loopholes in the law and governmental policies.

PARENTAL RIGHTS VERSUS STATE POWER

The awesome presence of the state in almost every area of activity in society has been justified in terms of two distinguishable, though frequently confused and misunderstood, doctrines known as police power and *parens patriae*. The former is the state's power "both to prevent its citizens from harming one another and to promote all aspects of public welfare" such as public health, safety, moral and general welfare, and aesthetic and family values. *Parens patriae* authority, on the other hand, is the state's "limited power to protect or promote the welfare of certain individuals like young children and mental incompetents who lack the capacity to act in their own best interests" (*Harvard Law Review*, 1980, pp. 1198–99). Both doctrines have been utilized extensively in Canada.

Parens Patriae Authority

The state exercises its *parens patriae* authority in two different, although closely inter-twined, ways. The first is by way of legislation or laws that protect and promote the well-being of the weak. As already noted, provinces in Canada have passed numerous family-related laws for this purpose (Canadian Council on Children and Youth, 1979). The authority of the provincial government to pass such laws is based on a constitutional allocation of jurisdiction found in the British North America Act, 1867 (now the Consti-tution Act, 1867), which remains part of the new Canadian Constitution. The language of the relevant sections in the Act is susceptible to misinterpretation, insofar as section 91 gives the federal government power over "marriage and divorce" and section 92 gives provincial legislatures power over "Solemnization of Marriage." But any doubt as to the pre-eminence of provincial jurisdiction over the family disappeared in 1938, when the Supreme Court determined that a number of Ontario's statutes on adoption, children's protection, deserted wives, children's maintenance, and children of unmarried parents were matters for provincial determination (Bushnell, 1984, pp. 203–10). In any case, most pro-vincial power is derived from the provincial jurisdiction over "Property and Civil Rights" (sections 92, 13), which confers broad powers on the province over matrimonial property, succession, child and espousal support, legitimacy, affiliation, adoption, custody, and guardianship. Thus, while it is true that the federal government, particularly through the Criminal Code, circumscribes the authority of parents in the treatment of their young, the more wide-ranging measures that effectively curtail parental rights have been provincial initiatives. Provincially legislated child welfare departments and children's aid societies have been empowered, in the child's best interests, to act against parents.

The second closely linked way *parens patriae* authority is exercised is through judicial action. Child welfare or protection laws provide for courts to adjudicate cases needing enforcement or interpretation of statutory provisions. *Parens patriae* authority resides in the courts of law as they decide upon the state's power to act on behalf of the helpless young. As such, *parens patriae* is almost automatically associated with the principle of the best interests of the child.

While the court's reliance on the principle of the best interest of the child has been a serious reason for concern, two other problems have been noted in relation to the court's exercise of *parens patriae* authority. One pertains to the resolution of cases where a *parens patriae* statute is silent on a relevant, contentious issue. May a court supply a missing provision in the statute? This was faced by the Supreme Court in *Beson v. Director of Child Welfare* (1982). In this case, the Besons adopted a child who had been a ward of the Director. Before the expiry of a six-month probationary period, the Besons were required by the Director to return the child, due to alleged child abuse. In the court, they sought to recover the child who, in the meantime, had been adopted by another family. In this unusual situation where there were, in effect, two pairs of adoptive parents, it was found that the provincial statute contained no provision for appealing the decision of the Director to remove a child from adopting parents prior to the expiry of the probationary period. It was not clear from the statute whether the intent of the legislation was to make the Director's decision final. Speaking for the Court, Justice Wilson concluded that *parens patriae* does allow the court to fill gaps in legislation.

The other, more serious, issue is likely to arouse arguments for years to come. May the court, in exercising its *parens patriae* authority, deliberately override explicit and clear statutory provisions? This issue is illustrated in *Children's Aid Society of Winnipeg v. M.* (1979), where a parent was seeking access to his child, who had been placed under permanent order of guardianship. Although the Manitoba Child Welfare Act allows for access in most cases, it expressly forbids access to children under permanent order of guardianship. Did the Court of Appeal, which ruled in this case, exercise *parens patriae* in overriding the no-access clause in the Act, or did it in fact exercise another doctrine, namely, the power of judicial review?

The power of judicial review will come under intense scrutiny in the future. The open-ended language and the often contradictory provisions of the Canadian Charter of Rights and Freedoms will require judicial interpretation. Because the Charter applies to both federal and provincial governments and their respective agencies, and because it invites (in section 24) all citizens to seek remedies in the courts for rights that are infringed upon or violated, the courts may be expected to spend much more time than before in reviewing the statutory or legislative basis of governmental policies and actions (Hogg, 1983, pp. 69–100; Russell, 1983, 30–54; see Hovius, 1982, pp. 31–58, for a different viewpoint).

State Police Power

Along with its *parens patriae* authority, the state has police power to pass laws intended to prevent harm to society and to promote peace, order, and societal well-being. In pursuit of this power, provincial governments have enacted legislation establishing educational systems and empowering officials to exercise such powers and privileges as are necessary to develop young people into competent citizens.

State supremacy in education is a comparatively recent phenomenon in Canada (Phillips, 1957; Rowe, 1964; Sissons, 1959). Predating this supremacy was the common-law idea that educational authority is derived from parental mandate for schools to fulfil parental desires and expectations. Known as the doctrine of *loco parentis*, this was the controlling principle in many educational cases resolved by the courts in the past. However, this doctrine grew under circumstances in which teaching was conducted on a tutorial basis or in small schools established through parental initiatives. Today, when schools operate as part of enormous systems under a legislative delegation of authority, the *loco parentis* doctrine seems to have waned.

It has been determined in New Brunswick (*Lapointe and Lapointe v. Board of Trustees*, 1979) and in Nova Scotia (*MacDonald v. Municipal School Board*, 1979) that parents have no right to have their child attend a particular school within a school district; it is a matter for the school board to determine. Also, parental choice of schools is restricted in districts where public and separate school systems exist. In Alberta, a father decided to send his children to a public school, although his school tax went to the Catholic system. When the school board charged him for his children's tuition because of their non-resident status (non-payer of public school tax) in the district, the father sued for discrimination on the basis of religion under the province's Individual Rights Protection Act. He lost his suit

(*Schmidt v. Calgary Board of Education*, 1976). In a similar case in Saskatchewan, a Catholic parent was not allowed to send his child to a public school because a separate school was available in the district. The father's use of the province's Bill of Rights Act to advance his case also failed (*Bintner v. Regina Public School Board*, 1966).

Still, parental rights in education have been legally protected in certain areas. Parents who have opted for home instruction have received court support in cases where educational authorities have failed to show that such instruction is not commensurate with what is offered in school. Thus in *Lambton County Board of Education v. Beauchamp* (1979), the court exonerated a mother who instructed her 10-year-old son at home using correspondence materials from the Christian Liberty Academy in the United States. An earlier celebrated case had established the right of parents to provide their children with the education of their choice in Alberta's *R. v. Wiebe* (1978). In this case, a number of Mennonite parents led by Mr. Wiebe spent two years seeking the school superintendent's permission to establish their own religious schools. Exasperated, the Mennonites went ahead and withdrew their children from the public school system. The superintendent charged Mr. Wiebe and 44 others with violation of the Schools Act provisions relating to school attendance. In support of the Mennonites, the court noted that the Schools Act, under which anyone, including this group, was required to obtain permission to establish a school, imposed penalties without first permitting recourse to the courts of law. Referring to the Mennonites' deeply held religious convictions, the court declared that the Schools Act denied the freedom of religion guaranteed under the Alberta Bill of Rights. However, *Wiebe* must be understood in light of a recent Supreme Court ruling in *Jones v. R.* (1986). Pastor Jones refused to comply with compulsory education regulations in Alberta and, without seeking a permit, opened his school not only for his own children, but also others in his denomination. His argument in the court that the Alberta regulation infringed his freedom of religion and liberty rights in the Canadian Charter was rejected by the court, which held that he was free to pursue his freedom of religion by opening his school subject to legitimate government regulation. Requirement of a permit, it insisted, was a minor infringement justified by the substantial government interest in the education of all children. It appears, therefore, that parental rights in education must conform to certain reasonable state regulations.

The issue of exemption from a school subject arose in *Chabot v. Les Commissaires d'Écoles de la Morandière* (1957). Chabot was a Jehovah's Witness whose children, required to attend religious instruction in a Catholic school in Quebec, were expelled for refusal to do so. In accepting his request to have his children readmitted to school, the court held that the regulation imposing religious education on all children regardless of parents' wishes was invalid, because it violated the right to religious freedom. In recognition of this vital point, Newfoundland's Schools Act allows exemption from religious instruction upon receipt of written requests from parents. However, whether this will be legally upheld upon challenge is not certain, in light of recent cases in British Columbia (*Russow and Lambert v. Attorney-General of BC*, 1989) and in Ontario (*Re Corporation of the Canadian Civil Liberties Association et al. v. Minister of Education et al.*, 1990; *Zylberberg et al. v. Sudbury Board of Education*, 1986). These cases have ruled against the provinces by striking down Christian religious curricula and school prayer, which may not be imposed on children of non-Christian parents. Equally problematic are cases in which parents object to non-religious courses. What if parents, as in *Valent v. New Jersey State Board of Education* (1970), request that children be exempted from non-religious subjects such as family life? Should parental wishes be granted if, on religious grounds, a request is made for exemption of children from a biology class that teaches the theory of evolution? Should parental wishes be regarded as decisive when, upon finding certain teaching materials morally offensive or contrary to their religious beliefs, parents demand the removal of such material from the school curriculum?

The prospects for even more litigation over parental objections to "bad" influence in the schools appear great. Parents may argue that Canadian courts have a duty to prevent schools from violating the parental right to have their children provided with an education consistent with the parents' beliefs and values. Already, in British Columbia, a parent has gone to court against a school board prohibiting her from using a school library during school hours to monitor the books made available to students (*Serup v. School District No. 57 Board of Trustees and R.*, 1987).

CONCLUSIONS

The issues surrounding the rights of children and parents are complex and often resist quick resolution. Empirical findings drawn from historical, sociological, and psychological studies of the family, within which parental and children's rights are embedded and exercised, have introduced complicating — although undoubtedly useful — considerations. Recent accounts indicating tremendous problems facing the Canadian family today are, indeed, particularly disturbing (Conway, 1990). The character of the family has considerably changed. From 1981 to 1991, common-law unions increased 103.6 percent; single-parent families, 33.7 percent; childless families, 28.2 percent; while the so-called nuclear family, only 6.2 percent. Divorces escalated to 50 percent of all marriages in 1987, though they have decreased since then to 41.6 percent in 1990 (Statistics Canada, 1992). In 1991, 13 percent of all families were led by a lone parent, usually a woman, and female lone-parent families had the lowest average income in 1990 (Statistics Canada, 1993). Women (and a much smaller number of men) and children remain subject to economic, emotional, and physical abuse (Conway, 1990). Reports show that around one million women in Canada are battered each year and that children (one in two females; one in three males) are victims of unwanted sexual acts, mostly (98 percent) by male assailants, 20 percent of whom are family members (Mandell and Duffy, 1988, p. 123; also, Badgley, 1984). Partly because of these distressing accounts, there is a compelling case for a rethinking of rights and responsibilities within and of the families in Canada today.

Parental rights within the family have traditionally been paramount. Parents were assumed to be the most rational, responsible family members, and the parental right to determine family arrangements assumed a fundamental character. Overriding parental decisions or terminating parental rights required the strongest of justification. But intervention by the state has, as we have seen, become more widespread. Quite clearly, if children are to grow as people, they have to be rescued from gross failures in parental care, such as abandonment, negligence, sexual and other assaults, and parental refusal to authorize life-saving medical care. Thus state intervention in a number of cases is justifiable.

Recent recognition of and provision for the rights of the young certainly complicate the issue of rights within the family. Children's rights are separate from, and frequently clash with, parents' rights. The clash occurs in education. Here, as in other areas, the criterion is whether the growth of individuals is made extremely unlikely or impossible by parental choices. Parental refusal to provide education promoting personhood of the young is thus a ground for intervention. Arguably, however, insofar as Mennonite or Amish parents provide their children with functional literacy and other basic skills they will need to make independent decisions during adulthood, the presumption in favour of parental autonomy prevails. Needless to say, this issue will continue to be contentious (Crittenden, 1982; *Journal of Philosophy of Education,* 1984; Schrag, 1982).

Whatever contentiousness remains, the urgent task is to ensure that families of any configuration are able to function and to establish an atmosphere for mutual caring and individual growth. Such a task, as Dizard and Gadlin (1990) conclude, requires that public institutions reflect the values of the family and actively encourage its viability. There is also a need for families to acknowledge the necessity of their linking with such institutions to receive vital institutional support. In Dizard and Gadlin's words,

> If the public realm can be made to reflect the values of familism, families may well find themselves more able to meet the emotional needs of their members.
>
> If we can acknowledge our manifold dependencies, if we can see those dependencies as the links between our private lives and the larger social patterns our private lives constitute, we might then be able to forge a society in which autonomous individuals are capable of consciously shaping their own families and, in so doing, constitute a world in which "caring, sharing, and loving" are broadly incorporated into both our public and private lives. (p. 224)

A final point needs to be stressed. No implication is made here that the traditional nuclear family is superior to any other family form or type, or that every mature member of society has a duty to establish a family. Neither is it implied that, as a desirable institution, the family should serve as the focus around which all governmental policies should be built. What is highlighted in this chapter is that the family as a societal unit has an intrinsic value of its own and deserves support and autonomy under parental leadership. Those who decide to form or preserve a family should be given every assistance in their endeavour to make family life work. In the long run, unless a viable alternative to the family is invented, and unless the human hankering for stable and intimate relationships is quieted, a governmental policy geared toward strengthening the institution of the family and promoting its quality may prove to be the best way of ensuring the rights of every family member.

DISCUSSION QUESTIONS

❑ Compare the three theories of the family discussed in the article. Which theory better serves as a basis for determining the appropriate relationships between and entitlements of family members?

❑ In what ways have parental rights changed in Canada from the 1800s until the present? Are the changes desirable? Why?

❑ Discuss the protection afforded children by the Canadian Charter of Rights and Freedoms and by the Convention on the Rights of the Child. To what extent should children's rights prevail against the parental right to determine the upbringing of children? Justify your viewpoint.

❏ Elaborate on the two doctrines used by government to justify its curtailment of the rights of parents over their children. Is the increasing parental resistance against government's use of its authority based on these doctrines justified? Argue your position.

❏ Identify some potential situations demonstrating conflict of rights between parents and children, parents and government, and government and children. How should each of these situations be resolved?

NOTES

1. The civil law system establishes an accepted set of principles enumerated in the civil code, and courts make decisions on individual cases in accordance with these principles. In the common-law system, court judgements on previous cases are scrutinized to extract general principles that are then applied to subsequent cases. Thus judges are bound to follow judgements in precedent cases decided upon by higher courts. In civil law, the codified principles, not the precedents, establish the guidelines for court decisions (Gall, 1977, pp. 39–40).

2. "Section 15. (1) Every individual is equal before and under the law and has the right to the equal protection and equal benefit of the law without discrimination and, in particular, without discrimination based on race, national or ethnic origin, colour, religion, sex, age or mental or physical disability."

3. "Section 7. Everyone has the right to life, liberty and security of the person and the right not to be deprived thereof except in accordance with the principles of fundamental justice."

REFERENCES

Anderson, M. (1980). *Approaches to the history of the western family 1500–1914.* London: Macmillan.

Aries, P. (1962). *Centuries of childhood.* New York: Random House.

Armitage, A. (1977). The Canadian scene: Family policy in Canada. In Canadian Council on Social Development, *Proceedings of the conference on family policy.* Ottawa: Canadian Council on Social Development.

Armitage, A. (1993). The policy and legislative context. In B. Wharf (Ed.). *Rethinking child welfare in Canada.* Toronto: McClelland and Stewart.

Badgley, R. (1984). *Sexual offenses against children.* Vol. 1. Ottawa: Minister of Supply and Services.

Bala, N. (1991). An introduction to child protection problems. In N. Bala, J. Hornick, & R. Vogl (Eds.). *Canadian child welfare law.* Toronto: Thompson Educational Publishing.

Barnhorst, D., & Walter, B. (1991). Child protection legislation in Canada. In N. Bala, J. Hornick, & R. Vogl (Eds.). *Canadian child welfare law.* Toronto: Thompson Educational Publishing.

Bates, F. (1978). Does the family have legal functions? *Canadian Journal of Family Law, 1,* 455–76.

Beson v. Director of Child Welfare for Newfoundland (1982), 30 R.F.L. (2) 438.

Bintner v. Regina Public School Board District No. 4 (1966), 55 D.L.R. (2) 646.

Blustein, J.U. (1979). Child-rearing and family interests. In O. O'Neill & W. Ruddick (Eds.). *Having children.* Oxford: Oxford University Press.

Bushnell, I. (1984). The welfare of children and the jurisdiction of the Court under *parens patriae.* In K. Connell-Touez & B. Knoppers, *Contemporary trends in family law: A national perspective.* Toronto: Carswell.

Canadian Charter of Rights and Freedoms. (1982). *A guide for Canadians.* Ottawa: Minister of Supply and Services.

Canadian Council on Children and Youth. (1979). *Legislations related to the needs of children.* Toronto: Carswell.

Chabot v. Les Commissaires d'Écoles de la Morandière. (1957). BR 707.

Children's Aid Society of Ottawa v. G.M. (1978), 3 R.F.L. (2) 226.

Children's Aid Society of Winnipeg v. M. (1979), 15 R.F.L. (2) 185.

Civil Code of Quebec. (1980). L.Q. c. 39.

Cohen, C.P. (1989). United Nations: Convention on the rights of the child. *International Legal Materials, 28*(6), 1448–54.

Conway, J. F. (1990). *The Canadian family in crisis.* Toronto: J. Lorimer.

Crittenden, B. (1982). The scope of parents' rights in education. In D. Kerr (Ed.). *Proceedings of the 38th Annual Meeting of the Philosophy of Education Society,* pp. 324–33.

Cruickshank, D. (1991). The child in care. In N. Bala, J. Hornick, & R. Vogl (Eds.). *Canadian child welfare law.* Toronto: Thompson Educational Publishing.

Dickens, B. (1981). The modern function and limits of parental rights. *The Law Quarterly Review, 97,* 462–85.

Dizard, J., & Gadlin, H. (1990). *The minimal family.* Amherst, MA: University of Massachusetts Press.

Eekelaar, J. (1973). What are parental rights? *The Law Quarterly Review, 89,* 210–34.

Farrell v. Wilton (1893), 3 Terr. L.R. 232.

Farson, R. (1974). *Birthrights.* Harmondsworth, England: Penguin.

Flandrin, J. (1979). *Families in former times.* Trans. R. Southern. Cambridge: Cambridge University Press.

Foster, W.F. (1990). *Child abuse in schools: Legal obligation of school teachers, administrators, and boards.* Paper presented at the Inaugural Conference of the Canadian Association for the Practical Study of Law in Education, April 29–May 2, 1990, Vancouver, BC.

Fraser, F., & Kirk, H. (1984). Cui bono? Some questions concerning the "best interests of the child" principle in Canadian adoption laws and practices. In K. Connell-Thouez & B. Knoppers (Eds.). *Contemporary trends in family law: A national perspective.* Toronto: Carswell.

Gall, G. (1977). *The Canadian legal system.* Toronto: Carswell.

Godfrey, G. (1976). Report of the committee on parental rights and duties custody suits. In F. Bates (Ed.). *The child and the law.* Dobbs Ferry, NY: Oceana Publications.

Goldstein, J., Freud, A., & Solnit, A. (1979). *Before the best interests of the child.* New York: The Free Press.

Hall, J. (1972). The warning of parental rights. *Cambridge Law Journal, 31,* 248–65.

Harvard Law Review. (1980). *93*(6), 1157–1383.

Hepton v. Maat. (1957). S.C.R. 606.

Himel, S. (1991). The lawyer's role: Representing children. In N. Bala, J. Hornick, & R. Vogl (Eds.). *Canadian child welfare law.* Toronto: Thompson Educational Publishing.

Hogg, P. (1983). The supremacy of the Canadian Charter of Rights and Freedoms. *The Canadian Bar Review, 60*(1), 69–80.

Holt, J. (1974). *Escape from childhood.* New York: Ballantine Books.

Hovius, B. (1982). The legacy of the Supreme Court's approach to the Canadian bill of rights: Prospects for the Charter. *McGill Law Journal, 28,* 31–58.

In re O. (1978). 3 W.W.R. 1.

Jones v. R. (1986). 2 S.C.R. 284.

Journal of Philosophy of Education (1984), *18* (1), 55–84.

Kain, E. (1990). *The myth of family decline.* Lexington, KY: Lexington Books.

Lambton County Board of Education v. Beauchamp. (1979), 10 R.F.L. (2d) 354.

Landau, B. (1979). Barriers to consent to treatment: The rights of minors in the provision of mental health services. *Canadian Journal of Family Law, 2*(3), 245–66.

Lapointe and Lapointe v. Board of School Trustees. (1979), 25 N.B.R. 91.

Levy, R. (1976). The rights of parents. *Brigham Young University Law Review,* 693–707.

M. (C.G.) v. W.(C). (1989). 23 R.F.L. (3d) 1.

MacDonald v. Municipal School Board of the County of Halifax (1979), 30 N.S.R. (2d) 443.

McKnight, J. (1976). Minority and parental rights in the united family. In F. Bates (Ed.). *The child and the law.* Dobbs Ferry, NY: Oceana Publications.

McMurtry, J. (1979–80). The case for children's liberation. *Interchange, 10*(3), 10–28.

Mandell, N., & Duffy, A. (1988). *Reconstructing the Canadian Family: Feminist perspectives.* Toronto: Butterworths.

Melden, I.A. (1977). *Rights and persons.* Berkeley: The University of California Press.

Mohr, J. (1984). The future of the family, the law and the state. *Canadian Journal of Family Law, 4*(3), 261–73.

Ozment, S. (1983). *When fathers ruled.* Cambridge: Harvard University Press.

Parr, J. (1982). Introduction. In J. Parr (Ed.). *Childhood and family.* Toronto: McClelland and Stewart.

Phillips, C. (1957). *The development of education in Canada.* Toronto: Gage.

Pollock, L. (1983). *Forgotten children.* Cambridge: Harvard University Press.

Re Corporation of the Canadian Civil Liberties Association et al. v. The Minister of Education and the Elgin County Board of Education. (1990), 71 (2d) 341 (C.A.).

Re Duffell. (1950). S.C.R. 737 .

Re Eve. (1980). 27 Nfld. and P.E.I.R. 97.

Re Hatfield. (1895). N.B. Eq. 142.

Re J. and C. (1985). 48 R.F.L. (2d) 371.

Re L.D.K. (1985). 48 R.F.L., (2d) 164.

Re Mackay. (1923). 3 W.W.R. 369.

Re Moores and Feldstein. (1973). 12 R.F.L. 273.

Re R.A.M., Children's Aid Society of Winnipeg v. A.M. and L.C. (1983), 37 R.F.L. (2d) 112.

Re Thompson. (1935). 10 M.P.R. 36.

Regina v. Wiebe. (1978). 3 W.W.R. 36.

Rowe, F. (1964). *The development of education in Newfoundland.* Toronto: The Ryerson Press.

Russell, P. (1983). The political purposes of the Canadian Charter of Rights and Freedoms. *The Canadian Bar Review, 61*(1), 30–54.

Russow and Lambert v. Attorney-General of BC (1989, 22 November). Unreported.

Schmidt v. Calgary Board of Education. (1976), 6 W.W.R. 717.

Schrag, F. (1982). Reply to Crittenden. In D. Kerr (Ed.). *Proceedings of the 38th Annual Meeting of the Philosophy of Education Society*, 334–36.

Serup v. School District No. 57 (1957), 14 B.C.L.R. (2d) 393.

Shorter, E. (1975). *The making of the modern family.* New York: Basic Books.

Sissons, C. (1959). *Church and state in Canadian education.* Toronto: The Ryerson Press.

Statistics Canada. (1992). *Report on the demographic situation in Canada 1992.* Ottawa: Ministry of Industry, Science and Technology.

Statistics Canada. (1993). *Families: Social and economic characteristics.* Ottawa: Ministry of Industry, Science and Technology.

Stone, L. (1977). *The family, sex and marriage in England, 1500–1800.* New York: Harper and Row.

Sutherland, N. (1976). *Children in English-Canadian society: Framing the twentieth-century consensus.* Toronto: University of Toronto Press.

Task Force on the Child as a Citizen. (1978). *Admittance restricted: The child as citizen in Canada.* Ottawa: Canadian Council on Children and Youth.

United Nations. (1989). *Convention on the Rights of the Child.* 28 I.L.M. 1448.

Valent v. New Jersey State Board of Education. (1970), 274 A. 2d 832

Wharf, B. (1993). Rethinking child welfare. In B. Wharf (Ed.). *Rethinking child welfare in Canada.* Toronto: McClelland and Stewart.

White, W. (1980). A comparison of some parental and guardian rights. *Canadian Journal of Family Law, 3*(2–3), 219–49.

Wilson, J. (1978). *Children and the law.* Toronto: Butterworths.

Wilson, J. (1980). *Up against it: Children and the law in Canada.* Toronto: Anansi Press.

Young Offenders Act. (1982). 29-30-31 Elizabeth II, chap. 110.

Zylberberg and Director of Education of Sudbury Board of Education; League for Human Rights of B'Nai Brith of Canada, v. Sudbury Board of Education (1986), 55 O.R. (2d) 749 (H.C.).

FURTHER READINGS

Aries, P. (1962). *Centuries of childhood.* New York: Random House.

Blustein, J.U. (1982). *Parents and children.* Oxford: Oxford University Press.

Cohen, H. (1980). *Equal rights for children.* Totowa, NJ: Rowman & Littlefield.

Connell-Thouez, K., & Knoppers, B.M. (1984). *Contemporary trends in family law: A national perspective.* Toronto: Carswell.

Dizard, J., & Gadlin, H. (1990). *The minimal family.* Amherst, MA: University of Massachusetts Press.

Eichler, M. (1988). *Families in Canada today: Recent changes and policy consequences.* Toronto: Gage.

Gies, F., & Gies, J. (1987). *Marriage and the family in the medieval ages.* New York: Harper & Row.

Goldstein, J., Freud, A., & Solnit, A. (1979). *Before the best interests of the child.* New York: The Free Press.

Holt, J. (1974). *Escape from childhood.* New York: Ballantine Books.

O'Neill, O., & Ruddick, W. (Eds.). (1979). *Having children.* New York: Oxford University Press.

Ozment, S. (1983). *When fathers ruled.* Cambridge: Harvard University Press.

Parr, J. (Ed.). (1982). *Childhood and family.* Toronto: McClelland and Stewart.

Sutherland, N. (1976). *Children in English-Canadian society: Framing the twentieth-century consensus.* Toronto: University of Toronto Press.

21

ARE THE EDUCATIONAL RIGHTS OF EXCEPTIONAL STUDENTS PROTECTED IN CANADA?

Léonard Goguen and Donald Poirier

In order to study the status of the educational rights of exceptional students in Canada, this chapter will examine the legal protection provided by provincial and territorial educational legislation, and by decisions generated by court actions. The influence and the ongoing impact of the Canadian Charter of Rights and Freedoms will also be discussed. However, before we focus specifically on the educational rights of those students described as having special needs, it is important to clarify the nature of such needs. The transition from *needs* to *rights* can then be more fully understood.

EXCEPTIONAL STUDENTS: STUDENTS WITH SPECIAL NEEDS

Statements about children's needs, or absence of needs, can take many forms: single parents could say that their children do not need two parents; parents of handicapped children could say that their children do not need to go to school because they have time to educate them themselves; teachers might see no need for change because slow learners appear to be enjoying their special classes. Various professions and organizations have become advocates of children's needs, including their protection, support, care, and education. The Canadian Council on Children and Youth (1978), in order to draw attention to the needs of children and to advocate on their behalf, published *Admittance restricted: The child as citizen in Canada*. This report specifies four basic needs of all children: the need for economic support, the need for health care, the need for protection, and the need for education. Since children alone cannot meet these needs, society, through the family and other institutions, is expected to meet them.

Exceptional children are often defined as students with special educational needs. Day et al. (1985) use the term "exceptional children" to refer to any atypical child, including disabled and gifted. They define the exceptional child as one

> who deviates from the average or normal child (1) in mental characteristics, (2) in sensory abilities, (3) in neuromotor or physical characteristics, (4) in social behavior,

(5) in communication abilities or (6) in multiple handicaps. Such deviation must be of such an extent that the child requires a modification of school practices, or special services, to develop to maximum capacities.

Winzer (1993) analyzed the various definitions of exceptional children and identified similar categories.

Like all children, exceptional children need education to help them achieve their full potential. Exceptional pupils' need for appropriate programs (such as individualized educational programs) matches the need of all children to have an education tailored to their abilities. However, because of their deviations or differences, exceptional children often require pecially adapted programs in order to develop fully. Guaranteeing the delivery of appropriate educational programs means that there must be access to special resources (conditions, programs, personnel, and funds) and procedures (screening, assessment, parental involvement, and appeal).

FROM A NEED TO A RIGHT

Why should we be concerned about rights? At all times, but particularly in difficult economic times, the educational needs of students must be protected so that they can all be treated equally, and so that the special needs of some students are not in danger of being neglected.

The rights of students in the school setting have been closely analyzed over the last twenty years by a variety of writers. Fisher and Schimmel (1982) analyze rights as freedoms and self-determination, with emphasis on the freedoms of speech, religion, and information. In Canada, several publications (Berkeley et al., 1978; Hurlbert & Hurlbert, 1992; Leduc & de Massy, 1981; Manley-Casimir & Sussel, 1986) have contributed to the topic of *freedom rights* in the school context. (See also chapters 19 and 20 in this volume). In this chapter, however, we will focus not on *freedom rights* but on *welfare rights*. Wringe (1981, p. 75) argues that educational rights are not freedom rights but welfare rights, deprived of which an individual can sustain serious or permanent harm.

The shift from recognition of a need to its declaration as a right has been influenced by various events in Canada. The United Nations Declarations, U.S. Public Law 94-142, as well as the actions of parents and educators, preceded the major impact of the Canadian Charter of Rights and Freedoms. The proclamations by the United Nations for the International Year of the Child in 1979 and the International Year of the Disabled in 1981 are within the framework of the welfare rights in the Canadian Charter. The United Nations included the right to education in its major declarations of welfare rights: the International Covenant on Economic, Social and Cultural Rights (1966), the International Declaration of the Rights of the Child (1959), and the Declaration of the Rights of the Mentally Retarded (1971). The United Nations Covenants, including the 1989 Convention on the Rights of the Child, although recognized as progressive and ratified by Canada, have no automatic legal effect on education in Canada for two reasons: first, international agreements and laws are not part of the internal law of Canada (Williams & de Mestral, 1979, pp. 29–31); and, second, education is a matter of exclusive provincial jurisdiction under the Constitution Act, 1867. When Canada ratifies such Conventions, it does so only after consultation with all provinces.

In the United States, appropriate education for handicapped children clearly shifted in focus from an expressed need to a recognized right with the enactment of Public Law

94-142 — the Education of All Handicapped Children Act of 1975. The essence of that federal law was to ensure a free and appropriate public education for all children with disabilities. It provided for identification activities, non-discriminatory assessments, placements in the least restrictive environment, individualized educational programs, parent consultations, appeal procedures, program reviews, and program evaluations. Before Public Law 94-142, the U.S. Supreme Court had already decided that students with mental disabilities must be given access to schools and to an education suited to their needs within the school system (*Mills v. Board of Education*, 1972; *PARC v. Commonwealth of Pennsylvania et al.*, 1972).

Over the last fifteen years, the implementation of Public Law 94-142 in the United States has generated a massive number of legislative amendments at the state level, policy developments at the state and school board levels, and research and publications on educational service delivery models to children. Canadian specialists, through various agencies and professional organizations, have been sensitized to the rights of the exceptional child expressed in the U.S. legislation. Some of the contents of revised provincial education acts have many similarities to the U.S. legislation, particularly in the provinces of Saskatchewan, Ontario, New Brunswick, and Alberta.

Canadian policy statements influenced by the U.S. Public Law 94-142 are found at various levels of government and may all have some bearing on protected rights, which exist to prevent the infringement or loss of primary rights. In addition to laws, regulations, and guidelines found at provincial levels, various other policies may exist as guidelines or instructions at district or local school levels.

In determining the extent to which policy statements other than laws and regulations may guarantee the right to education according to needs and abilities, a study of one particular case is enlightening. In *Bales v. Board of School Trustees* (1985), Aaron Bales' parents, basing their argument on mainstreaming, had requested that their 8-year-old, moderately disabled child be re-enrolled in an ordinary primary school with a predetermined individual educational program (p. 206). Justice Taylor of the Supreme Court of British Columbia considered as authoritative the provincial-level administrative policy book *Policies, procedures and guidelines for special programs—A manual of the British Columbia Ministry of Education*, known as the Red Book. Both the Red Book and the 1979 Department Circular No. 85, entitled "Towards clarification of the Ministry position on providing educational services to handicapped pupils," were taken into account in interpreting the Education Act and regulations. Justice Taylor recognized that the Red Book "adopts and strongly endorses the concept of mainstreaming as a matter of educational philosophy" and that Circular No. 85 provided "the ministry's official statement concerning mainstreaming or integration of handicapped pupils." However, he went on to say that "there is nothing in these documents, nor in the regulations themselves, which either expressly or by implication actually requires that school boards integrate handicapped children into regular schools or classes" (p. 216). Mainstreaming was expressed as a recommended practice, leaving the school board with the flexibility to decide on the planning and organization of programs for children with disabilities. Even though the contents of those policies were not in the act or regulations, they were considered in the Supreme Court judgement.

Parents and educators have been advocating on behalf of exceptional children for some time in Canada. Through organizations like the Council for Exceptional Children, the Canadian Association for Community Living (formerly the Canadian Association for the Mentally Retarded), the Canadian Association for Children with Learning Disabilities, or the Association for Bright Children, parents and professionals have lobbied legislators and provincial and board-level administrators. They have been instrumental in bringing about special services for exceptional children and their families. Parents, often supported by various organizations, have also been responsible for various court actions that have shed light on the interpretation of educational rights of the exceptional child in Canada.

THE IMPACT OF THE CANADIAN CHARTER

The proclamation of the Constitution Act in 1982, with its embedded Canadian Charter of Rights and Freedoms, will surely be a major factor in sensitizing legislators to the rights of exceptional children in Canada. These rights have been advocated in such documents as the special issue of the *Canadian Journal of Education* on Education in Canada and the Charter of Rights and Freedoms (Vol. 11.3, 1986) as well as in studies by Dickinson and MacKay (1989), MacKay (1984), and Poirier et al. (1988). The key words from the Charter relating to rights for exceptional pupils are contained in the Equality provision (section 15), which came into force in April 1985:

> every individual is equal before and under the law and has the right to the equal protection and equal benefit of the law without discrimination and, in particular, without discrimination based on . . . mental or physical disability.

The Charter has been described as the catalyst that triggered revisions in many education and school acts across the country. Legislative changes were made to assure equal protection and equal benefit to all children without discrimination on the basis of exceptionalities. As shown in Table 21.1, all Canadian provinces and territories have adopted legislation

TABLE 21.1

Proclamation of Mandatory Educational Legislation for Exceptional Children in the Provinces and Territories of Canada

PROVINCES AND TERRITORIES	YEAR OF PROCLAIMED MANDATORY LEGISLATION	
	PRIOR TO 1979	1979 TO 1993
Newfoundland		1979
Nova Scotia	1969	
Prince Edward Island	1971	
New Brunswick		1986
Quebec		1979
Ontario		1980
Manitoba		1980
Saskatchewan	1971[a]	
Alberta		1988
British Columbia		1989
Northwest Territories		1988
Yukon		1990

[a] Although mandatory legislation was established in 1971, a major revision to the Education Act of Saskatchewan was undertaken in 1978.

Source: Adapted from M. Csapo and L. Goguen. (1989).

mandating their departments of education to provide educational services to all children regardless of their physical or mental disabilities.

Two cases illustrate the impact and limits of the Charter in relation to provincial or territorial legislation regarding exceptional children. The Charter was specifically invoked in the New Brunswick case of *Jory, Cox and Lindsay v. Minister of Education* (1986). That case was brought to court by the parents of three children affected by Down's syndrome. In their statement of claim, the parents explained that they started their court action in order to apply pressure on the provincial government to provide "mentally handicapped and other children with special needs with a right to an appropriate education in the least restrictive environment." The case was settled out of court, when the New Brunswick government amended the Schools Act (1986) to provide that all children were to be placed in regular classrooms "to the extent that is considered practicable by the School Board having due regard for the educational needs of all pupils" (s. 45(2)).

Now that all provinces have mandatory legislation regarding educational services to exceptional students, parents may want to challenge legislative provisions allowing school boards to place exceptional students in special classes. Such was the case in *Rowett v. York Region Board of Education* (1988). In that case, an identification, placement, and review committee identified a child with Down's syndrome as an exceptional pupil and recommended that she be removed from a regular classroom and placed in a class for the educable retarded that was some distance from her home. The parents appealed, unsuccessfully, to the special education tribunal, and finally to the Ontario High Court of Justice. In their court action, the parents asked that the provisions of the Education Act be declared in violation of sections 2(d) and 15 of the Canadian Charter of Rights and Freedoms. The court rejected the parents' claim of a Charter violation and maintained the validity of the provisions of the Education Act. This was appealed and reversed in 1989 by the Ontario Court of Appeal. The Charter issue is still part of the case to be tried.

A DIFFERENT DECADE FOR EXCEPTIONAL STUDENTS (1979–1989)

Before 1979, only three provinces—Prince Edward Island, Nova Scotia, and Saskatchewan—had legislation stating that school boards must provide educational services to the exceptional student. The Prince Edward Island School Act (1988) calls for the provision of free educational instruction to every child from 6 to 20 years (section 44(1)). In the province of Nova Scotia, Regulation 7(c) of the Education Act (1979) has given all school boards the responsibility to provide instruction for children with mental and physical disabilities. In 1971, Saskatchewan established in its School Act (section 122) the right of all exceptional children to an appropriate public education. Carlson (1980, p. 61) reports that the passage of that legislation brought a significant growth in educational programs and services in the province of Saskatchewan. In 1978, the law was further revised to clearly extend the Department of Education's responsibilities to all disabled students, including those with multiple disabilities, through the funding of regional developmental centres and special education services to school boards (Education Act, 1978). In 1975, the four Atlantic provinces (Newfoundland, Nova Scotia, Prince Edward Island, and New Brunswick) entered into an agreement and created the Atlantic Provinces Special Education Authority to co-ordinate educational services to students with visual and hearing disabilities. This agreement was protected through legislative amendments in the school acts of each province, but the protections were not mandatory.

Table 21.1 identifies each of the provinces and territories with mandatory legislation for exceptional children, differentiating between the provinces that enacted the legislation before and after 1979. Whereas before 1979 only Nova Scotia, Saskatchewan, and Prince Edward Island had mandatory legislation, between 1979 and 1990 the other seven provinces and the two territories enacted mandatory legislation for the education of exceptional children. These provinces and territories and their acts are, in order of proclamation, Quebec (Loi sur l'instruction publique, 1979), Newfoundland (School Attendance Act 1979), Ontario (Education Act, 1980), Manitoba (Public School Act, 1980), New Brunswick (Schools Act, 1986), Alberta (School Act, 1988), Northwest Territories (Education Act, 1988), British Columbia (School Act, 1989), and Yukon (Education Act, 1989–90).

A look at some of the pre-Charter case law in this area may help us understand the impact of legislation providing for mandatory special educational services. In the case of *Shelly Joyce Marie Carrière v. County of Lamont No. 30* (1978), a 9-year-old with cerebral palsy applied to an Alberta court for a writ of *mandamus* requiring a school board to permit her to attend school. She had attended Edmonton's Glenrose Hospital School for two years at a cost of $28 000 to the school board. However, in June 1977, the Glenrose staff had decided that she was mentally retarded and did not belong in the hospital school, which served only children with physical disabilities, and so they had excluded her. Psychologists at the University of Alberta had subsequently performed a series of tests on her and concluded that she was not mentally retarded, but merely required individual assistance at school. The court directed the school board to accept the child into one of its schools or to arrange her education in a school of another district. The court also ordered the school board to assume responsibility for the cost of the girl's education, provided that she attended the school to which she was directed. Recently, a similar decision was reached in *Thompson v. Ontario* (1988), in which the Ontario High Court of Justice declared that the Ministry was obliged to pay for the schooling of a "hard to serve pupil" at an appropriate placement.

Another decision dealt with the right of an autistic child to attend school. In *MacMillan v. Commission scolaire de Ste-Foy* (1981), an autistic child had been placed in a Kindergarten classroom in an anglophone school for one year, with the help of a special subsidy of $3000 from the Quebec Department of Education. The following year, the school board decided that the subsidy was inadequate and gave the child's parents a choice between a special class for autistic francophones set up locally or an anglophone class in Montreal. Since the Loi sur l'instruction publique du Québec (1979, section 480) provides that school boards must integrate disabled children under 16 years of age into their regular schools, Judge Moison ruled that the law no longer conferred a power upon the board, but rather imposed an obligation. Judge Moison said that the board "shall" integrate disabled children under age 16, thus obliging the board to do so. By replacing the word "may" with the word "shall," the decision left no doubt that the amendment intended to impose a duty upon school boards to provide special education services to all children needing such services and that they were obliged to accept such children into district schools. The Quebec legislature had recognized the right of such children to receive special education. Such a simple change of words, it is suggested, had the effect of recognizing the right of all children to education in those provinces as well. In the *MacMillan* decision, Judge Moison also stated that although he was aware that his decision would impose a financial and administrative burden on the defendant board and on all the school boards in the province of Quebec, he would not be guided by this consideration in deciding the rights and obligations of the parties before him. A similar recent decision was reached in *Commission des droits de la personne et Marcil v. Commission scolaire de St-Jean-sur-le-Richelieu* (1992).

THE RIGHT TO EDUCATION TAILORED TO NEEDS

Since all the provinces and territories having enacted mandatory legislation regarding education for exceptional children, it is important to analyze what these laws specifically protect. Education rights tailored to special needs has been approached through both a categorical and a non-categorical definition of children in need.

The categorical definition of exceptional children recognizes various characteristics of the exceptional child or types of exceptionalities that create a need for special education, appropriate education, or individualized programs. In the provinces of Newfoundland and Nova Scotia, exceptional children are defined as students with mental and physical disabilities. In Alberta, a board may determine that by virtue of the student's behavioural, communicational, intellectual, learning, or physical characteristics, or a combination of those characteristics, a student is in need of a special education program, and entitled to have access to a special education program (School Act, 1988, s-31, 29 (1) & (2)). The provinces of New Brunswick, Ontario, Saskatchewan, as well as the Yukon territory, have definitions similar to Alberta's.

As for the different types of exceptionalities protected, three provinces (Saskatchewan, Ontario, and Alberta) explicitly include the *gifted* child within their definition of exceptional children who have special needs. Although the general definition of exceptional children in New Brunswick is similar to the ones in Alberta and Ontario, it is not explicit in the law or in policy statements, which further elaborate the definition to include gifted children.[1]

A universal right or non-categorical approach was taken by some of the provinces and territories. These do not target specific disabilities but guarantee education to all students or to children who need special resources. In the Northwest Territories, "students who are unable or unlikely to be served to advantage by the regular education program" are deemed to need special education (Education Act, 1988, s. 107. (1)). In Prince Edward Island, Quebec, Manitoba, and most recently British Columbia, non-categorical approaches specify that every school board should take the necessary measures for all children to have an education.

It is debatable which view of children with special needs — the categorical or non-categorical view — is less labelling. A detailed study of the specific provisions to special-needs students within schools in provinces and territories with a categorical versus a non-categorical orientation could provide further clarification.

The two concepts of *appropriate education* and *least restrictive environment* have been described in policies on educational provisions for exceptional children to ensure that education is tailored to the needs of an individual and is protected through Individualized Educational Programs (IEP). Exceptional children are defined as children who, on account of their characteristics, need appropriate special resources and services to meet those needs. Appropriate education is most often defined as a special program, or an individualized educational program. Least restrictive environment defines the setting in which the exceptional child should be receiving her or his education. The least restrictive environment is the one that would be most appropriate to the child's needs and abilities while allowing maximum contact with students who are not disabled.

Table 21.2 shows the orientation of provincial education legislation to either the IEP model or the Least Restrictive Environment (LRE) model. As can be seen in the table, four provinces and one territory have adopted the IEP approach. Other provinces and territories have, to varying degrees, some practices to prepare IEPs. The provinces of Alberta, New Brunswick, Ontario, and Saskatchewan, as well as the Yukon territory, have protected the IEP practice in their education or school acts.

The provision of educational services in the least restrictive environments has been a major trend in Canada over the last decade. Mainstreaming and integration in the service delivery policies and practices have become widespread (Csapo & Goguen, 1980; Day et al., 1985; Winzer, 1993). Four provinces (New Brunswick, Ontario, Quebec and Saskatchewan) and the two teritories have clearly based their legislative revisions on the concept of integration and mainstreaming within the least restrictive environment orientation.

In New Brunswick, the placement of the exceptional child within the regular classroom was emphasized by the legislative revision of 1986. Section 53.4 of the New Brunswick Schools Act states:

> A school board shall place exceptional pupils such that they receive special education programs and services in circumstances where exceptional pupils can participate with pupils who are not exceptional pupils within regular classroom settings to the extent that is considered practicable by the School Board having due regard for the educational needs of all pupils.

The 1986 legislation received a test in *Robichaud v. Commission scolaire numéro 39* (1989). In that case, the child had learning difficulties and had been placed in a classroom for special students. Together with her parents, she applied for a mandatory interlocutory injunction requiring the school board to place her in a regular Grade 8 class, after having developed, without delay, an individualized plan for her in consultation with her parents. The Court of Queen's Bench allowed the application. In his reasons for judgement, Judge Bernard Jean said that section 53.4 of the New Brunswick Schools Act provides for the integration of exceptional pupils such that they receive special education programs in circumstances where they can participate with those who are not special pupils. Furthermore, Judge Jean ruled that the special education programs provided for in the act were individualized special education programs. Accordingly, the court ordered the development of a program including the following elements: formulating a committee according to guidelines issued by the Department of Education; consulting with specialists; developing

---

TABLE 21.2
Provincial Provisions for Education Tailored to Needs

	PROVINCES											
PROVISION	**AB**	**BC**	**MB**	**NB**	**NF**	**NS**	**NWT**	**ON**	**PE**	**PQ**	**SK**	**YU**
IEP	X			X				X			X	X
LRE				X		X	X			X	X	X

Source: Adapted from Poirier D. et al. (1988), Table 4, p. 51.

a preliminary program in the week following the order; making teachers and pupils who were not exceptional pupils sensitive to the experiment to be undertaken; and allowing the participation of the parents of the exceptional pupil to be integrated. Although the New Brunswick Court of appeal reversed the decision of the trial judge on technical grounds, Natalie Robichaud was allowed to complete her school year in a regular classroom. Furthermore, the substance of the trial judge's decision was not contested by the court.

PROVISION OF FINANCIAL RESOURCES

The provision of financial resources to ensure the educational rights of exceptional children have been clearly enacted in all Canadian provinces with mandatory legislation. Where legislation directs children to attend school, the school board must necessarily provide a school. In *McLeod v. Salmon Arm School Trustees* (1952), the school board closed a school because the municipality did not contribute adequately to its funding. As a result, the students were without a school for the rest of the year. The British Columbia Court of Appeal stated that the school board had the duty to provide the pupils with accommodation even if it had financial problems. This does not mean that schools cannot be closed due to declining enrollments and economic restraints, as long as other schools are available to the pupils (*MacDonald v. Lambton County Board of Education*, 1982).

The *Shelly Joyce Marie Carrière* (1978) case dealt more specifically with funding of special education. In that case, Judge O'Byrne, after finding that the child was entitled to an education, held that the school board was responsible for all education costs and fees arising from the child's attendance at school. In the *MacMillan* case (1981), Judge Moison recognized that his decision ordering the school board to provide educational services to an autistic child would create financial hardship, but that these considerations would not prevent him from making such an order. Similarly, in *Commission des droits de la personne du Québec et Marcil v. Commission scolaire St-Jean-sur-le-Richelieu* (1992) Madam Justice Rivet ordered the school board to pay the parents some $20 000 incurred by them for special education services for their child. In all these cases, the courts were interpreting legislation with mandatory requirements. The result would have been different had the legislation been permissive and discretionary.

Human rights legislation was used in an Alberta case in an effort by parents to get full reimbursement of the fees they paid to a private school attended by their physically disabled child. In *Department of Education v. Deyell* (1987), the Alberta Department of Education had agreed to pay the full fees to a private school in the United States that could assist the child with his disabilities, but refused to pay the full amount to a private school within the province. While Madam Justice Veit agreed that schools are a service provided to the public, she ruled that grants provided by the government and the board of education to assist children with disabilities were not a service customarily available to the public. It would seem that the decision in *Deyell* was especially directed to private schools, as was the case in *Bourque v. Westlock School Division No. 37* (1987). The case might have been decided differently if the child had been attending a public school.

Section 15 of the Canadian Charter of Rights and Freedoms would have the effect of raising serious doubt about educational provisions where groups of students were excluded. The onus would then be on any province with permissive legislation to show the existence of a rational basis for such exclusions. Lack of money may not be a good enough reason (*Mills v. Board of Education of District of Columbia* (1972)).

ASSESSMENT PROCEDURES AND PARENTAL INVOLVEMENT

The most commonly debated procedures in the provision of education to exceptional children are those of parental involvement and the right to appeal decisions. As can be seen in Table 21.3, parental involvement in the screening, assessing, and (in some provinces) planning and deciding of programs has been addressed in the legislation of seven provinces and one territory. Alberta, British Columbia, New Brunswick, Nova Scotia, Ontario, Quebec, Saskatchewan, and Yukon protect parental involvement. The level of involvement varies from consultation in the identification process (New Brunswick) to parent consultation in program delivery (Ontario). Table 21.3 also shows that appeal procedures are predetermined in the educational legislation of five provinces and one territory: Alberta, British Columbia, New Brunswick, Ontario, Saskatchewan, and the Yukon.

When there is no court hearing and a parent has therefore been deprived of the right to be heard, the courts are prepared to intervene by invoking the common-law principle of natural justice or *fundamental justice* under section 7 of the Canadian Charter, which states that no one will be deprived of his or her right to life, liberty, or security of the person except in conformity with the principles of fundamental justice. Teachers and school boards should not worry about the imposition of natural justice or fundamental justice requirements. It does not mean that the courts will make decisions on behalf of the school boards. It simply means that proper procedure with respect to parental involvement should be followed in deciding on the placement of children in a particular school setting.

In the New Brunswick *Robichaud* case (1989), Judge Jean expressly ordered that the parents be "involved throughout the whole process." However, he took care to point out that the parents "must avoid imposing their will and they must study all suggestions objectively. They must not contest the plan by taking Natalie out of the program before all aspects have been examined by the group" (p. 385).

CONCLUSIONS

Educational rights of exceptional children in each of the Canadian provinces and territories may be protected through laws, regulations, and court cases but also through pro-

TABLE 21.3
Provincial Provisions for Parental Involvement and Appeal in Assessment

PROVISION	PROVINCES											
	AB	BC	MB	NB	NF	NS	NWT	ON	PE	PQ	SK	YU
Parental Involvement	x	x		x		x		x		x	x	x
Appeal	x	x		x				x			x	x

Source: Adapted from Poirier D. et al. (1988), Table 10, p. 77.

vincial/territorial and district-level policy statements. Whether is is through a categorical or a universal-right approach, the right of exceptional children to an education is implicitly protected in all Canadian provinces by section 15 of the Canadian Charter of Rights and Freedoms, which implies that all children have a right to attend school, regardless of mental or physical disability.

The needs of exceptional children raise an important issue that affects many levels of governance. Parents, teachers, school trustees, provincial governments, and the federal government say that they are all working toward the same goal — that is, fulfilling the needs of exceptional children. One way of accomplishing that goal is to transform those needs into rights by amending the respective provincial education or school acts, refining provincial and territorial policies and guidelines, and developing district-level policies and guidelines that guarantee the base, as well as the resources and procedures, to meet the specific needs of the exceptional child. Appropriate education for the exceptional child includes individualized programs, least restrictive environments, adequate funding, special programs, certified special education teachers, identification procedures, parental involvement, and appeal procedures.

DISCUSSION QUESTIONS

❏ What are the implications of the statement "parents have the right to choose the kind of education to be given to their child" when one is considering the best interests of a child with special needs?

❏ How do the other children in a school where special education students are being taught benefit from their presence?

❏ What special qualifications should be required for those teaching exceptional children?

❏ Are the special provisions for students requesting services beyond the regular program provided through a categorical or non-categorical perspective within the school board in your area?

NOTE

1. Those further interested in the specific educational rights of gifted children in Canada may consult Goguen (1989) and (1993).

REFERENCES

Bales v. Board of School Trustees, School District 23 (Central Okanagan). (1985). Administrative Law Reports 202.

Berkeley, H., Gatfield, C., & West, G. (Eds.). (1978). *Children's rights, legal and educational issues.* Toronto: Ontario Institute for Studies in Education.

Bourque v. Westlock School Division No. 37. (1987). 8 Canadian Human Rights Reporter. D/3746 (Alta. Q.B.).

Canadian Council on Children and Youth. (1978). *Admittance restricted: The child as citizen in Canada*. Ottawa: CCCY.

Carlson, L. (1980). Special education in Saskatchewan. In M. Csapo & L. Goguen (Eds.). *Special education across Canada: Issues and concerns for the '80s*. (pp. 137–45). Vancouver: Centre for Human Development and Research.

Champoux-Lesage, P. (1989). Special education in Quebec: Summary of present situation and future prospects. In M. Csapo & L. Goguen (Eds.). *Special education across Canada: Issues and concerns for the '90s*. (pp. 93–102). Vancouver: Centre for Human Developement and Research.

Commission des droits de la personne du Québec et Marcil v. Commission scolaire de Saint-Jean-sur-le-Richelieu. (1992). 16 Canadian Human Rights Reporter. D/85.

Conseil scolaire no 39 v. Robichaud. (1989). New Brunswick Appeal Court, unpublished.

Constitution Act. (1867). (U.K. 30 & 31 Vict.) c.3. (Formerly British North America Act, 1967, U.K. c.3.)

Constitution Act. (1982). (Enacted in Canada by the Canada Act, 1982. (U.K.) c.11 Sched. B.) Pt. 1. (Charter of Rights and Freedoms.)

Csapo, M., & Goguen, L. (Eds.). (1980). *Special education across Canada: Issues and concerns for the '80s*. Vancouver: Centre for Human Development and Research.

Day, C.F., Kirk, S.A., & Gallagher, J.J. (1985). *Educating exceptional children*. Canadian edition. Scarborough, ON: Nelson Canada.

Department of Education v. Deyell. (1987). 8 Canadian Human Rights Reporter. D/3668 (Alta. Q.B.).

Dickinson, G.M., & MacKay, A.W. (1989). *Rights, freedoms and the education system in Canada: Cases and materials*. Toronto, ON: Montgomery.

Education Act. (1978). Revised statutes of Saskatchewan. c.17.

Education Act. (1979). Consolidated statutes of Nova Scotia. c.E-2.

Education Act. (1980). Revised statutes of Ontario. c.129.

Education Act. (1988). Revised statutes of Northwest Territories. c.E-2.

Education Act. (1989–90). Statutes of the Yukon. c.25.

Education of All Handicapped Children Act. (1975). Public Law 94-142. United States Code Service, Rochester, NY: Lawyers Publication, vol. 20.

Elwood v. Halifax County-Bedford District School Board. (1987).

Fisher, S., & Schimmel, D. (1982). *The rights of students and teachers*. New York: Harper & Row.

Goguen, L. (1989). The education of gifted children in Canadian law and ministerial policy. *Canadian Journal of Education*, 14(1), 18–30.

Goguen, L. (1993). Right to education for the gifted in Canada. In K.A. Heller, F.J. Monks, & A.H. Passow. *International handbook for research on giftedness and talent*. (pp. 771–77). Oxford: Pergamon Press.

Hurlbert, E.L., & Hurlbert, M.A. (1992). *School law and the Charter of Rights and Freedoms*. 2nd ed. Calgary: University of Calgary Press.

Jory, Cox and Lindsay v. Minister of Education. (1986). Unpublished.

Leduc, C., & de Massy, P.R. (1981). *Youth, equal in rights and responsibilities*. Quebec City: Commission des droits de la personne du Québec.

Loi sur l'instruction publique du Québec. (1979). Lois refondues du Québec. c.1-14.

MacDonald v. Lambton County Board of Education. (1982). 37 Ontario Reports (2d) 221 (Ont. H.C.).

MacKay, A.W. (1984). *Education law in Canada*. Toronto: Emond-Montgomery.

McLeod v. Salmon Arm School Trustees. (1952). 2 Dominion Law Reports. 562 (B.C.C.A.).

MacMillan v. Commission scolaire de Ste-Foy. (1981). Cour supérieure 172 (S. Ct. Que).

Manley-Casimir, M., & Sussel, T.A. (Eds.). (1986). *Courts in the classroom: Education and the Charter of Rights and Freedoms.* Calgary: Detselig.

Mills v. Board of Education of District of Columbia. (1972). 348 Fed. supp. 866.

PARC (Pennsylvania Association for retarded children) v. Commonwealth of Pennsylvania et al. (1972). 343 Fed. Supp. 279.

Perner, D., & Roberts, D. (1989). Special education in New Brunswick: Approaching special regular education. In M. Csapo & L. Goguen (Eds.). *Special education across Canada: Issues and concerns for the '90s.* (pp. 103–16). Vancouver: Centre for Human Development and Research.

Poirier, D., Goguen, L., & Leslie, P. (1988). *Education rights of exceptional children in Canada.* Toronto: Carswell.

Public School Act. (1980). Consolidated Statutes of Manitoba. c.p.250.

Robichaud v. Commission scolaire numéro 39. (1989). 95 N.B. R. (2d) 375.

Rowett v. York Region Board of Education. (1988). 63 O.R. (2d) 767-768.

School Act. (1978). Revised Statutes of Saskatchewan. c.17.

School Act. (1988). Revised Statutes of Prince Edward Island, c.S-2.

School Act. (1988). Revised Statutes of Alberta. c.S-3.

School Act. (1989). Statutes of British Columbia. c.61.

School Attendance Act. (1979). Statutes of Newfoundland. c.61.

Schools Act. (1992). Statutes of New Brunswick. c.S.5.1

Shelly Joyce Marie Carrière v. County of Lamont No. 30. (1978). Unpublished decision handed down by Judge O'Byrn, Sup. Ct of Alberta, Judicial district of Edmonton, August 15.

Thompson v. Ontario. (1988). 63 O.R. (2d). 489.

Williams, S.A., & de Mestral, A.L.C. (1979). *An introduction to international law.* Toronto: Butterworths.

Winzer, M. (1993). *Children with exceptionalities: A Canadian perspective.* 3rd ed. Scarborough, ON: Prentice-Hall.

Wringe, C.A. (1981). *Children's rights, A philosophical study.* London: Routledge and Kegan Paul.

FURTHER READINGS

Csapo, M. (1989). *Children in distress: A Canadian perspective.* Vancouver, BC: Centre for Human Development and Research.

Csapo, M., & Goguen, L. (1989). *Special education across Canada: Issues and concerns for the '90s.* Vancouver, BC: Centre for Human Development and Research.

22

SEXISM IN EDUCATION

Nancy Sheehan

In 1990 one of the young women participating in the A Capella project of the Canadian Teachers' Federation is quoted: "I think there should be non-sexist education because if we don't stop this problem in the schools, it will continue on through life and everyone will be living in an unfair world, which isn't right" (p. xi).

Seventy years earlier, in 1920, the Dominion Elections Act extended the right to vote in federal elections to all women in Canada. The granting of the franchise meant that women could vote and hold office at federal, provincial, municipal, and school board levels in most areas in the country. In Alberta in 1917, two women were elected to the legislature — the first women in Canada to be elected to legislative office — and two others were named as judges.[1] In 1929, the much-acclaimed Persons Case, taken to the Privy Council in England by five Alberta women, resulted in women being declared persons and eligible for appointment to the Senate of Canada.[2] It appeared to some that women in Canada had not only achieved equality in all the responsibilities and duties of full citizenship, but that they were becoming leaders in political, educational, and social affairs at local, provincial, and even the national level.

Reality was a little different. Attitudes embedded in the social fabric take more than legislation to change. Issues of power, curriculum, and opportunity for women in the school system show that women are still not fully equal. This inequality has a long history, as girls and women have been denied opportunity and equal access to knowledge. In 1865, Egerton Ryerson, Superintendent of Schools in Ontario, and grammar school inspector George Young argued against admitting girls to grammar schools and to the study of Latin, claiming that this would affect the character and sensibility of the girls, but, more importantly, that girls would distract the boys from their studies. Although this attempt to exclude girls failed, it did so for economic reasons, not reasons of equality (Prentice & Houston, 1975, pp. 253–55; Royce, 1975, pp. 1–13). The issue of curriculum suited for and attractive to girls remained a thorny problem for Ryerson, as it has for educators throughout this century.

This problem has also been prominent at the postsecondary level. In 1875, Grace Lockhart graduated from Mount Allison College in New Brunswick with a B.Sc., the first woman in the British empire to be awarded a degree (Harris, 1976, p. 116). Although several more women received degrees from Mount Allison, the wisdom of admitting women to university was debated widely. At McGill University, Royal Victoria College was created in 1884 as a teaching, social, and residential college for women. It was "a separate but equal" answer to the clamour of women for higher education (Gillett, 1981). This solution of a separate college highlights the difficulties women have experienced in being admitted and accepted as serious students in arts and science and in professional programs at the university level in Canada. And today, although there is no overt discrimination against admitting women, they are still very much under-represented in engineering, math, and physics programs and at the Ph.D. and postdoctoral levels.

Female teachers have been denied power. In September 1885, the Calgary Protestant School District No. 19 found that it needed to hire a second teacher to assist Mr. J. Spencer Douglas. In contrast to Mr. Douglas, who with a first-class teaching certificate was making $60 a month, Miss Rosabelle Watson was hired to teach the younger children at the princely sum of $25 a month. Her teaching certificate was a second-class one (Bourassa et al., 1975, pp. 5–7; Stamp, 1975, pp. 10–12). This pattern was widespread. Male teachers taught the older children and were given administrative responsibilities as principal or head teacher; therefore, a first-class certificate was needed and a higher salary justified. For the women, who taught the younger children and had few administrative responsibilities, a second-class certificate was quite acceptable. Their gender, generally lower qualifications, and elementary grade responsibilities combined to produce much lower salaries. This pattern of more males teaching the senior grades and holding administrative positions with better salaries and qualifications remains the norm.

The rhetoric of the first three decades of this century that women in Canada (outside of Quebec) had achieved full equality and could become leaders in the society was not true in the field of education then, nor is it true today. This chapter looks at sexism in education over this century and attempts to analyze both change and continuity in the three dimensions of power, curriculum, and opportunity. It will attempt to address the rhetoric/reality conflict and, in the process, show the distance that women have traversed and the miles still to go.

WOMEN AND POWER

In Canada, as elsewhere, teaching has been and continues to be a classic case of the division of labour by gender. In general, women have held the lower-paying jobs at the bottom of the educational occupational ladder, and men have been favoured at the top. The literature on this topic and available statistics indicate several factors at work. Madeleine Grumet (1988) has argued that women were sought as teachers because of their ability to nurture, sustain, and provide a humane culture for children. They came into the schools seeking to extend their knowledge and nurturing abilities outside the home. Once in the schools, however, intimidated by their own lesser qualifications, surrounded by a bureaucratic, graded organization, and excluded from the decision-making process, women teachers were trapped. They found themselves in an occupation labelled as women's work, but over which they had little control or influence and in which they accepted the prevailing patriarchal norms.

FEMALE TEACHERS, MALE ADMINISTRATORS

The fact that teaching—particularly elementary teaching—was viewed as either preparation for or substitution for the mothering role meant that women teachers were more appropriately placed in elementary schools, that minimal qualifications were acceptable, and that salaries could be abysmally low. The notions that all women had fathers, brothers, and husbands to support them, that they did not have financial obligations, and that they were only teaching "for something to do" until marriage, absolved male school trustees from paying higher salaries to female teachers. In the end, it also reinforced the idea of the woman teacher as a "trousseau" teacher, rather than a career one, and it may have helped persuade some women who might have preferred a career to accept a marriage proposal.

If female teachers had a motherly role, then male teachers had a fatherly one, exerting their "natural" authority as high-school teachers, principals, inspectors, and superintendents. This fact, coupled with the proportionately fewer men who went into teaching, meant that male teachers had a better-than-average chance of progressing to administrative jobs. They were better qualified, and more males took first-class certificates or obtained degrees than did women. For example, in Alberta from 1914 to 1919, 991 women and 291 men entered the Normal School at Calgary. Of these, only 279 women (28 percent), as compared with 155 men (53 percent), were seeking first-class certificates. Although the numbers changed slightly for the years 1929 to 1933, the proportion of male/female teachers and certificates shows the same ratio (Alberta Department of Education).

In Ontario, the County Model School System (elementary schools where prospective teachers spent three months in a brief apprenticeship) helped both to feminize the teaching profession and to encourage women to become teachers with minimal qualifications. Teachers with ability and ambition—meaning particularly male teachers—were discouraged from attending these regional teacher mills (Phillips, 1957, pp. 577–78). The result was a marked difference between the academic quality of elementary and secondary teachers and the career attitudes of male and female teachers. By 1915 in Canada, 83 percent of all Canadian elementary school teachers were women (Wilson et al., 1970, p. 317).

The result was a female ghetto run by male administrators. According to one official, young men who did not aspire to administrative positions and were content to remain in teaching lacked in "Go, Grit or Gumption" (Patterson, 1979, p. 198). Although women could be paid less and might be appropriate for young children, some officials were concerned about the lack of male teachers. Catholic school boards in Quebec received higher provincial grants for a number of years if they employed male teachers, and the school board in Victoria, BC, in 1903 argued that boys needed more male teachers (Wilson et al., 1970, p. 317). Robert Patterson (1986) noted that in 1917, Alberta normal school officials, aware of a decline in male recruitment, commented that such trends did not "promise well for material from which to recruit our force of instructors, inspectors and supervisors" (p. 101). These gendered patterns in qualifications, grade level and subject, administrative positions, and salaries were visible evidence of general beliefs that have been difficult to change.

TEACHERS' ASSOCIATIONS

One factor that has contributed to better teaching conditions for both women and men has been the formation of teachers' organizations. However, even here the gendered pattern of leadership and administration has been slow to change. The Alberta Teachers' Association (ATA), an outgrowth of the Alberta Teachers' Alliance, is instructive in this regard. Unlike women in Ontario, who formed their own organization—the Federation of Women Teachers' Association of Ontario (FWATO)—or Saskatoon teachers who organized the Saskatoon Women Teachers' Association (SWTA), Alberta women did not form a separate organization.

The result was few women on the executive or board, little attention paid to specifically women's issues, and the adoption of practices that were eventually labelled discriminatory. The number of women officers on the ten-member board of the ATA fluctuated over the years, from none to a maximum of three during the 1920s. During the late 1930s and 1940s, there were very few women on the board. Many of those years saw no women elected. Mary Crawford of Edmonton, one of the women teachers involved in the formation of the Alliance in 1917 and 1918, was never on the board. She was, however, president of the Alberta Education Association (AEA) in 1921–22 (Chalmers, 1968, p. 301–18). This organization had originally "allowed" teachers to organize, and both the ATA and the AEA existed side by side through the 1940s, when the AEA folded (Ramsey, 1978, p. 7). It wasn't until 1949–50 that a woman became a member of the executive. It was she who argued for more classroom teachers and more women on the executive, on committees, and on delegations. She accused the ATA of discriminatory and wrongful use of money, in charging to the Association the travelling expenses of wives of executive members. Marian Gimby, an Edmonton high-school teacher who became the first woman president in 1951–52, opposed any increase in ATA fees until "the Association can find ways and means of assuring that the women teachers are elected to our AGM and our Executive in a reasonable proportion to their numbers" (Chalmers, 1968, pp. 209–13).

In British Columbia, this same pattern existed and the British Columbia Teachers' Federation (BCTF) was slow to adopt a policy supporting salary equity. Once it did, in 1943, the differential began to lessen. Pressure from the BCTF, difficulties in attracting teachers during the war and in the growth years of the 1950s, and court decisions in test cases around the province resulted in changes beneficial to women teachers. For example, female teachers who married were then able to remain teaching, and the salary differential for women decreased — from 55.6 percent of male salaries in 1945 to 23.0 percent in 1954–55, and to 21.2 percent for elementary teachers and 16.0 percent for secondary teachers in 1971–72. Like their counterpart in Alberta, the executive of the BCTF had no women members throughout its formative years. Only in the 1950s did BC women make it to the executive of their own teaching federation, and it was not until the 1970s that the federation established a Status of Women Committee (Khosla et al., 1979).

The two women teachers' associations, FWTAO and SWTA, did not fare much better in gaining status and salary for their women members. Although they gave women a voice, administrative experience, and solidarity, FWTAO members were affected by the accepted role of women in society. For example, not until 1960 did they fully support the right of women teachers to retain their jobs when they married or to obtain maternity leave (French, 1968, pp. 133–34). As in the larger teacher organizations, their concerns reflected the role and status of women within the society.

On the surface, much has been gained by women teachers. Salary equity based on experience and qualifications, paid maternity leave, the ability to compete for administrative posts, the acceptance of women as serious, committed career teachers, and the opportunity to be on association committees and elected to executives are some examples of the rhetoric and reality of increasing equality. The teaching profession, therefore, is both a microcosm of the larger society as well as an instigator of social change.

POWERLESSNESS

Today in the 1990s, despite the gains of the women's movement over the last three decades, schools are still segregated pools of labour, organized on the basis of gender. A Canadian

Teachers' Federation (CTF) (1993) study, *Progress revisited*, argues that education is an "internally segregated profession," whose stability is so pronounced that it must be said to be apparently intransigent (p. 3). It quotes an address to the CTF in 1988 that summarizes efforts to reduce gender imbalance as benefiting men more than women in the following respects: in numbers entering teaching; in maintaining a near monopoly of administrative positions; in increasing male representation among principals and department heads; in support for parental benefits translating into benefits for fathers; in increasing tolerance for part-time teachers affecting women's careers; and in a "generic-management" focus for administrative roles as opposed to a facilitative and supportive role more attuned to women's leadership values (p. 4).

A 1990 cross-Canada study reiterates the findings of the CTF study. It concludes that the situation of women and men in positions in educational systems across the country reflects one of tradition, rather than employment equity. Men dominate all line positions in education — in school boards and in secondary, junior high, and elementary schools (Rees, 1990, p. 91). Women predominate in the lower grades and in certain subjects in secondary schools, like home economics. They are under-represented in the upper grades, in subject areas with a mathematical or scientific basis, in administrative posts in schools, on teachers' association executives, and in ministries of education. And they make less money. Some provinces still sanction lesser qualifications for certification as an elementary teacher. Women benefit less from administrative stipends, lose in "years of experience" because of family responsibilities, are less likely to be able to pursue graduate study, and suffer from the predominance of the "old boys' network." A study conducted in British Columbia summarized the problem:

> Indicators of systemic barriers in the school system include:
>
> - Within the Ministry of Education, females represent 63.04 per cent of the workforce and hold 90.9 per cent of clerical positions. In contrast, men comprise 39.96 per cent of the workforce and hold 68.8 per cent of the management positions;
> - Females comprise only 19 per cent of principals and 27 per cent of vice-principals;
> - Only eight per cent of female professional staff are administrators and 92 are teachers, whereas 29 per cent of male professional staff are administrators and 71 per cent are teachers;
> - Women hold 41 per cent of all professional positions in the district offices, but are under-represented in administrative positions;
> - Theoretically, salaries should be the same for males and females in the same position, with the same qualifications and experience. However, the net impact of systemic barriers to training and career opportunities is reflected in the lower average salaries of female staff;
> - Secondary female teachers (35.22 per cent) are in a minority in a setting where female students represent 48.9 per cent of all students;
> - Female teachers are a small minority in several key areas—computer education (10.6 per cent), mathematics (20.9 per cent), science (17.8 per cent), social studies (25.3 per cent);
> - Male and female segregation in such teaching areas as agriculture, science, mathematics, computer education, home economics and industrial arts continues to reflect traditional roles and perpetuate stereotyping. (BC Ministry of Education, 1991)

The result of this reality is that women are less powerful than men. They have less opportunity to make a difference — to affect the curriculum, the organization, and the environment of the school, and therefore, to have their view of education taken seriously.

Since education is an essential piece of ammunition in the struggle of women for equality, this gap between rhetoric and reality is very serious. Socialization of men and women to "separate spheres" that begin in the family and carry over into school will not be corrected by an educational system in which male power and ideology continue to dominate.

WOMEN AND THE CURRICULUM

"**W**hat would you have a woman know?" was put to Mrs. Malaprop, one of the classic comic characters of English drama, in Sheridan's *The Rivals* (1775). It is a question that many have tried to answer over the years, and the answer has depended upon the particular society in which it has been raised. In Canada, in subtle and not-so-subtle ways, the curriculum and the resources in use in the schools have delivered two messages—one for the boys and one for the girls. In doing so, the curriculum has trapped both sexes, but more particularly and dramatically girls, in a specific and restrictive pattern of behaviour and opportunity. One study (Baker, 1985) documents that as girls mature to adolescence, they become less interested in competing with boys for high grades; they lose interest in math and science; their confidence in their academic ability diminishes; and their career aspirations decline. They see their lives in very traditional and romanticized terms (pp. 2–4).

CO-EDUCATION

Public schooling in Canada has always been for girls as well as boys. Compulsory education laws did not discriminate on the basis of sex. For the most part, schooling has also been co-educational, with boys and girls not only attending the same school but also sitting in the same classrooms. In a country with a sparse population, one-room rural schools, and a pioneer tradition of girls and boys doing the same type of farm chores, the notion that children should be educated separately had little moral justification and was economically inefficient.

Even in the growing cities, where large numbers of students and multi-roomed schools made it possible to organize single-sex classrooms, the notion of one public school held sway. The public educational system was for everybody—boys and girls, rich and poor, native-born and immigrant, children who spoke different languages, rural and urban inhabitants, and those of all religious persuasions. Only in Roman Catholic separate systems and some urban areas did single-sex schools and classrooms operate. In most provinces, Catholic separate schools began to become co-educational in the 1950s — except in Ontario, where some Catholic separate schools remain single-sex today. Research on the attitudinal and academic benefits of single-sex versus co-educational schools is mixed.

Florence Howe (1984), in *Myths of coeducation*, argues that co-education is based on the idea that if women are admitted to men's education, then all problems of sexual equity will be solved; thus, what is important is "access," and content and quality can be ignored (p. x). A recent study conducted in Ontario separate high schools indicates more positive attitudes about students' academic competence in co-educational schools than in single-sex boys' schools and, to a lesser extent, girls' schools (Schneider et al., 1988). A 1986 study of 75 Catholic high schools in the United States suggested that students in single-sex girls' schools were generally more interested in academics than those in co-educational schools (Lee & Bryk, 1986). Since the aims of schooling are varied and include both social and academic development, more study is obviously warranted.

Across the country, most schools and postsecondary institutions have been co-educational, compulsory education laws have been for both sexes, and there has been little legislation that restricted girls from taking specific courses, from obtaining matriculation, or from going on to college or university. And yet we know that in today's age of "liberation," girls' career aspirations are less than those of boys, and many of them expect to work for only a few years. They have erroneous information and an idealistic view of adult life. One Ontario study (Ellis, 1984) reported that the high-school girls surveyed believed that 40 percent of women who are university graduates never marry, that homemakers are less likely to become divorced than women who work outside the home, and that women spend very few years in the workforce (p. 95). For those who do decide to go to university, a recent study by the Secretary of State (1989) indicates that women continue to concentrate in "traditional" areas such as education, nursing, and social work, and fewer than before go to graduate school (pp. 4, 6, 8). From the early debates over the propriety of teaching Latin to girls, the suitability of certain courses for women has been questioned: How should women/girls be portrayed in textbooks and other resource materials? Is there a feminist knowledge that should be incorporated into all courses? Is there knowledge/course content suitable for one sex but not the other?

HOME ECONOMICS

Home economics makes an interesting case study of the position of women in the educational system. Introduced into Canadian elementary schools in the early years of the twentieth century, at the same time that women were campaigning for the vote, home economics was hailed as a step forward in the education of girls and women. It did provide a welcome addition to what was then considered a "male-oriented" curriculum. But a close look reveals that its advocates and supporters saw it not as a vehicle for freeing the new twentieth-century woman from traditional domestic responsibilities, but rather as a means of fitting her for her "God-given place in life," as custodian of hearth and home (Stamp, 1974, pp. 18–23). Its beginnings in Canadian schools were not always promising. In Calgary, domestic-science class was the solution to the question of what to do with the girls while the boys were involved in manual training classes. Several of the women teachers volunteered to teach sewing to the girls, and classes were begun. Unlike the manual training classes, there were no special facilities, no teachers properly educated in the subject, and no equipment, resources, or curriculum guides—factors that changed as home economics became an accepted part of the curriculum (Bannerman, 1981, p. 9).

From a feminist perspective, the advent of homemaking in schools had dubious consequences. Adelaide Hoodless, an Ontario resident known as the founder of home economics, argued that domestic science was a way of preparing women for their role as wives and mothers, relating school and life, and strengthening the home at a time when some thought the family was threatened by the new independence of women, evident in their campaign for the vote. Underscoring these arguments was a preoccupation with providing a scientific basis to housework and elevating a career in the home to a profession requiring specific knowledge and skills (Stamp, 1977, pp. 213–32). Thus domestic science had followers among both liberal and conservative women. Nellie McClung, for example, and the other four women who sponsored the Persons Case supported domestic science, as did the members of the Imperial Order Daughters of the Empire (IODE), who thought domestic-science classes in schools would provide well-trained domestic servants (Royal Commission, 1913). At a time when women were gaining the vote, the gender-specific nature of domestic science ensured the continuation of conservative views about male and female roles in the family and the workplace (Sheehan, 1987, pp. 233–34).

Two further points need to be made. Although domestic-science classes for girls were offset by manual training classes for boys, once these courses moved into the high school, this neat ordering fell apart. Not all boys were counselled into "shop" classes; manual training was not considered necessary for boys heading for university, the professions, or white collar jobs. However, all girls were to be homemakers. Girls were "counselled" into these classes by mothers, friends, and teachers. There was something obviously wrong with a girl who showed no interest in sewing and cooking classes. Girls were not actually forced to take home economics and it was not a matriculation subject in most provinces, but the combination of peer and parental pressure and the stress of being alone in a class of adolescent boys meant that only very intelligent, determined, and courageous girls took physics.

Domestic science in schools had other effects. It provided new opportunities for women since teachers needed to be educated in this new field. Next came the introduction of domestic-science classes in agricultural schools and then departments of home economics at universities. Trained personnel became available for industry, the health-services field, and the government (Bannerman, 1981, pp. 14–19). Although opportunities for women in the workplace were increased, the definition of what was acceptable remained unchanged. Even the terms "domestic science" and "home economics" had gender-specific connotations.

Although home economics may have opened career opportunities for some women, it also could act as a restraint, directing ambitious, scientifically minded women into traditional programs, "more appropriate to their sphere in life." After three-quarters of a century, the idea of an integrated curriculum brought an end to such total segregation. Some girls began to opt for industrial education instead of home economics. Although some critics thought that girls would lose out on knowledge and skills that would be helpful to them as individuals, the integrated curriculum, in fact, widened their opportunities.

TEXTBOOKS

Another aspect of the school to influence the place of women in society was the textbook. In the early schools resource materials other than textbooks were lacking, educational theories of the time dictated practices, and highly trained teachers were scarce; therefore the textbook took on great importance. It was the one undisputed authority upon which the child and the teacher could rely (Sheehan, 1979, pp. 77–84). The depiction of girls and women in the authorized textbooks used across the country until 1960 had three main aspects: women were invisible; women were frail, simple, helpless creatures; and women were confined to the home.

The best illustration of this treatment can be found in readers. They were used in all grades by all children, told stories that could be said to reflect societal values, and the same text selections were found in readers from Nova Scotia to British Columbia. Reading series such as the Canadian Series of Reading Lessons, as well as the Ontario, Canadian, and Highroads Readers were used in many provinces. Others, such as the British Columbia, Alexandra, Victoria, New Brunswick and Maritime Reading Series, were specific to one province or one region. Regardless of province of use or title of a series, the selections and tone were markedly similar. The stories portrayed a certain vision of the world in which women were seldom mentioned, except perhaps in nursery rhyme selections such as "Mary Had a Little Lamb" or the story of Joan of Arc or Florence Nightingale. Witches, queens, and princesses were present. Stories about everyday people and activities did not usually include girls and women. When they did, little girls were placed in embarrassing situations with their mothers, reacting with screams and shrieks (as in the story called "Maggie and Tom") or, as in "Maggie Tulliver and the Gypsies," portrayed as silly (Maggie thought she could run away and be happy with gypsies). For the most part, these sets of readers told the stories of heros, hunters, soldiers, Indians, explorers, inventors, and wise men—topics that tended not to refer to or include women.[3]

By the 1940s, the progressive education movement had had some impact and the readers changed to catch the eyes of children and to reflect their interests. Colourful covers, catchy titles, relevant pictures, and content developed to appeal to children were the obvious changes. The Dick and Jane books were probably most indicative of the new educational trend. Jane and her sister Sally played with dolls, helped mother in the kitchen, and asked big brother Dick questions to which he always knew the answers. Dick played with kites, boats, and cars; he helped father in the workshop or garage and rode spirited horses; once he even remained in the car when it was raised by a hydraulic lift. He was the knowing, caring big brother to his little sisters. Although Dick and Jane are probably the readers with the most stereotypical content, many other series throughout the 1960s gave a one-sided depiction of girls and women. They were silly (as in "Jane Helps," in which Jane set the table and forgot to set a place for herself), or a nuisance (as was Deborah, who insisted on going fishing with her brothers), or they were baking, cleaning, or sewing. Boys and men, meanwhile, were involved in building treehouses or tracking wild animals; they saw that the car was repaired, carried briefcases or tools, and were seldom found in the house. The illustrations that accompanied these stories were, if possible, more stereotyped than the content.[4]

The 1970s saw some attempt to change this. Under pressure from teachers' associations and women's groups and backed by research findings, ministries of education listened to advice, established gender guidelines, and began to screen resource materials. The authorized curriculum materials began to improve. Unfortunately, teachers don't use only authorized resources, and it is extremely difficult and time consuming to detect all instances of sexist portrayal, even for those teachers committed to gender-free classrooms. One recent example of a resource kit for use in schools is "The Olympics and Playing Fair," developed by the Canadian Olympic Association (1989). Unfortunately, the use of males only in the logo, in almost all photographs and cartoons, and in the majority of case studies; the negative stereotyping of girls and women when they are represented; and the absence of material about drug-related problems applicable to girls and women suggest that the kit is seriously biased and, if used, will continue to reinforce negative stereotypes about girls in sport.

In *Claiming an education: Feminism and Canadian schools*, Gaskell et al. (1989, pp. 35–39) argue that the society portrayed by textbooks is stereotyped and that the texts reflect the fundamental reality of the sexual division of labour. They question whether textbooks can do otherwise: should they portray an ideal world or the world of children's experiences? A number of issues impinge on this discussion. Should schools support the status quo? Or are there moral reasons why educators should insist that their resource materials be non-sexist? The notion of equity as a fundamental value of Canadian society must be addressed. Gaskell et al. (1989) conclude that in the hands of skilful, sensitive teachers, non-sexist textbooks that portray both traditional and progressive lifestyles may help the child relate to the world at hand and perceive a range of possibilities. The difficulty is that teachers are not always sensitive to gender issues and the concerns of young women. In a Nova Scotia study (Day, 1990) young women identified attitudes of teachers as problematic:

> "I feel that girls are discriminated against a lot. Women students had trouble with male teacher, asked guidance counsellor for help; he told them they were wrong." (p. 51)
>
> "A surprising number of male teachers made sexist remarks about women (women drivers, women in sports . . .).'' (p. 51)
>
> "A lot of Cape Breton boys and men have very chauvinistic views concerning women (girls) and like to treat girls as second class citizens." (p. 51)

On the other hand, the Canadian Advisory Council on the Status of Women survey of young women in Canada (Holmes & Silverman, 1992) reports that "an overwhelming majority of students of both sexes say young people have an equal opportunity to succeed in school . . . that only a small minority of young people are aware of inequality of opportunity for women" (p. 45). The survey indicates that an awareness of gender discrimination increases with age among young women but not young men (p. 46).

Should we be surprised that young women (and young men) are unaware of discriminatory values, attitudes, and organizational practices? From the earliest grades teachers organize (often unintentionally) classroom activities by gender. Line-ups, coatrooms/lockers, groupings in physical education class or in the playground are some examples. As Jenny Blain (1993) argues, "if the children want to be organized by gender, then many teachers will oblige" (p. 66). However, by failing to challenge the idea that boys and girls are different in ways that "extend beyond biology into friendships, behaviour, ability, aptitude and knowledge," sexism is reinforced (p. 64).

LANGUAGE AND CONTENT

In analyzing the curriculum, whether yesterday's or today's, it is not enough to look at course content, specific subjects, or the resources used to support the content. Also important is the hidden curriculum—the values, the message, and the socialization process that the school is expected to convey. The use of sexist language and the domination by boys of both classroom talk and teacher time are examples. Streaming girls into courses and programs that lead to job "ghettos" and upholding the objective values associated with math, science, and computer courses—values that according to Carol Gilligan (1982), are more characteristic of male than female thinking—are also part of the hidden message.

The use of male-exclusive language, Charol Shakeshaft (1986) acknowledges, is common among most educators and contributes to the male culture of the school. Studies of language demonstrate that "he," "him," "mankind," "chairman," "fireman," and so on, are coded by males and females to mean "male" only. Since these terms can be used in the generic sense as well as to refer exclusively to male populations, their use is, at the least, ambiguous. Shakeshaft continues: "Male exclusive language in the classroom relentlessly chips away at female self-esteem. If a girl always hears that 'he' means everyone, while 'she' means females only, that girl is learning that females are less important than males" (p. 501). Since, in these same classrooms, boys also receive more instructional attention than girls, and more praise and criticism, a double message is being delivered. Myra Sadker and David Sadker (1986) believe that students in the same classroom, with the same teacher, and studying the same material experience very different educational environments. Speaking of girls in U.S. schools, Sadker and Sadker ask: "What other group starts out ahead—in reading, in writing, and even in math—and 12 years later finds itself behind?" (p. 515). This is especially true in certain science subjects.

Knowledge of mathematics and the sciences, including computer science, is considered by most experts to be essential for all students in a global and technologically advanced economy. For some time, there has been concern over the low participation of girls in senior courses in these areas. Despite knowledge of the problem and heightened sensitivity for more than a decade, recent studies indicate there has not been much improvement. Results from the Second International Mathematics study conducted by International Educational Assessment (IEA), in which Ontario and British Columbia participated, confirm this (Robitaille & Garden, 1989). In the 50 countries participating in the study, all girls and boys were still studying mathematics at age 13. However, in both British Columbia and Ontario, girls constituted only 40 percent of the population of senior mathematics students (lower than in the United States, but higher than in England, Sweden, and Japan). A 1993 study in British Columbia (Gaskell et al.) notes that three times as many boys as girls take physics (1 in 25 girls) (p. 153). What we do not know, clearly, is why and when decisions to drop mathematics and physics are made and which girls are affected. The IEA study points out that most senior-high-school mathematics teachers are male — 80 percent in Ontario and 95 percent in British Columbia. Is the message to young women that mathematics is a male bastion in which they do not belong? Studies in the United States confirm that girls—even girls who do very well in mathematics—often lack confidence in their ability (Robitaille, 1989). A school atmosphere in which mathematics is deemed a male activity does not help improve the belief among girls that they can learn and perform well in that subject.

This issue of confidence has been documented in a study of Quebec girls and science programs conducted by Mura et al. (1987). In the study girls tended to think that the success they enjoyed in mathematics and science was more a result of effort than ability. The girls, their teachers, and their parents all assumed that girls had to work harder, reinforcing a long-held, popular belief that women have less ability than men in mathematics and in the physical and applied sciences that require advanced mathematics (pp. 133–50). The 1990 British Columbia Mathematics Assessment study, *Gender issues in student choices in mathematics and science*, identified three factors limiting the participation of girls in mathematics and physical science courses: problems of accessibility; narrow conceptualization of what constitutes mathematics and physical science courses; and the absence of gender as an issue in schools (p. 154).

The participation of girls and young women in computer science courses and, more generally, in using the computer is even lower than in mathematics/science. Betty Collis (1987) documents that this difference occurs from elementary grades through the senior classes, and becomes even more marked if extra-curricular activities are included. A lack of confidence, a popular belief that women have less ability, and the perceived irrelevance of computer knowledge are some factors. There is not much doubt that the great majority of computer teachers are male (often the mathematics teacher), that boys have been allowed to dominate the school computers, that the content of computer experiences has minimized or ignored the central use of language and communication, and that girls go through school feeling inadequate and not appreciating the need for computer knowledge for participation in a technologically dominant society (pp. 117–32).

The re-emergence in the 1960s and 1970s of a feminist movement has resulted in women's studies programs, in research that delves into women's experiences, and in publications directed to and about women. In a field like history, for example, enquiry into such non-traditional areas as the family, the life cycle, sex roles, relations between the sexes, women in the labour market, the lives of "great" women, and women in the traditional professions has been accepted as legitimate historical work. Women now have a sense of their past, of their struggles to achieve equality, of role models to follow, as well as an image of themselves as contributors in their own right to societal development. Unfortunately, very little of this scholarship is finding its way into history classrooms. The content of courses generally has not changed to include the relevant feminist research and literature of the last several decades (Bourne, 1989, p. 5). What is needed is not only course content that includes women, but also content that is caring, non-violent, ethical, humane, and relevant to the needs and concerns of girls and women as well as boys and men. Effort must be made to include in the curriculum and associated resource materials information and analyses based on current feminist research. The male dominance of the curriculum must change to give young women, as well as young men, a fair perspective of a just society for all. Social changes in the last half of this century include changes in the roles of women and men, career expectations, family life, and technology. These cannot be ignored by our educational system and must be addressed by changes to the curriculum, both overt and hidden, and to administrative practices.

WOMEN AND OPPORTUNITY

RHETORIC AND REALITY

From the beginnings of the Canadian educational system, women have had legal access to the same educational opportunities as men. Girls were welcomed to school, and indeed were bound by the same compulsory education laws as boys. For the most part, they were in the same classrooms taking the same courses. Access to postsecondary education, normal schools, technical institutes, agricultural colleges, and universities was available to women as well as men. There was no legislation that prevented women from becoming high-school teachers or administrators, from being on the executive of the teachers' federation, or from taking positions in the ministry of education. Nor was it written down that women must receive a lower salary or second-class certification, or be restricted to teaching in the elementary classroom. Once the franchise was extended to women, they could, theoretically, get elected to the legislature and even become minister of education; they could be school trustees and serve on the executive or board of the trustees association; they could, in fact, be influential in the educational system. Women had equality with men. That is the rhetoric of educational history.

The reality was, and is, somewhat different. The attitude that promoted domestic-science courses; the timetabling that had domestic science conflict with physics or mathematics or Latin; and the textbooks that ignored women or portrayed them as silly, weak creatures in awe of their strong, knowing brothers or confined them to domestic activities—all of these were potent influences on the young girl. They delivered a subtle message that girls and women were certainly different (if not unequal), that they occupied different spheres in society, and that they should not aspire to the same positions and roles as men. This message was reinforced by the fact that fewer women than men taught in high school or faculties of education, and even fewer occupied administrative positions in the schools or in colleges and universities. Once the women became teachers, the message did not change.

Confined to elementary schools, paid a lower salary, and seldom placed on committees or made delegates, women teachers not only learned to live with this bias, but they often believed it and passed it on to their own students. It is important to remember that the different knowledges, prejudices, resistances, and beliefs that both teachers and pupils bring to the classroom affect the delivery of knowledge in the classroom. The curriculum, administrative practice, and gender roles in the school deliver a message of discrimination. The school's socialization role has reflected and continues to reflect societal practice, rather than the stated objectives and legal requirements of the educational system.

THE CANADIAN CHARTER OF RIGHTS AND FREEDOMS

The situation described above may be about to change. One interpretation of the Canadian Charter of Rights and Freedoms is that women must have not only equality of opportunity and of treatment, but equality of benefit as well. Manley-Casimir and Sussel (1987) acknowledge that section 15, on "equality," section 28, on "gender-equality," and section 27, on "multicultural affirmation," add "to the procedural protections of equality before and under the law, the substantive protection of equal protection and equal benefit of the law" (p. 178). In terms of education, what does this mean for women students, women teachers, and women administrators at all levels of the educational enterprise? What does it mean for the administration and curriculum of our schools?

Several recent court cases across the country relate to both employees and students in public schools, particularly on issues of sex-based discrimination and sexual harassment. Although these decisions take time and are open to interpretation, the Supreme Court of Canada has ruled in *Robichaud v. The Queen* (1987) that employers are liable for sexual harassment perpetrated by their employees, and in *Janzen v. Platy Enterprises Ltd.* (1989) that sexual harassment constitutes sexual discrimination.

Several recent incidents of allegations of sexual harassment have been brought by students and teachers. In *Harris and Reicker v. Her Majesty the Queen* (1991), a penalty of suspension without pay was imposed on a teacher who had written romantic poems, letters, an essay, and notes to a student, and the principal who had "overlooked" the incident was demoted from principal to teacher, and also suspended. In *Avalon North Integrated School Board v. the Newfoundland Teachers' Association* (1990), an arbitration award imposed a suspension on a principal for sexually harassing two members of his staff.

Although it is too early for a definitive interpretation, the Charter may indeed be saying that "affirmative action" to achieve equality may be acceptable and not against the Charter. A recent study (Brodsky & Day, 1989) suggests that this may be wishful thinking. In fact, women are initiating few cases and men are using the Charter to strike back at women's hard-won protections and benefits. It is argued that unless access to the courts becomes a reality, interpretations are made that positively affect women, and the courts are willing to listen and learn, the equality section will not benefit those for whom it was intended.

The use of affirmative action in the United States has invoked anger and derision in many circles, while gaining approval in others. There have been numerous lawsuits. It is not a phrase Canadians have been comfortable with, and we have chosen the term "employment equity" instead. Regardless of terminology, it is a policy that must be used carefully in education. Women confront structural barriers that prevent the recognition of their skills and knowledge in the workplace, despite the manner in which they are treated in acquiring them. Affirmative action to establish equal benefit must apply across society, as well as in the educational system, and it must be associated with a revaluing of work and of what society deems important. In opening up opportunities for women, we must be careful that traditional activities associated with women—mothering, elementary teaching, nursing, and clerical work—do not become devalued (Gaskell et al., 1989, pp. 69–72).

CREATING OPPORTUNITIES

In the meantime, as we work through the provisions of the Charter, opportunities for girls and women within our schools need to be stressed. While most Canadians are committed to a society based on equity, this will not be achieved unless the schools and the curriculum lead as well as reflect societal practice. Although parental attitudes and stereotyping in the wider society play an important role in creating inequality, the school seems to reinforce rather than challenge inequities (Whyte et al., 1985, p. xiv). How do we rectify this? Obvious practices are hiring teachers sensitive to inequity; recruiting, mentoring, and appointing women as administrators; and using gender-neutral textbooks and resource materials. But we need to go further, particularly if we want girls to have opportunities in higher education and in positions requiring a technical or scientific background. Here are a few suggestions:

- A science or mathematics club for girls only, to meet over the lunch hour or after school.
- Visits by female role models — women who are scientists, mathematicians, senior administrators, and women who have families.
- An emphasis in science on topics that are of interest to girls — such as nature, the environment, and medical science.
- The use of computer software that is not violent or sports-oriented.
- The promotion of the importance of and the provision of equal resources for girls' sports and extra-curricular activities.
- The use of gender-free language.

The 1990 BC Mathematics Assessment Study suggests four general principles to follow to encourage girls in math and physical sciences. They are appropriate for all subjects and grade levels:

1. Systematic and gender-sensitive strategies should be developed to attract girls to mathematics and physical science subjects.
2. Diverse and flexible strategies for attracting girls and boys to mathematics and physical science should be developed.
3. Gender-sensitive strategies should be developed on many levels.
4. Gender-sensitive strategies should be developed at all grade levels.

Many schools across the country are endeavouring to improve their practices, and a wide variety of plans to make schools less sexist have been attempted. The difficulty, however, is that educators do not always recognize sexist behaviour in themselves. Strategies for non-sexist teaching need to be continuous and an integral part of daily instruction. Being socialized in a society that undervalues women's work and working in schools that are organized upon and reflect this bias mean that teachers have a difficult role. *Progress revisited* (Canadian Teachers' Federation, 1993) quotes one teacher: "In the classroom I encourage female students to reach for careers of their own—not just something until they are married. I am always fighting for some cause for my students or me. Men administrators, men teachers, think status of women is to be ignored or a threat" (p. 51). Both women and men teachers need to overcome stereotypical attitudes toward all their students and present a classroom experience and an education that will enable them to participate equally in all aspects of the society. In the words of Marjorie Cohen, as quoted in a BCTF journal: "Real liberation is not merely the opportunity to choose between set alternatives. Freedom is a chance to formulate the available choices, to create alternatives from which we can choose" (Pedrini, 1987, p. 12). Such choices should be available to all—young women as well as young men.

CONCLUSIONS

This chapter has focussed on sexism in Canadian schools throughout this century. Despite a rhetoric of equality and the stated objectives and legal requirements of the educational system, girls and young women have not benefited to the same extent as boys and young men. Administrative structures and practices that favour males, curriculum and resource materials that ignore females, and teachers who consciously or unconsciously pay more attention to males and their needs have been factors in this inequality. The language, course content, and atmosphere of the school have delivered different messages. Those messages reflect societal practice. The question that must be considered is whether schools can and should lead society and instigate social change, or whether they are mirrors of society, inculcating in students the values and practices of society as it is.

The last several decades have witnessed numerous attempts to make the schools less sexist. The feminist movement of the 1960s, the Royal Commission on the Status of Women, status of women committees within teachers' associations, women's studies courses, and programs and research have heightened awareness of the plight of women, given women a history, and initiated plans and procedures for addressing inequality. Although there have been improvements—such as attempts at gender-free language; non-sexist curriculum and resource materials; proposals that enable girls to see the value of, and participate in, mathematics and science courses; and the recruitment of more female administrators—the fact is that schools are still classic cases of the division of labour by gender.

The Canadian Charter of Rights and Freedoms, specifically the sections on equality, gender equity, and multiculturalism, may be used to force the schools to provide "equal benefit" to all students. Should future Supreme Court of Canada interpretations uphold the notion of "equal protection and equal benefit of the law," affirmative action may be acceptable. Although it is difficult to know what the future holds for the feminist movement, the Canadian Charter of Rights and Freedoms suggests that progress will occur, albeit slowly—and occur it must. The difference between rhetoric and reality as it affects girls and women in our educational systems and institutions must be erased if we are to have a just society.

DISCUSSION QUESTIONS

- ❏ Reforms in education have been proposed by eliminating sexist discrimination and by ensuring that education for each sex is appropriate. For example, some argue that schools should be "single-sex." These ideas do not easily fit together, but where does the proper balance lie?

❏ Teachers are considered to be important to the development of a society where gender opportunity is substantially equal. What changes should be made in teacher education, recruitment, promotion, and job descriptions?

❏ Some recent changes within society have permitted women to interrupt their careers for childbearing. What further changes are necessary so that both parents can enjoy a meaningful and demanding career for either or both parents? How do these proposals affect education?

NOTES

1. The first two women elected to the legislature were Louise C. McKinney, president of the Alberta Women's Christian Temperance Union, and Roberta McAdams, serving as a lieutenant in the armed services in England; the judges were Emily Murphy, Edmonton, and Alice Jamieson, Calgary.
2. The five women were Henrietta Muir Edwards, Emily F. Murphy, Nellie L. McClung, Louise C. McKinney, and Irene Parlby.
3. For example, the Alexandra Readers Series consisted of five volumes. Published in several editions, they were the authorized readers in Alberta between 1908 and 1922. The Canadian Series was published in 1922 and authorized through 1935 in all three Prairie provinces. Like the Alexandra Series, it went through many editions.
4. This synthesis is taken from three series published in the 1940s: Canadian Parade Readers Series, Highroads to Reading Series, and Canadian Reading Development Series. All three series were authorized for use in a number of provinces.

REFERENCES

A Capella. (1990, November). *A report on the realities, concerns, expectations and barriers experienced by adolescent women in Canada.* Ottawa: Canadian Teachers' Federation.

Alberta Department of Education. (1914–18, 1929–33). *Annual reports.*

Avalon North Integrated School Board v. The Newfoundland Teachers' Association. (1990, April 25). Arbitration award.

Baker, M. (1985). *What will tomorrow bring? . . . A study of the aspirations of adolescent women.* Ottawa: Canadian Advisory Council on the Status of Women.

Bannerman, N. (1981). *What's past is prologue: A history of home economics in Alberta.* Calgary: Alberta Home Economics Association.

BC Ministry of Education. (1991). *Gender equity: Distribution of females and males in the British Columbia school system.*

Blain, Jenny. (1993, January/February). Gender in line: Some observations from an elementary school. *Our Schools/Our Selves, 4*(2).

Bourassa, K., Hare, J., Mitchell, E., Richards, V., & Stiles, M. (Eds.). (1975). *From slate pencil to instant ink: Calgary's public, separate and private schools.* Calgary. Century Calgary Publications.

Bourne, P. (1989). Introduction: Women's studies. *The History and Social Science Teacher, 25*(1).

British Columbia Mathematics Assessment. (1990). *Gender issues in student choices in Mathematics and Science.* Victoria, BC: Ministry of Education and Ministry Responsible for Multiculturalism and Human Rights.

British Columbia School Trustees' Association. (1992, January). *Gender equity policy development in British Columbia school districts.* Employee Relations Committee/ British Columbia Ministry of Education and Ministry Responsible for Multiculturalism and Human Rights.

British Columbia School Trustees' Association. (1992, September). Gender equity: The commitment to change. In *Shattering the glass ceiling: A policy resource manual focusing on gender equity in employment.* (pp. 24–59). Employee Relations Committee/British Columbia Ministry of Education and Ministry Responsible for Multiculturalism and Human Rights.

Brodsky, G., & Day, S. (1989). *Canadian Charter equality rights for women: One step forward or two steps back?* Ottawa: Canadian Advisory Council on the Status of Women.

Canadian Association for the Advancement of Women and Sport/Association canadienne pour l'avancement des femmes aux sports. (1990, March). *Action Bulletin 1990–9.*

Canadian Olympic Association. (1989). *The Olympics and playing fair.* Ottawa: The Canadian Olympic Association.

Canadian Teachers' Federation. (1993). *Progress revisited: The quality of (work)life of women teachers.* Ottawa.

Chalmers, J. (1968). *Teachers of the foothills province.* Toronto: University of Toronto Press.

Collis, B. (1987). Adolescent females and computers: Real and perceived barriers. In J. Gaskell & A. McLaren (Eds.). *Women and education: A Canadian perspective.* Calgary: Detselig.

Davis, J. (1990, September). The education of a feminist union leader. *Our Schools/Our Selves,* 2(3), 30–54.

Day, D. (1990). *Young women in Nova Scotia: A study of attitudes, behaviour and aspirations.* Halifax: Nova Scotia Advisory Council on the Status of Women.

Ellis, D. (1984). The schooling of girls. In H. Oliver, M. Holmes, & I. Winchester (Eds.). *The house that Ryerson built: Essays in education to mark Ontario's bicentennial.* Toronto: OISE Press.

Eyre, L. (1991). Gender relations in the classroom: A fresh look at coeducation. In J. Gaskell & A. McLaren (Eds.). *Women and education: A Canadian perspective.* (pp. 193-219). Calgary: Detselig.

French, D. (1968). *High button boot straps.* Toronto: Ryerson Press.

Gaskell, J., McLaren, A., & Novogrodsky, M. (1989). *Claiming an education: Feminism and Canadian schools.* Toronto: Our Schools/Our Selves Education Foundation and Garamond Press.

Gaskell, P.J., et al. (1993) *Gender issues in student choices in mathematics and science, A study for the 1990 British Columbia Mathematics Assessment.* Victoria: Province of British Columbia.

Gillett, M. (1981). *We walked very warily: A history of women at McGill.* Montreal: Eden Press Women's Publications.

Gilligan, C. (1982). *In a different voice.* Boston: Harvard University Press.

Grumet, M.R. (1988). *Bitter milk: Women and teaching.* Amherst, MA: The University of Massachusetts Press.

Harris & Reicker v. Her Majesty the Queen in Right of the Province of New Brunswick. (1991, January 23). Arbitration award.

Harris, R.S. (1976). *A history of higher education in Canada, 1663–1960.* Toronto and Buffalo: University of Toronto Press.

Holmes, J., & Silverman, E.L. (1992, March). *We're here, listen to us! A survey of young women in Canada.* Ottawa: Canadian Advisory Council on the Status of Women.

Howe, F. (1984). *Myths of coeducation: Selected essays, 1964–1983.* Bloomington: Indiana University Press.

Janzen v. Platy Enterprises Ltd. (1989). 59 D.L.R. (4th) 352

Khosla, P., King, L., & Read, L. (1979). *The unrecognized majority: A history of women teachers in British Columbia.* Vancouver: BC Teachers' Federation.

Lee, V.E., & Bryk, A.S. (1986). Effects of single-sex secondary schools on student achievement and attitudes. *Journal of Educational Psychology, 78*(5), 381.

Manley-Casimir, M., & Sussel, T. (1987). The chartered path: The new rights reality in Canadian society. In R. Ghosh & D. Ray (Eds.). *Social change and education in Canada.* (pp. 170–83). Toronto: Harcourt Brace Jovanovich.

Mura, R., Kimball, M., & Cloutier, R. (1987). Girls and science programs: Two steps forward, one step back. In J. Gaskell & A. McLaren (Eds.). *Women and education: A Canadian perspective.* Calgary: Detselig.

Patterson, R.S. (1979). Teacher education in Alberta. In D.C. Jones, N.M. Sheehan, & R.M. Stamp. (Eds.). *Shaping the schools of the Canadian west.* Calgary: Detselig.

Patterson, R.S. (1986). Voices from the past: The personal and professional struggle of rural school teachers. In N.M. Sheehan, J.D. Wilson, & D.C. Wilson (Eds.). *Schools in the west: Essays in Canadian educational history.* Calgary: Detselig.

Pedrini, L. (1987). Bill 10: A challenge to women. *Status of Women Journal.* Vancouver: BC Teachers' Federation.

Phillips, C.E. (1957). *The development of education in Canada.* Toronto: Gage.

Prentice, A., & Houston, S. (Eds.). (1975). *Family, school and society in nineteenth century Canada.* Toronto: Oxford University Press.

Ramsey, R.D. (1978). *The ATA as a Social Movement 1918–1936.* Master's thesis. University of Calgary.

Rees, R. (1990). *Women and men in education: A national survey of gender distribution in school systems.* Toronto: Canadian Education Association.

Robichaud v. The Queen. (1987). 40 D.L.R. (4th), 577.

Robitaille, D.F. (1989). *Canadian participation in the Second International Mathematics Study: A discussion paper for The Economic Council of Canada.* Vancouver: University of British Columbia.

Robitaille, D.F., & Garden, R.A. (Eds.). (1989). *The IEA study of Mathematics II: Contexts and outcomes of school mathematics.* Toronto: Pergamon Press.

Royal Commission on Industrial Training and Technical Education. (1913). Report of the Commissioners (Part 2). Ottawa: Minister of Supply and Services.

Royce, M.V. (1975, March). Arguments over the education of girls—Their admission to grammar schools in this province. *Ontario History, 67.*

Sadker, M., & Sadker, D. (1986). Sexism in the classroom: From grade school to graduate school. *Phi Delta Kappan, 67*(7).

Schneider, F.W., Coutts, L.M., & Starr, M.W. (1988). In favour of coeducation: The educational attitudes of students from coeducational and single-sex high schools. *Canadian Journal of Education, 13*(4), 479.

Secretary of State of Canada. (1989). *Profile of higher education in Canada 1988–1989.*
. Ottawa: Minister of Supply and Services.

Shakeshaft, C. (1986). A gender at risk. *Phi Delta Kappan, 67*(7).

Sheehan, N.M. (1979). Character training and the cultural heritage. An historical comparison of Canadian elementary readers. In G.S. Tomkins (Ed.). *The curriculum in Canada in historical perspective.* Vancouver: CSSE.

Sheehan, N.M. (1987). National issues and curriculum issues: Women and educational reform, 1900–1930. In J. Gaskell & A. McLaren (Eds.). *Women and education: A Canadian perspective.* Calgary: Detselig.

Smith, Laverne. (1991) The gender composition of the pool of prospective school principles. *Canadian Journal of Education, 16*(2), 198–205

Stamp, R.M. (1974). Adelaide Hoodless, champion of women's rights. In R.S. Patterson, J.W. Chalmers, & J.W. Friesen (Eds.). *Profiles of Canadian educators.* Toronto: D.C. Heath.

Stamp, R.M. (1975). *School days. A century of memories.* Calgary: McClelland and Stewart West.

Stamp, R.M. (1977). Teaching girls their "God given place in life": The introduction of home economics in the schools. *Atlantis, 2*(2).

Whyte, J., Deem, R., Kant, L., & Cruickshank, M. (Eds.) (1985). *Girl friendly schooling.* London: Methuen.

Wilson, J., Stamp, R.M., & Audet, L. (1970). *Canadian education: A history.* Scarborough, ON: Prentice-Hall.

FURTHER READINGS

Apple, M.W. (1986). *Teachers and texts: A political economy of class and gender relations in education.* New York: Routledge and Kegan Paul.

Arnot, M., & Weiner, G. (1987). *Gender and the politics of schooling.* London, Melbourne, Sydney, Auckland, Johannesburg: Century Hutchinson, The Open University Press.

Gaskell, J. (1992). *Gender matters from school to work.* Milton Keynes, UK: Open University Press.

Rury, J. L. (1991). *Education and women's work.* Albany, NY: State University of New York Press.

Strong-Boag, V. (1988). *The new day recalled: Lives of girls and women in English Canada, 1919–1939.* Markham, ON: Penguin.

Tyack, D., & Hansot, E. (1990). *Learning together: A history of coeducation in American public schools.* New Haven, CT: Yale University Press; New York: The Russell Sage Foundation.

23

To Keep the Fire Going: The Challenge for First Nations Education in the Year 2000

Jo-Ann Archibald

Walk in our moccasins
the trail of our past.
Live with us in the here and now.
Talk with us by the fires
of the days to come.
(Indians of Canada Pavilion, Expo 67)

While researching this paper, I found the above-reported message and spent a long time thinking about its meaning. At Expo 67, one hundred years after Canadian Confederation, First Nations peoples across Canada were publicly showing that our cultures had survived attempts by religious and governmental groups first to suppress and later to assimilate First Nations into dominant Canadian society. *To walk in our moccasins* is a gentle and powerful metaphor when used within a cultural context. It requires that one set aside, but not deny, values, assumptions, and beliefs, and try to place oneself in the other person's situation, to reach a new understanding of the other's worldview, and perhaps one's own. I wondered if our people had wanted others to begin a process of understanding our cultural ways and if others could "walk in our moccasins." Then I began to remember the words of my Elders who often said that the power and wealth of our people come from the strength of our culture: to increase *cultural power, wealth, and strength*, one must give it (culture) away by sharing it with others.[1] Then I understood why this national celebration of our cultures was conducted in the spirit of sharing, which is a common tradition and value among First Nations.[2] Sharing a culture in the First Nations way is a reciprocal process requiring time and the good will to listen, to teach, and learn, and to participate in essential cultural protocol and practice. When these essential conditions are lacking, the result is that our cultures are put on display to be glimpsed at, perhaps admired, perhaps ignored, and ultimately not appreciated for their social and educational value.

There are good reasons for including First Nations culture in the public school curriculum. Educational value can result from learning about our histories so that a better understanding of the history and development of Canada occurs. By learning about our technologies and the ways that we have come to know and preserve our environment, a broader understanding of science may result. Our traditional principles regarding the land could improve environmental education. Social value can result by debunking stereotypes of First Nations people and culture, and lessen racism in doing so.

One cannot deny the need to improve the social conditions and understanding among First Nations and other groups within Canadian society. Images of armed Mohawk warriors in face-to-face confrontation with armed Canadian soldiers, of Quebec citizens hurling stones at Mohawk citizens, and of First Nations rail and road blockades will be long remembered from the summer of 1990. These cogent actions of civil disobedience and militancy reinforce the need, as suggested in the new British Columbia Ministry of Education Mission Statement, to work toward "a healthy society and a prosperous and sustainable economy" (BC Ministry of Education, 1989a, p. 3).

In British Columbia, the decade of the 1990s will be marked by many actions concerning land claims, ranging from negotiations and litigation to civil disobedience and militancy. There are 197 bands (social and political units) throughout BC, and all potentially have some form of land claim.[3] The social and economic conditions of the province and people will obviously be affected by these actions. Perhaps it is timely that the BC Ministry of Education's proposals for sweeping educational reform of its schooling system advocate development of an educated citizen who will be "cooperative, principled and respectful of others regardless of differences" (BC Ministry of Education, 1990a, p. 10) and seemingly advocate the importance of learning about First Nations cultures to promote mutual understanding and social tolerance. This major schooling reform is referred to as the *Year 2000* and proposes major curricular changes in three areas: the Primary Program (the first four years of schooling—Kindergarten to Grade 3), the Intermediate Program (the middle seven years), and the Graduation Program (the final two years of high school).

This paper addresses four issues pertinent to First Nations cultural curriculum: (1) the need for a rich and full conception of "culture"; (2) emerging First Nations involvement in the curriculum; (3) some cautions in regard to how culture is brought into education in the *Year 2000*; and (4) the need to prepare teachers to adequately teach cultural curricula to "keep the fire going." The *Year 2000* documents' guiding principles and pedagogy for First Nations cultural curriculum will be examined in light of these four issues.

The following section identifies BC Ministry of Education prescriptions regarding First Nations and the curriculum.

FIRST NATIONS CULTURE IN THE YEAR 2000

The "guiding principles" section of the Primary Program Foundation Document (BC Ministry of Education, 1990a) contains a position statement on "Education of Native Children" that is supposed to identify and clarify pertinent issues and intentions of the Primary Program. According to this statement, the cultures of the First Nations are to be acknowledged for their distinctiveness and contributions; the skills, knowledge, and attitudes (based on their culture) of First Nations learners are to be affirmed and built upon;

and the involvement of parents and Native community members in curricular and support service activities is advocated:

> The Primary Program specifically honours the unique contribution of Native peoples to our thought, culture and way of life, and respects their wisdom in living in harmony with nature. . . . When Native peoples play an active role in developing curriculum and selecting resources, they are able to accurately reflect their society and history. . . . The Primary Program honours what Native children bring to school and builds upon their knowledge, weaving this into the fabric of the school culture. (BC Ministry of Education, 1990a, p. 34)

The Intermediate Program (BC Ministry of Education, 1990b) "Position Statement on Native Learners," which is included with the "Philosophy and Goals" section and is considered one of the "key aspects" of the program, echoes intents similar to the Primary Program:

> The curriculum will assist Native learners in retaining and strengthening their linguistic and cultural heritage by promoting the infusion of language and culture into regular curriculum, and providing for active involvement by Native peoples in the curriculum development process. Appropriate locally developed programs will be supported, and an accredited Native language program will be an acceptable alternative to French as a Second Language. . . . The contribution made by Native peoples to the social fabric of British Columbia will be promoted by the Intermediate Program, and it is expected that this will lead to increased respect and appreciation for Native peoples, as individuals, as communities, and as a unique and valued facet of multicultural society. (BC Ministry of Education, 1990b, p. 28)

In the Graduation Program (BC Ministry of Education, 1990c), information on "First Nations Learners" is placed in the "Special Issues" section and is not designated as a "key aspect" or considered part of the philosophy or guiding principles sections. Curriculum relevance and support services will promote "equal access to educational opportunities for First Nations learners" (BC Ministry of Education, 1990c, p. 61) so that their retention levels and graduation rates increase. One must wonder why equal access is even advocated. Shouldn't all learners have equal access to public education? However, curriculum relevance will be fostered by offering Native studies and Native language credit courses. Support services will require the involvement of a multitude of school, social service, and business groups along with First Nations parents and community. The social benefit of this cultural curriculum and proposed community–school collaboration on cultural awareness activities will extend to the general public:

> The value and contribution of Native cultures and languages will be promoted by the Graduation Program. This will enhance the appreciation and understanding of all members of the BC population. Native history and culture will occupy a more prominent place in the curriculum. Educational programs (including local programs) that promote awareness for all learners will be supported by Ministry. Structured awareness programs organized by districts, and the Ministry will provide insights into Native history, culture, and issues . . . Further, the awareness levels of teachers, students, parents, and community members concerning Native people and culture will be raised through preservice and in-service activities, summer institutes, and community school partnerships. (BC Ministry of Education, 1990c, p. 62)

The *Year 2000* foundation documents encourage goodwill and respect by recommending that all students have the time and opportunity to learn about First Nations cultures, and by using positive terms such as "honour and affirm" (BC Ministry of Education, 1990a, pp. 34–35), "value and contributions" (BC Ministry of Education, 1990b, p. 28), and "prominent place in curriculum" (BC Ministry of Education, 1990c, p. 62). Cultural accuracy and appropriateness are implied by recommending involvement of First Nations in the Ministry's curriculum and instructional framework.

To assess the adequacy of the *Year 2000* guidelines and pedagogy for First Nations cultural curricula we first require an understanding of how First Nations conceptualize culture and of the history of First Nations educational experiences. Our Elders say that we must know about our (trail of our) past—where we come from—in order to know who we are today so we can walk forward with strength and dignity.

FIRST NATIONS CONCEPTIONS OF CULTURE

> Stories, you see, are not just entertainment. Stories are power, They reflect the deepest, the most intimate perceptions, relationships, and attitudes of a people. Stories show how a people, a culture, thinks. (Keeshig-Tobias, 1990)

It is our tradition, first to patiently receive important teachings from master teachers and our ancestors, and then to think and reflect about their messages. From my experience I have learned to "listen hard" for the answers, which only become evident once an understanding is reached about the cultural context and forms of teaching (pedagogy) that are utilized. Some might characterize this way of knowing as indirect and roundabout; I prefer to characterize it as quite direct and cyclical in nature. What I mean should become evident in this paper. But first, we must listen to the stories and voices of our ancestors as they speak about their concepts of culture.

The late Chief Dan George of the Squamish Nation was a well-respected leader, orator, and teacher of our cultural ways. Some of his "talks" were recorded in his book, *My heart soars*. One of his talks about culture focussed on family unity and spiritual connectedness to nature:

> I was born into a culture that lived in communal houses. My grandfather's house was eighty feet long. It was called a smoke house, and it stood down by the beach along the inlet. All my grandfather's sons and their families lived in this large dwelling. . . . In houses like these, throughout the tribe, people learned to live with one another; learned to serve one another; learned to respect the rights of one another. And children shared the thoughts of the adult world and found themselves surrounded by aunts and uncles and cousins who loved them and did not threaten them. My father was born in such a house and learned from infancy how to love people and be at home with them.
>
> And beyond this acceptance of one another there was a deep respect for everything in nature that surrounded them. My father loved the earth and all it's [sic] creatures. The earth was his second mother. The earth and everything it contained was a gift from See-see-am . . . and the way to thank this great spirit was to use his gifts with respect. . . . This then was the culture I was born into. (1974, pp. 36–38)

The late George Clutesi of the Tse-shaht Nation said, "We must not confuse ourselves with the belief that Indian culture is confined within the narrow limits carving totem poles, masks and other like media" (1990, p. 135). Cultural artifacts only become significant if their utilitarian and symbolic functions are understood within social, spiritual, historical, and economic contexts. In response to the questions about where culture came from and how it came about, Clutesi responded:

> It is Native, indigenous. It is aboriginal.
> It belongs to the great coastal water of British Columbia,
> To its rivers, streams, cataracts, lakes and surging seas.
> It is part of the soil, the hills and great mountains,
> Of the majestic trees and also the reed in the swamp.
> The birds that flit over or rest neath a clump of grass
> Caress the buds of flowers or soar to the clouds in the sky.
>
> It is part of the weasel so small and also the massive sea lion,
> The seal so sleek and the lordly sea otter.
> It is part of the lumbering bear and the fierce timber-wolf
> That roamed the land since time began.
> It is part of the winds that may whisper now
> But later in a tempest can roar.
> Of the wavelets whispering on strands upon a rising time.
> The breakers that pound and pound the rugged shores.
>
> ... For it was from these, the wonders of nature
> That he sought for the subjects of his arts. (1990, pp. 136–37)

Tillie Gutierrez, a Sto:lo Elder,[4] teacher and storyteller, shared at an Elders' meeting two childhood experiences that show her cultural connectedness with the environment. Those who grew up listening to Sto:lo stories became accustomed to the transformative relationships among nature, the human and animal kingdoms, and the spirit world:

> My granny used to tell me about the cedar tree. That's what we used for our fire. When she gave me a washdown she'd burn the cedar tree. Then she used the branches to cleanse me; she'd cleanse me over with it. Cedar and water would wash my body inside and out. It would cleanse my spirit, too.
>
> Granny used to say: if demons get around you, you use the cedar tree and the branches to cleanse. Burn it. When it's burning, there's a crackling sound, and you scare the demons away. That was one practice that I can remember.
>
> As time went on, I learned about Xals (the Creator). I had two grandfathers who used to tell me about it. And my dad also: When Xals (the Creator) came through, He started His creation throughout our land. He used one of our grandfathers and created him into a cedar tree. And He said that the cedar tree was the one that was going to look after us, shelter us, and cleanse our spirits with it. (Gutierrez, 1982)

The cedar tree was held in high regard by the Sto:lo because it provided basic needs for everyday life and was also used for spiritual and aesthetic purposes. The reverence for and protection of the cedar tree was learned and emotionally felt at an early age as evidenced by Gutierrez's next story:

> You know, when I was very small, I saw some other people come to Katz Landing there. They started building all these chutes. They were sliding blocks of cedar.

> My heart cried. I was small, but I felt it. You know, even right now I feel like crying over it because I was unable to do anything about it. I was just standing there, watching all these cedar blocks coming down. It looks exciting all right. But I wasn't excited about it. I was brokenhearted, because of that cedar coming down. They were shipping them out somewhere, I don't know where, and making shingles and what have you, and right there and then my heart was already telling me that we were getting robbed. And there was nothing I could do. (Gutierrez, 1982)

Tillie Gutierrez was witnessing the introduction of the economic use of the cedar by "outsiders." She sensed that this use was not culturally correct, and felt that the taking of the cedar and the loss of respect toward it was like losing one of her family.

In 1984, the Gitksan and Wet'suwet'en Nations began their land claims case in the British Columbia Supreme Court. Their opening statement, "The Spirit in the Land," delineates their culture by describing the roles and responsibilities of the (extended family) members, identifying the source of their laws, and telling how their histories and knowledge are created and perpetuated. Notice how power and wealth are sustained:

> For us, the ownership of territory is a marriage of the Chief and the land. Each Chief has an ancestor who encountered and acknowledged the life of the land. From such encounters come power. The land, the plants, the animals and the people all have spirit— they all must be shown respect. That is the basis of our law.
>
> The Chief is responsible for ensuring that all the people in his House respect the spirit in the land and in all living things. ... My power is carried in my House's histories, songs, dances and crests. It is recreated at the Feast when the histories are told, the songs and dances performed, and the crests displayed. With the wealth that comes from respectful use of the territory, the House feeds the name of the Chief in the Feast Hall. In this way, the law, the Chief, the territory, and the Feast become one. ... Through the witnessing of all the histories, century after century, we have exercised our jurisdiction. (Gisday Wa and Delgam Uukw, 1989, pp. 7–8)[5]

The First Nations conceptions of culture emphasize the interrelatedness of humans and animals, nature, and the spirit world; the past, present, and future responsibilities of creating and perpetuating knowledge and values; and the oral way of creating and sustaining understanding. These could be considered essential elements or criteria of a concept of culture. Of course there could be more and different criteria. The important point is that the essential elements comprising the concept of culture need to be identified, so that appropriate curriculum can be developed.

INSTITUTIONAL SCHOOLING: FEDERAL GOVERNMENT INFLUENCE

The historical experience of how First Nations culture was perceived and treated within federal and provincial schooling systems shows what we don't want and what not to do. Through our experiences, we learn the "hard lessons," and consciously act so that previous mistakes will not happen again.

From 1850 to 1950, the majority of our children were schooled in separate educational systems administered by religious denominations and the federal government Department of Indian Affairs (DIA). The British North America Act, 1867 (now Constitution Act,

1867), section 91(24), designated the federal government with power and responsibility "for Indians and land reserved for Indians."

During this period, many children between 7 and 16 years of age were separated from their families and sent to industrial boarding/residential schools (for ten or more months every year), where policies of cultural and language suppression were enforced (Kirkness, 1981; Haig-Brown, 1988; Barman et al., 1986; Titley, 1986).

The assimilationist approach of the federal government is exemplified by Duncan Campbell Scott, an influential decision-maker for Indian Affairs between 1909 and 1932, who reported:

> The happiest future for the Indian race is the absorption into the general population, and this is the object of the policy of our government. The great forces of intermarriage and education will finally overcome the lingering traces of native custom and tradition. (Cited in Titley, 1986, p. 34)

It is ironic that intermarriage has resulted in a vast number of people retaining their cultural identity, as evidenced by Bill C-31, which, since 1985, has reinstated the legal First Nations status of approximately 136 512 people across Canada (DIA, 1990). Scott certainly underestimated the power of our genes!

First Nations leaders throughout BC have voiced their concerns about the negative effects of education upon their children, families, and communities. Children were returning home as strangers to the cultural ways, and critical of the family and community way of life. The late George Manuel recommended the residential schools for devastating the family unit and denigrating the students' culture:

> Our values were as confused and warped as our skills. The priests had taught us to respect them by whipping us until we did what we were told. Now we would not move unless we were threatened with a whip. We came home to relatives who had never struck a child in their lives. These people, our mothers and fathers, aunts and uncles and grandparents, failed to represent themselves as a threat, when that was the only thing we had been taught to understand. Worse than that, they spoke an uncivilised and savage language and were filled with superstitions. After a year spent learning to see and hear only what the priests and brothers wanted you to see and hear, even the people we loved came to look ugly. (Manuel & Posluns, 1974, p. 65)

Because of the detrimental effects of the residential schools, First Nations leaders and parents demanded that schools be established on their reserves. Day schools were later established on some reserves. These schools offered the basic subjects of reading, writing, arithmetic, and religion. Dissatisfaction with the quality and availability of curriculum resources, the lack of qualified teachers, and teachers' indifference to acknowledging the culture of their students is evident in community presentations to the McKenna-McBride Royal Commission on Indian Affairs and in petitions and letters to government officials (Archibald, 1984).

PUBLIC SCHOOL INTEGRATION: PROVINCIAL GOVERNMENT INFLUENCE

In 1951, a change in federal legislation of the Indian Act enabled provincial and federal governments to negotiate terms for the provinces to educate First Nations students, while

DIA maintained financial responsibility. The federal government's philosophy of school integration was that if Indian and Canadian children grew up together they would get along better as adults. Provincial school integration for First Nations meant that our children attended the public school and learned the same curriculum as everyone else and were treated "the same" as other children. This form of integration was really assimilation because the culture of the First Nations child was considered a barrier to the child's academic progress and had to be overcome:

> It is difficult to imagine how an Indian child attending an ordinary public school could develop anything but a negative self-image. First, there is nothing from his culture represented in the school or valued by it . . . one of the main aims of teachers expressed with reference to Indians is "to help them improve their standard of living, or their general lot, or themselves," which is another way of saying that what they are and have now is not good enough; they must do and be other things. (Hawthorn, 1967, p. 142)

I attended an "ordinary" public school and I remember the feelings of displacement; I remember the awkward feelings of being different because I was an Indian. This awkwardness occurred because others did not understand or appreciate my cultural difference, and I did not know how to tell them. I dreaded the social studies and history lessons where we read about Indians.

Until the mid-1970s, if First Nations cultures were addressed in school curriculum, it was mainly through history textbooks. Harro Van Brummelen's (1986) review of textbooks used in BC public schools between 1872 and 1925 reveals the portrayal of "Indians . . . as cruel and revengeful, spending their time gambling, smoking and feasting . . . pictures made native people look backward at best, brutal and savage at worst" (pp. 28–29). Even though BC Native people were generally described as "friendly," their totem poles were described as "rude, imperfect monuments" (p. 28).

McDiarmid and Pratt's (1971) examination of textbooks used in Ontario and Manitoba during the mid-1960s indicates that the image of First Nations was still negative:[6]

> The main feature of the textbooks under review is their tendency to treat the Native as an impediment to be removed so that the goals of European progress can be realized. After dealing with this conflict, the authors ignore the later history of native people. (Manitoba Indian Brotherhood, 1974, p. iii)

In 1977, Walter Werner and associates completed a national study, *Whose culture? Whose heritage?*, which examined multicultural content of social studies curricula prescribed for elementary and secondary schools. Werner's team found that local community involvement from ethnic groups was not encouraged—curriculum was developed as a product by experts outside the culture. Images of First Nations were either romanticized or stereotyped. Information on their cultures consisted of bizarre, disjointed facts which, in effect, trivialized, objectified, and therefore dehumanized First Nations. The following information was taken from a Grade 3 curriculum:

- the Native Indian is not dirty, alcoholic, or lazy by nature
- they had high standards of personal hygiene
- they were very conscious of their personal appearance
- women were respected and often given more authority than the men
- they did not work for work's sake but did work hard and were capable of extreme endurance when there was work to be done

- they were highly intelligent and ingenious in accommodating and modifying new ideas and materials to their needs
- they had mental telepathy as a form of communication because it was possible in a culture unhindered by materialism
- they have generally been successfully integrated into present day society, and dirt and diseases are lessening as they are learning hygiene
- many Indian children own very few manufactured toys, but find sticks, tin cans, stones and old tires which are of little value to them and are readily replaceable; as he tires of his toy such as an old tire, he will leave it along the road for someone else to play with, for there is little individual ownership of toys. (Werner et al., 1977, p. 26)

This brief historical overview indicates that First Nations culture was not considered of social or educational value, and therefore was not considered worthy for inclusion in school curriculum or, if it was included in curriculum, was done very poorly. The content and pedagogy was of a "piecemeal" nature and tended to reinforce or create misguided "myths" about First Nations as evidenced by the Grade 3 curriculum example cited above. And teachers did not understand or were not prepared to teach about First Nations. Neither did First Nations people have any power to influence cultural curriculum.

After the mid-1970s, improvements in the quality of First Nations cultural curricula began to happen. These improvements ranged from gradual increases in the amount of school time designated for learning about First Nations, to a more accurate and positive portrayal of First Nations people and their culture, to increased involvement of First Nations in the curriculum process. Much of this change is attributed to the influence of the national Indian Control of Indian Education Policy (National Indian Brotherhood, 1972).

EMERGING FIRST NATIONS INVOLVEMENT IN CURRICULUM

The Indian Control of Indian Education Policy was created by the National Indian Brotherhood, a political organization, and accepted for implementation by the Department of Indian Affairs in 1973. The policy was in response to problems identified by First Nations provincial groups across Canada. Regarding cultural curriculum, the policy document recommended greater parental and community responsibility and administrative control; improved curricula with accurate and appropriate Native content and pedagogy; increased numbers of properly prepared First Nations teachers; and required cultural courses for non-Native teachers at the pre- and in-service levels (National Indian Brotherhood, 1972).

Throughout BC, numerous First Nations communities, organizations, and school districts have worked collaboratively on these recommendations with funding from the Ministry of Education and DIA (More, 1989). The collective action of First Nations groups who have assumed a role in the improvement of cultural curriculum, and in the *Year 2000* education reform process, demonstrates that our people will accept nothing less than Native control of our own education. In fact, this involvement shows that we are attempting to put into practice our cultural teachings on the need to take responsibility for one's life. However, the scope of our involvement and the extent of our power to do so regarding *Year 2000* initiatives are yet to be agreed upon.

The foundation documents state that active involvement of First Nations people in the curriculum process is important. I would say that our involvement is essential. The BC Ministry of Education's (1989a) *Policy directions* booklet states that "Policies will be developed to increase the participation of Indian communities in decision-making about education for Indian learners, and to assist in the preservation of Indian languages and culture through school programs" (p. 21). Rather than merely participate in the process, our people should take a leadership role regarding First Nations language and culture programs.

To live with us in the here and now implies and requires, among other things, respect, good will, co-operation and compatibility. Based on past experience, it appears that First Nations, Ministry of Education, and other public school stakeholders need to develop better ways to bring culture and education together—to live together.

The next section highlights some problems with the Ministry's guiding principles and pedagogy, and provides some recommendations for improvement.

BRINGING CULTURE INTO EDUCATION IN THE YEAR 2000: SOME CAUTIONS[7]

The "Guiding Principles" section of the BC Ministry of Education's (1990a) Primary Program document states:

> By affirming the cultures of their students, by honouring the wisdom of their elders, and by providing a variety of adult role models, teachers recognize, acknowledge and value the contributions of Native peoples to our society, and reinforce the children's culture by sharing and celebrating it with other children. (pp. 34–35)

Given what I have seen about the way First Nations culture has traditionally been interpreted in Canadian education, I have cause for some concern about the way that "culture" will be interpreted in the *Year 2000* documents. Adequate criteria and acceptable processes for developing the concept of First Nations culture are lacking in the documents. As suggested by the late George Clutesi, some teachers might define culture within the narrow limits of the dominant society's notion of "art and crafts." An example of an essential cultural criterion for the Sto:lo would be that mutualistic relationships among nature, the human and animal kingdoms, and the spirit world be recognized as fundamental to our way of knowing. Once essential criteria are determined, they become the basic elements of the concept of culture, and provide direction in selecting teaching approaches and curriculum resources. A teaching approach that would be culturally appropriate for the Sto:lo is the use of stories. However, teachers would need, first, to understand the story's form (structure) and know how to tell or share it in an appropriate context and, second, to prepare the learners so that each could acquire new understandings from listening to and thinking about the story's messages.

While intended to help teachers develop appropriate practice, the list of eleven instructional program planning considerations in the Primary Program Resource Document is too brief and general to be useful. As can be imagined from the sampling of considerations listed below, a piecemeal approach to teaching about First Nations cultures will most likely occur:

- establish two-way communication between the local Native community and school/ district personnel;
- make extensive use of the local Native culture/cultures throughout the curriculum, including methods of instruction, material, and instructors. Curriculum materials should reflect the cultures of the learners, and should be developed in concert with the local Native people. Materials and content which reflect the Native cultures need to be embedded in curriculum and integrated across content areas. Sharing information about traditional values, using Native craftspeople in the classroom, and inviting elders to share their stories are honouring the local community.
- reflect the cultures of the children by the use of photographs, art work, language and models of the cultures presented. (BC Ministry of Education, 1990e, pp. 133–34)

Certainly, inviting Elders to the classroom to tell stories is one way of honouring their wisdom and an appropriate cultural teaching method. In many of our cultural gatherings and in informal settings, Elders perform a significant teaching role through storytelling. However, when our stories have been improperly brought into a mainstream setting, such as the school, it is common that either their meaning has been misunderstood or their significance has gone unrecognized, resulting in the cultural lesson being denigrated to a "simple tale." I'll use a story to exemplify.

Barre Toelken (1979), an anthropologist, recounts his experience with a Navajo Elder, Little Wagon, whose grandson asked him where snow came from. Little Wagon told a story about an ancestor who found a beautiful burning material that he kept burning until the owners, the spirits, asked for it. The spirits wanted to reward the finder, but because the material was so precious they asked him to complete very difficult feats to test his endurance and worthiness. As his reward for successfully completing the feats, the spirits told him that each year when they cleaned house they would let the ashes swept from their fireplace fall into Montezuma Canyon. "Sometimes they fail to keep their word; but in all, they turn their attention toward us regularly, here in Montezuma Canyon" (p. 73). After a while the grandson asked why it snowed in another area. The grandfather told the boy that he would have to make his own story to answer that question. Much later, Little Wagon told Toelken that it was too bad that his grandson didn't understand stories. Toelken explains:

> I found by questioning him (Little Wagon) that he did not in fact consider it an etiological story, and did not in any way believe that that was the way snow originated; rather, if the story was about anything it was about moral values, about the deportment of a young protagonist whose actions showed a properly reciprocal relationship between himself and nature. In short, by seeing the story in terms of any categories I had been taught to recognize, I had missed the point; and so had our young visitor, a fact which Little Wagon at once attributed to the deadly influences of white schooling. (p. 73)

Another indication of a piecemeal approach is found in the "Integrated Studies" section of the Primary Program Resource Document, which shows how First Nations culture can be taught as part of a unit entitled "There's a Story in the Forest." This is the only example of teaching about First Nations culture provided in the document. The unit on the forests lists "People of the Forest: West Coast Native Culture" as one of thirteen topics. Some of the other topics include "Emily Carr Loved the Forest," "Forest Ecosystems," "Paul Bunyan," and "The Story of Lumbering." Only one teaching idea is suggested for the "West Coast Native Culture" topic: "invite resources people to demonstrate native cooking, weaving, basketmaking, etc." (BC Ministry of Education, 1990e, p. 328). Will teachers know how these activities relate to the forests and to West Coast First Nations?

Inviting the aforementioned resource people fulfils the guiding principle of exposing the children to adult role models, and if they are Elders, so much the better! This particular teaching activity also involves local community members and would result in displays that reflect the culture through artwork and, possibly, models. No doubt, the learning that arises from this integrated experience could be beneficial, and has been done many times. However, it results in superficial, unsatisfactory learning unless students understand the knowledge and beliefs that are inherent in the particular "craft," and its social, economic, educational, and aesthetic functions. A demonstration of basketmaking does not ensure that students will learn about the methods of collecting and preparing cedar roots without destroying the tree, or about the prayer of thankfulness and reverence offered to the cedar tree, or about the symbolic meaning and historic function of the designs on baskets.

Each First Nations cultural group has its own cultural protocols (social expectations and appropriate behaviour) for treating respected members of their community in formal contexts. Many of our Sto:lo Elders were hesitant about sharing their teachings in public school classrooms because they found that either teachers and students did not know how to listen and learn, or that they were "rude," or that they could not teach or share properly. Teachers and First Nations educators need to discuss with each other appropriate cultural protocols and practices that can be effectively implemented in both the formal classroom setting and the First Nations community.

The Intermediate Program and Graduation Program documents do not provide examples of how First Nations culture might be taught. Furthermore, if curricular integration is to be promoted, learning about the Gitksan and Wet'suwet'en feast system (as earlier described) would surely exemplify the "integrated nature of knowledge and the interconnected relationships that it between and among all things" (BC Ministry of Education, 1990b, p. 89).

Talk with us by the fires of the days to come. Our people have a rich conception of culture that can contribute to the understandings of all public school learners. First Nations children need to feel proud, not ashamed, of learning more about and sharing their cultures. However, these benefits can be achieved only if First Nations people are involved in meaningful ways throughout the curriculum processes, and if teachers are adequately prepared and willing to teach about First Nations cultures. First Nations involvement can extend to pre-service and in-service with universities and school districts. Herein lies a telling challenge. First Nations educators and community members must continue to develop educational resources that contain accurate information and culturally and educationally appropriate pedagogy. Our people need to remember, and to help others recognize, that when one speaks (learns) about First Nations culture it is we who are being studied and spoken about. We cannot become mere objects of history and contemporary issues! We must also remember that our traditional principles have been carefully handed down from generation to generation, and we have a responsibility to pass them on to those who come after us. In the days to come, our people will sit with those from the universities, school districts, and Ministry of Education to decide upon the best ways of transforming our cultural principles into current educational practice—of properly bringing together our culture and public school education. In the days to come, there will be room for more to join the circle, and then the fire will be kept going.

TO KEEP THE FIRE GOING

Many of our First Nations regard fire as a symbol of the power and core of our culture. It is the fire that helps us to survive by giving us warmth and comfort; to feed the fire is to feed ourselves; to keep the fire going is to keep our culture strong—to keep the land for the survival of future generations. To care for the fire is a sacred trust given to our people. Education can be the fuel to keep the fire burning. Teachers and parents have the serious responsibility of being the keepers of the fire.

I end this paper with a story told to me by my friend Thom Alcoze of the Cherokee Nation.

Creation had given the First Nations the gift of the land, to care for and to protect in return for their survival. She also taught them how to keep the fire going and said that she would check on them once in a while to ensure that they were doing their jobs properly. If the fire was going, she would know that they were also taking care of the land and themselves properly.

One day she decided to check on the keepers of the land. She could see no one by the fire and she could not even see footsteps on the earth to show that anyone had been by the fire to care for it. Eagle approached her for he could see that she was very sad and angry. Creation told him why and said that she was going to destroy the land because the people had broken their trust. Eagle begged her not to until he had searched throughout the land to see if he could find at least one fire surrounded by at least the footsteps of the keepers of the land to show that they were fulfilling their responsibilities. Creation agreed to give him until the first rays of sun appeared over the mountains the next day. If he was unsuccessful, she would destroy the land.

Eagle began his search and flew into the first light of dawn. Below him was the land of darkness. Eagle kept flying all over the land and could tell that the sun's rays were starting to creep closer to the mountains. Just as the rays were about to pass over the mountains, Eagle spotted a small fire. He could see footsteps leading to the fire and he could see a group of people, who were to become the new keepers of the land, standing around the fire.

DISCUSSION QUESTIONS

❑   The main theme that permeates this book is that assimilation and integration are no longer accepted and that participation is now the much-needed action to hold Canadian multicultural society together. How would you plan to integrate this theme into your future teaching?

❑   Tolerating other cultures often underlines the belief that one's own culture is superior to those cultures. How would one bridge tolerance and acceptance to participate fully in our multicultural society?

❑   Inviting different cultural groups to the classroom is one suggested method to promote understanding of our Canadian diversified cultures. Do you see any problems that may arise from this course of action, and if yes, what can be done to prevent the problems from happening?

❏   What would you do to ensure that presenting cultural artifacts not only brings about curiosity but also encourages learning, understanding, and accepting of the culture being presented?

NOTES

1. Wealth refers to honour, prestige, and respect attributed to people who follow cultural norms/values; it does not have a financial connotation.
2. First Nations refers to the aboriginal peoples of Canada. Other terms to be used in this paper include Native and Indian. Particular cultural examples will be mainly drawn from various First Nations in British Columbia. I will be using the collective voice of First Nations groups in this paper when referring to common cultural principles and practices. However, it must be noted that a "unitary" First Nations view has not been substantiated.
3. According to Helen Fisher, spokesperson for Indian Affairs, two-thirds of BC could be included in future Native land claims. Cited in the *Vancouver Sun*, Nov. 10, 1990.
4. The Sto:lo Nation cultural boundaries extend from Maple Ridge to Yale, BC.
5. The names of Gisday Wa and Delgam Uukw are not English names and therefore cannot be separated in the usual manner for citation.
6. It is assumed that BC used the same textbooks as Ontario during this time period.
7. Because of the diversity of Native Education educational provisions, it is difficult to generalize. It is easy to be lulled into a false sense of security by the substantial progress in arresting drop-out rates—even to an explosion of enrollment in higher education. Another hopeful sign is that more schools are being operated by bands. But Carl Urion (1993) worries that these changes may be enrollment or control changes that do not change the purpose or substance and that assimilation will continue.

REFERENCES

Archibald, J. (1984). *Locally developed native studies curriculum: An historical and philosophical rationale.* Unpublished Master's thesis. Vancouver: University of British Columbia.

Ashworth, M. (1979). *The forces which shaped them: A history of the education of minority group children in BC.* Vancouver: New Star Books.

Barman, J., Hebert, Y., & McCaskill, D. (Eds). (1986). *Indian education in Canada (Volume 1): The legacy.* Vancouver: University of British Columbia Press.

BC Ministry of Education. (1989a). *Policy directions: A response to the Sullivan Royal Commission on Education.* Vancouver: Province of British Columbia.

BC Ministry of Education. (1989b). *The primary program* (Response draft). Victoria: Province of British Columbia, Program Development.

BC Ministry of Education. (1990a). *The primary program* (Foundation document). Victoria: Province of British Columbia, Program Development.

BC Ministry of Education. (1990b). *The intermediate program: Learning in British Columbia* (Response draft). Victoria: Province of British Columbia, Program Development.

BC Ministry of Education. (1990c). *The graduation program* (Response draft). Victoria: Province of British Columbia, Program Development.

BC Ministry of Education. (1990d). *Year 2000: A framework for learning.* Victoria: Province of British Columbia, Program Development.

BC Ministry of Education. (1990e). *The primary program* (Resource document). Victoria: Province of British Columbia, Program Development.

Berthoff, A (1981). *The making of meaning: Metaphors, models and maxims for writing teachers*. New Jersey: Boynton/Cook.

Bowd, A., McDougall, D., & Yewchuk, C. (1982). Psychological perspectives on Native Education. In *Educational psychology: A Canadian perspective*. (pp. 276–95). Toronto: Gage Publishing.

Clutesi, G. (1990). *Stand tall, my son*. Victoria: Newport Bay.

Department of Indian Affairs (DIA). (1990). *Reinstatement of status information systems report: Entitlement status (S3–S4)*. Ottawa: Department of Indian Affairs, Membership Statistics.

Department of Indian Affairs and Northern Development. (1916). *The report of the Royal Commission on Indian Affairs for the province of British Columbia*. Victoria: Acme Press.

Geertz, C. (1973). *The interpretation of cultures*. New York: Basic Books.

George, (Chief) D., & Hirnschall, H. (1974). *My heart soars*. Surrey: Hancock House.

Gisday Wa and Delgam Uukw. (1989). *The spirit in the land*. Gabriola, BC: Reflections.

Gutierrez, T. (Speaker). (1982). *The teachings of the elders*. Sardis: Coqualeetza Education Training Centre.

Haig-Brown, C. (1988). *Resistance and renewal: Surviving the Indian residential school*. Vancouver: Tillicum Library.

Hawthorn, H. (1967). *A survey of contemporary Indians in Canada (Volume II)*. Ottawa: Queen's Printer.

Joint Committee of the Senate and the House of Commons on Indian Affairs. (1961). *Final Report: Education and development of human resources*, pp. 610–11.

Keeshig-Tobias, L. (1990, January 26). Stop stealing native stories. *The Globe and Mail*.

Kirkness, V. (1981). The education of Canadian Indian children. *Child Welfare*, 9(7), 447–55.

McDiarmid, G., & Pratt, D. (1971). *Teaching prejudice*. Toronto: Ontario Institute for Studies in Education.

Manitoba Indian Brotherhood. (1974). *The shocking truth about Indians in textbooks: Textbook evaluation*. Winnipeg: Manitoba Indian Brotherhood.

Manuel, G., & Posluns, M. (1974). *The fourth world: An Indian reality*. Toronto: Collier Macmillan.

More, A. (Ed.). (1989). *Native Indian education projects and programs in BC schools*, rev. ed. Victoria: Ministry of Education, Native Indian Education Branch.

National Indian Brotherhood. (1972). *Indian control of Indian education*. Policy paper presented to the Ministry of Indian Affairs and Northern Development. Ottawa: National Indian Brotherhood.

Parminter, A (1959). *The development of integrated schooling for British Columbia Indian children*. Unpublished Master's thesis. Vancouver: University of British Columbia.

Peterson, L. R. (1959). *Indian education in British Columbia*. Unpublished Master's thesis. Vancouver: University of British Columbia.

Petrone, P. (1990). *Native literature in Canada: From the oral tradition to the present*. Toronto: Oxford University Press.

Sealth (Chief) and His People. (1975). Seattle: United Indian of all tribes

Sheehan, N., Wilson, J.D., & Jones, D. (Eds). (1986). *Schools in the West: Essays in Canadian educational history*. Calgary: Detselig.

Titley, E.B. (1986). *A narrow vision: Duncan Campbell Scott and the administration of Indian Affairs in Canada.* Vancouver: University of British Columbia Press.

Toelken, B. (1979). *The dynamics of folklore.* Boston: Houghton Mifflin.

Tomkins, G.S. (Ed.). (1979). *The curriculum in Canada in historical perspective: Sixth Yearbook 1979.* Vancouver: Canadian Society for the Study of Education.

Tomkins, G. (1986). *A common countenance: Stability and change in the Canadian curriculum.* Scarborough, ON: Prentice-Hall.

Urion, Carl. (1993). First Nations schooling. In L.L. Stewin & S.J.H. McCann. *Contemporary educational issues: The Canadian mosaic*, second edition. (pp. 97–107). Toronto: Copp Clark Pitman.

Van Brummelen, H. (1986). Shifting perspectives: Early British Columbia textbooks from 1872 to 1925. In N. Sheehan, J.D.Wilson, & D. Jones (Eds.). *Schools in the West: Essays in Canadian educational history.* Calgary: Detselig.

Werner, W., Connors, B., Aoki, T., & Dahlie, J. (1977). *Whose culture? Whose heritage?: Ethnicity within Canadian Social Studies curricula.* Vancouver: University of British Columbia, Centre for the Study of Curriculum and Instruction.

Wilson, J.D., & Jones, D. (Eds.). (1980). *Schooling and society in twentieth century British Columbia.* Calgary: Detselig.

FURTHER READINGS

Dickason, O.P. (1992). *Canada First Nations: A history of founding peoples from earliest times.* Toronto: McClelland and Stewart.

National Indian Brotherhood. (1972). *Indian control of Indian education.* Ottawa: Author.

Snow, Chief John. (1977). *These mountains are our sacred places: The story of the Stoney Indians.* Toronto: Samuel Stevens.

Zaharia, F. (Ed.). (1992). *First Nations freedom: A curriculum of choice (alcohol, drugs, and substance prevention) K–8.* Vancouver: University of British Columbia, Mokakit, First Nations House of Learning.

24

CONTEXT, POLICIES, AND RIGHTS IN CANADIAN EDUCATION

Robert F. Lawson

The major sections of this book deal with context, policies, and rights. No three terms could better frame the study of education in contemporary societies. I shall base this concluding chapter on these concepts as they apply to the conservation and change of Canadian institutions. This suggests that formal education—its curricular centre, its institutional form, its transmission of values, its authority structure—is a product of society, and that its task is to promote both individual and social interests as though these are concentric. It also suggests that there is a tight connection between theory and practice, sometimes symbolized by the term *praxis*. Although this summary necessarily points you toward the theoretical or critical side, the practical questions should never be out of mind. The quickest way to test a general, abstract, or theoretical statement is to ask whether it usefully informs your professional life, whether it rings true against your life experiences generally, and whether it may serve as an idea around which other ideas can cluster. The practice of work, in our case of study and teaching, should be continually informed by thinking critically about that practice and understanding it conceptually—ultimately as theory.[1]

Throughout this book are examples of theoretical positions or inferences that may, on the one hand, illuminate the link between theory and specific information or, on the other, lead you to question the basis of a particular statement. Such statements embody an abstraction of history, of values concerning political process, of social organization, of the very concept of Canada. They become the often unwritten and unspoken principles on which educational arguments and finally decisions are made.

Out of the countless examples from previous chapters, a few questions will illustrate the many you might ask about theoretical linkage.

References to the inadequacy of equality measures suggest a standard and a change articulated but not yet realized. (See Ghosh.) How are institutions rationalized before and after such a change? What is the standard for equality of access, of outcome—i.e., how do you know when you've reached it? (See Lessard.)

Do the generalizations regarding stability and change (see Young), structural rigidity, pragmatism hold for other societies you are familiar with? How can Canada's history be described in terms of these characteristics?

How political is the process by which educational decisions are made? How is political choice for education distributed among policy-making groups, cultural professionals, and the general public? (See Poonwassie.) In a loosely coupled organization for policy-making, whose ideology finally prevails? Why do Canadian schools in the respective provinces have the curricula they do? What are legitimate grounds for criticism? (See Werner.) How has the curriculum, and authority for it, changed over the century? Can decision-making and practice be dichotomized? (See Eisner [1993], quoted in Werner.) Is there an essential difference between teaching and socialization practices that emphasize knowledge first, understandings and disposition first, or "doing" first? (See Esbensen, Magsino.)

Is there any problem with the coherence of a social formulation based on diversity, an economic formulation based on competition, and a political formulation based on equality? How would you refine and interpret the previous statement? What does unity mean in Canada?

CONTEXT

The context is Canada. In the spirit of Canadian history, educational history has drawn principles from an evolutionary construct and has relied on external influences—British and French culturally, the United States sociopolitically and technologically—to describe the foundations of the system(s). While useful in some ways, such attribution has failed to account adequately for specific educational initiatives in the provinces, for their source in the Canadian social environment and their effects in Canadian communities, and for contemporary changes in the beliefs that determine institutional behaviour. In turn, the institutions are continually modified by immediately pragmatic approaches to the administration of education, by local characteristics, and by contests among groups seeking influence over public education.

This only means that education and its social environment are unique to Canada, and further to Canadian localities. While it is often tempting to rely on big news elsewhere—changes in American law or in the European community organization, for instance—as impinging directly on Canadian institutions, such events are at best informative. Major political developments (e.g., the Anglo-American ideology of neoconservatism, addressed in Livingstone and Hart's chapter) may or may not be relevant to Canada, but are never immediately translatable to educational policy. Characteristics distinguishing modern Canada—"participatory democratic self-rule within the deep diversity of decentralized political cultures" (Charles Taylor, quoted in Livingstone and Hart) — are useful for characterizing the Canadian political premise, but still need particular interpretation for use as curriculum content or educational policy principle.

Preceding chapters have detailed particular changes that result in the Canadian context of today. These may be summarized as changes of belief, demographic changes, and changes in the institution of education itself.

Changes of belief refers to a change in our public attitude, in laws and policy statements, which may be a substantial elaboration of principles held historically but considered not to have been realized—for example, ethnic and gender equality (see Sheehan).

Demographic changes have been described particularly by Young. The effects of shifts in immigration source and emigration level and the change in urban demography have effects far beyond the visible. Not only are the city electorates increasingly distanced from those in rural areas, but regional differences are exaggerated rather than reduced. Note the breakdown categories frequently used for Canadian information: Ontario and Quebec; the

West and the Atlantic provinces; or Toronto, Montreal, and Vancouver and the rest of the cities (see McAndrew, Livingstone and Hart). As for the one real unifying Canadian characteristic and allegiance—this vast, formidable, largely frozen northern land—what does that now mean to the children growing up in the urban corridor close to the U.S. border?

Change in the institution of education includes the response of educational administration to democratic challenges from the public and from special groups, mainly toward openness of information and participation. Although authors in this book characterize the public's attitude toward Canadian education differently—i.e., the public has faith in education (see Ghosh); the public has lost confidence in education (Livingstone and Hart); education is still paternalistic, but the people like it (see Esbensen)—these differences can probably be summed up as greater scepticism about public institutions generally, leading to higher expectations for accountability in both the conduct and delivery of the system.

The change includes the educational ramifications of section 15 of the Charter of Rights and Freedoms and the more general mandate for educational access and content to address that equality now guaranteed by law to all citizens. Although there is no doubt as to the direction of change and its permeation of educational discourse, there is disagreement about its reach and efficacy in schools, and about what its reach and force should be. There is also theoretical confusion as to the utility of the Quebec alternative in the Canadian multicultural case. The differences between the situation of francophone Canadians in Quebec education and in anglophone or francophone systems elsewhere vary so substantially from that of the recent immigrant populations that their common analytic treatment is suspect. Finally, the use of multiculturalism as a panacea for stubborn school or curriculum problems veils the seriousness of those problems and compromises the multicultural mandate. There is very little agreement about the "new curriculum" in any case.

Perhaps the most significant structural change in the educational system is the attempt to extend the provision of education, particularly now to older learners. While the remarkable distinction is still made in the education system between the "school" and other forms of education, adult education has grown in response to the needs of urban citizens and Native Canadians in remote areas. New on the scene is the provision in many forms (formal classes, informal groups, political action, Elderhostels, clinics) for elderly learners. This "third age" education promises some creative solutions for reaching those educationally excluded or with unusual learning needs (see Lawson, 1992; Fry, 1989).

POLICIES

Historically and constitutionally, the provinces have complete control of and responsibility for education, except in matters pertaining to denominational rights and privileges, recognized by law in 1867. The policy implications of this distribution of power are probably more significant than those of any other legal or structural provision. Schools are reserved to the provinces as political organizations of Canadian culture(s). Together they represent politically the principle of social-religious-ethnic diversity fundamental to Canadian democracy.

Provincial differences in educational provision are basically attributable to accommodations for denominational schooling and language, and, to a limited extent, to the wealth of each province, although variations in structure and curricular detail are abundant. Not only is provincial financing proportionately larger than municipal and federal expenditures for education, but, since provincial treasuries channel much of the federal funding and provide for tax equalization, financial control has increased both the legal and functional powers of the provincial governments. Elections, commissions, and advisory committees provide for "input democracy" and for a democratic sanction, but they do not ensure public participation in such a way as to alter essentially the control pattern of provincial bureaucracies. (See O'Reilly's discussion of how the centre of policy-making for education shifted to a coalition of senior educational officials, as well as his reference to OECD, 1976.) Provincial and local administrators tend to make decisions based on their perception of what legislation and public opinion will allow.

Where authority is dispersed or disputed, and where teachers, through their professional associations, act directly in the policy process, there may be conflict among teachers, administrators, and local boards on specific issues, but general public debate is likely to be minimal. The general support the system and educators enjoy makes consultation and compromise the procedures of change; that is, it would be highly unlikely that an educational policy that promoted a radical departure from perceived educational practice would be accepted willingly by Canadian educators and the public. Even in areas of considerable controversy, such as language policy, policy-makers at all levels attempt to develop as wide a consensus as possible.

Canadian politicians have concentrated on preserving a rather delicate balance of interests among the provinces and among the major religious and ethnic groups. This has had the effect of reinforcing a conservative tendency in which innovative policies are seen as threatening the loose bond of agreement. Thus, it becomes very difficult to disturb the power arrangements that exist within Canadian society. Both politicians and institutional leaders tend to emphasize the administrative and bureaucratic forms that allow them to operate beyond the interest of their own group in ostensibly neutral terms. It remains to be seen whether O'Reilly's prediction of increasing political and interest-group diversity means simply that the bureaucracy will intensify its tendency to neutralize or override, or that at least some of those interests that have sought influence will be not only heard but negotiated with.

The unspoken but intentional exclusion of unofficial actors occurs directly as a result of this political norm, but also indirectly as a result of several social phenomena, which include the rapid industrial and urban growth in Canada over the last 40 years (increasing the tension between modern technocracy and remnants of rural attitudes about society and education), particularistic and social-class differences among the public, and the obvious self-interest of the most vocal groups. Expressions from the public on educational issues may be so unrepresentative or fragmented as to defy comprehensive planning in the interest of the community as a whole. The encouragement of public participation by some educational and political leaders is viewed as futile by many planners. The resultant suspicion on the part of the public that the processes are meaningless or even deceptive is as likely to create attitudes adverse to participation as to develop social support. It appears that the Canadian public has only a negative capability in policy influence. I agree here with the conclusions of Esbensen and Livingstone and Hart, among others in this volume, on the inefficacy generally of Canadian public participation in educational decision-making. However, both the *inference* from surveys that the public are content with such impotence, and the attribution of cause to a conspiratorial elite are questionable. Policy decisions finally rest on professional compromise and enough public acceptability to preclude outright resistance. It might be suggested generally that official actors gain influence where there is so deep and general a disagreement as to render open and active public participation a threat to social order.

In practice this means that when government accepts the responsibility to initiate change toward equalization of opportunity, or any of its correlates such as improvement of instructional technology, redesign of curriculum, or accessibility of postsecondary education, it will use the rhetoric of participation, but will ultimately use its bureaucratic mechanisms to close decisions.

Educational policy offering greater educational opportunity and greater individualization of programs has been brought about largely by the removal of constraints that formerly assured socialization, social selection, and cognitive development through the general education system, with results favourable to the existing order of society. The control exercised by traditional elites, either directly through educational selection and occupational recruitment or indirectly through public acceptance of the primacy of certain schools and learnings, has been contested. The weakening of educational constraints has not affected the "distribution" of power in the educational establishment. On the contrary, it is likely to be reinforced in such a transitional situation. However, the cultural monopoly of certain groups in the society has been threatened, and the exclusive rights and powers of those persons and institutions in education claiming preferred cultural or political status has been challenged.

EQUITY

It is of central importance for students of education to attempt to understand fully the social and educational consequences of democratic principles applied to education. The implementation of democratic principles requires substantial institutional change as well as normative changes in social or political behaviour. Democratic emphasis on diversity and openness has already exposed fundamental problems of authority, economy, content, and the unity of the education system itself. These problems result from ideological as well as practical challenges, and their solution requires the efforts of a creative leadership. Educational policy-makers have tended to respond to the new dilemmas of democracy by compromising, with various publics on substance, with each other on the organization and conduct of schooling.

In the Canadian model, equity policies result in acceptance of more categories (women, cultural minorities, people with disabilities) both officially and in social interaction, but always on neutralized meritocratic and authoritative terms. This means that gender and racial balance can be affected over time. Any shift is not likely to change the rules, or to affect inequality as a characteristic of the system; that is, inclusion of new social categories reduces discrimination based on those categories (e.g., race)—it does not alter automatically the inequality inherent in a privilege system.

Ghosh, in the introductory chapter, has detailed the social, demographic, and policy background against which educational decisions on equality and human rights in Canada are made. Almost every chapter in the book includes discussion of such issues, and for many chapters they are central. In fact, one could say that all educational discussions today hinge on equity issues, and the refinement of our understanding of those is refashioning our definition of democratic education. We are far from agreement, however. Neither the generalized extremism nor the uncoupled action on isolated school practices have brought us yet to the synthesis of institutional norms and organization, teacher and student behaviours, curriculum content, and authority structure that would signal a social resolution of the political problems (Lawson & Ghosh, 1986).

You might want to try detailing the changes in each of the above dimensions of education that might bring us closer to our multicultural ideals, testing your suggestions as to compatibility, practicality, and obstacles to implementation.

Comparatively, education's role in equity provision is mildly favourable, following Canadian political philosophy as that might be inferred from history and external affairs. Intellectual discussion is at once enlightened, pragmatic, and as open as one could expect. That, together with the actual interest arising out of Canada's well-advertised involvement in the Third World, and response to pressures and spokespeople from these countries lead to changes in education that appear to be in keeping with the times.

Because of the relative autonomy of institutions, education's reciprocal effect in the society is weak and its relationship to social policy generally not influential. Sensitivity to equity questions can be said to characterize Canadian education however, and schools have activated equity values through behaviour and content instruction—possibly more for race than gender, certainly more for both than for disabilities, personality difference, or poverty.

There are two matters that seem to me to be of overpowering importance in these discussions. One is only tangentially articulated in the book: the confrontation of race with class, in the scholarly literature, in the public debate, and in professional practice. One of the differences between American and Canadian multiculturalism is that in the United States multiculturalism is defined by race, primarily African-American, and secondarily by gender. Social class is now treated as a subset, a concomitant condition or effect of race or gender. Marxism dies at the hands of those who practised it. The danger in this is the assumption of intractability; that is, that divisions among people are genetically fixed, which effectively removes the problem from educational amelioration. Perhaps our elevation of this problem of nature (biological and social) should give way to the less dramatic but possibly more effective role of education to promote the political construction for a social mix (see *Time*, 1993). As John Higham (1993) has put it, "race and ethnicity do not always confer desirable identities; nor are these identities unalterable, uncontested, or monolithic . . . individuals renegotiate the loyalties they must choose among, or alter the dimensions of a predominant identity that begins to pinch. An effective civic education should widen instead of narrow the options that people can entertain."

The other matter *is* articulated in the book, by Jo-Ann Archibald. I have labelled it in my notes, "Archibald's wisdom," which in her article is the wisdom of her culture. I highlight this in summary here for reasons of both particularity and universality, of knowledge and beauty, of life and spirit. Given the interrelatedness of time, life, and ideas in the First Nations culture, it is not surprising that these concepts are linked in ways that once characterized cultures absorbed into the industrial organization of developed economies. What has been carefully preserved and handed down orally in that culture are the stories that quietly, pervasively empower the culture through their immanence in the thinking and feeling of individual members. That cultural education is, then, both collective and individual in its transmission and its effect. The stories represent beauty, knowledge, and power; they belong to the culture, but they may enrich others, and they represent, among other characteristics, what new methodologies are trying to recover generally: subjective, aesthetic, historically valid ways of knowing and teaching. When any culture gives up its right to its own historical property, when it loses its relationship to others in the universe of cultures, it is impoverished.

What does the experience of First Nations people tell us about cultural loss in Canadian education? Perhaps that our stories are as important as our science; that our elders are a source of knowledge not replaceable by institutional storage systems; that we, together with our forefathers, are the subjects of a continuing history. Archibald reminds us finally of the powerful simplicity of Indian ways of negotiating cultural transmission. The suggestion that the people need to "sit with" the educationists seems to cut through the new complicated, intellectualized, technical formulations of multicultural education.

CANADA

Why does this book speak to the interests of teachers outside Canada? For both sociopolitical and educational reasons. Canada has an experience with "difference" that few countries can match. Not only did the Canadian nation historically maintain peaceably the existence of the two charter European cultures, its politicians had to balance the cultural heritage with a North American environment increasingly distant from that heritage. The Canadian frontier moved westward and northward with an economic colonialism typical of the time, but with a relatively benign political force. The principle of accommodating later European groups extended to the waves of Asian and Caribbean immigrants after 1971. In all cases, Canadian identity was socially subordinate to the regional articulation of ethnic rights. As problematic as this has been for nation-building and for clarity of institutional policy, it means that the Canadian experience with diversity as a political principle and policy process is older and more extensive than that of probably any other country. What the variables of the Canadian context are, how the outcomes can be assessed, and what the issues mean to the lives of individual Canadians are questions rich in their implications for social decisions in Canada's family of nations.

NOTE

1.   For the theoretical construction, see Archer and Vaughan (1971).

REFERENCES

Archer, M.S., & Vaughan, M. (1971). Domination and assertion in educational systems. In E. Hopper (Ed.). *Readings in the theory of educational systems.* London: Hutchison University Library.

Fry, P.S. (Ed.). (1989). Special issue on psychology of aging. *Canadian Psychology, 30,* 505–615.

Higham, John (1993). Multiculturalism and universalism: A history and critique. *American Quarterly, 45*(2), 195–219.

Lawson, R.F. (Ed.). (1992). Special Issue: Education and the elderly. *International Review of Education, 38,* 295–466.

Lawson, R.F., & Ghosh, R. (1986). Canada. *Education and Urban Society, 18,* 449–61.

Time. (1993, Fall). Special issue: The new race of America: How immigrants are shaping the world's first multicultural society.

PART IV
APPENDICES

APPENDIX A

CONSTITUTION ACT, 1867* (ARTICLE 93)

Article 93 of the Constitution Act, 1867, states that:

In and for each Province the Legislature may exclusively make Laws in relation to Education, subject and according to the following Provisions:—

1. Nothing in any such Law shall prejudicially affect any Right or Privilege with respect to Denominational Schools which any Class of Persons have by Law in the Province at the Union:

2. All the Powers, Privileges, and Duties at the Union by Law conferred and imposed in Upper Canada on the Separate Schools and School Trustees of the Queen's Roman Catholic Subjects shall be and the same are hereby extended to the Dissentient Schools of the Queen's Protestant and Roman Catholic Subjects in Quebec:

3. Where in any Province a System of Separate or Dissentient Schools exists by Law at the Union or is thereafter established by the Legislature of the Province, an Appeal shall lie to the Governor General in Council from any Act or Decision of any Provincial Authority affecting any Right or Privilege of the Protestant or Roman Catholic Minority of the Queen's Subjects in relation to Education:

4. In case any such Provincial Law as from Time to Time seems to the Governor General in Council requisite for the due Execution of the Provisions of this Section is not made, or in case any Decision of the Governor General in Council on any Appeal under this Section is not duly executed by the proper Provincial Authority in that Behalf, then and in every such Case, and as far only as the Circumstances of each Case require, the Parliament of Canada may make remedial Laws for the due Execution of the Provisions of this Section and of any Decision of the Governor General in Council under this Section.

*The Constitution Act, 1867, was formerly the British North America Act.

APPENDIX B

Canadian Charter of Rights and Freedoms, 1982

Whereas Canada is founded upon principles that recognize the supremacy of God and the rule of law:

Guarantee of Rights and Freedoms

Rights and freedoms in Canada

1. The Canadian Charter of Rights and Freedoms guarantees the rights and freedoms set out in it subject only to such reasonable limits prescribed by law as can be demonstrably justified in a free and democratic society.

Fundamental Freedoms

Fundamental freedoms

2. Everyone has the following fundamental freedoms:
   (a) freedom of conscience and religion;
   (b) freedom of thought, belief, opinion and expression, including freedom of the press and other media of communication;
   (c) freedom of peaceful assembly; and
   (d) freedom of association.

Democratic Rights

Democratic rights of citizens

3. Every citizen of Canada has the right to vote in an election of members of the House of Commons or of a legislative assembly and to be qualified for membership therein.

Maximum duration of legislative bodies

4. (1) No House of Commons and no legislative assembly shall continue for longer than five years from the date fixed for the return of the writs at a general election of its members.

Continuation in special circumstances

   (2) In time of real or apprehended war, invasion or insurrection, a House of Commons may be continued by Parliament and a legislative assembly may be continued by the legislature beyond five years if such continuation is not opposed by the votes of more than one-third of the members of the House of Commons or the legislative assembly, as the case may be.

Annual sitting of legislative bodies

5. There shall be a sitting of Parliament and of each legislature at least once every twelve months.

Mobility Rights

Mobility of citizens

6. (1) Every citizen of Canada has the right to enter, remain in and leave Canada.

Rights to move and gain livelihood

   (2) Every citizen of Canada and every person who has the status of a permanent resident of Canada has the right
   (a) to move to and take up residence in any province; and
   (b) to pursue the gaining of a livelihood in any province.

Limitation

   (3) The rights specified in subsection (2) are subject to
   (a) any laws or practices of general application in force in a province other than those that discriminate among persons primarily on the basis of province of present or previous residence; and
   (b) any laws providing for reasonable residency requirements as a qualification for the receipt of publicly provided social services.

Affirmative action programs

(4) Subsections (2) and (3) do not preclude any law, program or activity that has as its object the amelioration in a province of conditions of individuals in that province who are socially or economically disadvantaged if the rate of employment in that province is below the rate of employment in Canada.

Legal Rights

Life, liberty and security of person

7. Everyone has the right to life, liberty and security of the person and the right not to be deprived thereof except in accordance with the principles of fundamental justice.

Search or seizure

8. Everyone has the right to be secure against unreasonable search or seizure.

Detention or imprisonment

9. Everyone has the right not to be arbitrarily detained or imprisoned.

Arrest or detention

10. Everyone has the right on arrest or detention
    (a) to be informed promptly of the reasons therefor,
    (b) to retain and instruct counsel without delay and to be informed of that right; and
    (c) to have the validity of the detention determined by way of *habeas corpus* and to be released if the detention is not lawful.

Proceedings in criminal and penal matters

11. Any person charged with an offence has the right
    (a) to be informed without unreasonable delay of the specific offence;
    (b) to be tried within a reasonable time;
    (c) not to be compelled to be a witness in proceedings against that person in respect of the offence;
    (d) to be presumed innocent until proven guilty according to law in a fair and public hearing by an independent and impartial tribunal;
    (e) not to be denied reasonable bail without just cause;
    (f) except in the case of an offence under military law tried before a military tribunal, to the benefit of trial by jury where the maximum punishment for the offence is imprisonment for five years or a more severe punishment;
    (g) not to be found guilty on account of any act or omission unless, at the time of the act or omission, it constituted an offence under Canadian or international law or was criminal according to the general principles of law recognized by the community of nations;
    (h) if finally acquitted of the offence, not to be tried for it again and, if finally found guilty and punished for the offence, not to be tried or punished for it again; and
    (i) if found guilty of the offence and if the punishment for the offence has been varied between the time of commission and the time of sentencing, to the benefit of the lesser punishment.

Treatment or punishment

12. Everyone has the right not to be subjected to any cruel and unusual treatment or punishment.

Self-crimination

13. A witness who testifies in any proceedings has the right not to have any incriminating evidence so given used to incriminate that witness in any other proceedings, except in a prosecution for perjury or for the giving of contradictory evidence.

Interpreter

14. A party or witness in any proceedings who does not understand or speak the language in which the proceedings are conducted or who is deaf has the right to the assistance of an interpreter.

Equality Rights

Equality before and under law and equal protection and benefit of law

15. (1) Every individual is equal before and under the law and has the right to the equal protection and equal benefit of the law without discrimination and, in particular, without discrimination based on race, national or ethnic origin, colour, religion, sex, age or mental or physical disability.

(2) Subsection (1) does not preclude any law, program or activity that has as its object the amelioration of conditions of disadvantaged individuals or groups including those that are disadvantaged because of race, national or ethnic origin, colour, religion, sex, age or mental or physical disability.

Official Languages of Canada

Official languages of Canada

16. (1) English and French are the official languages of Canada and have equality of status and equal rights and privileges as to their use in all institutions of the Parliament and government of Canada.

Official languages of New Brunswick

(2) English and French are the official languages of New Brunswick and have equality of status and equal rights and privileges as to their use in all institutions of the legislature and government of New Brunswick.

Advancement of status and use

(3) Nothing in this Charter limits the authority of Parliament or a legislature to advance the equality of status or use of English and French.

Proceedings of Parliament

17. (1) Everyone has the right to use English or French in any debates and other proceedings of Parliament.

Proceedings of New Brunswick legislature

(2) Everyone has the right to use English or French in any debates and other proceedings of the legislature of New Brunswick.

Parliamentary statutes and records

18. (1) The statutes, records and journals of Parliament shall be printed and published in English and French and both language versions are equally authoritative.

New Brunswick statutes and records

(2) The statutes, records and journals of the legislature of New Brunswick shall be printed and published in English and French and both language versions are equally authoritative.

Proceedings in courts established by Parliament

19. (1) Either English or French may be used by any person in, or in any pleading in or process issuing from, any court established by Parliament.

Proceedings in New Brunswick courts

(2) Either English or French may be used by any person in, or in any pleading in or process issuing from, any court of New Brunswick.

Communications by public with federal institutions

20. (1) Any member of the public in Canada has the right to communicate with, and to receive available services from, any head or central office of an institution of the Parliament or government of Canada in English or French, and has the same right with respect to any other office of any such institution where

(a) there is a significant demand for communications with and services from that office in such language; or

(b) due to the nature of the office, it is reasonable that communications with and services from that office be available in both English and French.

Communications by public with New Brunswick institutions

(2) Any member of the public in New Brunswick has the right to communicate with, and to receive available services from, any office of an institution of the legislature or government of New Brunswick in English or French.

Continuation of existing constitutional provisions

21. Nothing in sections 16 to 20 abrogates or derogates from any right, privilege or obligation with respect to the English and French languages, or either of them, that exists or is continued by virtue of any other provision of the Constitution of Canada.

Rights and privileges preserved

22. Nothing in sections 16 to 20 abrogates or derogates from any legal or customary right or privilege acquired or enjoyed either before or after the coming into force of this Charter with respect to any language that is not English or French.

Minority Language Educational Rights

Language of instruction

23. (1) Citizens of Canada

(a) whose first language learned and still understood is that of the English or French linguistic minority population of the province in which they reside, or

(b) who have received their primary school instruction in Canada in English or French and reside in a province where the language in which they received that instruction is the language of the English or French linguistic minority population of the province,

have the right to have their children receive primary and secondary school instruction in that language in that province.

Continuity of language instruction

(2) Citizens of Canada of whom any child has received or is receiving primary or secondary school instruction in English or French in Canada, have the right to have all their children receive primary and secondary school instruction in the same language.

Application where numbers warrant

(3) The right of citizens of Canada under subsections (1) and (2) to have their children receive primary and secondary school instruction in the language of the English or French linguistic minority population of a province

(a) applies wherever in the province the number of children of citizens who have such a right is sufficient to warrant the provision to them out of public funds of minority language instruction; and

(b) includes, where the number of those children so warrants, the right to have them receive that instruction in minority language educational facilities provided out of public funds.

Enforcement

Enforcement of guaranteed rights and freedoms

24. (1) Anyone whose rights or freedoms, as guaranteed by this Charter, have been infringed or denied may apply to a court of competent jurisdiction to obtain such remedy as the court considers appropriate and just in the circumstances.

Exclusion of evidence bringing administration of justice into disrepute

(2) Where, in proceedings under subsection (1), a court concludes that evidence was obtained in a manner that infringed or denied any rights or freedoms guaranteed by this Charter, the evidence shall be excluded if it is established that, having regard to all the circumstances, the admission of it in the proceedings would bring the administration of justice into disrepute.

General

Aboriginal rights and freedoms not affected by Charter

25. The guarantee in this Charter of certain rights and freedoms shall not be construed so as to abrogate or derogate from any aboriginal, treaty or other rights or freedoms that pertain to the aboriginal peoples of Canada including

    (a) any rights or freedoms that have been recognized by the Royal Proclamation of October 7, 1763; and

    (b) any rights or freedoms that may be acquired by the aboriginal peoples of Canada by way of land claims settlement.

Other rights and freedoms not affected by Charter

26. The guarantee in this Charter of certain rights and freedoms shall not be construed as denying the existence of any other rights or freedoms that exist in Canada.

Multicultural heritage

27. This Charter shall be interpreted in a manner consistent with the preservation and enhancement of the multicultural heritage of Canadians.

Rights guaranteed equally to both sexes

28. Notwithstanding anything in this Charter, the rights and freedoms referred to in it are guaranteed equally to male and female persons.

Rights respecting certain schools preserved

29. Nothing in this Charter abrogates or derogates from any rights or privileges guaranteed by or under the Constitution of Canada in respect of denominational, separate or dissentient schools.

Application to territories and territorial authorities

30. A reference in this Charter to a province or to the legislative assembly or legislature of a province shall be deemed to include a reference to the Yukon Territory and the Northwest Territories, or to the appropriate legislative authority thereof, as the case may be.

Legislative powers not extended

31. Nothing in this Charter extends the legislative powers of any body or authority.

Application of Charter

Application of Charter

32. (1) This Charter applies

    (a) to the Parliament and government of Canada in respect of all matters within the authority of Parliament including all matters relating to the Yukon Territory and Northwest Territories; and

    (b) to the legislature and government of each province in respect of all matters within the authority of the legislature of each province.

Exception

(2) Notwithstanding subsection (1), section 15 shall not have effect until three years after this section comes into force.

Exception where express declaration

33. (1) Parliament or the legislature of a province may expressly declare in an Act of Parliament or of the legislature, as the case may be, that the Act or a provision thereof shall operate notwithstanding a provision included in section 2 or sections 7 to 15 of this Charter.

Operation of exception

(2) An Act or a provision of an Act in respect of which a declaration made under this section is in effect shall have such operation as it would have but for the provision of this Charter referred to in the declaration.

Five-year limitation

(3) A declaration made under subsection (1) shall cease to have effect five years after it comes into force or on such earlier date as may be specified in the declaration.

Re-enactment

(4) Parliament or a legislature of a province may re-enact a declaration made under subsection (1).

Five-year limitation

(5) Subsection (3) applies in respect of a re-enactment made under subsection (4).

Citation

Citation

34. This Part may be cited as the *Canadian Charter of Rights and Freedoms.*

APPENDIX C

THE U.N. CONVENTION ON THE RIGHTS OF THE CHILD, 1989

Passed by the United Nations in November 1989, the Convention attempts to give better protection to the rights of the child than did the first declaration of 1959. Selected clauses relating to education are presented here.

Article 3

1. In all actions concerning children, whether undertaken by public or private social welfare institutions, courts of law, administrative authorities or legislative bodies, the best interests of the child shall be a primary consideration.

2. States Parties undertake to ensure the child such protection and care as is necessary for his or her well-being, taking into account the rights and duties of his or her parents, legal guardians, or other individuals legally responsible for him or her, and, to this end, shall take all appropriate legislative and administrative measures.

Article 5

1. States Parties shall respect the responsibilities, rights and duties of parents or, where applicable, the members of the extended family or community as provided for by local customs, legal guardians or other persons legally responsible for the child, to provide, in a manner consistent with the evolving capacities of the child, appropriate direction and guidance in the exercise by the child of the rights recognized in the present Convention.

Article 12

1. States Parties shall assure to the child who is capable of forming his or her own views the right to express those views freely in all matters affecting the child, the views of the child being given due weight in accordance with the age and maturity of the child.

2. For this purpose, the child shall in particular be provided the opportunity to be heard in any judicial and administrative proceedings affecting the child, either directly, or through a representative or an appropriate body, in a manner consistent with the procedural rules of national law.

Article 14

1. States Parties shall respect the right of the child to freedom of thought, conscience and religion.

2. States Parties shall respect the rights and duties of the parents and, when applicable, legal guardians, to provide direction to the child in the exercise of his or her right in a manner consistent with the evolving capacities of the child.

Article 18

1. States Parties shall use their best efforts to ensure recognition of the principle that both parents have common responsibilities for the upbringing and development of the child. Parents or, as the case may be, legal guardians, have the primary responsibility for the upbringing and development of the child. The best interests of the child will be their basic concern.

2. For the purpose of guaranteeing and promoting the rights set forth in the present Convention, States Parties shall render appropriate assistance to parents and legal guardians in the performance of their child-rearing responsibilities and shall ensure the development of institutions, facilities and services for the care of children.

Article 19

1. States Parties shall take all appropriate legislative, administrative, social and educational measures to protect the child from all forms of physical or mental violence, injury or abuse, neglect or negligent treatment, maltreatment or exploitation, including sexual abuse, while in the care of parent(s), legal guardian(s) or any other person who has the care of the child.

Article 23

1. States Parties recognize that a mentally or physically disabled child should enjoy a full and decent life, in conditions which ensure dignity, promote self-reliance and facilitate the child's active participation in the community.

Article 28

1. States Parties recognize the right of the child to education, and with a view to achieving this right progressively and on the basis of equal opportunity, they shall, in particular:

(a) Make primary education compulsory and available free to all;

(b) Encourage the development of different forms of secondary education, including general and vocational education, make them available and accessible to every child, and take appropriate measures such as the introduction of free education and offering financial assistance in case of need;

(c) Make higher education accessible to all on the basis of capacity by every appropriate means;

(d) Make higher education and vocational information and guidance available and accessible to all children;

(e) Take measures to encourage regular attendance at schools and the reduction of drop-out rates.

2. States Parties shall take all appropriate measures to ensure that school discipline is administered in a manner consistent with the child's human dignity and in conformity with the present Convention.

3. States Parties shall promote and encourage international co-operation in matters relating to education, in particular with a view to contributing to the elimination of ignorance and illiteracy throughout the world and facilitating access to scientific and technical knowledge and modern teaching methods. In this regard, particular account shall be taken of the needs of developing countries.

Article 29

1. States Parties agree that the education of the child shall be directed to:

(a) The development of the child's personality, talents and mental and physical abilities to their fullest potential;

(b) The development of respect for human rights and fundamental freedoms, and for the principles enshrined in the Charter of the United Nations;

(c) The development of respect for the child's parents, his or her own cultural identity, language and values, for the national values of the country in which the child is living, the country from which he or she may originate, and for civilizations different from his or her own;

(d) The preparation of the child for responsible life in a free society, in the spirit of understanding, peace, tolerance, equality of sexes, and friendship among all peoples, ethnic, national and religious groups and persons of indigenous origin;

(e) The development of respect for the natural environment.

Article 31

1. States Parties recognize the right of the child to rest and leisure, to engage in play and recreational activities appropriate to the age of the child and to participate freely in cultural life and the arts.

2. States Parties shall respect and promote the right of the child to participate fully in cultural and artistic life and shall encourage the provision of the appropriate and equal opportunities for cultural, artistic, recreational and leisure activity.

CONTRIBUTOR PROFILES

Jo-Ann Archibald is from the University of British Columbia, where she has contributed to the development of programs for students in Native Culture and Heritage.

Dennis Dibski is Professor of Education at the University of Saskatchewan, where he specialized in educational finance. Recently retired, he was one of the president's advisers to develop policies for financial management. His publications deal with educational finance. Dr. Dibski is a past director of the Canadian Education Association Short Course in Educational Leadership (1983–85).

Greg Dickinson is an Associate Professor in the Division of Educational Policy Studies, Faculty of Education, at the University of Western Ontario. Called to the bar in 1975, Professor Dickinson is a past director of the Faculty of Law's Clinical Legal Education program. His publications include two books, *Rights, Freedoms, and the Education System in Canada* (with A.Wayne MacKay) and *Understanding the Law* (with Steven Talos and Michael Liepner), as well as numerous articles on educational law. Professor Dickinson is principal editor of the *Education and Law Journal*.

Steen Esbensen is Professor of Early Childhood Education in the Faculty of Education at the University of Quebec in Hull. He is past executive director of the Canadian Society for the Study of Education and was executive director of the Social Science Federation of Canada (1988–90).

Ratna Ghosh is Professor of Education in the Department of Administration and Policy Studies in Education at McGill University. She has contributed extensively to books and journals dealing with education, sociology, international development, human rights, feminism, and multiculturalism.

Léonard Goguen is Professor at the University of Moncton, where he lectures on psychology and special education. His publications include several articles and chapters dealing with special education in Canada, both for children with disabilities and the gifted.

Douglas Hart is a senior research officer at the Ontario Institute for Studies in Education, Toronto. He has been associated with the OISE Surveys of Education Issues since their inception in 1978 and has co-authored six survey reports, including *Public Attitudes toward Education in Ontario 1988* (with David Livingstone and L.E. Davie).

William Knitter is an Associate Professor and former chair of the Department of Education at Concordia University. His current research interests include deliberative curriculum theory, the nature of interdisciplinarity in education, and epistemological issues in educational research.

Robert F. Lawson is Professor and Chair of the Department of Educational Policy and Leadership at Ohio State University. He was formerly Dean of Education at the University of Calgary. He has published widely in the field of comparative education.

Claude Lessard is Professor of Sociology of Education in the Department of Educational Studies and Educational Administration at the University of Montreal. He holds a Ph.D. in sociology of education from the Ontario Institute for Studies in Education, Toronto.

David Livingstone is Professor of Sociology at the Ontario Institute for Studies in Education, Toronto. His surveys of attitudes toward education in Canada are the benchmarks for the nation. He is the author of two books in sociology of education and editor of *Critical Pedagogy and Cultural Power*.

Marie McAndrew is Advisor to the Deputy Minister of Cultural Communities and Immigration of Quebec. She has prepared research reports on several provincial cultural and educational programs and presented over 40 papers on the subject of culture and education.

A. Wayne MacKay is Professor of Law at Dalhousie University. He is also a practising member of the Nova Scotia bar and has been the lawyer for parents and students in the trail-blazing cases of *Elwood* (on integrating students with mental disabilities) and *Lavoie* (on the minority-language educational rights of Acadians). His publications include *Educational Law in Canada; Rights, Freedoms and the Education System in Canada* (with Greg Dickinson); and numerous articles on educational law and human rights.

Romulo Magsino is Professor of Education and Head of Educational Administration and Foundations at the University of Manitoba. His works, reflecting his interest in rights and multiculturalism in education, have been published in several books and journals.

Suzanne Majhanovich is an Associate Professor of Curriculum Studies in the Faculty of Education, University of Western Ontario. Her publications include textbooks, articles on second-language curriculum, teacher development, and contributions to Ministry of Education curriculum documents on French as a Second Language and International Languages.

Paul Olson is an Associate Professor of Sociology of Education at the Ontario Institute for Studies in Education, Toronto. His work has included studies of international development in Latin America and community development in Canada.

Robert O'Reilly is Professor and Head of the Department of Educational Policy and Administrative Studies at the University of Calgary. Previously he was professor of educational administration and director of educational studies at the University of Ottawa. He has published widely in the field of educational administration and on legal issues in special education.

Donald Poirier is Professor of Law at the University of Moncton. His interests are children's rights and special education. He has published several articles on the question of education for children with disabilities.

Deo Poonwassie is Professor of Education at the University of Manitoba. A former associate dean of continuing education, he is associated with many innovative programs for distance education. His publications deal mainly with distance education and education for development, including international development.

Jud Purdy is an Associate Professor of Education, teaching history of education and policy studies at the University of Western Ontario. His research interests include religious education and constitutional history.

Douglas Ray is Professor of Education at the University of Western Ontario. He has published extensively in educational policy studies, especially in human-rights education, international development and co-operation, and multiculturalism.

Nancy Sheehan is Dean of Education at the University of British Columbia. As a historian of education, her research interests have been directed toward women's voluntary organizations and their influence on the school curriculum in the early decades of this century. Besides co-editing several books, she has published in Canadian and international journals.

Dien Tran is a researcher at the Faculty of Education, University of Western Ontario. He has designed computer-assisted instruction programs for various training purposes and is associated with international co-operation and human rights publishing.

Aniko Varpalotai is an Associate Professor at the Faculty of Education, University of Western Ontario. Professor Varpalotai's current research covers sociology of education; women's studies/gender relations; socialization; sociology of sport, physical education and leisure; qualitative research methods; adolescence and youth in Canada.

Walter Werner is an Associate Professor with the Department of Social and Educational Studies, University of British Columbia. His published works have been in the areas of educational change and global education.

John Young is an Associate Professor at the University of Alberta, where he holds a joint appointment in the departments of Education Foundations and Sociology. Professor Young's current research is in the areas of classroom analysis, multiculturalism, and voluntarism.

Gloria Rong Zhang is a doctoral candidate at the University of Toronto and is presently completing her dissertation on the integration of Chinese immigrants in Toronto. Before coming to Canada, she was a lecturer in the Foreign Language Department of Human Teachers' University in Changsha, China. She is also an ESL instructor for the Toronto Board of Education and has participated in several ESL research projects.

READER REPLY CARD

We are interested in your reaction to *Social Change and Education in Canada*, third edition, by Ratna Ghosh and Douglas Ray. You can help us to improve this book in future editions by completing this questionnaire.

1. What was your reason for using this book?
   _____ university course
   _____ college course
   _____ continuing education course
   _____ professional development
   _____ personal interest
   _____ other

2. If you are a student, please identify your school and the course in which you used this book. _____

3. Which chapters or parts of this book did you use? Which did you omit? _____
   _____

4. What did you like best about this book? _____

5. What did you like least about this book? _____

6. Please identify any topics you think should be added to future editions. _____
   _____

7. Please add any comments or suggestions. _____

8. May we contact you for further information?

   Name: _____

   Address: _____

   Phone: _____

(fold here and tape shut)

MAIL ➤ **POSTE**

Canada Post Corporation / Société canadienne des postes

Postage paid
If mailed in Canada

Port payé
si posté au Canada

**Business
Reply**

**Réponse
d'affaires**

0116870399   01

0116870399-M8Z4X6-BR01

Heather McWhinney
Publisher, College Division
HARCOURT BRACE & COMPANY, CANADA
55 HORNER AVENUE
TORONTO, ONTARIO
M8Z 9Z9